psychology
and
education
an introduction

psychology
and
education
an introduction

jerome kagan
Harvard University

cynthia lang

Harcourt Brace Jovanovich, Inc.
New York □ San Diego □ Chicago □ San Francisco □ Atlanta

ISBN: 0-15-572770-2
Library of Congress Catalog Card Number: 77-84312

Printed in the United States of America

Part openings by Marjorie Pickens
Figure illustrations by Vantage Art
Cartoons by Sidney Harris
Cover photograph by Joseph Standart

Acknowledgments and copyrights for textual material and for illustrations are
found on pages 600–05, which constitute a continuation of the copyright page.

preface

The education of children has been one of America's major concerns since the arrival of the Pilgrims. But the last twenty years have witnessed a dramatic increase in the amount of attention paid to the school experiences of American children. There are many reasons.

As our society has grown increasingly technological, it has become necessary for all people to have at least twelve years of formal education if they are to be successful and respected in their communities.

Moreover, America is committed to the ideal of good education for all its people, not just some. Attempts to equalize the educational opportunities for poor and minority students have led to many new and often experimental strategies and curricula. Behind these inventions is the hope that a child in a rural Alabama schoolhouse will be able to progress as rapidly as a child in a newly built regional school in a Connecticut suburb. But this is a difficult goal to attain, even when creative educators, psychologists, psychiatrists, and sociologists work together on constructive suggestions. The usefulness of many new educational programs is controversial. It is still not clear which ideas should be integrated into the system and which discarded.

Equally important, parents have come to realize—more clearly than they used to—that schools teach values. Obviously, parents want schools to encourage the standards that they promote at home. At the same time, different families uphold different value systems. Inevitably, there has been increasing debate about the values schools should foster.

The question, then, is how best to prepare teachers for a difficult and complex task. Strong convictions about the answer to this question account for our decision—and one that was not made lightly—to invest several years of concentrated effort in preparing a textbook in educational psychology—a field that already has many good books.

In particular, we felt that more attention should be paid to helping the prospective teacher understand the psychological nature of the child. This field of study has grown dramatically in recent years. Many significant advances have been made in what is known about the child's learning, thought, motivation, and emotion, and we explore those that are specially relevant to teaching. Specifically, Chapter 3 summarizes some major theoretical views about learning, Chapters 4 and 5 examine cognitive functioning, and Chapters 6 and 7 explore motivation and affect.

In these chapters—as well as throughout *Psychology and Education: An Introduction*—we emphasize the point of view that a profound relation exists between a child's cognitive processes and his or her motives and expectations and that cognition and motivation act in concert to influence school progress. We are friendly toward the Piagetian assumption that maturation sets certain limits on the child's cognitive functioning and that those limits, in turn, affect social behavior, motivation, and emotional experience; accordingly, we stress the changes in cognitive functioning that occur with age and experience.

We also believe that the teacher should have a cultural and historical perspective on education. The educational goals of a particular community are always tied to its needs and philosophy. It is useful and even occasionally therapeutic for teachers to appreciate how education has changed in our own culture and the form it has taken in other societies, both past and present. Chapters 1 and 2 explore these subjects in a more than casual manner so that prospective teachers will understand why it is so difficult to achieve a consensus on the goals of education.

A third aim of this book is to encourage an attitude of skepticism toward theoretical ideas—including commonly held views on intelligence, slow learners, and children from poor families—and toward the evidence that has given them momentum. In Chapter 8, for example, we suggest that future research may reveal that the concept of intelligence lacks theoretical utility. We are interested not in setting up straw men only to knock them down but in persuading prospective teachers to maintain a questioning approach to popular assumptions and current ideas. As comparatively new fields, developmental psychology and educational psychology can be expected to grow and change rapidly, and teachers need to be both discerning and receptive to changes in current thinking.

In addition, teachers need to be able to evaluate specific programs and practices. Each decade is marked by new educational approaches, some of which will be retained over time, others eliminated. Several major innovations of recent years are described and assessed in Chapter 13, which can also serve as a guide to teachers when they must judge future programs on their own.

We have tried throughout the book to apply basic knowledge and theory to the realities of teaching. We have been greatly helped in this effort by the fact that, during the preparation of this textbook, a good deal of our time was spent observing teachers and students in a variety of classroom situations. This practical experience is apparent in the sustained descriptions of classroom events in Chapters 5 and 12. It also informs the book in more subtle ways, and numerous examples of students' dilemmas, teachers' strategies, and personal interactions were drawn from this rich source of information.

On the other hand, we have declined to write a comforting book of recipes for teaching. We do not believe that there are any perfect prescriptions for teaching a subject. Individual teachers often develop techniques that can be usefully shared by others. But if teaching depended only on technique, anyone could buy a manual and go to work. Good teaching, we know, is not that easy.

One of our basic assumptions in writing this book is that teaching is, in part, an art. It involves competence in subject matter and the personality and character of the teacher. It also involves a sure grasp of fundamentals. We are convinced that a deep understanding of basic concepts about the development and the behavior of children is the best preparation a teacher can have. Equipped with this knowledge, teachers can choose the most effective practices for their classrooms as well as critically evaluate the techniques and theories developed by others.

Finally, this book represents a happy collaboration between a psychologist and a professional writer. The end product, we believe, offers the best scientific knowledge in a form that students can read with maximum interest and ease.

We are indebted to Doris Simpson, Carole Lawton, and Carla Carney for typing; to Mark Szpak for research assistance; and to Lauren Resnick, Judith Otto, Thomas Cone, Frances Donnagher, Frances Ness, Ruth Ann Richels, Wendy Postlethwaite, Richard Konicek, Cynthia Gilles, Tulie Warshauer, Elizabeth Holland, and Laurel Miller for their thoughtful contributions. For their helpful reviews of the manuscript, we would also like to thank Lois Burrill, The Psychological Corporation; Susan Eklund, Indiana University; Donald B. Holsinger, University of Chicago; Daniel Keating, University of Minnesota; Charles Kreitzberg, Educational Testing Service; Valerie Kreitzberg, Educational Testing Service; Pauline Leet, Franklin and Marshall College; Anthony Nitko, University of Pittsburgh; Ellis Batten Page, University of Connecticut; and Bruce Tuckman, Rutgers University.

JEROME KAGAN
CYNTHIA LANG

contents

the psychological nature of the child

two

3

the nature of learning: the processes of change

4

cognition I: units and processes of problem solving

5

cognition II: the development of competence   178

6

the development of affects and motives   222

9

classroom testing and evaluation   350

10

explaining school failure   390

11

classroom atmosphere and management   438

current problems and
tentative solutions
four

12

social class and ethnicity   486

13

tomorrow's education: meeting individual needs

In collaboration with Dr. Lauren P. Resnick

the goals of education
one

what are the goals of education?

1

Schools are such an integral part of our society that we rarely step back to ask why they exist or question what they do. If school-age children or adults were asked, "Why do we have schools?" they would be likely to answer, "To teach children the things they have to know," an answer that implies that there is general agreement about the "things to be known." But a brief examination of American education in the past and of schools in other cultures reveals that the content of education changes over time and varies with the specific challenges and problems faced by each society. The school's mission, then, is to serve its society by preparing young people to cope effectively with its problems and to contribute to the pool of human talents the society needs in order to function successfully.

Since every culture grapples with a special constellation of challenges, the goals of education vary from one society to another. Nevertheless, at the most general level, through history schools have been given two major assignments: *to equip the child and adolescent*

**Six cultures and their
educational goals**
  Sparta
  Athens
  Early Rome
  Tanzania
  China
  Israel
  A comparison with the United
  States

**The goals of contemporary
American education**
  To teach skills and knowledge
  To train character and
  personality

  To actualize the child's
  talents
  To achieve social harmony
  To narrow the income gap
  To create an awareness of
  group culture

**The school as a battleground:
current disputes**
  Which goals are primary?
  Desire for assimilation
  Attitude toward obedience
  Attitude toward stress and
  anxiety
  Impact of conflict on
  education

with skills and knowledge not easily learned in the natural
environment, and, in tandem with the family, to inculcate the values
and foster the desired character traits that will help the young person
meet the demands and problems of the society.

Obviously, the skills and knowledge to be mastered change
drastically with time and culture. Over the years in American schools,
languages such as Spanish and Russian have come to replace Greek and
Latin; rhetoric has given way to public speaking, bookkeeping to data
processing, woodworking to television repair.

Equally significant, though less obvious, are the changes that have
occurred in American values over the centuries. In Puritan New
England, piety, obedience to family, and loyalty to God were dominant
values, for the church was a strong and unifying force in the New
World. Both at home and at school the child was trained to respect
authority, inhibit aggression, be modest about sexuality, and be
formally religious. In the nineteenth century, however, the power of the

church declined, and rural families sent their children to the cities to work in the factories created by the industrial revolution. As piety and respect for authority came to be valued less, they were replaced by autonomy and individual achievement, attributes more appropriate to an increasingly secular, geographically mobile, and industrial America. Values continue to change and, as always, generate conflicts that reverberate through the wider society and are echoed in the schools, as we shall see in the last section of this chapter.

In addition to being taught to value independence, personal accomplishment, and autonomy, children born in modern America are encouraged to be rational, efficient, alert, and verbally fluent; they learn to control impulsive acts, value work, and care about money. In their earliest years girls and boys are taught to feed and dress themselves and to speak up when they are spoken to. In their teens they are encouraged to define and develop their special talents in school. As adults they look for jobs in which their personal initiative and the particular skills they have mastered enable them to make a unique contribution. The young person who has successfully incorporated the respected attributes of personal achievement and independence will probably feel considerable self-satisfaction and also be rewarded by society.

But what if this young adult were transplanted to a different society—to China, for instance—where the dominant values are cooperation and subordination of the individual's needs to those of the group? In modern China personal satisfaction and public reward accrue to those who put the aims and achievements of the group ahead of their own ambitions and accomplishments. Chinese children are taught to help rather than compete with one another. In school, children read together and study at the same pace. Instead of fostering the development of individual talents, teachers encourage each child to learn a core set of skills so that each can do the other's job.

The merits of these two ways of life can be debated. What cannot be argued, however, is that the young adult who excelled in the United States would be at a disadvantage in a society that applauds group effort and cooperation. His practical skills, it is true, might still be useful. But he would have difficulty adjusting because the psychological ideals he has learned to value are not those held by his new group. Thus, for example, a person who stays home may be admired and respected, but if he is forced to move, his new neighbors may regard him as poorly educated.

While such an example may seem remote, it does illustrate a situation that is common in America, where different ethnic and class groups hold conflicting values and the discrepancies affect the education of particular children. This subject will be discussed further in Chapter 12. The point here is that any evaluation of educational goals must always take into account the community that generated them.

Six Cultures and Their Educational Goals

It is easier to be objective about a distant civilization, since most people are too immersed in the life they know to be conscious of the details that set their society apart from others. Three of the communities presented here exist only in the deep past: Sparta, Greece, and Rome. The other three—China, Tanzania, and Israel—coexist with the United States in time, though not in philosophy. A study of all six cultures confirms our observation that the educational goals of a society reflect its values and are designed to serve its perceived needs.

Sparta

In the middle of the sixth century B.C. the Spartans conquered a barbaric group called the Messenians. Because they outnumbered the Spartans ten to one, Spartan authorities felt a pressing need to develop a large corps of professional soldiers that could keep the Messenians under control. As a result, the existing Spartan ego ideal of loyalty to the self yielded to the ideal of the warrior-ruler. Child-rearing practices became rigorous and austere. The educational goals changed: to raise boys who would be self-denying warriors and girls who would perform the traditional role of women among martial peoples, applauding bravery and military prowess and urging the young men on to great achievements in battle. One well-known story tells us that a Spartan mother instructed her son as he was leaving to fight in a battle, "Come back with your shield—or on it": for the soldier who threw away his shield was disgraced (Kitto, 1951).

The state took over the child's training at age seven and emphasized military skills and physical fitness. In the new Spartan education individuality was submerged, much as it is today in modern China. The state controlled the child in body and soul, discipline was constant, and obedience to one's immediate superiors was mandatory. Education was designed to produce both the skills and the character traits that made a good soldier. For growing adolescents in Sparta, there was little ambiguity of choice and their lives were carefully regulated (Castle, 1961).

Athens

The story of fifth-century B.C. Athenian Greece is different. While conservative Sparta was turning inward toward its domestic problems, Athens turned toward the sea. Athenians were unhampered by the need to control a conquered people, and the sea provided both their livelihood and access to fresh ideas. Their openness to new people and points of view was to be the basis of their cosmopolitan outlook. Beginning as sailors and merchants, they built a city-state. Their values encouraged Greek boys toward the goal of being good Athenian citizens—wise, loyal, devoted to Athens, and appreciative of the arts. They defined a good life as one that balanced physical, intellectual, aesthetic, and moral ideals. Without a pressing state crisis, such as the one that shaped Spartan education, the local government was less dictatorial about education. From seven to fourteen, boys attended private schools that emphasized music appreciation, athletics, and physical prowess; intellectual skills were secondary. In addition to developing the concept of the wise and loyal citizen, the Greeks valued a human characteristic that they called *arete,* best defined as personal excellence and outstanding performance in a socially valued endeavor. Those with arete led the society and had the respect of the community, even though the specific qualities that defined arete changed over the centuries from Homer to Plato. During the fifth century B.C. in Athens arete was demonstrated by unusual talent in music and poetry, rather than in soldiering or intellectual skills, and by display of the important characteristics of moderation and prudence.

But as Athens became larger, wealthier, and more powerful, the social and political climate changed. Old values celebrating loyalty to the small city-state and civil service as humanity's highest ideals began to weaken. The city required more complex political structures and men who could govern effectively and gain the confidence of the citizens. To fill this need, a new breed of young people emerged who cared more about personal status and political ambition than loyalty to the city. Former reverence for the gods faded among citizens who lived in a city that was a monument to human, not divine, achievements. Philosophers began to subject traditional beliefs to critical analysis.

These profound social changes altered educational priorities and led to the rise of a new group of teachers called Sophists. They were teachers of practical wisdom, less concerned with music, virtue, or athletics, and more interested in teaching young men how to win political influence. The Sophists rejected the earlier Athenian notion that the only way to attain wisdom was to practice it in everyday life; they argued that wisdom and morality could be taught through words. One Sophist, Isocrates, founded a school in 393 B.C. that might be regarded as the first high school of the Western world. Isocrates did not emphasize gymnastics and music but the acquisition of facts, oratorical skills, and knowledge of the literary classics with an eye to training gymnasts of the mind who would become good politicians. The specific qualities that defined arete had changed (Castle, 1961), but individual excellence and outstanding performance—the basic components of arete—continued to be highly valued.

We are compelled to admit that at the most glorious period of the empire the schools entirely failed to fulfil the duties which we expect of our schools today. They undermined instead of strengthened the children's morals; they mishandled the children's bodies instead of developing them; and if they succeeded in furnishing their minds with a certain amount of information, they were not calculated to perform any loftier or nobler task. The pupils left schools with the heavy luggage of a few practical and commonplace notions laboriously acquired. . . . Instead of happy memories, serious and fruitful ideas, any sort of intellectual curiosity vital to later life, school children carried away the gloomy recollection of years wasted in senseless, stumbling repetitions punctuated by savage punishments. (Carcopino, 1940, p. 106)

The details of the criticism as well as the tone are consistent with the ideas of contemporary critics. In fact, the author, Jerome Carcopino, is criticizing popular education in Rome. The passage is from the book *Daily Life in Ancient Rome,* written in the early years of the Christian era when Roman values had moved far away from the rugged farming life.

Early Rome

The society of the early Romans was markedly different from that of the Greeks, and so was their educational system. From the sixth to the third centuries B.C., before Rome became an empire, the Romans were neither ruling soldiers nor sophisticated citizens of a merchant nation but a rural and agricultural people, soldier-farmers who owned their land and supervised the peasants. The population was scattered over the countryside instead of being grouped in large cities. Each small estate was self-contained. Authoritarianism was the rule; the Roman father had absolute control over his wife, his children, his peasants. His authority was bounded, however, by the Roman religion, which fostered standards of steadfastness and moderation as well as customary rituals designed to seek the gods' approval for almost every public or domestic activity.

Since the population was scattered, most education took place at home. Mothers were responsible for the young children's training. Fathers took charge of their sons at the age of seven. The skills taught were simple and utilitarian, learned from working the land and from daily life rather than from a book; they included crop planting, crafts connected with farming, such as toolmaking and tool repair, and enough arithmetic to keep the farm accounts.

For the most part, it was an education based on the power of example: the child looked to his father and his father, in turn, looked to ancestral custom. The early Romans were practical and not particularly intellectual. Since the home unit was so inclusive, loyalty to the family was a primary characteristic, inculcated in children from an early age. They prized manual labor, the sturdy, useful skills of farming, a pragmatic outlook on life, and seriousness of purpose they called *gravitas*. Those were the qualities the Romans taught their children (Castle, 1961).

Tanzania

Tanzania is a poor rural nation situated on the east coast of Africa. Only about half its children attend primary school, and only one-tenth of primary-school graduates go on to high school. In accordance with the Tanzanian president's concept of education for self-reliance, in 1970 the government instituted a work-oriented program of education aimed at adults and children not in school. Classes, scheduled around the crop seasons, meet in school buildings, private houses, or simply in the shade of a tree. Primers are designed for a two-year course but are used flexibly. In addition to these classes, libraries, local newspapers, pamphlets, and radio discussions of national topics encourage a climate of literacy and an exchange of ideas.

The goals of the work-oriented program reflect the national values. One obvious goal is to increase literacy for all citizens, not just for

Figure 1–1
Tanzanian primers for adult-education classes teach Swahili and provide agricultural advice at the same time. These pages are from a primer designed for use in a cotton-growing area. (Viscusi, 1971)

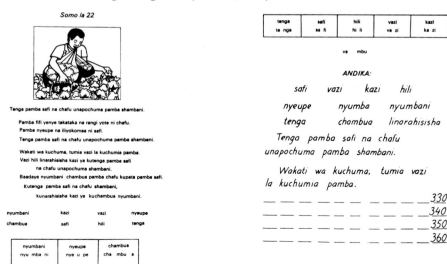

Figure 1-2
Illustrations from Tanzanian primers make practical points about cotton growing and home economics. The drawing of a mother bathing her baby in a basin of water has two aims: it attempts to discourage bathing in the river, where people encounter the menace of bilharzia (a parasite that enters the body through the skin), and it depicts a simple metal basin, which is readily available, rather than a Western bathtub, which is difficult to purchase and would raise unrealistic expectations for most Tanzanians. (Viscusi, 1971)

children. A second goal is to link education to practical knowledge: if people live in a banana-growing area, their primer will be based on facts about banana crops; if the area grows cotton, the primer discusses cotton (see Figure 1-1). Other useful subjects covered include hygiene and home economics (see Figure 1-2). The primers are prepared by lawyers, economists, agricultural workers, and nurses, as well as by teachers.

By 1973 well over a million people had enrolled in the classes. An unexpected but positive index of the program's success appeared some time after the classes had started: the government noticed a substantial increase in stamp sales and in the volume of mail. It turned out that as more people knew how to write, many more people were sending letters to one another (*Jenga Twelve*, 1972).

China

In contrast to small and recently independent Tanzania, China is one of the largest nations with one of the longest histories in the world. Like Tanzania, modern China has its own set of objectives: it must become more industrial and increase its food supply in order to feed its over 800,000,000 people (Mehnert, 1972). Chinese leaders have decided that to achieve these goals they must first persuade every man, woman, and child to identify with the state and devote all their loyalty to the nation. The educational system is monitored by the central government, and the national values are instilled with the same consistency and determination that characterized ancient Sparta. These include subordination of personal to group needs; cooperation; respect for productive labor; emphasis on intellectual skills and knowledge that are useful for the society; and an egalitarian spirit among all members of the society—between men and women and between children and adults.

These values, which appear to be generally shared by both urban and rural Chinese parents, are conveyed to children from an early age. Almost half the young children are in nurseries during their first five

Figure 1-3
A poem and picture from a Chinese children's book illustrate the value of cooperation. (After *Fun in the Garden*, 1965)

Turnips red and turnips white!
Turnips long and turnips round!
See the children all unite
To pull the turnip from the ground.
To the party they come prancing
Playing tricks, singing and dancing.

years of life. Here they learn to take turns and to cooperate with one another (see Figure 1–3). Relatively few toys are found in child-care facilities. Although partly a matter of economy, this practice also encourages children to rely on one another for stimulation. The toys they do have are there for a particular purpose. An American visitor to a Chinese nursery noted that the toy blocks seemed very heavy for small children. "Exactly," beamed the teacher when she was asked about them. "That fosters mutual help" (Dollar, 1973, p. 31).

Generous behavior occurs frequently among Chinese children. In a park in Hangchow, a visitor gave some candy to a ten-year-old boy. At once he gave the first piece of candy to his baby sister; he gave the second piece to his mother; he kept the third piece, probably because he had no one else to give it to (Sidel, 1972).

Another goal of Chinese education is to teach the philosophy of the late Chairman Mao Tse-tung. Banners, posters, daily reading sessions, and impromptu stories are all used to impress schoolchildren with the teachings of Mao. Six-year-olds play with sets of small blocks, turning them around to form different pictures, all of which show military scenes, such as a female member of the People's Liberation Army throwing a hand grenade or a schoolboy bayoneting a stick figure of a "foreign devil." Veteran workers come to class to tell stories of the past. In addition to teaching children about modern China, teachers and parents want them to learn about China's "bitter past" so that they can better appreciate the contrast between today's life and the oppressed life of the peasant prior to 1949 when Mao Tse-tung took power.

A third goal is to raise the children's consciousness with regard to politics and work. In Chairman Mao's words, "Education must serve proletarian politics and be combined with productive labor" ("Enlivening Studies," 1973, p. 10). Productive work is important in the life of schoolchildren, and, like the early Romans, they learn to respect physical labor. In the kindergarten three- to six-year-olds may be assigned the job of folding cardboard crayon boxes, work that is leased to the kindergarten by the local factory. Their earnings are used to buy extra equipment for the school. Children also plant seeds and grow vegetables. One group of middle-school students spends time in the school workshop making automobile accessories and electronic products. Politicians and teachers believe that through participation in such activities children will come to appreciate the beauty of manual labor and develop greater respect for the peasant (Kessen, 1975; Sidel, 1972).

Appropriate political thinking, a major subject in Chinese education, is taught in classes that we would call "social studies" and also is promoted indirectly in extracurricular activities. Primary-school children are elected to the "Little Red Soldiers" and adolescents to the "Red Guard." These student organizations confer prestige and promote Communist philosophy and ideals. Overt political activity by itself is

not enough; politically correct attitudes and behavior are equally important. In one middle school a thirteen-year-old boy said, "On the positive side, I have been active in political matters, but I had three points against me; I'm undisciplined, I talk too much, and I have a tendency to apply Chairman Mao's principles more to others than to myself" (Mehnert, 1972, pp. 101–02).

Political beliefs are also important in the children's lives during school vacations. In Peking the Children's Palace is one of the city's eight centers for activities during the winter holidays, and it is visited by 3,000 children a day. In addition to parties, movies, and lectures on science and technology, the Palace provides story hours in which actors recount revolutionary events.

In many schools Little Red Soldier groups organize children's teams. These teams spend some of their vacation time going to army hospitals to perform for the soldiers and visiting the families of army men to help with the household chores ("Vacation Activities," 1973).

In a more subtle but pervasive way political beliefs are taught in classroom practices. In the relationship between teacher and child the emphasis is on egalitarianism. Indeed, teachers are supposed to learn from their pupils, as illustrated in this story told to some American visitors:

A middle school student behaved badly in class, would not sit still, came late, and would on occasion actually leave school while it was still in session. The teacher would not know where he had gone and the relationship between the teacher and the student became very tense. His responsible teacher was the teacher of his English class, and when the English period came around the student always had some excuse to keep him out of class—he had a stomach ache or was constipated. One day when he left school early the teacher followed him home. He found the student repairing a clock. The teacher began to think it over: the more he criticized the student the less the student attended class. With the help of the leading comrade in the student leaders [Red Guard] the teacher began to realize he needed to change his attitude. The teacher, in a meeting, criticized himself. He realized he needed to praise the student. He told the student he respected his ability to repair clocks and said, "This is something I could learn from you." The student began to feel more receptive and the teacher gave him special make-up work in English. (Kessen, 1975, pp. 161–62)

Although the subjects taught in the primary schools in China are not unlike those taught in the United States (language, arithmetic, political thought, music, art, science, geography, history, and physical education), an overriding principle dominates the curriculum: the children's talents and abilities are developed not to help them acquire status or wealth as adults but to enable them to serve the people.

Israel

Israel—whose concept of nationhood is several thousand years old—celebrated its twenty-fifth anniversary in 1973. During the years before and after independence, Israel gathered in exiles from Germany, Eastern Europe, and Morocco, from city ghettos and country villages. They came from widely diverse cultures and spoke different languages. Those from Europe—who were the majority—remembered varying pictures of persecution. Israel's chief educational task, then, was to bring together its new citizens, heal their psychic wounds, and help them create and give definition to a new common way of life. Learning Hebrew was more than a way to bridge the language gulf among people from different countries; it also represented a renascence of Hebrew culture. Whatever their place had been in the old world, the exiles had all come from traditional societies. The new society was to be untraditional and truly egalitarian (Wolins and Gottesmann, 1971).

In order to understand the educational philosophy of Israel, we must appreciate the attitudes of the European immigrants who settled there during the decade from 1940 to 1950. The founders of the new nation were determined to alter the European stereotype of the Jew as an aesthete incapable of physical labor or military affairs, a recluse who devoted his time to the sedentary activities of scholarship and commerce. They devised a curriculum for young Israeli children that stressed physical skills and endurance. The schools—not unlike those in modern China—emphasized calisthenics, physical and psychological endurance, and agricultural and manual skills. The ideology of the original settlers of the kibbutzim, who today make up a very small proportion of the Israeli population, stressed egalitarianism among its members, especially between the sexes; commitment to the group, rather than personal aggrandizement; asceticism and self-denial, rather than hedonism. Work and productivity, rather than age, sex, wealth, or beauty, were the bases of dignity and status (Talmon, 1972).

Nevertheless, adults did not want their children to forget the bravery of European Jews who lost their lives resisting Nazi aggression. They created memorials to the Warsaw uprising on several kibbutzim, and schoolchildren made regular visits to these memorials—reminiscent of the Chinese insistence that the youth be conscious of the "bitter past" before the 1949 revolution. Finally, because the adults wanted to mold children who would not be entirely dependent on their families, infant houses were established with special caretakers called *metaplot* (singular: metapelet), where infants and children spent most of their time while their mothers and fathers worked.

This philosophy was consonant with the values of the European Jews, who made up three-quarters of the population at that time.

During recent years, however, there has been increased immigration into Israel of North African Jews, whose values do not always coincide with those of the Europeans. North African Jews did not experience the European massacres; furthermore, they came to Israel with a much more positive attitude toward the nuclear family. As a result, Israel is now undergoing debates on educational philosophy and curricula.

The formal curriculum of the Israeli school is similar to that of the American school. Language, mathematics, and science are central. The two required courses of the elementary schools—Bible and manual training—reflect the special needs of the Israeli society. Since Israel is a land of immigrants from many parts of the world, educators feel that their common cultural history should unite the new citizens. Hence, all Israeli children study the Bible, much as all American children study the history of the United States. In the first grade children are taught Jewish lore that is related to the holidays and to family and national occasions. Formal instruction in the Bible begins in the second grade, and studies in the oral law start about the fourth grade. Manual training is required because Israel needs adults who can work in the fields and factories and who value that kind of productivity (Bentwich, 1965).

In addition, as industrialization increases the country requires more highly trained technicians and specialists in different fields of knowledge than it did when the nation's greatest efforts went into making the desert bloom. Reforms have been implemented to bring more children into high school. The need for specialization is reflected in the four kinds of high schools: academic schools, which prepare students for the matriculation exam; agricultural schools; maritime schools; and vocational schools, which train students for jobs in electronics, metallurgy, mechanics, and other technical fields (Department for Aliya and Absorption, 1972).

The turn toward specialization (with workers each learning a particular set of skills, rather than all sharing common ones) is creating a conflict with Israel's goal of egalitarianism. Nevertheless, Israel has chosen the course of increased industrialization and its schools are teaching the skills and personality characteristics that are in harmony with that choice.

A Comparison with the United States

Three of the societies we have examined are distant from America in time; the three modern ones are distant philosophically. Still, a knowledge of their values and educational aims provides some perspective on our educational philosophy. In some cases, the contrasts outweigh the similarities. In China, for example, the ideal of individuals obtaining gratification from their contributions to the larger group is strikingly different from the ideal in the United States, where personal achievement is primary. China, like Tanzania, needs as many people as possible in the work force, for in rural, agricultural societies an extra pair of hands in the fields means greater yield and prosperity. In our own country, quite a different situation exists. As we become increasingly technological, we may have an oversupply of labor. The surplus would be even greater if men and women were automatically freed from school when they were fourteen and poured into the job market. Hence, in addition to providing extra years of schooling in which more advanced skills can be learned, high schools and colleges also function as holding areas for the work force (Broudy, 1972).

Of course, social and economic conditions alone do not determine educational policy. A nation's political philosophy also influences the priorities of its schools. A country can be poor and communist, such as China, or poor and capitalist, such as Kenya (which is next to Tanzania geographically, but remote politically), and the schools will teach different attitudes and values.

In spite of the obvious differences between the United States and the other six societies, there are also some similarities. Early Roman life was similar to life in nineteenth-century Vermont. In both places, farmers lived on scattered homesteads, a good deal of schooling took place at home, and education emphasized practical skills and religious and family-oriented values.

A profound parallel exists between modern America and Athens during the period of the Sophists. The Greek concept of arete is strong in the United States. Like the Athenians, modern Americans value individual success and outstanding performance, and they celebrate competition between individuals as a means of building character.

In both the United States and Israel, state intervention in educational policies became necessary in order to help assimilate new citizens. During the late nineteenth and early twentieth centuries, massive immigrations from Europe brought large ethnic groups to American cities, and America, like Israel after 1948, faced the task of integrating diverse groups of people into the nation's life. As the number of schoolchildren increased, the schools grew larger and their functions altered. Schools were now asked to perform a lion's share of the work in assimilating the new citizens, teaching them English, and exposing them to American customs and attitudes.

The Goals of Contemporary American Education

Like the societies described above, the United States has a particular set of problems it must solve. Let us consider the educational goals of contemporary America and how each relates to America's needs as a nation.

Goal 1: To Teach Skills and Knowledge

"If there is a unifying force in the American culture today, it is to be found in the silent logic of a technological/industrial society. It is virtually impossible to find any aspect of life that can be shaken loose from involvement with the system" (Broudy, 1972, p. 227). Technologically the most advanced nation in the world, America needs engineers and scientists who will maintain the complex machines that operate throughout the country, as well as create new and more efficient ones.

Literacy is obviously the one indispensable skill for every citizen. Adults who cannot read or write are at such a disadvantage that it is difficult for them to function in any vocation, even if they are physically strong or endowed with remarkable talents. Every year from the first grade through the last year of high school, therefore, schools teach reading and English composition. Mathematics is the second essential skill.

Other subjects follow: social studies, science, languages. For those who will go no further than high school, useful skills are taught, such as auto mechanics, home economics, radio and television repair, and accounting. Students who plan to have professional careers must prepare themselves by taking advanced courses in such fields as science, mathematics, law, or economics. But in all cases the skills that American children must master first remain—reading, writing, and arithmetic.

Goal 2: To Train Character and Personality

Besides being highly technological, America is a competitive and mobile society that values freedom and personal ambition. Although not everyone concurs that individual success should be ascendant over other values, schools, like other institutions in the nation, work on the tacit assumptions that each adult wants to attain status and wealth and that those who work hardest on their own behalf are the most likely to achieve these goals. Since that is apparently the philosophy of the American majority, some view the school system as a race where fifty million young people compete for a much smaller number of prizes. The American school considers competition the most effective mode for motivating individual effort. Starting in the first grade, the educational system ranks children on their abilities and academic productivity. Elementary and high schools conscientiously encourage individual

Hingham, Massachusetts: High School

Since 1872 the school committee has included a summary of the year's highlights in the annual town report. In this town's school history, it is possible to observe the changes in American educational goals over the last one hundred years. English, reading, arithmetic, and history are constants. The significant changes are in the subjects that have been dropped and in the new subjects that have been added—all are logical extensions of former areas, but most were unforeseen a hundred years ago. If a history of Africa was an unlikely course then, an introduction to data processing was unimaginable.

1872   There were 47 students in the new high school, out of a total population of 685, though the report adds, "It will be seen that the list is not as perfect as we could wish, many parents feeling that if they can escape the law in this respect, they are doing their whole duty; but this is not so, and our schools can never become what they should until parents recognize how important it is that their children be in regular attendance." They studied the following:

Drawing ("As this is one of the branches prescribed by law, we have introduced it into our schools.")

Music and elocution
Rhetoric
Latin and French
Natural philosophy and mental philosophy
Bookkeeping
Chemistry, botany, natural history, astronomy, geology, geography, and physiology
Constitution of the United States and modern history
Algebra and trigonometry
Reading, spelling, English literature, "and if necessary, penmanship"

1946   "The question uppermost in the minds of the parents," says the report this year, "is 'For what kind of trade, job or profession is my boy (or girl) best fitted?' " The subjects reflected this concern:

Bookkeeping is still on the list. Now, so are typewriting, shorthand, stenography, office machines, transcription, and business arithmetic. (Training for specific trades such as auto mechanics or printing was available in vocational high schools in a larger, nearby town.)
Biology and physics have joined the other sciences.
Spanish has joined French and Latin.

for the Last One Hundred Years

Philosophy has faded in the face of vocational concerns.

Drawing is no longer compulsory, public speaking has replaced rhetoric, and there is a course in home economics.

And, naturally, English, general math, history.

In addition to preparing students for work, the high school is now preparing them for leisure time: art, band, and chorus are given. In addition, the report includes a list of extracurricular activities: camera club, dramatic club, stamp club, model making, and wood-working.

1972   There are courses in English, mathematics, speech and reading, but more in all four fields than there were in 1946, including multi-ethnic literature, composition for personal growth, and a course called "write-on."

Business courses include an introduction to data processing and accelerated accounting; industrial arts has courses in technical drawing and graphics communication.

Ecology, conservation, oceanography, and electronics have swelled the already large science field.

German has joined French and Spanish; Latin is still offered.

The single home economics course has expanded to nine, including housing, interior decoration, child development, chef's club, and clothing.

Some of the extracurricular activities are now offered for credit, and there are eleven arts and crafts courses, including band, chorus, orchestra, textile design, ceramics, drawing and painting, music theory, and harmony.

The history section has burgeoned into social studies. There are courses on the Middle East, India, Africa, Russia, China, and South East Asia, as well as European history.

The courses speak for themselves. They indicate an emphasis on science, math, and business training; they reflect a world grown smaller, where the languages and histories of foreign countries are of some concern to seventeen-year-old students in a New England town. And they show that as well as preparing students for work, the schools are concerned with preparing them for a time of their own. Most significant, perhaps, is the variety of courses, underlining a strong need for specialized skills. In 1872 the new high school had 26 courses. In 1972, for the twelfth grade alone, 106 were offered.

effort and ambition. Other values emphasized are popularity and ease in relating to people. As American business and industry flourish, they contribute to a family mobility that exceeds that of any nation in the world and to a need for the traits of sociability and flexibility. Chapter 2 will elaborate on the role of the school in socializing children.

Goal 3: To Actualize the Child's Talents

Unlike the situation in many less well developed countries in the world, more than half of America's families have an adequate food supply, satisfactory housing, and available medical facilities. More significantly, many parents believe that their children stand a good chance of having as good a job and as satisfactory a life as they do. As a result, many middle-class parents believe that their children should be allowed to develop their own special talents to the best of their ability, even though their efforts may not lead to any practical or financial advantage. The schools have become sensitive and are responding to this desire. Although we recognize that the world can support only a few painters, most schools have an art program; they also have programs in music, crafts, drama, and athletics. Asked for an explanation, some teachers would probably defend the practice by

Benjamin Franklin wrote down what he considered the ideal curriculum for youth:

All should be taught "to write a fair hand" and "something of drawing"; arithmetic, accounts, geometry, and astronomy; English grammar out of Tillotson, Addison, Pope, Sydney, Trenchard, and Gordon; the writing of essays and letters; rhetoric, history, geography, and ethics; natural history and gardening; and the history of commerce and the principles of mechanics. Instruction should include visits to neighboring farms, opportunities for natural observations, experiments with scientific apparatus, and physical exercise. And the whole should be suffused with a quest for benignity of mind, which Franklin saw as the foundation of good breeding and a spirit of service which should be regarded as "the great aim and end of all learning." (Cremin, 1970, p. 376)

answering that every child should have a chance to paint just in case he or she has an exceptional talent. Others would say that painting is an emotional outlet for the child or that it fosters creativity and a richer fantasy life. But beneath these answers lies the premise that children should have an opportunity to improve their artistic abilities, whatever their talent and even though the skills may never be financially useful to them.

Goal 4: To Achieve Social Harmony

America has serious racial and ethnic conflicts, which derive from two disparities. First, the range in status and income between the poor and the wealthy is too wide. Second, various groups—racial, ethnic, and economic—hold some values that do not agree with those held by the majority of white, economically more secure Americans.

An important function of the school is to reduce the dissonance among value systems held by different ethnic subgroups. The social group that holds power in any society tends to deplore the speech, manners, and behavior of the less powerful or less affluent minorities. The school, therefore, tries to help children from ethnic minorities adopt an affirmative attitude toward the values of the majority culture. Although the schools are often criticized for co-opting minority students, their aim is to reduce discord in the wider society. At the same time, of course, the school works in the opposite direction as it attempts to accommodate to the values of the various groups, by teaching black history, for example, or celebrating Chanukah. The school thus walks a tightrope between acknowledging the vitality and legitimacy of the beliefs of its ethnic minorities and trying to expose all of America's children to a core set of attitudes.

Goal 5: To Narrow the Income Gap

In the United States the large disparity in incomes between the poor and the affluent is a grave problem. While many American families have two cars, two television sets, and savings in the bank, one-third do not have enough to eat. Philosophically this situation contradicts the national ideal of egalitarianism; in practical terms, it engenders conflict. Our nation knows it must find ways to enable more of the poor to improve their financial position and their status in society.

One purpose of American schools has always been to give less privileged classes the means to attain more status, power, and economic security. Part of our legend holds that in America all children have the opportunity to acquire skills that they can later market. The son of the shoemaker becomes an accountant, and his daughter becomes a doctor. As a result, the son of the shoemaker acquires new attitudes toward leisure and work and picks up new manners, speech patterns, and ways of dressing. He also takes on aspirations that would have seemed impossible to his father but appear realistic to him, partly because they are accepted as a matter of course by the men and women who have become his friends.

Education alone cannot eradicate all poverty, as critics of the legend have always surmised and as Christopher Jencks documents in his book *Inequality* (1972). Nevertheless, education has helped a proportion of children from poor families rise in society. Stated simply, the schools are only one place, although perhaps the best, where disadvantaged boys and girls can learn skills, personality traits, and attitudes that will allow them to attain a better financial position and more dignity, status, and power than their parents possessed.

In the middle of the nineteenth century when the communities in the eastern United States were beginning to think about public education and establishing high schools, one of the major beliefs held by the upper-middle-class families in power was that the schools would unite the working and middle class by exposing the children of all social classes to the same value system. One nineteenth-century American, Joseph White, wrote:

The children of the rich and the poor, the honored and the unknown, meet together on common ground. Their pursuits, their aims and aspirations are one ... they meet each other as they are to meet in the broader fields of life before them ... thus, and only thus, can the rising generation be best prepared for the duties and responsibilities of citizenry in a free commonwealth. (quoted in Katz, 1968, pp. 44–45)

Goal 6: To Create an Awareness of Group Culture

As we have indicated, one purpose of education is to teach children about their cultural heritage. In China children learn about the errors in Confucian philosophy. The early American Puritan schools, built by European men and women who felt cut off from the English way of life that had nurtured them, tried to provide the children with an awareness of their parents' cultural origins.

Since that time many American schools have been started with the same intent. Roman Catholic families have maintained parochial schools to emphasize spiritual values and provide ecclesiastical instruction, as well as to teach standard academic skills. In 1900 only about 8 percent of American elementary- and secondary-school children were not enrolled in public school. Major efforts by religious groups nearly doubled the proportion to 15 percent by the 1960s, though it has since declined to about 10 percent (Butts, 1973). Catholics, Protestants, and Jews have all provided religious schooling after public-school hours, so that their children can meet with religious leaders and other children of the same faith. As well as studying theology, the children learn and share the religious group's customs and values (and, in the case of Jews, the Hebrew language).

Inevitably, the public schools' emphasis on white, European Christian culture—its history, music, art, philosophy—contributes to social tensions in our society. The history of England is taught more often than the history of Mexico or Ghana. Eighth-grade orchestras play Beethoven, not Kenyan tribal music; literature classes read Shakespeare and Dickens, and art classes study Rembrandt and Picasso. Although these are not unreasonable choices for a country largely composed of white Christians of European descent, a child recently immigrated from Puerto Rico may have a difficult time identifying with an unfamiliar cultural heritage.

All children need to believe that they and their families have a rich and valued heritage. This has often been difficult for black and Spanish-speaking children since the study of their history has been preempted by the strength of the traditional western European saga.

Minority-group families are asking the schools to respond to this important need, and the result has been new manifestations of the old theme of cultural awareness. In black communities children learn about black history and the common suffering of their group, with the aim of reinforcing black values, language, idioms, attitudes, and hopes. In Boston's Highland Park Free School, where 98 percent of the children are black, the day begins with the students reciting the school's principles in Swahili: *umoja* (unity), *nia* (purpose), *kuumba* (creativity),

Figure 1–4
Young American students interested in establishing ties with their ethnic pasts may meet in community classes to study the language, history, and customs of their ancestors' countries.

and *imani* (faith). To further emphasize their sense of blackness, the children in the upper school are divided into four African tribes: Manikya, Kurumba, Fulani, and Bomitaba ("Schools with a Difference," 1973).

Other minority groups are showing an increasing interest in developing an ethnic cultural awareness. Also in Boston, classes in Latvian, Polish, Lithuanian, Greek, Armenian, Portuguese, and Italian communities are teaching languages and organizing trips abroad so that students can visit the countries of their ancestors (see Figure 1–4). Several public high schools have also begun teaching ethnic languages in response to demands from the community. Polish is being taught in some parts of the Pennsylvania coal-mining region. Teachers attribute the rebirth of cultural awareness to the fact that young people, with more chance to travel overseas and visit their ancestors' countries, are less willing to blend completely into the melting pot; they prefer to establish an ethnic identity (White, 1973).

The School as a Battleground: Current Disputes

Which Goals Are Primary?

American society has many needs and the schools, therefore, face many tasks: to teach technical skills and knowledge, inculcate and strengthen certain personality traits and values, permit self-actualization, achieve social harmony, narrow the income gap, and create a greater awareness of ethnic history and culture among America's minority groups. But there is more disagreement in America than in China as to which national goals are to be given priority.

Most middle-class Americans would award first place to a curriculum that helps their children to actualize special talents and teaches reading, science, mathematics, and composition. But some blacks and Mexican-Americans would order the priorities in a different way. A course of study that informs black children of their cultural heritage is a primary goal for many black families. Moreover, lower-class families are generally eager to have their children learn useful skills that will help them earn a living and gain a higher position in society than their families hold; they are less concerned with permitting the child to find and develop a special talent. In their view self-actualization is a luxury that they and their children cannot afford.

In American society disagreements exist about the relative importance of different values. Schools are often the scene of struggles

Conflict between the self-actualizing goals of a privileged parent and the skills-oriented goals of a less privileged one are apparent in PTA meetings of any school that includes both kinds of families. Concerned about too much pressure on her child and fearing that it may harm his emotional development, a privileged parent can be heard arguing in favor of more flexibility and less preoccupation with grades:

> "Sometimes I think this classroom is as bad as the one I was in when I was seven. All those desks lined up in rows, everyone reading at the same time, the teacher constantly telling the children to be quiet and pay attention. That's not what's really important in school. I want my child to have a nice experience. What I'd like to see is a room that's much looser, much freer. I know a school where the kids move around choosing what they're interested in and working on that until they've had enough and then going on to something else. The teacher is more of a friend. They use her like a resource, going to her and asking for help or advice."

A working-class parent, fearing that his child's cognitive growth may lose out in such a setting and that her school years may not produce the skills and abilities she'll need to get a good job, may strongly disagree:

> "Hold on—that may be what you want for your child, but it's certainly not what I want for mine. Our kids are really starting to take hold in class, and now you say you want to change all the rules. How can you say reading isn't important? My child is buckling down, these days, and working hard on the graded reader. As for wandering around from table to table, picking at what they want . . . I can see how well that would work out—she'd never stop wandering! Besides, she has plenty of friends. What she needs here is a teacher. And I mean a good teacher, somebody who takes no nonsense."

between contending groups. Being such conservative institutions schools are better able to mirror these conflicts than to resolve them. Currently, schools reflect three important ideological struggles being waged in American thought: the desire for assimilation; attitude toward obedience; and attitude toward stress and anxiety.

Desire for Assimilation

In contemporary America the public school system is again being asked to perform a task of assimilation. As we have seen, during the European immigrations the school was viewed as one of the chief mechanisms for socializing young children of European parents and turning them into adults who saw themselves—and were seen—as Americans. Today blacks and Chicanos in America are in a position somewhat analogous to that of the early European immigrants, even though the blacks have been here for many generations.

The white majority believes that the country will prosper optimally if ethnic minorities assimilate and adopt mainstream values, language styles, and customs. In the hope of achieving a more tolerant and harmonious society, the nation has decided—through the courts—that white and black children must attend integrated schools; busing is seen as one way to accomplish this. The traditional American ideal of the neighborhood school, while still strong, is being challenged by the national ideals of egalitarianism and social harmony.

However, assimilation does not go unopposed. Many black and Spanish-speaking families want their children to retain ties with their specific ethnic culture. Further, many Spanish-speaking children enter the school system with little English. Often their parents insist that primary-grade teachers speak fluent Spanish and know the cultural heritage and personality dispositions that Mexican and Puerto Rican children learn during their first six years in the family setting. In some places ethnic minority groups want to be given control of their schools, a request that raises fears among parents and educators who are afraid that such decentralization and local autonomy will lead to uneven standards of quality in the nation's schools.

Furthermore, the rocky history of school integration reveals that the middle-class majority is ambivalent about this goal. Some parents believe strongly enough in its worth that they will sacrifice other considerations. Some middle-class families would prefer to see their children grow up in a socially mixed school where they encounter heterogeneous attitudes and opinions, but they have reservations about how well their children will learn in such a situation. Still others, openly or in private, fear the "polluting" influence of unfamiliar customs in language, dress, and behavior and fear still more the erosion

of traditional attitudes, such as respect for authority, appreciation of the worth of school tasks, and optimistic attitudes about success in adult vocations.

As the preoccupations of a society change, so do its practices and the advice it welcomes. In 1836 Jacob Abbott, the Doctor Spock of his time, told American parents, "Keep children as much as possible by themselves—away from evil influence—separate, alone. Keep them from bad company. We may go much farther and almost say, keep them from company good or bad" (Abbott, 1836, p. 297). Today his advice seems insular and obsolete. Nevertheless, the current conflict over busing to achieve integration reminds us that now, as in 1836, parents worry about the consequences of their children interacting with peers who they believe hold values different from their own.

Attitude toward Obedience

From Puritan times to the present Americans have believed that children should be obedient to their parents and teachers. Obedience to authority was one of the most important character traits children could possess; regardless of how well they were doing in reading, writing, or arithmetic, they could be discharged from school for disobedience alone. Educators, physicians, public leaders, and essayists told teachers and parents in colonial America that they should train children in exact obedience to themselves and break them of their own will (Baxter, 1673). One hundred years ago most books on conduct for children

expressed the same theme. Adults would find fulfillment by accepting the established truths of morality and religion. But they could reach that goal only if, as children, they had been obedient to their parents and loved them (Wishy, 1968).

During the last ten or fifteen years, however, members of our society have become gradually less impressed by the legitimacy of adult authority. Young people rebel against their parents and professors and are encouraged by new psychological movements that emphasize that each person must construct his or her own principles of morality and answer only to his or her conscience. This view has begun to spread into the philosophy of some public schools, especially in middle-class neighborhoods on the east and west coasts. Although still a minority opinion in elementary schools, this new value raises questions about a child's unthinking obedience to authority and explores the merits of having the child "make decisions for himself." In the next chapter we will consider this issue in the context of American social and moral change. During the next twenty years the debate about obedience to authority is likely to be one of the major sources of tension in the value system of our schools and our society.

Figure 1-5
Artists, like other people, are concerned about the depersonalization of human life in our highly technological culture. *Wheel Man* (1965) is a sculpture in bronze, silicone, and silicone lacquer by Ernest Trova.

Attitude toward Stress and Anxiety

Another contemporary node of debate among educators concerns the child's proper emotional state in school. Two hundred years ago parents and schoolmasters agreed that the child should fear authority, for such anxiety was believed to facilitate obedience. But there has been a conspicuous change in this attitude; it has been superseded by a concern for the child's happiness. Today, partly as a result of the popularization of psychoanalytic theory, some families and teachers believe that anxiety is "bad" for children. It is assumed that fear—even mild fear—stifles creativity and leads to a restricted emotional life. One reaction to this view leads to minimal homework and examination pressures. Parents with a different attitude counter that such practices lead to student apathy and less efficient mastery of difficult school material. The pursuit of tranquility does not coexist comfortably with the national preoccupation with personal success, and youthful rebellions in the recent past were fueled, in part, by concern over this conflict (see Figure 1-5).

Impact of Conflict on Education

Struggles over assimilation, obedience, and happiness generate conflicts that show up at many levels. Administrators and teachers disagree about curricula and methods of grouping; parents provide an active—and critical—voice advocating changes in grading procedures and classroom atmosphere. There is greater discussion than ever over who controls the schools and who manages education in America. Parents, teachers, administrators, and educational critics debate spheres of influence: most parents are relieved that they do not have to teach the basics of chemistry to their children, yet they may be offended that the school presumes to teach their offspring the basics of sexuality.

Unlike people in some other societies, Americans believe that freedom of choice must be maintained. While struggles such as those we have discussed may cause dissension and unrest, they should not be viewed with dismay but seen instead as signs of health and vitality. Sparta, after all, had few open conflicts: the single-value system worked effectively for a while but contained so few options that when human nature rebelled at such a martial life, the nation was unable to make an adjustment and move in a new direction.

In this respect, the United States may be seen as strong and resourceful. Our situation allows for great flexibility: though the process of democracy is imperfect and certainly unwieldy, it allows people to implement productive new programs and take progressive turns as they attempt to bring their society closer to their national ideals. As the ties between the school and society, which are always strong, become more clearly recognized, it promises to be a challenging time for all the people who are interested in what the next generation of citizens will be like—most challenging, perhaps, for the teachers.

Summary

The goals of education vary, since each society decides what skills and character traits its citizens need. In studying ancient Sparta, Athenian Greece, and early Rome, we can see how the schools trained very different kinds of citizens. Today, in Tanzania, China, and Israel, educational goals again serve the needs of the country. They also provide a basis for comparison with the situation in contemporary America.

The United States values independence, personal achievement, and competition; its educational system appears to have six goals: to teach technical skills and knowledge, to inculcate specific values and promote certain personality traits, to actualize the talents of the child, to achieve social harmony, to narrow the income gap, and to create an awareness of group culture. Since there are national conflicts over which are the most important goals in American life, it is not surprising that the schools reflect these disagreements. In addition, as the needs of society shift, the demands on the schools change. Therefore, the schools are often battlegrounds for ideological struggles.

Currently, three main struggles are reflected in the schools: the desire to assimilate ethnic and class groups to a common set of values; the attitude toward children's obedience; and the attitude regarding stress and anxiety. Parents, administrators, teachers, and the students themselves are involved in these controversies in American education. Although they cause unrest, controversies such as these can be viewed as signs of health and vitality. America's national values require an atmosphere of choice. With many possible directions to choose from, it seems likely that our schools will follow more than one direction at a time. There is reason to hope that the choices will be made on the basis of what will best serve the country's needs.

Projects

1 Find five people each of whom attended high school in a different decade (one in the 1930s, one in the 1940s, and so forth). By talking with these people, determine how the curricula of their high schools was shaped by the political and social issues and the technological advances of their time.

2 Interview a military career person, a politician, and a farmer to determine whether the educations they received guided them into their fields and/or prepared them for these careers. Look for any parallels between their educational experiences and those a Spartan, an Athenian, and a Roman might have had.

3 Using the Tanzanian primer as a model, design some illustrations (or shoot and print some photographs) that could be appropriate visual aids for a similar primer in this country. What problems would you expect to encounter in trying to carry out this assignment?

4 Interview your parents and grandparents to discover whether those generations have differed in terms of upward mobility. What are your career goals? How do they differ from the goals of the last two generations of your family? Why?

5 Devise a project for six of your classmates; for three, plan it so they work competitively; for the other three, contrive the project so that they work cooperatively.

6 Make a list of the skills that you have learned in school, beginning with reading. Include academic skills, such as reading a computer printout or conjugating a French verb, and practical skills, such as woodworking and auto repair. If your schooling stopped this week, which skills—in each group—would you find useful? Which abilities will you find most useful if your education continues for several more years?

Recommended Reading

Castle, E. B. *Ancient education and today*. Harmondsworth: Penguin Books, 1961. A lively summary of the educational goals of ancient Sparta, Athens, Rome, and Judea, showing the relation between the values of the culture and the skills promotoed in the schools.

Kagan, J., and Moss, H. A. *Birth to maturity*. New York: John Wiley, 1962. A report on the results of a longitudinal study of a large number of adults who had been followed closely since infancy, showing that the stability of personality traits is very much a function of their degree of congruence with the sex-role standards of the society. Thus for this group of midwestern Americans, passivity, which was more appropriate for females than for males, was more stable from early childhood through adulthood for women than for men, while aggression, which has the opposite profile, was more stable for the males.

Kessen, W. (Ed.). *Childhood in China*. New Haven, Conn.: Yale University Press, 1975. A good description of the family, the schools, and the learning of language in the People's Republic of China, written by a group of child and educational psychologists who visited the country in 1973. Its portrayal of the homogeneity and conformity in the Chinese school system helps the reader appreciate the relation between the politics of a country and its educational policies.

Wishy, B. *The child and the republic*. Philadelphia: University of Pennsylvania Press, 1968. A readable history of attitudes toward the child in the United States from 1830 to 1900. It describes the shift from an emphasis on obedience to elders prior to the Civil War to the granting of much more independence to the child, and then, after the 1960s, to an emphasis on achievement, performance, independence, and autonomy, due, in part, to increased industrialization.

the role of the school in socializing personality and values

2

Children go to school for six hours a day. Each day they spend about two hours mastering the indispensable skills needed for life in American society—learning to read, write, and comprehend written material; to add, subtract, and multiply; and to present ideas, in good English sentences, written or oral. The remainder of their class time is spent studying history, geography, social studies, and science. Several times a week they attend an art or music class, and they participate in athletics. These are the explicit activities of the school.

But behind the formal instruction in composition, history, or science, there is a hidden curriculum. The categories on report cards labeled "conduct," "effort," and "work habits" only hint at the implicit function of the school, which is to socialize the child and, with the help of family and society, foster certain personality characteristics. Schools attempt to teach each pupil the values, motives, and character traits our society believes each citizen should possess. If you look carefully at any school, you can see that the personality traits and values being encouraged (often indirectly) reflect, in combination, the values of the nation, of the parents in the local community, and of the particular teachers in the school. They are expressed in simple practices usually taken for granted (for example, in American schools bathrooms are segregated by sex, in Israel they are not) or in traditional school festivities (such as graduation ceremonies where the important prizes go to students with the highest scholastic averages). They are part of the school's mission—teaching children to grow up American.

Major Changes in American Values since 1800

While a child's alphabet that begins "A is for Aardvark . . ." may refer to an animal unfamiliar to most American children, it is hardly more remote than the 1800 alphabet that began, "In Adam's Fall, We sinned all." In our current secular society such an association of ideas would puzzle American children, even those whose families are religious or attend church regularly. But a study of the primers of the early 1800s reveals that Christian virtue and obedience to parents were the central values nineteenth-century Americans wanted their children to acquire (see Figure 2-1). In fact, a primary reason for teaching children to read was to enable them to read the Bible.

The shift from religious to secular values occurred gradually over the past 175 years. With the rise of the Industrial Revolution, a conflict developed between the preeminence of the virtues of loyalty and obedience to God and family and the importance of success. In the volatile years before the Civil War economic and social changes forged

Figure 2-1

An alphabet from a Boston primer published about 1800 includes religious and secular jingles. In addition to teaching the letters of the alphabet, it encourages attention to the Bible ("Thy Life to mend, God's Book attend") and warns against laziness ("The idle Fool, is whipt at School"). (Johnson, 1904)

In Adam's Fall
We finned all.

Thy Life to mend,
God's Book attend.

The Cat doth play,
And after flay.

A Dog will bite
A Thief at Night.

The Eagle's Flight
Is out of Sight.

The idle Fool
Is whipt at School

As runs the Glafs,
Man's life doth pafs.

My Book and Heart
Shall never part.

Job feels the Rod,
Yet bleffes God.

Proud Korah'stroop
Was fwallow'd up.

The Lion bold
The Lamb doth
hold.

The Moon gives light
In Time of Night.

a new set of American values. Factories, machinery, the telegraph, steamboats, and railroads changed the fundamental character of American life, once based primarily on agriculture. People began to leave family farms to try their luck in the cities and towns where there were opportunities for making money. That migration brought about profound changes in American values.

Parents and schools became concerned with teaching children the skills and traits that would help them succeed in an urban, industrialized world. They emphasized individuality and self-reliance, characteristics that would enable the children to compete with strangers in the impersonal city. Activity and ambition were the goals that smiled out of the textbooks of the day. In a passage called "The Busy Bees" from the *Union Reader No. 2* (1861) by Charles W. Saunders, children are informed that in every hive, there is one large bee, which is called the queen and also some idle bees, that do not work; these are called drones. The working bees do not allow the drones to live. They sting them to death, and then drag them out of the hive. The children are then exhorted not to be idle, like the lazy drones, but to be like the busy bee that lays up a store of food against the time of need.

This change in emphasis was not unique to nineteenth-century America. The pattern occurs whenever young adults leave small agricultural villages and move to the cities to work. In the village, everyone is known and the family must work together under the direction of the parents in order to survive. The watchfulness of a small community encourages people to control impulses toward selfishness, egoism, stealing, and dishonesty. Parents must curb their children's asocial behavior or neighbors will gossip. Moreover, no one family can gain too much wealth or others in the village will be envious. But in the city, each person is more anonymous, and individual achievement and initiative in exercising freedom of choice are essential for successful adaptation. Inevitably these traits take precedence over dependence on and obedience to parents. This change in values, which began in the eighteenth century in Europe and is just now occurring in many rural areas of the new states of Africa and parts of Latin America, can be seen today in the still predominantly rural country of Brazil. A scientist compared the values and practices of two kinds of Brazilian families: those who had remained in the traditional culture of the countryside and those who had left the same area to make their way in the large industrial city of São Paulo. Compared to those in the country, the families who had lived in São Paulo for six or seven years were more appreciative and rewarding of individual achievement in their children (Rosen, 1973).

However universal this pattern may be, during the mid nineteenth century Americans had difficulty recognizing that their two favorite values might be incompatible, and they tried valiantly to equate moral

The Knight and the Scribe

Each society has an educational ideal that it tries to meet. For many centuries the ideal in Western society has had a touch of elitism about it. In the Middle Ages the ideal was personified by the *knight*, who exhibited bravery, skill at fighting, and gentlemanly manners while attaining prestige in the community. The knight's achievements were neither specialized nor intellectual but involved his total personality. According to the ideal he was expected to be physically strong, socially cultured, and morally sound but not expected to perfect his intelligence or acquire specialized knowledge. But as European cities grew and commerce expanded, a need for a new ideal developed. Sixteenth- and seventeenth-century Europe needed fewer courageous knights and more adults with intellectual skills: people who could speak different languages, negotiate with merchants in distant cities, and master the beginning technology involving deeds, contracts, ships, and printing presses. The profession of *scribe* began to emerge. Literacy, not physical strength, was his major talent. His literacy gave him status over peasants but not yet over knights. For several centuries, therefore, two ideals coexisted in Western society: the man of the world—brave, bold, cultured, strong, wealthy—and the man of the book—literate, learned, technically skilled. By the twentieth century, however, the world of commerce and politics had become so technical that even future men and women of the world automatically attended colleges and universities to listen to the modern counterpart of the seventeenth-century scribes.

Today, literacy, finely honed intellectual skills and a rich repertoire of technical knowledge are recognized as signs of status and prestige and are rewarded at the highest level by Nobel and Pulitzer prizes. New knowledge, techniques, and skills are vital if society is to combat its most serious crises—economic depression, energy shortage, overpopulation, inadequate food production, epidemic diseases, and environmental destruction. As a result, economists, physicists, geologists, chemists, sociologists, lawyers, and doctors have become the "knights" of society, and many talented young people who desire challenge choose these vocations. But the ideal grew out of society's needs; it was not the result of decisions by scholars. "Any satisfactory educational ideal for our own time must be appropriate to our kind of society and government" (Bouwsma, 1975, p. 211).

virtue with individual success (Yudkin, 1971). The consequences of that conflict have persisted to our day. The post–Civil War's answer, an adaptation of an earlier Calvinism adopted, ironically, by non-Calvinists, held that people who were virtuous became successful. In a series of popular stories of the nineteenth century, for example, the hero, a nine-year-old boy named Rollo, was self-reliant, suppressed his fears, respected authority, and always chose the morally correct act. His endeavors ended in success. "The great and constant lesson of the Rollo series is that merit lies in moral fitness and righteousness. Be good and all will be granted, be bad and you lose both the world and heaven" (Wishy, 1968, p. 61).

If success meant wealth, the argument continued, and if some people were poor (and, by definition, not successful), then their poverty was probably due to the fact that they were not virtuous. Some Americans still adhere to that belief. However, during the 1960s many members of the middle-class majority became persuaded that economic and social forces, which included racial discrimination in housing, schools, and employment, had created conditions that prevented many of the poor from rising from their position. These conditions adversely affected the motivations and expectations of success among poor parents, and they communicated these feelings to their children. The motivational problems of children from poor families, which are still not fully understood, will be discussed in detail in Chapter 12.

In addition to preoccupation with individual achievement, industriousness, and competition, another value emerged in the

Figure 2–2
A survey of textbooks from 1800 to 1952 showed a decline in themes of moral teaching and an increase in plots and themes about affiliation (close personal relationship). These changes reflect an important shift in emphasis in American values during the last century and a half. (After deCharms and Moeller, 1962)

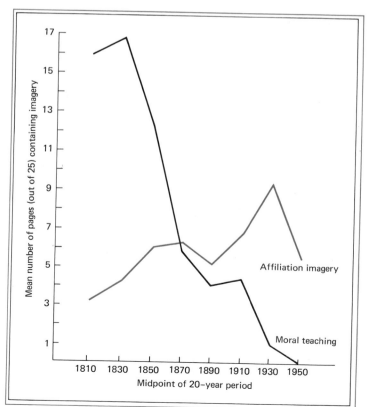

twentieth century—the importance of popularity and facility at interpersonal relationships. Sociality became a prerequisite for success. Whereas ambitious Americans had formerly moved from the country to industrial centers in the city, they now migrated many times, from one community to another, relocating in pursuit of challenge, wealth, and status. These upwardly mobile Americans needed new social skills in order to adjust periodically to new sets of strangers.

This shift in values can be discerned in a survey of textbooks from 1800 to 1952, which revealed a rise in achievement plots and themes from 1800 to 1900, followed by a decline. Moreover, themes involving close, affiliative relationships increased over this period (deCharmes and Moeller, 1962). This shift from morality to affiliation is illustrated in the graph in Figure 2-2.

Conflicts over the proper balance among achievement, friendship, and Christian morality are still apparent in the ways schools teach children to become American. In this chapter, we will consider the values Americans want their children to acquire and note where the current shifts appear to be taking place.

Primary Values Favored in Contemporary United States

Although no unanimous agreement on values exists among the people in one city or among the many regions of the country, it is possible to suggest some few personality traits and abstract values that most Americans hold in high regard and that they want to see inculcated in their children. We have identified eight themes that appear to pervade our culture: obedience to authority, autonomy and individuality, importance of language skills, competitive attitudes, group affiliation and social communication, emotional spontaneity, egalitarianism, and appropriate sex roles. Let us examine these one at a time.

Obedience to Authority

Like most societies, America believes in the wisdom of authority and age; it is convinced that if people are not obedient to older authority, society will disintegrate. Young people have always been expected to obey their parents, the police at the street crossing, their schoolteachers, and, eventually, their drill sergeants in the army and their employers. An early nineteenth-century book, *The Teacher's Assistant in English Composition*, states the assumption bluntly:

It is a very dangerous mistake to imagine that the mind can be
cultivated and the manners formed on any principle, but that of
submission to teachers and superiors; any other method is radically
absurd and unnatural; it is contrary to the rational order which does
and must prevail in all other cases of the same kind. The raw recruit
learns his exercise on the authority of the officer, because he knows
nothing of it till he comes into action. (Walker, 1810, p. 159)

As we indicated at the end of Chapter 1, the issue of obedience to
authority is one of the most profound moral questions in contemporary
America. A convergence of trends and events in the 1960s—the Viet
Nam war, erosion of the unity and stability of the family, wide distrust
of the government, and scepticism about traditional values—turned
historical authority-baiting into something more blatant. Draft resisters
burned their draft cards in public ceremonies; workers went out on
wildcat strikes against the orders of their union leaders; inmates
revolted against prison authorities; and students demonstrated against
the monolithic structure of college administrations. The concept of a
strong authority was not overturned, but it did become tainted.

The issue is apparent today and is sharply visible in schools. Both
educators and parents ask, "How obedient to the teacher should
children be?" Unquestionably, the all-powerful Puritan schoolmaster
has been consigned to historical caricature. Some schools, found mostly
in comfortable suburbs, encourage less submission to authority and
permit greater autonomy for the pupils. The moral education
movement, led by Lawrence Kohlberg of Harvard University,
encourages children to carve out their own set of moral principles and
be true to them, even though occasionally these principles may lead
them to disobey authority. We will consider the moral education
movement more thoroughly at the end of this chapter.

Autonomy and Individuality

Students in America are the spiritual heirs of the ancient Athenian
students, who were brought up to value *arete*—the concept of personal
excellence and outstanding performance. The favorite hero in
American mythology is the lone individual who runs ahead of the pack
and achieves success or glory through bravery and skill: the cowboy
who fights the elements and the outlaws in a show of individual
strength; the entrepreneur, such as Andrew Carnegie, who is born poor
but achieves success and wealth through ingenuity and hard work. The
Horatio Alger legend of the poor boy who makes good continues to be
an American credo. Americans commonly assume that each child can
work his or her way to the top—even as far as the presidency.
"Anybody can grow up to be president" is a notion that persists, even

in the face of evidence that the president has never been black, Jewish, female, or until the 1960s, Catholic.

The function of the school is to promote attitudes and abilities that will help the child achieve personal success. Thus American schools emphasize individuality, autonomous self-development, solitary decision making, and competition.

Each child and adolescent is expected to work alone and perfect his or her own set of language, mathematical, writing, scientific, and physical skills. American schools emphasize individual assignments and individual term papers and are reluctant to encourage or permit cooperative products. The notion that the child should learn his or her skills in a cooperative context would be rejected by most Americans. Moreover, the vocations with the highest status often require solitary judgments: surgeons, lawyers, architects, judges, and scientists are usually pictured as making independent, not cooperative, decisions, despite the fact that group effort is often involved in these vocations. Such an attitude is reasonable in our society, though a little less appropriate in others. In rural subsistence-farming communities, for example, it is expected that children will work the land with their fathers. The narrow range of skills they will need for adulthood has been identified and that is what they learn.

Reverence for individual excellence is associated with originality. Americans place a premium on the invention of new products and techniques because American preeminence in science and technology—our status and wealth as a nation—is due, in part, to our creative engineers, scientists, and businesspeople. Many Americans, when they first hear how the Chinese schools de-emphasize original work, assume that China will be hurt seriously by such an educational program.

Unlike Chinese students, American children are urged to decide issues for themselves, according to their own needs, talents, and personalities. The feast of extracurricular activities that is offered in most schools provides children with a chance to choose which interests to pursue. A child from a large family may want to spend after-school hours in an art workshop, where she can paint or throw clay by herself. An only child may be drawn to the teamwork involved in basketball and welcome a chance to participate in a group venture. Drama class may be a natural outlet for a histrionic ten-year-old—or for a shy, retiring child who is self-conscious in the classroom but feels refreshingly free on the auditorium stage.

In some schools the chance to choose extends to the classroom, where children decide what subject to work on and for how long. Originality and individual choice are celebrated with increasing frequency as we recognize that the adaptive traits of flexibility and openness to new ideas are essential in modern America. Unlike isolated villages in Latin America or Africa where the same beliefs prevail for generations, basic values change often in America, sometimes over a period as short as ten years. In order to avoid excessive bitterness or confusion, children and adults must at least be receptive to these ideas.

School contributes to the development of autonomy simply by its presence, for it provides an alternate framework for a child's education. Obviously, many skills learned in class could be learned at home. In the past, both in our country and in others, children have been taught at home by parents or tutors. Sending children to school is not just a more efficient way of teaching them (it may even be less efficient)—it represents the belief that children must learn how to adjust away from parental supervision. School takes them out of their families for six hours a day and gives them the experience of learning skills and attitudes from people other than their parents. In addition, some schools are openly experimenting with formal lessons in values that contribute to individual autonomy.

Individuality and the conditions that promoted it have been present in America since colonial days. But it was not until the second half of the nineteenth century that this value was pushed to the foreground. Then, the Industrial Revolution and the growth of entrepreneurial ventures accelerated the demand for highly specialized abilities. On the heels of these events, major personality theorists—Jung, Freud, Adler,

Maslow, and Erikson—maintained that individual mastery and the careful development of a unique and differentiated sense of self—an identity—were universal aspects of growth. These theorists, who were themselves products of the Western tradition, recognized which personal attributes were associated with successful adaptation in the West, and they assumed that the optimal pattern of development in this society was optimal for all human groups—now as well as in the past.

But it is not obvious that autonomous self-actualization is a universal rule of development or universally desirable. In parts of Africa, tribal traditions emphasize a collective effort rather than individual self-interest; and in modern China, as we have seen, the adolescent who contributes most to the commune is regarded as valuable and successful, not the youth who maximizes his or her own abilities.

Language Skills: The American Password

There are many talents a child can exercise—talents in athletics, singing, art, gymnastics, chess, memory, perception, mathematics. But Americans emphasize language skills—reading, composition, effective speaking—above most others. They respect language skills as other cultures have praised height, physical strength, hunting ability or possession by a benevolent spirit. The stress on language ability begins early, with the kindergarten fixture called "show and tell." And it continues through high school graduation ceremonies, when speeches by the most articulate students (not a display of art work or a wrestling match) are presented as the highlight of the celebration.

The effective production and comprehension of the written and spoken word are preeminent talents in our culture. In many vocations, especially professional ones, mastery of the necessary technical skills requires the ability to read and comprehend large amounts of information quickly and accurately. But the American preoccupation with language skills involves more than literacy. It implies an aspect of personality as well: a facility with spoken words and a psychological readiness to converse with acquaintances, future employers, and opponents at community meetings.

We can trace the importance of language skills back to the Sophists, the pragmatic Greek teachers who taught that what you believed or how you lived mattered less than the words you used in talking about it. Oral persuasion is equally vital today. In most white-collar jobs, the effective use of language is an important determinant of how much power and status accrue to the job holder. Architects and engineers have to be able to explain and defend their projects to boards of directors and city planning commissions. Lawyers need to be articulate with juries and with their clients. Politicians need to be more than

articulate—it helps if they are silver-tongued. Scientists rarely get ahead solely through their skill in the laboratory; they must inform fellow scientists of their work through preparation of papers and oral presentations at scientific conventions. Professors need to express their ideas and interpretations clearly and effectively, not only to students, but to colleagues and college administrators as well. Men and women in business must be skillful in presenting new ideas, products, and services to others. It seems hard to believe, but if you take a thousand ten-year-olds off the street and spend only fifteen minutes administering to each one a vocabulary quiz taken from one of the standard intelligence tests, the scores obtained by those children would predict their vocational status twenty years later (Kagan and Moss, 1962). The children with high scores can be expected to have more challenging, higher paying jobs as adults.

Our society's emphasis on language skills also operates in the processes that lead to higher education and promotion. The applicant's conversation during a college interview, the essay she writes on the application form and her statement of reasons for wanting to get into college all tap the degree and sophistication of her verbal ability.

The prominence of verbal skills in school, although consistent with American values, can lead to serious misclassification of pupils' general abilities. In many ways our culture and our schools regard children and adults who are quiet or who do not speak effectively as if they were

Figure 2-3
The effect of competition on test performance was demonstrated in an experiment in which fifth-grade children were divided into three groups and then given a vocabulary test. The two groups that competed for a reward—one to win candy and the other to be the leaders in a game—performed better than the group that was not competing for any reward. (After Clifford, 1972)

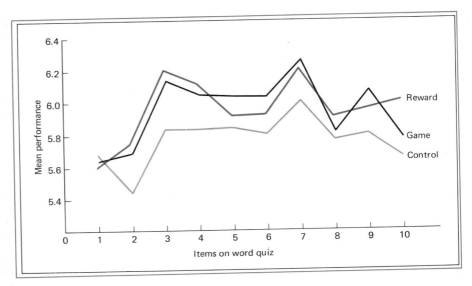

weak, ill, or crippled. Albert Einstein's early history reveals that he spoke late and had extraordinary difficulty learning to read (Hoffman, 1972). Yet he was one of the world's greatest physicists, with rare and remarkable intellectual powers. If Einstein were growing up in Chicago today, he might be placed in a class of learning disabled children because of his difficulties in learning to read.

Competitive Attitudes

Competitive attitudes are promoted in the service of training for success. Gold stars on charts depicting progress (both intellectual and behavioral), spelling contests, and relay races in gym testify to the schools' belief that competition is constructive and healthy. Raised with competition in as well as outside school, children become accustomed to it and even thrive on it. The following example is instructive: fifth- and sixth-grade children in thirty-six classrooms were given arithmetic problems. On tests of problems that required speed and accuracy rather than problem-solving reasoning, pupils performed better in an atmosphere of competition. The specific prize made no significant difference: a group competing to win candy performed about the same as a group competing to be the leaders in a game (Clifford, Cleary, and Walster, 1972). In a similar study of competition (Clifford, 1972), vocabulary tests were administered to three groups of fifth-graders. The first group received only corrections on its papers. The second group received Life Savers as a reward. The third group incorporated the quiz into a game board and moved colored markers as the tests proceeded.

The students in groups two and three, playing competitively for rewards, showed a somewhat better performance than group one and a substantially higher interest in the tests (see Figure 2–3).

Since families of different social classes and ethnic groups encourage competitive attitudes to differing degrees, not all children enter school with the same enthusiasm or preparation for competition. By the time they reach kindergarten, for instance, four-year-old white

Figure 2–4
Differences in cooperative attitudes between blacks and whites were shown when six- and seven-year-old children played a game on the Madsen Cooperation Board (shown here). They were instructed, "We are going to play a game now in which you can win prizes. You begin when I say 'go.' If the pen crosses this target spot [experimenter points to one of the target spots] you both get a prize or if the pen crosses this target spot [he points to other spot] you both get a prize. Either target spot and you both get a prize. However, if the pen doesn't cross either spot before I say 'stop,' then no one gets a prize. Are there any questions? Okay, here are the first two prizes. Ready, go!" Working in pairs, black children demonstrated more cooperation and less competitiveness than white children. (After Richmond and Weiner, 1973)

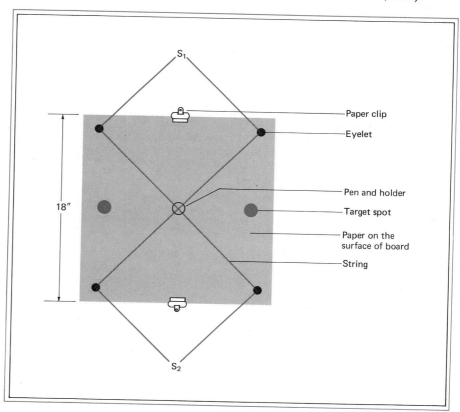

children of native-born parents have accepted competitive values more than have four-year-old Mexican-American children. In a study that compared children from both ethnic backgrounds, the children looked at pictures illustrating conflicts between social values (helpfulness, cooperation, concern for others, and sharing) and success values (competition, status, expertise seeking, and task completion). The inteviewer told an appropriate story and asked each child to indicate what the child in the story should do. The white children's answers expressed success values more often than those of the Mexican-American children (Wasserman, 1971). Similarly, six- and seven-year-old children played a game in which winning depended on cooperation. The game involved tracing a line on a board (see Figure 2-4). Black children working in pairs demonstrated more cooperation and less competitiveness than white children working in pairs. When the pairs consisted of a black child and a white child, the teams worked more cooperatively than the white pairs but less cooperatively than the black pairs (Richmond and Weiner, 1973).

Competition's place in the classroom is exemplified most graphically, perhaps, by the schools' attraction to the bell-shaped curve, a method of charting test results or final grades of an entire class (see Figure 2-5). Few teachers would be satisfied if all eighth-grade students received an A in American history: they would like to see a clear differentiation between their more and less competent history students, between their A students and C students. By charting grades on a curve

Figure 2-5
The normal probability or bell-shaped curve shows the proportion of cases that are found above and below the mean (0). While the test scores of an actual class do not fall into such an ideal and neat distribution, they can still be distributed in a curve that separates the proportion of the class that performs very well or very poorly and the segments of the class that perform moderately well or poorly.

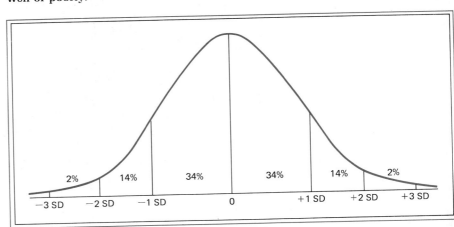

2%   14%   34%   34%   14%   2%

−3 SD   −2 SD   −1 SD   0   +1 SD   +2 SD   +3 SD

that is shaped like a bell, teachers guarantee that only some pupils will get an A, and only a few will get a D.

The teachers' partiality to the bell-shaped curve is not quixotic. It reflects a widely held American point of view. Many Americans believe that only a proportion of American adults can attain positions of high status, wealth, and exceptional competence. Some will have to be trash collectors, and some unemployed. This acceptance of *differential adaptation* to society is an outgrowth of Darwin's notion that some animals will be more successful at surviving the harsh challenge of nature than others. Among animals, differential success is attributed to basic biological differences—now known to be genetic—and, of course, luck. If a group of animals is caught in a freak flood, many will be drowned; no one can control these chance happenings. Those Americans who view society the way Darwinian biologists viewed the jungle believe that some children will grow up to be doctors, bankers, and scientists (rather than unskilled laborers) because of genetics and the child's luck in being born to economically secure parents. Indeed, in his recent book, *Inequality* (1972), Christopher Jencks concluded that in modern American success, defined in terms of wealth, is primarily controlled by intelligence (which he claimed is under partial genetic control) and luck. Although this conclusion has not been proved beyond doubt, it reflects a popular opinion. According to this belief, since only a small proportion of children can attain success, it is important to determine early who are most likely to do so. The fine differentiation our schools make in grading and scoring children from A+ to F is one way to separate the future leaders from the followers, the way predation, famine, and disease act to screen the fit from the less fit in the animal world.

Not all Americans agree that this is a valid view of society or a wise school practice. Neither the view nor the practice are inevitable. The People's Republic of China does not assume that some children must perform poorly. Rather, it assumes that, except for the few that are severely handicapped, all can learn to read and all can contribute to the society in a major way. The schools of modern China pay less attention to tests and grades because they do not feel the same need to distinguish the talented from the less talented.

Group Affiliation and Social Communication

While Americans continue to respect individualism, self-actualization, and competitiveness, our society also applauds traits of accommodation and sociability. The taciturn, staunchly independent farmer still exists from Vermont to Iowa, but he is no longer the prototype of an American citizen. Today our culture requires men and women who are able to reach out in a friendly way to the people around them, including strangers. Although friendliness has been a human virtue throughout history, it plays a more critical role in contemporary America because of the pace of change and the geographic mobility that is part of modern life.

Mobile citizens must have the skills that enable them to adjust to new situations, locations, and standards of behavior, dress, and language. Above all, they must have the ability to make new friends. To be sure, not all people move away from the community where they were brought up. But whereas before World War II it was common for families to live in one town all their lives, now forty or fifty million Americans live in towns where they have no long-term emotional ties, far away from the schools, churches, clubs, and friends to whom they developed childhood loyalties and with whom they identified. Many of them will move again and again.

In such a situation, the primary loyalties are to oneself and one's immediate family, and such feelings of loyalty continue as a powerful force. At the same time, it is impossible to live in a vacuum. Therefore, these families continue to plant bulbs that they know they will not stay to see in bloom and to make friends whom they know they will leave. There is no question that American mobility has changed the nature of friendship and loyalties. In *The Organization Man* (1956) William Whyte quotes an advertisement from a nursery catalogue:

Stock is transplanted in our nurseries from one to four times or more times. Each time, the longer, more easily damaged roots are reduced so that more small feeder roots develop near the stem. The more feeder roots, the more quickly the tree is established on your land. Also, the resulting compact mass of small feeder roots makes the tree easier to plant. (From 1954 catalogue of Musser Forests.) (p. 289)

Metaphorically, those are also the personality traits that schools, as well as families, attempt to inculcate in children: an openness to new situations, flexibility, and the capacity to make overtures of friendship on short acquaintance. To some observers, the pendulum has swung too far in this direction, giving rise to a national eagerness "to belong" at the expense of private and individual standards of morality and sincerity.

Emotional Spontaneity

Free and natural expression of one's feelings has been awarded an importance in recent years that would have been inconceivable to a nineteenth-century schoolmaster. In 1810 *The Teacher's Assistant in English Composition* warned about the folly of indulging the passion of anger:

> There never was a more absurd apology than that which is commonly made for passionate people that they are the best natured creatures in the world. It is true, when their anger is over, they are often heartily sorry for what they have done; but this is only defending them, by proving that they are not quite demons; and that though they are very absurd and injurious for a time they are not always so: but this will be found to be but a poor excuse, when we consider that, a moment's anger will often produce more mischief than whole years of good nature may be able to atone for. (Walker, 1810, p. 184)

During the early stages of America's history, the culture frowned on open, unrestrained displays of strong feeling. As the culture has moved away from a traditional and conservative stance to a highly fluid and mobile society, the quality of spontaneity has come to be esteemed. Excessive restraint and reserve, signs of respectability a hundred years ago, have become negative attributes. In the seventy-five years since Freud developed his theory of personality, Americans have grown to believe that children should be allowed to express some of their anger, resentment, and joy and to accept their sexual feelings, rather than feel compelled to suppress these emotions. This general belief has expanded to the view that children should enjoy their day at school and not be overly anxious about failure. Although no definitive scientific research shows that children learn history more effectively if they are free to express anger and exuberance, it is a growing conviction among many that children should not be frustrated, suppressed, or annoyed.

But spontaneity is not encouraged simply because it may lead to freer expressions of joy and less suppressed resentment. It is felt that children will be better adapted to our society if they are allowed to express their emotions; in short, they will develop personalities that will maximize their abilities to deal with people, move ahead in their jobs, have rewarding marriages, and cope with problems in the adult environment. The middle-class respect for spontaneity is not unanimous, however. How much spontaneity should be allowed in the classroom?

As the desire grows to see children enjoy their day at school, a new philosophy has developed that holds that children should be minimally afraid of authority. But the majority of teachers still value self-control and inhibition of feelings and think children are behaving in an immature way if they express too much anger, joy, or frustration. Teachers and parents alike are often concerned that the freedom to express feelings in the classroom may lead to loss of respect for the teacher (and parents are concerned that the teacher may lose respect for the child). The traditional view that children should be afraid of their teachers used fear as the school's main mechanism for insuring obedience. In the absence of a "proper respect for authority" (i.e., fear) both teachers and parents worry that the classroom atmosphere will disintegrate into chaos. We will consider the question of classroom atmosphere and management in Chapter 11.

Egalitarianism

Most Americans believe in egalitarianism: all citizens should be equal before the law, have equal access to economic opportunity, and be judged by their talents and products, not by their sex, race, ethnicity, or religion. That is one of the fundamental premises of American society. We believe status, wealth, and privilege should be awarded on the basis of hard work and ability. Moreover, higher status is only supposed to confer special satisfactions and an easier life; it should not make people morally superior to those with less status or entitle them to special legal privileges. The uneasiness some Americans feel over separating bright or retarded children from their average classmates, or segregating black and white children, stems from the fact that these practices violate our egalitarian ethic.

As we discussed in Chapter 1, the courts have ordered desegregation of schools and compulsory busing in order to move toward greater egalitarianism. Since these actions violate the personal liberties of families who do not want their children bused to schools across the city, the nation is experiencing substantial friction. These controversies over busing reflect the serious conflict between egalitarianism and individual freedom.

Appropriate Sex Roles

In the past our society, like most, believed that boys and girls should develop slightly different traits because they were biologically different and because they had different jobs to do. The practice of promoting different attributes in boys and girls is called *sex typing*. Sex typing begins at home during infancy and is continued in the schools. It was assumed that, ideally, boys would be handsome, emotionally cool and contained, courageous, and strong; girls would be passive, dependent, pretty, conforming, kind, emotional, expressive, and sociable. Even though these values have been changing rapidly, the pervasiveness of sex typing has undeniably affected children's behavior and influenced what they learned in school, how they behaved in the classroom, and how teachers reacted to them.

In the primary grades the school atmosphere can be called somewhat feminine. The teacher is usually a woman. Many behaviors

encouraged during these years—obedience, conformity, neatness, and order—are commonly viewed as feminine, since in our culture these attributes have been more easily acquired by girls. Boys tend to be more disruptive and disorderly. Hence, during the early years of school children tend to regard schoolwork as a more feminine than masculine activity.

In one study second- and third-grade children were taught different nonsense words to stand for maleness and femaleness. Then they were shown pictures of school-related objects, such as a blackboard, a page of arithmetic, a book, a school desk, and also some animals. Both the boys and the girls were more likely to label the school objects feminine than masculine. But the tendency diminished as the children became older (Kagan, 1964).

In the later grades more teachers are men, competition is even more openly encouraged, and a classification takes place concerning the academic material. Adolescents regard some courses of study (mathematics and the sciences especially) as subjects that can be used actively, have a practical purpose, and may have a concrete, instrumental effect in the world. Foreign languages, history, and the arts, on the other hand, are not seen as practical; they seem too abstract or speculative. Since a pragmatic, instrumental, and mechanical orientation to the world is central in the sex-role standard of males, adolescent boys may find themselves highly motivated to master the sciences but less highly motivated to pursue French or history, subjects that involve words rather than action.

At the same time, sex-role values work against girls in three ways: girls are ambivalent about entering into the competitive atmosphere in the classroom; they are less willing than boys to be conspicuous in their behavior and accomplishments; they encounter different teacher expectations in science and mathematics because the mythology holds that in these fields girls are less able than boys.

Older girls have a little less confidence than boys in their scholastic abilities, especially in science and mathematics. Years ago most able girls did not seek careers in "male" vocations. Today, of course, that is changing. One study analyzed changes in career plans occurring between the ninth grade and one year after high school among approximately seven thousand girls included in the Project Talent Data Bank. The study considered five career groups: natural sciences, professions, teaching, office work, and housewife. Brighter girls tended to change from initial careers in office work and as housewives to the natural sciences, professions, and teaching; those who shifted out of the career-oriented groups were scholastically less capable than those who maintained the same plans over time (Astin, 1968).

Let us now turn to the methods schools use to teach children to grow up American.

How American Schools Teach American Values

American schools influence the values of children through several mechanisms. One is the selection of curriculum and materials; the choice of subjects and textbooks reflects the values the school wants to emphasize. Certain values are promoted, often unconsciously, by the teachers' words and actions: what behavior they reward and punish, which children they favor and disfavor, and how they structure classroom learning. Children are also influenced by identification with their teachers and by the attitudes and behaviors of their classmates. Finally, some schools are openly encouraging the development of values by teaching moral development as a subject.

Value Bias in Materials and Curricula

Although designed to promote intellectual skills, textbooks influence a child's opinions and attitudes. The author of a primer may sit down to write a story, consciously using words that second-graders know. At the same time, he may unconsciously write a story illustrating values he holds or believes the schools hold. His story may show the importance of obeying authority, describe a child who suppresses (or at least never reveals) angry feelings, or portray a mother who does not leave the house from the beginning to the end of the tale. Subtle bias in textbooks and readers constitutes an important item in the school's hidden curriculum. Consider the values regarding competition, relationships with friends, egalitarianism, and sex typing revealed in the following few examples.

Competition is a frequent theme. In a story called "Duck in a Box" a child at an amusement park tries to throw a toy duck into a black box in order to win a big doll. This simple story of thirty-five lines not only contains the theme of competing (and persevering until you win) but also includes the idea of learning to accept second and third, as well as first, prizes. The man at the fair cheers the child on: "She didn't win, but she may win the next time. See what she can do." "You can still win, the next time you can do it." Finally Jan throws the duck into a red box: "Oh my," she says, "I did win something! But not the big doll" (Harris et al., 1972, p. 68).

Affiliation stories are common. In "The Story of Dobbin" Jack and Jerry receive a new toy horse. They paint their old horse, Dobbin, planning to give him away to the children's hospital, but when he is spruced up again, they realize how much they love him and decide to

keep their old friend and send the new horse to the hospital. The final lines of the story reflect the need for attachment transferred to an inanimate toy: "Dobbin ran and bounced so fast on his little red wheels that it seemed as if he were glad he was to stay with the twins for many more years" (McCracken et al., 1964, p. 128).

Egalitarianism is promoted in a number of stories in which black and white children attend school and play together. Their message, however, often reflects ambivalence. This is apparent in a series of stories designed to be multi-ethnic. In the first story a black boy sits down on his front steps to read. Before he can begin, a white boy tickles him with a branch. The black boy drops his book and chases the white boy. The story ends with the frustration of the black boy's intention to read. The next story shows a chase in which the white boy trips over the black boy's books and skins his knee. A comparison of the two boys reveals that the black boy is depicted as an athlete, less intelligent, impulsive, distractible, and the object of humor. In contrast, the white boy is presented as reflective, intelligent, and socially secure (Blom, 1971).

Sex typing is prominent in readers. In fact, it is probably even more conspicuous in readers than it is in real life. The men in children's readers behave in active, adventurous ways; women stay home and bake cookies. Boys are shown as clever, heroic, persistent. Like girls they are sometimes helpful—but whereas girls are expected to be helpful, boys win special commendation for cooperation and washing the dishes.

Dick builds a house; Jane plays house. Girls are shown as dependent, passive, not very competent, and often fearful. Although the range of emotions in readers is not wide, fear occurs often, and usually it is the girl who is afraid:

Sam led, and Helen went after him. Helen held his hand in a hard grip. She was timid in the darkness . . . Helen fell, and Sam helped her get up. (*Dick and Jane as Victims*, 1972, p. 53)

Boys are not supposed to be afraid or show any emotion weaker than manly confidence:

He felt a tear coming to his eye, but he brushed it away with his hand. Boys eight years old don't cry, he said to himself. (p. 53)

Preoccupied with looking neat, pretty, and well dressed, happy to help in the kitchen and stay out of trouble, girls are second-stringers and know it. The boys know it, too: not surprisingly, they prefer to leave the girls to their activities and move on to bigger and better things:

"Oh, no," said [the narrator]. "It is no secret. We are willing to share our great thoughts with mankind. However, you happen to be a girl." Smart Annabelle flipped her eyelashes at me. "Come on Albert," she said. But Albert stood still.

"Excuse me," he said, "I think I will stay and learn to build an Electro-Thinker." (p. 55)

Story themes involving active or aggressive play, pranks, and work projects are generally related to boys; quiet activities, folk tales, and stories involving warm, positive emotions (the Pollyanna pattern) are related to girls.

Boys and Girls in Textbook Stories

In a study of 2,760 stories in 134 books, boys and men were present in overwhelmingly larger numbers than girls and women. The greatest discrepancy was in the category of biographies (*Dick and Jane as Victims*, 1972, p. 10):

Male to female biographies	6:1
Boy-centered to girl-centered stories	5:2
Male-centered to female-centered folk and fantasy tales	4:1
Male to female adult main character	3:1
Male to female animal stories	2:1

How do boys and girls behave when they appear?

	Girls	Boys
Clever	33	131
Persistent	47	169
Heroic	36	143
Helpful	68	53
Domestic	166	50
Passive	119	19

Attitudes and life styles presented in books often conflict with the world as individual children know it. A book may introduce a family with children named Dick and Jane (they are named Theresa and Gonzales much less frequently), a little house in the suburbs (less often a city apartment, hardly ever an impoverished one), and a father who goes off to work (but not a mother). Human nature and physical nature are shown as cooperative and smiling. There are few evil impulses. In general, life is easy and comfortable, frustrations are rare and easily overcome. If idealization is rampant in the sunny world of textbooks, it is equalled by the blandness of the people who inhabit it. There are hardly any children from very large families or from one-parent homes; few children wear glasses or are too short, tall, slim, or stocky (Michelak, 1965).

Greater awareness of the values taught by texts has led educators to begin choosing particular books in order to convey values deliberately. In one Midwestern city, for example, where the school population was white and the pupils had no opportunity to know black children personally, a multi-ethnic reader was used to improve the children's attitudes about blacks. During a four-month period one group of thirty-four children in the second grade used the multi-ethnic reader, while another group of thirty-four used standard readers. Interviews with children before and after the four-month period tested their attitudes using black and white dolls, pictures of black and white boys and girls in groups, and lists of traits—cheerful, honest, lazy, forgetful, neat. The children were asked which dolls they preferred, which children in the pictures did not fit into the group, and which traits were characteristic of whites and blacks. The children who had used the multi-ethnic readers showed more positive attitudes toward blacks than they had before (Litcher and Johnson, 1969).

Value bias also shows up in the curricula of schools. A prevalent mythology holds that boys and girls are not inherently competent in the same subjects, and therefore the curriculum for boys should differ somewhat from the one for girls. Boys are supposed to be naturally better than girls in subjects that require spatial reasoning, such as geometry, physics, and chemistry. Girls are expected to excel at foreign languages, English, composition, and history. Historically, there has been a consistent public-school pattern of more boys than girls choosing science and mathematics (and, of course, sports) and more girls than boys choosing language and history (Mussen, Conger, and Kagan, 1974).

Yet when a series of California Achievement Tests measuring reading ability, arithemetic, and mental maturity were administered to Ohio schoolchildren in grades two through eight, 2,651 boys and 2,369 girls finished the three tests, and the results indicated no fundamental sex differences on any test, at any grade level (Parsley et al., 1963). But in high school the sex difference in these subjects does appear (Maccoby and Jacklin, 1974).

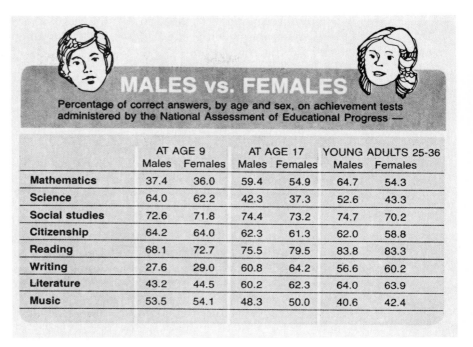

MALES vs. FEMALES

Percentage of correct answers, by age and sex, on achievement tests administered by the National Assessment of Educational Progress —

	AT AGE 9		AT AGE 17		YOUNG ADULTS 25-36	
	Males	Females	Males	Females	Males	Females
Mathematics	37.4	36.0	59.4	54.9	64.7	54.3
Science	64.0	62.2	42.3	37.3	52.6	43.3
Social studies	72.6	71.8	74.4	73.2	74.7	70.2
Citizenship	64.2	64.0	62.3	61.3	62.0	58.8
Reading	68.1	72.7	75.5	79.5	83.8	83.3
Writing	27.6	29.0	60.8	64.2	56.6	60.2
Literature	43.2	44.5	60.2	62.3	64.0	63.9
Music	53.5	54.1	48.3	50.0	40.6	42.4

Figure 2–6
Differences in achievement scores of boys and girls persist, in spite of changes in sex typing. Girls continue to score lower than boys in math and sciences and higher in literature and music. These differences appear to be largely, if not entirely, due to cultural factors. ("Girls Lag on Tests," October 20, 1975, p. 54. Reprinted from *U. S. News & World Report*. Copyright 1975 U. S. News & World Report, Inc.)

The reputed superiority of boys over girls in visual and spatial ability typically does not appear until junior high school. In one study of sex differences in spatial reasoning, the children were shown one picture of a geometric form and four variations on that form. Each child had to decide which one of the four pictures was like the original but rotated in a two-dimensional plane. On this kind of task, adult males do perform better than adult females. But among children in grades one through four, there were no sex differences. In grade seven, among the good math students there were still no differences. Only among the poor math students did the girls do less well than the boys (Karnovsky, 1973). Thus, although possible, it is not yet certain that sex differences in spatial reasoning or performance in mathematics and science are partly due to biological factors.

Although a school can certainly take the step of opening "shop" to girls and domestic science to boys, patterns of sex typing are not easily changed (see Figure 2–6). However, America is in the process of re-evaluating the roles of men and women, and the schools have an important function to perform by allowing both boys and girls to discover and develop their skills in an atmosphere that is free from sexual discrimination.

The Teacher and the Hidden Curriculum: Reward and Punishment

To a significant extent, how well a student absorbs the values taught in the classroom depends on the teacher's personality and the student's response to it. What is the nature of the teacher-pupil relationship? On close study you will notice that there is a current of approval and disapproval that travels in two directions. It runs from the teacher to the pupil, and the teacher's favor is a major element in socialization in the schools. But it also runs from the pupil to the teacher: how much the pupil likes the teacher will affect how much the teacher influences the pupil. It is useful to see how this reciprocal relation works.

What Kind of Pupils Do Teachers Like?

In order to discern which qualities teachers favor, a group of first-grade teachers were asked the following questions about students (Good and Brophy, 1972, p. 617):

Attachment: "If you could keep one student another year for the sheer joy of it, whom would you pick?"
Concern: "If you could devote all your attention to a child who concerns you a great deal, whom would you pick?"
Indifference: "If a parent were to drop in unannounced for a conference, whose child would you be least prepared to talk about?"
Rejection: "If your class was to be reduced by one child, whom would you be relieved to have removed?"

The teachers' answers suggest that they favor high-achieving children who actively seek them out and initiate contact with them (to be expected in a society that values personal achievement, flexibility, and sociability). Teachers are concerned about children who do not perform well—or they reject them. They are apt to be indifferent toward children who are essentially quiet, passive, and inclined to fade into the background. (We can see that children who have a good command of verbal skills and the incentive to use them are already ahead of the ones who do not.) While observations in the classroom show that teachers favor smart, obedient children, it is important to note that most of these children are already smart and obedient when they come to class. They do not develop those traits because teachers openly praise them, since observations in classrooms indicate that teachers do not praise them more than the other children (Good and Brophy, 1972). Here the influence of the child's home carries over to the school.

Obedience to authority is reinforced and disobedience punished daily in the classroom. A ceiling is also apparent on how active or disorderly children can be and still win the teacher's approval. In general, careful, conforming, cautious, and orderly students are preferred. Student teachers in California, for example, were given a situation test consisting of these two stories depicting elementary-school children engaged in classroom activities:

> Steve is working on a model for the space project. He decides to make a space capsule and works out a design for it. While he works, he scatters glue, wood and nails on the floor. When he can't find a piece of wood the right shape, he re-designs part of his model. When he catches his shirt on a nail, he pulls it loose carelessly. Although there is always a ten minute clean-up after a work project, Steve continues working on his model until the final bell rings.

> The children are learning how to handle and feed hamsters. The teacher asks David to help take them out of the cages for their food. Although David thinks it will be messy, he agrees to help. After putting on a lab coat, he gets some newspapers and covers the floor with it. He lines up the food dishes in front of the cages and carefully pours the food. He closes the food container tightly and returns it to the shelf. David follows the teacher's directions precisely in feeding each hamster. (Feshbach, 1969, p. 128)

Asked to select which kinds of behavior they preferred from these stories, student teachers gave their most favorable rating to actions associated with rigidity, conformity, and order; the least favorable was given to behavior denoting independence, activity, and assertiveness (Feshbach, 1969).

These stories, and the student teachers' reactions, testify to the conflicts concerning the values taught in school. A child who is capable of redesigning his space capsule to make use of the materials he has would seem to win high points for inventiveness, initiative, and solitary decision making. Unfortunately for Steve, however, these attributes are associated with a disregard for neatness and the established way of doing things—traits that are exemplified, on the other hand, by David's fastidiousness in feeding the hamsters. This particular conflict is central to a struggle going on in the schools today, where some middle-class parents want the teachers to change their priorities on these matters. For now, though, the sample of California student teachers can be taken as representative of teacher attitudes in general: a preference for active, intelligent, obedient, and conforming students. Furthermore, elementary-school teachers tend to evaluate overly aggressive and spontaneous behavior as more pathological than do psychologists (Tolor, Scarpetti, and Lane, 1967).

Primary-grade teachers are also more likely to feel negatively toward boys than girls—probably because boys are apt to be more aggressive, disobedient, disorderly, loud, and mischievous. Girls are inclined to be compliant, to talk more quietly, and are more eager to please. And, as might be expected, girls like school more than boys do. This is as true of girls in England as it is of girls in America (Berk, Rose, and Stewart, 1970).

What Kind of Teachers Do Pupils Like?

Obviously, the teacher's attitude towards a pupil will influence the pupil's behavior. Less obvious, but almost equally important in its effect on behavior, is the way a pupil views the teacher.

According to several investigations, the teacher's power to sway the student's beliefs and behavior rests with the student. A group of 256 eighth-graders were asked how they felt about some common classroom episodes that illustrated teachers giving positive and negative feedback, approving or disapproving of what a student had done. Here is one episode (Davison, 1972, p. 419):

> Suppose you were in this teacher's class and he (or she) was busy doing something in the hall, and your classmates became loud and you tried to quiet them. If this teacher saw you after class and praised you for what you did, how would you feel?
>
> A. I would feel *good* if this teacher did this.
> B. I would feel *neither good* nor *bad* if this teacher did this.
> C. I would feel *bad* if this teacher did this.

Before responding the students were asked to select the teachers they most (or least) preferred. The students responded more favorably to praise and rewards offered by "liked" teachers than by "disliked" teachers. Students were more unhappy when a "liked" teacher disapproved of what they had done than when a "disliked" teacher disapproved. In other words, for both positive and negative rewards, the effect is greater when it comes from a teacher that the student likes. When it comes from a teacher students dislike, apparently both praise and criticism are diluted and have less power over them (Davison, 1972).

One study suggests that students commonly agree on four qualities that make teachers attractive: a good teacher is sympathetic, supportive, firm, and fair. Working-class pupils emphasize firmness, whereas middle-class children emphasize warmth and nurturance. However, all concur that the primary quality is fairness. Students demand a sense of justice in teachers—even if the justice does not benefit them in specific cases (Taylor, 1962).

Approval by the teacher is the school's most effective way of socializing children, especially young children. As one investigator states, "One of the most powerful motivating factors available to the teacher is her own attention to the child, which she may give or withhold at will" (Sechrest, 1962, p. 334). How the teacher shows her approval is another matter; this brings us to a discussion of the *reward system*.

How the
Reward
System
Works

The teacher's personal approval is the major reward a young child receives for acceptable behavior. The teacher can demonstrate her approval in a number of ways. She may praise the child. With young children, she may use affectionate gestures, like hugging or a pat on the back. She may put gold stars on a chart showing which children behaved especially well that day. The chart may even have categories of good behavior: "worked hard," "helped his classmates," "cleaned up the best." She may give special privileges as a reward for good behavior, such as the freedom to pick out a game or activity. Or she may give him a treat, such as a piece of candy, a toy to play with, or a token that he can receive right away but redeem at a later, more convenient moment for a toy or a privilege. She may even use pennies. Chapter 11 will explore the ways that these strategies can be used, but for now we will examine the choice of rewards for different age groups, the effectiveness of the system, and how it relates to competitiveness.

There are advantages and disadvantages to all rewards. Candy is easy to give out, but a child may quickly tire of it. Many children like games better, but it is often impossible to stop the work flow in order to play a game right away. Tokens are one way to circumvent that problem. The child being rewarded is given a star or piece of paper that can be exchanged for a real prize later. It is often difficult to determine an appropriate reward. But it is clear that if a reinforcer is used, it must be something the child wants if it is to be effective (Stainback and Stainback, 1972).

As children grow older, material rewards become less important, and more abstract rewards, such as good marks on a report card, can be substituted as symbols of the teacher's approval. Acceptance of less tangible rewards with increasing age is a universal characteristic. In New Zealand Maori children were shown a game that involved removing beads from a spiral by unthreading them. Five- and six-year-old Maori children performed better when butterscotch Life Savers (which they got to eat afterwards) were substituted for beads; ten- and eleven-year-old children, on the other hand, performed the task equally well whether they were unthreading beads or Life Savers (Storm, Anthony, and Porsolt, 1965).

In high school the reward system operates in more varied ways. To some extent all eight-year-olds want their teachers' praise. But students in high school, feeling the impact of a wider world, want a variety of rewards. Some want to go to college or be members of the National Honor Society; others prefer to work on the year book or play football. Still others reject all the standard school goals and are concerned instead with breaking new ground. Just as adolescents rebel against the goals of their parents, which they view as traditional, they may also rebel against the teacher and the school policies. Inevitably, the less closely they identify their own interests with those of the school, the less effective is the teachers' favor or disfavor.

Effectiveness of the reward system and the distribution of rewards is obviously related to how eagerly—and how optimistically—students compete to win them. The competitiveness of students varies, at least to some degree, according to sex. Competition is expected to be the driving force in American schools, but as we indicated earlier, boys and girls are expected to respond to it in different ways. A boy who is highly competitive conforms to society's view of what a boy should be like. A girl who is highly competitive does not. As children grow older, the sex difference in conflict over competition becomes more marked. Adolescents tend to regard serious intellectual strivings as competitive, and perhaps aggressive; obtaining the best grade in a social studies class may mean defeating another classmate in open debate and on examination scores.

American high-school girls, fearful that they may appear unfeminine, are more anxious than boys about showing strong competitiveness. If a girl actively debates the merits of establishing a Karl Marx society in the high school, she is aware that she may be regarded as aggressive, even militant. She may rein in her enthusiasm, moderate her arguments, and feel comfortable that she has not acted inappropriately. However, if she loses the debate as a result, she may also realize that she might have won if she had tried her hardest.

The reward system is a central school mechanism for inculcating the values Americans want their children to learn. It revolves around the attention and approval of the teacher and the students' success in approaching the image society has of how boys and girls should develop.

The Teacher as a Role Model: The Effect of Identification

We have seen how a child's behavior can be shaped through praise. His behavior and values can also be influenced by the example of an adult whom he respects and wants to resemble. Such an adult is *motivationally relevant* to the child. Admiration for teachers depends less on what they say and more on what they are like as people.

The old admonition "Do what I say and not what I do" is not worthless. But the adult who demonstrates the behavior she wants the child to adopt is more effective, since children are apt to take a person's actions more seriously than his statements. But a child does not imitate

"She wants so much to identify with her kindergarten teacher, who is a wonderful, patient person—but he's 6 feet 2 and he has a moustache."

or adopt the actions or values of all the adults he knows. The reason a child's interest focuses on one teacher rather than on another involves the concept of *identification*.

Identification involves four interrelated processes. The essence of identification is that the child believes some real similarity exists between himself and another person. The similarity can be physical or involve values or emotions. A second-grade boy, for example, may identify more closely with his music teacher than with his homeroom teacher because they are both black. A high-school junior may feel a strong identification with her art teacher—rather than her regular teacher or her parents—because her art teacher not only touches a responsive chord about painting as an expression of emotions but also shares the student's feelings about political issues. When a child believes in a close similarity to a person, the child may share vicariously in the emotional state of the model. This is the second process involved in identification. A seventh-grader in a science class, on seeing a new comet through the telescope, may feel the same excitement of discovery that she imagines her science teacher does. The third aspect of identification involves the child's desire to have some of the teacher's attributes—competence, warmth, justice, enthusiasm, sensitivity—for himself. When these three processes take place, the

The Teacher as Role Model

Teachers

In Hellenic Greece young boys were taught their letters by a schoolmaster, but instruction in manners and moral supervision was provided by the pedagogue, a peculiar institution of ancient Greece. He stood in as the symbol of parental authority during the day: he taught the boy how to behave. It is ironic that such an important function was left in the hands of a slave (for usually the pedagogue was a slave of the household), and pedagogues were held in very low esteem. Seeing a house slave fall from a tree where he had been sitting and break his leg, an Athenian citizen remarked, "Lo, he is now a pedagogue" (Castle, 1961, p. 64).

In nineteenth-century America educators were very conscious of their role in forming a child's mind and character. Teaching books of the time, like *The District School* (1834) by J. Orville Taylor, indicate that the children were seen as malleable and impressionable:

> Teachers should well consider the nature of their business. You are now acting upon mind—mind that is young and flexible. Your example, your opinions, your address are to form on your pupils such characters as will make them either useful and happy or useless and miserable. You are acting upon minds which will act upon other minds, and your whole influence will be towards the for-

child is likely to adopt some of the behavior, values, and attributes of his teacher. He believes that by increasing his similarity to her in tangible ways—such as walking like her, talking like her, or sharing her enthusiasm for astronomy—he will also gain some of her less tangible characteristics—her warmth, popularity, and competence. In short, if the teacher is a hero or a heroine in the child's eyes and the child believes he shares some basic similarities with the teacher, he will strive to increase the shared base of similarities by adopting the values and behaviors of the model. But, if a child does not perceive any similarities between himself and the teacher, he will not be able to identify with her, and he will be less influenced by what she does. On the other hand, if a child recognizes similarities in a teacher he does not respect or admire, he will not try to be like that teacher either, for obviously he does not want to be similar to someone he does not admire.

Aside from quite individual similarities—such as a particular sense of humor or an interest in animals—there are several broad categories of similarities that are important for schools to consider when matching teacher to child. Ethnicity is an obvious one. A Puerto Rican child is more likely to feel a bond with a teacher who is dark-skinned, Spanish-speaking, and familiar with the food, music, and religious holidays of the Puerto Rican community than with a blond teacher with a Southern accent who grew up in a community that regarded dark-skinned people as inferior. (That is not to say that a particular Puerto Rican child may not develop a bond with a blond, Southern teacher because of a mutual interest in, say, folk music.)

and Pupils

mation of the character of society. You should, then, consider well the nature of your business. You should examine yourselves, and see if you are prepared for an office at once so honorable, influential and responsible. (p. 41)

Today the interaction between teachers and children is a key factor in the school's job of socializing personality. American parents provide examples for their children—they also expect the teachers to be examples. Now, however, we acknowledge that children in school have already developed unique personality silhouettes. They do not arrive passive and unformed. Therefore, the teachers do not inscribe or mold at will—they meet the children where they are. The personalities of the teachers and their appropriateness as models in the particular classrooms in which they teach are as important as their intellects or technical skills. (As a dramatic example, notice the move toward community control in black neighborhoods, where parents have insisted on removing white teachers from the public school, not because they were unable to teach reading and spelling, but because they seemed unsuitable models for black children.) In the subtle, intangible aspects of socialization teachers shape the behavior of their students as much by what they are as by what they openly do.

Social class is another category of similarity. Teachers from middle-class backgrounds tend to be more permissive and less puritanical in their outlook, take more pleasure in the emotional aspects of teacher-pupil relationships, and show less authoritarian attitudes toward children than do teachers from working-class backgrounds. Working-class children, used to a less indulgent and more rigid framework, may be put off initially by a middle-class teacher who does not provide them with the discipline and structure they expect.

A third category of similarity is sex. Since the majority of elementary-school teachers are women, there are few male models for young schoolboys and, as we have seen, a "feminine" atmosphere in the primary grades. This makes it a little more difficult for boys to identify with their teachers. Hiring more male teachers may help to improve the atmosphere for boys in elementary schools.

Peer Influences on Socialization

Children's behavior is influenced by the teacher's approval or disapproval, the reward system (which elaborates the teacher's reactions to him), and the process of identification. The peer group is a fourth factor in the socialization process.

Attitudes, values, and behavior of classmates play a strong part in shaping the individual; peer influence involves the same mechanisms that operate with the teacher: desire for approval and identification. In addition there are two new and related factors: *peer assignment of a role* to the child and the child's perception of his *relative ability* compared with others in his peer group.

Children want to be accepted by their peers and take steps to avoid being rejected by them. Peers, like teachers, also give rewards. Instead of taking the form of good grades, gold stars, or candy, peer attention and favor are shown by offers of friendship, by paying attention when the child speaks, and by membership in groups, gangs, or cliques. Some groups, like high-school fraternities, are formal; more often informal groups grow organically according to the likes and dislikes of the members. Conversely, peers show disfavor through a range of rejections, from disinterest and interruptions to open ridicule, ostracism, and cruelty.

Since not all children have the same need for approval, their responsiveness to group pressures varies. About five hundred elementary-school children were asked to give true-or-false answers to questions such as, "I sometimes say something just to impress my friends," "Sometimes I let someone else get blamed for something I've done," and "I sometimes feel like making fun of other people." A picture emerged of children with high or low needs for approval from peers. The children with a high need for approval, determined to show that they were worthy of acceptance, were reluctant to admit that they became angry. The low-need children were less concerned with what others thought of them and more able to admit that they cry and shout. High-need children are more easily led by the group and more anxious to conform to the group's standards (Tulkin, Muller, and Conn, 1969).

Just as a child identifies with some teachers, he also identifies with some children, especially older, more talented ones. In most classes, there is one child whose talent is exceptional. He or she is skilled at sports, good-looking, witty, and sophisticated. Since these attributes are valued, peers who possess them are respected and admired. The leader of the peer group exerts a powerful influence, and, as is true with teachers, his influence will be greatest on children who feel they are similar to him and admire him.

Peer groups also influence children by assigning them a role. In addition to its leader every stable peer group has a variety of role-players: a scapegoat, a wit, an athlete, a daredevil. Since the child wants to be part of the group, he is willing to accept the role given him, even if it is not the one he welcomes, because it gives him a unique position in the group. Once he accepts the assignment, his attitudes about that ability change. Suppose that a boy named John has a strong desire to be an athlete, but in his class or on his block most of the other boys are more athletic than he is. John, on the other hand, is better than most of the boys at debating. If the peer group comes to think of him as the debater (even though his verbal talents had not previously mattered as much to him as his athletic skill) gradually he, too, will place considerable value on his skill with words and his debating ability because these are the talents that have won him a special place and a secure position in the group. A child may go to great lengths to preserve his particular slot. For example, a high-school girl won the nickname "Sunshine" because she was an outgoing person. As time went on she came to feel that she should not show concern or anxiety about her grades or getting into college because she felt she would be letting down her friends by violating her role assignment.

Finally, the group gives a child yardsticks by which to measure himself. The peer group influences the child's perception of his intelligence, sex role, integrity, bravery, appearance, and a host of other culturally involved traits. It provides a mirror for a child. By giving or withholding acceptance, the group lets a child know how he is "doing." Children seem to put greater trust in their peers' evaluation than their parents' or teachers' probably because they believe their friends are more perceptive and will be more honest with them. A ten-year-old girl, for instance, does not have any absolute definitions for determining how bright, wise, honest, capable, and likeable she is. What she can do, however, is measure herself against the other children she knows and draw her own conclusions. Thus a child's specific peer group, which is, after all, a matter of chance, can have a powerful influence on his or her concept of self.

Another reason peer group influence can prevail over the influence of parents or teachers is that its ethos allows some leeway that adult standards do not. It permits children to rebel against adult demands for socialization. As part of a group of children his own age, a child feels he has "time out" from the process of growing up. He can safely indulge in activities—such as swearing or smoking—that he thinks his parents would frown on. Children, especially older ones in junior high school and high school, set up units that work like therapy groups. They hear each other out on secret resentments and encourage each other over matters that they believe would be nonnegotiable at home. Children who feel upset and anxious because they resent their parents, for instance, may feel less guilty when they hear friends describe their own hostilities toward their families.

Moral Development: New Curricula for Socialization

The current American bewilderment and concern about morality reflects an ironic turn of events considering that in the early years of this country one of the chief purposes of education was to promote Christian virtue. Today Americans are again deeply concerned about moral questions. In the past decade the Viet Nam war, the events of Watergate, the debate about abortion, and the increasing crime rate have drawn our attention to a national dilemma: Americans are unable to agree on a set of moral standards that the majority will accept as a guide to behavior. Confidence in our ability to discern right from wrong has eroded. Although many citizens long for earlier days when the line between good and bad behavior was drawn more clearly, even the most traditional thinkers agree that such a definite line is not possible at the present time.

If children are to be raised as moral human beings, they will need a set of moral principles that they respect and can count on. They should not be offered a set of standards that will be functionally obsolete when they turn to it in a crisis. This need has led to the beginning of a movement for moral education in the schools. The morality lessons of the 1800s insisted that children show unquestioning obedience to the rules of authority. Today's curriculum in moral training, whose leader is Professor Lawrence Kohlberg of Harvard University, encourages children to make moral decisions for themselves—a strategy that is consistent with our respect for autonomy. Kohlberg believes that morality is a set of rational principles for making judgments about how to behave; he rejects the traditional view that defines morality in terms of behavior. The basic principle is *justice*: the primary regard for the dignity, worth, and equality of all persons. Since it is not always obvious which particular action is the most just, each person must make a decision based on some criteria.

Kohlberg believes that all children pass through a series of stages as they mature and that during each stage they refine their concept of justice. There are six stages of moral development, from the least to the most mature. Diagnosis of the stage at which a particular child is operating is based on his reasons for behaving in a certain way, not on his behavior. Kohlberg believes that by presenting moral dilemmas to students and encouraging discussion about them, students can be helped to recognize the more abstract principles that lie behind moral judgments and, as a result, move from one stage to the next.

In the first, or least mature, stage children abstain from an asocial act because of fear of punishment from an authority figure. They refrain from stealing, for example, because they are afraid of adult punishment. This stage is characteristic of preschool children. In the second stage of moral development children behave properly in order to satisfy personal needs. They are willing to inhibit stealing if their abstention allows them to attain certain goals they want or to obtain a privilege (an ice-cream cone). In the third stage (which Kohlberg calls the "good girl" or "good boy" stage) the basis for moral behavior is a desire for approval from others. Children tell the truth or do not steal because they believe that the people whom they respect will approve of their moral behavior.

In the fourth stage preadolescents believe that the moral rules given by authority deserve respect and obedience. The reason for not stealing is that teachers and parents regard that action as wrong. The respect due to authority is a sufficient basis for adhering to the moral standard.

In the fifth stage the basis of morality is the general welfare of the community. Adolescents believe that moral behavior is necessary to maintain social order. Now adolescents hold a more abstract rule for judging the appropriateness of an act. They believe stealing is wrong because if all people took what they wanted there would be general social disorder. This is a much different reason for honesty than fear of punishment or rejection. Persons in the fifth stage realize that what is proper for one society might not be for another.

By the sixth and final stage adults have formed a personal set of moral principles that are abstract, logically consistent, and derived from their own experiences and thoughts. These principles involve respect for the worth and dignity of all persons. When a law or standard given by authority violates this principle, people believe they have a right to disobey. Thus people in the sixth stage might not steal because that act violates the dignity of the victim whose property is being taken. On the other hand, adults in the sixth stage might steal in order to save a life, if such an action were the only way to accomplish the merciful act and be honest to one's principles. Kohlberg admits that few people reach stage six. Presumably Socrates, who made decisions based on his own conscience, is an example of someone who reached the sixth stage. On the other hand, the attainment of the sixth stage

"Valuing" in Elementary School

In an eastern city school, a team of teachers worked with Kohlberg's principles to deepen their pupils' ability to make value judgments. The teachers used filmstrips, role playing, or stories that contained a situation requiring moral or value judgments such as this one:

> Gladys has waited all week to go to the movies. On Saturday, her parents gave her money so that she can see a special movie in town. Gladys takes the bus. When she gets to the theater there is already a long line with many children waiting to buy tickets. Gladys takes her place at the end of the line. Somebody shoves her accidentally and she drops her money. It rolls down the sidewalk and she leaves to get it. When she comes back, the girl who had been in back of her in line, whose name is Mary, does not want to let her back into the line. Should Mary let her in, or should Gladys go to the end of the line and perhaps miss seeing the movie? (Landsmann, 1973, p. 93)

After they were sure that the children understood the situation, the teachers reviewed the guidelines for discussion:

> We will ask each other for the reasons for our opinions.
> We will listen to each other's reasons by looking at each other.
> We will each give our own reasons.
> We will see that everyone has a chance to talk. (p. 93)

The children broke up into groups. The teachers helped them by raising questions such as these:

> What if Mary and Gladys are really good friends?
> Would it make a difference if Gladys had left the line to buy ice cream instead of leaving to pick up her money?
> Now pretend that I am the movie owner and you are Mary, the girl who took Gladys's place. I want you to tell me why you think it is right for me to give you the last ticket. (p. 93)

As the debate ended, nearly everyone agreed that Mary should let Gladys back in line. Two or three disagreed and explained why, and a few children were undecided. The teacher concluded:

> I think every teacher knows there isn't any "right" answer to a true social question, and we want the children to understand this. The object of all our discussions is to show that in making value decisions or a moral judgment there are lots of factors to consider and there is no [one] right answer that applies. (p. 94)

creates problems, since a man who assassinates a dictator or a president may believe that he, too, is acting out of highest moral principles, regardless of the law.

The following is an example of a moral dilemma that Kohlberg uses to assess the current moral stage of a child or adolescent. A man had a wife who was desperately ill, and he could not pay the druggist the full price for the drug she needed. So he broke into the pharmacy and stole the drug. The child is asked, "Should the husband have done that? Was it right or wrong?"

A younger child may reply, "It's wrong to steal because you'll go to jail." They would be classified as being in stage one.

Adolescents may say, "You can't really blame someone for stealing, but extreme circumstances don't really justify taking the law in your own hands. You can't have everyone stealing whenever they get desperate. The end may be good, but the ends don't justify the means." This answer is characteristic of stage five (Kohlberg, 1969).

Professor Kohlberg has begun working with teachers to develop a curriculum that can help to teach values in school. Kohlberg says:

> Behind all of these developmental goals lie moral and philosophical dimensions of the meaning of life which the adolescent currently questions and the schools need to confront . . . . The high school must have and represent a philosophy if it is to be meaningful to the adolescent. If the high school is to offer some purposes and meanings which can stand up to relativistic questioning, it must learn philosophy. (Kohlberg and Gilligan, 1972, p. 177)

Abandoning traditional obedience to authority as a basis for morality may threaten to drown us in ambiguities. Nevertheless, the traditional respect for the virtue and the power of authority and their sanctions have been called into question. People have only two places to look for moral guidance when they must act. They can turn to external sources, the behavior of others or directions laid down by authorities, or to internal sources, that is, their personal feelings and beliefs. When the former sources lose some of their legitimacy—as they have—then each person turns inward for guidance in making difficult, moral decisions. Among all the changes in values taking place in our country, one of the most serious is a growing recognition of the fragile morality of the society. This state may lead to an attempt to rebuild a coherent set of standards that most members of the community will support.

Summary

A major goal of schools is to inculcate the values that the society believes its future citizens should hold. In America there have been changes in values over the past 175 years. Around the middle of the nineteenth century, one major change was a shift in educational emphasis from virtue as an aim to an education that aimed for achievement; a second change, around the middle of this century, was an increased emphasis on sociability, close relationships with friends and family, and spontaneous displays of feelings. Currently, we teach children how to be American by conveying attitudes about eight main values: obedience to authority; autonomy and individuality; the importance of language skills; competition; group affiliation and social communication; emotional spontaneity; egalitarianism; and appropriate sex roles.

Children encounter these values at home, among their friends, on television, in books, in movies. The absorption of these values is not left to chance, however, and the schools present them in several ways. There is a value bias in the curriculum. Often the bias is inadvertent, but its effect is persistent. Second, values are presented in the "hidden curriculum" through the teacher's pattern of rewarding some types of behavior and punishing others. Teachers' values are also conveyed, indirectly, through a process called identification, wherein children see similarities between themselves and a teacher they admire, and emulate him or her in the hope of assuming more of those characteristics for themselves. Values are conveyed by a child's peer group. Like teachers, peers reward some kinds of behavior with approval and punish other kinds with rejection; in addition, peers also assign a role to a child, which he or she usually lives up to in order to maintain a special position in the group. Finally, some experiments are attempting to further moral development through lessons in valuing.

Projects

1 Plan a high-school graduation ceremony that would celebrate cooperation rather than competition.

2 On report cards, children are often evaluated on their verbal participation. A percentage of their grades may be based on participation. For a teachers' handbook, compose a paragraph that will help them to assess participation in other than verbal ways.

3 Write a brief children's story that incorporates but does not center on one of the following: a family with the father as the single parent; a family in which the mother works full-time; a family without children; a communal family; or a handicapped child.

4 Over the next week, make a list of the values that you see expressed in one of the following categories: magazine advertisements and television commercials; the movies; newspaper editorials and letters to the editor; a letter from your parents; advice from your friends.

5 Think about the years when you were growing up and about the teachers, older friends or relatives, and friends your age who had a special impact on you and with whom you identified. Looking back, can you see what factors were involved in the process of identification? What similarities did you notice? What traits did you admire and want to have for yourself? What visible characteristics did you copy?

6 Interview half a dozen parents of school-age children: ask them their

reasons for approving or disapproving of sex education in schools. Make up a page with their words in quotations. If you keep it until you become a teacher, how much of a change do you think you will find between their attitudes and those of your own pupils' parents? Do you think time or geographical location will affect the differences more?

7 Invite three friends to discuss moral education. Can morality be taught? Should the schools take up the issue or is it best left to individual families?

Recommended Reading

Jencks, C. *Inequality: A reassessment of the effect of family and schooling in America.* New York: Basic Books, 1972. A very important, controversial book dealing with the relation between education and economic status. Jencks and his colleagues challenge the belief that educational opportunity is an important determinant of socioeconomic status and imply that investment in education is not an effective way to produce a more egalitarian society.

Kohlberg, L., and Gilligan, C. The adolescent as a philosopher: The discovery of the self in a post conventional world. In J. Kagan and R. Coles (Eds.), *Twelve to sixteen: Early adolescence.* New York: W. W. Norton, 1972. In this article Kohlberg describes his theory of moral development and suggests that a basic aim of high-school social studies should be to stimulate principled moral judgment. Kohlberg believes the high school must be committed to standards of morality if it is to be meaningful to the adolescent.

the psychological
nature of the child
two

the nature
of learning:
the processes
of change

3

On Thursday, September 6th, Juan Benedetto started kindergarten. It was a cool morning for September, and he wore the new, navy blue sweater his grandmother had knit. With his mother he walked through the streets he knew, past the bakery, the dry cleaner's, and the grocery store, and turned into a schoolyard he had often walked by before. In the kindergarten room he saw only two or three children he knew in a crowd of twenty-three unfamiliar faces. He met his teacher, Mr. Winship. He was friendly, but Juan thought he seemed very tall and thin, not at all like his father. With his teacher's encouragement he sat at a table with some other children to play with a puzzle, but he kept glancing up at his mother to be sure that she was still there. When she did leave, half an hour later, he cried, putting his face down on his elbow and refusing to look up at Mr. Winship.

As the morning wore on, Juan stopped crying but continued to be very quiet. When Mr. Winship asked the children if they knew the alphabet, Juan could recite the letters up to G, but after that he scrambled them and gave up. Mr. Winship took out a big book with pictures of animals; he pointed to some of the pictures and asked the children if they knew the animals' names. Juan recognized the dog and the cat and several others that he had seen in the country: cow, horse, pig, duck, chicken. But many animals were unfamiliar to him. He felt better around snack time. He sat at the table and poured juice from the pitcher into his paper cup, ate three crackers, and enjoyed the story that came right after the snack. But in the free play period at the end of the morning, as Juan was pushing a truck up the ramp of blocks he had built, another boy snatched his truck away. Juan sat beside his ramp with his hands in his lap and began to cry again, so that when his mother returned a few minutes later, she found him much as she had left him.

    The last day in May was also cool, so when Juan left for school he was again wearing the sweater his grandmother had knit, only now two inches of shirt sleeves showed below the cuff. He waved goodbye to his mother at the entrance to the schoolyard, picked his way through the group of older children jumping rope, and sprinted into the school.

During the morning he wrote the alphabet with a large, red crayon on a piece of paper. One of the other children tried to take the crayon away when he was only up to Q, but he held onto it and after a slight scuffle finished the letters. At the beginning of the story hour he asked Mr. Winship to read from his favorite book, *Animals of the World*. As he read, Juan recognized all the animals even before he heard their names: cow, horse, pig, duck, chicken, sheep, lion, alligator, elephant, and the one with the long nose, the anteater.

What We Mean by Learning

The word *learning* is one way to describe all the changes that took place in Juan during the school year. However, it fails to convey the variety inherent in those changes and, for many people, implies that only one process was involved. In the language of the Eskimo many different words stand for snow. One word stands for wet snow, another for dry snow, still another for scattered snow. Ideally, psychologists, teachers, and parents should have a vocabulary with separate terms for the different types of behavioral changes that occur in a human being as he or she grows.

The goals of this chapter are to describe and compare the major psychological changes that are the result of growth and experience and to consider the necessary conditions that permit change to take place.

Old Brain and New Brain

"The brain grows from the inside out. That is, the parts closest to the neck—the parts sometimes called the 'old brain' because they are similar to the brains of lower animals—mature first. Many of these areas are mature at birth. This is necessary to the newborn's survival, since these brain areas control automatic functions—heartbeat, breathing, sucking and the like. There are also centers here for hunger and thirst and fear . . . . Another important structure in this area is the general arousal system . . . which is extensively involved in the processes of attention . . . mediates alertness and the focus of thought. It is the part of the brain that wakes the sleeping mother when her baby cries but lets her sleep when the telephone rings; that wakes her doctor-husband when the telephone rings, but lets him sleep when the baby cries. . . .

"As our species evolved, 'new brain'—the great folds of cortical tissue—developed. This is largely what Penfield (1964) calls 'uncommitted' at birth. Human infancy and childhood are long so that complex learning, or cortical mapping, will have time to take place." (Farnham-Digory, 1972, p. 5)

Much of the discussion refers to a child in school and the examples pertain to pupils, not adults. Nevertheless, while reading these chapters you should recognize that you are subject to the same processes. As you absorb and master the material, your cognitive processes are the same as those you are reading about. Your own cycle of comprehension/confusion/comprehension can throw light on a child's rhythm of understanding and puzzlement.

The abstract ideas that follow constitute basic theory in the field of education. Some of the concepts may appear to be remote from the actual work of a teacher in the classroom. You may be tempted to ask, "What does this have to do with a fourth-grade reading group in which some children can't seem to concentrate?" Illustrations will point out the connections. There will be still more in the next chapters, in which the concepts here will be applied to the processes of cognitive change.

Many technical terms are commonly used in discussing the psychology of learning. They will be defined as they are presented; it will be helpful if you become familiar with them. Since they are part of the everyday language of psychologists and teachers, you will encounter them often, both in this book and in discussions you have about teaching. These terms are used as a kind of shorthand: they permit faster communication. For example, acquired behavior that is instrumental in bringing about a specific effect is known as *operant conditioning*. By mastering the terms, you will be able to deal with the material faster, whether in conversation or in your own thinking.

Duration of Change: Transient versus Permanent

When psychologists talk about learning, they mean a change in an organism that lasts longer than a few moments. Some changes will last for weeks or months; others for several years; still others for a lifetime. If a one-month-old baby is pricked with a diaper pin, she pulls her leg away reflexively even if she cannot see the pin. That action is a transient, momentary change in her behavior; she may not have acquired any new knowledge from the experience that will affect her the next day. But if twelve months later the baby is burned because she touched a green lamp, she is likely to avoid the lamp for months, perhaps longer. The experience with the lamp led to a more permanent change in her behavior, and we say the child learned something. A major task of psychology is to explain how these more lasting changes occur: what happens when a child learns to call a long, green, scaly animal an alligator, to throw a baseball, to whistle, to do long division, or to make up a story?

The Three Classes of Change

There are at least three different kinds of change that occur as a result of the child's experience in the world. These are changes in *behavior*, changes in *knowledge* and *cognitive skills*, and changes in *emotional feelings*. For example, during his kindergarten year Juan learned not only to recognize and recite the letters of the alphabet but also to leave his mother in the morning without feeling frightened. The first is a change in cognitive ability; the second is a change in emotional feelings in a given situation. Juan also learned how to keep possession of his crayon—a change in his behavior in a given situation. Juan's experiences separated into these three categories are shown in the chart in Figure 3–1.

HOW KINDERGARTEN CHANGED JUAN			
	BEHAVIOR	COGNITION	FEELINGS
SEPTEMBER	Forfeited his truck. Listened passively as Mr. Winship read out loud.	Scrambled letters after G. Failed to recognize many animals.	Cried when his mother left. Intimidated when someone took his truck.
MAY	Held onto his crayon. Asked Mr. Winship to read his favorite book.	Able to recognize the letters of the alphabet. Able to name all the animal pictures.	Unafraid when his mother left. Angered when someone tried to take his crayon.

Figure 3–1
The three classes of change, as illustrated in a chart showing how one child changed after nine months of school.

It is important to recognize that behavior, cognition, and feelings are not isolated processes in the child. Often a change in one is accompanied by a change in another. Thus before Juan was able to overcome his fear, he had to learn that his mother was not abandoning him and that the children in school were not dangerous. His new awareness helped him master his fears. But even though behavior, cognition, and feeling interact much of the time (Chapters 6 and 7 will deal with this matter in detail), there are occasions when a change in one of them is primary. The perfection of a piano piece involves, for the most part, a change in motor coordination; the memorization of a poem primarily a change in cognition; the automatic sense of isolation when one is left alone in a house is primarily a change in feeling.

Universal or Culturally Specific Changes

We must also distinguish changes in action, cognition, and emotion that develop as a matter of course among most children from those that develop only as the result of specific teaching or observation. The ability to speak the language of one's community, to distinguish between a tree and a flower, remember the names of objects or people, or feel anger when frustrated eventually evolve in all healthy children as they mature in any normal environment. We call these changes *universal*. The ability to understand chemistry, play chess, do long division, or experience feelings of alienation—an emotion that appears to be specific to modern Western culture—does not develop as a matter of course. Those skills or feelings are *culturally specific:* they must be taught or passed along by adults or older children who have themselves learned chemistry, chess, and long division or labeled their feelings "alienation."

Obviously, even for culturally specific beliefs and skills, the child may not be able to acquire an ability until he has reached a certain level of maturation. The child must have the necessary motor coordination to learn to ride a bicycle, play soccer, or throw a spear. But even when the child is maturationally ready, culturally specific actions do not appear spontaneously.

In contrast, the universal changes are part of a program of maturation that is inherited. Given interaction with other people and objects, opportunity to move about, and the variety inherent in each day, one-year-olds will begin to stand and walk rather than crawl; three-year-olds will ask for a desired food rather than cry; six-year-olds will feel pride in a good performance; and adolescents will begin to behave like the adults around them. Even though these changes are common, we do not yet understand how they develop. One might say that humans are built to use their competences. Hence, when a new ability matures, the child naturally uses it. It is still unclear, however, how the new competence matured.

During the latter part of the seventeenth century John Locke also noted that observation (through the senses) and reflective thought were the main mechanisms through which change occurred:

All ideas come from sensation or reflection, ... first our senses ... do convey into the mind several distinct perceptions of things and thus we come to those ideas we have of yellow, white, heat, cold, soft, hard, bitter, sweet. I call this sensation. Secondly, the other fountain from which experience furnishes the understanding with ideas is the perception of the operations of our own mind within us ... and such are perceptions, thinking, doubting, believing, reasoning, knowing, willing and all the different actings of our own minds.... I call this reflection, the ideas that are forged being such only as the mind gets by reflecting on its own operations within itself. (Locke, 1965, p. 78)

The Mechanisms of Change

Whether the child is learning to talk or play baseball, certain mechanisms are necessary if the child is to become competent. We can approach the study of these mechanisms by asking the question, "What is the learner doing?" Although many complex and interrelated acts are involved in learning a new competence or acquiring new knowledge, they can be clustered around the answers to this question. Two fundamental actions of learners lead to change: the learner is *observing* and the learner is engaged in *reflective thought.* Let us first turn to the mechanisms operating in observation and see how they work.

Observation as a Mechanism of Change

The child gains knowledge—mental representations of experience—through observation; that is, through listening to and watching other people, looking at objects, noticing the results of his own actions, and, in cultures with books and newspapers, reading.

The infant first learns about his world through observation. During the first few weeks the infant begins to acquire mental representations of his parents' faces, his hands, and his rattle by looking at them. Experiments indicate that by eight to twelve weeks he knows what a face looks like and reacts to the unique configuration of a face in a special way (Kagan, 1971). The infant has acquired a permanent piece of knowledge through attentive study of the faces of people.

New behaviors can also be acquired through observation. A father and his four-year-old son walk down the street. Genetics can explain their common body structure and their curly blond hair. But the similarity in their appearance as they walk together goes beyond body structure and hair type. The father holds his left shoulder slighter higher than his right, stuffs his hands in his pockets, moves his legs in an easy, almost shuffling gait, and swivels his shoulders in a loose, relaxed way. The little boy, with his left shoulder slightly higher than his right and his hands in his pockets, moves his legs and shoulders in precisely the same motion. The similarity is striking to anyone watching the pair, and doubly so as they pass another father and son, this pair walking with short, brisk steps and swinging their arms vigorously as they go by. Although the sons may not have been aware of what was happening, both of them acquired their special postures primarily through observation (see Figure 3–2).

A high-school sophomore at the edge of the tennis court watches the tennis pro stand at the back line, toss the tennis ball up with his left

Figure 3–2
Two pairs of fathers and sons, walking along the street, reveal the kind of learning that takes place through observation. Each boy has watched his father's posture and manner while walking and, without being aware of it, imitates the walking style of the parent.

hand, and swing his right arm and racket in a serve. She is learning about the correct use of a tennis racket through watching the teacher.

But how does observation of events produce a change in action? Clearly additional factors are necessary, for no one could become a tennis champion just by watching an expert. Three factors are: imitation, or the behavioral expression of an observed act; accommodation to new events; and reinforcement for successful actions, thoughts, or feelings. Let us consider each of these in turn.

Imitation

Although most of the knowledge gained through observation never results in any action, some does. It happens when a child expresses in action some behavior he saw another person display; that is, he imitates it. For example an eighteen-month-old watches his mother dial a telephone. A few hours later he goes to the telephone and repeats that action. More pointedly, the adult can invite the child to imitate an action. The adult taps her finger on the table and indicates to the child that she wants him to repeat that behavior; the child smilingly reproduces that action. Imitation usually begins to emerge a little after the first birthday and increases in frequency through the second and third years. When the child imitates an action that he has seen, he generally duplicates the whole action as a unit, quickly and efficiently. This suggests that he has the ability to perform the act and is not imitating in order to learn how to perform the action.

Why does the child imitate? One possibility is that the child has a mental representation of his ability to perform an act he has witnessed. If he is certain he can perform it or certain he cannot perform it, he will probably not imitate the act. But if he is not quite certain whether he can or cannot, then he imitates the act to reduce that uncertainty. Hence four-year-olds will not imitate someone who builds a block tower (too easy) or someone who plays the violin (too hard). But they will imitate a ten-year-old who is playing with paints. Watching a model perform an act that is of moderate difficulty alerts and excites a child and provokes imitation.

The young child will also imitate an action in order to produce excitement. She sees another child kick a metal stand that moves and makes a noise when it is struck. The child wants to enjoy the fun and so imitates the action. In this case the incentive is not to resolve uncertainty over the ability to perform an action, but to produce an exciting change in the world.

That desire can also motivate the child to imitate himself. The one-year-old accidentally kicks his feet against the crib and makes an interesting noise. He notes that effect and repeats the action for several minutes until he becomes bored. Thus the most general principle is that the child notes what others do, as well as the results of his own actions. When the actions produce outcomes that are attention getting or exciting, the child will repeat that behavior. Psychologists usually restrict the word imitation, however, to those instances in which the original action was displayed by another person.

Finally, the child will imitate others in order to increase his similarity to a model. In this case the nature of the particular act is less important than the nature of the model. Almost any act that is characteristic of the admired model will do. A girl wants to wear earrings or to type because she wishes to increase her similarity to her mother. With age, this motive becomes the main reason for imitation.

Accommodation

Imitation, since it permits the child to practice some behavior, provides an opportunity for practice to lead to improvement. But in addition to learning through imitation the child expands his understanding of the world by relating new experiences to old ones and changing his concepts accordingly. This is the process of *accommodation*. It involves, four steps: focusing attention on an unusual event (an unfamiliar object, person, or occurrence); making a mental adjustment to its unique character; relating the event to previous knowledge; and generating a new mental representation that takes into account both the old and the new information.

Comprehension of new experiences through the alteration of previous knowledge is the essence of accommodation. A person's attention is attracted to what is for him an unusual, or *discrepant*, event. He tries to comprehend it in terms of what he knows. If he cannot, he then either forms a new mental representation or alters a previous one. In short, he accommodates to the new event. For example, a child sees an adult human dwarf for the first time. The dwarf has the face of an older person but the size of a child. She tries to resolve the inconsistency and may either create a new category or alter her old idea that all small humans are children. Or a child who is playing with magnets for the first time notes that paper clips adhere to the magnet. She begins to experiment with the magnet, placing it on all the loose small objects she can find. She is accommodating to the new experience.

Attention is the initial step in accommodation. The child uses his eyes, ears, and fingers. He may sniff things or put them in his mouth both to taste and to touch. But what kinds of events capture and hold a child's attention?

The fundamental principle controlling attention is that a person attends to events that are a little different from what he knows or expects. If they are totally unfamiliar to him or if they are too familiar, he will ignore them. What catches the child's attention is an event just over the edge of familiarity or a known event in a totally new context. Thus a three-wheeled car has the right degree of novelty to capture a child's attention.

Motivation is a second factor influencing attention. A child will attend to those people who he believes will gratify his basic needs and are thus motivationally relevant to him. A child pays attention to his teacher not because she is unfamiliar (except for the first week or two of the year) but because he wants to receive her praise and avoid her punishment. He has already learned that he is likely to achieve those goals if he watches her closely and listens to what she says.

In the section in Chapter 2 that dealt with the teacher as a role model, we stated that a teacher—or any other adult—may appear

motivationally relevant for a second and independent reason. If the child feels he is similar in some ways to the teacher and admires her, he wants to have some of her qualities for himself—her power, competence, warmth, or popularity. He will thus be strongly motivated to pay close attention to her words and actions.

The final stage of accommodation occurs when the child creates a mental representation of what he has observed, heard, or read. The high-school sophomore watches how the tennis pro swings his racket, and when her turn comes, she replays, with her body, the representation she has generated in her mind. The process involved in creating such a mental image has been one of the major enigmas in psychology. We can reasonably guess, however, that the mind represents the motor actions of another person or the symbolic description of those actions, and when the chance comes, it translates them into its own motor actions. It is as if the observer draws up a blueprint. She registers the first, middle, and last steps; then, letting her actions follow her blueprint, she monitors her progress and makes any necessary adjustments (for example, the young tennis player swings forward a little faster than she had planned, as she notices that the tennis ball has fallen an inch or two lower than she had expected). She keeps in mind the goal of the task and recognizes when she has completed it.

Of course, new knowledge is not synonymous with new behavior. If a child focuses his attention on a new event that interests him, registers its unique features, relates it to what he knows, and forms a new mental representation of the event, his mind has been affected but his behavior may not have been. The girl learning to play tennis can try out her knowledge by practicing, *if she wants to* (see Figure 3–3). Wanting to—being motivated—is a separate process. The girl may have a mental representation of how to serve and still remain seated on the bench. But she may not want to practice because she has a sprained ankle. Or she may be shy and afraid that being watched by her classmates will make her miss the ball. Still the sprained ankle or the shyness need not prevent her from acquiring the knowledge.

Since motivation is such a key factor in what a child learns tomorrow and what he choses to do with what he learned yesterday, it will be the subject of two chapters. For the moment it is enough to recognize the difference between the changes in knowledge gained as a result of observation and accommodation and the changes in actions that result from the active implementation of knowledge. These two processes influence each other continually. The child's actions produce

Figure 3–3
Observational learning occurs when a child's attention is focused on a new event: he accommodates to the novel aspects of it, forms a mental representation of the event in his mind, and then, if he is motivated, initiates some new action as a result of what he has learned.

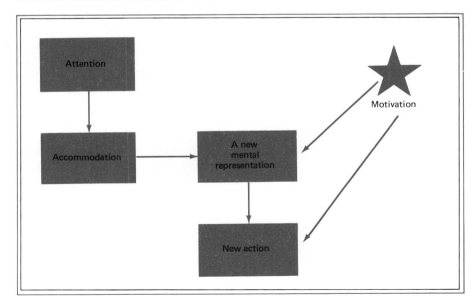

new experiences that he notes and to which he accommodates. The child's attentive study of another person leads to knowledge of new behaviors.

The Role of Reinforcement

Before we consider the nature of reinforcement, we must understand the idea of *association* and how it affects learning. Thus far we have seen that a change in knowledge occurs when a person attends to a new event and relates it to his prior knowledge. Some psychologists would say he "associates" the two pieces of information.

What is the dynamic at work in the process of association? For instance, a child reads in a book or hears someone say, "Birds belong to the class Aves." Those two ideas, *birds* and *Aves,* become associated because they occurred together and the child attended to them. Or consider a more significant example that happens in the classroom: the child is trying to solve an arithmetic problem but is failing and feels distressed. The feeling of distress engages his attention and interferes with his attempt to concentrate on the work. The child may begin to associate distress and an inability to concentrate with his experience of working on the arithmetic problem. On future occasions the prospect of

Figure 3–4
The theory of reinforcement is illustrated by the experiment of a pigeon in a lucite box: as he pecks randomly at his cage, he pecks at a red disk mounted on the side and immediately a kernel of grain is delivered to him. After this happens repeatedly, the pigeon deliberately pecks at the red disk, apparently to receive the reinforcement of food.

working on arithmetic problems in the context of the classroom may elicit anticipatory distress and mental confusion in the child.

Up until recently many American psychologists had assumed that most learning occurred as a result of association. Some of them believed that the only requirement for learning (through association) was observation of events that occurred closely in time or in the same place. Others insisted that observation of related events alone was insufficient and that an extra ingredient called *reinforcement* was necessary if any permanent change was to occur.

A reinforcement was typically defined as any event that produced a change in behavior. Early in the history of the theory, psychologists assumed that most reinforcements were events that gratified a drive or a motive: food to gratify hunger or praise to gratify a desire for positive responses from people. But it is now apparent that on some occasions when an act is followed by a change in the environment—whether the change is a piece of candy or the sound of a gong—the change can lead to altered behavior. Since a reinforcement is regarded by some as a primary basis for learning new actions and beliefs, let us examine how the process is supposed to work.

A pigeon is in a lucite box that has a red disk mounted on one side (see Figure 3–4). While making random pecking motions, the pigeon pecks at the disk. Each time he strikes the disk an automatic device immediately delivers a small kernel of grain. Soon the pigeon begins to peck at the disk more frequently. The pigeon's behavior in the box has changed, apparently as a result of the delivery of food following pecking at the disk. Some psychologists say a stimulus-response bond has been established between the stimulus of the red disk and the response of pecking. This is often called an *S-R bond*. The crucial aspects of the experiment were: (1) pecking at the disk—not at the floor or the walls of the box—was reinforced with the grain; (2) the reinforcement occurred immediately after the pecking, that is, in close temporal *contiguity* with the pigeon's actions; (3) the pigeon increased his pecking at the disk presumably to obtain more grain (Skinner, 1938).

During the last few decades the dynamics involved in this experiment with the pigeon, the red disk, and the grain have been expanded into a theory about how some changes take place in a child. The theory concentrates on changing a child's behavior.

Learning Theory

The reinforcement of desirable behavior is the central idea behind a set of assumptions called *learning theory,* a widely held view about how change occurs in the child. It has a long history that includes the work of Clark Hull and Neal Miller of Yale. The person most often associated with this theory of change is B. F. Skinner of Harvard. He is the leading proponent of the view that reinforcement is the major mechanism of change in behavior.

The term *learning theory* can be misleading, since it implies that it is the only theory of learning in existence. In fact, there have been and continue to be opposing views. There is some debate both about the way the principles of learning theory operate and about the importance of the role they play in promoting changes in a child.

The basic principles of learning theory are as follows: (1) an organism acts in a certain way in a specific context or situation; (2) that act is followed quickly by some change in the environment—the reinforcement—that the organism notices; and (3) the reinforcement leads to an increased likelihood that the organism will repeat the act again in the same or a similar situation.

Psychologists who want to account for the increased likelihood of a reinforced behavior suggest that the reinforcement produces a change in the strength of a hypothetical bond between external conditions and the response. The increase in the strength of the bond means that the next time the organism is in that situation and desires that reinforcement he is likely to repeat the act that originally led to the reinforcement. The objects or events that have the power to elicit a response that they do not ordinarily provoke are called the *conditioned stimuli.* The responses that come to be elicited are called *conditioned responses.*

In the case of a child who has learned that the sound of footsteps on the stairs means his father is coming to play with him, the child's running to the door is the conditioned response that is elicited by the conditioned stimulus—the sound of the father's footsteps. These assumptions form the heart of learning theory. In sum, reinforcements create or strengthen a hypothetical bond between the salient aspects of a situation (conditioned stimuli) and the particular reactions (conditioned responses) when the responses are followed by reinforcements that occur contiguously.

Psychologists make a distinction between two kinds of conditioning. The pigeon experiment provides an illustration of *operant conditioning*. The pigeon's act (pecking at the disk) operates to produce a result (the delivery of the grain). The second kind is called *classical* or *respondent conditioning*.

Classical Conditioning

In the early 1900s a Russian physiologist named Ivan Petrovich Pavlov experimented with his dog (see Figure 3–5). The dog was placed in a harness and a gong (the stimulus) was sounded. The dog did nothing special except make a few restless movements. Then, however, a variation was introduced: right after the gong was sounded, some food powder was given to the dog. In response to the food—and with the

Figure 3–5
Classical conditioning is illustrated by the example of Pavlov's dog: naturally salivating upon hearing a gong sound at the same time that he was given some food powder, the dog, in time, began to salivate when he heard the gong, even if no food powder accompanied it.

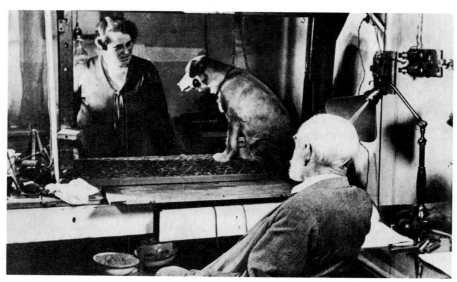

sound of the gong still ringing in his ears—the dog began to salivate. After this procedure had been enacted a few times, there was a new development: when the gong sounded, the dog began to salivate, even if no food was presented. An S-R bond had been established between the sound and the reaction of salivation because the sound, the reinforcement of food, and the salivation all occurred contiguously (Pavlov, 1927).

One distinction between classical and operant conditioning involves the role of the organism. In classical conditioning the organism takes a less active part in producing the reinforcement, for the response is reflex reaction to the reinforcement (salivation is an automatic response to the presentation of food). In operant conditioning the organism's action is instrumental in effecting a particular change in the environment, and the response is ordinarily not a simple reflex to the conditioned stimulus (presumably pecking is not an automatic response to a red disk).

In both forms of conditioning four principles apply to the behavior that has been learned, and these should be understood: generalization, discrimination, extinction, and frequency of reinforcement (which psychologists call schedule of reinforcement).

Generalization. The organism who has been conditioned to make a response in one situation has a tendency to behave the same way in a similar situation. We say that the organism *generalizes* the response. A child who has found a particular action appropriate in one situation behaves as if it is likely to be appropriate in a similar situation. Thus a learning theorist would say that if a child came to school from a strict home where she had learned to be afraid of her mother, it is likely that she would initially be afraid of the teacher because the response of fear would be generalized from her mother to her teacher. Generalization promotes efficiency, for it means that a child does not have to start from scratch to learn new responses to every new situation.

Discrimination. Naturally, the generalization holds up longer if the similarities in situations are strong. If they are not, children must modify their responses. If a child comes to school and discovers that her teacher is not strict, she will soon differentiate between her mother and the teacher and change her actions. She will no longer be afraid of the teacher. She *discriminates* between home and school.

Extinction. Children not only generalize and modify their responses; they can also abandon them altogether. The child who used to cry when her mother refused to give her extra dessert does not cry anymore. The twelve-year-old who used to start a fight when he was insulted by a peer does not fight anymore. Why does an accustomed pattern of behavior cease—or occur less frequently? Learning theorists say that when a particular behavior is not followed by a reward, it is less likely to persist. In technical terms, when the behavior no longer occurs, it has undergone *extinction*.

It is unclear whether the hypothetical S-R bond itself is "erased" by the process of extinction or whether only the probability of behavior has been changed. While the practical result may be the same, the question is a profound one, since it deals with a major issue: can knowledge once acquired ever be lost?

A behavior may also occur less frequently if it is punished (although in this case it is not called extinction). The twelve-year-old may exhibit less fighting behavior if each time he fought his father punished him by depriving him of privileges. The punishment, according to learning theory, led to the strengthening of an inhibitory response that was incompatible with fighting and acted to check the boy's inclination to fight.

Frequency of reinforcement. What is the optimal frequency of reinforcement? Is a change in behavior most effectively achieved if the response is followed by a reinforcement every time, every third time, every tenth time? Learning theory states that if a reinforcement occurs occasionally, rather than always, the response will be more difficult to extinguish. This would seem to make sense, for if a child always gets an A when he studies before an exam, it is likely that he will quickly give up the habit of studying if he suddenly stops receiving A's. But if he occasionally gets A's and other times receives a lower grade, he will continue to study, hoping that this will be one of the times when he will receive an A grade.

Evaluation of Learning Theory

The principles that have come to be called learning theory seem to have some validity. They are used to modify behavior, as we will discuss in Chapter 13, and are frequently applied in teaching. Consider the example of a boy who sits in front of a console of programed instruction in order to learn Spanish vocabulary. A sentence is presented, and he hits a typewriter key indicating his answer. If the answer is correct, a light and the next item appear, which are the reinforcements. He feels good and proceeds to the new sentence. Learning theory assumes that the reinforcements helped to stamp the knowledge in his mind and to increase his ability to sit attentively at the console and try new items.

Since learning theory assumes that reinforcement (the light and the next item) should occur in close contiguity with the behavior (pressing the key, being attentive, and rehearsing the correct word), it is a good idea to look more closely at the meaning of reinforcement.

The nature of reinforcement: reward or release? Reinforcement, a critical factor in learning theory, appears to have an influential role in changing behavior. However, there are important findings that challenge its validity and imply qualifications that must be taken into account if we are to assess its usefulness and effectiveness. Although reinforcement appears to promote a specific action because it acts as a reward, experiments suggest that perhaps the animal is not behaving as it does *in order to obtain* the reinforcement. For example, pigeons will peck at a disk even if food is already available in a nearby dish. This suggests that they are not necessarily pecking in order to obtain the food. In addition, some experiments show that pigeons will continue to peck at the disk even if each time they peck the food delivery is delayed. Thus by not pecking food delivery is accelerated. Some psychologists conclude from these findings that pigeons naturally tend to peck at disklike objects when they are excited or aroused. They do not necessarily do so to obtain food. The food—which has been called the reinforcement—acts to excite the hungry pigeon and the excitement causes him to peck, if a disk is available. Consider a similar example in children. An infant becomes excited and vocalizes when his mother makes funny faces and talks to him. The child does not necessarily vocalize in order to get the mother to make funny faces and talk. Rather, babies babble and coo when they are excited and a person is interacting and talking to them.

Some psychologists would say that the "funny face talking" was the reinforcement. But it is also reasonable to say that the mother's funny face released the babbling, as the red disk released the pecking for the pigeon. Thus objects or events that have been called reinforcements often act as ways to excite the child or the animal. At that point he displays the behavior he normally displays when he is excited or aroused in that particular situation.

A reinforcement is a special punctuation mark in the individual's experience that accents a particular thought or activity. Reinforcements tend to focus the organism's attention on the response he has just made. In Pavlov's experiment the food powder that produced salivation was unexpected, alerted the dog, and attracted his attention. Or consider a young child who is painting and has just drawn a chimney on a house when unexpectedly the teacher says, "That's good, John." That interruption breaks the chain of action and draws the child's attention to the response he has just made. As we discussed in connection with observation as a mechanism of change, such attention is critical for human learning. The power of reinforcement to focus attention is one reason it facilitates learning. As two leading psychologists recently put it, "Customarily . . . creatures are said to learn because of the rewards they get . . . we say that they learn when they are rewarded because rewards and punishments are the sorts of things creatures pay attention to" (Brown and Herrnstein, 1975, p. 159).

Limitations of the power of reinforcement. It is important to realize that some changes in behavior cannot easily be effected by reinforcements. It is difficult and perhaps impossible to teach an animal a behavior that is incompatible with his natural tendencies, regardless of the number of reinforcements he receives. For instance, when a rat is frightened by shock, his natural tendency is to run. Therefore, no matter how many times he is given a warning signal and then an electric shock, it is extremely difficult to teach him to avoid the shock by pressing a bar when the warning signal is given. But it is relatively easy to teach him to run down an alley to avoid the shock because that behavior is a more natural consequent of his fear (Bolles, 1972). Thus, each animal or person is more or less prepared by his biology to learn new behavior with ease or with difficulty.

Contiguity. Contiguity—a short time interval—between the behavior and the reinforcement may not be necessary to bring about a change. Let us return to the child at the typewriter console: instead of showing a red light and the next item each time the child makes a correct answer, suppose that the machine just continues to tally all the child's answers. When he is finished with the lesson, he goes to the back of the machine and pulls out a piece of paper that has recorded it. At home that evening, he takes out his book, studies the errors he has made in the lesson, and memorizes the correct answers. If he is *motivated* to learn Spanish, he can acquire the vocabulary words as well through this method as he will if he sits at the console and waits for the light to go on. His existing motivation provides an impetus to master the vocabulary; he does not need to depend on immediate reinforcement. In other words, immediate reinforcement can undoubtedly help a child learning vocabulary. But if motivation is present, it will make immediate reinforcement unnecessary.

The unique qualities of a child can minimize the importance of a short delay between the behavior and the reward in another way, too. Human beings have both memory and insight. In many instances, contiguity of events is not necessary, since a person can remember over a long period of time. In his own mind, he can fill in the gap between events, whether they are separated by hours, days, or years. The child studying Spanish can remember, five hours after school, that the Spanish word for flowers is *flores,* and he can review, mentally, the mistakes he made several hours earlier. He can also remember why it is important to learn the vocabulary words: not because he wants to see the light come on, but because he wants to be able to speak some Spanish to the Mexican-American children in his neighborhood.

Alternative methods. Reinforcement is not the only method, nor is it necessarily the most efficient one, to achieve certain changes in a child. This is true even with animals: in one experiment, a group of cats was

Figure 3–6
Although reinforcement is one mechanism for achieving change, it is not the only one, nor is it necessarily the most efficient. In an experiment, a group of cats was conditioned through reinforcement to press a lever in order to procure some milk. A second group of cats was permitted to watch the first group while it was being conditioned, and the second group learned to press the bar more quickly than the cats who had been trained through the mechanism of operant conditioning. (After John et al., 1968)

conditioned to press a lever in order to procure some milk (see Figure 3–6). The cats were put into a cage and a light flashed on. If they pressed a bar within fifteen seconds of the light being turned on, milk was automatically given to them. This was an instance of operant conditioning, for their reaction caused a change in the environment. A second group of cats was permitted to watch the first group while it was being conditioned. When put in the same situation, the cats who had observed learned to press the bar more quickly than the cats who had been trained through operant conditioning (John et al., 1968).

Predictions. Reinforcements also set up a problem in prediction. Children try to predict when adults will be angry with them or when their parents will return home. Experiments have shown that if the young child is given a piece of candy or a toy every time she selects the correct answer to a learning problem, she will often try to control delivery of the rewards until she has figured out the secret of the schedule. Once she understands the relation between her actions and the reinforcing candies or toys, she may stop trying to win them. The child becomes bored, not necessarily because she is satiated with the toys, but because her curiosity has been satisfied regarding what controls their appearance. She can predict when they will be delivered, so she stops playing games. It is not necessarily the reward that she wanted but the *certainty of knowing how to get it*. Children complain about games or events that can be figured out too easily. The well-worn dictum about not praising every action is valid because uncertainty makes the prediction problem more challenging for the child.

In summary, reinforcements have several functions. They can be inherently pleasant and emotionally exciting. A light touch, a sweet taste, a rhythmic ride on an adult's lap, all generate strong, pleasant sensations that the child likes to experience again and again. They focus the child's attention on the action he has just made, motivate him to figure out the schedule of occurrence, emotionally excite him, and elicit behaviors that are normally in the service of that excitement.

But although reinforcement can be helpful in facilitating change, it is neither the only mechanism nor in many instances the most relevant. Reinforcement is usefully viewed as one strategy that helps produce change.

Limits to Observational Learning

Observation alone cannot implement all kinds of change. If complicated motor activities are involved—as they are in tennis—observation is not enough. After watching the tennis pro, the high-school sophomore can walk on to the court and copy his actions in a rough way, but to achieve the pro's form and style, she will have to practice with her body. Hence, to perfect an ability, action must often implement knowledge gained through observation.

Observation often needs to be coupled with reflective thought for certain changes to occur. For instance, men had studied the skies for centuries, taking note of the stars and even, as in the case of Stonehenge, constructing elaborate and accurate astronomy observatories to use the stars to mark the earth's planting and harvesting seasons. Nevertheless, it took Kepler and Newton to explain the laws governing the motions of planets. Observation and recording alone, without reasoning, will not allow a child to know all that is necessary to survive in the world.

Thus, a useful way to view the changes in knowledge, thought processes, and behavior that occur throughout human development is to recognize that maturation of the central nervous system (by which we mean growth of insulating sheath around nerve fibers, establishment of connections between different parts of the brain, and, perhaps, alterations in biochemical systems) permits the child to coordinate his actions, pay attention for longer periods of time, remember more about an experience, detect inconsistencies, and be able to think and plan. As a result of these developments, a particular experience will be psychologically different for a one-year-old and a six-year-old. But during each maturational stage observation, classical and operant conditioning, and reflective thought produce the changes that have generally been called learning.

It is important to distinguish between the changes in mental ability that depend on maturation of the central nervous system (Piaget's theory is most concerned with these) and the specific changes in knowledge and mental activity that occur at a particular age as a result of observation, conditioning, and reflective thought. Robert Gagné, a psychologist who is closely identified with learning theory, has outlined the types of changes that can occur at particular ages.

Gagné's Theory

Although learning theory can more easily be applied to changes in behavior than to those in thought, Robert Gagné has tried to apply principles of learning theory to cognitive development. Gagné has proposed a cumulative learning theory. He attempts to bridge the gap between the very simple learning phenomenon usually associated with stimulus-response learning theory and the higher thought processes that are involved in a child's work at school. Gagné's eight learning types occur in a fixed order: he sees learning as cumulative because more complex types of learning depend on the previous mastery and the recall of similar types.

Learning type 1: signal learning. Gagné's first learning type corresponds to classical conditioning. A stimulus acts as the signal for a reaction. (In the example of Pavlov's dog, the gong is the signal that activates salivation.)

Learning type 2: stimulus-response learning. His second learning type corresponds to operant conditioning. A stimulus provokes a deliberate and specific response from the subject. (The sight of the disk leads the pigeon to peck at it in order to procure food.)

Learning type 3: chaining. Chaining involves the linking of two items of learning type 2. In one step of a chain, for instance, a child has an object that looks and feels a certain way: it is her "doll," but she doesn't know the word yet. However, in a nonverbal way she "knows" the doll. She may associate it with lying in her bed and hugging it. The next link is saying "doll" when she sees it, following the stimulus of seeing it plus hearing the name from her mother. In the final step, chaining, she is put into her crib for her nap, the thought of hugging the doll comes to her, she recalls the name (which she now knows), the two events link in her mind, and as she lies down she demands, "Doll!"

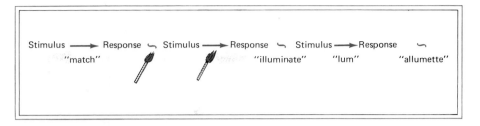

Figure 3-7
According to learning theorist Robert Gagné, one step in the sequence of
learning types involves verbal associations: the child uses some kind of coding
device to master foreign words or synonyms in the same language. For
example, a student learning that *allumette* is the French word for *match* is apt
to notice its resemblance to *illuminate.* That is, the syllable *lum* occurs in both
allumette and *illuminate.* So the student may think, "A match illuminates;
lum; allumette," after *lum* helps her remember that the French word for *match*
is *allumette.* (After Gagné, 1965)

Learning type 4: verbal associations. In this step Gagné is not
concerned with learning a label for an object, event, or idea (which
would be learning type 2) but with learning a word that is associated
with another word, as in learning a foreign language or mastering
synonyms within one language. He views verbal association as being
essentially a subvariety of chaining but with some special
characteristics. The process depends on a coding connection, and the
words must be "reeled off" in contiguity. For example, a student
learning that *allumette* is the French word for *match* is apt to notice its
resemblance to *illuminate* and uses the connection as the code (see
Figure 3-7). A person with wide verbal experience can form many
codes to help in verbal associations. Young children have relatively few
codes available to them and have greater difficulty making up a verbal
chain.

Learning type 5: discrimination learning. This learning type involves
two separate steps: first, perceptually discriminating among events and
second, attaching the proper names, or labels, to each of them. The
steps can be differentiated by considering the problem people
commonly have with identical twins (see Figure 3-8). After an initial
period of confusion, you learn that one twin has a small mole near the
cheekbone and the other does not. That is discrimination. It does not
solve the problem of remembering which name is attached to the twin
with the mole, so that twins are often faced with the announcement, "I
can tell you apart, but I can't remember who is called what."

Learning type 6: concept learning. This learning type involves
classifying stimulus situations in terms of properties such as color,
shape, position, and number. During the process a child comes to

Figure 3–8
Gagné's learning type 5, discrimination learning, can be illustrated by, first, telling twins apart and, second, attaching the proper name to each of them.

understand and recognize what a square is, what red is, what "in the middle" means. He shows that he knows the concept by performing accurately when asked, for instance, "Give me the middle block."

Learning type 7: rule learning. A rule is made up of two concepts joined by a verb. For instance, "The pronoun *each* takes a singular verb." To master rule learning, a child first needs to understand the two concepts involved. Then he must be able to show that he has mastered the rule—not by reciting it, but by using it. He might be able to fill in the blank in the statement "The pronoun *each* takes _____" with the correct answer. But the real test is whether he says, "Each of the boys goes to school" or "Each of the boys go to school."

Learning type 8: problem solving. Gagné's final learning type describes a child using rules in combination in order to deal with his environment. It involves defining the problem and clarifying what the solution should accomplish (sometimes stated as a *goal*); recalling rules that have been tried before and seem relevant; and regrouping the rules so that a new rule emerges and/or is learned. The example of a child making pairs from six colored squares illustrates Gagné's view of learning as a sequence of steps. Using learning type 5, the child discriminates among the colors; she distinguishes red from blue, both red and blue from green, and so forth. Next she uses the concept of "pairs"—learning type 6—to make sets of two squares each. Then she uses learning type 7, in this case a geometric method, to work out all the possible pairs of colors. She applies the rule—learning type 8—and comes up with the solution: fifteen. While the process of problem solving may take some time, the solution appears to occur in a "flash of insight." Unlike in learning types 1, 2, and 3, repetition does not appear to play a part (Gagné, 1965).

At this point, it should be clear that in Gagné's view, each step of learning uses the ideas mastered in the earlier steps.

Reflective Thought as a Mechanism of Change

So far we have discussed changes that depend on the child's direct experience. Does that mean that an adolescent who had never heard a conversation about corruption in government would never have that idea? Or that a child who was never reinforced for polite behavior would never behave in a polite way? Are there other ways to learn? Many philosophers and psychologists would say yes. They contend that the child, like the adult, is an actively thoughtful creature. He mentally works on the experiences he observes and the reinforcements he receives and transforms those experiences into new knowledge. It is possible, therefore, for an adolescent to conclude that some government officials are corrupt without ever having heard that opinion expressed and for a child to be polite to a friend even though that act was never reinforced by anyone. If we return to the original question—"What is the learner doing?"—we realize that in addition to observation he also engages in reflective thought.

Jean Piaget, a noted Swiss psychologist, gives a nice example of how an eight-year-old child playing alone discovers a new fact through reflective thought. There are seven pebbles arranged in a row in front of him. He counts them from left to right—1, 2, 3, 4, 5, 6, 7. He then counts the same pebbles from right to left and notes that the number remains the same. He then rearranges the pebbles into a circle and recounts them—again the same number. At that moment he discovers, by himself, a new idea; namely, the number of pebbles remains the same regardless of the direction in which they are counted or the pattern in which they are arranged. And at that moment it also strikes him that that fact is probably true for all objects, not just pebbles. He has generated a profound principle through reflective consideration of his experience.

Reflective thought involves accommodation as defined earlier, as well as the more sophisticated process in which the person generates thoughts or actions to match a standard.

Matching to a Standard

In accommodation the incentive for change comes from an event or thought that the child tries to relate to his existing knowledge. In that process he changes his prior knowledge, as in the case of a child's first encounter with a dwarf or a magnet. But the child need not have any idealized notion of what concept he should hold about the size of adults or what behavior he should initiate with horseshoe-shaped metal objects painted red at each end. In accommodation the child is practical. He cares only whether an idea or an action works to resolve uncertainty or facilitate the solution of a problem.

But in other instances the child holds a representation of some idea or act that he *wishes* to attain. This idealized structure can be called a

standard. The standard may be an effect to be gained through action, such as serving the tennis ball into the right court; an original design reflecting intellectual creativity, such as a theme for a poem or a plan for a simple engine; or a desired state of mind—perhaps tranquility after a demanding week of study. The child generates thoughts or behaviors in order to make his experience match the standard. He alters his ideas or behaviors in the service of approaching the desired goal. For example, a frustrated child loses his control and shouts at his mother because she asked him to stay home one evening. He holds the standard "Children should not shout at their parents." His action provokes him to generate explanations that will justify his angry behavior. He may come up with a hypothesis he never before entertained: "My mother is too restrictive, she deserves to be yelled at." Or "I'm an adolescent now and should not be told what to do." These cognitive inventions will be maintained if they resolve the child's uncertainty.

The same principle can apply to actions. For example, a child holds an ideal standard for the drawing of a tree, and her prior attempts fall far short of that ideal. She generates different strategies to improve the quality of her art. One day she hits upon the idea of imagining a tree in her mind. While she is drawing she uses that image as a guide. If that strategy improves her product, she will use it from then on, and a permanent change will have occurred in her psychological organization.

One of the most exhilarating moments for children occurs somewhere between the ages of seven and eleven when they discover that they are *thinking about their own thoughts*. One ten-year-old showed that she had passed into that stage when she climbed out of the bathtub and said, "I know it may seem like a funny thing to be thinking about, but do you ever wonder where people came from to begin with?"

Treating Thoughts Objectively

At the onset of this important stage of thinking, children begin to treat their thoughts as if they were objects in the outside world. They not only think, they think about what they are thinking about. They begin to play with ideas and possibilities in their minds, as they once played with blocks, trying one size on top of another to see which worked best for building a tower. They consistently try to generate efficient principles from their past experience. From then on, many of the changes that take place are due to a synthesis of prior experience (much of it acquired by observation) into more efficient and broader rules and concepts.

Diane is in the twelfth grade. One Sunday she notes three events. Early in the afternoon, she reads her history assignment and memorizes the facts concerning the initial rebellion of the American colonists, who were oppressed by the British on their own soil. Later, she watches a dramatization of *Elizabeth the First* on television. She is intrigued with the costumes and the headdresses of the people at court and with the emotions portrayed by the actress playing Queen Elizabeth, but she also notices the relentless political as well as religious rivalries between the heads of the Catholic and Protestant churches. Last, she watches the eleven o'clock news and hears that thirteen people have been killed by the IRA in a bombing in Northern Ireland. She notes similarities among these three events, and she suddenly generates two ideas that she had not thought about before:

1 Revolutions and rebellions take place when a minority group feels unjustly oppressed, in Ireland now as in America in 1775.
2 Strong religious rivalries influence politics. The disagreement between the heads of church in the Elizabethan costumes resembles the contemporary political trouble in Northern Ireland between the Catholics and the Protestants.

She realizes that historical events are not a series of unique causes and effects but are examples of a small number of themes that recur over time.

Thoughts as Change Agents for Action

Thought can also change actions. The fourteen-year-old girl learning to play tennis observes the tennis pro, practices her serve, and trains her reflexes and muscles. But she also thinks about improving her game. She reflects, "Why is it that so often the ball goes into the net instead of over the net? Maybe I'm swinging the racket down too far; or maybe I'm waiting too long, so that the ball has already dropped too low. I think I'll try to hit the ball sooner." So she does and finds that it clears the net. Her actions change as a result of her reflections.

Jean Piaget emphasizes the power of reflective thought as a significant cause of change in the child. Piaget believes that the child is in a continuing process of making sense of the world through his thoughts by dealing actively with objects, people, and ideas. The child is engaged in a constant game of discovering new puzzle pieces, fitting them into his ongoing idea of the puzzle, and changing the shape of the puzzle where necessary to allow for new pieces. Piaget believes that the ability to reason abstractly, to think about hypothetical situations in a logical way, and to organize rules into more complex and powerful structures are the goals of mental development.

Piaget's notion that major changes occur as a result of developmental maturation was initially based on his observations of his own three young children. Since Piaget is now in his eighties, he has had many years to reflect on his observations and work them into his own particular puzzle: how does a child's thought develop?

Piaget's Four Main Concepts

There are four important concepts in Piaget's theory: assimilation, accommodation, equilibration, and operations. The first three are processes. The fourth—operations—can be involved in these three processes. Since the operation is the major unit in Piagetian theory, it is useful to discuss it first.

Operations. An operation is a special kind of mental routine whose chief characteristic is that it is reversible. For instance, it is possible to break a ball of damp clay into two pieces and then reverse that action and put the pieces together to restore the original piece of clay. Or, six apples and four pears can be mentally combined to get ten pieces of fruit, and then the ten pieces of fruit can be divided into two different categories again: apples and pears. Or, a child can square the number 5 and get 25; she can also perform the reverse routine and take the square root of 25 and return to 5. The *knowledge* that one can do that is an operation. An operation resembles a rule with reversibility; it is a mental round trip. For Piaget the operation is the heart of mental activity, for it allows one to play with possibilities and to return to the starting point if those possibilities do not seem feasible. A pitcher can think out a plan for pitching to a left-handed batter, then change his mind and start over again with a new plan.

Piaget believes that the origins of operations begin early in infancy when the child interacts with objects. A child playing with a plate sees that one side has a design and the other side does not. He can reverse the plate over and over again, noticing that he can always return to either side. Piaget believes that a simple experience such as this lays down the foundation for the operational thought the child will achieve when he is in the second or third grade.

We should remember that not every new idea or piece of information is an operation; in fact, many are not. Facts or rules that are not reversible—fire burns, glass breaks, flowers smell—are not operations. However, the three processes whose descriptions follow can be applied generally to any new event or information.

Assimilation. Assimilation takes place when the child incorporates a new object or a new idea into his existing knowledge, that is, into his functional repertory. It is the act of fitting a new piece into the existing puzzle. For example, a child who has never seen a magnet before and does not know its properties will treat it as if it were like any other metal object he has seen in the past. A one-year-old will assume it is useful for banging and bang it like a stick. He treats the magnet as he does objects with which he is more familiar. Piaget would say, "He assimilates the magnet into his existing knowledge of small objects."

Accommodation. If assimilation is the process of recognizing what is familiar about a new event, accommodation involves taking into account the novel aspect of an event, enlarging one's existing knowledge, or creating a new category. The one-year-old with the magnet may bang the ends on a paper clip and discover that the paper clip sticks to the magnet. He is surprised initially; then he tries the magnet on a block of wood and discovers that it does not stick. He tries it on a nail and this time it does stick. Now he has changed from using the magnet for banging and moves on to a new game, using the magnet to test objects in order to discover if they will or will not stick to his new toy. He has accommodated to the unique quality of the object—the magnet's attraction to steel. In accommodation the child's existing ideas need to change or adjust in some way to an experience that he cannot fit into his existing rules.

Equilibration. Piaget's third process is like a balancing act: the mind finds the balancing point between what is familiar and what is unfamiliar about a newly encountered object, person, or event. Intellectual change, says Piaget, takes place at this balancing point, in resolving the tension between assimilation and accommodation; in finding the balance between using old thoughts and actions for a new situation (using the magnet as a banging object) and developing new thoughts and responses that are more suitable (using the magnet as a

way to attract an object). Equilibration is a specific process of adaptation; each time the child goes through the process of accommodating to a new event, his intellectual growth is nudged closer to maturity.

These three processes are evident in a ten-year-old confronting a sea urchin for the first time. He has categories for plants and for animals. He notices that the sea urchin looks like a plant, and initially he conceives of it as being a plant (assimilation). However, when he sees the sea urchin inch along the rocks, he relates that observation to his knowledge that plants do not move spontaneously, whereas animals do (accommodation). At that moment his category for animals is broadened to include this new plantlike form. That is the process of equilibration.

Piaget's Four Stages

Several psychologists have described stages of cognitive development through which a growing child passes, each stage characterized by particular cognitive functions. Piaget's four stages seem especially useful in helping us to understand mental development and to develop teaching approaches and techniques that will be most effective for children of different ages.

Piaget has called the four stages sensorimotor, preoperational, concrete operational, and formal operational.

The stages in the development of thought must be mastered in a fixed order (stage three cannot be reached before stage two), and no stage can be skipped (stage three cannot be reached right after stage one). Nevertheless, although the stages occur in sequence, they are not precisely keyed to a certain chronological age. We cannot watch a child to see if she moves from stage two to stage three precisely on her seventh birthday. Rather, she is constantly in transition. While you are reading about Piaget's four stages keep in mind that these characteristics are most useful if we remember that a child is not enclosed in a stage but passing through it.

Stage 1: sensorimotor. In his first year and a half of life a baby moves from actions that are purely reflexive (sucking, smiling, turning his head), to actions that he deliberately initiates in order to achieve an effect (shaking a rattle in order to make it produce a sound), and finally, to the threshold of true intellectual activity (where he carries on some kind of assessment and consideration of a problem). A baby has reached this threshold when his ball has rolled out of reach across the table, and instead of crying or kicking in a hopeful but random attempt to retrieve it, he pauses for ten seconds and then reaches out and pulls the tablecloth toward him, bringing the ball into his lap.

Stage 2: preoperational. In the second stage, which children pass through from about a year and a half to seven years of age, the child

has command of a number of cognitive abilities that the sensorimotor child lacked. He uses language and other symbols. A three-year-old child gives her doll milk to drink from a cup because it is her "baby." A child of three years may arrange all the magnetized plastic letters on the refrigerator door by color, but Piaget believes that he does not yet have a mental representation of a set of categories. He is not aware of any defining characteristics that unite all the members of a class of objects (the child does not think, "These are all the red letters."). The child in this stage cannot reliably take the viewpoint of another person in all situations. In psychological terms he is *egocentric*. If he is shown an oversized chair in a doll's house, he sees it as "small" from his own point of view rather than "large" in proportion to the doll and the other pieces of furniture. Although a preoperational child can deal with symbols, he does not have a larger grasp of concepts and has not organized his thoughts in coherent structures.

Stage 3: concrete operational thought. Some time between six and eight years of age, an American child passes into the stage of concrete operations (it may be later for children growing up in isolated, nonmodern communities). Now the child has a set of rules that she did not possess earlier and that help her adapt to her environment. These new operations, which Piaget calls groupings, have special logical qualities. Once the child has mastered these groupings, she is able to appreciate four fundamental truths. First, she knows that if A is equal to B in some quantitative attribute (let us say, weight) and B is equal to

C, then A and C must be equal. She realizes that equalities of magnitude among objects have a reversible quality. In a moment we shall see how that is relevant for the grouping called conservation. Second, the concrete operational child appreciates that categories, which Piaget calls *classes*, nest into one another in a hierarchical manner. Thus the class "all pets that are dogs" and the class "all pets that are not dogs" nest into a category "pets." Moreover, "all animals that are pets" and "all animals that are not pets" nest into a category "animals." Third, the child realizes that fixed relations exist among certain attributes and entities. If A is taller than B and B is taller than C, then A must be taller than C. In the stage of concrete operations the child knows this last fact about A and C must be true, even if she has never seen A, B, or C.

Finally, the concrete operational child appreciates that specific attributes or objects can belong to more than one class or more than one relation at one time. Consider the two classes, "animals that are pets" versus "animals that are not pets" and the classes "furry" and "feathered" (see Figure 3–9). The child in the concrete operational stage appreciates that a dog belongs in the category that intersects pets and furry. Similarly, she appreciates that an event can be part of more than one relation. Consider one set of relations involving size (from small to large) and another set of relations involving color (from light to dark). She knows, generally, that a pebble is both small and pale, a tree large and dark, a sail large and white.

Piaget has made famous a series of experiments with children that are specific examples of these groupings. Let us consider the most famous of the victories that the concrete operational child displays.

CONSERVATION The preoperational child cannot grasp the idea that a particular number of buttons, quantity of water, or amount of clay is

Figure 3–9
Classification on two dimensions: the concrete operational child, according to Piaget, can consider the classes "animals that are pets" and "animals that are not pets" and also the classes "furry" and "feathered." The child can appreciate that dogs belong to the category that intersects pets and furry; bears to the category nonpet, furry; canaries to the category pet, feathered; and ostriches to the category nonpet, feathered.

	ANIMALS THAT ARE PETS	ANIMALS THAT ARE NOT PETS
FURRY	Dog	Bear
FEATHERED	Canary	Ostrich

Figure 3–10
Conservation: a child in the stage of concrete operational thought can recognize that the amount of water in the short glass is the same as in the tall glass, even though the level of water in the tall glass is higher. Before he reaches that stage, a child will state with certainty, "There is more water in the tall glass."

conserved (remains the same) no matter how it appears or is arranged spatially (see Figure 3–10). If he takes a particular measure of water and pours it into the tall, thin glass, then takes the same measure, fills it up again, and pours it into the short, wide glass, he is deceived by the higher level of water in the tall glass. He does not believe the amount of water is the same. By about age seven, though, he knows the amount is the same. He has mastered the operation of conservation.

The operation of conservation is one of the hallmarks of the concrete operational stage. The child's new understanding about the game with glasses of water implies that the child is on his way to understanding that even though some perceptual qualities such as shape and height may change, the more abstract qualities of quantity, volume, and weight do not necessarily change with them despite alterations in appearance. He realizes that whether a piece of clay is rounded into a ball, flattened into a pancake, or rolled into a sausage, its mass, weight, and volume remain the same. Psychologists call this the ability to conserve. It is an operation because the child knows that the pancake and the sausage shapes contain the same amount of clay as the ball. One of the bases for this belief is that the clay can be returned

> I hear, and I forget.
> I see, and I remember.
> I do, and I understand.
>
> Ancient Chinese Proverb
>
> Although this traditional Chinese saying goes back centuries, its essence has been corroborated in the work of the twentieth-century Swiss psychologist Jean Piaget, who believes that by manipulating, arranging, and rearranging objects, children gain an understanding of the objects' capabilities and structures.

to a ball, that is, the operation is reversible. Another is the rule that a given mass retains its identity; that is, the weight or mass of an object is a constant quality of an object unless something is taken away or added to it.

CLASS INCLUSION   According to Piaget the concrete operational child can think about the whole and a part of the whole simultaneously. If you show her eight yellow buttons and four brown buttons and ask her "Are there more yellow buttons or more buttons?", she will answer, "More buttons." A preoperational child cannot take into account the part and the whole simultaneously and will answer, "More yellow buttons." This achievement is an example of the grouping that permits the child to know that classes nest into one another. The class "yellow buttons" and the class "nonyellow buttons" are part of a larger class "buttons." Conversely, all the buttons minus the nonyellow buttons yields the class "yellow buttons."

SERIATION   A concrete operational child can arrange sticks of differing lengths into a series according to their lengths. In that case he is using the quantitative dimension of length. He may arrange disks according to their diameter, plastic blocks according to their weight. These are all dimensional measures. (The next step would be to arrange objects according to two dimensions, such as height and diameter, using cylindrical metal weights from old-fashioned scales.) The ability to serialize is an obvious prerequisite to mathematics. When a child begins to understand the relation of numbers to one another, he can begin to do arithmetic (add 7 and 9 or subtract 2 from 4) as opposed to simply reciting numbers by rote or counting the objects in a single set (counting all the buttons on his sweater).

RELATIONAL TERMS   As a child begins to think about numbers in relation to each other, she also develops a more sophisticated understanding of relational terms such as darker, bigger, and heavier. When younger, she thought "darker blue" meant blue that was very dark: she saw the colors as absolutes. Now she knows that it means a blue that is merely darker than another blue—even if both are light shades of blue.

In short, a child in the concrete operational stage has developed a set of rules that help her deal with reality and that she can use to assimilate and accommodate new events. These rules allow her to conserve mass, weight, volume, and number; deal with parts and wholes; serialize; and understand relational terms.

Stage 4: formal operational thought. A child in the concrete operational stage can reason about the properties, facts, and relationships that have to do with objects and real events—such as the mass of the piece of clay or the category "yellow buttons." Hence an eight-year-old can detect the logical inconsistency in the statement, "They discovered the skull of Abraham Lincoln when he was a baby," or solve a problem such as, "If Anne had six apples and gave away two apples, how many apples did she have left?" In both cases, the child is required to reason about concrete phenomena—the age of Abraham Lincoln when he died and the fact that skulls can only be found after death; that six and two are quantity adjectives that can be applied to apples.

According to Piaget the child in the stage of formal operations, which is reached at about age twelve, can transcend concrete reality and consider what may be. Adolescents can operate on propositions that are about other propositions, not just about concrete objects. They can detect the logical inconsistency in the following statement: "If X or Y leads to Z, then it is false to assume that if Y does not occur, Z will not occur." The adolescent can assume hypothetical conditions and generate implications. Piaget described it as thought taking wings (Inhelder and Piaget, 1958). The adolescent is no longer just preoccupied with all the ramifications of what is real; he or she is capable of dealing with what is possible.

REASONING ABOUT HYPOTHETICAL SITUATIONS   The adolescent is also able to deal with the hypothetical even though it violates his view of the real world. The older adolescent appreciates that problems may be self-contained entities that can be solved by special rules. He will try to solve a logical problem that involves unicorns or people from Mars, even though he views them as unreal objects. For instance, if the adolescent is asked, "If all unicorns have yellow feet and I have yellow feet, am I a unicorn?", he will examine the logic of the statement and quickly answer, "No." The seven-year-old, on the other hand, will not know how to deal with the problem and will say that he cannot do it,

perhaps because he knows that the unicorn does not exist, and he has trouble reasoning about objects he does not believe in. However, if the seven-year-old is asked, "If all women wear shoes and I wear shoes, am I a woman?", he will quickly answer, "No." He can reason logically about situations that are real (and familiar), but the adolescent can reason logically about situations that are both real and unreal.

SYSTEMATIC AND EXHAUSTIVE SEARCH FOR THE POSSIBILITIES   A second characteristic of the stage of formal operations is the ability to approach a problem with a systematic plan, to exhaust all the possible solution hypotheses, and to *be certain* that all possibilities have been exhausted. Let us turn again to the example of the child who is given six plastic squares of different colors—red, green, yellow, blue, orange, and purple—and is asked how many possible pairs of colors can be made (see Figure 3–11).

A concrete operational child is likely to make as many pairs as she can by trial and error. She puts the red with the blue, leaves them, then picks up the yellow square and puts it with the green one. She may pick up the red one again and pair it with the purple square. In a few minutes she has made a number of pairs but has run out of ideas.

An adolescent in the stage of formal operations, however, is not likely to waste her time with trial and error techniques. She knows the rule: namely, to pair each color with every other color. She picks up one color (red), compares it with every other color on the table, and jots down the number of pairs—five. She then takes the next square (green), and pairs it with every other color, and again jots down the number—five. At this point, she may notice the repetition of five and think that she can use multiplication to solve the problem. Looking again, however, she realizes she has counted one of the color pairs twice: red and green is the same as green and red. She may then pick up a pencil and draw a geometric diagram with lines between each possible pair. When she has finished, she checks to be sure all the squares are linked once, and once only, and then simply counts up the lines. She knows the answer is correct, for she has followed the logical requirements of the problem.

Even in less logically constrained problem situations the adolescent tries to exhaust all possibilities. Consider the following question put to a seven-year-old and a fourteen-year-old: "A man walking in the forest came upon a large area of trees that were lying on the ground. How might that have happened?" The younger child is likely to give one answer, such as, "The wind blew them down." The older child is apt to generate and systematically explore all the possible reasons—a

Figure 3–11
A child in the stage of formal operations can systematically organize a plan of attack to solve a problem such as this one: how many possible pairs can be made from six colored squares? Whereas a younger child will randomly try out two or three pairs and then give up, an older child may draw a geometric pattern of connecting lines between the squares and then count up the lines to arrive at the solution: fifteen.

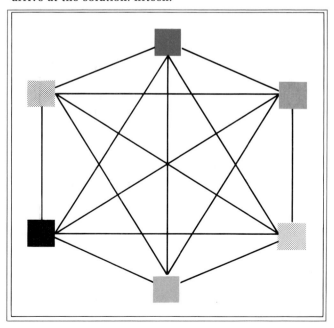

Yesterday, Today, and Tomorrow

SIX-YEAR-OLD CHILD: "Where is tomorrow right now? I know—yesterday, today was tomorrow."

ELEVEN-YEAR-OLD CHILD: "I wonder why it was so dark when we arrived in London, when we left New York in the morning? I guess because in London, the clocks are set differently. The farther east you go, the sooner the sun comes up, so the sooner the day starts. Let's call that seven o'clock. So when it's morning here, it's already afternoon in London. No, it starts farther east— in China, but no, even farther east, if you keep going around—in the Hawaiian Islands. But that's almost around to California! When the sun is going down in California, it's about ready to come up in Hawaii. Now, should I call that today or tomorrow?"

Both children are thinking about an abstract question—time, the provocative concept that attempts to relate nature's cycles and human awareness of them. However, each child deals with the question of time in a different manner, appropriate to her respective age. The young child views yesterday, today, and tomorrow as if they were concrete objects, with one taking the place of another at a specific moment. (She might even get out three blocks and use one to push another out of the "today" place into the "yesterday" place.) The older child uses familiar landmarks on the globe as points of reference but manipulates the concept of time in a theoretical way, trying to determine the nature of the relationship between the sun and the earth. Although she begins with a concrete problem—the unexpected darkness in London—she transcends the concrete situation of her trip across the Atlantic and considers it from a philosophical point of view as it affects the world.

hurricane, lumbering, vandalism, an earthquake—and check each carefully for its probable validity. This is one of the hallmarks of the stage of formal operations.

Finally, the adolescent in this stage examines his beliefs in sets and searches for inconsistencies among them. A fourteen-year-old will brood about the following two propositions: (1) God loves humanity and (2) The world contains many unhappy people. Troubled by the incompatibility he senses when he examines these two beliefs together, he recognizes the contradiction—if God loved humanity, he would not make so many people unhappy—and generates four possible solutions. He can deny that people are unhappy (but this is unlikely for its factual basis is so obvious to him). He can deny that God loves humanity (but avoids this for love of humanity is one of the definitive qualities of God). He can assume that the unhappiness serves a subtle purpose that God has for man: this may strike him as a reasonable and acceptable possibility and he may choose it. Or, finally, he can deny the existence of God. Able to examine the logic of his beliefs, the adolescent begins to question their validity and searches for a new set of values and premises.

As well as being rational and systematic, formal thought is self-conscious. Self-conscious reflection is one of the major steps in the development of cognition: the individual's awareness of his own thoughts, his curiosity about what produces them, where they will lead him, and how they are organized (Piaget, 1952).

Evaluation of Piaget's Theories

Psychologists disagree somewhat about various details in Piaget's arrangement of stages. First, there appears to be greater range in the ages when children pass through the stages than he suggests. A five-year-old American child may be able to understand the conservation of a mass of clay while a nine-year-old rural Latin American child cannot. In Switzerland not all children appear to reach stage two by the age of six; and the average child in Martinique is about four years behind children in Geneva (Ginsburg and Opper, 1969).

Nevertheless, Piaget's assumption that a child's intellectual growth can be conceptualized in terms of stages, each with distinct abilities, continues to be useful, and its acceptance has had revolutionary implications for teaching. In spite of the variety of ages at which a child may cross the threshold between one stage and another, it is commonly accepted that an individual passes through the stages successively. That is the important point. It recognizes that a child is not merely a shorter and less experienced adult. His mental functioning is different. This means that his level of *readiness* to acquire new skills must be taken seriously. A preoperational child cannot understand mathematics because he has not yet acquired the prerequisite operations: mental representation, serialization, conservation. An important part of the teacher's responsibility, therefore, is to discover where the child is in cognitive development and meet him there, devising appropriate strategies that will lead him toward an agreed-on goal.

Piaget says that there is an "American question" that he is asked in the United States and nowhere else: "If there are stages that children reach at given norms of ages, can we accelerate the stages ... how far can we speed them up?" (Elkind, 1968, p. 78). Most psychologists and teachers, like Piaget himself, are distrustful of this attitude. Certainly, Piaget's work has contributed to an understanding of how changes take place in a child's cognitive structure. But the understanding should not be exploited in an attempt to hurry the process. Nor should it be used to classify a child in a pejorative way. If a fifth-grade teacher realizes that some of her children are beginning to show evidence of formal thinking, while others are not, the knowledge may help her in planning individual instruction for each of the children. But the evidence should not be held against the student who is still mastering the steps of concrete operations.

In short, a child's behaviors, cognitions, and feelings all undergo change as she grows. The most important changes in his development are those that are part of his inherited, or maturational, program. Given almost any natural environment—a child will not mature if he remains locked in a closet—the child will pass through Piaget's stages of cognitive development, will come to experience the affects shame, guilt, joy, and love, and will become more skilled at running, climbing, and singing. These changes are inevitable, even though we do not completely understand how they occur. Piaget has outlined a possible scheme for the maturation of certain aspects of cognitive development given the normal experiences of most children in their natural environments.

Implications for Teaching

A school wants to see a child change in many ways—behaviorally, emotionally, cognitively. It wants her to become less restless and more cooperative, to be angry and sad less of the time and happy and excited more of the time. It wants her to gain a greater knowledge of the world and an increased skill at reading and mathematics. Throughout the remaining chapters we will refer again and again to the information presented in this chapter. We will conclude this chapter by considering a final question: what conditions are required for changes to occur most readily? Four conditions seem primary: competence, attention, time for practice, and opportunity to reflect.

Competence. Competence is a child's basic ability to understand and implement the task to be mastered. The child must have the proper skills to learn the task. A child's readiness is partly a matter of age (that is, level of maturity) and partly a matter of past experiences. Two-year-olds cannot learn to be cooperative all the time no matter how carefully they are handled, and six-year-olds have not mastered enough basic arithmetic to understand spherical geometry.

Competence is not always obvious from the child's daily behavior. The teacher must be conscious of a distinction between the child's potential competence, which is *hidden,* and his performance, which is *visible.* Competence refers to the ability and the knowledge that children have locked inside and can, under the right circumstances, display. Performance refers to what children reveal in the classroom on a test or in daily behavior. They usually know a great deal more than they show. For example, they know many more words than they

actually use. If you ask a six-year-old what the word is for a huge extinct reptile, she may reply, "tyrannosaurus." Yet from one year to the next the word tyrannosaurus may never appear in her spontaneous conversation. In other words, there can be a gap between a child's competence and performance. Since an obvious goal of education is to help children maximize the use of what they know, the factors that control this gap will be discussed at length in the next chapters.

Attention. A second prerequisite is that the child attend to those aspects of his environment that contain the essential information he needs. He must watch and listen to the teacher, notice the key words in the passage he is reading, or heed the crucial muscular actions involved in playing tennis. Since the level of concentration a child achieves has a strong impact on how he changes, the ability and willingness to pay attention is a major factor in school. As we saw in the example of the child learning Spanish vocabulary, motivation can be critical: if a child wants to learn he will pay attention and concentrate. If he is not interested in learning, he will watch the leaves out the window instead of the blackboard.

Time to practice. Many of the changes that the school promotes cannot be achieved in one lesson, or in one week. They require a period of time in which a child can first master, then polish her ability to perform a task. If she is learning multiplication, she must first learn the tables. Then she needs to rehearse them so thoroughly that she has no hesitation about using them quickly, as well as correctly. Obviously, that could not be accomplished in a week, even if she studied nothing else for seven days. A teacher needs to allow time for her to practice and provide reinforcement during the time so that her interest does not sag.

Opportunity to reflect. Finally, a child needs the psychic room to enjoy and pursue his own insights. In one sense, the need for freedom to reflect mentally is similar to the need for time to practice behaviorally. The child is continually examining and reviewing his knowledge in order to use it more efficiently and more precisely. He uncovers a similarity and uses it to form a new rule. For example, a child initially regards eggs and caterpillars as totally different entities: one is static, oval shaped, and smooth; the other is ambulatory, long and fuzzy. But when he realizes that they are both objects in an early phase of development—one to develop into a chicken and one into a butterfly—he regards them as having more in common than, say, eggs and snowballs, even though snowballs, like eggs, are static, oval shaped, and smooth. It is not an insight he has been taught: he generated it himself. A key function of a teacher is to provide an atmosphere and schedule in which such insights are encouraged.

This chapter has presented some ideas about the mechanisms of change in the child in school. Chapters 4 and 5 will discuss how these changes are brought about; they will deal with the cognitive processes involved as a child learns to think in progressively more sophisticated ways.

Summary

Although the word *learning* is generally used loosely, we apply it to three different classes of lasting change: changes in behavior, in feelings, and in cognition. A child's actions, feelings, and cognitions may go through changes that are universal, such as learning to speak one's own language, or culturally specific such as learning to play baseball or do long division.

Several different mechanisms are involved in change. We can approach the study of these mechanisms by asking the question, "What is the learner doing?" Two fundamental actions lead to change: the learner is observing and the learner is engaged in reflective thought.

Observation, the child's earliest mechanism of learning, may involve imitation: the behavioral expression of some action whose representation was acquired through observation. Children imitate particular actions for many reasons—they hold a mental representation of themselves in the role of the model, or want to resolve the uncertainty generated by a discrepant, or unusual, event. They also imitate to produce excitement or to increase their similarity to a model. Imitation allows the child to practice an action, improve it, and bring it closer to the ideal form—part of a broader mechanism called accommodation. Accommodation involves focusing attention on a discrepant event or experience, adjusting to its unique character, relating the event to what one knows, and finally, generating a mental representation of the event. The process may, but does not necessarily, lead to new behavior.

Reinforcement is a special factor that sometimes facilitates the acquisition of new behaviors and the elimination of old ones. Building on principles of classical conditioning and operant conditioning, learning theorists suggest that a child's behavior is altered by establishing a stimulus-response bond (S-R bond), that is, by means of reinforcement, or reward, which follows a behavior to a stimulus. Generalization, discrimination, extinction, and frequency of reinforcement are four principles that govern the relation of the S-R bond to behavior. Reinforcement has limitations, however, and is not the only method, nor is it necessarily the most efficient way, to achieve some kinds of change in a child.

One learning theorist, Robert Gagné, attempts to apply principles of learning theory to cognitive acquisitions, not just to behavior. His theory includes eight learning types, which occur sequentially: signal learning, stimulus-response learning, chaining, verbal associations, discrimination learning, concept learning, rule learning, and problem solving.

Reflective thought is also a strong change agent; it involves accommodation, as defined earlier, and a more sophisticated process in which the individual generates thoughts and actions to match a standard. Swiss psychologist Jean Piaget theorizes that there are three important processes involved in reflective thought: assimilation (incorporating a new object or event into existing knowledge); accommodation (taking into account the novel aspect of the event); and equilibration (resolving the tension between the familiar and the novel aspects of the new event). In addition, the child acquires a reversible ability that Piaget calls the operation. One important operation is the ability to understand the conservation of quantity, such as the fact that the amount of water in a tall, thin glass does not change when it is poured into a short, wide glass.

Piaget believes that a child progresses sequentially through four stages: the baby's sensorimotor stage is followed by the young child's preoperational stage. Between six and eight, children move into the concrete operational stage, when they master several important operations—conservation, class inclusion, seriation, and relational terms. In Piaget's final stage of formal operational thought, children not only can reason about concrete objects and real events but can speculate about abstract and hypothetical situations, attack a problem with a systematic plan, and self-consciously consider the validity of their own thoughts and speculations.

A school wants to see a child change in a variety of ways and implements various mechanisms to bring about changes. Whatever methods are used, four conditions seem necessary for change to take place; competence (the child's basic ability to understand the task to be mastered), attention, time to practice, and opportunity to reflect.

Projects

1 Find an eleven-year-old child and try out the experiment involving the pairing of colored squares described in this chapter.
2 Buy or borrow a toy advertised as appropriate for preschool children. Evaluate the toy in terms of its usefulness in fostering learning.
3 For a preoperational child, devise an experiment (such as the one described on page 115) to test Piaget's theory of egocentricity. Conduct the experiment.
4 Make a list of objects that could be usefully displayed in a fourth-grade classroom (for example, a photograph of a Kenyan woman working in the fields or a model of the life cycle of a chicken). Describe what a teacher could do to increase the changes that occurred in a child as a result of observing the objects.
5 Observe a group that is obviously a family, but about which you have no prior information (likely places to look: a restaurant, park, church, bowling alley, concert). List and detail observable similarities among this group that could be attributed to learning by imitation, such as posture, mannerisms, and behavior.
6 Outline a learning event that a high-school student may encounter in a science class and show, after Gagné, how the first step is a prerequisite to the second, and the second to the third.
7 Try to see the Truffaut film, *The Wild Child (L'Enfant Sauvage),* about the attempt to convert a boy, found living wild in the woods, into a civilized human being. Assess what the boy had already learned, as well as the new aspects of civilization that he encountered.
8 Recall a class that you attended in the past week in which you learned a new skill. In terms of what you have read in this chapter, analyze your thinking. What part, if any, did reinforcement play? Did the classroom situation encourage reflective thought or work against it?

Recommended Reading

Baldwin, A. L. *Theories of child development.* New York: John Wiley, 1967. An excellent discussion of the basic theories of development, especially the theory of Jean Piaget and the stimulus-response theories, including both social-learning and reinforcement-based theories.

Gagné, R. M. *The conditions of learning.* New York: Holt, Rinehart and
    Winston, 1965. A detailed description of Gagné's theory of learning
    and his educational philosophy.
Piaget, J. *The origins of intelligence in children.* New York:
    International Universities Press, 1952. A relatively clear statement of
    Piaget's basic theory and of the stages of intellectual development.

cognition I: units and processes of problem solving

4

Two major psychological forces facilitate children's mastery of a new skill, idea, or fact. The first consists of their *cognitive* abilities, which include their knowledge and the transformations they can perform on their knowledge. The second, their *attention to the task,* is a function of their motivation, which, in turn, is regulated by their expectancy of success on the task. Children who want to learn to read, either to please their parents or for the sake of the ability itself, may or may not act on that motive depending on their assessment of whether or not they will be able to perform well. If they expect to succeed and their motivation is strong, they will attend to the materials. If they expect to fail or seriously doubt their ability to accomplish the assigned task, children may turn away from the work, even though they want to learn the new skill. This chapter and Chapter 5 deal with the child's cognitive abilities; Chapters 6 and 7 examine the child's motives and expectation of success.

The Meaning of Cognition

Cognition is a general term used to cover the processes involved in extracting information from the outside world, applying prior knowledge to newly perceived information, integrating the two to create new knowledge, storing that information in memory, subsequently retrieving it for use, and continually evaluating the quality and logical coherence of one's mental products. Cognition, in brief, refers to acquisition, storage, transformation, creation, evaluation, and utilization of knowledge. The action of a living cell is a useful metaphor for cognition. The cell contains basic structures that are part of its fundamental inheritance. As a plant cell is built to convert the energy of sunlight into sugar and an animal cell is designed to convert amino acids into complex proteins, the human mind is constructed to convert experience into abstract representations. Even a day-old baby is prepared by her inheritance to attend to events characterized by change. In vision such events include objects that move and have a

well-defined contour (that is, the edge of a black line on a white background). For example, the two major loci of contrast in the human face are the eyes, which are bilaterally placed, horizontal, circular, and have a distinct contour. These four, salient elements attract the infant's attention, and by two months of age, the infant has converted that experience into an abstract representation of the human face. (We suspect that this is what happens because if we rearrange the eyes in a drawing of a human face so that they are vertical rather than horizontal or omit the eyes altogether, the infant's reaction to the face alters significantly; she will look at it less and will not smile at it. The ten-month-old is surprised by a picture of a face that does not contain two horizontal, bilaterally placed eyes [Kagan, 1971].)

Similarly, the human mind is constructed to treat the sounds of human speech, particularly consonants, in a special way. As early as one to two months of age the infant will easily discriminate *pa* from *ba* but has much greater difficulty telling the difference between *ah* (short *a*) and *ay* (long *a*).

Let us continue our analogy between the cell and the mind. The cell structures of the animal that are basic to its functions include DNA, RNA, minerals, salts, sugars, and fats. The mind, too, contains certain structures, or units—schemata, images, symbols, concepts, and rules (we shall describe them in a moment)—that participate in certain dynamic processes. The cell's processes include the construction of amino acids. The mind's processes include perception, memory, organization, activation of solution hypotheses, reflection, transformation, and implementation. This chapter will discuss the units and processes. But first we should consider an idea that will be discussed in detail in the next chapter: cognitive competence.

Cognitive competence means the potential capacity to apply certain "structure-process combinations" to a particular problem context. For example, we say that an animal cell is competent to manufacture the hormone insulin. In the presence of certain conditions—both internal and external—the chemical structures in the cell will be manipulated by particular processes to produce insulin. Both the context and the competence are important. The cell does not continually manufacture insulin. It tends to be manufactured when the sugar level of the blood rises to a critical level. As we know, some people, called diabetics, lost or never had the competence to make enough insulin. Similarly, the competence to learn a new word is activated when the child hears someone apply that word to an object or event that he knows. If he never hears the word (that is, if there is no context), he will, of course, not learn it. Nor will he learn it if he lacks the competence, no matter how many times he hears it. As some people are unable to produce enough insulin, some children with certain rare disorders of the central nervous system are unable to learn new words.

Let us turn to the units and the processes of the mind. To help distinguish between them, we can consider another analogy. In chess, pawns, kings, queens, bishops, knights, and rooks are *units* used to play the game. The moves—attacking, defending, castling, and checkmating—are *processes* used to manipulate the units according to certain rules. The relationship between the chess pieces and the chess moves can help us understand the material in the following sections.

Units Employed in Cognition

A child uses five different units in thought: schemata (singular: schema), images, symbols, concepts, and rules. This section will first define these units and then examine their development in the preschool child.

Schemata

A schema, the young child's earliest cognitive unit, contributes to the units that develop later. Neither an image, as described below, nor a photographic copy, a schema is a representation of the salient

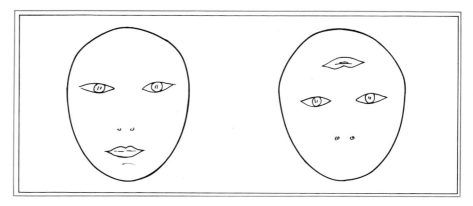

Figure 4–1
A schema, a young child's first cognitive unit, outlines the unique arrangement and preserves the essential aspects of an event; in this cartoon of a face (left) the features are in the appropriate places and although it is only a simple sketch, even a young child would distinguish it from the cartoon (right) in which the features are in the wrong places.

characteristics of an object or an event. Like a cartoonist's caricature, it preserves the outstanding and most essential aspects of the event in a unique pattern. A face, for instance, is an arrangement of features in a particular pattern (see Figure 4–1).

A simple experiment can illustrate what is meant by a schema. Look out the window for a few seconds, then turn away. Now ask a friend to look out the window and name some objects that appear in the scene outside and some that do not. You will probably be able to identify which objects are present and which are not with over 90 percent accuracy. Your ability to do this is derived from your schema for that scene: you can check off the items your friend names against the knowledge you hold in your mind.

Images

Compared to a schema, which is the elemental unit of the mind, an image is a more detailed, elaborate, and conscious representation—a finely delineated picture of a friend's face, say, or of a familiar park. Since conscious and controlled mental work is required to manufacture a detailed image from the more skeletal schema, probably the very young infant has no images. While everyone can see an object when it is in front of his eyes, only a few children and even fewer adults in the Western world are able to preserve a detailed visual image in their mind's eye after they have looked away from the object. Children who can maintain the image of a complex event and describe it in detail are said to have *eidetic imagery:* forty-five seconds after a picture has been taken away from their sight, they can still "see" it and report the details. About 5 to 10 percent of American children can do this. For some reason that is not completely understood, children and adults from nonliterate groups, such as the Ibo of Nigeria, have a frequency of eidetic imagery closer to 20 percent (Doob, 1964). Moreover, the occurrence of eidetic imagery among mentally retarded American children is also close to 20 percent, although again, the reasons are not clear (Siipola and Hayden, 1965).

Symbols

While an image or a schema is a partial replica of an object or an event, a *symbol* is an *arbitrary* way of representing an event or an object. An obvious example is the alphabet, each letter of which is a symbol representing a particular sound. There is nothing inherent in the shape of z to suggest that it should represent the buzzing sound we make. Nevertheless, in the English alphabet that is the case; ZZZZZZZZ is even used to symbolize snoring in cartoons. Although many similar sounds turn up in various languages, they are usually represented by entirely different symbols (see Figure 4–2). Numbers, letters of the alphabet, letters arranged in a particular pattern to stand for words, and

Figure 4–2
In this collection of symbols six of the "familiar" symbols are not English alphabet letters but symbols from the Cyrillic alphabet, used in the Russian language. Although the shapes of the characters are almost exactly like the ones used in our alphabet, they stand for quite different sounds, showing that symbols are entirely arbitrary designations for events.

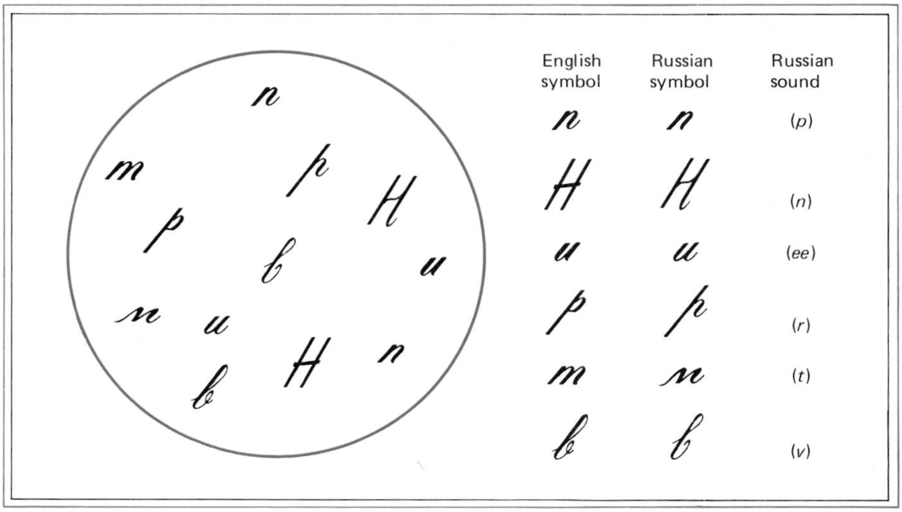

drawings used for international traffic signs (for example, an arrow symbolizing straight ahead) are all examples of symbols. Symbols are a component of a fourth unit of thought, the concept.

Concepts

The major difference between a symbol and a concept is that while the symbol stands for a specific object or event, a concept stands for a set of attributes shared by a group of objects or events. A concept represents what is common among a set of related objects or experiences (see Figure 4–3). If you ask a young child why she says that the woman in the grocery store is a mother, she may reply, "Because she has long hair and wears a skirt." Her answer suggests that she holds a concept of *mother* based on the attributes of long hair and skirts, which she has seen on many women. If she applied the word *mother* only to her own mother, we would know that she recognized the individual person, but we would not know if she possessed the concept.

Figure 4–3
The attribute game, played in various forms by schoolchildren of different ages, consists of recognizing the attributes of a concept and grouping them in sets. In this game, played with wooden blocks, a loop of string is used to define each set: one set consists of blocks that are *triangles;* a second set of blocks that are *green*, whatever their shape; and a third set of blocks that are *large*, whatever their shape or color. Therefore, *shape, color,* and *size* are the critical attributes being considered.

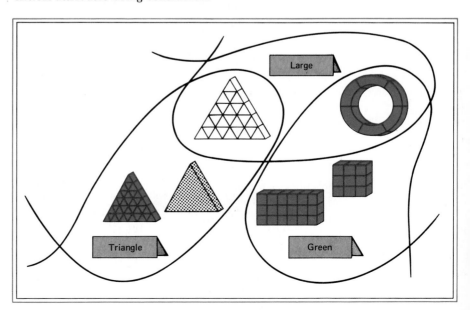

But when she applies the label to different people who share the same characteristics, we know she possesses a concept of *mother*.

A concept may represent the extracted characteristics common to a group of objects (long hair and a skirt viewed as attributes of *mother*), or it may represent shared qualities of experience *(friendliness, speed, refreshing, anxious)*. In these instances, the child recognizes a set of qualities common to various events that are summarized by the concept. The concept may be concrete *(mother)* or abstract *(friendliness)*. Furthermore, a child can understand a concept without possessing the word for it. He may not know the word *friendliness,* yet he may still appreciate that smiles, hugs, and a sense of well-being, coming his way from another person, are a common trio of experiences associated with certain people. He possesses the concept *friendliness.* It is also possible to possess a concept without being able to state its factual basis. People often find it difficult to describe beauty, for example, or to agree on what is beautiful, although each person knows when something he has encountered seems beautiful to him: the music of Mozart, the lily pads of Monet, the face of a grandmother.

One may ask why it is necessary to posit the notion of a concept. What does it explain and why do we need it? One of the most persuasive reasons for assuming there are such things as concepts comes from a phenomenon that is called *proactive interference.* If one reads to a ten-year-old trios of different words that are not part of the same concept (flower, pencil, apple; nail, grass, books; red, thirty-one, pipe cleaner) and after each trio the child is distracted by being asked to do something else for twenty seconds so that he cannot rehearse (repeat to himself) the three words, the child has no difficulty in remembering each of the trios read to him. He will recall the third trio of words as well as he did the first.

But if all the trios of words belong to the same concept (bear, tiger, chicken; cow, horse, mule; dog, squirrel, pig), he will remember the first trio of animals well, may miss one of the animal words in the second trio, and is likely to miss two or all three of the animal words in the last trio (Hagen, Jongeward, and Kail, 1975). Why does he have difficulty recalling the last three animal words, even though each is acoustically different and he had no trouble recalling the last three words (in the first example) when all words were unrelated to a concept? One way to interpret this phenomenon is to assume that the animal words were automatically referred to some abstract structure, such as a concept, and registered in that way. That is, the child created two simultaneous representations of the words as he heard them, one for the word and another for the concept to which it belonged. When it was time to recall the last trio of words, he mentally returned to the concept. The concept *animal* implied a host of different animal words that interfered with the ones he had heard, and hence he could not recall those that were read to him.

This phenomenon resembles that of a person who is trying to remember how to return from a house he has visited for the first time. On his way to the house he had noted a gas station on the corner where he made a right turn, but he had failed to rehearse the fact that it was a Shell station even though he read the sign. On his return he notes three different gas stations at three different corners. Since he represented the original event on a conceptual level—as a gas station—he has difficulty recalling which specific gas station he saw.

Attributes of Concepts

Concepts have several important qualities apart from their meanings. They differ in degree of abstraction, complexity, differentiation, and centrality of dimensions. Let us look at these attributes one at a time.

Degree of abstraction. Concepts can be described as relatively concrete or relatively abstract, depending on the tangibility or the intangibility of their dimensions. Books, tables, and children are concrete concepts because their dimensions are physical qualities one can see, hear, or touch. A book can be described by these dimensions: rectangular, flat, contains pages printed with words. Abstract concepts, on the other hand, have dimensions that are not tangible; their dimensions are often *other concepts*. Whereas the concept *book* can be described by physical characteristics, the concept *biography* depends on intangible attributes such as narrative, nonfiction, one person's history. We say a book is excellent because its themes, characters, and arguments hold together in a strong and convincing way—not because the binding holds

together. Or consider an example we will discuss at length in Chapter 8: *intelligence* is an abstract concept that rests on other abstract concepts such as language sophistication, alertness, and general learning ability. The more remote the constituent dimensions are from concrete experience, the more abstract is the overall concept.

Complexity. The number of dimensions needed to define various concepts varies too. Concepts that depend on many dimensions are regarded as more complex than those involving only a few. The concept of *pebble* for instance, rests on only a few dimensions—hard, dense, gray-black, small, rounded. But the concept *city* rests on many dimensions, both concrete and abstract—buildings, dense population, industry, automobile traffic, zoning, variety of stores, concert halls, schools.

Differentiation. Concepts also vary in the number of different but related instances or examples to which they refer. For example, our concept of *snow* is not highly differentiated, for we recognize only light, heavy, or wet snow. Among Eskimos, however, many more different kinds of snow are recognized as examples of the concept, and as previously mentioned, their language has many words for snow. *Stones* is a slightly more differentiated concept. *Cities* is a highly differentiated one, since cities can be as unlike each other as New York and Calcutta. In general, each concept has an ideal example and a host of related, less ideal examples. Most Americans think of the robin as an ideal example of the concept *bird* (wings, small beak, multicolored, relatively small, sings and chirps, flies a lot), while they regard the owl as a less ideal example (too big, too large a beak, doesn't sing and chirp, rarely seen in flight). When the concept is important to the culture, the way *building* is in our culture, there are many related concepts *(house, store, factory, hotel, cabin),* and we say the concept is differentiated. When it is less important, like *fishing net,* there are few related concepts, and we say it is less differentiated.

Centrality of dimensions. Apart from the number of dimensions a concept rests on, there is the matter of the centrality of certain dimensions. Some concepts have only a few (perhaps even just one or two) dominant dimensions that convey the concept, for example, *cup,* while others rest on many dimensions of equal importance. The concept *fruit* rests on many dimensions of equal significance: edible, sweet, grows on trees or bushes, small enough to hold, usually available in summer.

The central dimensions of a concept may be descriptive or functional. The central dimensions of a *tree* are descriptive—long vertical wooden trunk, leaves, placement in the earth. In the case of the concept *seat* the central dimension is functional. A seat can vary a good deal in its descriptive qualities—it may be a hard, marble bench; a soft, cushioned sofa; or an old, wooden chair. Yet all three objects function as a place to sit. Thus, in defining the concept *seat,* the function is more important than any of the concrete, descriptive characteristics.

Some concepts have both descriptive and functional central dimensions. For example, the concept *chromosome* can be defined in terms of its descriptive quality—composed of strings of genes—or its functional qualities—units that duplicate in our body cells and are responsible for what we inherit.

Rules

Rules are essentially statements that relate concepts. They can be classified in two ways. First, the relation between the concepts may be static or dynamic. A rule that describes a static relation between concepts is called a *nontransformational rule*. For example, "Stones are hard" states a relation between the concepts of *stones* and *hard*. This kind of rule describes a relation that is part of the meaning of the two concepts. A stone has several characteristics, one of which is its hardness. The quality of hardness applies to many objects, one of which is a stone. The rule does not require us to do anything in order to accept the relation—it is present in the meanings of the concepts.

But now consider the rule, "To build a wall, arrange a row of stones with cement in between, and add another row on top." The relation among *stones, cement,* and *arrangement of rows* is not clear until we act upon them and place them in a special relation temporally and spatially to one another. The relation among the concepts is dynamic; it involves action, not just definition of the concepts. A *transformational rule,* therefore, involves a set of procedures—behavioral or mental.

In addition to being classified as transformational or nontransformational, a rule can be classified as informal or formal. An *informal rule* refers to an imperfect or inexact relation between two or more concepts. That is, the relation between the concepts is true some of the time, or even most of the time, but not absolutely all of the time. "Wood is heavy" is an informal rule, true most of the time, but balsa wood is light. Most of our beliefs about the world consist of informal rules. "Snakes are dangerous," "Sand is dry," and "Men are tall" are three truisms that we continue to believe although we know perfectly well that there are also harmless snakes, patches of wet sand, and short men. By contrast, a *formal rule* states a relation between two or more concepts that is always true. "Oil floats on water" is a formal rule. So is the mathematical rule "$6 \times 10 = 60$."

There are, therefore, four kinds of rules (see Figure 4-4): informal nontransformational ("Stones are hard"); informal transformational ("To build a wall, arrange a row of stones with cement in between, and add another row on top"); formal nontransformational ("Oil floats on water"); and formal transformational ("$6 \times 10 = 60$"). Most of our everyday thoughts are informal nontransformational rules. Most of physical science, on the other hand, is composed of formal

	NONTRANS-FORMATIONAL	TRANSFORMATIONAL
INFORMAL	Stones are hard.	To build a wall, arrange a row of stones with cement in between, and add another row on top.
FORMAL	Oil floats on water.	$6 \times 10 = 60$

Figure 4-4
The four kinds of rules.

transformational rules. In school, each traditional subject emphasizes one of these kinds of rules: arithmetic and chemistry favor formal transformational rules; history and social studies favor informal nontransformational rules; poetry relies on informal transformational rules; and the axioms of plane geometry and much of anatomy are composed of formal nontransformational rules.

Development of Units of Cognition: Infants and Preschool Children

Infants and very young children—without knowing it, of course—initially acquire schemata and later a capacity for images. Although eight-month-olds possess schemata, they still live outside the world of concepts. Early in the second year children acquire some initial symbols. Combining the knowledge contained in their schemata, images, and symbols, they develop concepts and rules that they can ultimately use in solving complex problems. By the time children are four, they possess all the basic units used in mental activity.

Early Schemata and Images

Adolescents and adults continue to add new symbols, concepts, and rules to their repertory. A seventeen-year-old eats a mango for the first time and incorporates its new taste and texture into his concept of fruit, at the same time expanding and therefore altering his old concept. But, first, we shall consider the initial development of the cognitive units during the years between birth and school.

Some simple experiments persuade us that infants acquire schemata and can remember past experience. In one experiment two-and-a-half-month-old infants were shown an orange ball that moved up and down on a pulley for several minutes. When the infants were shown the same event twenty-four hours later, they became bored more quickly than a second group of infants who saw the event for the first time (Super, 1972). We can infer that the first group remembered the event and that the schema permitted that remembrance. A baby, regardless of where he is brought up, usually smiles at a human face from about three to four months of age. We conclude that by this time he has acquired a schema for a face, and his smile means he relates the face he sees now to his schema for the faces that he has seen before and knows. The best test for the possession of a schema is to determine if the person has the "knowledge" to decide whether or not a certain event occurred in the past.

Young children have a remarkable capacity to store schemata. If a four-year-old is shown sixty pictures cut from a magazine and typically looks at each one for one or two seconds, she is able to remember most of them over a twenty-four-hour period. The next day, if she is shown, one at a time, the sixty pictures she saw the previous day mixed in with sixty new pictures and is asked to say which are which, she is most often right from 80 to 90 percent of the time. It is unlikely she created an exact image for each one; the unit that permitted her to recognize so many of the sixty pictures is probably the schema. Schemata exist in all modalities, not just the visual. A group of ten-year-olds were read forty different sentences about ten or eleven words long. Seventeen days later they listened to 120 sentences—the forty old ones plus eighty new

ones—and were asked to say which sentences they had heard before. Children were typically correct 80 percent of the time (Kagan, in press).

A schema is mainly a cognitive phenomenon acquired through looking, listening, touching, and smelling. But children of all ages engage in a great deal of motor activity. Infants finger their clothes or kick at mobiles, two-year-olds build block towers, six-year-olds sculpt animals out of clay. It seems reasonable therefore that the young child also gains knowledge of the world through his motor activities. And this is probably true. However, a controversy persists: is the young child's motor activity always necessary for the acquisition of new knowledge, especially in infancy? Can an infant have any knowledge about his world that is not tied closely to action? Jean Piaget, the leading cognitive psychologist of the twentieth century, believes that the infant's knowledge is contained in schemes that are the product of his sensory motor actions. The sensory motor schemes are regarded as abstract structures that refer to the child's potential motoric interactions with objects. For Piaget, the infant's knowledge of a mobile is contained in the motor actions he can initiate toward it—his handling and kicking of it, for example.

The view being presented here, however, holds that the infant can acquire a schema of a mobile merely by looking at it, without touching or manipulating it at all.

There are two reasons we favor the view that infants and young children can develop and elaborate knowledge without necessarily engaging in motor activity. First, older children can learn about faraway countries, exotic fruits, and distant mountains just by listening to someone describe them: they do not need to climb the mountains or eat the fruit. Furthermore, studies of infants born with no limbs due to abnormalities in development during pregnancy show that at three years of age their cognitive processes do not seem impaired in any way despite the fact that they cannot crawl, walk, manipulate objects, or build things with their hands (Kopp and Shaperman, 1973).

Early Symbolization

Children's capacity to think with symbols emerges during the second year of life and grows rapidly after that. Since all language is symbolic, they must be capable of using symbols before they can use language. Studies of children's play with toys reveal that the infant younger than one year old does not treat objects symbolically. He will not treat a piece of clay as if it were symbolic of a cookie; he will not treat a toy cup as if it were a real cup and drink from it. But by the second year, most American children will do both reliably.

The capacity to think in symbols permits the child to use and understand metaphors. A metaphor is a symbolic substitution in which a quality that normally applies to one event or object is applied to another. Thus, to speak of a person in his "twilight years" is to apply the word *twilight,* which normally refers to the end of the day, to the end of a life.

Children three or four years old have the capacity for metaphor. If a four-year-old is shown a red and a blue patch of color and asked to say which is hotter or which color is more like summer, he will normally pick the red patch, signifying that he has abstracted one of the symbolic dimensions of heat, namely, redness. The use of metaphor reveals an important principle regarding the working of the human mind, for the mind often uses a unique logic that is not the logic of mathematics or science. When a child says red is more characteristic of summer than of winter or that a big doll is more characteristic of father than of mother, he is assuming that if two objects or events share one quality they probably share others as well. For example, fire is characterized by both heat and redness, while summer is characterized by heat. But the child presumes that since summer and fire share heat as a quality, they could appropriately share redness as well. Hence, he assumes that redness is characteristic of summer. That conclusion is not logical in the strict sense. Consider a logical analysis of what he is doing:

Premise 1: Fire contains both redness and heat.
Premise 2: Summer contains heat.
Conclusion: If it is summer, then redness is one of its qualities.

This is, of course, an error in logic. Consider an even more obvious example of such an error:

Premise 1: If it's a man, then it both speaks and breathes.
Premise 2: If it's a pig, then it breathes.
Conclusion: If it's a pig, then it can speak.

In this case it is obvious that the conclusion is not logical, yet this is the logic children, and adults as well, use in metaphor. Indeed, it may be that our basic emotional reactions to the new people we meet are based on illogical inferences, such as the ones in metaphors. If the child regards the teacher as taller than most adults, he is likely to assume that she is more competent, for to the child adults are both taller and more competent than children. Hence, to be tall implies greater competence.

Developmental Changes in Concepts

It is important to recognize that a concept is not a static element of knowledge but one that constantly changes. After two visits to London a traveler has a concept of the city, but with each succeeding trip the knowledge becomes more detailed and better integrated. An apparently simple concept such as *animal* changes its quality with development. Although the eighteen-month-old has a concept of animal, it is not the same as the six-year-old's concept. And although a six-year-old can

Children's readiness to master particular symbols, grasp the dimensions of concepts, or use transformational rules may vary not only according to their chronological stage of development but also with how familiar and interesting the material is to them. The material's significance was illustrated by a conversation between a psychologist, explaining the importance of a curriculum to teach double classification to disadvantaged children, and an anthropologist, who insisted that the children in question already knew how to perform double classifications:

"No," said the psychologist. "My test results—using colors and shapes—prove that they don't. The average disadvantaged child in my sample couldn't correctly classify red diamonds, blue diamonds, red squares, blue squares and materials of that sort."

The anthropologist shrugged. "I don't know about your squares and diamonds," he said. "But any ghetto child knows that black is good and policemen are bad, and that when he meets a black policeman he has a problem. *That's* double classification." (Farnham-Diggory, 1972, p. 38)

name several animals when you ask him to, he is far less likely to cluster animal words in recall or to activate the concept on a sorting task. Does this mean he has different concepts? Not at all. It means that the concept is at a different level of organization.

In addition to growing increasingly abstract, complex, and differentiated as a child develops, concepts change with time in three other respects. They are degree of agreement on the dimensions of a concept, articulation of the concept, and accessibility to language.

Degree of agreement, or consensus, refers to how much a child's understanding of the dimensions of a concept agrees with that of the children and adults in his community. To a two-year-old boy the concept *piggy* may mean a certain kind of stuffed animal, but no one outside the family would know that or understand what he wanted when he cried for a *piggy.* By age five, however, he understands that there is a concept *piggy* that refers to a large animal with an odd face that lives on a farm. Able to distinguish between his personal meaning and the popular meaning of *piggy,* he reaches the point where his concept has come into agreement with that of the community.

Articulation refers to the clarity of a concept and hence to its availability for active manipulation in thought. A three-year-old's concept of *hour* or *year* is vague; therefore she does not appreciate how long she will have to wait when her father tells her he will be back in an hour and, as a result, does not think of what she might do while he is gone. An eight-year-old has a much better understanding of the concept *hour* and knows how many things she can do in the hour she has before dinner will be ready. The eight-year-old not only understands the concept but uses her understanding when problems arise.

A young child is less adroit at using the concepts he knows because he tends to view some concepts as absolute rather than relative (see Figure 4–5). To him, dark means black or any very dark color. He has difficulty comprehending the idea of a dark yellow because he thinks that dark and yellow are mutually exclusive: "If it's yellow," he says to himself, "it can't be dark." If yellow and black are presented to him, he will have no trouble saying which is darker, but if he is shown turquoise blue and sky blue, he may be confused. In the same way, he thinks of 1, 2, and 3 as being small numbers and 99 and 100 as being large numbers. But if he is asked, "Which is larger, 1 or 2?", he may not understand the question. As we saw in Chapter 3, Piaget describes this kind of development in a child as the acquisition of relational terms: the child begins to understand that even among small numbers, one is smaller and one is larger, and even among light colors, one may be darker and one lighter.

One difficulty in teaching the young child to see both the absolute and relative qualities of concepts is that he must first appreciate that the same concept may rest on different dimensions under different conditions. Today, the concept of *lamp* rests on these dimensions: metal object, glass bulb, electrical cord. But two hundred years ago the concept *lamp* rested on different dimensions: hot metal base, wire handle, smell of oil, smoke. Seeing the point of view of another person requires one to understand that the other person may view a concept such as *lamp* in a different way. Young children have difficulty holding and relating both concepts, which is one reason why we call them "egocentric."

Figure 4–5
Understanding relational terms—bigger, smaller, lighter, darker—may initially be as confusing for young children as the riddle: "This man's father is my father's son" (A is the father of B). A child eventually understands that a concept changes in different contexts: he may be the largest child in his family but the smallest child in his class.

Accessibility refers to how easily a child can describe and talk about his concepts. A four-year-old cannot say very much about his initial understanding of the concept *love*, although he knows it has to do with a relationship between people who know one another very well. A fifteen-year-old can write a thousand-word essay on love: for him, the attributes of *love* are so clearly articulated and differentiated from other concepts that he can talk or write about it in terms of other concepts.

In short, as the child grows older, he not only acquires more concepts, but they become sharper in his mind, they come to resemble the meaning held by members of his community, and he becomes able to write and speak about them more clearly.

Implications for Teaching

Teachers can use the knowledge about the cognitive units contained in this chapter to help their students. Most of the knowledge that children learn in school consists of new concepts and rules, including the modification of existing concepts and rules that they bring to school. In learning a new concept, probably one step is more essential than any others: children must understand the central dimensions and be able to distinguish them from less central ones.

Focus on Central Dimensions

Suppose that a social studies teacher wants the pupils to understand the concept *democracy*. Saying that the United States is a democracy, or that a country with a president is a democracy, is not enough because the children may conclude that large countries with big cities like the United States are always democracies, or that all countries with a leader called "president" are democracies. Neither is true, of course: the central dimensions of a democracy are not its size nor the title of its leader. The dimensions that differentiate a democracy from other political structures are: it allows the will of the people to influence the actions of governing officials, and it permits dissent. Those are the two dimensions the teacher should emphasize and illustrate with the most typical examples. The children might be asked to consider whether, judged on those dimensions, Britain is not perhaps a better example of a democracy than the United States because the prime minister is always subject to a vote of confidence; if he does not receive a vote expressing the people's support, he resigns.

One of the most important things a teacher can do is be vigilant in pointing out the central dimensions of a new concept, whether she is explaining democracy to ten-year-olds or electrons to sixteen-year-olds. Why is it so important? If children see the central dimensions of a concept, they are more likely to be able to use that concept in a wide

variety of situations. Consider the concept *rate*. The twelve-year-old child is taught that when distance problems are posed, he should apply the rule, "distance = rate × time"; and he does this automatically once he learns the rule. But if he is faced with a problem about the flow of water through a pipe (which also has rate and time variables), he will not know what to do unless he is taught specifically that the total volume of water flowing through a pipe equals the rate of flow times duration of flow. If the child were first taught that rate and time are general characteristics of many phenomena, he would be more likely to generate a correct solution for all problems involving rate and time concepts. If he can be led to see that the central dimension of the concept *rate* is *the change in some unit over a period of time,* whether it is miles changing over minutes, quarts of water over hours, or kilowatts of electricity over days, then all the rules that involve rate have a similar form:

distance covered = miles per hour × time
electricity used = kilowatts per hour × time
water used = quarts per hour × time
interest paid = dollars per month × time

Or consider the concept *structure*. Its meaning is complex, yet many people who have never grasped its central dimensions use it as a catchword. *Structure* has two central dimensions: it is composed of units and they are arranged in a pattern. A protein has a structure because it is a specific arrangement of molecules. A sonata has a structure because it is a pattern of musical phrases. The social structure of a beehive is the arrangement of workers, drones, and queen.

Suppose a high-school teacher talks about perceiving structure in the school. If the student does not exactly understand the dimensions of the concept, she may think that the teacher means only the architecture of the building. If she grasps the central dimensions, however, she will know that *structure,* in this case, refers to the arrangement or pattern of faculty and students in the school.

Adjust to Change in Central Dimensions

A teacher should also help a child appreciate that a concept may have different central dimensions in different contexts. A teacher might initiate a lesson for first-grade pupils to help them see that the central dimensions of an object may change with the situation or its function. He presents a girl with a ball and an orange and says to her, "Tell me something about these objects."

"They're both round," says the child, "and the same size. I'd call them small. The ball is fuzzy and pale green; my brother uses one like that when he plays tennis. The orange has a bumpy skin and an orange color. And it smells sharp."

Although these are all attributes of the objects, the child can be led to a deeper understanding of the significance of the attributes of the ball and the orange if the teacher asks her to think of their *functions.* The child will realize that if she wants to use the orange for decoration, its color and shape are central, whereas if she's looking for something good to eat, its flavor and nutrition—invisible attributes—count more than its appearance.

A sixth-grade teacher can illustrate how central attributes change with a more complex example by designing a lesson on soybeans. One group of students could be asked to report on soybeans as used in cooking; another on soybeans as a means of feeding poor, undernourished populations; a third on soybeans as a crop. It would be discovered that taste and cooking properties would be the main attributes for the first group; nutritional content and cost would interest the second; and the way the plant grows, its yield, and how it is harvested would be emphasized by the third. In this way students learn that the particular problem, function, or situation determines which attributes of a concept are central.

Illuminate with Concrete Examples

Using concrete examples to illustrate abstract ideas is frequently a good way to acquaint students with a new concept. Since some young children do not yet appreciate that numbers can be applied to different magnitudes, it is useful to help them visualize quantification. A teacher may do this by having the class make a graph based on a survey of family cars. First, each student reports the kind of car his family has:

the sum is six Chevrolets, seven Fords, five Volkswagens, two Volvos, and one Buick. Then, each child cuts out a square of cardboard to represent his family's car. The Chevrolet owners color their squares blue, the Ford owners color theirs orange, and so forth. There are twenty-one squares of paper, colored according to the make of the car (not the car's real color—that was the first step in the abstraction). Next, the students take a big piece of cardboard and line up the squares on it, so that the longest line represents Fords, the next longest Chevrolets, and so on until they finish with the single Buick square. Finally, making the leap from representing cars by squares to graphing distribution, the children paste down the squares, so that they can hang up the cardboard and see that the lengths of the colored lines represent the makes of the different cars (see Figure 4–6).

Visualizing measurements of time is another way teachers can help young children with an abstract concept. For instance, instead of using a monthly calendar, the teacher can present a seven-day calendar showing "school days" and "no-school days." Such a calendar would have seven boxes, with the initial letter for the day of the week written over each box, beginning with Saturday and Sunday on the left and ending with Friday on the right. (The calendar should be large, clearly

Figure 4–6
A class of students made a graph depicting the makes of their family cars. They took a survey of the number and the kinds of cars, cut out squares to represent each one, colored the squares according to the make, lined them up on a piece of cardboard, and pasted them down to show, in the form of a graph, the distribution of cars.

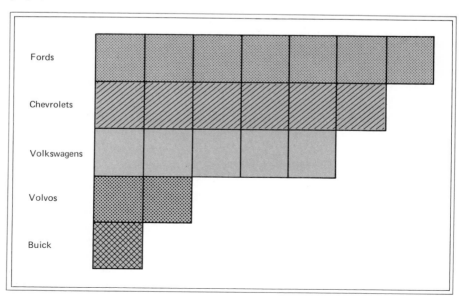

legible, and presented at the children's eye level.) After the children have learned the concept of a week and the distinction between school days and no-school days, succeeding weeks can be added to make a monthly calendar (Gotkin, 1967).

Another way teachers can help children conceptualize time is by planting a variety of seeds: some that sprout in ten days, some that sprout in two or three days, and some long-germinating seeds that take several weeks to grow. Checking the pots of plants over a number of days can help the children develop a sense of the duration of time based on how soon or how late the seeds germinate.

Secure the Concepts Needed for · New Rules

In teaching new rules, teachers should be sure, first of all, that the students understand the concepts on which the rules are based. Children cannot understand freedom of speech if they do not understand *freedom* and *speech*. After that, children should be encouraged to see that rules state principles that can be transferred from one, specific context to another, similar one. The teacher in a history or social studies unit on the Civil War may want students to understand the basic rules or principles that are believed to have been the source of the Civil War. She may begin by discussing the fact that the South's practice of slavery bothered the Northern conscience. The teacher may then mention other civil uprisings: in the latter half of the 1960s the morality of many American students was irritated by the presence of the United States in Vietnam and civil uprisings occurred. The peasants in China were angered by the moral corruption of the government during World War II, and a civil war occurred there, too. Gradually, the teacher adds examples until the students see the basic principle: "When a large body of people are morally outraged by a prevailing situation or policy, civil disturbances are likely to occur."

In short, a rule does not apply only to one particular problem in one particular area. In Chapter 3 we saw that the high-school senior, watching a presentation of *Elizabeth the First* and the eleven o'clock news about trouble in Northern Ireland, generated the rule, "Uprisings occur when people feel unjustly oppressed." Instead of teaching isolated and compartmentalized history courses (American history in the fifth grade, medieval history in the eighth, European history in the tenth) schools may organize a history curriculum around themes that reflect the principles mentioned here, along with others, such as, "When a group of people feel crowded, they want more land." Even in a one-year course on a particular period of history, however, the teacher can spell out the themes encountered and remind the students, by drawing analogies with current or recent conflicts, that they will come upon the themes again in other courses.

Teachers can also plan exercises to give students practice in developing and inferring rules. One fourth-grade teacher used this method: a child buried chess pieces in a large sand table and put a colored block above each one for a marker. The next child had to try to discover the first child's rules by digging up one or two pieces and then making guesses about the rest: "The king and queen were both marked with red blocks, and the pawn was marked with a blue block, so maybe the royal pieces are marked with red and the pawns are all marked with blue. But wait, maybe all the black chess pieces are marked with red, and all the white pieces marked with blue; I'll have to dig up a few more to find out which is the right rule."

In a social studies unit on Egypt a teacher may use the example of the Rosetta stone to encourage his students to develop codes of their own that depend on rules: for instance, A = one dot, B = two dots, and so forth. Or they may work up codes that are based on glyphs, with one little drawing standing for a letter or a syllable. One group can invent a code, a second group can have the job of deciphering it. (The first group may devise, along with the code, a "Rosetta stone" that will give clues to the rules of the code.) Codes are a dramatic and precise way of learning about rules.

The Processes at Work in Mental Activity

Before we begin the discussion of the processes involved in problem solving, a general distinction should be made between two types of cognition: undirected and directed. Undirected cognition refers to free associations, dreams, reveries, and the free flow of thoughts that occur continually as children stare out the window or wait in line for lunch (and as their parents wait for the bus to go to work). Little inquiry has been made into this important and tantalizing aspect of cognition because it is difficult to study a person's private, undirected thoughts: It is similar to what happens when one puts a movie on "hold" in order to look at one frame more closely: the last frame can be seen clearly enough, but the motion is interrupted and the significance of the flow itself is entirely lost. If you ask a child to report her free associations or to write them down, her loose undirected thought suddenly becomes organized, as the child automatically tries to present an orderly and coherent report of her thinking.

Since a child solving a problem depends on directed cognition, we will focus our attention on it. There are five processes involved: perception, memory, generation of possible solutions, evaluation, and implementation of preferred solutions. Although changes in the processes occur in early childhood, development of cognitive processes continues through adolescence.

Process 1: Perception

Children look out the window and are exposed to physical stimulation—shapes of trees, colors of chimneys, numbers of people, the speed of cars. From this mosaic they extract meaningful information: that is what we mean by *perception*.

Perception is best defined as the extraction of information from sensory stimulation. The difference between sensory stimulation, on the one hand, and information, on the other, can be appreciated by comparing a scene in a meadow registered, first, by a moving camera and, second, by a person. While the camera registers all colors, shadows, lines, and objects in the scene, the human being organizes the scene: he selects certain aspects and ignores the others. The person may make a bright red flower the central element and see the trees merely as background. But the roving camera plays no favorites: all elements emerge as equally important. Furthermore, the person, unlike the camera, relates what he sees both to what he saw a few minutes ago and to what he may see in the future. He integrates successive "exposures." The camera is faithful to the external world, but it is mindless. Each picture exists in isolation, with no ties to the past or future. But a person continually relates what he sees to what he knows. If a child sees a tree branch move on a windless day, she realizes it cannot be the wind and infers from her experience that it must be an animal. As a result she begins to scrutinize the area for some detectable sign of the animal.

Selectivity of Perception

The growing child learns to focus on certain aspects of the environment and to ignore others. He learns to focus his attention on the eyes of his mother to detect her mood toward him and, later, on the presence of a plus or minus sign on his page of arithmetic homework. He learns to detect what is relevant for the problem he is solving or the goal he wants to attain. Nonetheless, all humans are prepared by nature to attend to certain common aspects of the environment and to experience similar perceptions. All young infants are naturally attracted by objects that move, by objects with a great deal of black and white contrast, by patterns that have many rather than few elements, and by shapes that are circular rather than rectilinear.

Moreover, adults all over the world seem to react to colors in the same way. The answer to the traditional philosophical riddle "Does my brother see the same red that I see?" seems to be yes. Children and adults of several cultures will remember best the same shade of red and it happens to be the crimson characteristically printed on Christmas cards (Rosch, 1975). Young infants also react as adults do to the essential hue in the colors blue, green, yellow, and red. Evidently

nature has equipped all humans with the tendency to notice and prefer certain colors and shapes and to remember these better than less ideal ones.

But even though most children and adults are universally attracted by certain sensory qualities such as contour, movement, and circularity, when a person must discriminate between two objects, he uses different dimensions depending on what two objects he is comparing. The specific critical physical dimensions that help us to distinguish one event from another, that is, depend on the problem we are trying to solve. Suppose a boy is in the forest trying to determine whether a moving object is a bear or a man. In that situation, the critical dimensions are whether the shape wears clothes and makes the sound of a human voice. But if the same boy is on a dark street in a large city and hears footsteps behind him, he will wonder if the figure behind him is a man, a woman, or a child (since it's unlikely to be a bear). Clothes and human speech are no longer critical in helping the child identify the figure in the darkness, and he will listen, instead, to the sound of the footsteps and the pitch of the voice. Similarly, if a child wants to know whether the teacher is a man or a woman, he will attend to bodily shape and dress; if he wonders whether the teacher likes him, he will attend to her facial expression and her tone of voice. In sum, the specific problem the child is trying to solve will determine what dimensions are significant.

Interpretation of Events

Several important facts about perception make it a complex cognitive process. First, a person usually makes judgments about objects and events that involve more than the raw, sensory input. For example, when a child judges the strength of a chair from how it looks, assessing whether or not it can hold her, clearly her judgment about the strength of the chair is not entirely derived from the visual stimulation coming from the chair and registering on the retina of her eye. Rather, it is a highly complex inference made from the sensory information she receives.

Or, seeing an ambiguous form on a road that can be either a tire or a pair of black trousers, most children and adults will tend to perceive the object as a tire, since a tire is more likely to be lying in the middle of the highway than an article of clothing. Again, they make a judgment that goes beyond the visual information coming to them (see Figure 4–7).

Second, spontaneous changes in perception often occur without any change in the external stimulus, an effect known as *figure-ground reversal*. An example appears in Figure 4–8, in which the Rubin figure can look like an old man's face (on the left) or a person with his hand out (on the right). We can perceive one or the other, but not both at the same time. These facts, along with others, suggest that perceptions or hypotheses are inferences that are based on a combination of our past knowledge and what we are experiencing at the moment (Gregory, 1974).

Figure 4–7
In I the central figure is seen as a number because it is surrounded by numbers, while in II it is seen as a letter even though the visual stimulus in the center of each circle is the same.

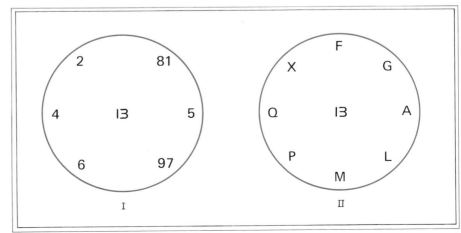

Figure 4–8
The Rubin figure, which can look like an old man's face (on the left) or a person with his hand out (on the right) is an example of figure-ground reversal. We can perceive one or the other but not both simultaneously.

Developmental Changes in Perception

Between early childhood and adolescence several important changes occur in the nature of perception. An older child can be specific in searching for additional information: she knows more about the world. She knows that if the branch that is moving on a windless day is low, the movement may be caused by a deer; but if the branch is high, she would do better to look for a squirrel. She may also recognize the squirrel on the basis of little information; perhaps just a glimpse of his curved tail will be enough instead of the complete view of the animal that her three-year-old sister needs.

An older child can *focus* her attention in a systematic way for a longer period of time, and she can also more easily *shift* her attention. Scanning the branches for a glimpse of a squirrel, she may suddenly decide to check the sky for the possible sight of a bird, shifting her eyes in time to see a hawk, while her younger sister continues to stare at the branches in the hope of spotting the squirrel. Because she approaches the problem with greater knowledge, can focus her attention longer and more selectively, and can shift the focus of her attention more readily, a seven- or eight-year-old child makes a better detective than a younger child does. She can interpret clues and knows the most fruitful locales to scrutinize in order to find them.

There is some controversy about the actual process involved in an older child's superior perceptual ability. Adults report more information about an event than children do. Shown a picture of a city street, an adult always reports more about what was in the picture (Morrison, 1971). Nevertheless, it is unclear whether the adult actually perceives more when he looks at the picture or whether, as appears more likely, he is simply better able to classify, name, and remember what he saw.

Although the child's ability to detect differences between similar events generally improves with age, the specific rate of improvement varies for different kinds of objects and stimuli. Professor E. J. Gibson and her students at Cornell University did an interesting experiment to determine which kinds of detections were easy and which were hard for children of different ages when the stimuli were nonsense designs. The child was shown the stand in Figure 4-9 and told to look at the single model design on top, then scan the row underneath of thirteen similar designs and choose only the one that was an exact copy of the model. The row contained one identical copy plus many similar ones. Some of the variations in the row had a break in the line; others changed the straight line to a curved line or a curved line to a straight line; still others reversed or rotated the design; and some had subtle changes in the perspective of the design. Children rarely treated the designs with a break in the line as identical, suggesting that a break in a continuous line is quickly detected. Children four years of age made quite a few mistakes in judging a design that was a rotation, a reversal, or a straight-line-to-curve change. But by age eight these errors were minimal. Designs in which the perspective was changed were most often mistaken by children four through eight (see Figure 4-10).

If we regard the designs as similar to letters of the alphabet (like the

Figure 4-9
The stand displays various forms in a matching task (one example is shown below: children were told to look at a model design on top, then scan the row of thirteen similar designs underneath and choose only the one that was an exact copy of the model). Some variations had a break in the line; others changed the straight line to a curved line or a curved line to a straight line; others reversed or rotated the design or changed the perspective slightly. Children rarely treated the designs with a break in the line as identical to the model. Four-year-old children made mistakes in judging a design that was a rotation, a reversal, or a straight-line-to-curve change, but by age eight such errors were minimal. Designs in which the perspective was changed were most often mistaken by children from four to eight years of age. (Adapted from Gibson, 1969)

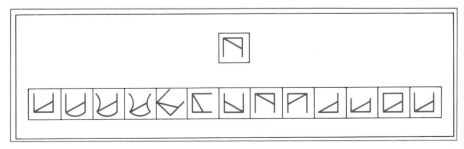

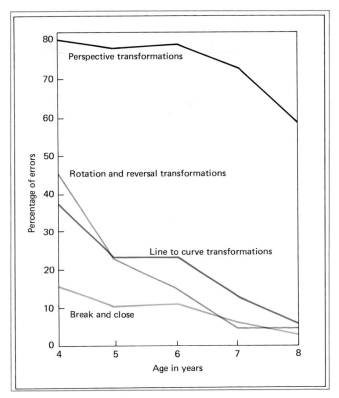

Figure 4–10
This graph charts the mistakes in perception by age of child and category of error: designs in which the perspective was changed induced the greatest number of errors, persisting through age eight. The errors kindergarten children make in letter identification tend to be in accord with this prediction. (After Gibson, 1969)

letter B, for example), the results suggest that young children would rarely regard ꓭ as B, would be a little more likely to regard B or Ɇ as B, and most likely to regard ꞵ as B. The errors kindergarten children make in letter identification tend to be in accord with this prediction (Gibson, 1969).

Process 2: Memory

The process of memory—storing information and retrieving it—is an elaborate system that functions somewhat like a computer data bank.

For many years it was assumed that all perceived events were registered or stored with equal strength and that faulty memory was due to a failure in retrieving what one knew. But recent research suggests that differences may exist in both the permanence and the quality of registration of events that a child sees or hears. Therefore, it is useful—at least tentatively—to distinguish among three kinds of memories.

Three Kinds of Memory

Sensory memory refers to the retention of information in the mind for only a moment—usually a fraction of a second. For example, after a person sees an object, such as a picture of an animal or a rock, a representation of it remains vivid for only about one-fourth of a second. In hearing, sensory memory remains for a little longer, often as long as two seconds. But if that memory is not stored or in some way related to knowledge the person already has, it vanishes (Neisser, 1967).

Short-term memory refers to the retention of information for a maximum of about thirty seconds, usually for an even shorter period of time. Remembering a telephone number from the directory long enough to dial it is an example of short-term memory.

Long-term memory refers to knowledge potentially available for a long time, perhaps forever. In order to transfer information to long-term memory, a person must make a conscious effort to file it away.

Recognition and Recall

The memory of an event is usually measured either by *recognition* or by *recall*. In a recognition test, for example, the child is shown a picture of a franc and asked whether it is a French or British coin. True-false and multiple-choice questions use recognition to measure what is remembered. In recall, the child must retrieve all the necessary information from his memory: he might be asked to define the word *franc*. Essay questions test recall. Obviously, almost everyone's recognition memory is better than his recall memory. Furthermore, the difference between recall and recognition is more dramatic in younger than in older children. A ten-year-old who has been shown a group of twelve pictures is usually able to recall spontaneously about eight of them, but he is able to recognize all twelve as pictures he has seen before, even if they are included in a larger set of photographs. A four-year-old will also be able to recognize all twelve, but he will only be able to recall two or three of them (Mussen, Conger, and Kagan, 1974).

If the number of pictures is increased to fifty and there is a delay of one week between the first and second viewing, ten-year-olds will be able to recall fewer than ten pictures but will be able to recognize about forty of them. If they hear forty sentences on one day, two weeks later they will be able to recall less than five but will be able to recognize over thirty-five of them (Kagan, in press).

Factors Affecting Memory

The ability to remember information is affected by the coherence of the material, the degree of organization imposed on it, and the strategies used for storing it in the mind. Some material is more available to recollection than others (Harris and Burke, 1972). Material that is coherent, that is, has some internal rule or structure (a series of numbers that increases by twos: 14, 16, 18, 20) is more easily recalled than material that has no structure (a string of unrelated numbers: 16, 20, 14, 18).

Some psychologists believe that information is transferred to long-term memory through a process of association: information held in short-term memory is linked to units that are already stored in long-term memory. If the incoming information fails to become associated with the existing knowledge, it will not be transferred to long-term memory. A name or an idea is much more likely than a number to become a part of permanent memory, and a name with a clear association is more easily transferred to long-term memory than a name without an association. For example, if you are introduced to Mr. Ernest Jones, a writer, it is more likely you will remember his name (associating it with the writer Ernest Hemingway) than if the person was introduced as either David Jones, a writer, or Ernest Jones, an architect.

Some information or experience fades very rapidly, and it is extremely difficult for the person either to recall that information or to

> If a class is trying to think up a name for a gardening group, which name are the students more likely to remember, and why?
>
> GROW (Gardeners' and Readers' Organic Workshop)
>
> MMBCC (Mr. Murphy's Botany Class Club)

recognize it. It is not clear whether this happens because there are two qualitatively different kinds of memory or because there is only one kind of memory, but some information is rehearsed better (that is, the child recites information to himself several times) before it is stored.

Developmental Changes in Memory

Older children are better at retrieving stored knowledge not only because the information is more organized but also because they have more reliable strategies. An eleven-year-old who has had to memorize the capitals of the eastern states is likely to systematically search her memory to guarantee that she has covered all the states. A six-year-old could not do that. As we shall see later, one of the major reasons recall memory improves with age is a growing awareness of what is required to remember information and of how to adjust one's effort to the difficulty of the task. Young children just do not appreciate what is required to remember a lot of information. A group of schoolchildren was asked, "If you wanted to phone your friend and someone told you the phone number, would it make any difference whether you called right after you heard the number or got a drink of water first?" Kindergarten children said with equal frequency that one could either phone or get a drink of water, while first- through fifth-graders said they would make the call at once (Kreutzer, Leonard, and Flavell, 1974).

Sensory memory seems to be the same for children and adults. However, adults have better short-term and long-term memories. Better techniques for storing and holding information, a richer store of concepts, schemata, and rules to aid storage and retrieval, as well as an increase in their ability to focus attention, all lead to better recall as the child grows. By age ten or eleven, the American child seems to have consolidated the essential skills necessary for remembering large amounts of information. The simple ability to recognize a given event as having occurred in the past may not improve very much from preschool years to preadolescence; but an important change does take place in recall, apparently based on the child's spontaneous tendency to organize incoming information into relevant units, transfer that information to long-term memory with greater deliberateness, and retrieve it more effectively. By age eleven or twelve children seem to understand what is required to memorize something and retrieve it. This knowledge of the task's requirements, not a better brain or a larger basic capacity to hold information, seems to be responsible for the improvement in memory among older children.

It is important to realize that memory does not exist in the abstract. A child's memory capacity is always for *specific types of information.* A child who can't remember four numbers may be able to remember six words. Three-year-olds are usually able to remember two or at the most three unrelated words. But if a three-year-old watches an adult hide five different objects under five different-colored boxes and the whole scene is hidden for five seconds, the child is able to find any one of the five objects the adult may ask her for (Kagan, Kearsley, and Zelazo, in press). Under these conditions she is able to remember any one of five different locations.

Consider one more example of the importance of the material that is being remembered. As we said earlier, if the material to be remembered is coherent, the child will remember more than if it is not—as long as he detects the coherence. If a ten-year-old child hears twenty unrelated words and is asked to recall them immediately, he usually remembers about six or seven. If the twenty words belong to four different conceptual categories (parts of the body, methods of transportation, food, and clothing), he can remember nine or ten words. But the

improvement only occurs if the child detects the categories in the list of words. If he does not, his memory will not be better for the categorized list (Frender, 1975).

Thus, it is misleading to talk of a child's memory without specifying exactly what it is he is trying to memorize and recall. Memory is for specific information. A teacher who decided a child had a poor memory merely because he could not remember his multiplication tables would probably be mistaken, for it is likely that the same child has a good memory for other classes of information, such as baseball pitchers.

Finally, it should be noted that for children four through ten years of age there is a great deal of variability in memory for words or pictures. By early adolescence, however, most children learn the strategies of rehearsal, organization, and detection of category and coherence (see Figure 4–11). Hence most eleven- and twelve-year-olds are able to remember as many as twelve independent items of information. In one study children from six to thirteen years of age were shown two pictures and asked to remember their order. Then a third picture was added to the first two, a fourth to the first three, and so on until twelve pictures were laid out and the child had to remember the order of all of them. American children were able to remember the order of all twelve by the time they were nine or ten years old, some by age six. By contrast, Indian children growing up in isolated farming villages in Central America were not able to remember

Figure 4–11
Young children often have trouble remembering instructions they have heard or knowing where they are in a problem, partly because they do not "rehearse." In one experiment seven-year-olds were asked to look at three dolls; then the dolls were covered with boxes and the children were asked to arrange three more dolls in the *opposite* direction. Initially, some children could not remember the directions of the original dolls; but after they had been taught to rehearse what they had seen (saying to themselves, "right side up, right side up, upside down"), they had no trouble arranging a new set of dolls the correct way. (After Kagan et al., unpublished)

all twelve pictures until they were twelve or thirteen years old (Kagan et al., unpublished).

Process 3: Generating Possible Solutions

When a child solves a problem, he perceives and interprets the relevant events, then stores them in memory. The next process involves generating hypotheses, or possible solutions to the problem. To do this, a child must possess the necessary knowledge (the appropriate cognitive units), be able to use that knowledge, not be overly anxious about making a mistake, and, finally, possess an intangible but necessary ingredient—insight.

The first step in solving a problem is developing a hypothesis: the mind suggests possible ways a puzzle or a problem might be solved. An example of this phenomenon emerges toward the end of the first year of life. At this age a child shows, for the first time, what has been called *separation anxiety:* when the child's caretaker leaves him in an unfamiliar setting or with a stranger, the child begins to cry. Rarely occurring before nine months of age, separation anxiety increases rapidly between nine and eighteen months and tends to decline after the second birthday. Since the child has been exposed to departures before, why is it that we only see this behavior toward the end of the first year? One possibility is that the child is now able to ask questions (that is, pose a hypothesis) about the separation event. He wonders, "Where is Mother going?" "When will she return?" "What will the stranger do to me?" Since he is unable to answer those questions, he becomes anxious and cries. Perhaps the most compelling example of the need to posit a hypothesis comes from a behavior usually seen a little later (around eighteen months of age) that is called Stage VI of object permanence. Years ago, Jean Piaget observed that if an eighteen-month-old child watched an adult pretend to hide a toy dog under a piece of cloth (while in fact the adult held onto it), the child would go to the cloth expecting the dog to be there. When it was not, she would not only show facial surprise but would also begin searching for the dog, as if she had the idea that the dog had to be there. Clearly, we have to posit some early cognitive query that explains the child's surprise and her conviction that the object is somewhere.

At first the query is wordless; later, the hypothesis—the child's query about the disappearance of the dog—may be verbalized: "Dog all gone?" Later still, other hypotheses, far more varied, arise. Consider again the problem of a schoolchild who confronts a sea urchin for the first time. It is a representative example, as well as familiar to us from Chapter 3, since a frequent intellectual problem confronting a child is how to categorize a new object. Looking at the sea urchin for the first time, he quickly reviews the categories he knows to see which one is the most appropriate setting for this creature. As we saw before, the initial question he asks is, "Is this a plant?" However, when the sea urchin begins to move across the floor of the aquarium, he must revise his hypothesis, since plants do not spontaneously move across the ocean floor; so his next hypothesis, stated with understandable scepticism, will be, "This is an *animal?*"

The sea urchin's self-propelling motion addresses a key issue in generating possible solutions: the importance of central attributes. "Small," "round," and "prickly" are all true descriptions of the sea urchin. But in deciding whether to classify it as a plant or an animal, the child needs to focus on a more central dimension, some attribute that is common to animals, but not to plants. When the small, round, prickly object moves off the rock and propels its way across the aquarium floor, the child has the answer.

Another common problem the child must solve is how and when to apply appropriate rules. He learns rules first in the context of specific situations—paper is for writing and not for stuffing pillows, bricks are used to build houses and not for sitting on.

In most examinations in school, teachers ask children to remember the rules they have been taught. In some instances, however, children are asked to generate a new hypothesis, perhaps a new use for an object, such as using paper to seal up a broken window or a brick to hold up a chair. When children generate an original and appropriate solution to a problem, we usually call them *creative*.

Unusual
Solutions:
Creativity

Creativity does not have the same meaning as intelligence. We call
children *intelligent* if they have a rich and varied storehouse of
schemata, images, symbols, concepts, and rules, but we call them
creative if they use these units in both an original and a constructive
way. While all intelligent children are not necessarily creative, most
creative children are intelligent. But their creativity stems from another
characteristic: they are not unduly fearful about making mistakes. One
major hallmark of the creative person is his disregard for the
humiliation that may result from an error. His willingness to take a
chance gives him the freedom to attempt experiments that may fail and
to consider possible though unexpected solutions without worrying too
much about the outcome (Wallach and Kogan, 1965).

Process 4: Evaluation

Evaluation is the stage in a child's thinking when she stops to assess
what she has perceived and the possible solutions she has generated,
anticipates where her train of thought is taking her, and estimates how
well her approach will solve the problem. It is the careful stage in
problem solving rather than the creative part described in process
three. Care is required in the original reading or understanding, in
considering all the possible solutions, and in checking the final answer.
(Clement Attlee is reported to have said that no matter what problem
came up, Churchill always had about ten possible answers: the trouble
was, he did not know which was the good one [Guilford, 1959].)

Variations
in
Reflective-
ness

Children do not show the same tendency to evaluate their thoughts and
answers; some children accept and report the first solution they
produce, after only the briefest consideration of its appropriateness or
accuracy. We call these children *impulsive*. Others devote a much
longer period of time to weighing the merits of their solutions and
rejecting the ones that seem incorrect or unproductive. These children
are called *reflective*. One basis for the difference in styles is anxiety
over making mistakes. The reflective child seems more concerned about
making errors than the impulsive child. As a result, the reflective child
takes longer and makes fewer errors, even though children of both
types may be equally intelligent.

The Matching Familiar Figures Test (see Figure 4–12) is one way of
assessing whether a child is reflective or impulsive in dealing with
intellectual problems. (The test does not necessarily reveal whether the
child will be reflective or impulsive on the playground or in situations
that are not involved in the testing of his intellectual competence.) The
child is shown a picture of a plane and six other pictures of planes: one
is identical to the original, the other five are very similar but have small

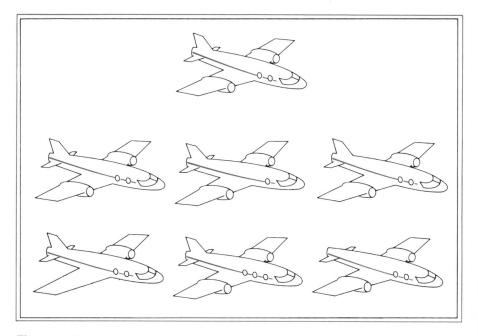

Figure 4–12
In the Matching Familiar Figures Test children are shown an original picture and six other pictures—one identical and five slightly different. In attempting to pick an identical copy, reflective children tend to study the pictures carefully for fifteen or twenty seconds, while impulsive children (who make more errors) tend to make snap decisions before they have scanned all the pictures.

variations. The child is told to look at the six and pick the one that is exactly like the original. Reflective children tend to study the pictures carefully for fifteen or twenty seconds and then select the right picture. Impulsive children are inclined to make their choice before they have scanned all the pictures carefully, and they make more errors.

The carefulness of reflective children is apparent in many tasks: they wait longer before they describe a picture or answer an adult's question; they make fewer errors in reporting words they heard on a list, in reading English sentences, and in answering inductive reasoning tests. This difference among children is evident as early as five years of age and seems to remain constant across different kinds of problems (Kagan and Kogan, 1970). It is a difference that is most relevant to school tasks that require careful analysis and thought in order to avoid making mistakes. In the beginning of the first grade an impulsive child will make more errors in reading *b* for *d* or *p* for *q* than his reflective classmates. In the third grade he checks his answers less often when he has finished an arithmetic problem. On an eighth-grade essay examination he may not check the logic of his argument and the relation of his answer to the original question.

Transformational Rules in Early Mathematics

In medieval Egypt mathematics scholars learned a different set of transformational rules for multiplying than the ones used by American students (Zaslavsky, 1973):

1 Take the first factor and halve it, rounding off fractioned numbers to the lower number (that is, 13½ becomes 13). Continue to halve and list the numbers in descending order in column 1.
2 Take the second factor and double it, then double that number and repeat the process until you have as many numbers in the second column as you have in the first.

3 Put a check mark beside all the uneven numbers in column 1.
4 For each uneven number in column 1, take the number across from it in column 2 and put it in column 3. Then add them together. The sum of these numbers will be the product. For example:

Column 1		Column 2	Column 3
27✔	×	16	16
13✔		32	32
6		64	
3✔		128	128
1✔		256	+256
			432

Although the tendency to be reflective or impulsive is stable over time and across varied tasks, it can be modified. In the Matching Familiar Figures Test some impulsive children were simply told to inhibit their responses and take more time answering. After several thirty-minute sessions of such training, they showed longer response times to similar problems than untrained impulsive children. Children also tend to be influenced by the teacher's behavior, becoming more reflective with reflective teachers and more impulsive with impulsive teachers (Yando and Kagan, 1968).

Process 5: Implementing the Most Appropriate Solution

The fifth process, which sometimes completes problem solving, is the application of a rule. Consider a typical arithmetic problem: "Two brothers worked for 8 hours each. The first got $2 an hour and the second $1 an hour. How much did they both make?" Assuming she comprehends it, the pupil must hold all the vital elements of the problem in her memory. Then she will generate possible solutions and arrive at the best one: to multiply 8 × 2 and add that to 8 × 1. Then she must implement that solution by applying the transformational rules of multiplication and addition to arrive at the answer: $24.

Or, to return to the sea urchin, in attempting to classify the object the child may have said to himself, "Some sea plants are small and round; this object is small and round and lives in salt water, therefore it may be a sea plant." After his initial hypothesis, however, he watches

the aquarium a little longer and generates new hypotheses. He may think to himself, "If I poke it a little with a stick and it moves away, then it would be an animal, not a plant, since only animals move of their own accord." This transformational rule—"If I poke it and it moves, it's an animal"—is different from the nontransformational rule—"The object is small, round, and lives in salt water"—in an important way. The transformational rule involves testing—either in the child's mind or in action—the outcome of a transformation or change in some event. The additional information produced by the change (in this case, poking at the animal) permits the child to decide which of two conclusions is more likely to be correct. In the case of the child and the sea urchin the rule involves a physical action. In another circumstance it may involve a mental problem. Performing experiments in physics and chemistry are common examples of transformational rules used in schools.

Developmental Changes in the Use of Rules

A child may stubbornly resist *retiring* his old rules if they have been effective in the past, causing a delay in the generation of new rules. For example a three-year-old believes that all metal objects sink in water, and he resists renouncing that belief in favor of the more exact rule that states that the density of an object determines whether it sinks or floats. In Piagetian language the child tries to assimilate a new experience into old ones, without making a comparable effort toward accommodating to what is novel about the experience he has encountered. Like scientific theory in the adult word, a child's rules are not displaced or replaced just because they are criticized, but only when he recognizes a better set of rules.

In addition, you will remember Piaget's notion that when a twelve- or thirteen-year-old child enters the stage of formal operations, he becomes capable of applying abstract transformational rules to mental units. He can solve algebraic equations or imagine what a shape would look like if all sides were doubled in length. Moreover, he can work with *hypothetical* transformational rules. For example, consider the problem, "A father is four times the age of his son. His son is twenty years younger than his mother. His father and his mother are of equal age. What is the age of each?" In order to solve the problem the child must be able to use a transformational rule that assumes a hypothetical value for the ages, such as x = the age of the son, $4x$ = the age of the father, and $x + 20$ = the age of the mother. He solves the problem by setting up the equation, $4x = x + 20$; and computing the value of x, he arrives at the solution: the son is 6.6, the father is 26.4, and the mother is 26.4.

A ten-year-old would not think of transforming the father's age to a multiple of the son's age and transforming the mother's age to a sum of the son's age plus twenty, but an adolescent has the ability to learn that rule and to use it at the right time.

Implications for Teaching

Teachers can use their knowledge about the processes of problem solving, noting individual developmental levels and giving exercises that encourage the processes of perception, memory, generating possible solutions, and evaluation.

Gauging Perceptual Competence

Studies of perception indicate that children differ in how easily they can discern differences among letters and numbers. Some do not detect or pay attention to open versus closed designs (the letter *C* is an open design, the letter *O* a closed one) and straight-line versus curved designs (*V* is straight-line, *U* is curvilinear). Since this is so, teachers of first- and second-grade children may find it more effective to teach the alphabet in some order besides the traditional one of *ABC*, such as pairing letters of similar shapes in order to maximize the contrasts to the children:

z versus *n*	r versus *k*
c versus *o*	u versus *v*
c versus *d*	n versus *m*
m versus *w*	

In the same way, words that are differentiated by only one letter can be taught in a cluster: rat, cat, hat, bat, sat, and so forth. Teachers may

want to make flip cards that emulate the technique used on educational television shows, where the constant part of the word (in this case, *at*) remains the same and only the first letter changes.

There is also an important principle that affects auditory perception: young children have more trouble than older children in attending to more than one event at a time. Therefore, if they are distracted when the teacher is talking, they may miss critical parts of what she says.

TEACHER: "Why don't you take out your [word list] and write the [first] five?"

If an adult missed the bracketed words, he might be able to reconstruct the sense of the request by basing his guess on a word he did hear, *write;* but a young child is less able to do so.

The teacher should appreciate this limitation in young children and be sure to have everyone's attention when she is giving instructions. Some schools encourage the presence of extra adults for reading lessons to help ensure the children's attention, since it is difficult for one teacher to hold the attention of twenty young children for very long.

Strategies to Improve Memory

To aid the process of memory, teachers need to help develop efficient coding devices. As Gagné suggests (Chapter 3), the mind may develop a shorthand, or code, to help in memorizing a synonym or word in a foreign language. Using the example given previously, the student notices the resemblance between *allumette* and *illuminate* (both in meaning and in sound) and uses it as a bridge from the English word *match* to the French equivalent *allumette*.

Students of music are often taught that the word *face* and the expression "Every good *boy does fine*" stand respectively, for the notes on the lines (F, A, C, E) and the notes on the spaces (E, G, B, D, F) of a staff of music. Such memory aids are called *mnemonic devices*. In medical school students learn similar tricks to help them remember the names of bones and muscles (such as the mnemonic aid for recalling the names of the bones in the wrist: "Never *lower* Tenley's *pants*, Mother *might come home*"). Children, too, can be taught to remember dates, places, presidents, and capitals through efficient use of memory aids. In ancient Greece one of the teacher's main tasks was to guide students in the use of strategies for remembering long speeches or recitations. Speakers used to imagine the room or hall in which they were going to make a speech in the future and associated paragraphs of the speech with parts of the room. When it was time for the person to give the speech, the speaker would look around, and the sight of windows, doors, or columns in the room would help him to recall elements of his speech (Yates, 1966).

A child's ability to remember information depends a great deal on the strategies she uses to organize it and "lay it down" in memory. The use of strategies such as rehearsal, grouping the information to be remembered (such as taking a number like 762773021 and mentally blocking it into three sections: 762 773 021), and a systematic search of memory during testing all help recall. Around the age of seven, American children are able to recall a longer string of words or numbers than they could have a few years earlier, probably because they automatically and unconsciously use tricks to organize information they want to remember.

Several studies verify the usefulness of teaching deliberate strategies to help children organize and remember new material. In one study children from five to nine years of age were given pictures of common objects randomly arranged. They all belonged to four conceptual categories—animals, furniture, vehicles, and clothing. Each child first named each picture and then was given two minutes to study all the pictures (even move them about, if she believed that would help her remember them). The pictures were then removed and the child had to remember as many pictures as she could. A second group of children was told the names of the four categories, and a third group of children was actually taught how to sort the pictures into the conceptual groups. Young children, five and six years of age, who were taught to organize the pictures into groups did so, but the five- and six-year-olds who were *not* taught did not move the pictures around into categories. Older children, though not specifically taught to rearrange the pictures, were much more likely to do so, and this strategy was associated with an improved memory for the pictures (Moely et al., 1969).

In another experiment children of three ages—kindergarten, second grade, and fifth grade—were shown a set of pictures in a specific order and then asked to point to the pictures in the same order. Older children, who were more apt to rehearse the names of the pictures silently as they touched them (evidenced by distinct movements of their lips), remembered the sequence better than younger children who did not (Flavell, Beach, and Chinsky, 1966).

The role of short-term memory is important in learning to read. Consider the simple word *boy*. The child may know the sound of each letter, but if he says to himself, "Bee-Oh-Why," the combination of sounds does not produce the word *boy*. So the child must learn—by memorizing—that the letter *o* in that particular set is sounded like *aw*, the *y* is sounded like *ee*, and the *b* is sounded like *ba*. Secondly, he has to be able to hold the sound of the *b* in short-term memory while he is working on the *o* and the *y*. If he cannot, he will not be able to read the word, for when he finally gets to recognize the *y*, he may have forgotten the *b* and will have to begin again. The main implication for teachers of children who are learning to read is to make sure that the child is at a stage of maturity where he can hold previously processed information in memory while he is working on a new item of information.

Encouraging Creative Solutions

Creativity is an essential ingredient in generating good solutions. Although a subtle and amorphous quality, it can be encouraged by developing an atmosphere in which a correct answer is not always essential and in which inventiveness, originality, and daring are rewarded instead. Brainstorming sessions are one possibility: for instance, a teacher could ask the children to name all the uses they can think of for newspaper. Children can also be shown pictorial designs and asked to say what the designs remind them of; or they can be shown designs in a series of three and asked to make up a story using the ideas suggested by the designs. Or one child can begin a story based on one design, a second child can build on his beginning and develop the idea, and a third can be responsible for inventing an ending to the story. Once they are old enough to consider hypothetical situations, children can respond to questions such as, "What would the world be like if there were no water?" In posing such a situation, however, teachers need to make the question accessible to the students; that is, they need to draw it close enough to what the students are familiar with, perhaps by continuing, "Would there be people? No? Why not?"

A freer atmosphere of thought can be developed in teaching a wide range of subjects, so that the children are able to think more broadly about the material they are studying. In social studies, for instance, instead of simply answering the question, "Describe the life of the

Sioux Indians," the children may be ready to think about this question: "Make a list of the ways in which their environment might have influenced the living and working customs of the Sioux Indians." The creation of a school atmosphere in which the children feel free to generate a wide variety of solutions is a major factor in teaching children to solve problems.

Modifying Reflective and Impulsive Tendencies

As we saw earlier, there are also specific remedies for overly impulsive or reflective children that can improve their ability to evaluate. Overly impulsive children need to be helped to consider their answers more carefully and slowly, while overly reflective children should be encouraged to be less fearful of making mistakes and more relaxed about venturing an answer to a problem.

For overly impulsive children the teacher can set up lessons in which accuracy is rewarded, and speed unimportant. She can continually remind the child that slowing down and being careful are the strategies he should pursue, rather than dashing through the material in an effort to complete it quickly; she may even encourage him to count to five before giving the answer. For the overly reflective child, she can emphasize that it is all right to make a mistake and remind the child that perfection is not the only goal in her class. She can set up lessons that encourage her to take some chances and make a guess and reward her for taking risks rather than for being correct. On tasks such as the Matching Familiar Figures Test, children can practice reflective or impulsive strategies. For impulsive children the teacher would emphasize finding the one correct picture that matches the standard model, encouraging them to take care to look past the general resemblances and discern the different details. Another way to help the impulsive child is to ask him to guess what an object is simply by feeling it, as though seeing it with his hands; in this way he learns to exercise care in perception and decision.

We have now considered the basic units and processes in problem solving. In Chapter 5 we shall consider a more complicated aspect of cognitive development and its application to teaching.

Summary

Cognition directed toward solving a problem is composed of five basic units, which are used in the processes at work in mental activity. The units are the schema, which is a representation of an event; an image, which is a detailed representation created from the schema; a symbol, which, unlike a schema or an image, is an arbitrary way of representing the event, as the number 4 stands for a collection of four things. The fourth unit is the concept, which stands for a common set of attributes shared by a group of schemata, images, or symbols. Concepts differ in degree of abstraction, complexity, differentiation, and centrality of their characteristic dimensions. Rules—the fifth unit—are essentially statements about concepts, and they can be classified in two ways. First, a rule may be regarded as either a nontransformational rule, stating a relationship between the concepts involved; or a transformational rule, involving a set of procedures enacted upon the concepts. Second, rules may be classified as informal, stating a relation between two concepts that is nearly always true; or formal, stating a relation that is always true. Therefore, there are four kinds of rules: informal nontransformational, formal nontransformational, informal transformational, and formal transformational. As children grow older, developmental changes take place in their grasp of images, symbols, concepts, and rules and in their ability to use these units in their thinking.

In directed cognition, the deliberate thought used in problem solving, five processes are at work. In perception children organize, select, and interpret material by means of their senses, increasing and sharpening their perceptions and interpretations as they grow older. Memory constitutes an elaborate system of storing and retrieving information. Three kinds of memory may be distinguished: sensory memory records vividly but for only a fraction of a second; short-term memory retains information for perhaps half a minute; long-term memory is the storage process for information to be retrieved at a later date. In remembering, children may recognize an event, that is, realize they have encountered it before when they see it again; or they may recall it, that is, entirely reproduce the event without any perceptual aids.

In the third process, generating possible solutions, children draw on the experience and knowledge they already possess and use it to formulate a hypothesis, or possible answer to a problem. In using the rules that they know in a new way, creativity plays an important part. Evaluation is the careful part of problem solving; it occurs when children stop to assess their thought and the relative merits of their solutions. Children who are overly impulsive may leap to a conclusion without adequately evaluating it; overly reflective children may be so fearful of making a mistake that they have difficulty arriving at a solution. The fifth process, implementing the most appropriate solution, requires the application of rules to the particular problem at hand.

Projects

1 Make a list of five simple concepts that might be discussed in kindergarten (for example, *color, time, weather*). Choose one of the concepts and plan some activities to be used over a period of time that would help five-year-olds understand it. For instance, the teacher may suggest growing seeds to teach an understanding of time.

2 Interview either a blind or deaf person and ascertain how this person understands a concept—such as *music* or *color*—that is usually understood by seeing or hearing the attributes of that concept.

3 Make up a ten-item test of the information presented in this chapter. Write five questions that test recognition, five that test recall. Administer the test to your classmates.

4 In one of the following psychological journals, find a recent study on creativity or perception in school-age children, and analyze and evaluate the study: *Child Development, Exceptional Children, Journal of Educational Psychology.*

5 Hold an informal workshop with four classmates on the changeover to the metric system. Gather the information that explains the conversions and devise ways to help each other master the new system. Work with various measuring devices: yard sticks, liter containers, and so forth.

6 Suppose you were conducting a lesson on electricity using a battery-run engine and photographs showing the technique of wiring the battery and the engine. What cognitive units and processes would the lesson activate in participating students?

7 Starting with a high-school biology lesson in a textbook, list the concepts it depends on and outline the rules it describes. How many of the rules could be applied to a different biology lesson?

Recom-
mended
Reading

Donaldson, M. *A study of children's thinking.* London: Tavistock, 1963. Summarizes interesting research on problem solving in school-age children. The problems are derived from Piagetian theory. The main conclusion is that the errors made by children under eight or nine years of age are often due to failing to understand the problem, adopting an inappropriate problem-solving set, and other factors having little to do with factual knowledge or the ability to reason.

Flavell, J. H. *Cognitive development.* Englewood Cliffs, N.J.: Prentice Hall, 1977. An excellent and concise summary of cognitive development from infancy through adolescence. The text deals with recent advances in understanding of memory, in formal operational thought, and in communication. It discusses the executive processes surrounding rehearsal and organization as related to memory processes.

Wallach, M. A., and Kogan, N. *Modes of thinking in young children.* New York: Holt, Rinehart and Winston, 1965. Describes research on creative thinking in children. New tests of creativity were developed by the authors and administered to children in order to determine the personality factors that were correlated with creative ideas.

cognition II: the development of competence

5

In Chapter 4 we discussed the units and processes used in acquiring new knowledge, transforming or recalling old knowledge, and solving problems. We saw that the basic units of cognition—schemata, images, concepts, symbols, and rules—develop gradually. Infants possess only schemata for the objects and events they perceive and manipulate, such as their mothers' faces or a rattle. Four-year-olds possess all five types of units. They can generate images of their mothers, know that a dog belongs to the category *animal,* treat *red* as more symbolic of summer than of winter, and have a rule for getting water from a hose. But the richness, the complexity, and the consolidation of the units continue to expand with age.

The processes of cognition also change with each passing year. As they mature, children detect and organize information more quickly, can remember more independent facts, generate more appropriate solutions to a problem, and pause longer to evaluate the validity of their ideas. Although a twelve-year-old obviously possesses more knowledge than a six-year-old, the older child's greater competence at problem solving derives not only from a larger inventory of concepts and rules but also from the ability to activate and reorganize existing knowledge. Twelve-year-olds are more efficient at using what they know.

This chapter continues to examine the development of cognitive competences. We will explore the growth of the executive functions, consider the role of maturation in cognitive abilities, and make a distinction between competence (what the child is potentially able to do) and performance (what the child actually does). Finally, we will see how these factors affect the child's readiness for an essential school task—arithmetic—and how teachers may use the information and ideas suggested in these chapters to design an elementary arithmetic lesson for their students.

Cognition at Work: The Executive Process

There are two ways to view the thought processes of an individual. One regards the mind as a collection of schemata, images, concepts, symbols, and rules that have been learned in the past. Each of these units has acquired a set of connections with other units and associations with certain problems. When a problem is encountered, the appropriate units are activated and the problem is solved. If the child does not have the proper set of units to solve a new problem, she must be taught them; or she may discover them by working on other problems. This theoretical position makes thought a more or less mechanical process and does not require us to assume a monitoring process that guides and integrates thought.

An alternative view places the units and processes of cognition under the supervision of an executive process that begins to grow early in development, perhaps as early as the second year. The executive functions keep track of what the mind has learned, know where to look for the best solution, and recognize when a problem has been solved.

Although some psychologists prefer not to posit a sophisticated monitoring system like the executive process, a simple experiment suggests the need for such a postulation. Ask an eight-year-old and a four-year-old to listen to you carefully and then say, "cat, cow, pig, dog." Wait twenty seconds and then say, "cat, pig, dog," and ask the children which animal was not mentioned. Most eight-year-olds—but far fewer four-year-olds—will answer "cow." This simple event is difficult to explain without assuming the operation of a complex psychological process that keeps an orderly record of past experience and knows how and where to search for an answer. The older child was not warned that he would have to remember the second animal name, yet twenty seconds later he was able to retrieve the word *cow*. For this reason we believe it is useful to assume a set of executive processes that begins to emerge, gradually, during the preschool years. The processes blossom around seven years of age in children from modern countries but not until ten or eleven years of age in children growing up in extremely isolated, subsistence-farming communities in the nonindustrialized areas of the world. In such locations children encounter less variety of experience, are given fewer challenges early in life, and have a less adequate formal education. Let us now discuss the separate functions of the executive in more detail.

Functions of the Executive

Reflecting on One's Actions and Their Consequences

By age four most American children have begun to reflect actively on what they are doing. While they are performing, children think about their behavior, as if an executive was monitoring their thoughts and actions. This process is seen in an experiment in which three- and four-year-old children were asked to draw a tree, a person, and a house. One week later each child was shown four similar drawings of one of the objects—four people, four trees, or four houses (only one of which was the child's)—and asked to pick out the one he drew a week earlier. Many of the three-year-olds could not remember which picture they had drawn, even though they could recognize photographs of different objects they had seen a week earlier, while the four-year-olds did remember their drawings. One reason the younger children could not recognize their own drawings is that they did not actively think about what they were doing when they were drawing.

Once children begin to reflect on their behavior, they try to relate the results of their actions to their knowledge. If they misbehave and the result is punishment, they reflect on that sequence of events and generate a new piece of knowledge—namely, that mischievous acts will lead to punishment. They are now able to exert control over their actions. Parents around the world note that it does not pay to punish a child until he has reason (the Utku of Hudson Bay call this awareness *ihuma*)—until the child is capable of knowing right from wrong. Parents discover that a child becomes aware of the consequences of his actions between three and five years of age. This is the time when children first experience guilt because they are now capable of realizing that their actions affect others and that they have the power to inhibit such actions; they begin to appreciate that they are responsible for their behavior.

Recognizing the Problem

Another important function of the executive is recognizing that a problem exists in a situation that is not directly and immediately relevant to the child. If a three-year-old wants to use the faucet and cannot reach it, she knows that she has a problem. She is aware of a goal she wishes to attain and she appreciates, to a limited degree, that she can implement some solutions to her problem. She may look for a chair to move up to the sink so that she can climb up and turn on the faucet. But when asked by an adult to find the correct figure in the Matching Familiar Figures Test (see Figure 5–1), that same

Figure 5–1

In the Matching Familiar Figures Test three-year-olds may be unable to solve the problem because they do not understand the purpose of a task that is not immediately relevant to them.

three-year-old may not grasp the purpose of the task and will not know what she should do to solve the problem efficiently.

In addition, the young child does not realize that the stated facts in a problem need not have anything to do with reality and that a given problem can contain all the information required to solve it. Consider the following problem: "Three children—Anne, Sara, and Charles—attend three different schools, called the East School, the North School, and the South School. If Anne goes to the East School and Sara to the North School, where does Charles go?"

A five-year-old might reply "My brother Charles goes to the Cleveland School" because he failed to appreciate that the problem was limited to the information presented and was not to be solved by referring to one's actual experiences. The nine-year-old would realize at once that the relevant information was stated in the problem and that he should not confuse people he knows with Anne, Sara, or Charles.

The preschool child does not have a generalized ability to recognize a problem as an isolated set of premises, a prerequisite, of course, for mastery of arithmetic.

Appreciating the Difficulty of a Problem and Adjusting Effort Accordingly

A related function of the executive is to understand how hard a problem is going to be and to use strategies appropriate to the difficulty of the task. Young children do adjust their efforts when the problems they confront are familiar and relevant. A two-year-old is more careful in placing a sixth block on a tower of five than a third block on a tower of two. But if she confronts a less familiar problem, such as being asked to draw three people on a small piece of paper, she may not take time to plan the drawing and will draw two so large that there is no room left on the paper for the third.

Consider an example that illustrates this aspect of the executive. In one study (Rogoff, Newcombe, and Kagan, 1974) children aged four, six, and eight were told they had to remember a large number of pictures for either a few minutes, a day, or a week. The experimenter first made sure that all the children understood that a week was much longer than a day and that a day was much longer than a few minutes. Then the children were shown a group of forty pictures, one at a time, to see how long each child would study the picture before he handed it back to the examiner. If effort was being adjusted to the difficulty of the task, then those who knew they had to remember the pictures for a week should have looked longer at each picture than those who believed they had to remember the pictures for only a few minutes. The four-year-olds did not adjust their effort to match task difficulty, for those who had to remember the pictures for a week did not look at them any longer than those who had to remember them for a few minutes. But the eight-year-olds did study the pictures in accord with how long they had to remember them. The six-year-olds fell in between (see Figure 5–2).

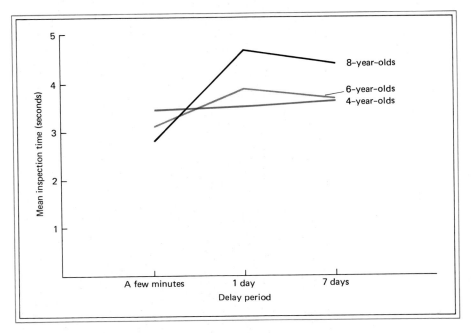

Figure 5–2
When groups of children were shown a set of forty pictures and told they would need to remember them for a few minutes, a day, or a week, four-year-olds failed to adjust their effort according to the task: those who would need to remember the pictures for a week did not study them any longer than those who would need to remember them for a few minutes. Eight-year-olds, however, did study the pictures in accord with how long they would need to remember them. (Adapted from Rogoff, Newcombe, and Kagan, 1974)

     As the child matures he recognizes the relative difficulty of problems and accommodates his effort accordingly in a greater number of situations.

Maintaining Flexibility

A fourth function of the executive is to give up inefficient and incorrect solutions quickly and to replace them with better ones. Preschool children are likely to stick to an initial solution even if it is not effective or to withdraw from the problem entirely. Older children are better able to cast aside a strategy that is not working and try a new one. A three-year-old who is trying to fit together two pieces of a puzzle will persevere with the pieces even though they obviously do not fit. The older child more readily looks for another puzzle piece.

**Using
Strategies**

We have already mentioned the fifth function of the executive in our discussion of memory in Chapter 4. Very few people can remember more than seven or eight independent items of information in short-term memory if they do not have the opportunity to rehearse the information, organize it in some way, or transfer it to long-term memory. Consider this series of numbers: 9, 3, 1, 5, 2, 4, 7, 3. The series has no pattern, and its eight digits represent the limit of short-term memory among most older children and adults. But consider this string of numbers: 1, 2, 4, 8, 1, 6, 3, 2, 6, 4, 1, 2, 8, 2, 5, 6. If a person noticed that, ignoring the separation of each digit by commas, the string was organized so that each number after the first was twice that of the preceding number (2×1 is 2, 2×2 is 4, 2×8 is 16, 2×16 is 32, and so forth), he could remember an infinite string, for all he has to remember is the first number and the rule of doubling. Of course, if the child does not know the rule of doubling or does not know how to multiply, he cannot solve the problem.

But even when five- or six-year-olds know certain rules, they often fail to use them. They fail to detect patterns or activate rules when faced with a problem for which they know a relevant rule. Most six-year-olds know the rule of alternation (right-left-right-left or up-down-up-down). But many six-year-olds do not detect or activate that rule in a memory problem. In one experiment children had to remember the position of a series of dolls, that is, whether the dolls were right side up or upside down. When the arrangement of dolls was

random—up-down-down-up-up-down-up—six-year-olds could remember the positions of the first four or five dolls, and eight-year-olds, the positions of the first six or seven. But when the arrangement was alternative—up-down-up-down-up-down—the older children, who are more likely to notice the alternation, could remember an infinitely long string because all they had to remember was the orientation of the first doll and the rule *alternate*. Six-year-olds, even though they possess the rule of alternation, are less likely to detect the pattern and therefore will be able to remember only the positions of the first four or five dolls (Kagan et al., unpublished).

One quality of unusually intelligent children is their ability to see an organizational pattern in a problem, an aptitude that makes the difference between good and poor performance in mathematics and geometry.

The ability to activate proper rules and strategies for a problem is correlated with increased speed in retrieving knowledge. Suppose a four-year-old and an eight-year-old were observed eating dinner. If half an hour after dinner you asked each of them what he had eaten, the eight-year-old would respond much faster than the four-year-old, who would appear to be groping for the information we know he has. If a four-year-old and an eight-year-old are shown thirty pictures and one week later are shown thirty pairs of pictures and asked to identify those seen a week earlier, the four-year-old will take a little longer than the older child to make his decisions. It is as if the extra four years of maturity are accompanied by a basic speeding up of the process by which stored information is retrieved. In everyday language we say that the eight-year-old seems to think more quickly. This is potentially important for many intellectual problems, especially school tasks that require the child to hold the problem's essential information in short-term memory and then to reach back and pull out the proper rules to solve it. Since we know that if it is not rehearsed, information in short-term memory tends to decay or become lost after twenty or thirty seconds, the ability to retrieve rules and concepts quickly means that vital information is less likely to be lost.

Surmounting Distraction and Controlling Anxiety

It is also the task of the executive to keep attention focused on a problem and to resist being distracted by outside noises, irrelevant thoughts, the pounding of one's heart, or the behavior of other people. This includes controlling anxiety, which may mount quickly when a problem is difficult, and preventing the anxiety from becoming overwhelming. When children four and five years of age are unable to solve a problem, they often become fearful and inhibited. At that point they may stop thinking. Older children, although anxious, are better able to contain the fear and devote mental energy to the problem.

Finding Elegant Solutions and Avoiding Failure

The older child seems to have a more generalized desire to avoid making mistakes and to solve certain problems with elegance and efficiency. As a result he is more careful and seeks the best possible solution. The younger child has a less clear idea of what constitutes a more efficient or a more aesthetic solution and seems less concerned about making a mistake. Hence, on the Matching Familiar Figures Test, the young child responds quickly and often makes mistakes, while the eight-year-old considers each set of figures longer before he makes his first response and, of course, makes fewer errors.

One reason the young child seems less concerned with error has to do with his conception of the self. The three-year-old child is aware of the attributes of other people—parents are big and strong, babies are small and they cry—but he does not yet see *himself* as an *object* to which qualities such as smart or big may apply. Once a child has generated a concept of himself as an object with distinctive characteristics, he wants to acquire the attributes that are in accordance with the standards he has learned, and he guides his actions to match those standards. This growing "consciousness of self" is also part of the growth of the executive.

If the child's culture values accuracy and avoidance of error, he becomes careful to avoid mistakes on all problems. "To be competent and not make mistakes" becomes the standard by which he judges himself. This standard begins to emerge in a tentative form at about the

same time other standards such as sex and age role emerge (usually at age three), but its growth covers many years.

One sign of the emergence of self-consciousness is boastfulness: the child begins to brag about his actions or abilities. In one study psychologists observed preschool children—aged two and one-half to five and one-half—in group settings and recorded their speech. At about age three there was a major increase in statements that indicate pride in mastery, such as "Look at my big house" (Schachter et al., 1974).

Another sign of the child's growing self-awareness is seen in his attitudes toward his cognitive abilities. For example, preschool children do not have a well-articulated conception of their memory capacity; older children do. In one study preschool, kindergarten, second-grade, and fourth-grade children were asked how many items they thought they could remember from a list of ten pictures. The preschool and kindergarten children made higher estimates than the second- and fourth-graders: 57 percent of the preschool children said they could remember all ten items, while only 21 percent of the fourth-graders thought they could (Flavell, Friedrichs, and Hoyt, 1970).

Consciousness of self may emerge earlier in modern countries than in rudimentary agricultural villages partly because parents in the former tend to focus on a child's characteristics, talents, and liabilities. They say to the child "You are bad, good, pretty, or handsome" more often than parents of children living in isolated, subsistence-farming villages. The family's focus on the child as an object with distinct qualities may hasten the development of a self-concept, which, in turn, facilitates the emergence of the standard to perform with elegance.

Having
Faith in the
Power of
Thought

When a child is not satisfied with her solution to a problem and perseveres in thinking about it, she is showing faith in the power of thought to generate a better solution. Such a belief presupposes an abstract process—the executive—that is aware of the intellectual talents of the self and can direct the self in mental work. If a young child's initial solution does not work, she stops thinking about it because she is not yet mature enough to appreciate that thought can be useful.

Relating
Information
to a Larger
Structure

As children grow from preschool to school age, they begin to relate events and ideas spontaneously to a larger conceptual structure. A six-year-old boy, for example, consciously identifies *dog*—a particular instance of a concept—as part of a larger category of *pets* or *animals*. Aware of the linkages among events and the larger conceptual classes to which they belong, he is capable of deliberately relating events to one another in a coherent network. We say he has *access* to relations among concepts.

Let us try to elaborate on the meaning of this new awareness. Consider the set of conceptual relations that is familiar to most young children: the relation between the concepts *dog* and *animal*. Although the two-year-old has a conceptual structure for *animal*, he does not know the hierarchical relation between *dog* and *animal*. But by age six or seven the child generates a cognitive structure that represents the relation between the concept *(animal)* and one example of it *(dog)*. Furthermore, he is conscious of it. Similarly, a three-year-old child can speak grammatically without being aware of the rules of language, but an eight-year-old knows and can state some of the rules of correct grammar. Knowledge comes first, awareness of that knowledge appears later. The relation between an example of a specific animal and the larger concept becomes articulated.

The same competence applies not only to inclusion concepts, such as pets and animals, but also to concepts that vary on a continuum, such as size and weight. The three-year-old knows which of two boxes or animals is bigger but does not easily see the parallel relation between the two smaller objects and the two larger objects. He does not recognize that the end of the day and the end of the tunnel he digs both share the quality of increasing darkness, even though he may know that the end of the day is dark and the end of the tunnel is dark. But by seven or eight years of age he can abstract the similarity they share. This ability emerges without deliberate teaching. The child distills these structures naturally from experience. His mind is continually at work, shaping, excluding, and synthesizing its units in an attempt to create the most efficient structure. The ability to extract similarities is like a seed that gradually sprouts until the flower explodes.

Once the child can state the relation of part to whole, many other changes appear. For example, in drawing a man or a tree he will be aware of the larger plan while making each stroke. Hence, the drawing will be more accurate and better balanced. In completing a puzzle, he will be conscious of the relation of the piece he is manipulating to the larger design.

Another consequence of the new competence appears in reading comprehension. Some early readers can decode words but do not understand the sentence, perhaps because they do not relate the part (the word) to the whole (the sentence). But children who have access to relations among concepts are more able to plan, for they are simultaneously aware of the goal and the specific activities they must implement.

Understanding the appropriate relation of part to whole is an important factor in the new affective (emotional) and motivational phenomena that emerge around the same time—between four and eight years of age. For example, it is during this period that phobias are most common. A five-year-old may develop a fear of large animals or snakes. In some cases the feared object is symbolic of a feared parent. Indeed, Freud wrote a famous essay about a boy named Hans who developed a fear of large horse-drawn wagons because he related them to his father.

The phenomenon of identification with a parent also emerges at this time. Recall from Chapter 2 that identification occurs when the child recognizes similarities between a model, usually his parent, and himself. In this case the child knows the larger category (the family) and two instances of that concept (the parent and himself) and recognizes the relation between them. The child and the parent share a common quality: membership in a particular family. Sex and ethnic identification also occurs, as the child begins to recognize the relation between the qualities he possesses (his sex, his skin color, his accent) and larger concepts (male, black, Spanish). He begins to see himself as a member of a category. Note that at age four a child does not have complete access to that relation—that is, he is not conscious of it. But in time, he will be. In addition, the eight-year-old can compare the degree to which he possesses a quality or a skill with the degree of that quality or skill possessed by his peers. He can *seriate* that quality according to degree, just as he can arrange a collection of boxes from larger to smaller. The self-concept grows rapidly at this time, for he arrives at conclusions about himself by relating his attributes to those of his peers. Put in other words, he sees "the self" as part of a larger network. As we shall discuss in Chapter 6, motives that involve symbolic goals, such as power, status, and recognition, also grow after age six or seven, once the child can articulate the relation between an activity (such as studying) and a goal (such as status). If the relation is not recognized, we say that the motive is unconscious; if the relation is recognized, the motive is conscious.

One of the functions of the executive—appreciating that a problem is being posed—may also be the result of the ability to see appropriate relations. Children can recognize the relation of their specific test questions to a larger network of school purposes and actions. This is one way of saying they understand the meaning of the test, for meaning can only be defined in terms of a set of relations.

The Growth of Cognitive Competence

There is remarkable change in the cognitive competence of children as they move from infancy through late childhood to adolescence. Since the world of American children is so frequently punctuated with new events and people, it is tempting to assume that the dramatic improvement in intellectual capacity results from this extraordinary variety of experience and from the knowledge it produces. But imagine a small, isolated village of 900 people located on the side of a mountain in northwest Guatemala, where clusters of three or four thatched huts sit on rutted, steeply inclined trails, and groups of six to twelve children remain within a hundred yards of their homes for the first five or six years of their lives. Despite the lack of variety—the same huts, children, trees, and chickens—these children display patterns of intellectual growth that are similar to those of American children. Although their rate of growth of cognitive skills is slower, they appear to possess many but not all of the basic competences that American children display. They can analyze drawings, remember lists of words or pictures of objects, reflect on the products of their actions and thoughts, make inferences from information, as well as think symbolically and conceptually. Such similarities force us to assume that the maturation of the executive psychological processes is universal and that it must be related to parallel changes in the central nervous system.

In modern societies, like our own, many of the executive functions tend to grow most rapidly between five and seven years of age. In isolated agricultural communities in South America, Africa, and Indonesia, where children experience less variety in their lives, where schooling is absent or minimal, and where parents do not continually encourage these functions and deliberately mold a consciousness of self, executive functions emerge a little later, usually between nine and eleven years of age. For example, if children have to remember the order of a series of twelve familiar pictures, American children are able to activate effective strategies of organization and rehearsal by the time they are eight or nine years old. Indian children in isolated communities do not usually remember all twelve until they have reached adolescence (Kagan et al., unpublished). Clearly, the growth of these cognitive competences involves an interaction between biological maturation and experience.

Maturation and Experience

It is difficult to separate the complementary influences of biological maturation and experience on intellectual growth. Maturation and experience go hand-in-hand, as temperature and humidity do in producing snow. In order for snow to fall, the temperature must be below freezing, but a temperature of 20° by itself is not enough. If there is no moisture, there will be no snow. Both are necessary, and neither one is more important than the other. So it is with maturation and experience.

Maturation refers to the gradual and inevitable changes in size, physiology, and psychological functioning that normally occur in all individuals from birth through adulthood as a result of inherited processes. The seven-month-old infant moves from lying on her stomach to sitting up, partly because the maturation of her brain and its control of the muscles has reached a stage where this complex act is possible. If her mother had placed her in a sitting position for an hour each day from the time she was one month old, she might have been able to sit up a little earlier, for experience can speed up maturation to some degree. But no matter what her mother did she would not have been able to sit up without support at two months of age. By eighteen months the average child begins to talk. By twenty-four months a baby in Chicago has learned to say "Hello, Mama," another in Paris says "Bonjour," and on the coast of Kenya a third says "Jambo." Each has learned a specific response in English, French, or Swahili. But none of these children could speak meaningful words at six months because their brains were not sufficiently mature. And, as Piaget has discovered, the ability to understand conservation of volume or mass does not emerge until six or seven years of age. Maturation sets a boundary age on the emergence of certain skills. Hence we say that the child is not "mature" enough to perform certain acts or master certain concepts when he is younger than that age.

But although a skill or an act is influenced by maturation, it does not appear automatically. The environment must provide the proper opportunities and experience. If these do not occur, the emergence of the various maturational milestones can be delayed, and in extreme cases they do not appear at all.

Experience fills the child's mind with the schemata, images, symbols, concepts, and rules that he will need to solve problems and familiarizes him with a variety of contexts so that he will be able to use his knowledge in a broad array of problem situations. If the young child is not ready to implement certain cognitive processes, environmental experiences that are helpful to some older children may be minimally influential. Reading books to a one-year-old is not likely to alter his ability to read during the next year or two. But a father who reads to his one-year-old familiarizes the child with books and may

inculcate a positive attitude toward reading that may help the child when he is ready to learn the skill several years later.

The Example of Reading Readiness

Reading readiness, as it is called, illustrates nicely how maturation and experience cooperate to provide a fruitful time, a stage when the child will be most receptive to reading instruction. A three-year-old can perceive the differences among the alphabet letters and can understand symbols. However, reading involves more than detecting the distinctive aspects of a letter or thinking symbolically. The child must also appreciate that the printed word stands for a sound that represents a familiar event or object in his world. This ability matures a little later, around four or five years of age. Although three-year-olds may recognize the initial of their own first name (all across the country children with the names Angelo and Ann, Peter and Polly, spot a letter that they know relates to them in the "A & P" signs), it may be a year or two before they realize that other names also have initials.

Are There Critical Periods?

The optimal time for teaching a child a particular school skill is an important issue in readiness for school instruction. Some psychologists believe that children can be taught some version of any subject, at any age, provided that it is put in terms they can understand. As psychologist Jerome Bruner describes it:

"When I was ready to read, they taught me to tie my shoes—when I was ready to tie my shoes, they taught me to read."

At each stage of development, the child has a characteristic way of viewing the world and explaining it to himself. The task of teaching a subject to a child at any particular age is one of representing the structure of that subject in terms of the child's way of viewing things. The task can be thought of as one of translation.... Any idea can be represented honestly and usefully in the thought forms of children of school age and ... these first representations can later be made more powerful and precise the more easily by virtue of this early learning ... Actually, any subject can be taught effectively in some intellectually honest form to any child at any stage of development. (1960, p. 33)

Bruner favors extracting the essential principles from a difficult and abstract subject and applying them, in familiar terms, to simpler material that the child already knows. Through this method, he says, we can teach principles such as " ... categorization and its uses, the unit of measure and its development, the indirectness of information in science and the need for operational definitions of ideas ... the attitude that things are connected and not isolated ... the idea of multiple determination of events in the physical and social world" (Bruner, 1960, pp. 26–27).

Bruner's work has expanded our sensitivity to how much a child can learn at an early age. His view is enthusiastically supported by advocates of early learning who believe that a child's intelligence grows at its fastest rate during the first five years. Anxious to take the greatest advantage of these years of growth, they are critical of an educational system that permits children to overindulge in finger painting and block building instead of harnessing their intellectual energy in the service of cognitive development. As a result, many elementary-school teachers have attempted to translate advanced material into primary-grade terms.

Nevertheless, it is probably a slight exaggeration to say that any subject can be taught at any age. A child in the preoperational stage who does not completely understand the principle of reversibility will have difficulty fully grasping some scientific principles, such as how water can turn to steam and condense again into water or why 8 balls can be divided into sets of $4 + 4$, $6 + 2$, $5 + 3$, and $7 + 1$. Although many scientific and mathematical ideas can be recast in terms the child understands (set theory can be understood by a young child who realizes that a cat, a dog, and a cow belong to a particular "set" that must exclude a stuffed teddy bear), we do not yet know whether all ideas can be simplified without losing their essential meaning.

If a pupil is asked to learn a task before she is prepared to understand it, she may experience so much difficulty and anxiety that later, when she is maturationally ready, her interest will have "soured" and she may resist learning the task. On the other hand, if the task is put off until too late, she may not have the energy, motivation, and

resources that were available to her earlier. For instance, an American student may begin to study French in the first, fourth, or eleventh grade. If she begins in the first grade, she is simultaneously developing skills in two languages, which may be confusing. If she does not study French until the end of high school, she will have little time to develop a proficiency in a second language before she graduates. But if she begins in the fourth grade, she can use the facility with written language that she has acquired through her work in English, and she has many years ahead of her for polishing her French.

Each teacher faces a cost/benefit analysis: when will her pupils learn a subject most easily and with the least amount of wasted effort or discouraging failure?

There are pitfalls in trying to determine too precisely the period when a child can learn a new task most easily and efficiently. Sometimes educators fall into the trap of thinking that there is only one optimal period and that if the child has missed it, he will never again have as good a chance for learning the task. A preoccupation with optimal periods leads to an excessively rigid view of education. Besides, there is little evidence to support such a view and some evidence to show that children at different stages of development can meet and master many kinds of tasks. Children can learn their first language as late as twelve years of age, and adults can learn a second language at forty.

We must also appreciate that intellectual competences do not suddenly appear in full strength. The ability to create a schema for an object and to recognize that object a few minutes later is present in an infant as young as twelve weeks of age. But the number of events that a twelve-week-old can recognize is very limited, whereas an eight-year-old's ability to recognize past experience is extraordinary. The ability to treat one object as symbolic of another can be seen in an eighteen-month-old who treats a piece of play-dough as a cookie. But he displays this capacity for symbolism in a limited number of situations, whereas the ten-year-old can treat a large number of objects symbolically.

Initially, children's basic abilities are displayed in the context of only a small number of problems. As they grow older, the number of problem contexts increases. When the functions of the executive emerge in full flower, the contexts in which they will be displayed increase substantially. A good way to conceptualize cognitive development is illustrated in Figure 5–3 in which the ordinate (vertical axis) represents the number of contexts and the absicca horizontal axis) represents age. One curve may be for the ability to impose a categorical organization on twelve events, the other the ability to recall five independent events. It appears that in America many basic competences are displayed in a large number of appropriate contexts by the time the child is nine or ten years of age. For example,

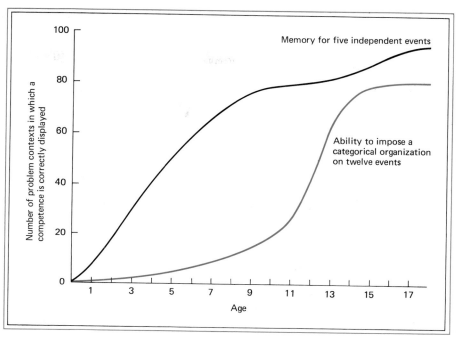

Figure 5-3
One hypothetical way to conceptualize cognitive development is reflected in this figure. With age, the number of problem contexts in which a particular skill is used increases. When the executive processes emerge in full flower, the number of contexts increases dramatically.

a five-year-old may be able to remember five names of his friends or five different locations where candy was placed, but be unable to recall five different unrelated words. By age ten, however, most children will be able to remember five units of information regardless of whether they are words, numbers, or capitals of countries. Those who favor the belief that cognitive development occurs in stages (Piaget being the best example) usually mark the appearance of a new stage when the child first displays—in a large number of situations—the abilities that characterize the stage. Piaget argues that children enter the stage of concrete operations at about seven or eight years of age, when they will apply the principle of conservation to clay, water, and number in many situations. By contrast, the five-year-old will apply the principle, but only in a few situations. Similarly, the five-year-old realizes that numbers can stand for different magnitudes, but he can work with only the first three or four, not with all numbers. By the time he is eight he knows that numbers form a series representing differential magnitude for any set of numbers.

Thus a stage—or the growth of a competence—should be regarded as a wave moving toward the shore. The wave begins yards out from the sand and gathers momentum until it breaks. The point of breaking is the time when a particular ability is generalized or activated in a wide variety of situations.

The Significance of Rate of Development

The idea illustrated in Figure 5–3 is related to the notion of rate of development. What do we mean when we say that a child is "behind" or "ahead," "intellectually slow" or "intellectually precocious"?

One interpretation of these terms focuses on the time when a specific competence first begins to emerge (point A on the curves in Figure 5–4). For example, we say that the child who begins to talk at twelve months is "ahead" of the child who begins to talk at thirty months.

Figure 5–4
The diagram illustrates the two meanings of the terms *intellectually slow* and *intellectually precocious*. One interpretation focuses on the time when a competence (such as manipulating concepts) first emerges—point A. The second interpretation focuses on the child's quality of performance on tasks using this skill after the curve has leveled off—point B. In some cases (green line) the child whose first display of the competence emerges later ends at a higher level ten years later than the child who first displayed the ability very early.

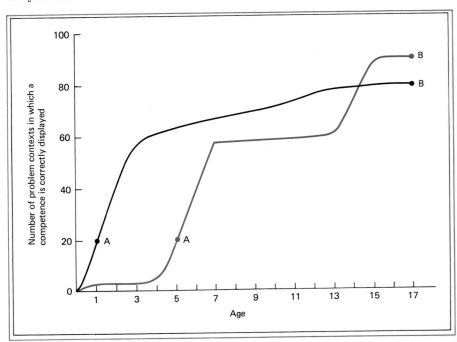

A second interpretation of the terms *behind* and *ahead* focuses on the performance of a competence after the curve has leveled off—years after its emergence (point B on the curves). Although all ten-year-old children can talk, some have large vocabularies and can give and understand elaborate speeches; others have small vocabularies and are less able to offer or understand long and complicated sentences.

The importance of discriminating between these two meanings of *behind* and *ahead* becomes obvious when we realize that there is no obligatory correspondence between the two meanings. The child who begins to speak early will not necessarily be the adolescent who is more proficient at language. Children who walk early will not necessarily be better athletes in high school. Early displays of symbolism do not automatically imply a greater imagination during early adulthood. In other words, early emergence of a natural competence does not necessarily predict a higher level of competence ten to fifteen years later.

But that conclusion applies mainly to those cognitive and motor processes that are part of a maturational program (competences natural to our species, such as language, symbolism, memory, inference, and evaluation) and is less likely to be true for abilities that are taught and improve with practice (culturally specific competences, such as playing the piano or baseball). It seems to be least true for specific factual knowledge, such as size of vocabulary. Indeed, a three-year-old who has a large vocabulary and is "ahead" of most of his peers in the number of words he knows *is* likely to have a larger vocabulary than other children ten years later. Since schools tend to evaluate a first-grade child on the latter skills—knowledge of words, numbers, and ability to read—rather than on memory, symbolism, or evaluation, the first-grade child who is behind his peers on these culturally specific abilities is likely to remain behind through high school, although, of course, some children reverse the trend and "catch up."

Inevitable Variations among Children

Although we will deal with the concept of intelligence in a later chapter, it is appropriate to say a few words here about individual differences in the application of cognitive processes to problems. There is no question that some children consistently solve problems faster and learn new ideas more quickly than others. But we do not know all the reasons for these obvious differences. Some major factors are the amount of knowledge children have, the richness of the repertory of concepts and rules they have learned, and the opportunities they have had to test out their competences in a wide variety of contexts.

But even when children grow up in the same environment, they will differ in how they apply their competences. Even if all are exposed to the same experience, some will learn more from it than others. For this reason, many people assume that biological differences must make some children more receptive than others to learning new information. There is good reason to believe that children differ on several related dimensions that are likely to influence their receptivity to learn new ideas. (We will reserve for Chapter 8 the question of whether or not these differences are inherited.) First, young infants differ in their alertness to anything unusual. Some infants respond to the slightest change in familiar objects or events—a rearrangement of their bedroom or a change in their mother's hair style. Since noticing an event that is discrepant from one's knowledge and trying to assimilate it is the most important cause of change in existing cognitive units, children who are ready to be alerted by subtle change will "learn more" and create more sophisticated systems of knowledge than children who are less receptive to change.

Second, some children can detect inconsistencies in the way adults use concepts. A child who is accustomed to hearing adults call certain flying objects *birds* and notices that one day his mother calls a bird in the back yard a *bluejay* will detect this difference and ask why. His question and her answer allow the child to acquire a more finely differentiated concept of *bird*.

Most important, children differ in their need to understand—in their desire to reduce ambiguity and resolve inconsistency. There are some children who continually question: "Why didn't you spank the dog for messing today? You did yesterday." "Why didn't you say grace today at dinner? You did yesterday." "Why did you lock the garage today?" Detecting discrepancy and inconsistency is a major impetus to thought and causes the child to attempt to understand the inconsistency. In that process the child's mind grows. Children who seem to be exquisitely sensitive to the slightest variation in the familiar are often those we call "smart." Although we do not yet know the reasons for their sensitivity, it is likely to be one basis for the attribute we call "intelligence."

Competence versus Performance

The cognitive competences described thus far should be viewed as potentials. Even if a child has a competence, there is no guarantee that she will use it to solve a particular problem. As a result, psychologists draw a distinction between *competence,* which is the possession of certain skills and knowledge, and *performance,* which is overt problem-solving behavior. If a child's performance is adequate, we can infer that she possesses the requisite competence for the task.

But if her performance—what she shows she can do—is inadequate, we are less justified in inferring that she lacks the relevant ability, although she may. A first-grade student asked to subtract 8 from 16 may fail to solve the problem because she has never encountered the rule for borrowing. But in attempting to assess competence (what the child is potentially capable of doing) by scrutinizing performance (what the child actually does), teachers are obliged to keep in mind that a number of factors can prevent competence from being smoothly translated into performance.

Obstacles to Successful Problem Solving

This section examines the obstacles to adequate performance in problem-solving situations. They can occur alone or in combination. They are failure to understand the problem; failure to remember the elements of the problem; lack of the relevant knowledge to solve the problem; belief in a contradictory rule or fact; fear of making a mistake; low motivation; and low expectancy of success.

Failure to understand the problem. Teachers often mistakenly assume that failure to solve a problem (an addition problem in arithmetic, for example) after exposure to instruction reflects a basic inability to learn the rule. But the child may fail because he does not understand the problem.

Suppose a four-year-old is given a red block to hold while a blue block lies on the table in front of him. If we say to him, "Fix it so that the red block is on top of the blue block," he simply moves his hand over and sets the red block on top of the blue block. However, if he is asked a second time and is holding the *blue* block, he may be confused; he may put the blue block on top of the red one. Does he fail because he does not know how to put one block on top of another? No, he has shown he can do that. He fails because he did not understand the instructions completely. If you show him a red block on a blue one, then put both blocks on the floor and repeat the instruction, he will solve the problem correctly.

Often children fail to understand a question because of the vocabulary or the grammar used. One question on a standard intelligence test asks, "What must you do to make water boil?" Many poor children in ghetto areas do not answer correctly because they are not familiar with the grammatical form, "must you do." If the question is rephrased to read, "What do you do to make water boil?" they often answer correctly, "Put it on the stove."

Misunderstanding a problem can also stem from the child's difficulty in dealing with an idea that is hypothetical or nonsensical. A ten-year-old, entering the stage of formal operations, can easily consider questions such as, "A 500-pound canary flew 4 miles one day and 3 miles the next; how many miles did he fly all together?" But many six-year-olds would be confused; although they can add 4 and 3, their experience tells them that canaries do not weigh five hundred pounds and they may therefore reject the problem.

Failure to remember the elements of the problem. In order to generate an adequate solution, the child needs to be able to remember all the elements of the problem. Consider an example of a test used to measure a child's ability to perform Piagetian class-inclusion tasks. The examiner puts six blue buttons and four red buttons on a table and asks, "Are there more blue buttons or more buttons?" A child has, at the least, three facts to remember while she solves the problem: (1) the number of blue buttons, (2) the number of red buttons, and (3) the fact that the examiner said "more blue buttons or more buttons" and *not* "more blue buttons or more red buttons." Many inexperienced first-grade teachers do not realize that a six-year-old often has trouble remembering long, complex instructions ("Put away your workbook, take out your reader, turn to page 10, do exercises 3, 4, and 5"). Interpreting a child's failure to solve a problem or carry out a request as lack of intelligence or hostility, a teacher can overlook a more innocent explanation: the child forgot what she was told.

Lack of relevant knowledge. A child may understand the problem, remember it, and still be unable to solve it because she lacks the appropriate concepts or rules. Consider this problem: "A circular lake has a circumference of twelve miles. What is the distance from one side to the other?" If the child does not know that $C = 2\pi r$, she will not be able to figure out the answer or even know where to begin.

Growing up in different social classes, children have different experiences and, as a result, may not generate the same solutions to a given problem. As we will see in Chapter 8, some questions on intelligence tests do not make an allowance for such variations in experience. For example, one question on a leading intelligence test asks, "What should you do if a boy (or a girl) smaller than you starts to fight with you?" A middle-class child usually replies that he would not hit the smaller child. However, a child from an urban ghetto, who may well have been raised to defend himself whenever attacked, is more likely to reply, "I would hit him back." Each child answers the question in accord with what he has been told; but only the first answer is given credit on the intelligence test.

Belief in a contradictory rule or fact. Great discoveries in science are rare because most scientists have a strong faith in what they were taught as students. Darwin's bold hypothesis that animals and plants had evolved gradually and were not all created at the same time by a divine being strongly contradicted the dominant belief of the nineteenth century.

In the same way, a child's firm belief in one rule will obstruct his ability to generate a new explanation that contradicts it. Suppose that a child has been taught to believe that all life—plant and animal—is sacred. He would be puzzled by the new forest service directive proclaiming that forest fires arising spontaneously (as a result of lightning storms) should be allowed to burn and destroy old trees, in order to permit the forest to regenerate new plants. In mathematics classes, when children are mastering the concept of numbers to the base one or the base two, they initially have a difficult time generating correct solutions because they tenaciously hold to the "common-sense" rule that 16 is 16; only after some time do they grasp the notion that both 16 and 2^4 are equally arbitrary symbols, and the only difference is that one statement is sanctioned by more common use.

Fear of making a mistake. School-age children wish to avoid the criticism from teachers and classmates that may follow a mistake. They also want to avoid private feelings of humiliation when they do not live up to their own standards of competence. Their easiest path is to volunteer answers only when they are certain of being correct and withdraw from the competition when they are unsure. Every class has some children who are intelligent but too cautious and always know more than they are willing to say. They censor good ideas because they would rather forego the possibility of success than risk failure.

The first-grade reading group was finishing a story about a famous figure in sports who had been a success when still very young.

"On the first day of the training season," Daniel read, "he pointed out Ruth as the newest 'babe' of the Orioles, known for its young players."

The teacher interrupted, "Why was he called Babe Ruth?" No answer. She asked again: "Why, children? It's easy—it's right in the part Daniel just read." The children reread the story, then looked up, still puzzled. Finally the teacher realized the problem.

"What is a 'babe,' Daniel?" she asked. "Anyone?"

"I don't know," he said.

"It's a baby," she answered, and the children said, "Oh!"

In order to answer the teacher's question about the nickname of the famous baseball player, the students needed to know that "babe" had the same meaning as "baby"—and they didn't.

Low motivation. Even a child who has all the necessary knowledge will not use it if he is not strongly motivated. Each child possesses an elaborate and varied pattern of motives that may work together or pull him in different directions. The set of forces we call *motives* play as important a part in his performance as do the units and the processes at his command.

Low expectancy of success. Children seek to avoid the unpleasant feelings that accompany failure. At the same time, they look forward to the pleasant feelings that accompany their success. Over a period of time, children become conscious of their ability—or lack of ability—to perform certain tasks or solve certain problems. Naturally, their motivation for tasks that bring success is much greater and they approach them more eagerly. In general, when a child has a high expectancy of success for an intellectual task, he will perform better than he will on a task for which his expectancy of success is low. We will discuss this in detail in Chapter 7.

Implications for Teaching: How Children Learn Arithmetic

The Nature of Mathematics

The need for numerical representation of things and people provides the bridge between the logical world of mathematics and the practical daily life of human beings. A clear example is seen in a custom of the Ibo tribe of Nigeria. The Feast of the New Yam, marking both the harvest and the new year, is also an opportune time for a census. Every grown man brings one yam for each member of his household. The yams are then counted and the number is announced by the priest—and joyfully received by the community if the population has increased since the last new year (Zaslavsky, 1973). In early cultures, yams, cowrie shells, sticks, and pebbles have all been used as simple counting instruments. Our word *calculus* is the Latin word for *pebble*. The practical needs to measure the passage of time and to determine the count of some objects for trade, taxes, dowries, and debts were major incentives for people to start developing the large body of logic that we now know as mathematics.

Mathematics is a conscious intellectual discipline; it does not develop naturally among peoples as does language. All societies invented a spoken language. But not all cultures invented mathematics. Historically, mathematics probably developed when people changed from a nomadic, pastoral life to an agricultural life. They needed to record the passage of the seasons so that they would know when to plant. When they began to raise crops in surplus and to trade one kind of goods for another, they needed some system of keeping accounts.

Grade-school children in America, however, are not asked to reinvent the subject from scratch: they are asked, instead, to master the international language and ideas of mathematics as it now exists. The language transcends the daily practical uses to which we put it and possesses elaborate but exact rules of its own. This is a difficult concept for a child to grasp. Although he can use the numbers and rules to compute all kinds of possible arrangements for bushels of apples or dollars received in allowance, the concept that he must eventually grasp is that the rules hold true in the abstract: the numbers play their exact and intricate games even when there are no apples and no dollars involved. Mathematics deals with the relations among numerical concepts, not with apples or dollars. The goal of teaching mathematics is, ideally, to develop children's appreciation for its elegance and beauty. But the elegant rules of mathematics do not derive from concrete events in the natural world; they are created by human minds. Ultimately, they can only be understood intellectually, not by rote learning.

Concept of Number

Since mathematics is a set of rules involving the relations between numbers, the first thing the child must understand is the meaning of number. As we have indicated several times, children do not master a concept all at once, but gradually. Moreover, the concept *number* is different from most other concepts the young child has acquired. The concepts *animal, food, clothing,* and *furniture* are defined by a set of

concrete similarities among objects, such as physical appearance (has fur and four legs), function (can be eaten, can be worn), or location (the things in a house). The concept *number* is not based on similarities in concrete qualities and for that reason is more difficult to understand.

The child must appreciate two basic characteristics of numbers. First, they form a progression or series that stands for differences in magnitude—this is called the *ordinal property of number*. In order to appreciate that three dogs is more than two dogs, the child must first understand the meaning of *more* or *less* applied to concrete objects. The average American child does understand the meaning of bigger, longer, larger, or heavier by the time he is four years old. A four-year-old who is shown two red sticks of slightly different lengths and asked which is longer or which is shorter will usually answer correctly (Brainerd and Fraser, 1975). Once he understands the meaning of differential magnitude, he is ready to appreciate that numbers can also represent different magnitudes. Three objects is more than two objects, for any set of objects. The ability to arrange a set of objects to form a series from smallest to biggest, thinnest to fattest, shortest to tallest, is called *seriation* and is obviously related to the ability to grasp the idea that numbers, too, progress from smallest to largest (see Figure 5–5).

Second, the child must understand that number can be applied to objects as a property of a set of objects, regardless of the specific nature of the objects, and that that property does not change, even though the specific objects or their arrangement may change. This is called the *cardinal property of number.* The number *three* refers to a specific property of a collection of objects, whether they are three dogs, three cats, or a cat, a dog, and a mouse. Before the child reaches the first grade, he can play games classifying different objects according to particular properties. In the attribute game described in Chapter 4, he can take wooden blocks and place them inside loops of string placed on the floor. One loop is for any block that is red, another is for any block that is square, a third is for any small block, and the fourth is for big blocks. He realizes that in the loop reserved for red blocks he can put a

Figure 5–5
Seriation is another concept a child can learn by manipulating concrete objects. She can arrange sticks, from longest to shortest, or plastic disks, from smallest to biggest, or cylindrical weights, which increase both in height and in width. The ability to seriate is a critical step in learning arithmetic and the ordinal property of number.

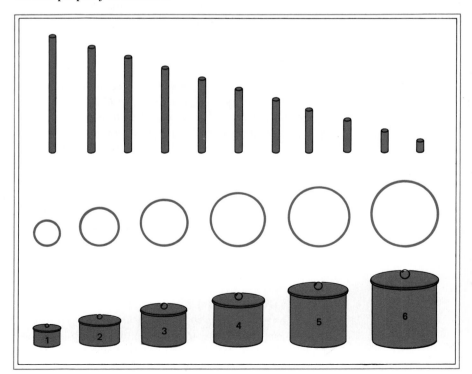

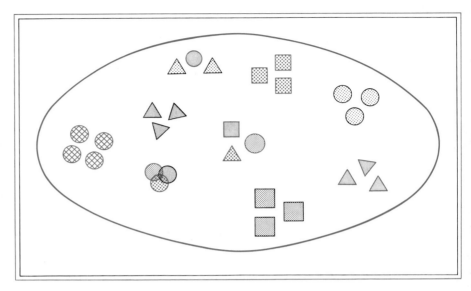

Figure 5–6
**First-grade children have won an important victory in mathematics when they
can recognize that number is a property, as well as size, shape, and color.
Here, with the exception of one grouping, all the sets conform to the
requirement of number (three) despite variations in other attributes.**

circle, a triangle, a square, or a big or small block as long as it has the
property red. He cannot put a green circle there. In another loop, for
which the critical property is big, he can put a green block or a circle,
if either is big. *Red, square,* and *big* are properties that objects share,
and we call them concepts. As he matures the child realizes that two
loops may overlap, and in their mutual space he may put a block that
has two properties, red and square.

A three-year-old child can play the attribute game without knowing
how to count or use numbers at all. But as she matures she learns to
count, first by simply reciting the numbers in sequence the way she
sings "Frère Jacques." One day, staring at her mother's sweater, she may
tap each button with her fingers and say one, two, three, four. At that
point she is on the edge of realizing a new important fact about the
attribute game—numbers are concepts too. Number is a property of
things in the world. If she wishes she can make a new loop of string
and put piles of blocks inside (see Figure 5–6). Now if she is making a
set of threes, it does not matter about their size, color, or shape. But
there must be three blocks in each pile she includes inside the loop.
Three, like red and square, is a property. When the child has that
insight she has won a major victory toward the mastery of mathematics

As early as three or four years of age some children understand the

Ordinal Numbers: The Other Kind of Counting

A child may be able to count, using cardinal numbers (1, 2, 3) but have no understanding of ordinal numbers (first, second, third). The teacher can begin by having the child take ten sticks and seriate them. Next, he can write names on ten little cards, using the names for the ordinal numbers ("first," "second") rather than the numerical abbreviations ("1st," "2nd") to help the child distinguish between cardinal and ordinal numbers. Then he may ask, "Which is the shortest stick of all?" When the child points to it, he says, "The first one?" "Yes." "Then let's put 'first' under it." He gives the child that label. "Now, which is the second shortest stick?"

After playing the game a few times with several children, the teacher can reverse directions—asking them to seriate from longest to shortest and use "first" for the longest stick, so that the children do not permanently attach the label "first" to the shortest stick. He can emphasize that the names on the cards are like placecards: they do not describe any of the sticks themselves but the place each one has in a given order.

concept of number as a property, at least for small numbers like two or three, even though they may not have mastered it for larger numbers (Gelman and Tucker, 1975). In one experiment children three and four years old were able to say how many stars or circles were drawn on a card when there were only two or three, but they had great difficulty when there were five stars or circles on the card. The child gradually extends his mastery from small numbers to large numbers until the concept crystallizes for all numbers.

It appears that most four- and five-year-old children find it easier to learn the ordinal property of number than the cardinal property. In one experiment (Brainerd, 1974) children were trained to assign one of the first five numbers (1, 2, 3, 4, 5) in either an ordinal or a cardinal way. In the ordinal training the child was shown a card and a series of shapes such as the following:

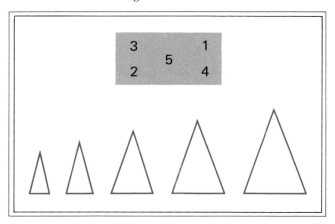

He was asked which one of the numbers on the card went with each of the triangles and was corrected if he was wrong. The child had to assign the number 1 to the smallest triangle, 2 to the next largest, and so on.

In the training for the concept of the cardinal number the child saw cards such as these:

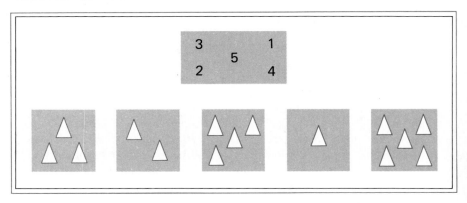

The child was asked to say which one of the numbers on the card went with each of the squares and was corrected if wrong. Each child received a total of fourteen training trials with sixty instances of feedback over two sessions.

The children showed greater improvement in mastery of the ordinal concept of number than in the cardinal concept, and when tested with different objects one week later they again performed better on the ordinal test questions (see Figure 5–7).

Figure 5–7
After being trained to assign numbers in an ordinal and cardinal way, five- and four-year-old children showed greatest improvement in mastery for the ordinal concept on posttests, one given immediately after the training and another given one week later. (Data from Brainerd, 1974)

MEAN NUMBER CORRECT ANSWERS			
	PRETEST	IMMEDIATE POSTTEST	POSTTEST ONE WEEK LATER WITH DIFFERENT OBJECTS
ORDINAL TRAINING	2.2	8.9	8.1
CARDINAL TRAINING	1.8	6.9	5.1

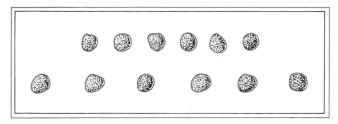

Figure 5–8
Children in the preoperational stage have difficulty conserving number and may insist that there are more pebbles in the bottom row because the row extends over more space. As they develop and realize that number is invariant, they will be able to deal with arrangements of objects intellectually, through counting, rather than simply perceiving "a whole lot" of pebbles.

Conservation of Number

Although the five-year-old may understand that a set of three toy dogs retains the property of three, even if a different toy, such as a cat, is substituted for one of the dogs, he may not retain that idea across all changes—or, as they are sometimes called, transformations. If six pebbles are placed in one row and, below it, another six pebbles are spaced farther apart, five-year-olds, who are in the preoperational stage, will say that there are more pebbles in the bottom row (see Figure 5–8). However, if only three pebbles are used, they will say that the number of pebbles is the same in both rows (Winer, 1974). If six toothpicks are laid out in a straight line, and then all are placed in a circle, the child may not acknowledge that the number of toothpicks remains the same. Psychologists say that the child will not "conserve number across all transformations." Gradually, however, children appreciate that number is a property of a particular set of objects and does not change, even when the specific objects or their spatial arrangement changes. This cognitive victory is sometimes called *conservation of number.*

Readiness for Arithmetic

The three concepts, then, that must be mastered before a child can understand arithmetic are the ordinal property of number, the cardinal property of number, and the conservation of number. The teacher can determine whether the child has these capabilities by using the games and exercises described and illustrated in this chapter.

The teacher should keep in mind that each of the three rules is first mastered for small numbers and is usually associated with the child's ability to count. Later it is mastered for larger numbers and, finally, for all numbers. Mastery of the ordinal and cardinal properties of numbers, as well as of conservation of number, is not achieved all at once.

During the period from three to ten years of age there can be enormous disparities among the child's performances on different problems involving numbers. For example, one experimenter gave children five through eight years of age problems involving the conservation of liquid and number, using pictures as well as real objects. In some of the problems the amount of liquid or the number of objects was initially equal before one of them was changed. In other problems the two containers of liquid or sets of objects were unequal before one of them was transformed. Children who could solve conservation of liquid problems when the two amounts were initially equal did not necessarily answer correctly when the two amounts were unequal. Similarly, some children who solved conservation of liquid problems failed conservation of number problems.

The experimenter concluded, "The results make it clear that it is highly improbable that children's responses in various conservation situations are guided by a single generalized mental structure. Rather there appear to be different logical concepts which come into operation depending on certain task characteristics. These underlying cognitive processes seem to be rather separate and to a certain degree independent of one another" (Winkelmann, 1974, p. 847).

As we have indicated, one of the most significant aspects of teaching is determining where a child is and what steps she should take next. It is a process that resembles the one evoked in many Japanese prints, in which a small figure slowly crosses a quiet, garden pond; we see the figure with one foot poised on a stepping stone and the other foot reaching toward the next stone. The figure makes his way to the other side of the pond with balance and harmony. Balance and harmony are equally critical in teaching children. They benefit most from their lessons when teachers are willing to help them take the next, appropriate step in good time—beginning where they already stand—rather than hurrying them along from one arbitrary task to another.

Facilitating the Child's Introduction to Arithmetic

There are exercises that the teacher can initiate that may help children master the concepts they will need in arithmetic. There is some controversy as to whether the ordinal property or the cardinal property should be taught first. Some psychologists argue that seriation and the ordinal property should always be taught before the cardinal property (MacNamara, 1975) because, as we indicated, young children know how to count long before they understand the notion of a cardinal number. Perhaps it is best to work at both simultaneously.

Early exercises involving the cardinal properties of number and conservation may include classification and sorting such as the kind involved in the attribute game. The teacher can give the child six toothpicks and ask him to place them in a row. Then the teacher puts

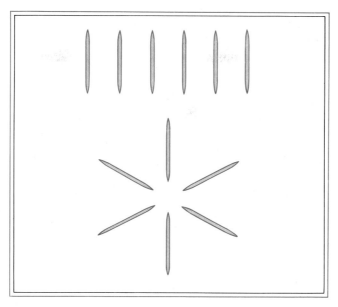

Figure 5–9
One early exercise to help children understand number as a property is a game
played with toothpicks: the teacher helps the children arrange sets of the same
number of toothpicks into different designs and shapes. Counting the
toothpicks in each set helps children learn about the invariance of number.

six toothpicks in a circle (see Figure 5–9) and asks if the sets are the
same. Gradually the child overcomes his initial tendency to regard the
sets in a qualitative way (seeing the sets as different because the shapes
are different) and becomes capable of regarding them quantitatively
(seeing that regardless of the different shapes there are still six
toothpicks in each set).

Children can practice making equivalent number sets, such as
matching six flowers in one row to seven vases in a second row (see
Figure 5–10). Young children continue to be influenced by spatial
perceptions for quite a while and will believe there are as many
flowers as vases because the rows are equal in length. Then, picking up
one flower and putting it in one vase, they arrive at the point where
they can match flowers to vases. Finally they make equivalent sets
simply by counting six flowers and counting six vases. By working first
with concrete objects rather than with abstract numbers, the child can
better understand the one-to-one correspondence necessary in number
equivalence.

Once a child has mastered the prerequisite concepts and rules, he is
ready to perform operations with numbers. The ones he will meet first
are the complementary rules of addition and subtraction.

Figure 5–10
Making equivalent sets is another early mathematics exercise. Although a child may be misled into thinking that the sets are equal because the lengths of the rows are equal, she can learn about equivalence by putting each flower into a vase. She would see that there was one vase left over. Later, as she becomes more familiar with the idea of equivalence, she can simply count out six flowers and then count six vases, skipping over the step of matching a flower to a vase.

Addition and Subtraction

Addition and subtraction may profitably be taught together as related operations. It is useful to begin with concrete objects, and it may be helpful to define a space (a circle drawn on a piece of paper or a loop of string placed on top of a table or a desk) that indicates the boundaries of the problem. Inside the space the teacher puts 5 beans or blocks. Then she pushes 2 to the left and 3 to the right and counts them. The children see that together the pile of 2 beans and the pile of 3 beans make 5 beans. At this point some children who are familiar with mathematical signs may be ready to write down a mathematical sentence: $2 + 3 = 5$. Next, the teacher rearranges the piles of beans so that now the pile with 3 beans is on the left and the pile with 2 is on the right. Again the children add them up, getting the answer 5. But now the teacher must point out that when they write down a sentence, they write it differently: $3 + 2 = 5$. This helps the children see that $2 + 3 = 5$ and $3 + 2 = 5$ are equivalent but not identical sentences.

Subtraction proceeds the same way: the children begin with a pile of 5 beans in the circle and take 2 beans out, leaving 3 beans. Then they write a sentence: $5 - 2 = 3$.

After that, addition and subtraction operations can be performed

with other sets, using 4 beans and 1 bean, then 5 beans and a special "pile," 0 beans.

Borrowing: An Illustrative Lesson Plan

Let us consider a specific lesson plan designed for second-grade students and see how the executive functions discussed earlier operate in the child's behavior. In this lesson the children initially need to know the symbolic meaning of numbers, the concept of the ones and tens place, and the basic process of subtracting (Warshauer, 1975).

The children sit in a circle. The teacher's materials consist of counters (small blocks), various transparencies on which the problem is shown in different forms, an overhead lamp, an egg carton cut down to contain ten compartments, and two lengths of yarn. The teacher begins the lesson.

TEACHER: Last night I started to make cookies at home. I got halfway through the recipe and found out I did not have any sugar. The grocery store had already closed. Now, can anyone tell me what I could possibly do? I couldn't go to the store. Where could I go? Where could I get some sugar?

STUDENT: Your next-door neighbor.

TEACHER: That's just what I did. I went to my next-door neighbor, and she had some sugar. Now, what did I do to get some sugar?
STUDENT: You asked for some.
TEACHER: OK. Now, what's another name for "asking for some" if you're going to take it back in a little while? What do you call that? Carlos?
STUDENT: Borrowing.
TEACHER: That's exactly what I did. I borrowed some sugar. Today, you're going to borrow in math. Let's see if you can do as well as I did last night with the cookies. Now this is the problem we're going to be working on. We have a set of 16 and we have a set of 8. We're going to subtract 8 from 16. The first thing I want you to do is put these two sets on the floor.
The teacher puts up transparency number 1.

$$16 - 8 = \Box$$

TEACHER: Andy, instead of counting out all 16 blocks, what would be an easier way? Maria, what could he do? What does he have on the floor that can really help him? Carlos?
STUDENT: The egg carton.
TEACHER: The egg carton! You've got 10 right there. Drop the blocks in fast, then you can add the rest of the ones you'll need.

Good. Now you've got a set of 10. How many more do you need to make 16? There you have to count because we don't have an easy way for that. Come on, Andy. OK, Andy, do you want to sit up? Now, can I have Carlos put a piece of yarn around one set and can I have Amy put a piece of yarn around the other set? Separate them a little bit so we can see better, so we know that we're working with two sets.
Using egg carton, counters, and yarn, the children make up the two sets of equations on the floor.

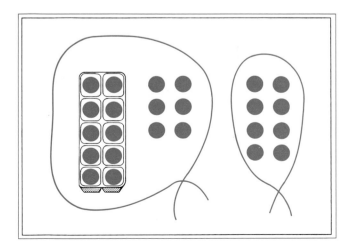

The teacher puts up transparency number 2.

16 =	_____ tens	_____ ones
−8 =	_____ tens	_____ ones
	_____ tens	_____ ones

TEACHER: OK, we've got two sets. Let's look at the numbers very closely. You've got 16 in this set. How many tens do you have in 16? Look at the floor and think about it a minute.

STUDENT: 1 ten.

TEACHER: 1 ten, so I have to cross off the *s* in *tens*. How many ones do we have? Michael?

STUDENT: 6 ones.

TEACHER: OK. We're going to take away 8 from 16. How many tens are there in 8? Carlos?

STUDENT: None.

TEACHER: Right. So we put a zero in the tens place. How many ones? Andy?

STUDENT: 8.

TEACHER: Good. 8 makes 8 ones. Now, there's a question at the bottom here. Can we subtract the ones right now? Look at the floor. Do we have enough ones here *(points to the 16 set)* to take away the number of ones we have here *(points to the 8 set)*?

The teacher puts up transparency number 3.

$$\begin{array}{r} 16 \\ -8 \end{array}$$

TEACHER: If we don't have enough ones, who can we borrow some ones from?

Children concentrate on floor illustration of 1 ten, 6 ones.

TEACHER: *(Again)* Where can we get more ones to make 6 ones larger than 8 ones?

STUDENT: Wait, let me think. *(Pauses)* From the tens.

The teacher puts up transparency number 4.

16	=	_1_	ten	_6_	ones
−8	=			_−8_	ones
		... becomes ...			
16	=	_____ ones			
−8	=	_____ ones			

TEACHER: From the tens! Good. When we borrow from the tens to get a set of ones, we take the blocks in the tens and add them to the 6 ones. Would you, Maria, dump out the carton of tens and add them all to the ones? Take them out of the egg carton to show that we no longer have 1 ten, and put them all in the circle. Craig, we don't have any more tens, do we?

STUDENT: Nope.

One of the children takes the counters out of the egg carton and puts them with the 6 ones, placing all the counters in a single row on the floor.

OOOOOOOOOOOOOOOO

The teacher fills in answers on transparency.

16	=	0	ten and	16	ones
−8	=			−8	ones
16	=	16	ones		
−8	=	−8	ones		

Another child places the 8 ones that are being taken away right underneath as many of the 16 ones as he can, setting up a one-to-one correspondence on the floor.

OOOOOOOOOOOOOOOO
OOOOOOOO

Another child takes the pairs of counters that are matched up.

TEACHER: How many ones are left? Count them, everybody. How many ones are left?

STUDENT: 8!

TEACHER: Good, 8. Now, how many is 16 take away 8?

STUDENT: I know, 8! *(Giggle)*

The teacher puts transparency number 1 back up and fills in the answer.

$$16 - 8 = \boxed{8}$$

TEACHER: In order to get this answer, what did we have to do that was special that we don't have to do in a problem like 8 minus 6?

STUDENT: Borrow from the tens place.

TEACHER: Good. Now, do you think you can do one more problem like this?

STUDENT: Yeah.

TEACHER: OK. This time it isn't all going to be written down. You'll have to use a lot of your head. Here's the new problem.

Let us look at the executive functions that were at work in this lesson and see how the teacher tried to encourage them.

First, the children had to recognize the inherent problem presented by "16 minus 8." Second, the children had to be flexible; they had to understand that the rules they already possessed were not appropriate for this new problem. Third, they had to have faith in the power of thought (recall the child who said, "Wait, let me think"). Fourth, they had to activate strategies: the child who lined up the eight blocks as far as possible in a one-to-one correspondence with sixteen blocks used a previously learned technique to help him solve the new problem.

It is also clear that the teacher tried to encourage these processes. She structured the learning situation to aid recognition of the problem. She used concrete materials to keep attention focused and distraction low, and she set soluble problems to reduce apprehension. She began by describing a familiar situation, "borrowing sugar," that she knew was accessible to the children. It helped them accommodate to the unfamiliar mathematical situation, "borrowing from the tens." She reminded the children that reflective thought is useful when an answer to a question is not immediately obvious.

Summary

As the child develops, he gains greater competence, as well as acquiring more images and symbols, concepts and rules, with which to work. One view of cognition places the units and processes under the supervision of an executive process, an abstract function that begins to grow during the second year. The executive monitors and coordinates the child's perceptions and memory and reasoning processes; relates past experiences and future possibilities to what the child knows in the present; and permits the child to know where to look for the best solutions and when a problem has been solved. The functions of the executive are: (1) reflecting on actions, (2) recognizing a problem, (3) appreciating the difficulty of a problem and adjusting effort accordingly, (4) maintaining flexibility, (5) using strategies, (6) controlling distraction and anxiety, (7) preferring to achieve elegant solutions and avoiding failure, (8) having faith in the power of thought, and (9) relating information to a larger structure.

The growth of cognitive competence depends on both maturation and experience. While some psychologists, such as Jerome Bruner, believe that schoolchildren of any age can learn any subject in some form, it seems likely that certain periods of a child's life, while not critical, are more propitious for learning a particular task than other times are. Naturally, variations exist among children in the development of cognitive competences.

Psychologists distinguish between competence—the child's basic ability—and performance—what the child shows he or she can do. Common obstacles to adequate performance include failure to understand the problem, failure to remember the elements of the problem, lack of the relevant knowledge, belief in a contradictory rule or fact, fear of making a mistake, low motivation, and low expectancy of success.

The chapter concluded by examining how children use units and processes and begin to acquire competence in arithmetic. As a prerequisite for mathematics, children must grasp certain concepts: the ordinal property of number (seriation), the cardinal property of number, and the conservation of number. We showed how these concepts are used and how the executive functions work in a sample lesson on an early mathematical operation, borrowing.

Projects

1 In a narrative, analyze a recent situation in which you were unable to solve a problem or found the process very difficult. Was your difficulty due to lack of competence, or were there obstacles in the way of your performance? If it was the latter, which of the following do you think interfered: failure to understand the problem; failure to remember the elements of the problem; lack of relevant knowledge; belief in a contradictory rule or fact; fear of making a mistake; low motivation; low expectancy of success.

2 (a) Team up with a classmate and pose a problem (such as designing a cereal box that encourages recycling or reusing the package). Instruct the classmate to do his or her thinking aloud. Observe and record the executive functions that were operant in resolving the problem.
(b) Pose the same problem to an eight-year-old child, note the executive functions operating in the resolution of that problem, and explain the differences.

3 Review a fourth- and fifth-grade textbook in the same discipline by the same publisher. Does the fifth-grade text accommodate to the students' maturation and experience? If so, in what ways?

4 Write a few paragraphs that can help a teacher who wants to encourage a child who is afraid of making errors.

5 How would you apply the concept of rate of development to yourself and your siblings, using one or two specific skills—reading, playing sports, or learning a second language—as criteria?

6 Design simple games that could help beginning arithmetic students grasp the ordinal and cardinal properties and conservation of number.

7 Observe a second-grade arithmetic lesson in which borrowing is being taught. Take notes so that afterward you can write out a description of the lesson plan and how it proceeded. Then write a comparison between the lesson you observed and the one described in this chapter.

Recom-
mended
Reading

Bruner, J. S. *Toward a theory of instruction.* New York: Norton, 1966. Discusses the relation between the psychology of the child and the educational process.

Kagan, J. *Understanding children.* New York: Harcourt Brace Jovanovich, 1971. Contains essays on cognition and motivation. The essay on cognition presents a summary of the units and the processes in problem solving.

Piaget, J. *Six psychological studies.* New York: Random House, 1967. Contains several essays that summarize the author's most important ideas on the thought of the young child. It gives his views of the relation between language and thought and of the development of perception and logical structures and discusses the concept of equilibrium.

Zaslavsky, C. *Africa counts: Number and pattern in African culture.* Boston: Prindle, Weber & Schmidt, 1973. A history of number systems in Africa, including the African concepts of time and superstitions about numbers.

the development of affects and motives

6

I n the last two chapters, on the growth of cognitive processes, reference was occasionally made to emotional states, such as fear and satisfaction, and to motives, such as the desire to solve a problem with elegance and to avoid error. Although emotions—usually called *affects* by psychologists—and motives are different from cognition and overt action, these four processes are inextricably related in every person. We now turn to the development of affects and motives and their relation to the child's progress in school.

The Nature of Affect

Affects are based on changes in feeling states, although they are not identical with those feeling states. We must first distinguish between a person's typical feeling state and changes in that state. Much of the time our feeling state has a neutral quality, like a car motor that is idling, and we are not aware of how we feel.

Consider an analogy. When filmmakers shoot a scene, they record a few minutes of "room tone"—the particular hum of the room without anyone speaking, opening a door, dropping a book, or firing a pistol. Our basic feeling state is like room tone—the background hum to which we are accustomed.

Changes occur against the background of the typical feeling state. As a spoken word breaks the room tone, a change in internal feeling alters the background state. That change may be registered in awareness. Sometimes it is a sharp, conspicuous change that we are actually aware of, and sometimes it is barely discernible: the spoken word that breaks the room tone can be anything from a shout to a whisper.

Every change in the feeling state, presumably, is accompanied by a parallel change somewhere in the central nervous system. The central nervous system is composed of structures in the brain and along the spinal column. Under special circumstances these structures change their normal rate of discharge and cause alterations in the distribution of the blood, metabolism of sugar, hormone levels, stomach activity, sweating, and muscle tension. These bodily reactions can affect our receptivity to certain experiences and our disposition to behave in certain ways. For example, when the hormone adrenalin is released, we are less likely to feel hungry and will find it more difficult to sleep.

If these changes inside our bodies are subtle and below our level of conscious awareness, they may not influence our thoughts. Thus alteration in the state of the central nervous system or in any organ as a result of a fatiguing day at work may lead a person to lose his temper more easily in the evening, even though the person does not detect any change in his bodily state. But if the internal bodily changes are more intense or distinctive, we are forced to attend to them, and we call them *feelings*. We try to interpret them, as we do changes in the pitch or the loudness of someone's voice or in the color or the brightness of a light source. We try to figure out the reason for the change and its implications and, if necessary, make a relevant response.

Consider a man whose normal heart rate is about 100 beats per minute. One afternoon, as he thinks about an important meeting at the end of the day, his heart rate jumps to 105 beats per minute (due to the actions of the parts of his brain that control heart rate). Although he does not detect the slight change in his internal state, nonetheless it is different from his normal one. We shall call it an *uninterpreted change in bodily state*.

Now let us suppose that just before the meeting his heart rate jumps to 115 beats per minute. This time the man perceives that his heart is beating much faster than normal. He pays attention to that change and tries to interpret it. He asks himself why his heart rate has increased. He considers several possibilities: that he is ill, that the office is too hot, that he is still angry at the cabdriver who was rude to him in the morning. He rejects each idea in turn. Finally, he considers the possibility that he is apprehensive over the upcoming meeting. He decides that this is the correct interpretation and now regards himself as anxious or tense. At this point his feeling state is quite different from what it was before he interpreted it. Once the person detects and interprets a change in his feeling state, he tries to maintain, eliminate, or control it in some way. We shall call this second state an *interpreted feeling state*.

Interpreting Feeling States

There are, then, two kinds of changes in a person's internal bodily state—those that are not perceived and remain uninterpreted and those that enter conscious awareness as feelings and are interpreted. In the past, most scientists regarded both kinds of changes as a component of

Event	Some Common Affect Names (from less to more intense)
Unexpected or discrepant event that cannot be assimilated, understood, or handled.	interest — alertness — vigilance — apprehension — worry — anxiety — fear — terror
Violation of a standard in a person's action or thought without the realization that he or she had a choice and with the belief others know of the violation.	embarrassment — shame — humiliation
Violation of a standard in a person's action or thought with the realization that he or she had a choice.	guilt — depression
Frustration of action by an agent for which person does not take into account whether agent intended the frustration.	irritation — anger
Frustration of action by an agent for which person believes agent intended to hurt him or her.	anger — contempt — scorn — hatred
Attack on standards by an agent for which person does not think about the intentions of agent.	irritation — anger
Attack on standards by an agent for which person believes agent intended it.	anger — contempt — scorn — hatred
Loss of beloved object or person.	sadness — loneliness — depression
Realization of loss of goal and inability to obtain goal with no agent to blame.	sadness — apathy — helplessness — depression
Anticipation of mastery of, success at, or attainment of desired goal.	happiness — joy — excitement — elation
Attainment of anticipated goal.	contentment — happiness — excitement — joy — pride — elation — ecstasy
Release from a negative affect such as fear, anxiety, or sadness.	relief — happiness — joy — elation
Sexual stimulation.	excitement — arousal — passion
Sexual arousal by person with whom identification exists.	love

affect. More recently, some psychologists have suggested the usefulness of restricting the word *affect* to the changes that are interpreted.

People are likely to interpret certain combinations of events and feelings in the same or a similar way. For example, most people who saw a bear rushing toward them while they were on a walk in a forest would experience a detectable increase in heart rate. They would interpret that particular change in feeling state in that situation as *fear.* If a husband grabbed a pen from his wife while she was writing a letter, she would also be likely to experience an increase in heart rate. But in that situation most wives would interpret the change in feeling state as *anger.* It is assumed, then, that a small set of common, perhaps universal, relations exists between events, feelings, and interpretations and that all people are susceptible to them.

A word or a phrase is often assigned to the interpretation we impose on our feelings. We have come to classify these words as emotions or affects (see boxed insert on page 225). Every language has many words that name affects. Almost all societies have words for affects, such as *happy, afraid, sad,* and *mad.* Other affect words occur in only one or a small number of societies, such as the Western term *alienated* or the Japanese word *ameuru,* which stands for a special kind of interdependent feeling between two people. Each word represents a special combination of internal feelings, external events, and thoughts. Listing the names that a society has invented for its human emotions is a little like listing the names of all the tastes and colors that can be experienced. Moreover, every time someone advances a new interpretation of a set of feelings produced in a specific situation, a new affect word may be added to the list. Indeed, about twenty-five years ago the psychoanalyst Erik Erikson invented the term *identity crisis,* and it has become part of the vocabulary of many thousands of Americans. Although there is a large number of specific affect words, it is reasonable to assume that a small set of basic patterns or internal feeling states form the basis of a small set of primary emotions.

These basic feeling states can be likened to the primary tastes of sweet, salty, sour, and bitter. In combination, they produce a broad array of flavors ranging from the taste of lobster to the taste of blueberry jam. In the same way the affects we call lonely, happy, anxious, guilty, and angry may be produced by different combinations of the basic feelings states. However, unlike tastes, the primary set of internal sensations that forms the nucleus of an emotion has not yet been discovered.

Characteristics of Feelings

Internal feelings can be characterized as varying along several dimensions. These include salience, perceived origin, direction of change, and duration of change.

Salience. The intensity and attention-getting quality of a particular set of feelings is called *salience*. We referred to this dimension when we suggested that the word spoken against the room tone might be a whisper or a shout. Nausea is a distinctive feeling that cannot easily be ignored; tension in the muscles of the legs is far less noticeable and therefore can be disregarded more easily.

Perceived origin. The quality of the sensation will differ depending on its source—head, stomach, heart, or genitals—since each origin is linked to special receptors and structures in the central nervous system. The feeling that accompanies a headache or flushing of the face is rarely confused with the sensation that attends stomach cramps or tension in the muscles of the legs.

Direction of the change. Some changes in feeling tone are perceived as increases in sensory activity or arousal, others as decreases (compared) to background feeling). Loss of a loved one usually leads to a decrease in the arousal level of internal feeling tone; frustration and victory lead to an increased intensity of arousal.

Duration of the change. Some changes last for a moment; others for minutes or hours. A heart rate increase usually lasts a few seconds, while tension in the muscles may last several hours.

The combination of these four characteristics—there may be more—produces a certain quality of feeling, the way that loudness, pitch, and timbre of a piano chord combine to produce a certain quality of sound. For example, the perception of a sharp increase in heart rate that lasts a few seconds while standing in a crowded elevator may be dismissed as unimportant. If the increased heart rate lasts during the three minutes it takes to get from the lobby to the twentieth floor, a person is less likely to dismiss it and may interpret his condition as being due to a lack of oxygen or an irrational fear. If the person in the elevator had felt, instead, a tightening of the stomach, he would have selected a different interpretation, perhaps hunger. Thus each person is continually monitoring the complex sensory messages that pierce the screen of consciousness and provoke an explanation.

But we must distinguish between the private interpretation of the person and the interpretation of an outsider, who can only guess what the person feels by evaluating the situation and the person's overt reaction. Let us return to our consideration of children. Imagine a twelve-year-old the night before an examination. Her muscles feel tense and she has difficulty getting to sleep. Many psychologists believe that anticipation of a dangerous or threatening event in the immediate future is accompanied by a particular change in internal sensations, and they call that state fear or anxiety. The girl who is going to take an exam may, in fact, interpret her feelings as fear. On the other hand, she

**Human Faces Express a
Wide Range of Feelings**

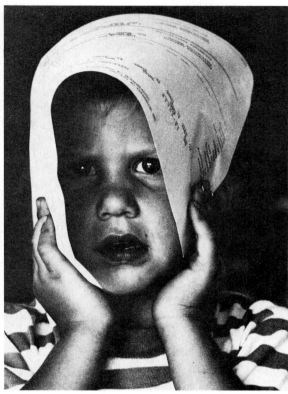

may decide that she is ill and not afraid. Or she may ignore the changed feelings and not try to interpret them at all. Thus, although the teacher, parent, or psychologist may interpret the girl's muscular tension and poor sleep as indicative of anxiety over the coming test, the girl may not. Similarly, the child who recognizes that he has insulted a friend experiences a change in internal feelings. The psychologist is prone to call the resulting emotion shame or guilt. But the child may not apply that interpretation to this combination of feeling change and events. He may recognize that he feels different but may decide that he feels sorry for the friend. Thus the affect experienced by a child is often different from the one inferred by an observer. Sometimes the observer is correct, sometimes not. A teacher may interpret an adolescent's sudden reluctance to volunteer in class, tardiness in homework assignment, and surly mood as an expression of anger, perhaps toward the teacher. But the change in his behavior may be an emotional reaction to an act of dishonesty toward a friend. In this case the adolescent feels guilty about the violation of a standard.

Development of Affect

As indicated in Chapter 5, cognitive competences develop as maturation of the brain and experience interact. Since affects involve cognitive interpretations of feelings, the age at which certain affects appear depends on the child's level of cognitive development. Let us describe some of the highlights of this developmental process.

The Infant

The infant is unable to think about changes in internal sensations; he experiences only uninterpreted changes in feeling states.

The newborn infant reacts directly to changes in physical stimulation and to internal drives, experiencing feelings we call hunger, satiety, pain, touch, warmth, and cold and reacting to them in an appropriate way.

His body is programed by nature to respond in certain ways to events that produce changes in feeling states. For example, a sudden bright light or a sudden loud noise is likely to cause increased heart rate and motor inhibition, while a more gradual onset of light or sound produces decreased heart rate and increased motor activity.

As early as two to three months of age, the infant reacts to experiences in terms of what he knows. He smiles at unfamiliar events he can assimilate; he becomes sober or cries at strange events he cannot

assimilate; he shows excitement when he displays mastery. By twelve
months he seems capable of anticipating future events and thinking
about the relation between what he knows and what he is experiencing.
As a result, he reacts more frequently with distress to strange events
that he cannot assimilate or to events that are potentially dangerous.
Psychologists have shown that from seven to eight months through the
second year, the child shows a variety of "fears" to many unfamiliar or
unusual objects, such as a stranger or a jack-in-the-box. He can also
experience a state some may call sadness, if he temporarily loses a
person to whom he is attached and anticipates that the loss may be
permanent (Scarr and Salapatek, 1970).

Some psychologists believe that the emotional labels contentment,
fear, joy, and excitement that we apply to adults are also useful ways to
describe these infant states. Others believe that these states are not
exactly like the feelings older children have when the same affect
words are used. The feeling state of a three-month-old when a thunder
clap makes him startle and cry (a state some may call fear) is unlikely
to be the same as the feeling state of a ten-year-old after he has almost
been hit by a car and says to himself, "That was scarey."

As we saw in Chapter 4, the eighteen-month-old child has become
able to think symbolically. His ability to treat objects as things other
than what they really are prepares him to experience a new set of
affects. By eighteen to twenty-four months of age he becomes excited in

anticipation of some challenging event or following successful mastery of it because he has established standards of performance. He can interpret the loss of a toy grabbed by a sibling as "caused" by the sibling and, therefore, is ready to experience anger. He also begins to learn the labels his community applies to his feeling states, and he starts to evaluate his feelings as *good* or *bad*. Once he has learned what actions, thoughts, and events are considered good or bad, he becomes capable of feeling distress when he violates a standard. But he is also capable of feeling the joy that comes from meeting a standard. There is a significant difference between the excitement and laughter of a six-month-old kicking his mobile and the pleasure of a two-and-one-half-year-old who has finished building a tower of six blocks. The older child, but not the six-month-old, knows he has accomplished something difficult and he values his achievement. He knows he has met a personal standard of excellence.

The Young Child

By twenty-four to thirty months of age a new competence emerges. The child is now able to infer the private feeling state of another person—an ability not present in the twelve-month-old. As a result the child is capable of feeling empathy for another. Some evidence for this new development comes from an experiment in which two-year-old children were given either opaque or clear ski goggles and asked to wear them at home. Sometime later each child came to a laboratory with his mother, who was then asked to put on the opaque ski goggles. Children who had worn the opaque ski goggles at home—but not those who had worn the transparent ones—behaved as if they believed their mothers were blind. One child pushed the goggles back on his mother's forehead and said, "Wear like that 'cause you can't see me." The two-year-olds who had worn the opaque goggles at home told their mothers to open their eyes and made more requests that their mothers remove the goggles. Thus by two years of age some children are able to infer some private psychological states in other persons (Novey, 1975).

Sometimes a three-year-old who sees another child in distress, especially if she has caused the distress, will go to the child and nurture him—give him a toy, put her arms around him, or behave in a way that implies that the three-year-old recognizes the distress state of the other. The child may or may not experience any change in her own internal feelings when she attributes a distress state to the other. Hence we cannot know her "emotion" merely by observing the child's behavior. Even if she goes over and gives the distressed child a toy, we cannot be sure she has *felt* any internal changes. If she has, then we would say that the child is experiencing an affect one may call empathy. If she

does not experience any change in feeling, psychologists will not attribute an affect state to her, even though the child inferred the distress state of the other child and went over to care for him. The cognitive ability to infer the state of another is a prerequisite for the affect empathy, but that new ability alone is not sufficient to produce an affect state.

Three-year-olds are able to infer feeling states merely by listening to a brief description of an event that happened to a hypothetical person. In one study (Borke, 1971) children from three to eight years old were told stories appropriate to one of four emotions—happy, sad, afraid, angry. At the end of the story the children were shown four faces, each depicting one of the emotions, and asked to select the face that was most appropriate to the feeling of the person in the story. The three-year-olds performed well when the feeling of the child in the story was happy but did not perform well when the story portrayed fear. The older the children, the more appropriate were their selections (see Figure 6–1).

The ability to infer the feelings of another person is accompanied by the ability to anticipate that an aggressive act can cause pain or distress to another child or adult. Once the child has reached this state of maturity, he becomes capable of directing hostility and aggressive behavior toward specific targets. He teases, taunts, and strikes with purpose because he now knows the effect of his actions on another. Often day-care teachers misinterpret pushing in an eighteen-month-old

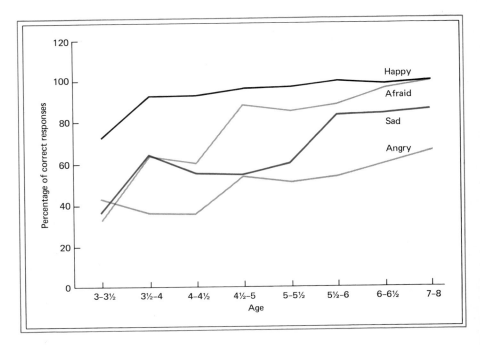

Figure 6–1
Children three to eight years old were told stories appropriate to one of four emotions: happy, sad, afraid, and angry. At the end of each story each child was shown faces and asked to select the face that best showed how the child in the story felt. Three-year-olds performed well when the child in the story was supposed to be happy but less well when the child in the story was supposed to be afraid. The graphs above show the percentage of correct responses for children at different ages. The older the children, the more appropriate their selections. (Adapted from Borke, 1971)

as reflecting anger or hostility. That behavior, although it appears provoked by anger, is typically an attempt to arouse a response in another child or to have an effect upon him.

Children are able to experience the affect we call shame when they are mature enough to recognize standards of conduct as good or bad and to realize that others will disapprove of behaviors or thoughts that violate those standards. An eighteen-month-old possesses standards for some behaviors, but she is not mature enough to anticipate that another person will disapprove of violations. Hence, she is not ready to experience shame. Around age two she may be aware that she violated a standard (by teasing her sister, perhaps) and may feel ashamed as a result. But she still does not realize that she had a choice.

A profound advance that emerges around four years of age is related to the process discussed earlier, in which the child becomes aware of her own talents and liabilities and realizes she has the power of choice and control regarding her actions. Once that competence matures, the child is vulnerable to the affect of guilt if she violates her standards. On the other hand, she is able to feel pride if she conforms to them.

As the child acquires standards by which to evaluate her actions, thoughts, and attributes, she becomes susceptible to the affect anger when someone threatens those standards. Anger may be generated if someone calls her stuck-up or dumb because she is mature enough to recognize that these names are a devaluation of her idealized conception of herself.

The child of four or five also becomes capable of the affect of identification with models, which was described in Chapter 2. She recognizes that she and a model (the parent, perhaps) possess some of the same attributes, and she experiences vicarious feelings appropriate to the victories and the defeats of the model. To do this, the child must have a conception of her attributes, distinct from the attributes of others, and appreciate her similarities to the model.

During the early school years the child becomes capable of comparing her qualities with those of her friends and becomes vulnerable to those emotional states we commonly call feelings of inferiority or superiority.

The Adolescent

As adolescence approaches, the child displays the cognitive functions that Piaget has called formal operational thinking. One major characteristic of this new competence is the ability to examine one's beliefs and detect inconsistencies among them; to appreciate that one may hold two incompatible beliefs. For example, a six-year-old believes that her parents are considerate and kind; but she also believes that they argue too much and are irritable and inconsistent. But she does not detect the incompatibility between those beliefs—she keeps them separate. The adolescent, mature enough to perceive the inconsistency, experiences an affect we may call dissonance. The adolescent who makes that discovery may feel disappointed as she is forced to recognize that her parents are not the idols she thought them to be but people with some of the same frailties she recognizes in herself. That disappointment may be followed, in some adolescents, by a feeling of relief and exhilaration. Heretofore some adolescents conformed to parental prohibitions because they idealized their parents. Now that they see them more realistically, they feel greater freedom to violate parental strictures that are incompatible with their own motives. Many great plays and novels are built around the theme of the sudden adolescent disillusion with a parent who had been worshipped during childhood.

The adolescent is also vulnerable to a slightly different affect modern Western psychologists call ideological confusion or alienation, which occurs when the person recognizes he has no faith in his values or when he sees serious inconsistencies or flaws in his beliefs.

The interpretation that is applied to the feeling states is critical. An urbane, well-educated middle-class adult may experience "emptiness," apathy, and lethargy over a period of months and interpret that set of feelings as an identity crisis. An illiterate laborer who has never read any psychology books—and, indeed, never heard of the word *identity*—may experience the same feelings and decide that he is bored with his job. The difference in interpretation is important, for the actions each will take depend on the interpretation. The well-educated man is likely to examine his beliefs and commitments, the laborer to quit his job.

The young adolescent also experiences changes in sexual feelings due, in part, to changes in hormonal level that influence sexual excitement. The affect that Western psychologists call love refers not only to sexual excitement but also to the cognitive capacity to feel enhanced because of being valued by another and the desire to enhance another at the expense of the self. The adolescent is willing to put the feelings of the person he loves ahead of his own, believing that his own happiness can be enriched by the joy of another. This affect goes far beyond empathy and is similar to the emotions involved in loyalty to family, country, and philosophical ideals.

One Conception of Affect

As indicated earlier, many psychologists believe there is a basic set of universal emotions common to all humans. The question is how to determine what they are. A group of psychologists, pursuing Charles Darwin's suggestion that the face reveals emotions (1892), has postulated that the face is the primary source of human emotions. They believe that different patterns of sensory feedback from distinct facial expressions determine the fundamental human emotional state. Carroll E. Izard (1971) suggests that there are nine basic emotions: interest, joy, surprise, distress, disgust, anger, shame, fear, and contempt.

Silvan S. Tompkins (1962–1963) believes there are only eight basic affects, each of which has a low and high intensity level:

1 interest—excitement
2 enjoyment—joy
3 surprise—startle
4 distress—anguish
5 fear—terror
6 shame—humiliation
7 contempt—disgust
8 anger—rage

In Tompkins's view an emotion consists of a combination of neural activity, muscle activity, and a subjective experience. Each of the eight basic emotions is innately associated with a distinct facial muscle pattern that produces a unique facial expression. The reader should note, however, that among others guilt, passion, tension, depression, relaxation, contentment, and loneliness are absent from this list.

Partial support for the theory that the face is the primary source of emotions comes from the fact that adults from varied parts of the world are able to recognize many of these emotions from photographs of people who are presumably displaying those affect states (Izard, 1971).

Children, too, show some ability to infer human emotions from photographs of faces. In one study American and French children were

Figure 6–2
In a cross-cultural, emotion-recognition study, French and American children were shown three photographs of faces displaying three different emotions, such as fear, joy, and surprise. They were asked to point to the person experiencing one of the affects. As the graph shows, there were no important differences in average scores between French and American children, and correct recognition of various affects improved with age. (Adapted from Izard, 1971)

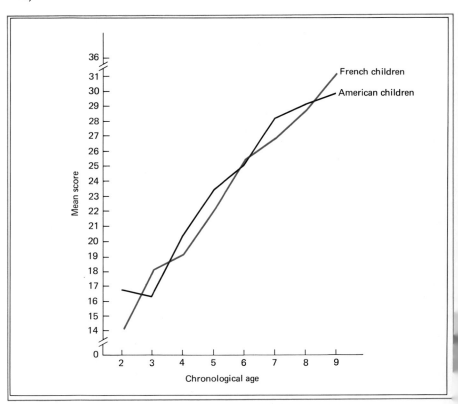

given two tasks. The first was an emotion-recognition task. The child was shown three photographs of faces displaying three different emotions. The examiner then said, "Show me the person who is experiencing _____," completing the sentence with one of the nine basic affect words. Figure 6–2 shows the results of the recognition test. As you can see, children's correct recognitions of various affects improved with age and there were no important differences between French and American children. However, there was a difference in accuracy among the various affects according to age groups. Anger and joy were recognized easily by five-year-olds, while contempt and disgust were not (see Figure 6–3). Most older children recognized all the emotions. In a second, emotion-labeling task, in which the child was shown a single photograph and asked to say how the person in the photograph might be feeling, accuracy improved substantially after five years of age (Izard, 1971).

Developmental Changes in Children's Conceptualization of Emotion

Whether or not the face reveals the fundamental human emotions, as Izard and Tompkins believe, there are nonetheless developmental changes in the way the child thinks about emotions, especially with respect to the perceived origin of the emotions and the events believed to produce specific emotions.

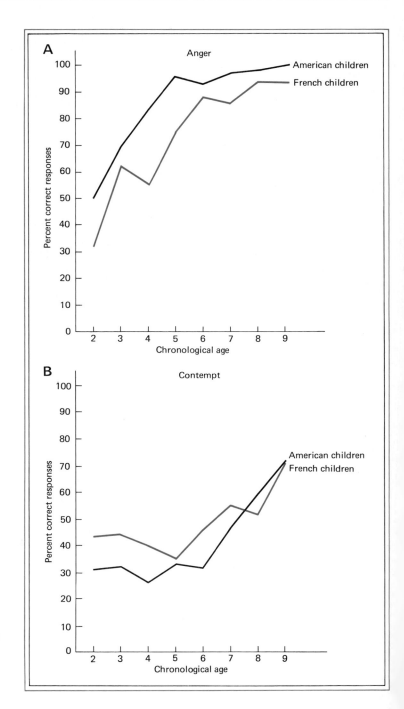

Figure 6–3
In the emotion-recognition task given to French and American children, not all affects were recognized with the same accuracy. Anger was easily recognized by five-year-olds (graph A). Contempt was not, though it was recognized by the older children (graph B). Interestingly, more young French children than American children recognized expressions of contempt. (Adapted from Izard, 1971)

Investigators interviewed fifty-six children divided into three age groups: six, nine, and twelve years old. The children were asked questions such as "Have you ever felt _____?" "When do you feel _____?" "What does _____ feel like?" "Where do you feel _____—inside your body or outside?" "What do you want to do when you feel _____?" The eight words used to fill the blanks were *hungry, thirsty, sleepy, sad, happy, angry, scared,* and *nervous.* With increasing age children were less dependent on the external environment for signs of emotional arousal. For example, the older children said they felt hungry when they had not eaten for a while; the younger children said they felt hungry "when dinner is on the table." Further, with increasing age there was an increasing tendency to ascribe the source of the emotion to the interior of the body and to acknowledge that the emotion was related to one's thoughts (Lewis, Wolman, and King, 1971).

American children of all ages tend to be in remarkable agreement regarding the events that produce various emotions. In another, similar study (Demos, 1974), an investigator asked children aged six, nine and twelve what kinds of events led to certain emotions, what they did when they felt that way, and where they felt the emotion. The ten emotion words explored were *happy, mad, ashamed, proud, worried, scared, sad, excited, lonely,* and *loved.*

The children agreed on the sources of these ten affects. Happiness was a result of "getting something you wanted," "being with people you like," or "achieving." Feeling mad followed injustice, disappointment, attack, or annoyance. Shame occurred when the child was disappointed in himself, did something wrong, or was ridiculed. Pride followed achievement and accomplishment, surpassing someone in a competition, or doing one's duty. Worry occurred when one was threatened, anticipated failure or something else bad, or was caught in a mischievous act. Fear was a reaction to strange noises, dreams, irrational surprises, physical danger, and punishment. Sadness was the response when a child lost a loved person, a pet, or a valued object; did not achieve a goal; or did something wrong. The child was excited following achievement or when something special was to happen in the near future; lonely when he had no one to play with or was rejected. Love meant being hugged or kissed, being with people he liked, or being appreciated.

The greatest agreement among the children occurred for the words *happy, mad,* and *sad;* followed by *excited, scared,* and *proud;* and *worried, lonely,* and *love.* Least agreement occurred among children of different ages for the affect *ashamed.* Although the breadth of understanding depended more on the specific affect word than on age, the quality and complexity of understanding was dependent on the child's maturational level. With increasing age there was an increase in the complexity and subtlety with which the child understood the ten different affect words. Older, but not younger, children said emotions were in their thoughts.

Although both the six-year-olds and the twelve-year-olds agreed that attaining a desired goal made one happy and being annoyed made one mad, young children did not name injustice as a cause of anger, whereas older children did. Although all the children agreed that a disappointment would make them sad, older children said they would be sad if they saw the suffering of another person. Six-year-olds were far less likely to regard that event as a source of sadness. Overall, however, the similarities in the understanding of affect words outweighed the differences.

The children were also asked about the association between emotions and either color or line designs. They were shown eight colors on a page—yellow, green, red, brown, black, purple, blue, and orange—and asked which color was most representative of a specific affect. The children did not agree on any one color as most symbolic of a specific emotion, with one exception: the color black was selected by the majority of children, at all ages, as most representative of the emotion mad. However, when the colors were grouped according to brightness (red, yellow, orange) and darkness (black, brown, and blue), the positive affects, happiness, joy, excitement, and love, were associated with the bright colors, while the negative affects, sad, mad, ashamed, worried, and scared, were associated with the darker colors.

The children were shown drawings of eleven line designs and asked which design was most representative of each affect (see Figure 6–4). When lines 4, 6, and 11 were grouped together because they were relatively straight and unchanging and lines 5, 8, and 9 were grouped because they were upward curving and dynamic, the children chose the straight, unchanging lines as representative of the negative affects and the curved, dynamic lines as representative of the positive affects. As with the colors, the children did not point to any one line as representative of a specific affect, with the exception of line number 2, whose sharp, angular line nearly half the children associated with the emotion mad. *Anger* seems to be a particularly salient affect word for most children.

In this study an important finding emerged that has implications for school. As the children became older they said that competence and achievement were sources of pride and failure at a task a source of worry and anger. As they approached adolescence, competence in and out of school became a major source of emotion for American children. Every society assigns one or two major missions for its children to accomplish. In rural agricultural societies, boys must learn how to plant, weed, hoe, and reap the corn and bean crop; among the Eskimos, they must learn how to hunt seal. In America and Europe the child's primary mission is to be competent in school. Success or failure in school becomes a major influence on the affective life of the child.

Figure 6–4
Six- and twelve-year-old children were shown drawings of eleven line designs
and asked which design was most representative of each affect (happiness, joy,
excitement, love, sad, mad, ashamed, worried, scared). When lines 4, 6, and 11
were grouped together because they were relatively straight and unchanging,
and lines 5, 8, and 9 were grouped because they were upward curving and
dynamic, the children chose the straight, unchanging lines as representative of
the negative affects and the curved, dynamic lines as representative of the
positive affects. They did not point to any one line as representative of a
special affect, however, with the exception of line number 2, whose sharp
angularity nearly half of the children associated with mad. Anger seems to be a
particularly salient emotion for children. (After Demos, 1974)

Implications for Teaching

How does knowledge about affective development relate to the tasks of
the school and the practices of the teacher? One of its values is to help
teachers understand the emotionally based causes of students' behavior.
Anger and aggression may be based on frustration of their goals, a
direct or indirect attack on their values, or a threat to their beliefs
about themselves. Excessive fearfulness can come from anticipated
failure on a test, peer rejection, or failure to understand why their
parents quarrel at home.

Second, it is useful for the teacher to appreciate the cognitive bases of emotional experience. Although most school-age children have sufficient cognitive maturity to possess a wide range of emotions from joy to guilt, some first- and second-graders do not yet appreciate that they can choose to act—or not to act—in a way that violates a standard. They fear punishment for a violation they have committed but do not realize they had an alternative.

Encouraging spontaneity. A small but growing movement called *affective education* seeks to liberate children who are inhibited and frightened so that they can express excitement and happiness spontaneously and feel less anxiety and fear. But excitement and happiness do not materialize from thin air. Even making the child less anxious over tests and less fearful of the teacher does not automatically lead to excitement and happiness. Fear and anxiety are caused by factors that cannot always be understood, such as the unpredictability of the outcome of an event, the anticipation of a threat, or the inconsistencies between one's behavior and one's belief or among one's beliefs. Alleviating these dissonances reduces fear, certainly. But excitement and happiness are often the results of other processes. Indeed, one can produce asocial, aggressive children who are neither anxious nor fearful. An important source of happiness, excitement, and satisfaction, as previously indicated, is the child's sense of competence

and mastery. Children thrive on surmounting challenges—if they can meet them and if they perceive them as real. Even young children respond to challenges: several studies show that children two and one-half through six years of age smile spontaneously when they solve a difficult problem but not when they solve an easy problem (Kagan, 1971).

Reducing negative affects. Teachers can help children overcome negative emotions. Sometimes a child perceives a threat, an attempt to frustrate him, or a devaluation where none was intended. The teacher can help the child understand that he has misdiagnosed the situation. For example, a child may be mad at a classmate who would not let him ride her bicycle. If he learned that his classmate refused because of her fear of her mother's disapproval—and not because of animosity toward him—the basis for anger would be neutralized. In the same way, a child can feel guilty as a result of misdiagnosis. A ten-year-old may feel at fault because his mother and father quarrelled at breakfast about whether or not he should have permission to go on a camping trip that weekend. Feeling that had he not asked for permission to go on the trip the fight between his parents would not have occurred, he blames himself for causing the quarrel. If he can be helped to understand that the argument resulted from basic tension and frustration between his parents and that his request was incidental to the quarrel, he may feel less guilty.

A situation that permits or provokes a response from the child usually leads to an increased intensity of feeling, whereas a situation that does not lead to any clear action (as an extreme example, the death of a close friend or a relative) often leads to apathy or withdrawal. If the teacher can succeed in helping the child commit himself to action in the service of a future goal, she may rouse him out of apathy and withdrawal. Nature has prepared children and adults to generate feelings in preparation for a future event. If the event is one the person thinks he can handle, then he will be excited. The best way for a teacher to promote more positive affects among children is to set them goals they find challenging but believe they can reach.

Motives

Let us now turn to a discussion of a related phenomenon: motivation. Although affects and motivation interact closely, they are not the same process. Among the many factors that distinguish human beings from animals, the human's ability to generate a cognitive representation of a future event is one of the most important. A person can think of tomorrow's sunrise, next month's full moon, next winter's snowfall. A very small class of these representations of the future refer to events that a person wants to experience. We commonly call these representations of desired future goals *motives*. A motive is a state of mind created by the tension between the unsatisfactory reality of the present and the presumably more satisfying state in the future.

Characteristics of Motives

A motive has several distinguishing characteristics. First, there is the discrepancy between the present reality and the hoped-for future. The person holds both representations in his mind, side by side, like the before and after pictures of a redecorated room. The mind compares the two—the existing state (being unable to solve a mathematical equation, for example) and the anticipated state (triumph at solving the equation). Second, the person often, but not always, feels uncertain of his ability to achieve the desired state. Third, a motive is often, but again not always, linked to a potential set of actions or a set of ideas that may help the person pursue and attain the desired state.

Fourth, the motive is linked to a representation of an emotional state that is expected to accompany gratification of the desire. The child imagines both the accomplishment of his goal—the solution of the equation—and his feeling of triumph at having achieved it. These four characteristics distinguish a motive from most cognitive representations (see Figure 6–5).

Obviously, a person may possess many motives at one time, some compelling and at the center of his attention, others peripheral. In other words, motives exist in a hierarchy. Motives that are easily activated by external events and thoughts are said to be high in the hierarchy; those that are less easily activated are low in the hierarchy.

Psychologist Abraham Maslow (1968) outlines the hierarchy of human needs in this order: (1) physiological (such as the need for oxygen, food, water); (2) safety; (3) love and belonging; (4) self-esteem and respect; and (5) self-actualization. Maslow theorizes that a person's needs must be satisfied in that order. Thus a child who comes to school without breakfast (need number 1) cannot concentrate on spelling—but neither can the child who feels he has no "place" in the class and does not belong in the group (need number 3).

Activating Specific Motives

It is important to realize that a motive, like a change in feeling, is not invoked in all situations. A child does not have the motive to hurt everyone all the time, just some people or groups at particular times.

	PRESENT	FUTURE	REACTION
COGNITIVE REPRESENTATION	Darkness	The sun will rise.	Indifference, no uncertainty
MOTIVE	Dry fields	The rain may come.	Deep concern, uncertainty

Figure 6–5
A young man on a farm in Vermont goes out for a walk at ten o'clock one night in August. As he thinks about the next day, two thoughts come to mind—one is that it will be daylight (the sun will rise) and the other is that it may rain. Both ideas are cognitive representations of a future event, but the latter is part of a motive. In his mind's eye he sees the field as it looks in the daylight, without having any strong reactions one way or the other. Nor does he *wish* for daylight; he simply expects it. But when he thinks of the possibility of rain, he envisions the contrast between the dry fields and the rain-soaked fields—the corn and the vegetables soaking up water through their roots—and hopes it will come. He also anticipates the feeling of relief he would experience if rain came.

An adult does not wish to win all competitions, just those he selects as relevant to his own enhancement. Some situations, of course, are so compelling that they provoke the same motives in most people. The applause and praise awarded to the valedictorian on graduation day is likely to motivate most adolescents in the audience—at least momentarily—to be academically successful. Most people who saw someone being brutally insulted would want to take action against the perpetrator. However, people have different hierarchies of motives and, in most everyday situations, are less likely to be motivated in the same way.

The hierarchical arrangement of motives means that in a given situation all children may not behave in the same way because different motives are likely to dominate each child's thought and behavior. At a Christmas party, three children may each have a different ascendant motive and therefore see the party in a different light. The child with a strong motive to compete sees the party as a chance to win the games. The child with a strong motive to dominate a situation sees the party as a place to boss others. For the child who is easily motivated to be sociable, the party is a chance to visit with his friends. Even though they may all feel competitive, domineering, and sociable to some degree, for each child only one of the three motives is ascendant. A party, a classroom, a park, or a store do not typically push forward one dominant motive for everybody. The individual's personal history will determine whether hostility, dominance, sexuality, mastery, or some other motive will prevail.

Motives are often in conflict with one another. The mother giving the Christmas party may want to help her children with the preparations and festivities of the holiday but, on the other hand, begrudge the time taken away from her other work. While a motive may lead to a change in behavior or some form of action (the mother does, in fact, bake cookies for the party), it does not always lead to an action (when you are rudely insulted, you may want to punch the aggressor in the nose, but you may keep your hands in your pockets). The relation between a motive and action will be discussed further at the end of the chapter.

Development of Motives: Infants and Young Children

Let us now consider some of the motives that develop during the early years of life. While most children develop motives to possess property (toys, other objects) and to experience sexual stimulation, we will concentrate on the motives that seem to set the stage for the motives of the child in school.

"As I see it, Pinocchio was motivated by a need to prove himself, while both Hansel and Gretel were driven by an inborn rebelliousness."

Although we do not know the first time the infant has a motive, it is probably no earlier than the second half of the first year. It should be appreciated that the act of crying when hungry does not necessarily entail any motive, for crying can be an automatic reaction to discomfort or unfamiliar events. The sequence of an unusual event leading to fear and then to crying need not involve any representation of possible food or a familiar person or place. When a four-month-old cries following her mother's exit through the bedroom door, it is unlikely that the child has any mental representation of a desired state or any anticipation of the future. The discrepant event elicited the crying directly. But when a two-year-old cries at the same event, it is more likely that the child is generating a motive that represents his mother's return to him. The two-year-old will probably initiate some action following the separation. He may go to the door or search for his mother. This important difference distinguishes the older child from the baby under eight months: the older child is likely to generate a representation of a state that involves eliminating the intruding event, escaping from it, or resolving the uncertainty.

Motive for Presence of Caring Adults

During the first year the child begins to associate specific adults with the alleviation of his distress and the provision of pleasant feelings. Hence, one of the first motives to emerge is the representation of those adults when he is in distress.

Motive for Mastery

The motive for mastery, also developing during the first year, is perhaps one of the most pervasive human motives. The child begins to show goal-directed mastery in her play toward the end of the first year. The early appearance of the motive for mastery is apparent in a twelve-month-old child who sees a dozen blocks on the floor and starts to build as if she had a mental representation of the final product. This "idea" seems to guide her behavior and provides a standard that, when attained, permits an affect that looks like satisfaction in a one-year-old and pride in a six-year-old.

The motive for mastery is a mental representation of some idealized level of performance. With age the motive is applied to an increasing number of contexts—from language, athletics, reading, spelling, and arithmetic to sexuality, painting, bowling, and parenting. The idealized representation is called a *standard*. The child creates standards for feelings, thoughts, behaviors—as well as a standard for a tower of blocks. Those standards are, first, to be attained and, later, maintained.

A child attempts a task for which he has set a standard when he knows that he has sufficient skill to embark on it but is a little uncertain as to whether he will be able to complete it. Thus the child who wants to make a collection of all the local wildflowers or swim under water for three minutes is motivated to make his action meet that standard in part because he is not absolutely sure he can. ·

Undoubtedly, the esteem of others also plays a part in reinforcing the motive for mastery, as we will discuss next. Nevertheless, it is important to identify the desire the mastery for its own sake as a primary motive in both children and adults.

Motive for Positive Evaluation from Others

During the second year, when the child becomes capable of representing symbolic dimensions of events, another important motive emerges. The child now has a motive for a caring adult's positive evaluation. This motive is not necessarily for a particular demonstration of approval, such as a hug or a commending "Well done," but for any one of a number of different acts a caring adult can display that inform the child that he is positively valued. The adult can wink, smile, tickle, say something affectionate, grant a demand, hug, kiss, or offer to play. The child can have representations for any and all of these actions, which signify that he is valued.

How does this happen? Let us try to trace the steps of this process. The child's desire to believe that he is valued by a person whom he needs, likes, and respects is central in human development. First, the child must recognize that the person has the potential for providing contentment, joy, and protection against distress—that the person is a source of "attentive care." The adults who care for the child display gestures, facial expressions, and other behaviors when they are alleviating the child's distress or providing him with pleasure. As a result, the child gradually acquires an awareness of various actions of others that accompany attentive care. "When my father smiles like that," a child may say to a friend, "it means he is going to give me a present." This awareness may or may not be conscious in the young child.

By the time the child is three or four years old, he classifies instances of attentive care from others as "good." How does he come to relate the evaluative category "good" with the category "attentive care"? We must make one assumption. Shortly after the child begins to develop some language, he learns the words *good* and *bad,* or their close synonyms. In the child's mind the word *good* becomes linked with care, approval, and valued actions; the word *bad,* with pain, distress, withdrawal of attention, disapproval, and prohibited actions. *Good* and *bad,* in other words, become linked to two separate categories. One is the presence or absence of attentive care, the other is conformity or nonconformity to adult standards.

The child links attentive care from adults with conformity to adult standards as a result of the natural tendency to treat categories as similar if they share a major dimension. Since attentive care and conformity to the standards of caretakers are both associated with demonstrations of approval (a smile, a hug, a present) and both are linked to the word *good* by the child, attentive care also becomes associated with conformity to standards. We now have a trio of linked categories: attentive care, *good,* and conformity to parental standards. There is also an alternative trio of linked categories: adult indifference, *bad,* and violation of parental standards. Once the link between attentive care and conformity to standards has been forged, children will react to a violation of a standard or to a withdrawal of care as if they had fallen from grace. If they have violated a standard—hit a peer, for example—they are quick to assume that adults will withdraw care. If attentive care is withdrawn when they have not violated a standard, they may conclude that they must have done something bad; otherwise why was the attention withdrawn?

Motive to Regard Self as Valued, Competent, and Virtuous

As the child approaches the fourth and fifth years of life, he develops a conception of himself, an awareness of the dimensions and characteristics that summarize his individuality. This concept of self

includes his knowledge of the specific acts, feelings, and thoughts he can experience and implement. (He knows he can run, eat, talk, and dream; but he cannot fly, solve geometry problems, or speak Spanish.) It also includes his knowledge of his age and sex role and encompasses, finally, a sense of his basic goodness and badness. The child, like the adult, cannot avoid evaluating his characteristics as bad or good, desirable or undesirable. It is a natural tendency of the human mind. His decision depends on his answers to three questions, and the answers depend on three different sets of experiences.

How valued am I? The first question addresses the child's perception of his value in the eyes of others, especially members of his family. The child believes, unconsciously to be sure, that since he is of his parents' flesh and therefore more closely related to them than to any other person, they are obligated to him. Naturally, they should value him. If he believes they do not, he begins to question his capability to be valued and loved by another. If he feels rejected he does not initially question his parents' ability to value him, oddly enough, but instead assumes that there is something wrong with him. In this evaluation the information he uses comes from his family's behavior toward him: whether they act as though they care or do not care for his welfare and happiness. Later he will come to similar conclusions about his peers.

How competent am I? The second evaluation a child makes pertains to his competence, ability, or talent. Naturally he focuses on the instrumental competences that the culture values: endurance, running speed, speaking proficiently, or reading well. Initially, of course, the child has no absolute definition that states exactly how fast he should read or how quickly he should be able to solve arithmetic problems. He is forced to look to other children—peers and siblings—for a standard he can use to judge his own level of competence.

The relevant information comes from the performances of other children. On the basis of that information the child assigns himself a rank, as we saw in Chapter 2. If he judges himself to be less talented, he may think that he will be less valued by the teacher; but a child who believes he is not competent can still believe that, as a person, he is valued by his family.

How virtuous am I? Finally, the child asks how good or bad he believes himself to be. He bases his judgment primarily on his evaluation of his actions and behavior as well as on the reactions of others to him. Over time he learns standards of actions and thought that his culture regards as morally proper. Although the list will vary depending on the culture, it is likely that most societies include such qualities as kindness, honesty, generosity, obedience, sincerity, and sympathy. The child evaluates his own actions and thoughts according to those standards. As early as three years of age, American children will agree on what acts and qualities are good or bad, and their choices are not surprising. Disobedience, violence, lying, and violations of parental prohibitions are unequivocally bad; their opposites are good. In addition, parental warmth, affection, and nurturance are good (Kagan, Hosken, and Watson, 1961). Further, across a broad range of cultures good-bad is the primary dimension people use to categorize objects, events, and qualities (Osgood, Suci, and Tannenbaum, 1957).

Clearly, if a child answers all three questions negatively, he will feel vulnerable and anxious. A negative answer to one of the questions, however, can be buffered by a positive answer to another. A change in the social environment can supply the child with new evidence. A different peer group, for instance, can lead to changes in the assessment of talent. A thoughtful and academically talented high-school boy who moves from an inner-city school where bravado and the show of strength are applauded more than academic talents may find his self-esteem improving in a middle-class suburban school where his abilities are admired rather than belittled.

Adolescence brings an increasing preoccupation with one's value, virtue, and competence, especially in our society. Adolescents articulate these qualities more directly, and if they feel they lack them, they seek an explanation. An American adolescent who is unhappy may blame her state of mind on her family. She may decide her father is too indifferent, her mother too restrictive. Part of the folk theory of our culture, such convenient explanations are supported by magazine articles, television shows, and public discussions of child development. Whether it is actually true or not, the adolescent who believes her family is to blame acts on that belief. She may express her anger toward them, perhaps by refusing to study if she believes such behavior will upset her parents. On the other hand, she may feel threatened by her interpretation and try instead to create a better relation with the family, perhaps by doubling her effort in school.

However, since the second World War there has been an increasing tendency to blame personal failure on "external social conditions" such as poverty and discrimination and even on chance. Consider, for instance, how ideas have changed during the last one hundred years concerning the causes of children's failure in school. A century ago it was assumed that hereditary factors doomed some children to degeneracy and academic incompetence. A quarter of a century ago family practices were regarded as the primary cause of school failure or success. Today the blame is commonly put on the neighborhood, and the social structure of the school, even though Americans continue to believe that parents' behavior and attitudes toward their children are important influences on their development.

Some realistic, factual bases underlie the current practice of placing blame on external conditions. With so many young people applying to good colleges, some who are competent will be rejected because of factors that have nothing to do with their ability. For example, they may come from a metropolitan area with many applicants, while the college wishes to promote a broader geographical distribution. A similar situation exists for those who graduate from college. Arbitrary cutoff scores determine who gets into medical, law, or graduate school and who does not. Overshadowing such particular cases is the mood of impersonality created by large bureaucracies, schools, and cities, where almost everyone feels expendable. Few people believe they have the power to make decisions that can produce a significant effect. This attitude leads to feelings of helplessness and, eventually, quiet apathy. As a consequence, constructive attempts to alter one's situation are inhibited. Although some social realities underlie these beliefs and the affect states they generate, young people tend to exaggerate them. Teachers can play a useful role in combating these distortions.

The Hostility Motive

The desire to cause another person pain or distress—the motive we call *hostility*—is related to the emotion anger and the behavior we call aggression, but the relation among the three is complex.

There is no good reason to assume that the infant has any mental representation of inflicting harm on another. But before children are

three years old, they display behavior that implies that they entertain the idea. Three-year-olds, with premeditation, will strike a child who has hit them or taken their property. But we must distinguish between an intention to strike and an intention to hurt. Otherwise, kicking a ball is an aggressive act, and sticking out one's tongue is not.

In order to assume a child has a hostile motive, several conditions must be met. First, the child must have a concept of the self. We suggested that this emerges soon after the first year, well before any evidence of hostility. Second, the child must know that others react as he does; he must be able to infer, to some extent, the emotional state of another person. Specifically, he has to appreciate that another will feel pain when hit just as he feels pain when he is hit. Then he can initiate actions that he has learned cause pain and distress. The action he chooses will depend on the child's experience. It may be yelling, not eating, or refusing to brush his teeth. What is required is the knowledge that a particular action can cause distress.

The third condition is that he must be provoked. Provocations generally fall into two main categories: either goals are blocked or standards are threatened. Let us consider each of these.

There is a period when the blocking of goals leads the young child to react with a tantrum or a hit. The action can be called aggressive, but it is not necessarily hostile in intention, resulting as it does from the young child's tendency to strike out motorically when provoked by the internal mosaic of feelings that we call anger. But once the child realizes that his hitting can hurt another person, he may deliberately strike out when he believes he is being, or is going to be, frustrated in reaching his goal.

The second main provocation of hostility is a perceived threat to one's standards. Whereas a young child is most likely to be provoked to anger and hostility when his goals are overtly blocked, a few years later—usually by age five—he will show anger and even aggression if he is accused of being something he considers undesirable or called a name, such as "sissy," "dummy," or "baby." Four conditions over and above the two already described (a concept of self and an ability to infer another person's emotional state) are required for the child to perceive a threat to his standards.

Figure 6-6
Hostility can be generated by the presence of another individual of very different appearance or with different standards, who seems to threaten one's own standards simply by existing. It's as if each person says, "If *that* person is right, *I* can't be right." In the classroom a child may feel threatened by a teacher of a different ethnic group or even one with a different personality. Of course, hostility does not move in only one direction: teachers, too, are often threatened by pupils whose behavior, values, language, or appearance strike them as foreign.

First, he must hold a standard that summarizes ideal and nonideal qualities. Second, his concept of self must include these symbolic qualities. Third, the provocation must cause distress, and fourth, he must believe that the one who provokes him means to hurt him. If he falls down and experiences pain but no one pushed him, he is not angry. Nor is he necessarily angry at a doctor who causes him pain or a teacher who makes him worry over a test—instances in which an agent does cause distress—because in both cases the child does not believe the agent intended to harm him. In order to infer the intention of another, of course, the child must have reached a certain level of cognitive mastery. At that point, we should expect threats to his standards to cause anger and hostility. Sometimes a threat to standards can be provoked by the mere presence of a person whose standards are obviously different (see Figure 6–6). The meek are angered by the haughty, the haughty by the timid, the homosexual by the zealously heterosexual.

In all these provocations an action, a routine, or a belief of one person is disrupted by that of another. Often, hostile intentions are incorrectly attributed to a person. A child wets his bed, for example, and the mother becomes upset, even if the child did not wet his bed in order to upset his mother. A teenage girl talks loudly at the dinner table and angers her father, even though she was not trying to do so. Although hostility might have been a partial cause of these actions (bedwetting and loud talking can be initiated with the intention of upsetting parents) it need not have been the cause. Fear or fatigue may have been responsible. Distressing the parent need not have been part of the child's plan.

Motives for Control, Power, and Status

The desires to maintain control of one's possessions, to resist the domination of other people, and to gain others' respect appear to be present in all societies. These motives do not emerge at the same time or develop at the same rate.

Control   The desire to maintain control of the situation one is in—to be allowed to continue an activity and retain possession of prized objects—appears first, usually early during the third year. Imagine a two-and-one-half-year-old child—we will call her Sally—who is playing with a toy drum. A second child, Oscar, comes up, takes the drum, and pushes her away. Sally may (1) withdraw (to her mother or to a more secluded and protected location), (2) stay and passively submit to Oscar's raid, or (3) resist and perhaps even counterattack. The choice

Sally makes in this situation will be the product of her temperament, size, and socialization. But Sally is likely to have a mental representation of the lost property and the lost territory; her motive is to resume playing the drum or regain the space where she was playing before she was invaded.

By her third birthday Sally may have acquired a more abstract motive. She will have a mental representation of herself controlling situations with Oscar that transcends the specific representation of herself with the drum. This motive is likely to occur first with her parents, for parents most often interrupt Sally's activity. Notice that the interruption can also provoke anger, as we discussed in connection with the motive of hostility. A common developmental sequence emerges, in which intrusion into Sally's activity leads to anger, which leads to the motive to regain control. In fact, goal blocking may not produce anger at all but may lead directly to the motive to recover control of the situation.

One reason this new sequence is most likely to occur first with parents is that the five-year-old knows that her mother and father do not intend to cause her distress, and that knowledge undercuts the basis of hostility.

Power

In the next step in the developmental sequence, Sally learns the specific qualities of humans who have the potential ability to exert control over her in the future. Initially, Sally is controlled by adults (primarily her parents) and larger, stronger children (older siblings and peers). Sally does not create a category for these classes of people, only schemata for specific people. As yet, she has no rule, "Larger, older people can control me."

But as she approaches five and six years of age, she identifies attributes of those who actually or potentially control her behavior. At this point, Sally develops a motive *to acquire* those attributes for herself. She believes that those qualities, which include size, posture, and dress, as well as other, psychological, traits, will give her the power to resist control and to control others. We shall call the desire for these attributes a motive for power. This motive involves a more mature level of cognitive ability than the one required for the motive to control. In a sense, the difference is reminiscent of our differentiation between a schema and a concept, described in Chapter 4. The child has a schema for controlling an event but a concept of the dimensions of those who have the potential to control. The motive to possess the attributes of those who control is important in the process of identification, as described in Chapter 2. Hence by the time the child is ten years old, she has two concurrent motives: one for controlling a specific context or person, and another to possess the qualities of those who control.

Status   Each culture awards respect and prestige to certain categories of people. In our society these include Supreme Court justices, Nobel laureates, and Pulitzer Prize winners, as well as doctors, professors, poets, and astronauts. These people have status in our society. An implicit understanding exists that people with status have the potential to influence—and even control—the behavior of those with less status. When children realize that certain roles offer people respect and control, a motive to fill one of those roles emerges. We call that desire the motive for status.

In sum, there is a pyramid of related motives having to do with the situations in which one person can actually or potentially dominate, influence, or force a submissive posture on another person. Each social group values particular competences and awards status to people who have them. Thus the American school gives status to students who are very competent at academic and athletic skills. The child or adolescent who desires status can gratify that motive by perfecting those talents. The child who does not have those abilities feels a little intimidated by the children who do—and may come to feel angry and hostile toward them.

Now that we have identified some of the fundamental motives that emerge during the first twelve years of life, we need to consider two further questions: what is the relation of affect to motive and of motive to action?

Motive and Affect

Feelings, as we indicated at the beginning of this chapter, are an important part of the human experience, and affects compete strongly for attention and for control of one's actions. Sensations from the stomach, the heart, the muscles, the skin, and other parts of the body form an omnipresent source of information that the mind continuously monitors. Although these feelings are internal, they are often linked to external events.

When a motive—such as sexuality, escape from pain, or hostility—is associated with a salient feeling state, the feeling will recruit the person's attention, and the associated desire will dominate the motive hierarchy. Only when the dominant motive has been gratified, and the intense feeling state associated with the motive has subsided, can motives associated with less intense and less distinctive feelings—such as the motive for mastery—ascend in the hierarchy of motives and gain control. This is one way of describing Maslow's hierarchy of motives. But it is not always true that survival needs are the most basic. Fear can often suppress hunger; rage and sexual excitement can mask pain.

Hence, the hierarchy is not always a function of immediate biological necessity—it can also be the function of the salience and the duration of internally generated feelings.

Motive and Action

The link between a motive and a subsequent action is like a dotted line: the possibility is apparent, but the realization depends on what else occurs in the spaces. We have just examined one condition necessary for a motive to lead to an action: the motive must be currently ascendant in the person's hierarchy. Suppose that a tenth-grade boy wants to improve his geometry and is about to take the initiative by asking the teacher to go over the work. At this point, the motive for mastery is ascendant. But several events intervene. First, the teacher turns to the boy and says that he is sorry, but he will have to take fifteen minutes more to tutor another student. The boy feels disappointed and slighted by the teacher. Further, the intruding student is the boy's chief rival, and the boy suddenly feels resentment toward the teacher as well as disappointment. Now disappointment combined with resentment succeeds in subordinating the original motive for mastery. When the teacher is ready to see him fifteen minutes later, he confronts a student whose original interest in attending to geometry has been superseded by hostility toward the teacher. Or suppose that the teacher is an attractive woman, and the boy's original motive is temporarily subverted by fantasies about the woman. In either case, until the boy succeeds in setting aside his resentment, or his romantic fantasies, they will take his attention away from his original purpose.

Possession of the necessary competence is a second condition for a motive to lead to an action. A child may envy the fluent Spanish of the teacher and wish to speak in the same voluble way but will be unable to if she has taken Spanish for only a week.

A third condition for a motive to be activated is that the child have minimal conflict or inhibitions associated with the gratification of his desires. Anxiety is a continual threat to the expression of goal-directed behavior. Anxiety over motivated actions (such as the wish to express resentment toward parents) grows during the first decade of life. As a result, during the period from three to ten years of age the relation between a child's motives and his behavior is apt to be increasingly disguised. However, during adolescence the relation becomes more direct (when, for instance, the adolescent persuades himself that it is childish to be afraid of showing resentment toward a parent).

Many conflicts that derive from contradictory wishes can influence behavior in the classroom. For example, children want the teacher's approval—but they also want to appear mature, independent of adults, and indifferent to their praise. Or a girl's wish to perform well in mathematics may be in conflict with her desire to conform to traditional sex-role standards, which hold that unusual competence in mathematics and science are masculine traits. The urge to compete and win recognition through superior grades conflicts with the desire to be cooperative. Or the wish to excel may be opposed by the fear that continually high performance will prove impossible to maintain. When the motives for praise, recognition, mastery, and power, which impel the child to work in school, conflict with opposing desires, the result is often anxiety and inhibition of appropriate action.

Finally, expectancy of success determines the activation of behavior to satisfy a motive. In school most children want to learn to read, but some do not expect to succeed and therefore do not commit their energies to the task. If a child continually expects her desire for friends to be frustrated, the motive will eventually become subordinate in her hierarchy, and she will attempt to gain friends less often. As early as age three, children learn the pain of failure and want to avoid it. Their aversion stems from fear of disapproval or punishment and from anxiety over failing to meet their own standards of performance.

Expectancy of success is a major factor in the performance of a schoolchild. In Chapter 7 we will examine the role of expectancy of success and the primary motives operating in school.

Summary

The discussion of the nature of affect begins by distinguishing between an individual's normal feeling state and a perceived change in feeling state. Changes in the nervous systems cause changes in stomach activity, muscle tension, sweat, and pulse rate. If the changes are sufficiently intense, the person detects them, attends to them, and interprets the change. An almost limitless list of specific human affects exists. Joy, anger, fear, relief, disappointment, are names we have given to a few common ones. The internal sensory feelings that form the basis of emotions are characterized by salience, origin, direction of change, and duration of change.

As cognitive competences mature in the infant and the young child, various affects emerge, including delight and anticipation of pleasant events in infants two or three months old, shame in the three-year-old, and dissonance in the adolescent.

One conception of affect assumes that the face is the primary source of human emotions, and psychologists have suggested that sensory feedback from distinct facial expressions (joy, terror, disgust, excitement, and so on) form the basis of the primary emotions. A substantial level of agreement regarding the emotional meaning of facial expressions exists among children from different cultures. Level of developmental maturity plays a part in children's interpretations of facial expressions and in their understanding of the complexity and subtlety of words used to describe affects.

Teachers can draw on the information accumulated by psychologists about the affective nature of humans. It can help teachers to understand the emotionally based causes of student behaviors and appreciate the cognitive bases of emotion. Advocates of affective education are concerned with encouraging spontaneity in children and attempting to reduce student anger by helping the children to understand its sources.

Although affect and motives are closely related, a motive is a mental representation (often unconscious) of a state that the person wishes to experience. Motives have several distinguishing characteristics: a discrepancy between the present reality and the hoped-for future; often an element of uncertainty about its attainment; often a link to a potential set of actions or ideas that may achieve the goal; and a link to a representation of an emotional state accompanying gratification. Each person possesses many motives simultaneously, arranged in a hierarchy with some ascendant over others and some in conflict with each other. Psychologist Maslow suggests the following hierarchy of needs: physiological, safety, love and belonging, self-esteem and respect, and self-actualization.

Motives, like cognitive competences and affects, emerge in a developmental pattern in infants and young children. Common childhood motives that also provide the foundation for the motives of the schoolchild include the motives for presence of caring adults; for mastery; for positive evaluation from others; for self-regard as valued, competent, and virtuous; for hostility; and for control, power, and status.

A motive may or may not lead to action. The four conditions required for activation of a motive are ascendancy in the person's hierarchy; possession of the necessary competence to achieve the goal; absence of conflict over the gratification of the desire; and an adequately high level of expectancy of success.

Projects

1 Observe in a nursery school or a day-care center to determine whether three-year-olds are capable of empathy. Keep a record of pertinent data and use it as evidence to present your findings in class.

2 In a schoolyard or on a playground, photograph the outward manifestations of emotional states in children.

3 Collect three inexpensive art prints, such as the 3 x 5 reproductions available in museum shops, that may be used in a secondary-level humanities course entitled "Emotions in the Arts." Ask three friends to describe the emotions the prints evoke in them—and why.

4 Prepare a reading list of fifteen novels for a high-school literature course. Suggest emotions that characterize the protagonist in each book.

5 Learn more about Maslow's theory of a hierarchy of needs. Taking the needs in ascending order, tell how a school may help a child satisfy each one.

6 Make a list of ten accomplishments that you enjoyed in the past five years (for instance, getting into college, defeating an opponent in a sports contest, building a desk). Tell which of the following motives dominated each accomplishment: motive for mastery; motive for positive evaluation from another; motive to regard self as valued, competent, virtuous; hostility motive; motive for control, power, status.

Recommended Reading

Coles, R., and Kagan, J. *Early adolescence: 12 to 16.* New York: W. W. Norton, 1972. Includes chapters on the motivation and conflicts of young adolescents, summarizing their moral reasoning, sexual preoccupations, and physical growth. One essay is by an adolescent who describes her own feelings about this period of development.

Holt, J. C. *How children fail.* New York: Pitman, 1964. A famous book that argues that conditions in the classroom tend to make children anxious and confused and, as a result, impede the development of motivation to perform well in school.

Izard, C. E. *The face of emotion.* New York: Appleton-Century-Crofts, 1971. A summary of the author's theory of emotion, which holds that the feedback from the muscles of the face provides an important basis for emotional experience.

Kagan, J. *Understanding children.* New York: Harcourt Brace Jovanovich, 1971. The initial essay summarizes the role of uncertainty in the motivational development of the child and the process of identification.

motivation and expectancy of success in school

7

O bviously, some obstacles to satisfactory school progress are cognitive. The child may fail to understand a problem because she is unfamiliar with the language used to present it, because she forgot the information contained in it, or because she never learned the concepts and the rules necessary for solving it. But there are three additional factors—usually called affective—that can also obstruct learning and problem solving. They are insufficient motivation, fear of possible failure, and low expectancy of success. Scientific studies are proving what teachers have known intuitively: even though a child possesses the requisite understanding and knowledge, she may not use what she knows to solve a problem if she is not motivated or if she expects to fail. Among elementary-school students of the same intellectual ability, those who are highly motivated obtain higher achievement test scores on basic skills than those with less motivation (Barton, Dielman, and Cattell, 1972). A child's motivation is closely monitored by her subjective estimate of whether she will succeed or fail if she invests effort.

Major motives operating in school
- Desire for the teacher's approval
- Desire to be similar to the teacher
- Desire for mastery of academic skills
- Desire to resolve uncertainty
- Desire for control, power, and status
- Desire to gratify hostility

The relationship between expectations and performance
- Internalizers and externalizers
- Teacher attitudes
- Optimal level of expectancy

Differences between boys and girls
- Individual variations in motivation
- Sex typing of school material

Changes in adolescence
- A different set of motives
- Dissonance in America
- Design for school change

Implications for teaching
- Ascertain each child's hierarchy of motives
- Design productive incentives and rewards
- Tailor individual programs
- Direct instruction to each child's level
- Collaborate with the child on setting goals
- Reduce student anxiety
- Generate mild uncertainty

Children of all ages fear criticism from their teachers and classmates for failing to master their lessons and, like adults, dread the feelings of shame and humiliation that arise when they violate their personal standards of competence. Establishing standards of competence and feeling embarrassed when one is discovered performing below one's standards are processes that begin early and are universal in human development. When one of the authors was walking through a small isolated Indian village in northwest Guatemala, he came upon a three-year-old boy whose attention was completely absorbed in a small pile of mud and water. He was trying to shape it into what appeared to be a tortilla. When the stranger was within a few feet, the boy noticed him and blushed and bowed his head in a way that suggested shame and embarrassment. The stranger asked if the boy was making a tortilla. The boy nodded but indicated that it wasn't a very good one.

Unsure about the potential success of a new, untried hypothesis, a child may censor a good idea or resist complete involvement in a task because he would rather forgo success than risk the unpleasant emotion that follows failure. As a result, students who are more certain of their ability to do well in their courses perform better than students who do not expect to succeed (Battle, 1966). And, of course, the cycle is self-perpetuating, since the better they do, the more confident they become. Further, since successful performance produces a greater expectation of success on the next occasion, a child who starts out with a low expectation but succeeds because of ability, motivation, or persistent effort is likely to alter his expectancy upward. In short, success breeds confidence, failure breeds pessimism.

Major Motives Operating in School

Chapter 6 discussed the development of emotion and motivation in a general context. Let us now apply the principles contained in that discussion to a particular situation—the child in school. In order to understand the academic progress and behavior of the school-age child, we must have a fine appreciation of the child's wishes, hopes, and fears. Let us consider six motives that affect the child's behavior in school.

The Desire for the Teacher's Approval

You will recall from Chapter 6 that the child has a strong motive for the positive evaluation of people who are significant in his life. Parents, of course, are the first adults from whom he seeks approval. Then, when the child enters school, the teacher becomes another important person whose approval is desired.

In the early grades the motive for the teacher's approval is paramount in most children. Her good opinion is reflected in many symbols—gold stars on work papers, smile faces drawn on quizzes, high marks on report cards, privileges ("Today Phyllis gets to erase the blackboard"). While the power of these symbols of approval from adult authority never entirely disappears, other motives ascend the hierarchy as the child grows. But for the young child, still firmly connected to the rhythm of behavior and approval in his home and still unable to appreciate the potential intrinsic joy of mastering mathematics and science, the teacher's attitude is central in determining how he performs in school.

The motive is not equally ascendant for all children, however. What characterizes a first-grade child with a strong motive for approval? *Children who are just a little uncertain about their value and virtue—or their lack of value and virtue—are likely to be the most susceptible.* Children who are very sure that they are valued by their

parents seem to require less corroboration of their worth and try less hard to win the teacher's recognition. Nor will the motive be ascendant for children who are equally certain that they are *not* valued. Since they believe they cannot win the teacher's approval anyway, they may not exert much effort to gain it. It is the mildly uncertain children who will raise their hands most often, rush to show the teacher what they have done, and work hardest in school for the teacher's praise. Such children usually come from homes where parents award praise and approval when the child demonstrates progress or mastery on some task but show mild signs of disappointment or temporary disfavor when the child fails to live up to the standards set by the family.

The Desire to Be Similar to the Teacher

As we saw in Chapter 2, a child may want to be similar to a model—a teacher, an older peer, or a classmate—whom he admires and whose traits he wants for himself. He will adopt the actions, values, and motives of that person, especially if he perceives some similarities to him. A Puerto Rican child who loves music will perceive such psychological similarity to a Puerto Rican music teacher. If she is also poised and warm—traits the child admires—then in order to attain these positive qualities he may adopt her more tangible characteristics, such as the way she gestures to make a point or her particular way of saying "You see?" at the end of a sentence. He may also adopt her positive attitude toward perfection of a skill and persistence in the face of obstacles and frustration.

The Importance of Perceiving Similarity

The motive to be similar to an admired model is universal in children, whether the model is a teacher or a classmate. The three-year-old Indian boy trying to make a tortilla was practicing the actions of the admired parent in the hope of creating greater psychological similarity between the parent and himself. Indeed, if children did not want to be similar to adults, parents would have a difficult time socializing them through the use of reward and punishment alone. But for the child to actively attempt to modify his behavior and attitudes to match the model, he must need to believe he is similar to the model in some meaningful way.

The importance of perceiving similarity to a model is seen in a study of ninety Minnesota Boy Scouts (Rosenkrans, 1967). Initially, each Boy Scout was asked to fill out a personal information sheet. He was then told that the purpose of the investigation was to find out how well boys his age could plan things. To that end the Scout was going to see a film showing a boy playing a war-strategy game, after which the Scout himself would play a similar game.

Before the film, the Scouts were shown different photographs of the boy in the film (the model). Some boys were shown a picture of the actor wearing a Scout uniform and were encouraged to notice similarities between themselves and the actor:

> As you can see, he's a Boy Scout just like you. He likes camping and hiking and other things that you do in Boy Scouts. He lives here in the Twin Cities. It looks as though he is a lot like you. It says here that he loves [and mentions two of the interests that particular Scout had put on his information sheet] just as you do. (p. 309)

Other boys were encouraged to see dissimilarities and shown a picture of the actor dressed in regular clothes rather than in a Scout uniform:

> This boy doesn't live in Minnesota. He lives in another state far away from here. He doesn't go to the same kind of school you do. He doesn't even like to do the same things you do. It says here that he doesn't like [and mentions two of the interests from the Scout's information sheet]. It also says he isn't interested in camping and hiking. I guess that's why he never joined the Boy Scouts. (p. 309)

Then each of the Scouts watched a film of the model playing a war-strategy game, maneuvering the pieces and, in some versions of the film, breaking the rules. The film was the same for all Scouts until the end, when some Scouts saw a film in which the model was rewarded, some saw a film in which he was punished, and some saw a film in which there was no consequence at all.

After the film each Scout played the war-strategy game alone, and his actions—how he maneuvered the pieces and whether or not he broke the rules—were observed. The Boy Scouts who saw strong similarities between themselves and the model imitated him much more than those who perceived little similarity—and the impact of *similarity* was more significant than whether or not the boy in the film was *punished* or *rewarded*.

If students notice close similarities between themselves and a model, they are likely to pay more attention to what the model says and be more receptive to the model's communications. A study was made of two groups of college women. The first group was studious and avoided social occasions; the second studied much less and socialized a great deal. Each student in the two groups was told that she was going to be asked to judge which of two poems (described as the top winners in a contest) was most creative. First, the hypothetical poets were described. Half the women in the social group were told that poet A was social, poet B, studious; the other half were told the opposite. The same pattern was followed with the studious group. They then listened to a tape recording of the poems being recited by two different women, whom the students believed to be the poets A and B themselves. After hearing the poems, the women were asked to remember as much of each poem as they could. Those in the studious group remembered more of the poem that they believed was written by a studious poet, and the social students remembered more of the poem by a social poet. The study implies that we are likely to be most attentive to, and therefore learn more from, people who we believe are similar to ourselves (Chang, 1965).

Model's Apparent Satisfaction with Work

In addition to perceived similarity between child and model—based on ethnicity, sex, or parallel interests (such as a love of camping among Scouts)—the model's apparent gratification in and enjoyment of his work are important determinants of whether the child will try to adopt the model's qualities.

One study contrasted the impact of a model's *happiness* as opposed to the *rewards* he received. Sixty second-grade boys watched a film in which a woman came into a room carrying several toys and told a boy (the model) that if he played with the toys the right way, he would get a prize; otherwise, he would not. She left the room, giving the child a chance to play with the toys; then she returned. At this point, the film, like the one in the Boy Scout experiment, had different endings. In one ending, the woman returns and gives the model a positive reward (an attractive locomotive), and he is happy. In another, she gives a positive reward, but the model is unhappy. In the third version, she gives a negative reward (an old, torn book), and the model is unhappy. In the fourth, the reward is negative, but the model is happy anyway.

After the film each of the sixty boys was given a chance to play with toys like the ones in the film, while observers noted how much they imitated the film model. Boys who had seen the version in which the model was happy after he received the reward imitated the model's actions with the toys more than did the boys who had seen film versions in which the model was unhappy, *independent of the positive or negative qualities of the reward itself.* The results suggest that the emotional state of the model is central in determining whether the child will behave as the model did (Lerner and Weiss, 1972). Since the child wishes to have the model's desirable attributes for his own, it is not surprising that the model's apparent happiness can influence the child to emulate that model.

The child's desire to model his motives and actions after an adult he respects and admires is one of the most powerful forces in his education. Since it hinges primarily on the kind of person the teacher is—in contrast to the quality of the teacher's training—beginning teachers should realize that their ability to motivate children rests in part on their personal characteristics. There are some qualities that all children admire—honesty, warmth, fairness, and competence—and some that appeal to one child but not to another. Some admire a "tough" attitude; others a permissive one. Some admire those who are emotionally spontaneous; others prefer more controlled adults. Thus a teacher cannot be a perfect model to all students. Teachers often sense this fact unconsciously and want to be assigned to schools where the practices and the values of the children are in accord with their own. When there is a great deal of agreement between the qualities of the students and the teacher, the conditions for identification are optimal and the students are more likely to adopt the values the teachers promote. This is an old principle, for centuries ago—before schools were constructed—parents were advised to be careful in selecting tutors for their children and to pay special attention to their personal characteristics. The same is true today.

The Desire for Mastery of Academic Skills

The motive for mastery, sometimes called *achievement motivation,* is perhaps the most significant motive parents and teachers want to promote. The motive for mastery is the desire to improve one's talents for their own sake. If the motive in a particular subject area is low in the hierarchy, the child will not perform well, even if he has the ability.

The basic source of the mastery motive is the desire to match one's behavior to a standard, the generation of which was discussed in Chapter 3. A child gradually acquires ideas about the world he lives in,

and he uses this knowledge, as a captain uses a sextant on the open sea, to help him find his way around new territory. From his own experience he knows that milk is white, dogs bark, summer is warm. He also comes to believe in facts and rules that he has not experienced directly—elephants flap their ears when they are angry, the Eiffel Tower is tall, some mountains have snow in summer. In addition, through observing other children in the classroom and around the neighborhood, each child comes to appreciate the appropriate level of competence for each school skill.

In time, these experiences consolidate into a standard about how things are and how they work. The standard gradually becomes idealized, and children try to match their behavior to that idealized image. For instance, in a geography course, a child wants to design and color a map that will be as precise and thorough as the map she has seen in the textbook or an atlas. When in a chemistry lab she wants to perform experiments without spilling the materials or breaking the glassware. In math class she wants to solve division problems quickly and without help. If she is a little unsure of her ability to meet each standard, the motive for mastery in that context will be ascendant. If she is certain she will be unable to meet the standards, or certain that she will, the motive will be less likely to rise in the hierarchy. The child motivated for mastery is one who is pretty sure—but not absolutely sure—that she can meet the standards she has generated. You will recall that this process resembles one of the bases for imitation discussed in Chapter 3.

The Desire to Resolve Uncertainty

We have alluded several times to the role of uncertainty in a child's constellation of motives. Resolving uncertainty does not mean dispelling it completely, however, but rather monitoring and adjusting the amount of uncertainty experienced at a particular time. Hence a person usually seeks uncertainty, like Saint George tackling the dragon, when he is fairly confident that he can deal with it. The converse is also true: an individual avoids uncertainty when he is relatively sure that he cannot deal with it.

Sources of Uncertainty

Uncertainty, and the motive to resolve it, stem from several sources. A child notices a gap between an unfamiliar event and a familiar one, like the child in Chapter 3 who encounters a sea urchin for the first time. The need to account for an unfamiliar event is one source of the motive to resolve uncertainty. The resolution involves a balancing act (Piaget's concept of equilibration) between an initially discrepant or conflicting event and one's knowledge.

Uncertainty develops in school when the child has a motive for academic mastery and gauges his progress by comparing his ability with one or two peers. As long as the child thinks he is progressing at the same rate as those other children, there is no increase in uncertainty. However, if the child believes that the others have moved closer to the goal than he has, he begins to feel uncertain and may conclude that his progress is too slow. One response is to make an extra effort to close the gap; another is to withdraw effort. A common reaction is to remove the motive for school mastery from a high position in the hierarchy—to delegitimize school. This is an easy choice for children whose friends and families do not place a high value on schoolwork. Hence, it is more often the choice for lower-class than for middle-class children. Conforming to the values of their friends and adults in the neighborhood, they protect themselves from distress at the same time. Having made that choice, they invest less effort in schoolwork.

But for children from homes and neighborhoods where school mastery is highly valued, it is not easy to demote the motive for school mastery, since that threatens congruence between the children's values and those of their friends and family. For them, increased effort is the most feasible strategy. But if that effort fails, the children are in a double bind. They do not believe they can attain the goal, but they are unable to persuade themselves that it is unimportant. Now they are seriously threatened. They can blame themselves by assuming they are not talented. They can blame the teacher for being unfair, the parents for not being supportive enough. Or, they can cast the blame on all three.

A similar script can be written for the child who is uncertain about being accepted by classmates. Potential peer rejection generates uncertainty. One reaction to the uncertainty is to claim that peer acceptance is unimportant. Delegitimizing friendship is more difficult for most children than delegitimizing schoolwork unless, of course, the family also devalues the importance of peer acceptance.

If the child can neither gain friends nor reject friendship, she will become tense and anxious. She may believe there is something wrong with her and withdraw, or conclude that her classmates are cruel and become hostile toward them. Hostility to peers develops more easily if the child can detect a basis for prejudice. She may decide that her race, ethnicity, or class is the reason for prejudice toward her. Hence, a child in a minority group may conclude that the majority of the other students do not like her. Once she believes that, hostility can ascend in the motive hierarchy. But a child needs evidence in order to feel angry and hostile, rather than simply lonely or rejected.

We should consider two other important sources of uncertainty: the need to predict the future and the need to define the self. Attempts to resolve these questions fuel the motive for school mastery.

Adult or child, every person prefers to feel that he has some control over the circumstances in his life and can deal with events that come his way. Since he cannot realistically expect only good fortune, he wants to be able to anticipate when unpleasant events will occur and what form they will take, so that he can prepare for them. A woman who invests in the stock market, for instance, may be testing her ability to predict the rise and fall of prices, and her financial investments are directed as much by this motive as by the desire for increased wealth.

The desire to predict what is going to happen next—to resolve uncertainty of the future—is an important motivational force in the early grades. A child spends a great deal of time in his first few school years trying to predict what will happen in class and on the playground and how he will be evaluated. By about the fifth grade he may have a good idea of what happens in school and how the teacher will regard him. Uncertainty over the future is partially resolved, and as a result, interest in school may diminish for some children. This can happen to older students as well. Take the case, not uncommon, of a high-school senior. During the early weeks of the school year he was intrigued by the array of equipment, chemicals, and experiments in his chemistry class. He did his homework enthusiastically and carefully and worked in the lab. By Christmas he had an idea of what chemistry involved. The novelty had worn off—a common occurrence in all new adventures. He could predict what would happen in each class and he became bored.

The desire to match various behaviors and emerging competences to an ideal that one is uncertain of attaining, and the wish to predict the

Heartland to Border: The Uncertainty Run

A proprietor's confidence is at its peak in the heartland, as is an intruder's at its lowest. That confidence, however, will wane as the proprietor approaches his border, vanish as he crosses it. Having entered his neighbor's yard, an urge to flee will replace his urge to fight, just as his neighbor's confidence and fighting urge will be restored by the touch of his vested soil. (Ardrey, 1966, p. 90)

In describing the complementary pulls exerted on animals—the need for the safety of the heartland but also a craving for the excitement of the border—writer Robert Ardrey catches one of the dynamics that also operates for children in school. Like all individuals, children are curious about what they do not know. They may be excited by the challenge of mastering something new, and, at the same time, apprehensive about the danger. The danger they encounter when they go too far from what they know, and which diminishes their confidence, is the fear of failure.

For each child, in each academic subject, there is some ideal spot along the run from heartland to border where he should be each day. The teacher's task is to discover, as near as possible, the strategic place where a child can be optimally excited and minimally afraid. To locate it, he needs to diagnose the child's ability and his past experience. Then the teacher should assess what motives are ascendant in the child's hierarchy and devise ways to activate them. While reducing a child's anxiety may be one aspect in guiding him from the known to the unknown, arousing his interest is another.

future, appear early in every child's school life. As children approach adolescence, a third node of uncertainty emerges—the desire for self-identity. Each person wants to know his basic characteristics. The preadolescent generates a concept of himself in much the same way that he generated concepts of food, clothing, and animals when younger. A concept, you will recall, is defined by a set of common qualities and relations. So, too, with the concept of the self. The preadolescent wants to know the core dimensions that define him.

The qualities that define people vary with history and society. In many societies the concept of self is based primarily on the social position of one's family and one's sex and age. In thousands of rural subsistence-farming villages scattered throughout the world, adolescents view themselves as members of particular families. Twelve-year-old Maria, for example, sees herself as a Puzul, one of twenty families in the village of San Miguel, Guatemala. She is Catholic, she is adept at cooking, cleaning, and caring for children, and she will be a wife and a mother in a few years. The dimensions that define her are given by the culture. She does not have to discover unique ones to determine her identity.

Uncertainty and identity in America. Modern America is relatively unique in that a family's name is not an important attribute of the child's concept of self. (Of course, for the few children whose families have distinctive status—the Kennedys, the Roosevelts—family name and position are part of their identity.) Furthermore, as large metropolitan areas grew and families moved from town to town, place of residence became unimportant to one's concept of self. Finally, our society does not assign a fixed set of activities to boys or girls. The one exception is school mastery, and that is expected from both boys and girls. Thus, unlike Maria Puzul, who is given her defining dimensions by her society, the average American child is given only one and must discover the rest.

As Americans have placed less value on external characteristics—family name and position, place of residence, sex, religion—they have put more emphasis on what you *do* and on what you *believe*. The American adolescent must discover his defining dimensions by mastering skills, discovering how others react to him, and developing an individual set of opinions that will constitute his philosophy of life. None of these is given. School experiences are more important for self-definition in modern America and Europe than they are in most other parts of the world. American children and adolescents are motivated to work hard in school partly to resolve uncertainty over who they are. In order to discover his talents and limitations, the child, and later the adolescent, must attempt difficult tasks. Unfortunately, learning about one's talents usually requires

comparison with others. Most students cannot know if they are good at history or science unless they know how good their classmates are.

Our culture uses grades, nationally normed test scores, awards from science organizations, prizes in art exhibits, and varsity letters to provide the adolescent with information regarding the extent of his skill or talent. This situation encourages each child to eye his classmates on either side, constantly evaluating who is ahead in the race, rather than encouraging him to focus on his own development. Adam may be a very good basketball player, but in gym class he plays with a boy who is clearly headed for the Harlem Globetrotters. The future Globetrotter's extraordinary physique and skill eclipse Adam's prowess (and diminish his pride and self-confidence) even though he is, in fact, a good basketball player.

A somewhat slow, uncertain child will notice that three-quarters of the class is always ahead of her in reading and conclude that she must be incompetent. If her class were arranged so that she did not focus so intently on the other students, she might appreciate, instead, how much progress she has made since the beginning of the year. The basketball player, too, will benefit if he can recognize what a skilled player he is, instead of being preoccupied with the shadow of the future Globetrotter. As we will discuss at the end of this chapter, one of the advantages inherent in a program of individualized instruction is that it decreases each child's focus on the group contest and increases his awareness of his own personal growth.

The Desire for Control, Power, and Status

As we indicated in Chapter 6, the motives for control, power, and status are similar, for they share common goals: the wish to be in command of one's own behavior, and the wish to be free of others' coercion or domination—now and in the future. The child wants to ensure that other people will not try to dominate him either through fear or through enhanced status.

The motives for achieving control of situations, attributes of power, and signs of status are influential in school. Although a child influenced by these motives may work as hard as another child with an ascendant motive for mastery, he is working for different reasons. The motives for control, power, and status, usually not important in the early grades, emerge as ascendant in junior high and high school. A common example is the boy who feels dominated, even bullied, by larger, stronger boys because he is small, weak, or shy. In an effort to resist their power over him (even if he cannot beat them on the playground), he may be highly motivated to excel in academic subjects in order to gain power and status. He knows that adults respect good grades and that "smart" students have status in the community as well as in the classroom. He gains concrete signs of power and status in the form of a place on the honor roll, academic prizes, and high grades.

One study demonstrated the influence of this motive in high-school students. One hundred and sixty high-school juniors heard twenty words played one at a time on a tape: sixteen of the twenty words belonged to one of four classes of motives. The motives and words were:

Motive	hostility	friendship	mastery	power-status
Words	fight	love	goal	leader
	hatred	closeness	success	boss
	anger	friend	work	director
	murder	buddy	determination	power

After they had listened to the words, the students were asked to write down all the words they could remember. They then heard the same words a second time, played in a different order, and again wrote down all the words they could remember. The students who recalled more power-status words, implying that a concern (or motive) for power-status was ascendant for them, had higher grades and were more likely to be on the honor roll than students who recalled fewer power words (Jordan, 1973). There was no difference between better or poorer students in recall of mastery words.

Less frequently, power and status can have an inhibiting effect on mastery. There is a small number of children and adolescents who, for

Control, Power, and Status

Lawyers, who usually charge on the basis of time, have their own ways of establishing their importance. At the lowest level, they have clocks that face toward them, status being set by the kind of clock it is. A round, wedge-topped battery-operated clock that sits flat on the desk and is only visible to the lawyer himself seems to be this year's favorite.... At this stage of power, the lawyer wants to know how long the client has been there, but would just as soon the client didn't know. More important lawyers announce that their time is expensive by having the clock face the cli-

ent.... Some older lawyers have no clocks at all, the implication being that everyone they see is on a retainer basis anyway, and if they're not, there's a secretary outside to keep the log. (Korda, 1974, p. 31)

While the proper timekeeper for a lawyer at each rung in his career may be a sophisticated, if not precious, form of showing status, children in school also display status symbols in their clothes, jargon, dance steps, after-school activities, and sometimes even in the seats they choose in a classroom.

complex reasons that cannot be specified, are bullied, teased, and rejected by their classmates. If this continues for a long time, the adolescent may begin to view those with power and status negatively—as people who are cruel and secretly disliked. They become undesirable role models. Suppose such an adolescent with an ascendant motive for mastery becomes an achieving high-school student and as a result is elected to positions of status by his peers and placed in a position of power by the teacher. Now this adolescent finds himself in the role he had classified in a negative light earlier. He may begin to inhibit effort in order to remove himself from the position of status and privilege that he had regarded negatively. Although this is not as common a reaction as its opposite, namely, to achieve in order to gain status and power, it does occur.

The Desire to Gratify Hostility

Hostility—the wish to cause another person pain or distress—is not a motive that parents or teachers are anxious to encourage in their children. Nevertheless, it exists in children as well as adults and plays a role in the classroom.

As we saw in Chapter 6, hostility arises when a child believes that she or her standards are threatened or when her attempts to reach a goal are blocked—and another person is believed to be the cause of her frustration. Hostility can influence work in school when a student believes that she can gratify resentment against someone by failing or succeeding in her courses. For example, a child may feel hostile toward her parents and refuse to work hard in order to disappoint them. This is most likely to occur if parents show that they are easily distressed when the child does not perform well academically. If a child is angry at a teacher, either because she has threatened her, frustrated her needs for acceptance, or does not conform to standards she admires (perhaps because the teacher belongs to a different racial or ethnic group), the child may inhibit effort as a way of expressing her resentment.

One investigator asked fifth-grade boys (thirty-six achievers and thirty-nine underachievers) to make up stories to pictures. The stories were scored for evidence of themes of hostility toward an authority figure. Underachievers expressed more hostile fantasy toward authority than did achievers. It is not clear that the underachievers' hostility caused their poor performance (instead, they might have been more hostile *because* they were performing poorly in school). Nevertheless, the study suggests that some preadolescents may find the demands of their parents or the school threatening. They may seek to gratify their hostility indirectly by demeaning adult values—academic achievement being a paramount adult value. The investigator writes: "Grades provide communication between adult authorities, parent and teacher.

The underachiever may be conveying the message, 'I can do better, but I will not' " (Morrison, 1969, p. 169).

On the other hand, hostility can lead to improved performance. If a child wants to win her parent's acceptance and remove her older brother from the limelight of family favoritism, she may strive hard to improve her grades in an effort to outdo her sibling. Or a child may compete with a classmate, hoping to win either the teacher's praise or the esteem of the class as a whole. Some highly creative people are often motivated to show how uncreative their peers are. They try to be original in order to gratify hostility toward their rivals (Watson, 1969).

These six motives exist in all children. But, of course, they do not exist in the same hierarchy for all, nor do children have the same opportunities to gratify these motives. As a result, there are dramatic differences in behavior among children. But perhaps the most important determinant of whether the child will act to gratify his motives, and the greatest influence on the motive hierarchy itself, is what we have referred to as "expectancy of success"—an expectancy that one can gratify the motives that are ascendant.

The Relationship between Expectations and Performance

Consciously or unconsciously all children have an idea of how well they can perform a task. That expectancy influences the amount of effort they expend and how well they actually do in school.

Low expectation of success affects school performance as early as kindergarten. Measures of general intellectual ability, as well as the children's confidence in their talents, were obtained on 120 kindergarten children (Wattenberg and Clifford, 1964). One of the measures of self-confidence was based on spontaneous comments the children made as they drew pictures of their families, scored to reflect each child's positive or negative attitude toward his personal ability. Adults familiar with the children also rated each on expectation of success. Reading achievement scores for these children were obtained two years later, at the end of the second grade. The kindergarten children who appeared more confident of their abilities and were viewed as having a greater expectancy of success had higher reading test scores (the self-confidence ratings had no strong relation to the child's general intellectual ability).

If a child has a strong motive to master a school task (such as reading) but does not expect to succeed, she is unlikely to make the effort to learn the skill and will behave as if she did not care about school. Such a child is Andrea. Sure that she will fail, each time the reading period begins she acts out a series of behaviors she has developed whose purpose is to keep her from starting the reading assignment: she starts a fight, throws a paper airplane, teases the child in front of her, or goes to sleep. After a year or two of such behavior, a change gradually occurs in the status of the original motive. She cannot continue indefinitely wanting to learn to read and being unable to read: the conflict is too painful. As a result, she is forced to alter the salience of the original motive. She persuades herself that reading is not important. She tells herself that only "teacher's pets" learn to read well and that she's not going to do what the teacher wants. Gradually a new motive—to resist the teacher's inducement to develop reading skills—becomes ascendant over the original one and subordinates it.

Internalizers and Externalizers

Once the motive "to resist" gains ascendancy over the motive "to master," Andrea may blame the painful school situation, and her failure, on events outside herself: the teacher's hostility, the difficulty of the books, or bad luck. In other words, she *externalizes* the reasons for her public failure. Other children in the same position will blame themselves, assuming that they are not smart enough, did not work hard, or were lazy. These children *internalize* their reasons for failure. This is an important difference that distinguishes individuals. Some children and adults feel that many important events that affect their lives are not under their control but are due instead to people and forces outside themselves—the prejudice of others, economic conditions, bad politicians, even astrological events.

Obviously, no one externalizes blame for all events, only for selected ones. Nor does anyone internalize the reasons for all events. These two attitudes—internalization and externalization—represent extremes, for in most situations the individual actions and the behavior of others act together. A child who is elected president of his class because he is a good student attains that prize not only through personal effort but also because his peers value his qualities. As with most psychological terms, the terms *internalize* and *externalize* are too broad and too stereotyped but are nevertheless still useful as a way to explain the attitudes of children in particular school situations.

A series of experiments indicates the close relation among a child's expectancy of success, feelings of internalization or externalization and school performance. Fifth-grade children were asked to make specific designs with colored blocks. While some of the designated designs could be formed from the blocks, others could not. Some children continued to persevere in their attempt to solve the insoluble problems, while the performance of other children deteriorated. The children who

YOU AND SCHOOL

	YES	NO
1 Do your marks get worse when you don't work hard?	(·)	( )
2 Does studying before a test seem to help you get a higher score?	(·)	( )
3 Are you surprised when you get a good mark?	( )	(·)
4 Do you think studying for tests is a waste of time?	( )	(·)
5 If you get a bad mark, do you feel it's your fault?	(·)	( )
6 Are you surprised when the teacher says you've done an assignment well?	( )	(·)
7 When a teacher gives you a low mark is it because he doesn't like you?	( )	(·)
8 When you really want a better mark than usual, can you get it?	(·)	( )
9 Do you think students get low marks just because luck is against them?	( )	(·)
10 Do your lowest grades come when you don't study your assignment?	(·)	( )
11 Do your test marks seem to go up when you study?	(·)	( )
12 Is a high mark just a matter of "luck" for you?	( )	(·)
13 Do you think you deserve the marks you get?	(·)	( )
14 Do you usually get low marks even when you study hard?	( )	(·)
15 Are tests just a lot of guesswork for you?	( )	(·)

Figure 7–1
Questions such as these were given to children in fourth, fifth, and sixth grades to determine whether they tended to think they were responsible for how well they did in school or to believe the cause of their success or failure was outside their control. Children who were "internalizers" performed better than pupils who were "externalizers" on academic tests. The dots in the Yes and No columns indicate the answers that signify internalization. (Clifford and Cleary, 1972, p. 650)

persisted, even after a run of failures, were internalizers; they believed that the reason for their failure lay within themselves. But the children whose performance deteriorated—the externalizers—tended to attribute their failure to causes outside themselves—bad luck, a poor teacher, the difficulty of the task (Dweck and Reppucci, 1973). In another study, children in fourth, fifth, and sixth grades in Iowa were given a questionnaire to measure their tendency to internalize or externalize (see Figure 7–1). They were then tested in spelling, vocabulary, and mathematics. The children who internalized the most performed better on the tests than the pupils who internalized less (Clifford and Cleary, 1972).

In a third study, fifth- and sixth-grade boys were measured for internalization, then given puzzles to solve—some of which were insoluble. At the same time, each boy was shown a bowl of poker chips, along with two panels of buttons labeled "win-take" and "lose-give back," and instructed to indicate (by pushing the buttons) how many chips he thought he should take for solving the puzzle and how many he thought he should give back for failing to solve the puzzle. It was like a self-determined credit rating, reflecting whether he thought he had won by a big or a narrow margin. Those who internalized most gave themselves greater rewards (in chips taken) when they solved a puzzle and milder penalties (in chips given back) when they failed than the boys who internalized least (Weiner et al., 1972).

Internal-ization Linked to Expectancy of Success

Children with strong internalization attitudes not only perform better on tasks they view as related to individual qualities, they also have a higher expectancy of success. Children who externalize have a lower expectancy of success. There is a metaphor that captures this dynamic: imagine a seesaw, with apprehension of failing on a new task at one end and desire to meet and master the challenge of the task at the other. Standing astride the middle of the seesaw, and helping to determine the outcome, is the child's expectancy of success. If a child is strongly motivated to read and also expects to master the skill, the weight at the center of the seesaw shifts, and we see a child showing behavior consistent with "mastering" rather than with "resisting" the task (see Figure 7–2). He attends to the teacher, concentrates on the book, studies a little longer after the end of the reading period in order to gain practice. If the child does not expect to master the task, his behavior shifts to resistance.

Several behaviors may be triggered in the service of mastering a new skill—concentration and perseverence are the two most useful. They function like the low gears of a car, doing the hard, unspectacular, but necessary, uphill work. A child who believes that he will master a new skill, or solve a problem, is more likely to concentrate and persevere than the child who does not.

Teacher Attitudes

The teacher's actions can contribute to the child's expectancy of success. While teachers communicate to some children that they expect them to succeed, they may signal to others quite the opposite message.

Figure 7–2
A high expectancy of success can tip the balance in a child's performance, persuading her that the difficulties of the task are outweighed by the probable rewards of meeting the challenge and solving the problem.

In an intriguing study in a middle-class suburb younger siblings in the first grade were each classified according to whether an older brother or sister had been a good or a poor student in the school. In twenty-seven cases the first-grade teacher had taught the older sibling, while for fifty-two others (the control group) the teacher had no knowledge of the older sibling's school performance. Thus, some of the teachers might have had a "halo"—or prejudiced expectancy—that the younger sibling would perform like the older one. Each child's academic achievement was assessed by scores on the Stanford achievement subtests for vocabulary and arithmetic, as well as by their grade-point averages. First-grade children with a teacher who had taught an older sibling who had been a good student (which would lead the teacher to have a positive expectancy for children from that family) had higher scores than children with teachers who did not know the older sibling. Further, children with a teacher who had taught an older sibling who had not done well in school scored lower than the control children. Like other tantalizing but not yet conclusive studies, these results suggest that the child's performance can be influenced by the teacher's expectation for him (Seaver, 1973).

But you may wonder about the order of these events. Does a child perform poorly because she began with an expectation of failure? Or does she only develop an expectation after she has performed poorly for many years? It is not always clear whether the child's expectancy was low when she began school and so she did not try hard or whether she performed poorly during the first months, and as a result developed an expectancy of failure. But in either case, when expectancy of failure is strong, the child stops investing effort and subsequently falls behind her peers. As a result, she becomes more convinced that she will fail and becomes caught in a downward spiral.

Optimal Level of Expectancy

Too high an expectancy of success, like expectancy of failure, can also block outstanding performance. An adolescent who is completely certain he can master social studies is likely to exert minimal effort. The task does not provide sufficient challenge to promote concentration and perseverance. In this case the mood will not be one of futility, as it was for Andrea, but of boredom.

It is not uncommon for college students who view intelligence as a basic dimension of their concept of self to seek the most difficult and challenging courses, even though they might not be interested in the content, and to shun courses that are less challenging but more interesting. This type of student will often major in mathematics or physics—the most difficult subjects—rather than in sociology or psychology, which are easier to master. Often during the junior year some will change their major to a social science becaue they realize they are more interested in the content of those courses, even though they may not have resolved the uncertainty about their competence at the difficult subject.

There are, of course, differences among students in the degree of challenge they like and seek. Some are bold; others cautious. In a series of studies children played a game of ring toss, standing at varying distances from a peg on the floor. A successful toss from a great distance was worth many points, while one from a short distance was worth only a few. Some students chose to play it safe, standing close to the peg and winning a small number of points that were practically guaranteed. Others preferred to take the chance of scoring high from a distance with the concurrent risk of failing. The investigators found a correspondence between the children's behavior in this game and in other situations. Those who played the game cautiously—or daringly—approached other problems in a similar way. Furthermore, the game could be used to help students learn to gauge their abilities more accurately and to abandon excessively cautious or excessively risky strategies (Alschuler, 1970; McClelland, 1965).

As we have indicated many times, the optimal task is one in which the student is *a little unsure* of his ability to learn a new skill. The goal is slightly out of reach, but the child believes that, with effort, he has a reasonable chance of success.

Differences between Boys and Girls

In the old section of a city, sometimes you can still see a school
building that was designed with separate entrances: over one door,
chiseled in stone, is the heading "BOYS"; over another, usually at the
opposite side of the building, is chiseled "GIRLS." It seems very
old-fashioned; yet when we observe an elementary-school class at
work, it often appears that boys and girls do, indeed, go separate ways
in school.

Take a look, for example, at one fourth-grade language arts class.
Both the boys and the girls show a great reluctance to sit together:
already a division is apparent. Furthermore, their behavior is strikingly
different. Both the boys and the girls have comments to make. But
different ethics dominate the two groups. Although there is some
giggling and whispering among the girls, for the most part they seem to
play the teacher's game her way, eager to make suggestions that will
catch her interest, anxious to win her smile or word of approval, and
relaxing into sheepish grins when they do. Girls tend to be more
attentive to teachers and school material. One study of 132 first-graders
found girls more apt to focus their eyes on the text or the teacher,
observe the chalkboard, and work on follow-up exercises. The boys

were more apt to play with nonassigned materials and disregard instructions (Samuels and Turnure, 1974).

While the girls are primarily paying attention to the discussion, the boys are using it as a springboard for their own comments. They view the language arts class, like many other classes they attend, as a jumping-off point for a second circle of talk, interruption, and activity that includes the teacher and the girls but is not a class discussion. The boys have a routine down pat; they take turns playing straight man and comic, feeding each other lines and answering cues.

In our society boys have a different hierarchy of motives than girls. In school, control and power are more often ascendant motives for boys, while the wish to be accepted and evaluated positively by the teacher is more often ascendant for girls. In order to assess the extent of their power, boys may test limits with the teacher and their peers. Girls, on the other hand, concentrate on gaining approval. Since boys do not want to appear weak and dependent (which would make them seem less powerful), they put on a facade. Both boys and girls want to avoid failure and the appearance of incompetence because it implies weakness and potential rejection by parent and teacher. But the former threat—weakness—seems to be more salient for boys, the latter—rejection—more salient for girls. In general, sex differences in motives involve the relative position of similar motives, rather than one sex having a motive that the other lacks.

Individual Variations in Motivation

Naturally, there is variation in the hierarchy of motives of boys and girls. Some boys want the teacher's acceptance; some girls want to have power over their peers. Compare two classmates: Carl lives with foster parents he dislikes and depends on his friends at school for a sense of belonging, since he feels out of place at home. Because he is gratifying hostility toward his foster parents by performing poorly, a motive for mastery needs to be encouraged in other ways. To improve his performance, he has to have a good reason. The teacher can help here by investigating his interests and trying to tie some of the schoolwork to a particular hobby.

Peter, the only child of older parents, usually turns toward the teacher because he is accustomed to relating to adults. But this year, in a new school, he is attempting to break into the boys' inner circle and, hence, wants to be accepted by them. The teacher may be able to find a group project that depends on one of Peter's skills so that the boys may elect him as its project director.

Children share common attitudes concerning the sex role of the teacher. In the United States girls usually excel over boys in early reading progress. The predominance of female teachers in the primary grades may lead boys to view schoolwork as feminine. In West Germany, where male teachers predominate, boys are superior to girls in reading achievement (Preston, 1962). The tradition that views the teaching of young children as a woman's job is changing. The increase in male teachers in the early elementary grades provides male role models for boys, increases the probability that they will perceive similarities between themselves and the teacher, and, therefore, makes it more likely that they will be more motivated to do well in school.

Sex Typing of School Material

As we saw in Chapter 2, schoolwork itself is subject to sex typing. A long academic tradition contends that some school materials are viewed as masculine, others as feminine. (In ancient Greece the Pythagorean school regarded *even* numbers as feminine, pertaining to the earthly, and *odd* numbers as masculine, relating to the celestial [Zaslavsky, 1973]). Children tend to react differently to so-called masculine and feminine subjects. In a study of sixth-grade students some tests were introduced as "tests to tell how good you would be at girls' subjects, like home economics," some as "tests to show how good you would be at subjects that both boys and girls do equally well, like band music," and some as "tests to tell how good you might be at boys' subjects, like shop or industrial arts." The boys scored highest on the masculine tests and lowest on the feminine tests; the girls' scores were noticeably lower on the masculine tests than on the feminine ones (Stein, Pohly, and Mueller, 1971). Mathematics and science are generally regarded as "boys' subjects" by both boys and girls, which may be a reason girls feel less compelled to perform well in these areas, while literature and languages are regarded as "feminine" by boys, who may be less strongly motivated to perform well in these subjects.

Changes in Adolescence

Much of this book has concentrated on children in elementary school; educators believe that if children can master the initial requirements of school, many problems that arise during high school can be prevented. Moreover, more is known about the problems of younger children. We have less certain knowledge of the adolescent, who is an evasive subject; and the values, expectancies, motives, and fears that dominate adolescence are more difficult to measure.

Several important differences distinguish high-school students from primary-grade children. The high-school student possesses all the functions of the executive and potentially, at least, has the cognitive capability to learn what is required. The few children who may have begun school with serious cognitive deficiencies have probably been detected during elementary school and do not attend the typical high school. But the content of high-school subjects depends more on prior knowledge than do the skills taught in the primary grades, so that a student who has deficiencies in specific areas of mastery—such as algebra or history—faces special difficulty.

The high-school student, with over eight years of school experience, has crystallized his perception of his abilities and, as a result, has a less alterable expectation of success or failure than does a younger pupil, who is just being exposed to school demands.

Peer-group values influence the adolescent more powerfully than they do the younger child. Eight-year-olds relate primarily to their parents and teachers, seeking their acceptance. Adolescents relate primarily to their peers; peer acceptance carries more weight than teacher approval and, for some, matters more than family opinion. Values of the older child's peer group are often the most important determinant of his behavior both in and out of school. If the peer group values academic competence, the adolescent feels free to invest effort in schoolwork. But if it does not, and the youth does not want to be alienated from his peers, the conflict may induce him to alter his hierarchy of motives.

A Different Set of Motives

Finally, when the adolescent does invest effort in school, it is for different reasons than those that propel primary-grade children. Younger children do not always understand why they are being asked to learn addition, reading, or writing. But they take on faith the importance of these tasks that seem so arbitrary because adults they admire and depend on insist that these skills are valuable. As one seven-year-old said, "You go to school because your parents tell you to, and so you won't be dumb." Motivations for parental acceptance, identification, and inherent mastery sustain effort during the elementary-school years.

But the adolescent does not take the adult's word. Instead, she demands to know the connection between schoolwork and her personal agenda. She needs to have a concrete reason for investing effort. To be sure, society supplies her with one outstanding pragmatic reason: academic mastery will enable her to enter college and therefore choose a vocational role that she wants. Even for those who are not headed for college, education is supposed to make it easier to find a good job. For adolescents who are strongly motivated to attend college or are enthusiastic about a specific vocational role, and who can see the connection between their own goals and school assignments, motivation will be high.

But many adolescents, perhaps most, have not placed a specific job or college attendance at the top of their motivational hierarchy. Nor can the school rely on the desire for teacher acceptance or on identification with teachers as ascendant motives in adolescence. In short, the dominant motives of fifteen- and sixteen-year-olds are not closely tied to school mastery. What, then, occupies their attention? Adolescents in contemporary America apparently are preoccupied with three concerns. First, they are trying to match their behavior to the standards of independence and autonomy promoted by the society. They would like to regard themselves as independent of their families and free from the need of praise and support from adults. Obviously, this concern is incompatible with school progress, since the school situation places adolescents in a dependent posture.

Second, they are trying to match their behavior to a standard of a mature sex role. Therefore, they need to invest effort in general social relationships and in establishing heterosexual bonds in order to meet the standards for masculinity and femininity learned since they were young children. Again, these preoccupations and the behaviors initiated to gratify them are not compatible with academic work.

Third, they are attempting to bring conflicting beliefs and behavior into balance. This is perhaps the central motive of adolescents in America. You will recall from our discussion in Chapter 3 that when adolescents reach the stage of formal operations, they discover the

"It just so happens that all my heroes are anti-heroes."

ability to detect inconsistencies in their beliefs and feel compelled to resolve them. A young child does not recognize the logical incompatibility of believing that her father is a wonderful person who also loses his temper irrationally. But as an adolescent, she will recognize the incompatibility between those two qualities and try to resolve it: she may excuse her father's temper, or else devalue her earlier respect for him.

Dissonance in America

Americans confront a special note of dissonance, deriving from the long period of transition between childhood and adulthood. Adolescents in many parts of the world are exempt from this problem. In rural nonmodern villages, young children have few serious responsibilities, and life seems to proceed with little uncertainty. Then, at about age ten or eleven, they begin to participate in the work of the family in order to prepare for adulthood. This apprenticeship lasts for about half a dozen years, until marriage, but during this period adolescents perform adult jobs and understand clearly why they are investing their energy in planting crops, breeding livestock, irrigating fields, caring for infants, and cooking. In modern countries, however, the transitional period between childhood and adulthood is longer and is dominated by activities that do not resemble adult work. American adolescents are in a psychologically frustrating position. They want to be adults because they perceive adults as having more freedom, power, competence, independence, and pleasure (a perception that, though partly distortion, is universal in all cultures). Childhood is characterized by a lack of power, freedom, and competence. The adolescent would prefer to dissociate himself from that dependent and powerless role. Recognizing, at puberty, that he or she is reproductively fertile is like a punctuation mark that signals an "end" to childhood. But although the thirteen- or fourteen-year-old is no longer a child, he is clearly not yet an adult; he knows he will not acquire adult attributes—financial independence, marriage, and family—for at least another decade.

The situation is exacerbated because at the same time that adolescents want to rush to adulthood, they are asked to invest effort in activities that do not seem characteristic of adult life. Examinations, term papers, fire drills, assemblies, class plays, and yearbooks are not what adults do. A small proportion of adolescents realize that although these activities do not have the flavor of adulthood, they are proper preparation. But many do not appreciate this fact. Instead, their ascendant motives are desire for independence, sexuality, power, and friendships, not term papers on the Civil War. The harsh incompatibility between the new conception of one's self as someone on the brink of adulthood and the daily activities that seem more appropriate for children produces psychological tension.

A century ago the majority of children left school at adolescence and entered the world of work. Only a small proportion of youths, usually from more affluent families, continued in school, and they recognized that school was a relevant preparation for adulthood. It is a historical precedent to have over ninety percent of our youth between thirteen and seventeen years of age enrolled in school and engaged in activities only remotely tied to the adult world.

Design for School Change

It seems reasonable that changes in school practices that would relate school to the adult world might increase the motivation of many adolescents and help resolve some of their uncertainty over their ambiguous position—caught between the worlds of the child and the adult and unable to be in either.

First, the school might institutionalize activities that allow adolescents to participate in the adult world. Most day-care centers, for example, could use extra help, for few can afford to hire all the personnel they need. Most primary-grade teachers would welcome high-school students to tutor children who are having a difficult time learning to read or do arithmetic. Elderly widows and widowers who sit alone in nursing homes are often despondent and hungry for some variety in their lives. They would appreciate contact with adolescents who might read to them, put on plays, or teach them a new skill:

A fifteen-year-old girl writes poignantly of the conflict between independence and uncertainty.

> Parents of adolescents must be as clever and perceptive as possible. It is their responsibility to decide whether the child is mature enough to carry through with what he wants to do, that is, whether or not to let him do things like going out alone, staying out late, and travelling alone. If they let him do anything without question, he could easily feel abandoned and that nobody gives a damn. From there, he could feel that growing up was too much for him to handle, that it was just not worth all the trouble.... Parents should support by being willing listeners and not trying to measure the adolescent by their own values....
>
> Much of the confusion between me and my parents comes when I make ridiculous demands on them and they are personally offended. I am not aware of the ridiculousness of my demands nor of the seriousness with which they are received. My demand is unsure, backed up by shaky, unfamiliar emotions. If the emotion in my parents is motivated by a feeling that they are threatened, and they take my demand too seriously, I am thrown off balance. Furthermore, if my parents' reaction is irrational, I may wonder whether there is a tremendous lack in me which produced the demand that threatened them so. Parents have more control over their overreactions than children, and parents should guard against losing perspective. (deVaron, 1972, pp. 337–48)

phrases in a foreign language, perhaps, or handicrafts. Some industries and businesses could accept a few participant-observers. The local newspaper might be willing to take several adolescents for a day or a week to learn how newspapers work. A school might set aside one day each week to permit interested adolescents to participate in outside activities. The youth would benefit and so would the larger society.

Within the school salutary changes could be initiated. Opportunities for adolescents to be more independent and autonomous would allow them to practice behaviors that they know are characteristic of adults. They should participate in some decisions regarding the curriculum, as well as in some form of self-government. Without giving total sovereignty to the students, teachers could share power with them.

It must be remembered that although the adolescent may call for more power, independence, and autonomy, he is still uncertain of his ability to cope with those prizes. Secretly he wants to be restrained a little. The adolescent is testing adults to see if they have any faith in his capacity to assume some of the attitudes and the responsibilities of adulthood. Therefore, the schools should give some rope to the adolescent, but it would be poor practice to let go of the tether completely. The adolescent wants to know that if he oversteps his capacity to handle freedom responsibly, there will be an adult present to intervene and prevent him from hurting himself and others.

Adolescents recognize how important it is to develop competences in order to dispel the uncertainty and anxiety that characterize these years. Recall that the affect joy occurs when a skill is mastered. The school's primary task is to create optimal conditions for children and adolescents to develop new talents and to perfect old ones. The act of mastery itself, highly engrossing, routs uncertainty and anxiety from the forefront of consciousness. Perfected talents help to articulate each adolescent's perception of self, persuading him that his external profile has moved just a little closer to that of the adult.

High-school teachers, like those in primary grades, should try to have every student participate in at least one activity that uses and perfects his best talents. Artistic and athletic activities within each classroom, as well as in the school as a whole, could be initiated if schedules were made more flexible. Perhaps every class might prepare its own yearbook, photography display, or class play. Obviously, a school with a small number of students, say five hundred, can make adjustments such as these more easily than a large urban or regional high school of several thousand students. In the smaller school more student participation is possible (Barker and Gump, 1964) because fewer candidates compete for each role. In a large school where there are too few institutional activities for the number of students, teacher ingenuity is needed.

Implications for Teaching

A teacher can influence a child's motivation in many ways. Ironically, several effective teacher characteristics cannot be controlled: ethnicity, sex, and, to some degree, personality are givens that do not change. If the teacher is a white woman, children will react differently than they would if the teacher was a black man. However, one influential aspect of a teacher's personality can be governed, and that is his or her own degree of satisfaction and sense of well-being. There are strong indications that this quality contributes even more to a teacher's effectiveness as a model than sex or ethnicity. And teachers can consciously arrange their classrooms and their actions with students to increase their motivation and skills.

Ascertain Each Child's Hierarchy of Motives

Teachers should get to know their students well enough that they can identify the hierarchy of motives each one carries through the school day. One child needs to be in the limelight of the teacher's attention;

another prefers to work alone but thrives when she can master a new topic. A third wants to be the leader of a small group, controlling not only his progress but that of his classmates as well. A fourth is stimulated by any new idea but is reluctant to work on it for very long.

It helps to use each child's special goals to motivate him in school, permitting him the goal he wants as a reward for effort and good performance. Put the child who likes the limelight in the front row if he gets a good test score in math (but not as a punishment if he misbehaves, because then he is getting what he wants—the limelight—for behavior that is counterproductive to learning mathematics). Give the second child enough space and time to pursue her own course toward solving the problem. Allow the third child a chance to direct a small group in some activity as a prize for a good week's work. Have the fourth child think up a project for the next day's science class—but also encourage her to plan the entire project (by listing the necessary materials and drawing up a set of objectives) so that she will learn to follow through her initial interest.

You may prefer to ignore hostility. Some hostility will be present in any classroom, even if it is not directed at you. Nevertheless, hostility is probably not a motive you want to fan into a fire in a child. To channel it quietly is preferable. If you suspect that a student is gratifying hostility to his parents by performing less well than he can (the child who is sending the message, "I can do better, but I will not!"), you may be able to overcome his determination to fail by arousing other motives in his hierarchy, perhaps an urge to master a new, untried area, such as high-school computer mathematics, or a desire for status in the student body.

Design Productive Incentives and Rewards

Some school material is naturally exciting. Most high-school students, for instance, are stirred by the first sight of a laboratory desk equipped with beakers, bunsen burner, and jars of chemicals, and kindergarten children are intrigued when they first encounter a set of colored cubes and a tray with graduated squares from one to ten. The rewards of working with these materials—at least the first few times—are intrinsic and immediate.

But a great deal of school material lacks the initial excitement of beakers or cubes, even though it is necessary and may lead to more advanced and interesting studies. Therefore, the teacher is challenged to think up incentives and rewards, using some appropriate balance between the carrot that entices and the stick that prods. A child's motive to win the teacher's praise and approval can be gratified in many possible ways—smiles, encouraging comments, stickers on papers, and good grades. In junior high and high school appeals to the student's motive for status or power can be productive. Art exhibits, science prizes, public reports at monthly current events sessions, stories in the newspaper or literary journal, exhibitions displayed in hallway showcases, are examples of rewards that can gratify a motive for status and resolve uncertainty over the developing concept of self. Incentives and rewards that are pleasantly toned are preferable to negative threats, although sometimes they, too, are necessary. (This will be discussed further in Chapter 11, "Classroom Atmosphere and Management.")

Each child, like each adult, wants to think that he is especially competent or talented in some area. As long as the teacher emphasizes the importance of only one or two skills in primary grades (they are typically reading and arithmetic), only a proportion of the children will be able to experience success and build up their expectancy of future victories. Those who enter school less well prepared for those subjects are going to experience failure in the beginning. Because they will always be comparing their ability and scores with the good pupils, they may grow to believe they will fail. Therefore, the teacher should try to encourage a wide variety of talents—music, art, bodily coordination, singing, acting. This is expecially important in the primary grades, when a child's expectancies are not yet firm and his beliefs are more malleable.

Ideally, each child should have at least one activity for which his level of talent places him in the top third of the class—among the ten or so best pupils in his room. Such a success buffers the distress he may feel if he is in the bottom third in reading or arithmetic. The teacher should try to find each child's special talent and promote it.

A child's belief in his talent is relative to the group he takes as his referent. Hence, one strategy is to create work groups of five or six

There are different ways that children's feelings can be touched to help them learn. In *Spinster* (1958), novelist and teacher Sylvia Ashton-Warner describes working with Maori children in New Zealand. To help them read, she made up key vocabularies for each child and wrote the words on cards.

> Ghost . . . kiss; captions of the instincts. There must be many more words like this, analogous to these two; captions of other instincts, other desires, resentments, horrors and passions. (p. 163)
>
> I print these words on separate cards and give them to him. And Rangi, who lives on love and kisses and thrashings and fights and fear of the police, and who took four months to learn "come, look, and" takes four minutes to learn:
>
> | | |
> |---|---|
> | butcher knife | Daddy |
> | gaol | Mummy |
> | police | Rangi |
> | sing | fight |
> | cry | kiss |
>
> So I make a reading card for him; out of these words, which he reads at first sight, his first reading, and his face lights up with understanding. And from here he goes on to other reading. His mind is unlocked, some great fear is discharged, he understands at last and he can read. (p. 177)

When a child did not know a word on one of his cards the next day, she did not scold the child—she ripped up the card, saying that the word couldn't have been very important to him or he wouldn't have forgotten. The words vary from place to place, but the idea holds: some words are evocative for children, and the words that ring like gongs are the ones we can use to entice children to read.

children. If a child compares himself to others in a *small* group, he is more likely to think he is competent than if he takes the whole class as his frame of reference.

The more each child shares actively in the "prizes" that a school values, the more vital and ascendant his motive for mastery will be. Organizing children into small groups, in which they can take turns displaying various strengths and stating ideas, is another way of saying, "Let's not always see the same hands."

Tailor Individual Programs

By designing assignments that are individualized to the child, teachers can reduce the intense aura of competition that persists in many classrooms. Individualized instruction emphasizes each particular child's progress. She compares her capabilities now to what they used to be. Every child can benefit from noticing her advances in her own rear-view mirror: seeing the ground she has already covered compared to where she started. Programs that explicitly allow her to chart her progress can amplify her motive for mastery instead of thwarting it.

Linking Schoolwork with Familiar Realities

As one psychologist points out, *interesse,* the Latin source for our word *interest,* means "to be between" (Kolesnik, 1963). Often a child believes that there is no connection between the familiar realities of her own life and the material that she meets in books at school. One way that a teacher can stimulate the child's interest in the material is to encourage her to bring it into register with what she knows, pointing out that the child herself is between the familiar and the new, making explicit the links between schoolwork and the child's world.

In one example a child in a fifth-grade social studies class reads about the early explorers in North America. She is mildly interested: it is an adventure story and she knows it is part of her own country's history, ancient though it seems. However, her interest jumps when the teacher asks her to think of influences from these explorers and colonialists that continue to this day. She realizes that the name "Amsterdam Avenue" in New York City, the English language she speaks, French bread, and the pumpkin pie she eats every Thanksgiving are directly related to the earlier actions of the people she is reading about.

Direct Instruction to Each Child's Level

One of the main implications of this chapter is the significance of diagnosing each child's level of competency in each subject area and prescribing assignments accordingly. For example, the teacher can use a pretest to analyze how well a child can multiply and then assign work sheets that give him a chance to practice on problems that are a little more difficult than the ones he can do easily. After he appears to have learned the new material in multiplication, the teacher administers a posttest (see Figure 7–3). If the child shows he has mastered the assignments, he proceeds to a more advanced level of work.

Even in a classroom where such systematized individual instruction is not possible, the teacher can make an effort to determine the ability level of each pupil in each subject area and assign tasks that will pique his curiosity and challenge his ability, without being too difficult or so far removed from what he knows that he regards them as impossible.

Collaborate with the Child on Setting Goals

There is value in giving the child a hand in choosing her own schoolwork. This encourages her interest in the work by appealing to her motive for control. In most schools children believe that the course of study is set up before they arrive in September. Enlisting children in the process of deciding what topics are to be studied and what procedures are to be followed is likely to increase their interest and help persuade them that their success can be a product of their own efforts.

The same principle applies to setting goals. There are a number of ways teachers can encourage children to play a part in determining what they are going to accomplish. A tenth-grade teacher holds a group meeting, where a small number of students decide on the plan of action for studying the neighborhood for a social studies course. Each Friday a fourth-grade teacher sets up a system of individual contracts between herself and each child that outlines what the child will accomplish during the following week.

Since success leads children toward establishing more challenging as well as more realistic goals, whereas failure usually leads them to set goals that are too conservative (as a defense) or unrealistically ambitious, setting goals that can be realized leads to more successes in the future. In addition, this process encourages pupils to think that they have some control over what occurs in the class, instead of believing that they act solely on the teacher's sufferance.

Figure 7–3
One kind of individualized instruction is based on pretests and posttests. First, a child takes a pretest to determine his level of ability. Next, the teacher assigns work that is a little more difficult than what he already can do. She gives him a chance to practice with exercises (in this case, multiplication problems), providing help if he needs it. Finally, the child takes a posttest measuring his mastery of the new material.

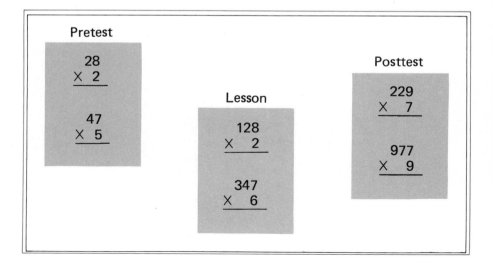

Reduce Student Anxiety

Too often, the teacher sees her function as teaching facts. Actually, this objective is less important than convincing the child that when she is faced with a difficult problem, she can call upon her knowledge and certain strategies to begin the work. Anxiety, based on the fear that the child will not be able to solve a problem—or even know how to begin it—is a persistent handicap to learning. Sometimes simply familiarizing students with the materials they will use and the people they will be with reduces wariness and buffers fear. A study with preschoolers showed that spending time with new games and new teachers, without even practicing with the games, improved their performance, whereas children who had no preliminary play period performed less well (Zigler, Abelson, and Seitz, 1973).

Since anxiety can lead a child to withdraw from a problem, it is often helpful to give a child more than one task to work on at a time. Then, if he is overwhelmed by one assignment, he can abandon it—for the moment—and turn to another that seems less forbidding. By dealing adequately with the second task, he may gain the composure and confidence to return to the first problem.

Generate Mild Uncertainty

While reducing undue anxiety is one goal, sometimes the teacher should create constructive uncertainty. Some years ago, at the

In one middle western elementary school, students rely on the daily newspaper, rather than textbooks, for most of their classes. First-graders read the headlines, older students learn mathematical skills by adding football won-lost columns or averaging bets at the race track. A story about how bail is used to reduce jail crowding leads to an exercise: "Jail and bail—how many new words can you make by changing the initial consonant?" Students also play the stock market, learn geography from weather maps, and write essays on the meanings of editorial cartoons. In the first year of the program, the principal says, the students—many who come from poor families in this industrial city—averaged a year's extra growth in most categories ("Education: Learn All About It," 1974). Why?

A combination of factors—probably all motivational rather than cognitive—are likely to be contributing to the students' increased interest in schoolwork and, almost inevitably, better performance. Newspapers provide information that is both local and topical, and "today's news" imparts an aura of immediacy and relevance that textbooks cannot achieve; the news is also spicier than the stories in most texts. There is no question that the newspapers were a good idea, but the Hawthorne effect may also be operating—a refreshing change in classroom practice usually leads to increased attention and better performance because it recruits the students' attention.

Hawthorne plant of Western Electric, researchers measured the rate of worker productivity, then increased the illumination in the plant, and measured again, discovering that worker productivity had risen (Roethlisberger and Dickson, 1939). Unfortunately, they had not used a control group. Later, the study was tried again with a control group who was told the lighting would be increased (though in fact, it was not). This time the productivity increased in both groups, although the lighting actually changed in only one. In a third study the lighting was decreased and still production increased. The "Hawthorne effect" has become the name for an effect achieved merely by a change in circumstances. The source of change in these cases was probably the unexpected attention paid to the workers rather than the specific nature of the change (altering the light).

Most teachers discover that the classroom is invigorated if the environment is changed from time to time so that the children are a little unsettled and not quite sure of their positions in the class. Mild uncertainty vitalizes the need to know oneself as well as the motive to predict the future. Some teachers use this principle when they grade a bright child a little lower than she deserves. Others claim that the main advantage of altering curriculum, changing readers, or having the children switch seats from month to month is that it stirs things up. Faced with the task of resolving new though gentle uncertainties, the children tend to draw on reserves of perseverence and curiosity that they may not otherwise use.

Summary

In addition to cognitive units and processes, several affective factors—motivation, fear of making an error, and expectancy of success—form a web of influence that helps to determine a child's performance in school.

A motive, as defined in Chapter 6, is an idea (often unconscious) that represents a state that the person wishes to experience. Motives exist in a hierarchy; although the most essential ones (the needs for food, shelter, warmth, and safety) are ascendant for everyone, others vary in ascendancy from person to person. Each person possesses many motives. The six basic motives that function in the classroom are: (1) the desire for the teacher's approval, (2) the desire to be similar to the teacher, (3) the desire for mastery, (4) the desire to resolve uncertainty, (5) the desire for control, power, and status, and (6) the desire to gratify hostility.

A child's expectancy of success also strongly affects his school performance. Children who expect to do well tend to perform better than the children who do not expect to succeed. On another dimension, there are children who take personal blame for failure; they are called internalizers. Pupils who blame their failures on forces outside their control, such as bad luck or unfriendly teachers, are called externalizers. Internalizers tend to perform better than externalizers.

The same motives are not ascendant in all children. Differences in the hierarchy of motives distinguish boys from girls, children from adolescents, and one individual from another. Teachers can use their awareness of the motives functioning in school and the role played by expectancy to help children to learn. They can ascertain each child's hierarchy of motives, design productive incentives and rewards, tailor individual programs, direct instruction carefully to each child's level, collaborate with the child on setting goals, reduce student anxiety, and generate mild uncertainty.

Projects

1 You are an English teacher in an urban secondary school, and one of your male students has shown a talent for writing. Achievement is low in his hierarchy of motives; the desire to be recognized as a leader is high. How will you cultivate the student's talent for writing?

2 Examine a high-school home economics text to see whether it promotes sex-role stereotyping. If it does, how may it be revised so that it will motivate male students to study home economics? List five ways in which this may be accomplished.

3 Team up with a classmate. One of you visits an open third-grade classroom; the other a traditional third-grade classroom. Compare and assess how each classroom accommodates to the motives of schoolchildren.

4 Compose a letter to a former teacher in whose course you did not achieve as you had expected, suggesting what he or she might have done to motivate you to do better work.

5 A junior-high-school teacher gave his boys' class of poor readers copies of a sex, blood, and thunder paperback to read out loud in small groups and found that their interest in the story was an incentive for them to read better. Next, he gave them copies of D. H. Lawrence's novel *Women in Love* in which key passages were marked. Using the same technique to increase student interest, devise a plan for a class in (1) third-grade social studies, (2) fifth-grade history, and (3) seventh-grade geography.

6 What steps can a third-grade teacher take to reduce the pupils' ascendant motive to gain her approval and strengthen their motive for mastery?

7 With seven classmates, role-play this situation: you are a search committee composed of three parents, the school superintendent, the school principal, and three teachers. You are charged with hiring a first-grade teacher to fill a vacancy in your urban school. The first grade is composed of ten black, six Hispanic, four Chinese, and four Caucasian children. These roles are defined:

(a) The superintendent, knowing the fiscal concerns of the school committee, is interested in hiring a relatively inexperienced teacher, since his or her starting salary will be lower than that of an experienced teacher.

(b) The principal is concerned with the academic credentials of the candidates. His school has a reputation for having a well-trained faculty.

(c) A second-grade teacher on the committee has been dissatisfied with the achievement level of the pupils who have come from the first grade in the past two years.

The other five roles may be defined by the people playing them. The task is to discuss and decide what kind of candidate will be most acceptable.

Recommended Reading

Barker, R. G., and Gump, P. V. *Big school, small school.* Stanford, Calif.: Stanford University Press, 1964. Summarizes a research project showing that children who attend a small high school tend to participate more in school activities and feel more involved and less alienated than those who attend a large high school.

Rosenthal, R., and Jacobson, L. *Pygmalion in the classroom.* New York: Holt, Rinehart and Winston, 1968. A description of a research project showing how teacher expectations for children may influence their intellectual performance.

Watson, J. D. *The double helix: A personal account of the discovery of the structure of DNA.* New York: Atheneum, 1969. An exciting description of the competitiveness, the expectancies, and the motivation that surround the winning of a Nobel Prize.

the child in school
three

intelligence and intelligence tests

8

All societies tend to place a high value on certain sets of skills, behaviors, feelings, and thoughts, while devaluing others. The Bushmen of the Kalahari Desert require superior hunting skill of their adult males. South Pacific islanders require outstanding navigational skill. Other societies value physical endurance or the ability to survive for a long time without water. The choice depends on such factors as the society's requirements for defense against enemies, its form of economy, and the density and the composition of its population.

Even societies that need and value mental talents do not always prize the same profile of competences. The prerevolutionary Chinese valued mastery of the written form of their language; the Sophists of Athens, mastery of oratorical skill. The Indians of modern Guatemala value both mental alertness to opportunity and physical strength and vitality required for working hard in the fields. A great deal of variation exists, then, in the traits that are valued and promoted, whether they are mental, physical, or emotional. For reasons that are partly historical, modern America has come to emphasize intellectual abilities over emotional and physical qualities. Let us consider some reasons for this emphasis on "intellectual talent."

The Basis for American Emphasis on Intelligence

Technology. As a society becomes increasingly technological, it needs more adults who can understand, manage, and master its machines, mathematics, and scientific laboratories, as well as its treatises and practices of medicine and law. All these domains require primarily intellectual skills. Since the smooth functioning of society depends on these vocations, adults who demonstrate the appropriate talents are likely to be given positions of status, wealth, and dignity. Moreover, a technological society creates institutions to foster intellectual talents and tries to select intellectually proficient youth who can be guided into the necessary vocational roles after a proper education. But the current emphasis on molding intelligent children is a relatively new historical development. It may come as a surprise to learn that many nineteenth-century Europeans regarded an intellectually precocious child as ill, and experts advised parents to take precautions if their child appeared too studious. They were to take his books away from him and offer diversions so that his brain would not become inflamed (Chavasse, 1869).

Egalitarianism. Our desire to create a society in which all citizens are of equal value and dignity is another reason the United States stresses intellectual ability. While we are striving to reach that difficult goal, it is important that we judge people according to personal accomplishment and not on the basis of sex, ethnicity, religion, or socioeconomic status. In an egalitarian society all should have the opportunity to improve their economic and social positions. Hence, we prefer to award wealth, power, and status to those who demonstrate a will to improve their talents. We like to believe that, theoretically, any child can be president, senator, surgeon, or Nobel laureate.

This belief is buttressed by our knowledge that children who are highly motivated to improve their intellectual skills will attain better grades and be more proficient in school and college, and that a family that encourages intellectual growth will, probably, produce children who are more capable. Moreover, many Americans have been friendly to the idea that experience, rather than heredity, is a major determinant of intelligence—an idea that goes back to John Locke. This means that, potentially, most citizens can attain the intellectual skills necessary to function in the society and few are disqualified by their biology. This belief is central to an egalitarian society, although difficult to prove scientifically.

Fairness. Americans want to believe that even though some citizens will eventually have more wealth, status, and power than others—a fact that disturbs our egalitarian ethic—the unequal distribution should be as fair as possible. It is important to us that just choices are made about who shall have access to privilege and resources. Although many people in our society would like to promote those who are honest, cooperative, and humanitarian to positions of responsibility, unfortunately it is difficult to measure these traits objectively and fairly. Since our society has developed objective tests for assessing intellectual qualities, the decision to use intelligence as a basis for awarding privilege seems fair to the majority of citizens.

Preference for abstract qualities. Finally, America, like most countries in the western hemisphere, tends to view people in terms of abstract qualities that are not highly dependent on specific situations. Many of the adjectives we use to describe people are general; they are words such as *extrovert, honest, moral, hostile,* and *intelligent.* We do not have different words that take into account the particular context in which the person is honest or angry. The cultures of the East—China and Japan specifically—take quite another view. Their words for describing human qualities and actions usually vary according to the specific situation in which the person is acting. Thus, if an adolescent is disobedient to his father, a different set of words is used than if he is disobedient to a stranger. We have only one word—*disobedient.* Our word *intelligent* implies a general ability to show mental talent and skill in all situations at all times and hence is in accord with the other terms we use to describe human behavior and qualities. As we shall see later, however, there is no guarantee that such a general mental ability exists, and our semantics may be forcing people into a mold that nature did not intend.

For many reasons, then, Americans and Western Europeans have made intelligence a central human characteristic. We need intellectually proficient people to run a complicated and technological society. We would like to believe that most children have the potential

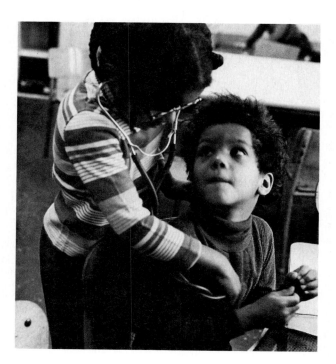

ability to become technically skilled if they work hard and their parents provide them with the proper early encouragement and experience. In a society concerned with fairness and justice we feel more confident about our ability to detect, with some precision, those children who have intellectual ability than we do about detecting children who may have other traits we admire, such as honesty, sincerity, and responsibility. Finally, we would like to believe that people possess general qualities that cut across a variety of situations, rather than a set of more specific talents that apply to particular contexts.

These are only some of the reasons the concept of intelligence has become so important in American society and is such a popular explanation for the obvious differences in "success" among adults. Intelligence—not endurance, obedience, physical attractiveness, hunting skill, or athletic prowess—is the quality American parents believe they and their children must have in order to attain a happy and successful life.

Five American Assumptions about Intelligence

In America the conventional attitudes about intelligence rest on five assumptions:

1 Intelligence is a generalized ability to learn new things quickly, to solve different kinds of problems efficiently, and to adapt to unfamiliar situations with flexibility and skill. Intelligence is viewed as a generalized coping ability.
2 A person with intelligence, as defined above, is likely to attain more wealth and status—our most popular definition of success—than one with less intelligence. Hence, if someone is not successful, low intelligence is a possible explanation. Some people consider it the most likely explanation.
3 Adequate intelligence permits a child to profit from proper family treatment, environmental opportunity, and good schooling. If a child works hard in school, has parents who encourage him, and has basically adequate intelligence, he should succeed.
4 Differences in basic intelligence are partly due to differential heredity. A person's intelligence must be related to the integrity of the neurons and the biochemistry of his brain. Since genes influence the anatomy and physiology of the brain, they must also influence intelligence.
5 I.Q. tests measure the "intelligence" referred to in assumptions one through four.

It is the last assumption—not the first four—that has created much of the current controversy about intelligence.

Scores on tests that measure various intellectual and academic abilities are used for two purposes. Most commonly, test scores are used to predict some relevant behavior. Thus, the score on a reading readiness test predicts how easily a child will learn to read, or the score on a French placement examination predicts how easily a high-school sophomore will learn advanced French. But notice that these scores are not used to *interpret* why a student attains a low or a high score in the future. Hence, a second use of tests is to obtain information that may *explain* why a person behaves or is performing in a certain way. A child who is retarded in speech is given a hearing test. If his score reveals that his hearing is defective, it is used to *explain* why he is retarded in speech, not to predict that he will remain speech deficient. Most educators agree that scores on academic achievement tests—for reading, arithmetic, or spelling—are not to be used to explain why a child does or does not do well in a school subject; they are only to be used to predict future achievement. There is one educational test, however, whose function is controversial, namely, the intelligence test. Some educators use the intelligence test score only as a tool for predicting school progress, and it serves that purpose well. But other educators and psychologists believe that it fills both functions; it not only predicts the child's future progress but also purports to explain why. A low I.Q. score is interpreted to mean that the child has low intelligence, and that characteristic is regarded as an explanation of poor school performance. The controversy over I.Q. tests centers directly on this issue; namely, is intelligence a characteristic of people—like deafness—that explains academic achievement and later

---

Scientific Concepts: Vital and Obsolete

Electron: "one of the constituent elementary particles of an atom being a charge of negative electricity equal to about 4.8027×10^{-10} electrostatic units . . ."

Phlogiston: "the hypothetical principle of fire or inflammability regarded by the early chemists as a material substance . . ."

There was a time when chemists believed that phlogiston was a substance separate from the material that was burning, but they no longer believe that today. The concept of the electron, however, is still accepted as valid. Some concepts remain vital and scientifically useful for a long time. Others become obsolete as new information underlines their liabilities. The concept of intelligence is defined today by many psychologists as a single-faceted general ability to make correct judgments in many areas and to learn new skills quickly. Currently it is the popular way of explaining differences in problem-solving among individuals. Will it have the future of *phlogiston* or *electron*?

success in life, or is the intelligence test score merely a way to predict school progress?

In contemporary America a good education has become the most important requirement for attaining a job with status, dignity, and financial rewards. Since the more intelligent the child, the better his grades in high school and the better his chances for being admitted into a good college, most Americans believe that high intelligence, as revealed in the I.Q. score, endows a child with the basic gift he needs to succeed.

Although many people believe that the quality "intelligence"—as discussed above—is best defined and measured by the score on an intelligence test, and educational decisions are made on the assumption of that equivalence, some psychologists question that assumption. It is useful, therefore, to probe more deeply the meaning of the word *intelligence*. We must address a number of questions. First of all, does it refer to something real? How should it be defined? Is intelligence measured accurately by intelligence tests? Is intelligence under hereditary control?

Although the word *intelligence* is used freely, it is defined quite differently both by laymen and by those who have spent their lives investigating this evasive quality. For example:

David Wechsler: "The capacity of an individual to understand the world about him and his resourcefulness to cope with its challenges" (1975, p. 139).
Jean Piaget: "Intelligence is an adaptation" (1952, p. 3).
Schoolchild: "It doesn't have anything to do with schoolwork, no matter what they say. It's common sense—knowing what's the best thing to do next."
Artist: "It means that you can learn new things fast."

Some words refer to things we can see, feel, or hear in the outside world. We can touch concrete objects such as a spear or a book, and we can see the neurons of the brain under a microscope. In these cases we think we know what objects the words refer to. But many words refer to abstract ideas—not concrete objects—words such as *spirit, happiness, magnetism,* or *electron.* Of course, people everywhere use abstract words to help them understand their world. In our society the words *optimism, fear, energy, alive, gravity,* and *love* stand for concepts that have been invented to describe and explain meaningful events in our lives. Intelligence is one of those abstract ideas.

Originally, the word *intelligence* came from two Latin words—*inter* ("between") and *legere* ("to choose or gather")—and meant "to choose between." Although there was always a fair range of disagreement as to its meaning, as intelligence tests became popular the word gradually came to be defined as what intelligence tests measure. Let us turn to these tests, see how they work, and decide what light they can throw on the concept of intelligence.

Intelligence Tests

Their History

Sir Francis Galton, who lived and worked in London in the late 1800s, was one of the first important investigators who tried to measure intelligence. He thought a person's intelligence should be reflected in his ability to react quickly in a simple situation (he called this *reaction time*) and in his possession of visual and auditory acuity. Galton constructed tests that measured speed of reaction and sensory acuity, thinking they measured intelligence. But as it turned out, these tests were not very good at predicting adult success in the society and soon lost favor. Galton was followed by an American named James McKeen Cattell, who believed that how fast a person could tap his finger on a table, how accurately he could judge time intervals of seconds or minutes, and how keenly he could hear and see reflected his basic intelligence. Although both of these tests revealed information about the functioning of the person's nervous system, they did not predict how well children would perform in school or how successful they would be in the larger society.

Soon after the turn of the century two Frenchmen, Alfred Binet and Theophilus Simon, persuaded the French Ministry of Education to let them develop some tests that would serve a particular purpose. The schools of Paris were overcrowded, and Binet and Simon believed they could devise a test that would identify the mentally retarded children who were unable to profit from normal school instruction and required special education. If these children could be diagnosed properly and distinguished from those who could perform well in school, the efficiency of educational instruction would be enhanced.

To do this, Binet and Simon picked tests that they thought represented the kind of intellectual activities that children engaged in during the school years—processes such as memory, perception, reasoning, and verbal ability. They assumed that a child who could not pass tests of these processes, in contrast to the majority of children who could, could not be expected to do schoolwork at a high level of performance and might be mentally retarded. They chose questions that dealt with memory, vocabulary, perceptual discrimination, and knowledge of numbers. They omitted questions that did not seem relevant to the subjects taught in school, such as physical coordination or artistic ability. This early test, therefore, was very practical and not very theoretical. The assignment Binet and Simon took was a little like the assignment given the psychologists who had to select the men who would be trained to be America's astronauts. The psychologists knew what skills and personal qualities were best suited for a flight to outer space, and they devised tests accordingly. They did not think they were inventing tests for some abstract quality of humans or for any theoretical concept. They were merely trying to decide, on an objective basis, which men would be the best candidates for taking a trip to the moon.

Questions were included in the original intelligence test only if they discriminated between children who were actually doing well in school and those who were failing. If a question was answered correctly by a seven-year-old who was doing well and incorrectly by one who was doing poorly, it qualified as a good item for the test. If all the children of a given age passed a specific question or if they all failed that question, it was discarded from the test at that age level because it did not help to differentiate good from poor pupils.

In one sense, this early intelligence test was a collection of questions tapping a child's alertness, acquired knowledge, motivation, and language skill—qualities a wise and experienced teacher may detect during the first year of school. An experienced teacher can tell if a six-year-old child has an adequate vocabulary, can draw circles and triangles, is attentive, can count, and can remember complex instructions. The intelligence test made what had been a subjective, informal, and unscientific judgment of the teacher into something objective, formal, and scientific.

Binet published his first test in 1905. In 1916 Lewis M. Terman, a psychologist at Stanford University, translated it into English and adapted it for American use. The test was revised and standardized in 1937, in 1960, and most recently in 1972. Since the Stanford-Binet

---

While intelligence tests had the appearance of being innovative and a fairer and more equitable way of distributing wealth, power, and status, they did not lead to many changes, for the children from high-status families obtained higher I.Q. scores and those in poverty obtained lower scores. As one psychologist has said:

Needless to say, the tests could not have been so accepted if the people in power at that time saw the tests as potentially destroying their children's power. But the I.Q. tests of that time had the rather happy property of being a conservative social innovation. They could be perceived as justifying the richness of the rich and the poverty of the poor; they legitimatized the existing social order. (White, 1975, p. 12)

Intelligence Test used today is similar to the one developed by Binet over seventy years ago, it is important to remember why it was created in the first place. The test was not devised to prove a theory about mental functioning or to see if an abstract entity called intelligence actually existed. Rather, the test was created for a specific, practical purpose—to determine which children could be expected to perform well and which poorly in French schools in 1905. But during the intervening seventy years, the intelligence test—and how well children do on it—has come to have a different, theoretical significance.

Two Kinds of Testing Systems

There are two fundamental ways to assign a human being a score on a particular quality or skill. One, less often used, establishes a level of performance as the criterion and measures how close to or far from the criterion each person comes. That is called a *criterion-referenced system*. For example, one may set a criterion of eight minutes (which would reflect adequate ability) as the time for running a mile. (Until recently, the record for running a mile was four minutes, although it has since been broken.) One would then assign scores based on different running times. The person who ran a mile in twenty minutes would be rated incompetent on this particular task; the person who ran the mile in eight minutes would be rated competent. The person's age, nationality, race, and physical condition would be disregarded. Running a mile in twenty minutes would be considered incompetent whether the runner was a six-year-old or a sixty-year-old. In a way, when we decide that a four-year-old who is not speaking, or a two-year-old who is not walking, is retarded, we are using implicit absolute criteria. We know that most children are speaking by age three and most walking by age two, regardless of where they live in the world.

We do not use such absolute criteria in assessing mental ability, although they might have been established. For example, suppose schools decided that every person should have an active vocabulary of one hundred thousand words. Then each child, adolescent, and adult would be given a score based on the degree to which he fell below or above the fixed figure of one hundred thousand.

Instead, the scores assigned each individual are relative to those obtained by children of the same age who are taking the test. This is called a *norm-referenced system*. Our intelligence tests measure knowledge of vocabulary, reasoning with words, factual information, memory for numbers, and ability to solve puzzles and analyze pictures. The correct answers are totaled, and a child's final intelligence quotient

Figure 8–1
The distribution of I.Q. scores for the population used in standardizing the Stanford-Binet approximates a bell-shaped curve. The center of the curve is at 100, and the distribution of scores falls almost equally above and below 100. (Adapted from Terman and Merrill, 1937)

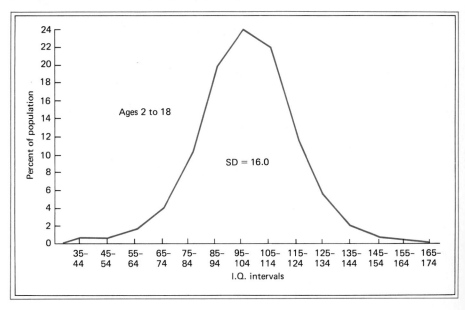

(I.Q.) is determined by how well he performed in comparison with the performances of other children his age in his society.

In order to standardize the I.Q. test, creators of the modern I.Q. tests first established sample populations of children at various ages, administered the items of the intelligence tests, and arranged the scores so that they resembled a bell-shaped curve (see Figure 8–1). Then they made up scoring instructions for the test items so that there would be the same average score *at each age*. The performance of the average eight-year-old is given an I.Q. of 100; that of the average nine-year-old an I.Q. of 100, and that of the average ten-year-old an I.Q. of 100—even though the ten-year-old *answers more questions* than the eight-year-old. Thus, equal I.Q. scores do not mean equal intellectual ability. They simply mean that all three children have the same relative intellectual ability when compared with other children their age. All the possible scores for all ages are given in a numerical table. The examiner can find the child's I.Q. by knowing the child's age and the number of questions he answered correctly.

If a child has an I.Q. score of 100, then about 50 percent of the children in her age group will have a higher score than she, and about 50 percent will have a lower score. If she has an I.Q. of 126, 94 percent of the children her age will have a lower I.Q., and 6 percent will have a higher I.Q. A score of 64 will be higher than about 1 percent of the children her age and lower than approximately 99 percent of the children in her age group.

How Intelligence Tests Work

Almost all intelligence tests are administered individually—the child sits alone with a trained examiner who gives a series of test items. Similar tests are sometimes administered to a group of children simultaneously. These are usually called *mental ability tests*. However, children who attain high scores on the individually administered intelligence test almost always get a high score on the group-administered mental ability test. Hence, the two types of tests are measuring similar—if not identical—processes. Moreover, both individual and group intelligence tests are based on a norm-referenced system. Let us consider some of the items used on major intelligence tests and see how IQ scores are derived.

The Stanford-Binet Intelligence Test

The Stanford-Binet Intelligence test includes several basic categories of test items. Naturally, the items themselves vary—at age six the child may be asked to add 2 and 3, whereas at age ten he may be asked to add 37, 95, and 18. For younger, preschool children, the scale involves nonverbal items, such as placing simple blocks properly in a three-hole

form board, but the tests for older children emphasize verbal skills. In general, test items fall into these categories:

Word definitions   An easy word may be *curtain;* a difficult one, *ubiquitous.*

Verbal analogy problems   "What is the similarity between hail and snow?"
"Grass is green: mud is_____."

Adaptive problems   "What would you do if the lawn mower you were using to mow the grass broke down?"

Arithmetic problems   "How many 5¢ candy bars can be bought for 30¢?"

Memory   "Repeat this series of numbers: 1, 3, 8, 5, 2."
"Look at this bead chain, then draw it from memory":

General information   "Who wrote *Robinson Crusoe?*"
"How many pennies are there in a quarter?"

Absurdity detection   "What is silly about this sentence?: A boy says to his brother, 'If I get home first, I'll write my name on the door, but if you get there first, you erase it.' "

Missing-parts pictures:	A child is shown a picture in which a part is left out (a number on a clock, the ear of a donkey) and asked what is missing.
Spatial problems	A child is asked to draw a path through a maze.
	"If you unfolded this piece of paper, how would it look?" (See Figure 8–2.)
Comprehension	"What should you say in a strange city when someone asks you how to find a certain address?"

The Wechsler Intelligence Scale for Children

Whereas the Stanford-Binet yields a single I.Q. score based on answers to different questions at different ages, the Wechsler Intelligence Scale for Children (WISC), designed by David Wechsler, gives three scores: a verbal I.Q., a performance I.Q., and a full-scale I.Q. It uses the same set of questions for children of different ages. The child's performance on each subtest is scored in terms of the mean for his own age group. Like the Stanford-Binet, the Wechsler scale measures a child's relative intellectual ability. If an eight-year-old receives an I.Q. of 79, it means (if one consults the appropriate table in the manual) that he is at the tenth percentile. That is, he has done better on the test than about 10 percent of the eight-year-olds in the standardization group and more poorly than 90 percent.

In addition to WISC, for ages six to sixteen years, there are tests for ages four to six and a half (WPPSI—Wechsler Preschool and Primary Scale of Intelligence) and for age sixteen and over (WAIS—Wechsler Adult Intelligence Scale).

In the verbal scale in the Wechsler I.Q. test there are six subtests: information ("How many weeks are there in a year?"); comprehension ("Why should we keep away from bad company?"); digit span ("Repeat

Figure 8–2

An example of a nonverbal item from the Stanford-Binet test might be the drawing below with the question "How would this piece of paper look if it were unfolded?"

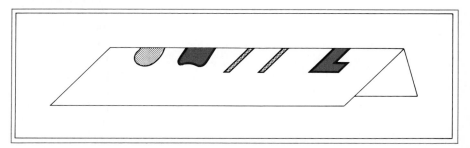

The Meaning of Correlation

A *correlation coefficient*—or, simply, *correlation*—is a number that represents the degree of relation between two sets of events. Applied to test scores this means the degree to which two different sets of scores rise and fall together. Consider the scores of thirty children who have taken two different I.Q. tests. If the children who obtained high scores on one test also obtained high scores on the other, and the same similarity held for low scorers, then the correlation between the tests would be very high. A perfect correlation is 1.00. If the scores are inversely related, the correlation is negative. The correlation between height and weight, for instance, is usually between +.60 and +.70. Often the correlation between scores on two I.Q. tests is +.90—close to perfect. When the scores on one test have no relation to the scores on another—as might happen if I.Q. scores were compared with scores on a test of hand strength—the correlation would be .00. Generally, I.Q. scores correlate with school grades about +.50, which is regarded as a moderately high correlation. I.Q. scores correlate negatively with family size. The term *correlation* is often used and should be understood.

this series of numbers backward and forward: 2, 7, 3, 9, 6); similarities ("In what way are air and water alike?"); arithmetic ("Multiply 49 by 23"); and vocabulary ("Define *irritate* and *highway*").

The performance scale attempts to minimize verbal ability. In one test a child is shown three or more cartoon panels in random order and asked to arrange them so that they tell a sensible story. In another she is shown a picture of a familiar object with a missing part, and she must detect what it is. In a block design test she is given a series of blocks and asked to construct a geometric design that will look like the one pictured in front of her. In an object-assembly test she is given parts of a puzzle and asked to put them together so that they form the shape of a hand or a horse. In a coding test she must learn a code symbol for each number and put the correct ones in the blank spaces under a series of numbers.

Although both scales try to measure different skills (memory, speed of solving a puzzle, verbal analogies, arithmetic), there is usually a high correlation between the two. Moreover, children's I.Q. scores based on the full-scale Wechsler test are very similar to those based on the Stanford-Binet test. The correlation is usually about .80.

Group Tests of Mental Ability
Although many educators and psychologists believe that the quality measured by the individually administered Stanford-Binet or Wechsler intelligence test differs from that measured by the group tests of mental ability, examination of the test items reveals a great deal of similarity between the knowledge and the competences necessary to pass both

types of tests, and children who do well on one usually do well on the other. Thus some psychologists believe that even though the two types of tests are given different names, they are not measuring fundamentally different qualities. Group testing is obviously more efficient, although individually administered intelligence tests are more sensitive. There are three main disadvantages to a group test: the child must read the instructions (which could handicap a poor reader, who may misunderstand the directions); the examiner cannot take the anxiety, motivation, or mood of the child into account; and she cannot stop the test for awhile to reassure the child or motivate him if he becomes discouraged.

The Stability of a Child's I.Q.

Since I.Q. scores are used both for comparison (to state how well a child performs on certain tasks compared with other children his age) and for prediction (to state how well he can be expected to perform as he continues in high school), it is important to ask how stable an individual's I.Q. is over a long period of time.

The stability of I.Q. scores is to be regarded as quite different from the stability of precocity or retardation in displaying the universal milestones of cognitive development discussed in Chapters 3, 4, and 5. Between the ages of eight and thirteen months most American infants show that they know an object still exists even if it is out of sight, are temporarily inhibited when they meet someone or something new, and show separation anxiety, although some are a few months ahead and some are a few months behind as a result of environmental experiences, health, or basic rate of development. Study of a group of children living in a village of five thousand people in the highlands of Guatemala revealed that the Indian infants display these competences at the same time as American middle-class infants (Kagan et al., unpublished). But during the ages from five to nine years, when tests of memory for familiar pictures were administered to the Indian and American children, the Indians were several years behind the Americans. The memory tests required the child to display competences that, as we saw in Chapter 5, eventually appear in all children: namely, the spontaneous tendency to rehearse information that is to be remembered and the tendency to try to impose some organization on material to be recalled. The Mayan Indian children display these abilities at about eleven or twelve years of age. Thus precocity—or retardation—with respect to the appearance of universal cognitive abilities is not predictive of the level of cognitive functioning three to five years later for a different set of capabilities. Stated concretely, early display of object permanence does not predict early display of the tendency to impose organization on information. There does not seem to be much stability of what we might call precocity of intellectual development.

Age	4	5	6	7	8	9	10	11	12
3	.83	.72	.73	.64	.60	.63	.54	.51	.46
4	. .	.80	.85	.70	.63	.66	.55	.50	.43
5	. .	. .	.87	.83	.79	.80	.70	.63	.62
6	. .	. .	. .	.83	.79	.81	.72	.67	.67
7	. .	. .	. .	. .	.91	.83	.82	.76	.73
8	. .	. .	. .	. .	. .	.92	.90	.84	.83
9	. .	. .	. .	. .	. .	. .	.90	.82	.81
10	. .	. .	. .	. .	. .	. .	. .	.90	.88
11	. .	. .	. .	. .	. .	. .	. .	. .	.90

Figure 8–3
How stable is I.Q.? In general, I.Q. scores resemble each other more closely when the testings take place at short intervals. For example, the correlation between testings at ages five and seven is .83; between testings at ages five and twelve the correlation is .62. (Sontag, Baker, and Nelson, 1958, p. 28)

But when we look at I.Q. scores, we find that, from age three or four on, there is stability of the intelligence quotient (see Figure 8–3). Indeed, I.Q. is the most stable psychological quality psychologists have been able to measure thus far. (Naturally, a child's score may vary by five or more points within a short time period, for she may be tired or ill on one occasion and well rested on another. She may feel more confident in the fourth grade than in the seventh, or vice versa. An I.Q. score should be viewed as an approximate measurement of a child's ability to answer the particular test items.) As may be expected, the I.Q. is more stable over short time intervals than over long ones. For example, if a child is tested at age five and again at age seven, the correlation between the two I.Q. scores is likely to be higher than if the child is tested at ages five and twelve. (Although there are infant tests for children under two, which mainly assess sensorimotor responses such as building a tower of two wooden cubes, these scores are not very useful in predicting the school-age child's I.Q.). Moreover, the I.Q. score becomes more stable with increasing age: the correlation between I.Q. scores at ages three and five is around .70; the correlation between I.Q.'s at ages eight and ten is .90 (Sontag, Baker, and Nelson, 1958).

Correlations of I.Q. with Other Factors

The I.Q. score reflects a child's ability to answer particular questions tapping cognitive processes and knowledge. It does not necessarily reveal an individual's ability to make intelligent choices on the playground or solve personal family problems. Complex emotional and motivational factors influence the latter choices. Nevertheless, there are some interesting correlations between I.Q. scores and personality, sex, and socioeconomic class.

With respect to personality, children whose I.Q. scores continue to rise from early childhood through adolescence tend to be more energetic, independent, and competitive than those whose scores decrease (Sontag, Baker, and Nelson, 1958).

Although intelligence tests were purposely designed so that they would not favor one sex over another (and in any age group the scores of boys and girls tend to be similar), girls nevertheless tend to perform a little better on tests of verbal ability, whereas boys perform a little better on tests of spatial relations and arithmetic. Moreover, in the 1950s, more girls than boys showed a pattern of declining I.Q. score over age (Sontag, Baker, and Nelson, 1958). It seems reasonable to speculate that the girls felt a conflict between the traditional demands for passivity and the personality traits associated with higher I.Q. scores, namely competitiveness and independence. Today, fewer women automatically celebrate traditional female traits, and we may stop seeing a preponderance of declining I.Q. scores among school-age girls.

The socioeconomic class of a family is highly correlated with the child's I.Q. after age three. That is, allowing for many individual exceptions, children from poor families generally have lower I.Q. scores than children from middle-class families. The power of social class to predict I.Q. score was seen in dramatic form in a study of over twenty-five thousand black and white infants from lower- and middle-class families who were assessed regularly from birth through four years of age. Physicians and psychologists had gathered extensive information on the mothers' health during pregnancy, the difficulty of delivery, and the integrity of the infants at birth—biological factors that should influence the infants' brains and, therefore, their intellectual development. But these factors were far less important than the family's socioeconomic class in predicting the child's I.Q. score at age four. The mother's education—not her health, trauma during delivery, or the child's birth weight—was the best predictor of her child's I.Q. (Broman, Nichols, and Kennedy, 1975).

Why do school-age pupils from poor families do less well on intelligence tests than middle-class children? One possibility, of course, is that poor children are basically less competent, meaning that in most situations they have greater difficulty learning new ideas or skills. But let us examine some other reasons poor children may get lower scores on I.Q. tests.

Poor children face two problems in taking a standard intelligence test. The first concerns their attitude toward test-taking, and the second involves the content of the test. Minimal interest in the test, low motivation to do well, low expectation of success, and belief that the test score can make little practical improvement in their lives all may hinder their performance. Although not confined to children from poor families, these attitudes are more common among them.

Many studies have manipulated the motivation of children taking an I.Q. test to see if it affected their performance. Some of these studies found that motivation had no effect on I.Q. score. Others have found that motivation made a difference. For example, in one such study poor and middle-class children were given practice sessions in taking I.Q. tests. In three one-hour sessions the examiner explained what was involved in each of the different types of subtests. He gave rewards to the children who did well during these sessions and coached the test administrators, training them to be responsive to the poor children as well as to the middle-class students. In a period of three days the I.Q. scores of the children from poor families improved an average of fifteen to twenty points (Haggard, 1954). Nevertheless, whether or not poor children in this study got lower scores because of low motivation is still uncertain.

Bias in the Content of Tests

The second factor that hinders poor children involves the content of the tests. A repeated criticism of all intelligence tests is that many questions include words and concepts that are more familiar to middle-class children than to poor ones or to black, Puerto Rican, or Chicano children. The answer to "What does *franc* mean?" for example, is less likely to reveal how intellectually competent a child is than to reflect whether or not his parents have talked about French currency.

Many years ago a psychologist standardized two general information tests similar to the tests on today's Wechsler I.Q. scale. Information Test A was standardized on urban schoolchildren from a city of about forty-seven thousand people. It included questions such as "Who is President of the U.S.A.?" "What is the largest river in the U.S.A.?" "How can banks afford to pay interest on the money you deposit?" Information Test B was standardized on children from rural areas in New York State. Some of its questions were: "What is butter made of?" "Name a vegetable that grows above the ground." "Why does seasoned wood burn more easily than green wood?" The two tests were given to both urban and rural schoolchildren. The rural children did significantly more poorly than urban children on Test A but performed better than the urban children on Test B, demonstrating the importance of the children's familiarity with test material (Shimberg, 1929).

As the test-taking population in American schools extended to include many children from different ethnic backgrounds (as well as from families with less obvious, but still crucial, differences in socioeconomic level), attempts were made to reduce the amount of acquired knowledge necessary for good performance and to increase

1839 Vocabulary Test

Most of the criticism of "culture-bias" that is directed at standardized intelligence tests is aimed at the vocabulary subtest. We have seen, both in this chapter and in Chapter 5, how familiarity with particular words reflects the chances you have had to encounter them. Test yourself on this vocabulary list, taken from a nineteenth-century American school manual (Howland, 1839):

1 abba
2 abluent
3 antipodes
4 appal
5 besom
6 clothier
7 cooper
8 cordwainer
9 crier
10 currier
11 draper
12 gauger
13 glazier
14 haberdasher
15 mechanic
16 whitesmith

16 One who works in polished iron and makes tools and instruments.
15 A person who has the knowledge of some art.
14 One who sells small things.
13 One who sets glass in windows.
12 One who measures vessels.
11 One who sells cloth.
10 One who blacks and dresses off leather.
9 One employed to proclaim things.
8 One who makes boots and shoes.
7 One who makes barrels and tubs.
6 One who finishes cloth.
5 A broom.
4 To be frightened or grow faint.
3 Those people on the other side of the globe who have their feet opposite ours.
2 That which washes clean.
1 A word used for father.

the emphasis on abstract reasoning. Some subtests asked questions that required reasoning about spatial rearrangement of designs ("How would this piece of paper look if it were unfolded?"), memory ("Repeat this string of digits: 1, 7, 6, 8, 35, 20"), and the ability to create designs from a set of blocks. While tasks of spatial reasoning or memory for numbers do not depend on previous knowledge, a child's performance on them may be influenced by previous practice. The children who have spent their early years cutting and pasting shapes of paper or memorizing nursery rhymes may have an advantage on such tests.

An objective eye can easily pick out aspects of a standard I.Q. test that are biased to favor the life experience of middle-class children in one way or another. The vocabulary sections are the most obvious example. (They are also the subtests in which scores show the greatest difference between middle- and lower-class children.) Consider five questions taken from the Wechsler scale:

1 Who wrote *Hamlet?*
2 Who wrote the *Iliad?*
3 What is the Koran?
4 What does *audacious* mean?
5 What does *plagiarize* mean?

Questions such as these tap acquired knowledge. Clearly, some groups of children have more access to knowledge of this kind than do others.

On the other hand, as we will discuss further in Chapter 12, it is possible to construct tests that favor children from poor families, just as standard tests favor children from middle-class families. Consider five questions that would be more familiar to black than to white adolescents:

1 In C. C. Ryder, what does C. C. stand for?
2 What is a *gashead?*
3 What is Willy Mays' last name?
4 What does *handkerchief head* mean?
5 Whom did "Stagger Lee" kill in the famous blues ballad?

The head of a university black-studies program has developed the Black Intelligence Test of Cultural Homogeneity (BITCH). Multiple-choice questions include (Williams, 1973, p. 109):

1 *Nose opened* means (A) flirting, (B) teed off, (C) deeply in love, (D) very angry.
2 *Blood* means (A) a vampire, (B) a dependent individual, (C) an injured person, (D) a brother of color.
3 *Mother's Day* means (A) black independence day, (B) a day when mothers are honored, (C) a day the welfare checks come in, (D) every first Sunday in church.
4 The following are popular brand names. Which one does not belong? (A) Murray's, (B) Dixie Peach, (C) Royal Crown, (D) Preparation H.

Blacks are more likely than whites to know the correct answers (1–C, 2–D, 3–C, 4–D).

Knowledge of the vocabulary on the WISC or the Stanford-Binet scale does predict school grades, while knowledge of the vocabulary on the BITCH does not. For those who regard the I.Q. vocabulary test as only a practical method for predicting school success, the bias on the test is no criticism or weakness, for it permits the prediction to be accurate. However, for those who regard the I.Q. score as a reflection of the child's fundamental intellectual capacity to cope with any new challenge, the bias on the test is potentially a serious matter, for it does not seem reasonable to assume that a high score on any vocabulary test indicates superior mental capacity. A person's score on the vocabulary scale of the WISC or the BITCH is likely to reflect whether he has

Figure 8–4
"Name the days of the week" was one of the questions on Stanford-Binet tests administered over the past sixty years to children from many countries. More English-speaking children answered the question correctly before age eight than non-Western children. All children improved with age, and most passed the test by age eleven. (After Smith, 1974, p. 28)

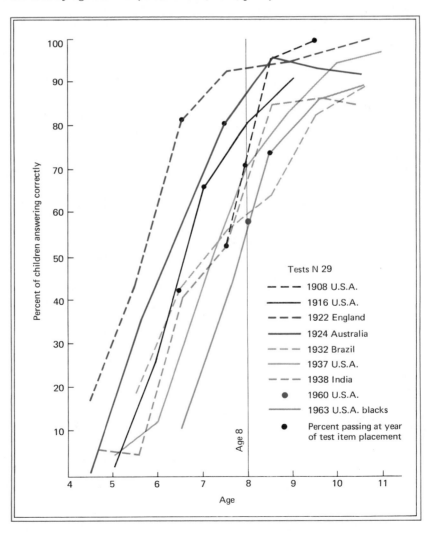

previously encountered the words to be defined; differences in vocabulary scores on the standard I.Q. tests are closely tied to the educational attainment of the child and the child's family.

The Stanford-Binet Intelligence Test has been used by psychologists to test children in many countries since the popularization of the test seventy years ago. One researcher examined the test performance of four- to eleven-year-old children from the United States, England, Australia, Brazil, India, and other countries over the last sixty years. Included on the test were items asking the children to name the days of the week (see Figure 8–4) and to use three words to make a sentence. Generally, more English-speaking children from America, England, and Australia passed test questions prior to age eight than did children from a non-Western culture such as India. Furthermore, the performance of all children improved with age, and most children passed the test items by age eleven. Answers to the questions requiring verbal skills—rather than skills at memorizing or copying—showed the greatest cultural differences, suggesting that many parts of the Stanford-Binet scale are biased to favor English-speaking children (Smith, 1974).

Although vocabulary questions are most subject to cultural bias, others are not immune. Consider this problem and the reactions of three seven-year-olds: "Donald went walking in the woods. He saw a pretty little animal that he tried to take home for a pet. It got away from him but when he got home, his family immediately burned all his clothes. Why?" Tom lives in the country; he will probably know the clothes were burned because the animal was a skunk. Rachel lives in the city, but she has been reading picture books and stories about animals for years; she, too, may know the answer. But Joel lives in the city in a household that has not been able to spend money on picture books; he cannot answer the question—not because his reasoning is poor, but because he has never heard of skunks.

We may conclude that Joel may have trouble in school, may not finish high school, and may not get a good job as an adult because of difficulties arising from the same situation that prohibited him from knowing, at age seven, what a skunk was. But we cannot conclude from this information alone that Joel is intellectually less capable than Tom or Rachel.

What Do I.Q. Tests Measure?

The original purpose of Binet's test, which was to predict which children would be successful in school, is still valid today. The I.Q. score of a ten-year-old does predict grades in elementary school, high school, and college and therefore predicts final adult vocational status. But the causal relation between I.Q. and eventual vocational status is

still not certain because of the controversy surrounding the determinants of I.Q. scores. Specifically, the argument centers on whether a person's genetically determined qualities make an important contribution to his I.Q. Even though all agree that biology helps determine the structure and function of each person's central nervous system and therefore must influence his intellectual functioning, it is still not necessary that it make a contribution to I.Q. score. Similarly, biological differences affect our hormone levels, but there is no evidence to suggest that they make any contribution to the degree of marital satisfaction or success.

It is argued by some that doctors, teachers, and lawyers are innately more "intelligent" than cabdrivers or house painters; that is, they have biologically different nervous systems. Others insist that their high I.Q.'s are a result of being brought up in families and neighborhoods in which it was easier for them to learn the knowledge, skills, and strategies required to pass the tests.

No one questions the fact that the Stanford-Binet and Wechsler tests measure a quality that is useful, for it predicts success in school. It is a little less clear that what the tests measure should be called "native intelligence." Oddly enough, the inventor of the most widely used intelligence test—the Wechsler Intelligence Scale—takes a more culturally relative view of I.Q. scores and intelligence than do many

psychologists who theorize about the significance of intelligence. David Wechsler suggests that intelligent behavior has four characteristics. The first is awareness. An intelligent act is monitored by the executive we mentioned in Chapter 5. The act is conscious and volitional, not reflexive. The second characteristic of an intelligent act is that it has purpose and meaning; it is not a random action. A third characteristic is rationality; the act is logically related to a coherent and consistent set of cognitive units. These three qualities are characteristic of the behavior of almost all humans from about age four on. But Wechsler's fourth characteristic is the critical one for this discussion. "To merit being called intelligent, behaviors must be judged worthwhile. Worthwhile is what the consensus of group opinion deems valuable and useful. . . . The assessment of intelligence inevitably is a value judgment" (Wechsler, 1975, p. 138).

Thus Wechsler is implying that a clever robbery that has awareness, intention, and rationality is not intelligent because it is not socially worthwhile.

Hence, the creator of the modern intelligence test appreciates what some teachers and parents do not; namely, that intelligence tests measure facts and cognitive skills the majority of the community deems valuable at this point in history. This does not mean that the I.Q. score is unimportant; it only means that perhaps it should not be regarded as some fixed, absolute quality of a person.

Guilford's View of Intelligence

J. P. Guilford of the University of Southern California has spent a
lifetime of research promoting a different view of intelligence and a
different set of tests to measure intellectual processes (Guilford, 1967).
The most important aspect of Guilford's conception is that he does not
view intelligence as a single, generalized ability but as a large set of
quite separate abilities. In addition, Guilford distinguishes among the
operations, or the mental processes; the contents, or the materials the
person manipulates; and the products of the manipulation of
information (see Figure 8–5). The five basic mental operations are
cognition, memory, divergent production, convergent production, and
evaluation. The four contents are figural, symbolic, semantic, and
behavioral; and the six products are units, classes, relations, systems,
transformations, and implications. Multiplying five operations by four

Figure 8–5
**Guilford suggests that intelligence consists of 120 different mental abilities—the
combinations of operations, contents, and products—rather than a single,
generalized ability. (After Guilford, 1967)**

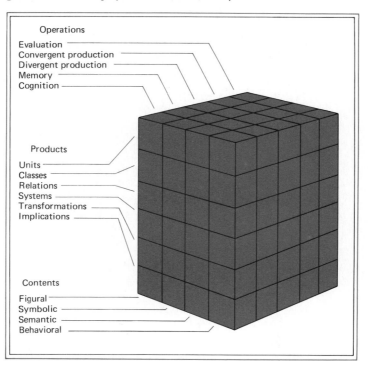

contents by six products yields 120 different intellectual units, or types of abilities. Let us consider the three categories in turn.

Operations

1 *Cognition*—the recognition that a newly encountered event or experience is related to one's past knowledge, the vast informational storehouse possessed by the person. Cognition is the process by which one recognizes that a tree, a person, or a musical melody is something one has experienced before. Cognition applied to a symbolic content may include presenting a word with two blanks in it and asking the child to guess what the word is:

sc__n__   (the word is *scene*)
tr__v__l   (the word is *travel*)

Cognition occurs when a person is given partial information and activates prior knowledge.

2 *Memory*—involves recalling past information and can involve different contents: words (semantic), pictures (figural), symbols, or the behavior of others. For example, in one test the person first studies fifteen nonsense syllables and must then write as many of them as he can remember in any order.

3 *Divergent production*—involves fluency and flexibility of thinking, that is, an easy flow of ideas and the readiness to change directions in one's problem-solving approach. A test for divergent production with figural content involves giving the child a simple form (such as a circle) and asking her to draw as many real objects as she can, adding as few lines as possible. She may draw a man, a baseball, or a hat. Or, in a test for divergent production with semantic content, she may be asked to think of all the possible ways one can use a brick or a wire coathanger. Or she may be given the question "What would happen if people didn't have to sleep anymore?" and asked to generate all the possible events that may result from this change in the world. Divergent thinking is the ability to generate many products from existing information; the more products a child generates, the higher her score.

4 *Convergent production*—related to deduction. The person is given information and has to deduce the one correct answer. In one task the person is given a pile of sixteen geometric forms, which differ in size and color, and asked to sort them into classes. He must detect the classifying principles inherent in the set: size and color. In convergent production the person has all the information and must detect a principle, a concept, or a category.

5 *Evaluation*—defined as the tendency to compare some information with known information according to particular criteria and to decide if the criteria are satisfied. In other words, the person assesses the quality of the solution he has produced to see if it meets the requirements of the problem. A test for evaluation includes giving the child the words *cat, cow, mule,* and *mare* and asking him to decide the best (that is, the most valid) category for them: (a) farm animal, (b) four-legged animal, or (c) domestic animal. Although all the alternatives are correct, the best answer is c. "Farm animal" is a less satisfactory category, since a cat is found in other places besides the farm, and "four-legged animal" is too broad a category. Items such as these measure the child's ability to evaluate the best or most elegant answer.

Contents

Each of the five mental processes, or operations, can be applied to four basic kinds of content.

1 *Figural*—pictures, designs, and scenes
2 *Symbolic*—letters, numbers, and signs.
3 *Semantic*—words and sentences.
4 *Behavioral*—the behavior of other people.

Guilford believes it makes a difference whether a person is trying to remember a scene (figural content), the multiplication tables (symbolic content), a poem (semantic content), or how a tennis player places his feet and swings when he is serving a tennis ball (behavioral content).

Products

The application of a process or processes to one of the four contents yields a cognitive product. Guilford suggests six different kinds of products:

1 *Unit*—a segregated whole; the things that nouns normally stand for, such as a book, a dish, a blow, or a smile. Hence, remembering the equation for the area of a circle involves using the operation of memory on symbolic content to produce a unit, namely, the equation πr^2.
2 *Class*—a set of objects with common properties; a concept such as edible foods, circular shapes, or hairless animals. Generating the names of all the foods one knows uses the process of cognition on semantic content to produce a class of objects.
3 *Relation*—a connection between two things. To recognize that men are usually more boisterous than women involves using the process of cognition on behavioral content to produce a relation; or to reason that the wind on a lake is greatest in late afternoon after the sun has warmed the water is to use divergent production on a figural content to produce a relation.
4 *System*—a complex pattern or organization of independent parts or units. An essay or an outline for an article is a system. Proving the Pythagorean theorem involves applying the operations of divergent and convergent production on symbolic content to produce a system.
5 *Transformation*—a change or revision of one's knowledge. Suppose one believes that all birds can fly and reads that a penguin is a bird that cannot fly. The change in knowledge involves the operations of cognition and memory on semantic content to produce a transformation.
6 *Implication*—a prediction or expectation from given information. If one has had the experience many times of being misled into wrong answers by multiple-choice test items, then one may decide to be more careful when a test is announced. This decision is an example of the process of memory acting on semantic content to generate an implication or prediction.

Using Guilford's Tests

Guilford believes that each person has a unique profile of intellectual abilities. His tests yield a multifaceted view of each individual's particular abilities, rather than a single score. Some people think more creatively with words and sentences, others with numbers, still others with pictures and diagrams. The philosopher, the mathematician, and the architect represent optimal realizations of these types of ability. Guilford's profile is like an elaborate medical report that states that the patient's skin color and weight are good and the circulatory system is fine but that there is a malfunction in the gastrointestinal system. The Stanford-Binet test or the WISC is like a report that averages out the health or deficit of many systems and concludes that, in general, the patient is in pretty good—or poor—health.

Only some of Guilford's suggested 120 intelligence factors have been established. The others are a matter of speculation. Critics of Guilford's theory point out that a definition of intelligence that includes 120 cognitive functions may be too complex to be helpful. Certainly, the Stanford-Binet test, and tests modeled after it, are easier to administer and score than Guilford's tests, which require hours (and are only available for older adolescents and adults). Moreover, scores on Guilford's tests do not predict grades in college better than the I.Q. test. Americans value efficiency of thought and predictive power, and a concept of intelligence that can be summed up in a single score that predicts something of practical significance seems more useful than Guilford's more complex view of intellectual ability. Nevertheless, Guilford's approach, even disregarding his 120 factors, may ultimately prove a more useful and valid way to view cognition because it separates the units of thought manipulated in problem solving from the processes used in that manipulation—an idea we proposed in Chapter 4.

Is Intelligence Inherited?

The intense controversy concerning the meaning and measurement of intelligence is related to an even more delicate subject—to what degree are differences in intelligence due to inherited qualities? Since height, color of hair, eyes, and skin, and susceptibility to disease are controlled by heredity to some degree, it is not unreasonable to assume that some aspects of intellectual functioning are also genetically influenced. (This is, in fact, one of the five American assumptions about intelligence mentioned earlier.) Most psychologists believe that a child's heredity and experience interact in a complex way to affect his level of intellectual ability. But they cannot agree on how great an effect each factor has on the child's cognitive abilities. Although a person's height is partly inherited, the known genetic influences on height can be altered by medical care and diet while the child is growing up. In America many short men and women have children who are much taller than they are as a result of improved health conditions.

Studies of Twins

The major source of evidence favoring a significant genetic determination of I.Q. score is based on studies of genetically related people—parents and children, siblings, and especially twins. The closer the genetic relation between two people, the more similar their I.Q. scores. Some studies compared the I.Q.'s of identical twins and fraternal twins living in the same home as well as the I.Q.'s of identical twins separated in infancy or early childhood and raised in different homes. Identical twins have exactly the same genes, while nonidentical, or fraternal, twins do not. If the environments of fraternal twins are as similar as the environments of identical twins (that is, if identical and nonidentical twins are "treated" similarly), then a greater similarity of the I.Q. scores of identical twins would seem to be due to genetic factors.

In general psychologists have found a greater similarity in I.Q. scores for identical twins than for fraternal twins, and have concluded that differences in intelligence are seriously influenced by heredity (Wilson, 1975). Data from one study of twins are presented in Figure 8–6. The correlation between the I.Q. scores of parents and their natural children averages about .50. For fraternal twins the correlation between the scores is also about .50. For identical twins the correlation is higher, an average of .90. Even the I.Q. scores of identical twins who were reared in different homes have a correlation of about .75, which is higher than the correlation between fraternal twins living in the same family. These findings are persuasive evidence for a significant genetic influence on I.Q. scores.

Thus we have a paradox. The consistent finding of greater similarity in I.Q. scores among children with similar genetic makeup than among genetically unrelated children (but reared in the same household) suggests that heredity makes a contribution to I.Q. score. Yet considerations given in the preceding discussion on the nature of I.Q. tests have led some psychologists to wonder how genes can influence whether or not a child knows the meaning of a word such as *franc* or can detect a missing element in a picture of a face.

One possible way to explain some of the similarity in I.Q. between genetically similar children, especially twins, is to postulate that the environments of identical twins are more similar than the environments of nonidentical twins.

Naturally, fraternal twins, being the same age (and sometimes the same sex), can be expected to do many things together. But compared to fraternal twins, identical twins spend more time together, enjoy more similar reputations (since the people they know perceive them as very much alike), are more likely to be in the same classrooms, have more similar health records, and in other respects share a more common physical and social environment than do fraternal twins (Smith, 1965). Thus, the highly similar I.Q. scores of identical twins reared together may be due, in part, to greater similarities in experiences than was supposed in the past.

Early twin studies overlooked a second factor. If the similar scores of identical twins raised apart is to be used as evidence for genetic influence, the twins must be brought up in substantially different home

Figure 8–6
Over one hundred pairs of twins were given tests on the Wechsler scale at ages four, five, and six. On all ten subtests the scores of identical twins were more similar than the scores of twins who were not identical, as seen in the higher correlations for the scores of identical twins. (Adapted from Wilson, 1975, p. 131)

SUBTEST	IDENTICAL TWINS	NON-IDENTICAL TWINS	NON-IDENTICAL TWINS OF SAME SEX
Information	.81	.51	.47
Vocabulary	.71	.50	.27
Arithmetic	.65	.52	.57
Similarities	.73	.58	.40
Comprehension	.80	.62	.40
Animal house	.82	.40	.42
Picture completion	.69	.26	.38
Mazes	.61	.45	.43
Geometric design	.72	.25	.36
Block design	.68	.43	.34

environments and encounter very different values and treatments. This situation does not always occur. Since officials responsible for placing children in foster homes make an effort to place them in similar settings, it is likely that most of the twins, though placed separately, were still placed in families with common religious, racial, class, and linguistic backgrounds. In some cases, they were even placed with members of the same family. As a result, although one twin may have been raised a few miles away from the other, their homes were alike.

Let us consider one study of identical twins reared in separate homes (Shields, 1962). In this study only four out of nineteen pairs of separated twins grew up in homes with large differences in social classes. In two of the four pairs, one sister finished high school, the other only completed eighth grade. In the third pair, one girl completed five years of schooling and her twin sister finished three years of college. In the fourth and most dramatic case, one sister had an I.Q. of 92 and finished the third grade, while the other twin had an I.Q. of 116 and received a college degree. This background information makes it a little more difficult to conclude that the similarities in I.Q. scores of identical twins reared apart must be primarily a result of common heredity.

The Genetics of Intelligence and the Norm of Reaction

In order to appreciate the potential influence of heredity on differences in I.Q. we will have to discuss an important concept in genetics called the *norm of reaction*. The norm of reaction means that a particular set of genes—called the *genotype*—can have different outcomes in different environments. For example, for the case of a genotype for height, two identical genotypes may develop differently in different environments. As illustrated in Figure 8–7, genotype B produces short people in an environment with poor nutrition and tall people in an environment with good nutrition. Genotype A produces people who are generally taller than those with genotype B in a poor-nutrition environment but shorter than those with B in a nutritionally enriched environment.

If we regard verbal ability as a genetic trait—like height—then it, too, may have a norm of reaction. Hence, changes in the environment may alter the profile of intelligent behavior. For example, some children may have a set of genes that facilitates the easy mastery of written verbal material, and therefore they do well in a society such as ours, which emphasizes reading. But if the cultural tradition shifted to only oral transmission of information, these same children might perform less adequately. This idea implies that, in the environment of modern American schools, the differences among children in I.Q. and school grades may be partly due to genetic factors.

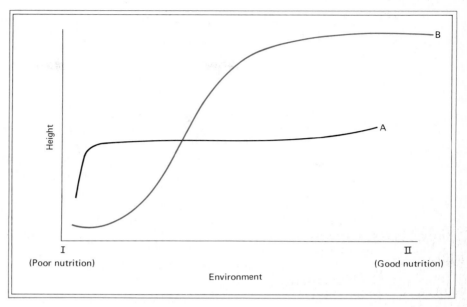

Figure 8–7
In genetics the norm of reaction means that a particular set of genes—the
genotype—will usually have different outcomes in different environments. In
this hypothetical illustration genotype B produces short people in environment
I (poor nutrition) and tall people in environment II (good nutrition), while a
person with genotype A is generally taller than one with genotype B in
environment I but shorter in environment II.

The Racial Hypothesis

Some psychologists have gone farther and suggested that the difference
in average I.Q. between groups of black and white children may also be
partly due to heredity. A key article on this subject was published in
1969 by psychologist Arthur Jensen. The article discussed what Jensen
considered to be strong evidence for a genetic influence on intelligence
and concluded that the genetic component was high. Jensen gave 80
percent as the likely proportion of intelligence governed by inheritance.
He went on to suggest that since heredity seems to influence differences
in the intelligence of individuals, then the average I.Q. difference
between black and white Americans—about ten to fifteen points—may
be due to differences in the genetic endowments of the two races.
Understandably, the monograph touched a raw nerve in American
sensibilities. It is useful to look at the data Jensen presented and try to
evaluate what it means.

Although white Americans have a mean I.Q. of 100 and black Americans have a mean I.Q. of 85, the difference is reduced to ten points or less if the comparison is made between whites and blacks of roughly the same social class. Ten points is about the same difference found among brothers and sisters of the same family.

More important, if black children are adopted by middle-class white families during the first two or three years of life, their I.Q. scores during the school years do not average 85 to 90 (which is the typical I.Q. of a black child being raised by his biological parents) but instead average 105, or a little above the average score for white children in the United States. Moreover, both black and white children who have been placed in white adoptive homes since age two or three have similar I.Q. scores, while black children adopted by black parents have a slightly lower I.Q. (94) than black children raised in white homes. Finally, the higher the educational level of the adoptive mother, the higher the adopted child's I.Q. These data imply that the lower I.Q. score of the black child in the United States is primarily a function of social and experiential variables, rather than genetic ones (Scarr and Weinberg, 1976).

Considering the dramatic differences in background, wealth, and experience of the average black or white child in the United States, and the previous discussion, one can question whether the ten-to-fifteen point difference in I.Q. is due in any serious way to heredity.

But actually the strongest objection to the inference that black-white differences are due to genes comes from the fallacy of assuming that if genetics accounts for the differences in a trait *within* groups of people, it necessarily accounts for the differences in that trait *between* groups of people.

Let us take a known genetic trait—height. In rural Guatemala poor children are shorter than those who are less poor. The differences in height within the two groups are likely to be partly genetic. But the difference between the two groups is not genetic, because if the poor children are well nourished in the first years of their lives, they become much taller than those who are not. And in America, as we have seen, a large number of children grow taller than their parents as a result of improved health conditions. Thus, differences between two groups on a trait that is known to be controlled by heredity may be due to environmental factors.

Consider two handfuls of corn taken at random from a large barrel that contains a variety of genetic species of corn. Each handful will have genetic diversity, but equivalent genetic diversity. We plant each of the handfuls of corn in a different place in a garden. If the garden environments are different in quality, the corn in the good environment will be taller than the corn in the poor environment and that difference is "environmental." However, the differences in height in each place in the garden are completely the result of genetic differences, for all the

American society has vacillated between environmental and genetic explanations of the enormous human variation in the attainment of wealth and status and in the display of socially appropriate behavior. During the 1950s and early 1960s most educators and psychologists believed in an environmental explanation of poverty and criminality, in part because learning and psychoanalytic theory stressed the importance of experience on personality and intellectual development. In the 1970s genetic explanations regained popularity. There were several reasons. One was that some social interventions based on the environmental theories (such as President Johnson's War on Poverty programs) had failed to have a beneficial impact. There had also been stunning scientific advances in biology supporting the hereditary explanation.

Ironically, the same shift in emphasis from experience to genes also occurred a century ago in the United States. In the 1840s most educated Americans believed that all men possessed equivalent capacities for good or evil and that their environmental experiences determined who would be a pauper, a criminal, or an upstanding citizen. Physicians believed that the tensions of the cities were the prime cause of mental disorder; it was assumed that insanity was most prevalent in the northeastern United States because it was the most urbanized part of the country. But by the mid-1860s—twenty-five years later—the shift to biological explanations had already occurred:

> The causes of the evil (the existence of such a large proportion of dependent and of destructive members of our community) are manifold, but among the immediate ones the chief cause is inherited organic imperfection—vitiated constitutions or poor stock. (Katz, 1968, p. 181)

Then, as now, social events that led many to feel frustrated over the inability of humans and society to reform humanity, rather than new scientific evidence, was the primary basis for the shift in opinion. That frustration made some citizens receptive to the view that perhaps the poor and the criminal cannot be reformed. Such a view is more readily associated with a biological explanation of maladaptive behavior.

corn is growing in the same environment. In this experiment it would be incorrect to conclude that the differences in height of the corn in the two places in the garden are due to genetics because we know that the original handfuls of corn came from the same barrel.

Moreover, geneticists have shown that if one studies the inherited profile of enzymes in the races of man, the variability in the occurrence of these enzymes *within* a particular racial group is much greater than the variation *between* racial groups (Lewontin, 1975). If this fact about genetic variability for enzymes is also true for psychological qualities such as intellectual ability, it is likely that black and white children are biologically very similar with respect to the *spectrum* of intellectual ability.

In sum, it is possible that the current I.Q. differences between blacks and whites may eventually be explained primarily in terms of social

The current, presumably sophisticated discussion of the intellectual abilities of black and white children has a close analogue in debates among colonial Americans. Thomas Jefferson, like Arthur Jensen, believed that the memory ability of blacks was equal to that of whites but that the black was deficient in reasoning and imagination; he regarded that difference as inherited. It is interesting that Jefferson did not suggest that other, equally obvious psychological differences between Negro slaves and free whites were innate. Personal untidiness and thievishness were regarded as learned because they were viewed as "moral qualities," and it was believed that the creator gave all humans a sense of right and wrong.

It is easier to argue for the influence of heredity on intellectual qualities than on moral ones. Morality and character seem to be products of our will: we can be honest and kind if we choose to be. But insight or creative imagination seem beyond our volition. Hence, we are tempted to assume that they are due to forces—such as genes—beyond our control. As a result, it is more difficult to defend a completely environmental explanation of low I.Q. scores than a partial biological one.

class, experience in home and school, and biased I.Q. tests, rather than by genetics. But at present, firm proof favoring either position is not available, and so we must be cautious and tentative. As one team of psychologists describes it with fine irony:

> There is no clear answer to this question because such an answer could only be obtained in an experiment that is impossible to conduct. That experiment would involve testing the intelligence of equally healthy black and white children, reared in exactly the same environment (including the prenatal environment). This environment would have to be the same in all respects related to intellectual growth and totally devoid of prejudice directed against any race. Unfortunately, man has not developed to the point where a society of that description is available to those wanting to investigate this issue. (Kimble, Garmezy, and Zigler, 1974, p. 73)

On the other hand, although some psychologists find it difficult to understand how the actions of genes can influence scores on I.Q. tests, we cannot ignore the indisputable fact that the more similar the genetic makeup of people, the more similar their I.Q. scores. This fact implies that differences in heredity influence differences in intellectual ability. Future research will have to solve this paradox.

In the beginning of this chapter we suggested that perhaps the concept of intelligence was not a useful scientific idea. People are always inventing concepts. Some of them survive, most do not. In the early eighteenth century scientists believed that the concept of phlogiston was useful to explain what happens when objects burn in air, but when oxygen was discovered, it soon became obvious to everyone that phlogiston was a useless concept and it was discarded. In the Middle Ages the devil was regarded by many Europeans as a major force struggling for people's souls, and many interpreted the attainment of wealth, power, and status, as well as freedom from illness and mental disease, as a reward for a life of piety. It was believed that the rich prospered because they were virtuous and free of the devil. As we saw in Chapter 2, a similar idea prevailed in America less than three hundred years ago. Today very few people use possession by the devil as an explanation for failure to obtain worldly prizes. The concept of devil, which was useful in the fifteenth century and thought to stand for something real, has turned out to be a fiction and of no use in explaining differences among humans. Now what about intelligence? Is intelligence a theoretically useful scientific idea—as electron, gravity, and atom are—or is it a misleading one like phlogiston? Only time will tell!

In the meantime teachers can find the results of intelligence tests useful if they are clear on what the tests can and cannot tell us about the child.

Implications for Teaching

What I.Q. Tests Can Do

Since I.Q. tests sample skills that are like the ones being taught in school, they predict, better than chance and more effectively than most other tests we have devised, the kind of school performance teachers can expect from particular students five or ten years hence. As a general rule, the more verbal the subject matter, the higher the correlation; the less the school subject depends on language sophistication (geometry and mathematics, for instance), the lower the correlation. The correlation between a child's I.Q. score and his score in reading comprehension is about .73; but the correlation between his I.Q. and his score in geometry is only .48. This makes perfectly good sense, since the I.Q. tests concentrate heavily on verbal skills.

I.Q. scores can be of some use to teachers in planning for their students. Teachers can expect superior academic performance from most students with scores of 120 or above. Children with an I.Q. below 70 will generally perform poorly. What about the large majority of children whose scores fall somewhere in between? Invariably, they will exhibit very different kinds of ability. Children who have an I.Q. of 100 may not resemble each other very much. One may excel at reading but

"We realize you do better on your I.Q. tests than you do in anything else, but you just cannot major in I.Q."

be poor in math; the next may have a keen mind for spatial designs but show little aptitude for composition. A third may be a steady, unspectacular student who works along conscientiously, while the fourth may seem to fluctuate between clever, impulsive responses in discussions and disinterested, incorrect answers on work that is routine.

While knowledge of a child's I.Q. score may predict something about her performance, every experienced teacher has a list of stories with surprise endings, based on the times he has looked up a student's I.Q. only to discover that either the student who was approaching schoolwork efficiently and competently had an average score or that the student who was lagging behind, failing to engage herself in the studies, and getting poor grades had a high I.Q. score. Motivation and expectation of success may be as important as I.Q. score. This is especially true for the vast majority of children whose I.Q.'s range from 85 to 120.

Most teachers and administrators agree that it does a child little good to know his I.Q. score, and as a matter of policy, schools do not like to reveal them. While this view is understandable (a low score may discourage a child, a high score intimidate him), some parents object to having this secret information kept as a part of a child's permanent record when they cannot know it themselves. Congress has recently passed a law that requires all schools to make public to parents all test scores of their children. And some parents have banded together to halt testing of this kind completely, preferring that no scores be known to the school rather than allowing the school to use the scores to separate "bright" children from "dull" ones in a way that parents feel is detrimental to some of the children.

What I.Q. Tests Cannot Do

There are limits to what intelligence tests can do to facilitate the task of the school. One constraint concerns the sensitivity of the test in assessing the basic mental abilities of children from poor families. If a middle-class child who is failing to learn to read but is familiar with the language of the test gets an I.Q. score of 75, it is likely that he is suffering a serious biological or psychological impairment. But if a poor ghetto child obtains a score of 75, it is a little more likely that he has the ability to master the school's requirements and that his low score is due to the bias in the test, rather than to a fundamental impairment in his mental ability.

Another major limit of intelligence tests is that they overlook some skills and do not assess crucial motivational factors, such as the determination to succeed. They do not measure talents for drawing, singing, science, organizing groups, quarreling, or mediating between friends. Among college students, scores on the Scholastic Aptitude Test (SAT), which correlate highly with I.Q. scores, do not predict quality or number of actual accomplishments in music, art, or science, even though they do predict college grades (Wallach, 1976). Moreover, in a study of productive mathematicians and chemists, the I.Q. scores of those who were doing good research—in the opinion of their peers—were not higher than those who were not doing outstanding professional work (Wallach, 1976). It seems, therefore, that among adolescents and adults whose I.Q.'s are above average—those with low I.Q. scores are unlikely to be in college—differences in I.Q. (say between 110 and 140) are not correlated with creative accomplishments or productivity in one's profession.

Surprisingly enough, I.Q. tests do not always predict how fast a child will learn a new idea or new association. A large group of Mexican children living in Mexico City were compared with a group of American children in Austin, Texas. On the Wechsler I.Q. scale the Mexican children had generally lower I.Q. scores than the Americans. However, in a test in which each child had to learn to associate a nonsense syllable with a geometric form (for example, learn to say *guz* to a picture of a circle), the Mexican children learned faster than the Americans. Many teachers assume that intelligent children are able to learn any new idea fast, yet in this case the higher I.Q. score did not mean that the child was going to learn a new idea or rule more quickly.

In the same group of children a subgroup of six-year-olds was tested both on the Wechsler scale and on a complicated object sorting test. Sixty familiar objects chosen to maximize variations in the material, color, shape, and size, were spread across the table in front of the child. He was asked to examine the objects and then to sort them into groups of his choosing. He could have as many or as few objects in a group as he wished, but he had to sort all the objects. Later he was asked the conceptual basis for each group. The child's performance was scored not only for the number of groups he produced but also for the degree to which the concepts he named were commonly held (*fruits* or *pets*) or idiosyncratic and very personal (*I like these* or *they make me happy*). There was no relation between either the kind of concepts or the number of concepts produced and the I.Q. scores of the children (Holtzman, Diaz-Guerrero, and Swartz, 1975).

Finally, I.Q. tests do not measure one significant component of problem solving, whether in schoolwork or daily life, namely, the reflectivity of the child. As we indicated in Chapter 4, many children are characteristically impulsive (they answer questions too quickly without thinking) or reflective (they take a lot of time to review their choice). While styles of impulsiveness and reflectivity are somewhat stable, they are modifiable; the overly impulsive child can gradually learn to be more reflective and make fewer mistakes on complex problems. If a child receives a score of 95 on an I.Q. test, no one reading the test score can tell whether it was below average because the child did not know the material or whether he made more mistakes than he need have because he did not reflect long enough on each question.

There are an almost infinite number of abilities a growing child can possess. While the abilities to read and do arithmetic are

unquestionably essential for anyone living in this culture, just as the ability to navigate a raft or to hunt is essential in other societies, other skills and talents can vary from person to person. It is not necessary that everyone be equally good at speaking French, performing chemistry experiments, understanding economics, or fixing the engine of a car. Perhaps by decreasing the emphasis on a single kind of intelligence, the schools will find students responding by developing more varied abilities and, as a result, a greater willingness to master the few, essential ones.

Summary

Although almost everyone in the United States agrees that intelligence is a central human quality and a major explanation for differential success in school and adult vocation, there is far less agreement on what intelligence actually is and how it is determined. This word is most often intended to mean a generalized mental ability that permits a person to learn new ideas quickly, to solve a variety of different problems efficiently, and to adapt to unfamiliar situations flexibly. Francis Galton and James McKeen Cattell, early students of intelligence, used tests of sensory acuity and reaction time to measure intelligence. But Alfred Binet developed the intelligence test that became the model for the tests used today. These tests have been highly successful because they do what they were intended to do—predict school success.

There is no doubt that intelligence test scores can discriminate between students who will perform well or poorly in school. This may be no coincidence, for they were originally based on the academic skills mastered by good students in school. The Stanford-Binet, modified by Lewis Terman, and the Wechsler I.Q. scales are widely used in America. Both are based on a norm-referenced system: they give a person an intelligence quotient (I.Q.) that states how his performance compares with that of other children his age. Both tests emphasize memory, verbal reasoning, vocabulary, and arithmetic. In addition to these I.Q. tests, which are administered individually, there are a number of group tests of mental ability that can be administered to many children at one time. While they are a little less accurate, they are more efficient for making gross estimates of the ability of large numbers of students. An individual's I.Q. is moderately stable, though it may fluctuate as much as fifteen points from testing to testing. Factors of health, fatigue, motivation, and anxiety can affect a final I.Q. score. There is also a high correlation between a child's I.Q. and his social class. Although children from middle-class families have generally higher I.Q. scores than poor children, it is not clear that they possess better nervous systems or a healthier biological basis for the mental processes mediated by the brain. It is possible that middle-class children simply have greater opportunity to learn the skills necessary to obtain high I.Q. scores. Poor children may also obtain lower scores on intelligence tests because they have lower motivation and lower expectancy of mastering essential skills.

J. P. Guilford presents an alternative model of intelligence. He suggests there are five basic mental operations (cognition, memory, convergent production, divergent production, and evaluation), which can be applied to four kinds of content (figural, symbolic, semantic, and behavioral) to produce six possible kinds of products (units, classes, relations, systems, transformations, and implications). Guilford's tests take longer to administer and produce a multifaceted, detailed profile of each person's abilities. It may ultimately prove more useful to assess many separate skills than to insist on a single score for a hypothetical generalized ability.

There has been considerable debate about the heritability of differences in intelligence, and a number of studies have claimed to isolate a strong genetic influence. The proven similarity in I.Q. scores among biologically related members of a family, and between identical twins, is the best evidence. However, some scientists believe these studies have seriously underestimated the effect of environment and overestimated the influence of heredity. The suggestion that the lower I.Q. scores of black children is due to genetics is not proven because the test content is biased to favor middle-class white children. Further, genetic control of a characteristic (such as height) within a group does not necessarily imply that variations of that characteristic between two groups are the result of different genetic endowment.

I.Q. scores can be useful in predicting how well children will perform in school and how quickly they will master academic skills. But I.Q. tests overlook important psychological attributes, such as a child's reflectivity or special talents for music or drawing, and they do not assess motivational factors, such as the child's determination to succeed.

Projects

1 List ten people whom you consider intelligent, and in each case, cite the reason for your opinion. Are there common characteristics among these people? If so, what are they?

2 Suppose that you are preparing a manual to help people administer I.Q. tests to groups of students. Write the section of the manual that advises the administrator about environmental factors that may influence the test scores.

3 With four classmates design an I.Q. test. Each one writes five questions to measure the intelligence of a different interest group (for example, chemical engineers, television addicts, Gestalt therapists, health food fanatics) so that five subcultures are represented in the questions. Give the test to your class. Grade the tests and discuss student reactions to the questions.

4 (a) Survey five people of different ages and backgrounds and find out their definitions of intelligence.

(b) Draw a chart showing the cluster of common points of agreement among them and the divergence of differing opinions.

5 Write your definition of intelligence.

Recommended Reading

Guilford, J. P. *The nature of human intelligence.* New York: McGraw-Hill, 1967. An important book that presents the author's theory of intelligence, which states that cognitive processes and products, and the materials the child works with, must all be taken into account in a discussion of intelligence.

Holtzman, W. H., Diaz-Guerrero, R., and Swartz, J. D. *Personality development in two cultures.* Austin: University of Texas Press, 1975. Summarizes a comparison of children growing up in Austin, Texas, and Mexico City and reveals that different kinds of intelligence are shown by the children in the two cultures.

Jensen, A. R. How much can we boost I.Q. and scholastic achievement? *Harvard Educational Review,* 1969, *39,* 449–483. An essay that stirred considerable controversy, stating that since most of the variation in intelligence is inherited, it is not realistic to assume that environmental intervention can change a child's intellectual ability.

Kamin, L. J. *The science and politics of I.Q.* New York: Halsted Press, 1974. Attacks the Jensen position by examining the history of the intelligence test and data that have been used by scientists to argue intelligence is inherited. Kamin finds the data deficient in many respects.

Wechsler, D. Intelligence defined and undefined. *American Psychologist,* 1975, *30,* 135–139. An interesting article by the creator of one of the most famous intelligence tests that argues that intelligence can only be defined in terms of what is valued by society.

classroom testing and evaluation

9

The measurement of human qualities has existed for several thousand years, and long after people have left the classroom, they will continue to be evaluated. Occasionally people receive unambiguous evaluation ("This man is number one in sales in our firm"). More often, though, the evaluations are phrased in less practical terms ("As a cellist, she has matured since her last concert and shows promise of greater command and subtlety to come").

Although children and adults in our society are always being evaluated, there are important differences both in the purposes of evaluation and in the methods used. This chapter is concerned with the evaluation of the student's mastery of academic skills.

The Purpose of Testing in Schools

Why do teachers and school systems devote so much energy to testing children? It is estimated that two hundred million standardized achievement tests are given each year in the United States, aside from teacher-constructed tests, and the cost of these tests is over one hundred million dollars. There are three major reasons for evaluating children. The first and perhaps the most important reason is to allow the student to evaluate his or her rate of progress toward mastery of the academic skills being taught. The results of testing also give teachers information regarding the quality of their instruction and, finally, enable the entire school system to compare the average performance of its students with that of students in other parts of the country.

Let us begin by discussing how evaluation benefits the student. Testing of students serves at least five functions, although some tend to be underplayed in classrooms.

How Testing Serves the Students

Diagnoses readiness. A test can determine how well prepared a student is for a particular course of study. Reading readiness tests given to preschool or kindergarten children evaluate how well the child has

Evaluation of how well people perform continues long after formal education has been completed. However, it is often presented in more subjective terms than those used in academic tests:

Newspaper criticism
"That the Philharmonia's players are very good indeed is not news—though I have reservations about some of the violins and about the timid violas—but rarely have they played so consistently well as at this concert. Perhaps that long-promising orchestra is really about to turn the corner and to find a profile and an audience." (Steinberg, 1974)

Personal recommendation
". . . and Phyllis's concern with the arts and practical experience as a craftsperson would certainly contribute to her understanding of the Council's goals. In recommending her for the job of administrative assistant, however, I would stress her capacity for planning, her attention to detail, and her ability to implement projects so that the outcome closely reflects the initial intent."

Peer evaluation

"Not bad, for a woman."

mastered the alphabet and can recognize simple words. Before a high-school student begins to study algebra, he needs to know basic arithmetic. The teacher can test for the presence of basic number skills and prescribe review exercises, if necessary. Tests help the teacher make a wiser, more appropriate choice of curriculum for a particular child. When tests are used in this way, they are called *diagnostic tests*.

Diagnostic tests can isolate areas of special difficulties so that the teacher knows where to begin to help overcome weaknesses in a subject area. Diagnosis is one of the most useful and, often, most underused purposes of testing. (We should mention here that the term *diagnostic* also refers to the use of special psychological tests designed to determine the underlying causes of a child's difficulty in school. These tests are not usually given by classroom teachers but by school or counseling psychologists.)

Assesses progress. Testing is also used to evaluate student progress. Such evaluations serve two purposes. One is to determine whether a particular subject area was understood and to award a grade or score to the performance. These are called *summative evaluations* and usually refer to the final test given at the end of a course or a school year. Summative evaluations, such as final examinations, are often used for certification.

Evaluations also provide feedback to the student—and to the teacher—as to how well a student is mastering the material as he goes along and what problems are being encountered. These are called *formative evaluations*. Teachers often give short quizzes during a particular course that is broken into small units of instruction so that pupil and teacher can find out what material is not well understood. The results of a formative test tell the teacher which points of instruction need modification or clarification and can also act as a kind of quality control for presenting the course in the future. Formative tests, therefore, help both students and teacher focus on the particular skills necessary for movement toward final mastery. The important difference between a formative test and a summative test is not when it is given, but how it will be used.

Increases motivation. Most teachers want to encourage their students to study the material with more effort. Students who know that they will be tested on classroom work and outside reading focus their attention more intensely than if they have no incentive to remember or understand the material.

Promotes depth of understanding. Teachers want their students to rehearse the material and to assimilate it in a profound way. Students

who are strongly motivated to perform well on a test usually study with greater concentration and are, therefore, more likely to remember and comprehend the material. In advanced courses in high school and college, studying for a test often leads the student to gain an insight into a difficult subject area. The chemistry student who has listened to the lectures and done the homework but has not grasped the principle of oxidation-reduction may, through intensive study for a test, come to understand what the principle means. Many students have attained a richer appreciation of a complicated idea through studying for an examination.

Provides reinforcement. The teacher wants to reward students by letting them know that they have mastered the topic. While critics of traditional testing may question whether the glow of success that follows a good grade is effective, many students do experience a sense of satisfaction after passing a test successfully. Like a period at the end of a sentence, a test can mark the end of one year's study and allow students to consolidate what they have learned and proceed to a new section of work.

How Testing Serves the Teachers

Teachers have their own reasons for being interested in the results of tests. The necessity for tests compels teachers to decide which aspects of the material they are going to emphasize and to ask themselves, "What do I think the students should know when the semester is over?" If a history teacher emphasizes names and dates in his lectures but constructs a test asking for a discussion of political trends, the test scores will reveal the discrepancy. If he wants his students to perform well, he will have to choose which features of the course he values most.

Tests also help teachers discriminate among students. Through quick, informal judgments, teachers sense who are the able or motivated students and who are the less capable or apathetic. Good tests can confirm or refute these personal impressions, provide valid indications of the progress of each student, and reveal the student's particular areas of difficulty.

Finally, tests are one way teachers communicate with students. A test says, "This is what is important for the course and what you are expected to know by the end of the year."

How Testing Serves the School

While test scores are most often used for individual evaluations, standardized achievement tests can also indicate how well a school compares with other schools in the same city or region and how the school's present performance compares with its past record. A rising average achievement over ten years says something about the school, its population, or its educational process. A declining average achievement implies changes in school population, curricula, quality of teaching, or administrative policies. Administrators use test results as a basis for setting policy and making adjustments in the priorities and the goals of the school system.

The Disadvantages of Tests

Some criticisms of testing are difficult to refute. One concerns the objectivity of scoring certain kinds of tests. Many years ago an investigator who was curious about the range of possible marks for identical papers sent two student essays to two hundred English professors in different parts of the United States. Each essay received a range of grades from A to E (Starch and Elliot, 1912). More recently, in a study of how teachers' gradings fluctuate, one teacher marked the same ten essay examinations two months apart. The correlation between grades assigned the first time and the second time was low, only about .45. A teacher grading the same essay test does not always agree even with herself, to say nothing of agreeing with other teachers (Teigs, 1952).

Classroom tests also have the disadvantage of freezing the current of sympathy and trust running between the students and the teacher. A teacher may try to establish rapport in classroom discussions by willingly admitting ignorance to some questions and encouraging diversions when they seem provocative and fruitful. But as a result, when he announces an upcoming test, the students may feel betrayed: the class is now polarized into two factions—the tester and the tested. Furthermore, tests produce anxiety among some students, and the anxiety itself can prevent them from demonstrating the knowledge that they have gained.

A fourth criticism of testing centers on how the results are expressed; in other words, grades. Instead of concentrating on the potentially interesting aspects of the subject, students become preoccupied with grades, worry about competing against their classmates, and learn to evaluate themselves and their schoolwork in terms of their rank. Teachers, in turn, can spend prodigious amounts of time assigning grades—and defending them to dissatisfied students.

One may agree that testing is necessary and still object to the traditional forms of grading; we'll return to the matter of grading later in the chapter. Let us now consider the relative merits of classroom tests compared to more subjective personal evaluations.

The Advantages of Tests

The perennial criticisms of testing and test scores nourish a longing for a better system of evaluation. Many students, parents, and even teachers voice a plea for more personal methods of measuring each student's achievements, based, perhaps, on private interviews and individual scholastic projects.

Unquestionably, teachers include classroom performance and personal impressions in their overall evaluation. But it is for just that reason that objective tests make a unique contribution to the educational process. The four main reasons good written classroom tests uniformly administered have an advantage over more personal evaluations are that they are fair, efficient, valid, and reliable.

Fairness and representativeness. Good written tests offer students a representative sample of questions and the same questions for everyone. The oral tests used until one hundred years ago offered neither. In those tests the examiner selected a student and picked out a question to ask her. One student might have drawn an easy question, the next student a difficult one. Written tests offer all the students the same questions, easy and difficult together. The test is a standardized situation in which all the students are being compared on the same items—an impossibility if each student is judged on independent and

unrelated projects. Furthermore, they are offered a large selection of questions, not just one or two, which gives each student a greater number of opportunities to show what she knows. And by making the tests written and objective, as compared with a face-to-face interview, teachers reduce the danger that they will succumb to the *halo effect:* allowing previous impressions of the student's performance to interfere with their assessment of her current performance.

Efficiency. Written tests are also more efficient, for an entire class can take a test in the same time needed to question a few students individually on a few items. As the need for evaluation grew and it became important to complete the process efficiently, written tests appeared more attractive, as teachers could administer a test to many students simultaneously, rather than question them one at a time.

Validity. A test is valid when it measures what it is supposed to measure. Consider a simple example. Suppose a census taker wishes to know the number of people who live in all the homes on a particular block. The question asked of the person who answers the doorbell is "How many people live in this house?" The validity of the answer depends on the correspondence between the answer given by the respondent and the number the census taker would obtain if he actually entered the house and counted the number of people who lived there. If the question was intended to mean how many people actually use the house as their living quarters, regardless of their genetic relationship to the family, but the respondent thought that the interviewer only meant blood relatives and therefore omitted mentioning two visitors from Europe who were living in the home for that year, the question would not be valid, even though the respondent gave what he regarded as an honest answer. Thus the validity of a test depends on how it will be used. Answers to questions can be valid from one perspective but not from another. The validity of a test or a question on a test always refers to the intention of the person giving the test.

Consider the following problems:

(a) $427 \times 7 = ?$
(b) $6x = 42, x = ?$
(c) $\dfrac{x-2}{42} = \dfrac{1}{x-3}, x = ?$

Only the first problem can be regarded as a valid test of knowledge of multiplication. A student who knew multiplication but did not know algebra would not be able to solve problems b and c.

Although teachers must always be sensitive to the representativeness of the questions they ask, there is likely to be little disagreement with a teacher's decision to give a dozen multiplication problems involving two-, three-, and four-digit numbers and regard it as a valid test of a child's ability to multiply. But when it comes to more ambiguous skills, there is often much disagreement about the validity of a test. Robert Ebel, a psychologist who specializes in measurement and evaluation, gives this example of the problem:

> Applicants for positions in the police force of a city were shown this sign
>
> | Throw trash |
> | in the |
> | the trash cans |
>
> and asked to comment on it. If the applicants noticed the repetition of the word "the" they were given credit for perceptiveness and their chances of acceptance were improved. But there is little evidence, and really not much reason, to expect that people who are good at noticing printing errors in signs will also be good at noticing essential details at the scene of a crime. (1972, p. 444)

Hence, the test item may not be valid for selecting police officers, although it may be a valid test item for secretaries or proofreaders.

As a rule, two strategies are used to evaluate the validity of a test. In the first, an expert or group of experts examines the contents of the test and judges whether they are a sensitive way to assess mastery of the material. For example, a group of teachers compose a twenty-item true-false test for knowledge of the Civil War and show it to three professors who are experts in the field. If the professors feel the questions are drawn from the most important facts and principles of the Civil War and will assess mastery, then the test is said to have *face validity* (the term comes from the phrase "on the face of it"). To a limited degree, face validity is common-sense validity. Although in many cases it is easy to judge the face validity of a test accurately, in many others experts cannot agree. Consider an example in mathematics. Many new mathematics curricula were written during the last ten years, each with different emphases. Suppose a teacher wanted to construct a valid test for her eighth-grade students to evaluate their mastery of mathematics. She biases the test in favor of word problems

---

Testing emerged as part of the educational process far back in human history. The tests given by ancient Greeks to identify citizens who would be good at government jobs were very much like our civil service exams today, except that they were not exclusively mental. They included physical tests that measured a man's ability to run, wrestle, throw a discus, and perform a folk dance—an important test item because it combined musical and athletic skills, two attributes highly prized by the Greeks (Doyle, 1974). Most of our general achievement tests do not measure artistic or athletic ability, since in contemporary America these skills do not usually facilitate the acquisition of wealth, professional knowledge, or access to prestigious institutions. Instead, we test for knowledge and reasoning ability with words and numbers.

Oral testing, an old tradition, is still alive in the "orals" taken by graduate students who complete their course of study by answering questions posed by members of their department. When universities were first established in medieval Europe, the examinations consisted of public debates on controversial questions. As one may expect, considering how subjective the questions were, dissatisfaction with oral examinations developed. In the sixteenth

century Jesuits concerned with scholarship insisted on the use of written exams. They wrote down a set of rules for giving these examinations that are similar to the rules used today.

In early American schools oral exams were once again popular. But in 1845 Horace Mann, a major figure in American education, substituted written tests in the Boston schools. Like the Jesuits, he argued that written examinations would give better, more reliable, and more impartial evidence of a student's knowledge; furthermore, they provided a permanent record of a child's achievement. As a result, written exams began to be introduced in American schools. Perhaps the oldest and most venerable—the Regents' Examination of New York—began in 1865.

With the passage of laws making secondary education compulsory, the number of high schools increased from five hundred to ten thousand (Hofstadter, Miller, and Aaron, 1959). As a result, many more students wanted to go on to college. College admission committees needed to discriminate among these students, and as an efficient alternative to written evaluations, the practice of grading increased in order to help the colleges select the students they wanted.

rather than computation. One expert may judge the test a valid measure of the skills a student has mastered in eight years, a second expert may not. Hence, there will be disagreement about the face validity of the test.

But in addition to measuring past mastery, the teacher wants to use the test to predict future performance in high-school mathematics. In this case the test would be evaluated for its *predictive validity*. If the teacher's test accurately predicted who did well and who did poorly when they entered high school, we say that the test had predictive validity. Many psychological tests have predictive validity even though experts disagree on their face validity. For example, there is a famous personality questionnaire called the Minnesota Multiphasic Personality Inventory, which consists of a large number of questions about a person's feelings, beliefs, and actions. The answers to these questions do better than chance in predicting who will be schizophrenic or depressed even though psychological experts quarrel about the reasonableness (that is, the face validity) of diagnosing a person psychotic on the basis of his answers to these written questions. Most standardized tests have both face and predictive validity. Most teacher-constructed tests have face validity—in the eyes of the teacher—but their predictive validity is rarely evaluated.

Reliability. A test is *reliable* if it measures what it is supposed to measure *consistently*. If a child takes a test and a few days later, without further study or discussion, takes the test again, his two scores should be very similar. Or, if a child takes two tests that have different items but involve the same skills and knowledge, his scores should also be similar. If they are, we say the test is reliable. A valid test must be reliable. However, a reliable test may or may not be valid. Recall our earlier example of asking a person how many people live in a home.

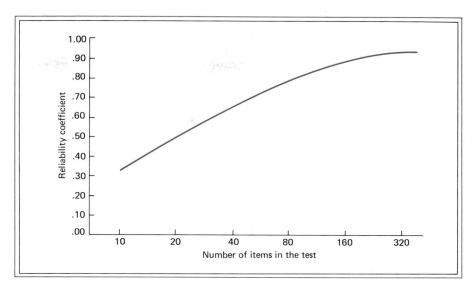

Figure 9–1
**Reliability is one of the major requirements for a test. Although perfect
reliability is rare, the longer a test is, the greater its reliability. (Adapted from
Ebel, 1962)**

The respondent may give the same answer every day—hence, his
answer is reliable—but if he does not include the two nonmembers of
the family who live in the house, it will not be valid.

One way psychologists assess the reliability of a test is to give it to a
large number of children on two different occasions and compute a
correlation between the two sets of scores. If the correlation between
the scores of the children on the two administrations is .90 or better, the
test can be regarded as highly reliable. For our best tests, such as
standardized intelligence tests, the reliabilities often approach .90. In
general, although perfect reliability rarely occurs, the longer a test is,
the greater its reliability (see Figure 9–1).

The Design of Tests

What Do Tests Measure?

Normally, when one asks the question "What do tests measure?" the
reply is that they measure the knowledge the student has acquired.
However, this answer raises a broader question. Should the tests we
give try to evaluate all the educational objectives that have been
formulated over the years? The list is a long one and includes the

following aims: transmitting our cultural and intellectual heritage; improving the discipline of the mind; promoting moral and spiritual values; developing democratic citizenship; fostering good mental health; inculcating a positive attitude toward knowledge; cultivating aesthetic sensitivity; providing instruction and practice in the skills of note taking, essay writing, research, reasoning, mathematics, and oral expression.

Obviously, no one test can measure all these goals. A serious effort has been made to identify educational objectives, especially at the college level. Benjamin Bloom and his colleagues (1956) have tried to specify educational objectives in the form of a taxonomy, or classification scheme. They believe that educational objectives should include both cognitive skills and affective competences. Let us consider the first group of objectives, cognitive skills.

Cognitive Objectives

Bloom's taxonomy of educational objectives identifies six cognitive skills, which are arranged in order of complexity (see Figure 9–2). The

Figure 9–2
The taxonomy of educational objectives is an attempt to describe a hierarchy of six steps in the cognitive domain. In theory, any level in the hierarchy depends on the preceding levels. (Adapted from Bloon. et al., 1956; Stanley and Hopkins, 1972)

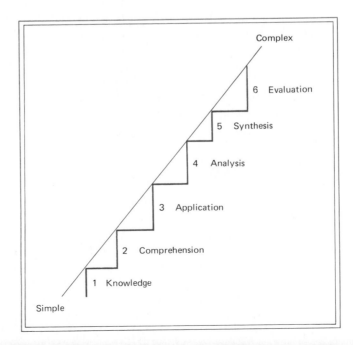

first—and simplest—is knowledge. In theory, each level must be mastered in turn.

1 *Knowledge*—the ability to recall specific facts, methods, or procedures, such as mathematical rules or scientific principles. This objective involves little more than retrieving stored information ("When is George Washington's birthday?"). It is related to Guilford's factor of recognition, discussed in Chapter 8.
2 *Comprehension*—the ability to understand the basis of the question. A teacher can test for comprehension by determining if the student can paraphrase a specific question or explain the essence of the question to another person. A student who has memorized the formula "Force equals mass times acceleration" but does not comprehend it will be unable either to put it in different words or to explain it. When we say that we want the student to study for understanding, we are implying that we want her to comprehend the basic issues and the meaning of the facts that she is learning.
3 *Application*—the ability to use one's knowledge correctly when required. This means that the student must be able to generalize a fact or a principle to another situation. If the student has learned that distance equals rate multiplied by time in the context of an automobile traveling 60 miles an hour for 3 hours, he should be able to apply that knowledge to a question having to do with an airplane traveling 600 miles an hour for 2.5 hours. Or, a student should be able to relate his knowledge of the conflicts that produced the

Revolutionary War and the Civil War to those producing fighting in the Middle East and southern Africa.

4 *Analysis*—the ability to separate a particular idea into its components. It requires the student to be able to distinguish a fact from a hypothesis or a theory, recognize unstated presuppositions and assumptions, and even recognize the bias or prejudices of a writer. This ability is demonstrated when a person perceives that a liberal or a conservative politician giving a speech on law enforcement has slanted his argument so that it is in accord with his political beliefs. Often test writers will insert irrelevant material into a problem in order to assess whether a student can discriminate the essential from the unessential. Consider the following physics problem: "Two balls, one black and one white, each weighing two pounds, were dropped from a 100-foot tower at high noon. How many seconds did it take each to hit the ground?" To solve this problem, one has to know the distance to the ground and the equation that relates distance to time. The information that the balls were dropped at high noon and were colored black and white is irrelevant—and the student must be able to recognize that fact.

5 *Synthesis*—the ability to put together cognitive units and knowledge to form a coherent whole. If a student consolidates his knowledge, gained through reading many books on a particular topic, into an organized and logical essay, he is demonstrating the ability to synthesize.

6 *Evaluation*—the ability to judge the value and the quality of a particular idea or solution, to reflect on an answer or hypothesis, and to recognize the best of several reasonably good answers. This final cognitive objective is partially related to the matter of reflective and impulsive approaches to problem solving, as discussed in Chapter 5.

Most teachers emphasize the first educational objective—knowledge—on their tests. Such tests are relatively easy to construct and grade, compared to tests measuring comprehension, application, analysis, synthesis, and evaluation. However, these objectives are important too, and the taxonomy can serve as a useful guide for teachers who believe that tests should tap abilities other than knowledge more frequently and sensitively than they do.

Criterion-referenced and Norm-referenced Tests

There are two kinds of tests that evaluate a child's performance following instruction. The first establishes some absolute standard, or criterion, regarding what a child should have learned in a particular unit of study and measures how closely he meets that standard. Such a test is called a *criterion-referenced test*. The score the student obtains reflects the proportion mastered of what the teacher thought the student should have mastered. If the teacher feels that every child should be able to solve a particular set of twenty addition problems after six months of instruction, the proportion of the twenty problems that the student solves, whether it is 10 percent, 30 percent, or 100 percent, will determine the final grade.

The second is a *norm-referenced test,* in which the score assigned to a child is compared to those of the students in his class, rather than measured against an objective standard. The teacher may take all the scores on a particular twenty-item arithmetic test and determine which child obtained the highest score, whether it was five, six, twelve, or all twenty correct. That child would then receive the highest grade, regardless of his actual score. In a standardized test, each child's score will reflect his standing in a larger group. Obviously, there is a difference between local norms, for which students in one school or one city are taken as referent, and national norms, which include students in many regions. In general, criterion-referenced tests are more often used in individualized instruction where the teacher is very clear about the criterion of mastery she wants a particular child to attain.

There are problems, however, with the use of criterion-referenced tests in all curriculum areas. The most crucial one is that it is sometimes difficult for the teacher to set the criterion that establishes the minimal level of competence. It can also be difficult to write the test. Even simple changes in the phrasing of a test question can influence a child's performance. Thus, although on a theoretical level the idea of criterion-referenced testing is appealing to many, in practice it is limited.

Standardized Achievement Tests

It is important to distinguish between tests made up by a classroom teacher for either formative or summative evaluation and standardized achievement tests. Standardized achievement tests, which are usually available commercially, differ from teacher-constructed classroom tests in many ways. First, they have been carefully prepared and pretested on a large number of children in order to eliminate or refine improperly worded items or questions that are too difficult or too easy. In addition, the reliability and, on rare occasions, the validity of these tests have been established. Standardized achievement tests, which usually have fixed time limits, provide explicit instructions to administrators and students so that, no matter where students go to school, they will take the test with the same general understanding and mental set. Sometimes they are designed to be scored on a computer. Often they include a graph for plotting a student's test results.

Finally, tables of norms for interpreting the scores have been established for the tests. The test manual lists the norm, or average score, obtained by a large group of children of a particular age or grade level, so that teachers can evaluate how a particular child's score compares with that of the norming sample that originally took the test.

The most commonly used standardized achievement tests in the United States include California Achievement Tests, Comprehensive Tests of Basic Skills, Iowa Tests of Basic Skills, Iowa Tests of Educational Development, Metropolitan Achievement Tests, SRA Achievement Series, Sequential Tests of Educational Progress, and Stanford Achievement Tests (see Figure 9–3). Several of these tests have been administered in enough states and in enough schools to give some idea of national norms; some, however, were developed primarily for certain states or regions and the original standardization groups came from those localities.

Figure 9–3
Standardized tests, such as the Stanford Achievement Test excerpted here, are used to test achievement at different levels in specific areas: language usage, knowledge of current affairs, literary comprehension, arithmetic skills, social studies, and scientific skills and principles. They measure achievement on commonly accepted educational objectives, rather than on individual classroom work, and are most useful for comparisons with national standards. (Madden et al., 1972)

TEST 2.
Reading: Part B

SAMPLE
We saw a happy boy and a sad girl.
The girl was

A crying   flying   purple   asleep,
   ●   O   O   O

but the boy was

B sick   laughing   hurt   angry.
   O   O   O   O

Tim's legs were very tired.
He had just run up a long, steep

1 fence   hill   wall   chimney.
   O   O   O   O

Leslie is Bill's sister. Leslie is a

2 girl   man   shoe   boy.
   O   O   O   O

TEST 6.
Mathematics Applications (Continued)

Use this chart to answer questions 15-17.

The Ages of Children in Our Room

Years Old	Number of Children
7	///
$7\frac{1}{2}$	///// /////
8	///// ///// /
$8\frac{1}{2}$	///// /

15 In which age group are there the most children?

   7   8 $7\frac{1}{2}$ $8\frac{1}{2}$
   O   O   O   O

16 How many children are in the $7\frac{1}{2}$ year old group?

   3   12   10   5
   O   O   O   O

17 How many children are in the room all together?

   17   13   30   25
   O   O   O   O

Transformed Scores

Norms on standardized achievement tests are usually not given in raw score form—that is, in terms of number of questions answered correctly—but are transformed to a more meaningful scale. Typically, the norms are expressed in relation to age or school grade and are called *grade-equivalent scores*. An achievement test in reading, for instance, will present the average score for groups of first-graders, second-graders, and so forth. Unfortunately, the norms for some standardized tests are based on all the children who took the test, no matter where in the country they took the test or how big the school they attended. The norms would be more immediately valuable to the teacher if they were given for particular areas of the country or for schools of particular sizes, since a school in a large eastern metropolitan city, for example, is likely to have a different curriculum than a school in a rural town in the Southwest.

Since curricula are always changing, the norms must be kept up-to-date. Both vocabulary and content of specific mathematics and science curricula have changed during the last quarter of a century. The norms of an achievement test published twenty-five years ago may be inappropriate for children in school today, and the teacher should be aware of which tests have been normed most recently.

Although grade-equivalent scores are often used to report results on achievement tests, the practice holds some hidden dangers. If a third-grade child takes the reading test appropriate for third-grade children and obtains a very high or a very low score, the grade-equivalent score he is assigned is obtained by estimating what his

And the Gileadites took the passages of Jordan before the Ephraimites: and it was so, that when those Ephraimites which were escaped said, Let me go over; that the men of Gilead said unto him, Art thou an Ephraimite? If he said, Nay; Then said they unto him, Say now Shibboleth: and he said Sibboleth: for he could not frame to pronounce it right. Then they took him, and slew him at the passages of Jordan: and there fell at that time of the Ephraimites forty and two thousand. (Judges 12:5–6, King James Version)

Perhaps an oversimplified test, this interrogation nevertheless addresses several components of testing. It is standardized: everyone who wanted to cross the Jordan had to pronounce *Shibboleth*. It assumed that the correct response indicated an underlying trait (in this case, nationality). It discriminated among the participants. But two major requirements of a test were not, in all probability, definitely established: reliability and validity. Can we be sure that all Ephraimites, and no Gileadites, pronounced the word with a sibilant first consonant? And how valid an indication of nationality is the pronunciation of a consonant pair? (Stanley and Hopkins, 1972)

score would be had he been given a more or a less difficult test. This procedure makes certain assumptions about the rate of growth of reading ability. These assumptions are not always accurate, and as a result, the predictions can be inaccurate. Teachers should be cautious when interpreting grade-equivalent scores from raw scores that are far below or far above the child's actual grade level.

Computing Transformed Scores

The vast majority of classroom tests are used by teachers in a norm-referenced, rather than a criterion-referenced, manner because the teacher wants to know something about each child's ability relative to the other children in the classroom. A raw score of 75 on a test does not convey that information. Hence, over the years psychologists interested in measurements have developed a series of procedures that convert the raw scores obtained by a group of children into *transformed scores* that inform the teacher, child, and parent about a particular child's standing relative to his classmates.

Ranks and Percentile Ranks

The simplest procedure is to assign a rank of 1 to the student with the highest score, a rank of 2 to the student with the next highest score, and so on until every child in the classroom has been assigned a rank. The lower the rank, the higher the child's relative standing. The disadvantage of this simple ranking procedure is that the ranks of children from classes of different sizes cannot be compared. Obviously a child with a rank of 10 on an arithmetic test in a class of 20 students is not as able as a child who obtained a rank of 10 on the test in a class of 40 students.

But there is a way to convert the ranks to a new score that permits such a comparison. This procedure converts the ranks of the two students to a hypothetical rank—the rank each would have if the students were in classes that contained 100 pupils. This is called a *percentile rank*. A student whose score outranked 20 classmates in a class of 30 has a score that is better than two-thirds of the scores of the other students. In order to determine what his rank would be if he were in a class of 100 rather than a class of 30, we take the ratio of the number of students scoring below him to the size of his classroom (that is, 20 over 30) and multiply that ratio by 100, which yields a percentile rank of 67. A student whose score in arithmetic outranked 20 classmates in a smaller class of only 25 would have a higher percentile rank of 80, obtained by taking the ratio of 20 over 25 and multiplying it by 100. Here is how the computation looks as a formula:

$$\text{percentile rank} = \frac{\text{number of students with lower score}}{\text{total number of students in class}} \times 100$$

The percentile rank of a given score indicates what percentage of the scores was lower than that score. Hence, a percentile rank of 92 means that a particular score was higher than 92 percent of the other scores in that classroom.

Standard Scores

Another procedure that assigns transformed scores involves the concept of the *standard score*. It has a major advantage over percentile rank because it provides an estimate of how large a difference exists between two raw scores.

Suppose two students obtain percentile ranks of 50 and 70, respectively. The percentile rank difference of 20 can, in one classroom, reflect a difference of only one extra question answered correctly, while in another classroom it can reflect a difference of five extra questions answered correctly. Thus, under some conditions, the percentile rank can distort the real discrepancy between two scores.

Standard scores avoid that distortion. A standard score is obtained by converting a student's raw score on a test into a new value that indicates the difference between that individual score and the *mean* score for the class. It expresses that difference in a unit that is called the *standard deviation*. But before we describe the standard score further, we must first consider what is meant by the mean. The mean (or average) score is obtained by adding all the scores on a particular test and dividing that sum by the number of children who took the test.

Thus, the formula for the mean is:

$$\text{mean} = \frac{\text{sum of scores}}{\text{total number of scores}}$$

If the sum of 20 scores in a classroom came to 1,560, dividing that sum by 20 yields a mean score of 78. The mean score would be 78 even if none of the actual scores was 78.

A related measure is the *median*. It is the actual score obtained by the child who is at the middle of the group. If you arrange the scores of twenty-one children from the highest to the lowest, then the score of the child eleventh in rank will be the median score. If there is an even number of children—twenty—then the median will be the number half way between the two middle scores. A median score means that 50 percent of the children have scores that are higher, and 50 percent have scores that are lower. If the scores of five children are 62, 71, 76, 81, and 90, the median is 76.

A third measure is called the *mode*. The mode is the score made by the largest number of students.

Now let us return to the standard deviation. What we want is a measuring rod that provides us with a standard way of talking about the distance between each child's score and the mean so that we can use it for any set of scores in any classroom for any test. That measuring rod is the standard deviation, which reflects the variability of dispersal of the scores around the average score.

Consider the three sets of scores below, called distributions A, B, and C, each of which has a mean of 70.

Child	A	B	C
1	69	40	20
2	69	50	30
3	70	60	40
4	70	70	100
5	70	80	100
6	71	90	100
7	71	100	100
Sum	490	490	490

You will notice that when the scores from these three distributions are put on a graph, as they are in Figure 9-4, the distance of each score from the mean of 70 is slight in distribution A, a little larger in distribution B, and very large in distribution C. In each set of scores the sum of all the distances of each score from the mean determines the variability. The lowest variability occurs in distribution A because most of the scores are close to the mean, and the standard deviation is between 1 and 2. In distribution C, where most of the scores are far from the mean, the variability is larger and the standard deviation is over twenty times as large.

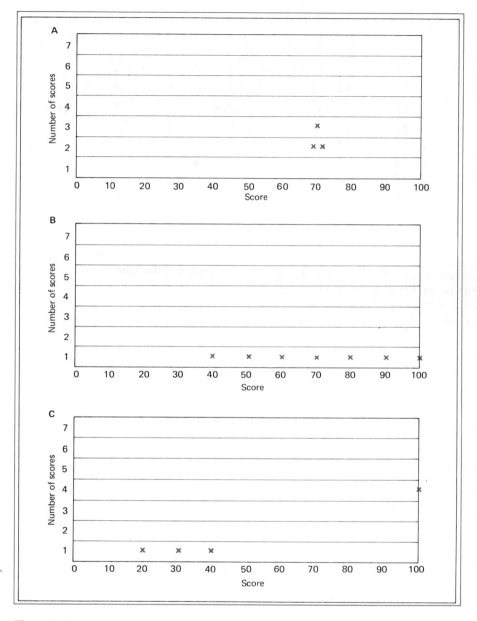

Figure 9–4
Three sets of scores, each with a mean of 70, showing different dispersals of the scores around the mean.

But we have not yet shown, as we promised, that the standard deviation can state information about the relative rank of the student in terms of standard scores. Before we do, one more issue must be appreciated. It involves the form of the distribution of the scores on a particular test. Consider the pattern of the three sets of scores in distributions A, B, and C in Figure 9–4. You will notice that in distribution A the most frequent scores are in the middle. Moreover, the distribution of scores is symmetrical: if we drew a line down the center at the mean of 70, the number of cases below the mean would be the same as the number of cases above it.

These are some of the characteristics of a *normal distribution,* a mathematical concept in which the mean, the mode, and the median are exactly the same and the scores cluster around a single score (see Figure 9–5). Moreover, the mean, the mode, and the median divide the curve into symmetrical halves. Finally, the tails of the curve draw closer and closer to the horizontal axis but never quite meet it.

In practice, no distribution of scores will correspond exactly to the ideal of a normal distribution. Nevertheless, distributions of scores often approach the ideal and, for our purposes, can be used to make the same inferences about the scores. If the distribution of scores resembles a normal distribution, then we know that about 68 percent of all the scores will fall between one standard deviation below and one standard deviation above the mean and that 96 percent of all the scores will fall

Figure 9–5
When a distribution of scores approaches the theoretical normal distribution, as this drawing shows, about 34 percent of all the scores lies between the mean and one standard deviation below the mean; another 34 percent falls between the mean and one standard deviation above the mean. On either side of the mean, about 14 percent of the scores falls between one and two standard deviations away from the mean, and about 2 percent falls between two and three standard deviations away from the mean. A final .14 percent of the scores is found more than three standard deviations above and below the mean. The percentages shown here hold true for any normal distribution, although the size of the standard deviation itself varies from curve to curve.

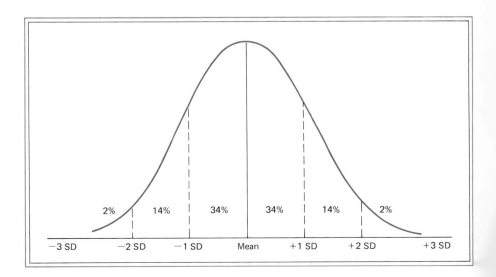

| 2% | 14% | 34% | 34% | 14% | 2% |

−3 SD   −2 SD   −1 SD   Mean   +1 SD   +2 SD   +3 SD

between two standard deviations below the mean and two standard deviations above the mean, as in Figure 9–5.

Any child with a score greater than two standard deviations above the mean would be in the top 2 percent of his group; any child whose score is two standard deviations below the mean will be in the bottom 2 percent of his group. On the Stanford-Binet Intelligence Test, for example, we know that the mean score for a large number of children approximates 100 and that the standard deviation is about 15 points. If the child obtained an I.Q. score of 145, we can ask how many standard deviation units that I.Q. is from the average. Since the difference between 145 and 100 is 45 and the standard deviation of the test is 15 points, we know that this child's score is 3 standard deviation units above the mean; this means that his I.Q. score is in the top 1 percent of all I.Q. scores.

Hence, the standard score, often called a *Z-score*, is computed by taking the difference between the mean and a particular child's score and dividing by the standard deviation. Here is the formula:

$$\text{standard score (Z-score)} = \frac{\text{student's score minus the mean}}{\text{standard deviation}}$$

If a child received a score of 90, the class mean was 78, and the standard deviation was 13.6, the computation would read as follows:

$$\text{standard score} = \frac{90 - 78}{13.6} = 0.9$$

We must remember, however, that when a distribution of scores deviates from the normal distribution in a serious way, one cannot be sure what percent of the cases falls between one standard deviation below or one standard deviation above the mean.

Many published tests present norms in terms of standard scores; we can now say what that means. A standard score represents the deviation of a particular child's score from the mean in *standard deviation units*. Thus if a child's standard score was $+1.6$, it would mean that his score was 1.6 standard deviations above the mean. A standard score of -0.6 would mean that his score was 0.6 of a standard deviation below the mean. A score between $+1$ and $+2$ standard deviation units is typically higher than 90 percent of all scores. A score that is -0.6 standard deviation units is higher than about 30 percent of all scores.

T-Scores and Stanine Scores

You will notice that standard scores can have negative numbers and decimals. Since most teachers like to avoid both negative signs and decimals, the standard scores are often converted to another transformed score called a *T-score*.

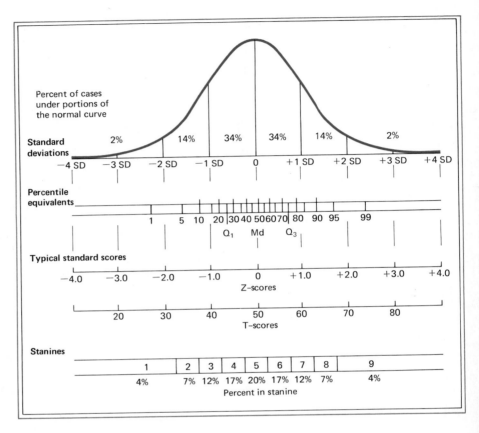

Figure 9-6
A comparison of scores in different forms. (Adapted from Test Service Bulletin No. 48, 1954–1955)

The T-score is obtained by multiplying the standard score by 10 (which eliminates the decimal) and adding 50. Thus a standard score of +2.0 is comparable to a T-score of 70. Both scores are two standard deviation units above the average score. The T-score distribution has a mean of 50 and a standard deviation of 10 points. Some tests, like the Graduate Record Examination, adjust the standard scores so that the mean will be 500 and the standard deviation 100. Hence, a score of 400 is one standard deviation below the mean and is equivalent to a T-score of 40, which is also one standard deviation below the mean.

Another transformed score is called a *stanine score*. The stanine has a mean of 5 and a standard deviation of approximately 2. Each single stanine is about one-half of a standard deviation unit. Hence, a stanine score of 7 represents a score that is one standard deviation above the mean and therefore is greater than about 84 percent of the scores. A stanine score of 3 is roughly equivalent to a T-score of 40 and to a Z-score of −1.0; each of the three scores is approximately one standard deviation below the mean. (For a comparison of scores in different forms, see Figure 9–6.)

Implications for Teaching: Teacher-constructed Tests

When teachers have to make up their own tests for either formative or summative purposes, they must make three important decisions: what should the students know, how can their knowledge be measured, and how will the teachers and students use the results of the test?

What Should a Test Contain?

First of all, the teacher should consider some of the questions raised in the section on the design of tests. Before beginning to write particular questions, she should review the material covered and make an outline of the relevant topics (she can look over the section headings of the textbook or make up a list of categories for vocabulary, concepts, and

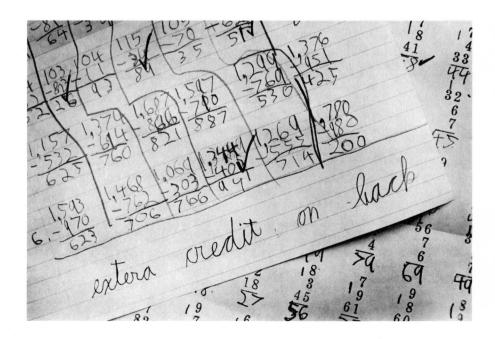

principles and their uses), keeping in mind the cognitive objectives described earlier. Some material can be defined specifically: a list of spelling words, multiplication tables, the twelve major dates in one hundred years of English history, or the forms of three irregular French verbs. In other cases, the material is less easily defined. A unit on the Civil War, for instance, contains many ideas, interpretations, and facts—economic, political, and social conditions before the war as well as the names of leaders, milestone dates, and major battles. It is harder to specify the information to be mastered for literature, history, social studies, or government than it is for mathematics and science.

In writing test questions, it is also important to be faithful to your word: if you have assured students you are interested in the dynamics at work in the years prior to the Civil War and administer a test entirely composed of questions on dates, names, and battles, the students are likely to feel betrayed. The important point is that the test reflect the teacher's conception and that the students be aware of what the teacher thinks is important.

Power or Speed?

For some subjects the teacher may only be interested in the depth of the child's understanding of the material and therefore will not care how fast a pupil can finish the test—only whether he knows the issues and facts. These tests are called power tests. On other occasions, however, she may want to know if the students have thoroughly mastered certain skills so that they can quickly apply their knowledge to new problems. She may impose a time limit on the test: such tests are called speed tests.

Norm-referenced or Criterion-referenced?

As we described earlier, tests can be used either to rank the pupils or to ascertain to what degree each pupil has mastered the material considered essential for mastery in that area. If the topic to be tested is mastery of the multiplication tables to 12×12, a norm-referenced test would rank the students depending on how many correct answers each student gave. But if the teacher believed all students should know the tables completely to 12×12, this would be his criterion, and all the answers would have to be correct for the student to obtain an A. If the teacher chooses to score the test in a criterion-referenced manner, there is less need to include especially difficult items designed to discern between very able and average students. It is necessary, however, to provide an adequate work sample to assess whether the child reached the criterion for mastery: three multiplication problems would not be enough.

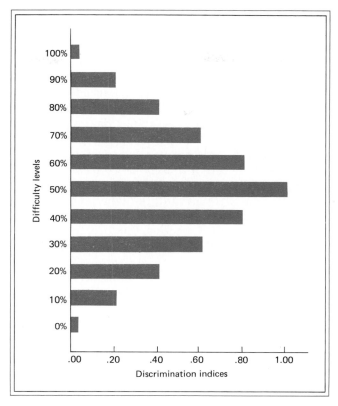

Figure 9–7
In choosing items for a classroom test, the teacher should remember that moderately difficult items are more discriminating than either very easy items or very hard ones, as shown in this graph. (After Ebel, 1962)

Teachers who treat the scores to tests in a norm-referenced manner usually are interested in discriminating among very able, average, and less able students and must include questions that will achieve the distinction. Moderately difficult items are more discriminating than either very easy items, which all but one or two of the students can be expected to answer correctly, or very hard items, which all but one or two of the students can be expected to answer incorrectly (Ebel, 1962). This point is illustrated in Figure 9–7.

What Form Should Questions Take?

Having defined the content of the tests and the time constraints, the teacher must now choose the form of the test questions. The two basic forms are essay and short-answer questions.

Essay
Questions

The essay question is useful if the teacher wants to evaluate the students' ability to organize and to synthesize information and to challenge them to formulate and present arguments. The essay involves all the cognitive processes discussed in Chapter 4 and those in the taxonomy of educational objectives. Essays allow students more freedom than short-answer questions in deciding how to approach a question, what material to include, what points to make, and how to organize the information. Unquestionably, essays favor students with good verbal and writing skills and may distort the degree of mastery and knowledge possessed by students who have a difficult time expressing themselves in expository writing. The disadvantage of the essay test is that it is more difficult to write and grade reliably and tends to penalize those children who may have learned a great deal of specific material but have difficulty synthesizing it.

In writing essay questions, the teacher should guard against questions that are too general ("Discuss the Civil War"). The more precisely worded the question, the more likely that the answers will reflect differential mastery of the material. At the same time, a carefully worded question directs the students' attention to the aspects of the subject the teacher considers important and protects against misunderstanding of what is wanted in the response. The teacher should write out his own model answer for each essay question, listing the major points and facts believed essential and the secondary points and facts that have a place in a good answer. Individual answers are then judged against that model.

If a teacher wanted to see how well the students could generalize their knowledge about Lincoln's views and their place in the Civil War, he might ask:

> Instead of writing the Gettysburg Address on the back of an envelope,
> Lincoln was writing a speech to the nation one year after the Civil
> War had begun. Considering Lincoln's stance and the forces dividing
> the country, write an outline of his speech.

This question addresses several cognitive objectives. The students must remember Lincoln's attitudes (knowledge), distinguish forces at work in the nation that year (analysis), and compose a speech that takes both of these factors into account (synthesis). While such a question does not attempt to address a number of aspects that might have been included in a reasonable answer to the general question "Discuss the Civil War," it does narrow the students' focus and demands a more specific and considered response.

Over the years there has been considerable discussion about the best way to evaluate essay questions since, unlike multiple-choice items, there is usually room for a good deal of ambiguity. There have even been some experiments in using computers to grade.

The computer bases its grade on elements such as frequency of uncommon words, prepositions, commas, and length of the answer, Oddly enough, while computer grades are not based on the essential characteristics of good organization, sound argument, and clear language, they correlate with the grades of independent judges (Page, 1966).

Some teachers believe that answers to essay questions need to be read several times: first, to get a range of the content and presentation and second, to make tentative categories with the poorest in one pile, the best in another, and the others in an intermediate pile. The third reading verifies whether or not the individual papers have been rightfully categorized.

When reading essay tests, it is useful to read every student's answer to the first question and grade that question (without looking at the names, if possible). Then continue to the second essay question. This strategy avoids the halo effect, where a good impression created by one answer colors the interpretation of the succeeding answers. Remember, too, to include some positive comments on your remarks to each student. Inadvertently, teachers often write only criticisms, which discourage students and inhibit their future writing efforts. Students deserve to know where they have performed well, as well as where they have been less successful.

Short-answer Questions: Recall and Recognition

Short-answer questions hold some advantages over essay questions. Answers can be more quickly and readily scored and, in some instances, can be scored by using a key. Short-answer questions are an excellent way to test for knowledge. In addition, if the teacher has enough ingenuity and command of the subject matter, they can be

designed to test comprehension and not just rote memory. They can also make imaginative use of cartoons, maps, graphs, charts, and the like (see Figure 9–8).

There are two kinds of short-answer questions: recall and recognition. *Recall questions* require the child to supply the answer himself; *recognition questions* only require the child to select the correct answer when it is presented along with incorrect answers.

Recall questions can be written two ways: as a query ("Who discovered America?" "How much is a franc worth?") or as a

Figure 9–8
Maps, cartoons, drawings, and charts lend themselves to short-answer tests. One teacher chose this political cartoon to ask a question about national parties. The cartoon has a useful distractor built into it, as the over-burdened mother may lead some students to misjudge the question as one relating to overpopulation and choose India as the correct answer. (Kurfman, 1962)

"... Had so many children she didn't know what to do ..."

In the twentieth century the situation illustrated by the cartoon has pertained most often to which of the following countries?

A. France
B. Spain
C. Canada
D. India

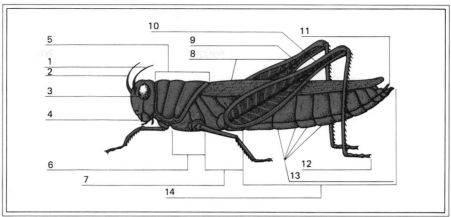

Parts of the Grasshopper

Figure 9-9
A recall question uses a detailed drawing of a grasshopper to test the students' knowledge of the parts of the grasshopper and their functions. (After Baker and Mills, 1943)

completion item ("The Capital of Ohio is _____." "An elementary particle consisting of a charge of negative electricity is called a (an) _____." [Stanley and Hopkins, 1972, p. 224]).

Either way, they can present some difficulties in scoring, since a wide range of answers may result and the teacher may be hard pressed to evaluate their correctness. "*Columbus* discovered America." Correct, but what about "*the Vikings*"?

Completion items should be worded so that the answer is not given away in the stem: if *an* instead of *a (an)* were written in the question above, it would indicate that *electron* is the answer and fail to discriminate among students who were vacillating between *electron* and *neutron*. Completion items should not be too mutilated, or they become ambiguous: "The (1) is the largest (2) in the world" would elicit innumerable answers in a science class.

Recall questions are not limited to testing simple knowledge. Given the detailed drawing of a grasshopper, as shown in Figure 9–9, along with a real specimen of a grasshopper, high-school biology students were asked to locate each part using a hand lens on an actual specimen, find the corresponding part in the accompanying illustration and label it. Then they were asked to consider how each part functions in the life of the grasshopper (Baker and Mills, 1943).

Recognition questions take three forms—true-false, multiple-choice, and matching—and are usually easier than recall questions. Because there is no uncertainty as to the correctness of answers, and less chance for misinterpretation than in recall questions, true-false and multiple-choice tests are popular and regarded by many teachers as the most flexible. Moreover, if care is taken in constructing questions, then true-false and multiple-choice items can, on some occasions, tap subtle and complex cognitive processes.

The *true-false question* presents a statement that must be assessed for its accuracy. True-false tests can include many items and still be completed in a short span of time—an advantage, since reliability increases with length. They are often used to measure rote recall and learning: "The Battle of Hastings was fought in 1066." T F

However, true-false questions can be used to test broader principles and more sophisticated knowledge: "In the laboratory preparation of carbon dioxide one of the essential ingredients is limewater." T F

They can also test the students' ability to apply rules and principles: "The radius of a circle whose area is 75 must be less than 5." T F

Critics of true-false questions say that the scores may be inaccurate because the students guess, tending to guess "true" when they do not know. However, there is a distinction between blind guessing, when a student chooses capriciously, and informed guessing, when the more a student knows, the more likely he is to guess correctly. If there is only one item on a test, the student has a fifty-fifty chance of getting a perfect score if he guesses. On a five-item test, however, he has only a 3 percent chance. On a ten-item test, his chance is down to .1 percent, and on one hundred items, his chance of guessing his way to even a moderately good score is less than one in a thousand!

One measurements expert suggests that the best way to write true-false items is to first write all the items as true and then to turn about half of them round to make them false. This procedure prevents distortions in the question (Tuckman, 1975). Each item should query a single major point, without two or three hitching along and blurring the issue. "Early in his career, Will Rogers said, 'I never met a man I didn't like'" is an example of a true-false item with "hitchhikers"—Did Rogers say it? Did he say it in those exact words? Was it early or late in his career? (Tuckman, 1975, p. 83).

A good true-false test should test propositions that are important and should test understanding as well as rote memory. The questions should not echo the language and examples of the text or lectures so that the student confronts a fresh situation. The correct answer should be easy to defend to critics who disagree with the interpretation. Questions should not call for answers that are a matter of common knowledge—or available only to students with expert knowledge.

The *multiple-choice question* has two main parts. The stem comes first and defines the domain of the question. It is followed by several responses from which the student must select the best alternative. The incorrect responses should be plausible and relevant so that students who do not possess the necessary knowledge may select one of them rather than the correct answer. Consider the following question (Bloom et al., 1956, p. 136):

If a person is planning to bathe in the sun, at what time of day is he most likely to receive a severe sunburn? He is most likely to receive a severe sunburn in the middle of the day (11:00 to 1:00) because:

A. We are slightly closer to the sun at noon than in the morning or afternoon.
B. The noon sun will produce more "burn" than the morning or afternoon sun.
C. When the sun is directly overhead, the sun's rays pass through less absorbing atmosphere than when the sun is lower in the sky.
D. The air is usually warmer at noon than at other times of the day.

While all these statements are true, only one—C—states the reason for getting sunburned at noon.

Good tests also avoid verbal tricks and questions that depend on words like *always* and *never*. The questions should be clearly written to avoid ambiguity ("President Johnson was a popular president"), and the stem of the question should pose the problem without giving away the answer. The more similar the alternatives, the more discriminating the item, as seen in the following examples (Hawkes, Lindquist, and Mann, 1936, pp. 146–47):

I. Engel's law deals with
   A. the coinage of money
   B. the inevitability of socialism
   C. diminishing returns
   D. marginal utility
   E. family expenditures
II. Engel's law deals with family expenditures for
   A. luxuries
   B. food
   C. clothing
   D. rest
   E. necessaries
III. According to Engel's law family expenditures for food
   A. increase in accordance with the size of the family
   B. decrease as income increases
   C. require a smaller percentage of an increasing income
   D. rise in proportion to income
   E. vary with the tastes of families

To answer version I correctly, the student need know only that Engel's law concerns family expenditures; to answer version II, she must know that the expenditures involve food. Version III gives more information in the stem of the question and requires a more detailed understanding of Engel's law than either I or II (Stanley and Hopkins, 1972).

All the alternatives should be approximately the same in length and precision so that the answer is not given away. They should also be

"Today my class had (choose one): (a) a party, (b) a fire drill, (c) an I.Q. test, (d) a riot."

grammatically consistent with the stem. Moreover, the answer intended should be the one that most experts consider the most valid. Often it is a good idea to try out multiple-choice tests on a colleague.

The *matching question* presents the students with two columns of items and asks them to draw a correspondence between the appropriate ones. The items may be names and characteristics or actions ("John Quincy Adams . . . the son of a president"), or words and definitions:

(1)	ubiquitous	(a)	harmful
(2)	enigmatic	(b)	equivalent
(3)	deleterious	(c)	widespread
(4)	tantamount	(d)	purposeful
		(e)	puzzling

These questions are useful in assessing how well students can discriminate among similar pieces of knowledge. They also cover a good deal of ground in one question. Their inherent disadvantage is that as the student answers the items he knows, he reduces the ones he must guess to only a few, improving the odds in his favor. This can be offset by providing one or more unnecessary items in one of the columns, as above (Tuckman, 1975).

In general, the best strategy for most teachers is to use a combination of essay and multiple-choice questions and, on occasion, standardized achievement tests. If the teacher is going to combine test scores for final evaluation in a norm-referenced system, there is a way to convert the scores from the tests that the students have taken into a standardized scoring system. This is presented in Figure 9–10.

All the teacher needs to do is establish the rank order of each student's score on each of the tests. Suppose a student had five tests in

TOTAL NUMBER OF PERSONS RANKED

RANK	5	6	7	8	9	10	11	12	13	14	15	16	17	18	19	20	21	22	23	24	25	26	27	28	29	30	31	32	33	34	35	36	37	38	39	40	41	42	43	44	45	RANK
1	63	64	65	65	66	66	66	67	67	68	68	68	69	69	69	69	70	70	70	70	70	71	71	71	71	71	71	71	71	71	72	72	72	72	72	72	72	72	72	73	73	1
2	55	57	58	59	60	60	61	62	62	62	63	63	64	64	64	64	65	65	65	65	66	66	66	66	66	66	67	67	67	67	67	67	67	68	68	68	68	68	68	68	68	2
3	50	52	54	55	56	57	57	58	59	59	60	60	60	61	61	62	62	62	62	63	63	63	63	63	64	64	64	64	64	64	65	65	65	65	65	65	66	66	66	66	66	3
4	45	48	50	52	53	54	55	55	56	57	57	58	58	59	59	59	60	60	60	61	61	61	61	62	62	62	62	62	62	63	63	63	63	63	63	64	64	64	64	64	64	4
5	37	43	46	48	50	51	52	53	54	55	55	55	56	56	57	57	58	58	58	58	59	59	59	60	60	60	60	61	61	61	61	61	61	62	62	62	62	62	63	63	63	5
6		36	42	45	47	49	50	51	52	53	53	54	55	55	55	56	56	56	57	57	57	58	58	58	58	59	59	59	59	59	60	60	60	60	60	61	61	61	61	62	62	6
7			35	41	44	46	48	49	50	51	52	52	53	54	54	55	55	55	56	56	56	57	57	57	58	58	58	58	58	59	59	59	59	59	60	60	60	60	60	60	61	7
8				35	40	43	45	47	48	49	50	51	51	52	53	53	54	54	55	55	55	56	56	56	57	57	57	57	57	58	58	58	58	59	59	59	59	59	59	60	60	8
9					34	39	42	44	46	47	48	49	49	50	51	51	52	52	53	53	54	54	55	55	55	56	56	56	57	57	57	57	58	58	58	58	58	59	59	59	59	9
10						34	39	42	44	45	47	48	49	49	50	51	51	52	52	53	53	53	54	54	55	55	55	55	56	56	56	56	57	57	57	57	57	58	58	58	58	10
11							33	38	41	43	45	46	47	48	49	49	50	51	51	52	52	52	53	53	54	54	54	54	55	55	55	55	56	56	56	56	56	57	57	57	57	11
12								33	38	41	43	44	45	46	47	48	49	49	50	51	51	51	52	52	53	53	53	54	54	54	54	55	55	55	55	56	56	56	56	56	57	12
13									32	38	40	42	44	45	46	47	48	48	49	50	50	51	51	52	52	52	53	53	53	53	54	54	54	54	55	55	55	55	56	56	56	13
14										32	37	40	42	43	44	45	46	47	47	48	49	50	50	50	51	51	52	52	52	53	53	53	53	54	54	54	54	55	55	55	55	14
15											32	37	40	41	43	44	45	46	47	47	48	49	49	50	50	50	51	51	52	52	52	52	53	53	53	54	54	54	54	55	55	15
16												31	36	39	41	42	44	45	45	46	47	48	48	49	49	50	50	50	51	51	51	52	52	52	53	53	53	53	54	54	54	16
17													31	36	39	41	42	44	45	45	46	47	48	48	49	49	50	50	50	51	51	51	52	52	52	53	53	53	53	53	53	17
18														31	36	38	40	42	43	44	45	46	46	47	47	48	48	49	49	50	50	50	51	51	51	52	52	52	52	53	53	18
19															31	36	38	40	41	43	44	44	45	46	46	47	48	48	48	49	49	50	50	50	51	51	51	51	52	52	52	19
20																30	35	38	40	41	42	43	44	45	45	46	47	47	48	48	49	49	49	50	50	50	51	51	51	52	52	20
21																	30	35	38	39	41	42	43	44	45	45	46	46	47	47	48	48	49	49	49	50	50	50	51	51	51	21
22																		30	35	37	39	41	42	43	44	45	45	45	46	46	47	47	48	48	48	49	49	49	50	50	50	22
23																			30	35	37	39	40	41	42	43	44	45	45	45	46	46	47	47	48	48	48	49	49	50	50	23
24																				30	34	37	39	40	41	42	43	44	44	45	46	46	47	47	47	48	48	49	49	49	49	24
25																					29	34	37	38	40	41	42	43	44	44	45	45	46	46	47	47	48	48	48	49	49	25
26																						29	34	37	38	40	41	42	43	43	44	44	45	45	46	46	47	47	48	48	48	26
27																							29	34	36	38	39	41	41	42	43	44	44	45	45	46	46	47	47	47	48	27
28																								29	34	36	38	39	40	41	42	43	43	44	45	45	46	46	46	47	47	28
29																									29	34	36	38	39	40	41	42	43	43	44	44	45	45	46	46	47	29
30																										29	33	36	38	39	40	41	42	42	43	44	44	44	45	45	46	30
31																											29	33	36	37	39	40	41	41	42	43	44	44	44	45	45	31
32																												29	33	36	37	38	40	40	41	42	43	43	44	44	45	32
33																													28	33	35	37	38	39	40	41	42	42	43	44	44	33
34																														28	33	35	37	38	39	40	41	42	42	43	43	34
35																															28	33	35	37	38	39	40	41	42	42	43	35
36																																28	33	35	37	37	39	40	41	41	42	36
37																																	28	32	35	36	38	39	40	40	41	37
38																																		28	32	35	37	38	39	40	40	38
39																																			28	32	35	36	37	38	39	39
40																																				28	32	34	36	37	38	40
41																																					28	32	34	36	37	41
42																																						27	32	34	36	42
43																																							27	32	34	43
44																																								27	32	44
45																																									27	45

Figure 9–10
This table can be used to convert rankings to a standard score scale with a mean of 50 and a standard deviation of 10. First determine the number of persons ranked. Then go to the table and find the rank of the individual. A rank of 3 indicates a person who is third from the top. The point at which the row indicating rank intersects the column indicating number of persons ranked is the standard score. For example, a person with a rank of 6 in a group of 17 has a score of 55. A person with a rank of 20 in a group of 30 has a score of 46. (Air Training Command, 1952, p. 8)

history over the course of the semester. The teacher ranks the student on each of the five tests. Each rank can be converted into a T-score by using the table. The average T-score for each student can then be computed and all the students evaluated on a common scale.

The Use and Review of Test Results

Writing test items is time-consuming; major testing services, such as the Educational Testing Service in Princeton, New Jersey, do not expect their writers to produce more than perhaps ten items in an eight-hour working day (Gage and Berliner, 1975). Teachers should not grow discouraged, then, when they feel that writing satisfactory questions is a difficult task. One way to make the job a little easier is to use the test results in order to learn something about test construction. The teacher should look at the proportion of children who passed each item in relationship to some criteria. For example, she should look at the items passed by those who are usually good students versus those who are poor students or those who have had no instruction. Items passed by good students who have had the instruction but failed either by the poor students or those who have not attended the lectures are good items. If a particular item is passed by both good and poor students or passed by neither, then it is less useful. Informal study of the distribution of scores can discriminate good from poor items.

Item-analysis information is helpful to the teacher in preparation of new tests, but it should also be used to provide feedback to the students. The teacher should go over each item with them so that they will know where they made their mistakes.

Grading

A grade on a test should convey some information about the student's performance, whether it is for the benefit of teachers, parents, college admission boards, or the student himself.

Recently, the strongest protests against grades have focused on the psychologically harmful effects of low grades, rather than the inaccuracies of the grading system. Although high marks may motivate and reward students, there is little evidence to show that low marks motivate. They are far more likely to confirm a student's low expectation of success and verify his image of himself as a poor student. In an attempt to avoid the overtones of failure inherent in grades of "D" and "E" or "poor" and "failing," some schools use a three-point system: outstanding, satisfactory, needs improvement.

Most recently, a wave of reform has resulted in the pass/fail system. At the start of the course the teacher states the criteria for passing and, at the end, gives a grade to indicate that the student has met the criteria

or has failed to meet them. In a further effort to remove the onus of failure, this system is sometimes called credit/no credit. If the student does not meet the criteria, the record simply states that no credit was given and does not specify whether it was because of illness, emergency, or poor work.

In the debate about the pros and cons of pass/fail, it is important not to lose sight of its chief characteristic. It is a two-point system. While the 100-point system is compulsively detailed in scope, the two-point system suffers from having almost no ability to discriminate among the degrees of mastery attained by a group of students. The reliability of grades and the amount of information they convey decreases as the number of categories decreases. The two-point system is down to a bare minimum.

Although used in some form in a number of colleges, high schools have been reluctant to adopt the pass/fail system for fear that college admissions officers would find it unacceptable. The more pertinent issue, however, is not whether colleges learn enough from a pass/fail grade—but whether anyone learns enough from it. Perhaps the fundamental issue concerns the nature of the message conveyed by a grade. In the long run, which is more satisfactory: A message that sends a detailed amount of information concerning the student's performance? Or a message that refrains from sending an unambiguous message of praise or blame?

Summary

Testing is an essential part of the classroom process. Besides assessing how well students have learned and can use new material, tests are used to diagnose readiness and isolate special areas of difficulty; to assess progress (summative and formative evaluations); to increase motivation; to motivate students to master the material in depth; and to provide reinforcements for effort. Testing helps teachers to clarify their own goals for the course and to discriminate among students. Tests also provide an objective comparison of the achievement of an entire school compared with other schools.

Testing also has disadvantages. Scoring is seldom as objective as it purports to be. Tests can cause a break in the trust between teachers and students and cause anxiety in students who obtain low scores. They may lead students to be inordinately concerned with grades. Unless carefully constructed, they encourage only rote learning. In spite of these drawbacks, many believe that achievement must be measured and that written tests are the most objective and efficient means of measuring achievement. They are fair, efficient, valid (measuring what they are supposed to measure), and reliable.

Tests measure knowledge and skills at more than one level. Benjamin Bloom has developed a taxonomy of educational objectives that describes six levels: knowledge, comprehension, application, analysis, synthesis, and evaluation. At the first level, the student need only indicate what he knows; at succeeding levels he must indicate how well he can use his knowledge.

Tests can be constructed to assess any level of knowledge, or its use, in two ways. Criterion-referenced tests establish absolute requirements for mastery: each student is marked on how close he comes to meeting these fixed requirements. Norm-referenced tests, on the other hand, are based on relative performance: each student's score is a reflection of his performance compared with those of his classmates. While criterion-referenced tests are theoretically attractive, it is often difficult to construct tests whose criteria really reflect optimal mastery of a given subject.

Standardized achievement tests for specific areas, published commercially, complement teacher-constructed tests. Since they measure achievement on commonly accepted goals, they may be less precise than teacher-constructed tests in determining achievement in a particular class but more effective in indicating a student's performance compared to national norms. The Iowa Tests for Basic Skills, the Stanford Achievement Test, and the California Achievement Tests are among the most widely used.

There are a number of ways to use statistics to interpret test scores. These procedures include determining the mean, median, mode, standard deviation, and percentile ranks.

Teacher-constructed tests require that the teacher make several choices: what material to cover, whether it will be a test of power or speed, whether it will be scored as a norm-referenced or criterion-referenced test, and what form to give the questions. Various types of short-answer or multiple-choice questions ask for simple knowledge or demand sophisticated and analytical reasoning. Essay questions require a spontaneous answer and give students both opportunity and motivation to organize and write cohesive arguments.

The purpose of testing is often overlooked. It should take place as part of an overall program of evaluation and, more important, teachers should use the results of tests to improve the performance of individual students and the school as a whole.

Projects

1 Suppose that you, as a teacher, were using a pass/fail system instead of letter grades in a course in a secondary-level discipline (choose one with which you are familiar). Develop ten criteria for passing.

2 Design four different tests—a short-answer test, a multiple-choice test, a matching test, and an essay test—each of which tests for the same information.

3 What are the educational objectives of the course for which this book is the text? Organize them according to Bloom's taxonomy of objectives for the cognitive domain.

4 What knowledge or skills are being taught in this class that would constitute criteria for good teachers? Can you devise a test to measure their mastery?

5 Construct an objective test that will measure knowledge of ten major concepts or rules taught in this class, and another test that will measure how well students can apply them.

6 How would you evaluate an essay question that asked you to discuss three main principles of good teaching? Can you revise the question so that it demands more precise reasoning?

7 In addition to written tests, what kinds of reports or individual projects would you like to see in classroom use? In view of the individual nature of the projects, what criteria would you choose in grading them, and what grading system would you think most appropriate?

Recommended Reading

Bloom, B. S., Engelhart, M.D., Furst, G. J., Hill, W. H., and Krathwohl, D. R. *Taxonomy of educational objectives: The classification of educational goals.* New York: David McKay Co., 1956. An important book that summarizes the classification of the educational objectives that teachers may take into account when they are evaluating student progress.

Ebel, R. L. *The essentials of educational measurement.* Englewood Cliffs, N.J.: Prentice-Hall, 1972. An excellent text on the construction of tests and educational measurement.

Tuckman, B. W. *Measuring educational outcomes: Fundamentals of testing.* New York: Harcourt Brace Jovanovich, 1975. Gives excellent advice to the teacher on the construction of tests.

explaining school failure

10

S cattered throughout every school are children who have great difficulty learning to read, do arithmetic, or write compositions. Their grades are in the lowest 10 percent of the class, and although some may be held back for a year, many are promoted to the next grade even though the teacher knows they have not mastered the necessary skills. Some of these children stay in the regular public-school classroom; others are placed in a special school or in special education classes within the regular public school.

Although all these children are having difficulty mastering the school's tasks, they have different intellectual, motivational, and behavioral profiles and are failing for a variety of reasons. For some, school difficulty may be due to an accident that required the child to stay at home for a semester or longer. Others may be hampered by an emotional problem in the home.

Known physiological causes	**Implications for teaching:**
Sensory disabilities	**strategies and curricula**
Neurological disorders	Planning curricula that work
Differentiating among	Phonics drill cards
children with intellectual	Initial Teaching Alphabet
impairment	What about perceptual
	training?
The puzzle of relative	Providing a better
retardation	self-image
	Arranging the school day
The central problem: learning	Encouraging a reflective
to read	attitude
Biological factors in reading	Using relevant reading
failure	texts
Psychological factors in	Capacity for recovery
reading failure	

This chapter does not discuss children who have temporary physical or emotional problems, nor children who are chronically ill or have been psychotically disturbed for a period of time. Chapter 7 dealt with the conflicts and the motives that can affect school performance. This chapter considers the nonmotivational factors that may be responsible for the children who fail to master the school's requirements. A small group of these children have known and often serious physical defects, such as sensory impairments involving sight and hearing, or inherited or acquired disorders of the central nervous system that can affect intellectual ability. But our primary concern is with a larger and more puzzling group of children whose academic retardation cannot be clearly linked to a specific impairment of the brain or the sensory system and who demonstrate some ability to master school material.

Let us consider initially the first, smaller group of children.

Known Physiological Causes

Sensory Disabilities

There is a small number of children who, although they have physical defects, do not have serious cognitive deficiencies. This group is composed primarily of children with sensory handicaps. They are blind or partially sighted, deaf or hard of hearing.

Visual Disabilities

The legal definition of blindness is based on both visual acuity and field of vision. A person is considered blind if the corrected vision in his best eye is 20/200 or less (in other words, he can see at twenty feet what someone with normal vision can see at two hundred feet) or if the widest angle of vision in view when he turns his eyes from left to right is not greater than twenty degrees (often called "tunnel vision"). By this definition, there are about 2.14 blind people per one thousand in the United States (Scholl, 1967). Nicholas Hobbs, a psychologist at Vanderbilt University, has estimated that about seventy thousand students (children and adults) have a visual impairment that interferes with schoolwork, and some twenty-four thousand are in special educational programs (Hobbs, 1975).

A little more than 10 percent of the blind are under the age of nineteen. However, not all the people in this group are totally blind; they range through five categories of visual impairment, from completely blind (the person cannot see hand movements three feet in front of him) to a visual acuity of 20/200 (the person can read large type but does not have enough vision for all the daily activities that require sight). Since imperfect vision can lead to school failure, children who manifest learning problems should have a thorough eye examination.

A sight-impaired child's readiness to master school skills will depend not only on the acuity of his vision but also on the extent of his previous learning experiences. Even if he does not have serious intellectual deficits, his development might have suffered as a result of his visual handicap, so that he may have large gaps in his experience by the time he reaches school age. A blind child can learn language spontaneously. But a good deal of early childhood learning is based on vision; he cannot see the shapes and colors of common objects, such as a ball, a dog, and a bed, or their arrangements in relation to each other ("in front of," "underneath"). Nor can he pick up the facial expressions of approval and disapproval, interest and boredom, on which sighted children grow to depend. Just as the game of peek-a-boo is based on a visual trick, the young child's understanding that an object can be out of sight and still exist depends on sight. If he is to master such understanding, the blind child must develop it through sound and touch instead.

If a child is totally blind, his education will be primarily through the auditory and tactile senses. He will need to learn to read Braille and write it with the writing machine. If he is partially sighted, he may be able to master print as well.

Blind children may benefit from spending some time in a class with other blind children, specialists suggest, because they gain a more accurate assessment of their abilities. In this situation they are viewed neither as "poor, blind children" nor as superhuman beings because they can read Braille. The trend to include blind or partially sighted children in the public school system has progressed to the point where now more are enrolled in public schools—where they divide their time between special and regular classes—than in schools for the blind (Jones and Collins, 1966).

Auditory Disabilities

While a deaf child can perceive all the subtle visual cues that a blind child misses, as well as the panorama of color and shape that makes up the visual world, she is isolated in a serious way because she cannot hear sounds. She acquires language with great difficulty, and as a result she is handicapped in mastering the symbols of language—printed words.

About 5 percent of school-age children have hearing levels outside the normal range, and one or two out of every ten children in that

group require special educational attention (Silverman, 1960). Hobbs (1975) estimates that there are three hundred and fifty thousand hard-of-hearing children, eighty thousand of whom are in special programs. There are five categories of hearing impairment, based on a person's ability to hear the frequency and loudness of sounds (Rushford, 1964). The categories range from profoundly deaf (the person hears nothing whatsoever) to mild hearing loss (the child hears speech and learns language spontaneously).

A leading cause of mild hearing loss in young children is an inflammation of the middle ear—the small space behind the eardrum between the end of the auditory canal and the inner ear—where the pattern of sound waves is translated into nervous impulses. Often following a serious cold, the inflammation leads to an accumulation of fluid behind the eardrum and prevents the small bones of the middle ear from responding faithfully to the pattern of sounds. One investigator in the northeastern United States found that during the cold season 30 percent of prekindergarten children had a slight hearing loss due to inflammation. If the child is subject to many colds and infections, the inflammation can be continuous and serious hearing loss may occur (Clark, 1976).

A seriously deaf child's handicap will be apparent long before he reaches school. He will not learn to speak, will not obey verbal directions, and may seem out of touch with those around him. However, a mildly hard-of-hearing child may enter school with a handicap no one knows about, and his below-average language skills and lower achievement may lead to the mistaken diagnosis that his retardation is due to brain damage or other psychological factors. Thus, in addition to having their eyes examined, children who are performing poorly in school should have their hearing tested.

Although deaf children face substantial obstacles, they can learn to understand language, to speak, and to write, and they can master the academic skills that depend on language. Lip-reading (also called speech reading and visual listening) can be used to master language initially and, once learned, to understand the communications of any speaker within view. Deaf children also learn to rely on touch (placing their fingers on a speaker's lips and throat to feel the movements and vibrations made by different words) and electronic hearing aids to amplify their residual hearing. In addition, they can use the kinesthetic sense (learning to feel and regulate the muscle action of their own bodies) to control their breathing, voice quality, and speech rhythm; and they can learn sign language.

Neurological Disorders

A third physical disability is lack of motor coordination due to injury to the central nervous system, usually at the time of birth. Two of the neurological disorders that can result from such an injury are cerebral palsy and epilepsy. Cerebral palsy is characterized by involuntary motions of one or more of the limbs, the head, or the mouth, or by poor balance or muscle tremors. Multiple handicaps are common in children with cerebral palsy. It is estimated that about half these children have I.Q. scores below 70, but about a quarter have I.Q.'s above 90, and some are very gifted. However, even a cerebral palsy child with an I.Q. above 90 may have such serious speech and motor difficulties that he cannot make his wants known and, as an adult, may be unable to achieve economic and social independence (Robinson and Robinson, 1965).

Epilepsy includes convulsive disorders, with periodic seizures or temporary loss of consciousness, or both. Seizures range from very mild to severe. Most of the time they can be controlled by medication, sparing the child not only the seizures, but also the fear of the social discrimination of alarmed observers (Hobbs, 1975).

Children with neurological disorders differ in their degree of impairment. Some may never learn to read; others may become extremely proficient. Fortunately, only a small percentage of children are in the former category, and they usually obtain very low I.Q. scores (below 50).

A distinction must be made, of course, between the degree of intellectual impairment and the cause of impairment. There are many different factors that can produce a profound inability to read or learn math, from a genetic defect (as in the case of mongolism, or Down's syndrome) to brain damage resulting from a serious measles infection. The fact that the child has a biological defect does not necessarily mean that he will be unable to learn to read or that he will have an I.Q. under 50. But if the child has a very low I.Q., it is likely that the cause is physiological.

Differentiating among Children with Intellectual Impairment

Unfortunately, distinctions among children's intellectual capacities are usually blurred, since many schools have used the I.Q. score as a yardstick for classifying children rather than the child's profile of abilities or the presumed cause of the child's cognitive impairment. As a result, children with varied physical and physiological handicaps, and different ability profiles, are placed in the same class simply because their I.Q. scores are equivalent.

The educational system's preference for using I.Q. scores as the major instrument for classification has led to some misleading categorizations. Children with I.Q. scores under 70 were generally classified as mentally retarded, and Hobbs estimates that over six million children fall into this category. This number includes, first, children whose I.Q.'s are under 25 and who are called *profoundly retarded*. These children need constant care and may never learn to talk, eat alone, or dress themselves. The next group is the *trainable mentally retarded*, whose I.Q.'s fall between 25 and 49. While they may never learn the skills and the abilities necessary to be completely independent adults, with help they can learn to care for themselves and make some contributions to the protected environment in which they will have to live. They may not learn to read, but they can learn to follow directions, take care of their personal needs, get along with others, and move about the community (crossing streets and using public transportation) with safety. For a long time educators held that these children were not educable and argued that their training should not fall under the supervision of public education. However, over the last twenty-five years that attitude has changed, and educators and parents have pressed for their inclusion in the public schools. As a result, most states have passed laws requiring public schools to enroll them, though in separate classes (Johnson, 1967).

Recently, the American Association for mental Retardation revised its definition of *retarded* to exclude people whose I.Q. scores range from 50 to 89 (the group formerly classified as *mildly retarded*), suggesting that special factors cause the learning problems of these children. Since they constitute the most overlabeled and least understood group of students with learning difficulties, we devote the next section of the chapter to them.

The Puzzle of Relative Retardation

The largest group of children failing in school does not seem to have serious physical or physiological defects. They are capable of the basic cognitive processes outlined in chapter 4, but their level of functioning on some of these processes and on school tasks is low relative to the average child in the classroom. Hence, they are called *relatively retarded*. But an American child who is called relatively retarded in Chicago because his I.Q. is 88 and his reading and arithmetic achievement are in the lowest 10 percent of the class would be considered advanced if he were transferred to a rural community in Brazil, Kenya, or Indonesia. There, he would be more proficient at memory, reasoning, reading, and arithmetic than the average village child his age. This would not be true for a child with serious brain damage due to encephalitis: this child will show a more similar profile of abilities no matter where he is living and in most places will be regarded as having a serious intellectual impairment.

Relatively retarded children fail to meet the school's requirements, as set by the performance of the average child. They obtain the poorest grades and the lowest achievement test scores and, in some cases, have

Absolute Incompetence and Relative Mastery

One of the most serious misunderstandings in our language involves the word *incompetent.* We apply the word to two quite different qualities. First, we use it to refer to the complete inability to master a certain skill, solve a problem, or learn a segment of knowledge. Consider these examples: "A bird is incompetent to bark," "A rat is incompetent to fly," "A baby is incompetent to read," and "A man is incompetent to see light in the ultraviolet range." In each of these cases, the organism cannot perform or master a task because of basic limitations imposed by its biology.

Second, and more commonly, we use the word to refer to a person's proficiency relative to another person or to some consensual norm. In this case, we mean that the individual in question performs at a level that is below the average. An example is a six-year-old from an economically disadvantaged section of the city who reads but reads much more slowly than a middle-class child the same age who lives in the suburbs. The city child does possess some of the required competence and is gaining additional skill daily but is *less capable than another.* However, this usage of the word *incompetent* often carries with it the totally negative connotations of the first usage—that is, an absolute inability. It would be helpful if we could use a term other than *incompetence*—perhaps *relative mastery*—when we refer to comparative inability in order to distinguish between these two quite different meanings.

the worst reputations for classroom behavior. They pose a persistent problem to the public school system, not only because of their numbers, but also because of their effect on the rest of the class and the teacher.

Many labels have been pinned on these children. The bottom 10 to 15 percent of the class has been called *learning disabled, minimally brain damaged, slow learning, functionally retarded, emotionally disturbed,* and—along with gifted children—*exceptional* (a semantically logical but confusing use of the word). Theoretically each term implies a different cause and a different form of rehabilitation. But since the specific causes cannot always be discerned precisely, the labels are often used loosely and even irresponsibly. More recently, if the child came from a minority group—black, Mexican-American, Indian, or Puerto Rican, for instance—he might be called *culturally retarded* or *culturally disadvantaged.* These labels tried to shift the emphasis from an apparently deficient intellect to an apparently deficient environment—poor families, pessimistic philosophies, and value systems different from those of the majority. (We will discuss these factors further in Chapter 12.)

One hundred years ago, when the nation was primarily involved in farming and small business ventures, relative retardation in academic skills often went unnoticed. (Even today, if a child comes from a family and a community in which nearly everyone has less than a high-school education, his slow reading pace may not show up markedly in comparison to his brothers, sisters, uncles, aunts, and neighbors.) But the growth of compulsory education legislation between 1852 and 1918

The historical trend has taken exceptional students out of the regular classroom and away from the rest of society. Until the early 1800s, it was thought that little could be done for retarded children, and they were housed in "colonies" to keep them safe and separate. However, innovators such as Horace Mann and Samuel Gridley Howe stimulated a concern for exceptional children and efforts to improve their conditions and education.

The first half of the nineteenth century saw the growth of many residential schools, such as the famous Perkins Institute for the Blind, started in 1829. These schools provided some education and training for children who might otherwise have received none and instead have spent their lives dimly understanding what passed in front of them as they lived at the edges of community life on farms, in villages, and in the competitive, crowded city neighborhoods that developed around the turn of the century.

The change in attitudes after World War II also brought more open ideas about children with learning problems and led to the growth of concerned parent groups and agencies (such as the American Association for Mental Deficiency) devoted to the welfare of these children. Undoubtedly the civil rights movement of the 1960s added to the awareness of rights for students who did not conform to the ideal of an "average," especially since so many of them (incidentally, it was thought at first) belonged to minority groups.

Today the trend has shifted the other had the effect of including thousands of children who would not otherwise have attended public schools.

Today, the child who performs below average in school is more conspicuous and a more serious source of concern to the community

" 'B plus' in motivational initiative, 'A' in conceptual visualization . . . so how come you can't read?"

Problems and the Community

way. Increasingly, society is ready to hold the public schools responsible for providing education for all children. What emerged as a social movement gained muscle as a number of court cases made the point in judicial terms: children had been improperly placed—and held—in special classes. Cases were filed on the questions of illegal tracking (grouping children according to ability) as a result of culture-biased tests (*Hobson* v. *Hansen,* 1967); language barriers to adequate performance, where Mexican-American children from Spanish-speaking homes were placed in special education classes on the basis of Stanford-Binet and Wechsler tests administered in English (*Diana* v. *California Board of Education,* 1970); and lack of parental participation in placement decisions (*Arreola* v. *California Board of Education,* 1968).

While focusing on a major aspect of special placement—the misclassification of children because of language or cultural differences—the court cases contributed to a growing cynicism about special classes as a useful and appropriate way of teaching most children with learning problems of any kind. Special classes still may be the best solution for the severely retarded, seriously crippled or disturbed, completely deaf or blind. But for the majority, alternative help and support to meet special needs, rather than isolation in special classes, begins to look like a more appropriate answer to the educational and social requirements posed by the situation, and as groups of parents press for this approach, school systems begin to comply.

and his family. If he comes from a professional family or lives in a wealthy suburb, his learning difficulties will be noticed early, and he will be tested and evaluated in an effort to find out why he is failing. He is also likely to feel the hot breath of expectations from his parents, which contributes to his frustration at not being able to perform in school. If he comes from a poor family, his parents—themselves caught between unemployment and insufficient skills—may be doubly frustrated and angry when the schools are unable to teach him reading and arithmetic. The current widespread worry about children who cannot read reflects the realities of American life. It is no longer 1900, when a Louisiana fisherman's son or an Iowa farmer's daughter could anticipate occupations that did not require the ability to read at the rate of five hundred words a minute. Today's parents know that their children must learn these skills or lose in the competition for college and challenging jobs.

The Central Problem: Learning To Read

When we sift through the roster of behaviors and misbehaviors, test scores and achievement records, of failing children, at the heart of the problem we usually find that most are having difficulty reading and (or else) doing arithmetic and that the problem began during the primary grades.

Reading and arithmetic are not the only important school skills; others include thoughtfulness in generating good answers to questions in social studies, memory for dates in history, precision in drawing maps in geography—to name only three. But reading and arithmetic are the essential skills most teachers worry about. If a child fails to master them, everything else he may want to learn in school becomes a major problem. It is as if the school years were like a children's game: everyone who crosses from one side of the yard to the other must read and answer three questions written on a plank of wood. Without the ability to read the child is thwarted, and we have an angry, frustrated crowd of children who cannot play.

In explaining school failure, it is useful to focus the discussion on a specific cognitive task rather than on broad, amorphous categories of intelligence or retardation. First, as we have indicated, there is no agreement as to what *intelligence* means. Moreover, *retardation* is a general term and does not specify whether the retardation is in memory, reasoning, arithmetic, or spelling. A child who is retarded in one area of mastery may not be in another. But difficulty in reading sentences and understanding them is a specific skill and probably the most important one the American child learns. Hence, let us examine some possible causes of reading failure and the evidence favoring each of them.

Biological Factors in Reading Failure

The Inheritance of a Specific Reading Disability

A very small group of children with average intelligence seem to be intellectually capable at many cognitive processes but cannot read. This special group is sometimes called *dyslexic,* the term deriving from Greek words meaning "poor reader." One child psychiatrist defines this deficit as follows: "Specific dyslexia may be defined as the failure to learn to read with normal proficiency despite conventional instruction, a culturally adequate home, proper motivation, intact senses, normal intelligence and freedom from gross neurological defect" (Eisenberg, 1976, p. 1).

Recently, some psychologists have suggested a genetic cause for the difficulty some children of average I.Q. have in learning to read and spell. The suggestion is based on evidence of family history: children of average I.Q. with reading difficulties are a little more likely than other children to have parents who also encountered difficulty in reading and spelling when they were in elementary school (Gibson and Levin, 1975). However, this correlation can be due to the fact that the parents, as children, were poorly motivated and in turn, failed to encourage their own children in school mastery. Therefore the notion that specific problems in reading and spelling may be inherited must still be regarded only as a possibility; more research is needed on this issue.

Differences in Intelligence

Another explanation for reading failure—albeit a simple one—rests on the assumption of differences in basic intelligence among children. This view holds that children vary in their basic intellectual capacity and that the variation is partly genetic. Like general health, intellect is seen as either very good, adequate, or poor. Accordingly, a child with a limited intellectual endowment can be expected to have difficulty functioning well or efficiently in the classroom. As we saw in Chapter 8, this has been a popular interpretation of the relation between intelligence and school success. Stated bluntly, students who cannot learn to read are believed to have *less intelligence*.

A little neglect may breed great mischief ... for want of a nail the shoe was lost; for want of a shoe the horse was lost; and for want of a horse the rider was lost.

Poor Richards Almanac, 1758

The majority of children do not fail in school because of inadequate cognitive abilities but because they fail to master one essential skill: reading. There is no doubt that the failure to read generates many additional problems. The nonreading child cannot delve into history books or read a chemistry text, master the written form of a second language, or read maps in geography. Failure to read precipitates the child into an academic bottleneck and produces substantial, demoralizing feelings of frustration, anger, and humiliation. In turn, these feelings hamper further efforts to read, diminish a child's expectations of success in the class he is in now, and dampen his enthusiasms for material he will meet next year.

It is too much to say that if we solve the reading problem for a child, he will have no further difficulty in school. But it is the single, most critical educational hurdle. It is worth not only taking greater efforts, but also designing more varied methods, for helping children learn to read.

For want of a nail the shoe was lost,
For want of a shoe the horse was lost,
For want of a horse the rider was lost,
For want of a rider the battle was lost,
For want of a battle the kingdom was lost.
And all for the want of a horseshoe nail.

Serious problems plague that interpretation, however. First, about three to four times as many boys as girls fail to learn to read in American schools. Since much of the power and intellectual productivity of the adult world has been in the hands of men, not women, it is hard to believe that more males than females are of low intelligence. Second, many more children from economically poor families than from economically advantaged families are in special education classes. One study suggests that minority children—who are often poor—constitute well over half of those enrolled in this country's special education classes (Dunn, 1968). As we will see in Chapter 12, there is no firm evidence indicating that children born to poor parents inherit less basic—or native—intellectual ability than those from more affluent families. Rather, the evidence indicates that they are at a cultural and motivational disadvantage. Moreover, the standard method of determining which children are to be classified as relatively retarded is the I.Q. test. But if the score on an I.Q. test is culturally biased, as we suggested earlier, then the statement "Children fail to learn to read because they have a low I.Q." is not satisfying. For if the same factors that produce the low I.Q. are also producing the failure to learn to read—namely cultural conditions of rearing—then to say children cannot read because they are of low intelligence is a little like saying children cannot read because they cannot read.

Delayed Cerebral Maturity

A third potential cause of early academic failure in reading involves the concept of cerebral immaturity. In general, the left hemisphere of the brain receives sensory impressions from and controls movement on the right side of the body, while the right hemisphere deals with the left side of the body. Moreover, each hemisphere functions a little differently, the left appearing to play the major role in language skills, the right in nonlanguage tasks. It is believed that, as it develops, the left hemisphere gradually gains dominance over the right, especially with respect to the detection and comprehension of language. Hence, delayed maturation of the brain can lead to a delay in left-hemisphere dominance. This delay may be associated with difficulty in learning to read (Critchley, 1964; Satz and van Nostrand, 1972).

Dominance of the left or right hemisphere with respect to language is often assessed by putting earphones on a child, simultaneously presenting a different word to each ear, and then asking the child which word she hears. If she consistently reports the word played to her right ear, she is regarded as having left-hemisphere dominance for language; if she reports the word played to her left ear, she is regarded as having right-hemisphere dominance for language. It is believed that this is because there is a stronger neurological connection between each ear and the opposite side of the brain (that is, the right ear and the left hemisphere, the left ear and the right hemisphere).

The results of experiments comparing normal and reading-retarded children are inconclusive. In one study, for example, five- and six-year-old children with serious delays in speech were compared with normal children. They heard forty different word pairs, differing in one phonetic element (such as *leg* versus *led*), as well as forty pairs or trios of numbers. Although the language-retarded children differed from the normal children in reporting the numbers (they reported more digits heard in the left ear than in the right), they did not differ in reporting the words. Both normal and language-retarded children reported two-thirds of the words they heard in the right ear, indicating normal left-hemisphere dominance for language. But the difference in the reporting of numbers implies a possible difference in brain functioning between the two groups (Sommers and Taylor, 1972).

Some psychologists believe that a child whose left hemisphere was slower to mature will be slower in mastering the competences necessary for reading. (Some of these competences belong to the executive functions discussed in Chapter 5.) They believe the child will eventually develop these skills, but perhaps a year or two late. Presumably if one can identify these children in kindergarten, the schools can either begin some simple tutoring in reading skills or, at the least, refrain from coming to the premature conclusion that the children are permanently unable to master school skills. In one study diagnostic tests were initially given to a large number of boys entering kindergarten (Satz, Freil, and Rudegair, 1974). Two years later the scientists assessed the boys' reading levels at the end of first grade. Eighteen children (4 percent of the entire group) were diagnosed as being severely retarded in reading at the end of first grade, and the kindergarten tests had predicted low levels of mastery for all eighteen. Of the three most sensitive tests one measured knowledge of the alphabet; another seemed to measure reflectivity and impulsiveness. The third required the coordination of perception and memory. In this test the child first had to learn a number for each finger on his hand; the examiner then touched one finger or several fingers (the child could not see his own hand), and the child had to say the number assigned to the finger or fingers touched by the examiner. To do this, the child had to detect which finger or fingers were touched, remember the number that corresponded to each finger, and finally coordinate these pieces of information. Eventually all children perform well on these tests, but the five- and six-year-olds who have difficulty with them are likely to become children who have reading problems.

Another argument put forward to support delayed maturity as one explanation for early reading difficulty is the fact that in the United States young girls' scores on reading readiness tests and primary-grade reading achievement tests are typically higher than those of boys (Balow, 1963; Dykstra and Tinney, 1969). Since girls develop faster than boys physically, it is not unreasonable to assume that their psychological development may also be precocious. Hence, girls may be temporarily more prepared for reading instruction than boys. A study of reading achievement scores in Germany, however, revealed that boys' scores were higher than those of girls (Preston, 1962). Moreover, in the German sample there was no preponderance of boys over girls who scored in the lowest 10 percent on the reading tests (in the United States, you will remember, more boys than girls generally obtain very low scores on reading tests).

These results suggest either that the reading superiority of American girls is not due to earlier biological maturation, or else that cultural factors have the power to overcome slight differences in biological maturity between the sexes. In either case, the German data imply that American teachers should not accept the boys' greater difficulty in mastering reading as inevitable.

We will have to wait for future research to determine how much retardation in the attainment of left-hemisphere dominance for language is a major cause of *reading* and language deficiency. At present, the hypothesis that reading disabilities are due to a lag in the development of the normal dominance of the left hemisphere of the brain and its associated cognitive functions seems reasonable, although it is certainly not proven beyond dispute.

Brain Damage

Another possible cause of serious retardation in reading has a good deal of consensus. The notion is that many children who are failing in school have a minor, but permanent, locus of brain damage—also called *minimal brain dysfunction* or *MBD*.

It is assumed that this "defect" leads to a special quality of disability. One source of persuasive support for this idea comes from a national survey of American schools, which revealed a remarkably constant proportion of children that teachers had classified as having a specific learning disability. The proportion was 2.6 percent, or about one out of every thirty children (Silverman and Metz, 1973). The fact that teachers all over America seem to recognize a difference between children having general academic difficulty and those with a specific and serious learning disability implies the presence of a special condition, perhaps biological in origin, in a small proportion of children. It is unclear, however, where or how extensive the damage to the brain is, or when or how it occurred.

Hard signs and soft signs. Let us be precise about the meaning of the phrase *minimal brain dysfunction*. A few children are confidently diagnosed as having brain damage on the basis of "hard" neurological signs such as severe motor tremors or paralysis; serious irregularities in the brain wave patterns recorded on an electroencephalogram; and delayed or absent speech, associated with an inherited form of retardation, a medical history of encephalitis or meningitis, or serious problems at the time of delivery. Children with such clear signs of brain damage make up only a small proportion of those who are failing in school. Typically these children do less well than children with no brain damage on school tasks and on standard psychological tests (Reitan and Boll, 1973).

But most children who are failing in school do not show these hard signs of brain damage. Physicians and psychologists have noticed, however, that many academically retarded children show a pattern of behavior characterized by hyperactivity, impulsiveness, inattentiveness, perseveration (needlessly repeating words, gestures, or questions), and clumsiness, as well as poor performance on mental tests. These are called "soft signs." On the basis of these soft signs, some neurologists have assumed that the children have some subtle or minimal brain damage that cannot be detected with existing medical techniques that reflect brain processes more directly. As Hobbs describes it, "Subtle brain pathology is inferred exclusively from behavioral signs" (1975, p. 74).

It is important to distinguish between these two kinds of signs, although either may be associated with poor school performance. It is reasonable to regard the hard signs as symptomatic of some neurological damage that may obstruct school progress. The more prevalent soft signs, however, are another matter. Although they cannot be traced to definite neurological damage, they have been popularly viewed as symptomatic of unspecified brain damage.

One psychiatrist wanted to see if hard and soft signs were correlated in the same children. She looked through the files of fourteen hundred patients (from infancy through young adulthood) she had seen in her practice. She selected eighty-eight children (sixty boys and twenty-eight girls) who had been diagnosed as having neurological damage based on the hard signs of spasticity and disorders of gait and matched them with eighty-eight children of the same age and sex who had been referred for psychiatric consultation but had no evidence of brain damage. The first group of children with hard signs did not display soft signs with greater frequency or intensity than the second group, with one exception. The children with hard signs perseverated more—they repeated the same words and questions over and over. But they did not show the other soft signs in excess (Chess, 1972).

In addition, some soft signs, especially hyperactivity, are open to misinterpretation by overworked teachers and worried parents, who may mistakenly slip into calling an energetic child "hyperactive" if the child is not doing well in school. When one hundred so-called hyperactive children were referred to a clinic and given a thorough medical and psychological examination (as well as an electroencephalogram), only thirteen were diagnosed as hyperactive by the observers, and fifty-eight of the children were not even judged overly active by any of the staff (Kenney et al., 1971).

Some psychologists believe that if the children with so-called minimal brain damage do indeed have a neurological disorder, it is probably not minimal. Rather the child is likely to have suffered undetectable damage to a very specific part of the brain or to possess a biochemical disturbance rather than an anatomical defect in the nerve cells or fibers (Benton, 1973). One psychologist has suggested that children diagnosed as having minimal brain damage, based on hyperactivity, inattentiveness, and poor cognitive test scores, are suffering from a deficiency in the metabolism of an important chemical in the brain called monoamine oxidaze. He suggests that there is the slim possibility that this chemical defect may be inherited (Wender, 1973).

Objections to minimal brain damage as a common explanation for learning disability. The fact that it is difficult to specify the locus of brain damage does not, of course, imply that no damage exists. But there are problems with this as an explanation of school failure. First, it is assumed that the damage to the brain usually occurred prior to, during, or soon after birth. But there is typically a poor relation between the signs of brain damage during infancy and the signs of brain damage during later childhood (Kalverboer, Touwen, and Prechtel, 1973). Second, some neurologists argue that most infants—animal and human—recover from minimal damage to the brain during infancy (Stein, Rosen, and Butters, 1974). Indeed, one boy had his entire left hemisphere removed when he was five-and-a-half years of age. Yet when he was twenty-six his I.Q. was 116, he was finishing college with a dual major in sociology and business administration, and he was working as a traffic controller. Since he was able to master academic tasks lacking an entire left hemisphere, it is a little hard to defend the argument that most children who have difficulty learning to read have "minimal" brain damage (Smith and Sugar, 1975).

A third problem has to do with the fact that most academically retarded children show no signs of brain damage. A careful study of middle-class, predominantly white, elementary-school and junior-high-school students who were seriously retarded in reading and spelling involved a core group of seventy-six children with an average age of ten living in a suburban community. These children were matched with seventy-six other children of the same sex, grade, and I.Q. who were performing adequately in school. Only three of the seventy-six academically retarded children—about 4 percent—showed definite signs of abnormality in brain function; the rest did not (Owen et al., 1971).

In addition, the profile of the test performances of children with presumed brain damage is puzzling. First, children who have been referred to a clinic for learning or behavioral disorders, most of whom are severely retarded in reading, are usually similar in their performance on a variety of tests, regardless of whether they show signs of brain damage or not. Second, children who are reading at grade level, despite a firm diagnosis of brain damage, are markedly more proficient on a variety of intellectual tests than are children diagnosed as having brain damage who are retarded in reading (Mattis, French, and Rapin, 1975). Finally, children retarded in reading who are supposed to have brain damage do better on tests requiring complex cognitive processes, such as memory, spatial reasoning, inference, and perceptual analysis, than they do on questions that tap knowledge of simple facts or vocabulary, questions that do not require dynamic cognitive processes. This is puzzling, since damage to the brain should produce greater impairment of memory and reasoning than of vocabulary knowledge.

One team of investigators examined three groups of children between the ages of eight and twelve, all of whom were attending special education classes. One group of forty-two children was diagnosed as brain damaged on the basis of hard signs, such as abnormal muscle tone and irregular gait. A second group of one hundred and twenty-nine children showed no hard signs but two or more soft signs, such as speech disturbance, clumsiness, and poor coordination. A third group of twenty-seven children showed either no soft signs, or fewer than two soft signs. Although this last group had a higher I.Q. than the first two groups (an average of 87 versus 73 and 71), the first two had roughly equivalent I.Q. scores. More important, the profiles of performance of the first two groups were surprisingly similar. Both the hard- and soft-sign children performed best on the subtests of the intelligence scale called similarities ("How are a fly and a tree alike?"), picture completion ("What is missing in the picture of a plane?"), and short-term memory for digits ("Repeat these numbers: 2, 9, 7, 6, 3"). Both groups did least well on the subtests dealing with comprehension ("What should you do if your mother sends you to a grocery store to buy a loaf of bread and the grocer says he doesn't have any more?"), arithmetic, knowledge of vocabulary words, and mazes. Hence, both hard-sign children and soft-sign children did better on the tests that required integration and complex cognitive processes, such as spatial and inferential reasoning and memory, than they did on the tasks that measured acquired verbal and arithmetic knowledge and the ability to plan ahead in solving problems (Bortner, Hertzig, and Birch, 1972).

Impact of home environment. It seems to make a difference whether the presumably brain-damaged infant grows up in a middle- or a lower-class home. One study found that eight-month-old infants diagnosed as developmentally retarded as a result of minimal brain

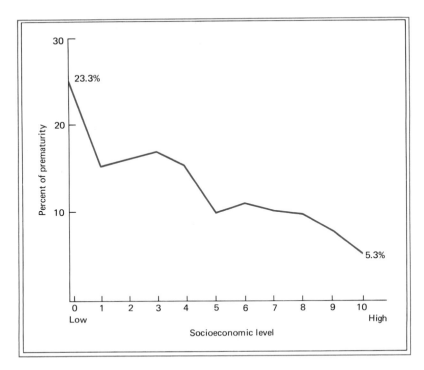

Figure 10–1
Using prematurity at birth as an index of the general health of a population, researchers notice that there is a greater proportion of premature births in families with low incomes. Some investigators suggest that this may indicate a higher incidence of damage at birth as well and that minimal damage to the nervous system may be one reason that there is a higher rate of school failure among poor children than among middle-class children. (Data from Crump et al., 1959)

damage who grew up in lower-class homes were more likely to attain low I.Q. scores (under 79) at age four than were eight-month-old infants diagnosed as brain damaged and retarded who grew up in middle-class homes (Willerman, 1973). If the retarded eight-month-olds from the two social class groups were equivalent in their neurological status and both did have minimal brain injury, then these findings suggest that a psychologically supportive and biologically healthy environent can offset the psychological deficit present during infancy. As indicated earlier, animals who are subjected to certain forms of brain damage during infancy seem to show little or no sign of psychological damage several years later if the environment allows proper development. Hence, perhaps it is the combination of injury to the brain and an environment that does not encourage the skills required for school success that leads more lower-class children to be classified as academically retarded.

Mothers of low-income families are less well nourished, more often ill, and more often under psychological strain, and they bear more children at younger ages than middle-class mothers. As a result, infant mortality and prematurity are highest among the poor (see Figure 10–1). The same factors that produce higher infant mortality and prematurity may also increase the risk of damage to the central nervous system for the children who survive (Birch and Gussow, 1970). But the presence of signs of minimal brain damage are much more predictive of academic retardation in a lower-class than in a middle-class child.

H∃LP the Learning Disabled Child

Bumper stickers such as this one have certainly helped to spread the message of learning disabilities. But how much does the concept help the failing child?

The notion that a child has a specific learning problem may be more accurate than the idea of low intellect. *Learning disabled,* yet another label ascribing blame to the child himself (and carrying in the word *disabled* the strong suggestion that the problem is primarily an organic one), has not really clarified the picture of cause and effect in school failure. The United States Office of Education for the Handicapped states it this way:

> Children with special learning disabilities exhibit a disorder in one or more of the basic psychological processes involved in understanding or using spoken or written language. These may be manifested in disorders of listening, thinking, talking, reading, writing, spelling or arithmetic. They include conditions which have been referred to as perceptual handicaps, brain injury, minimal brain dysfunction, dyslexia, developmental aphasia, etc. They do not include learning problems which are due primarily to visual, hearing, or motor handicaps, to mental retardation, emotional

disturbance or to environmental disadvantage. (Quoted in Hammill, 1974, p. 28)

One critic of the concept of learning disabilities points out that the definition is cluttered with so many ambiguous words and phrases that the statement leaves unresolved which basic processes are "disabled" and overlooks the strong association of motivational and environmental factors, which are important since the majority of nonachieving children referred to learning disability specialists live in center cities, have borderline I.Q.'s, and display disruptive school behavior. He suggests that if the ambiguities and redundant phrases were taken out, the definition would stand:

> Children with special learning disabilities exhibit problems in listening, thinking, talking, reading, writing, spelling and/or arithmetic. (Hammill, 1974, p. 31)

That would cover nearly all children having difficulty in school. Although currently a popular shorthand for children who cannot read and do arithmetic, the phrase *learning disabilities* falls short of specifying why they cannot and at the same time is too broad to describe adequately the *learning needs* of any particular child.

In summary, there is evidence, though it is not completely convincing, that a proportion of children who are having trouble learning to read, write, and do arithmetic are suffering from either a slower development of the brain, a defect in the chemical metabolism of the brain, or anatomical damage to very specific parts of the brain. But it has been difficult to prove any of these hypotheses conclusively or to locate the site of the damage or the specific biochemical abnormality. Moreover, symptoms such as hyperactivity, clumsiness, and inattentiveness—the soft signs—are not necessarily due to damage to the central nervous system; they may derive from purely psychological factors.

The ambiguity of the available evidence has led one group of psychologists, pediatricians, reading experts, and teachers to conclude that, at least for the present, the concept of minimal brain dysfunction does not offer a satisfactory explanation for the preponderance of reading failures. As a medical diagnosis, it is inexact. It is no more illuminating if rephrased in the more popular form, *learning disabilities*. In Hobbs's words:

> The term *learning disability* has appeal because it implies a specific neurological condition for which no one can be held particularly responsible, and yet it escapes the stigma of mental retardation. There is no implication of neglect, emotional disturbance, or improper training or education, nor does it imply a lack of motivation on the part of the child. For these cosmetic reasons, it is a rather nice term to have around. However, no one has ever been able to find evidence of the implied neurological impairment. (1975, p. 81)

At the end of a scholarly and exhaustive review of the research on the relation between reading failure and brain damage, two leading experts concluded that only a small percentage of dyslexic children really fall into the minimal brain-damaged category (Gibson and Levin, 1975).

Psychological Factors in Reading Failure

There are several nonbiological factors that may contribute to reading difficulty, especially in our culture, since it includes a great deal of heterogeneity in class and ethnic backgrounds. One group of factors involves the motives, conflicts, and expectancies already discussed in Chapter 7. In addition, some educators believe that special characteristics of the English writing system, differences in language environment between home and school, and the teacher's strategies influence how easily reading is mastered. Let us consider each of these in turn.

The English Language: A Decoding Dilemma

Some psychologists have suggested that because the English language contains letters or combinations of letters that can stand for different sounds (for example, *a, e, i, o, u,* can have different sounds in different words), the child learning to read English encounters problems that are not encountered by children learning to read other languages. One study of reading achievement in Japan revealed a rate of school failure less than 1 percent (Makita, 1968). The nature of the Japanese written language may make it easier for children in Japan to learn to read.

Reading in Japan. Japanese children learn two kinds of script. One is called *kanji* and is composed of ideographs (it was originally borrowed from China; kanji stands for the character of ancient China). Each visual form stands for a whole object or an idea and not simply a phonetic sound (see Figure 10–2). Hence, if the visual form we call *B* were a Japanese ideograph, it might stand for *house* or *boy,* not just a sound that is part of a word. At the end of the sixth grade, students are expected to know about one thousand kanji symbols—half the number in daily use in Japan. A fairly large number of the children with reading difficulties have trouble with kanji.

Kana, the other script learned in Japan, consists of forty-eight visual forms, each of which stands for a different sounding syllable, such as *be, bi, bo,* or *bu.* Primary instruction traditionally begins with kana.

Figure 10–2
The ideographs used in the *kanji* script of Japan are derived from pictorial representations of objects. Although they have changed over time, it is possible to see how they originated. Kanji ideographs, unlike the Japanese *kana* characters, cannot be deciphered by any phonetic code: they must be memorized one at a time. Hence, mastering kanji is more difficult than learning to read kana.

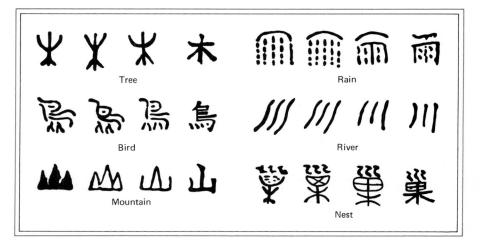

Tree Rain Bird River Mountain Nest

DIFFERENCE OF CHARACTERISTICS BETWEEN ALPHABET AND KANA SCRIPT

ALPHABET		KANA SCRIPT	
Letter	*Sound*	*Letter*	*Sound*
a	[a] [e] [ei]	い	[i]
b	[b] or silent	ろ	[ro]
c	[k] [s]	は	[ha]
d	[d] [t]	に	[ni]

A consonant or a vowel.	A syllable. A combination of a consonant and a vowel with which the uttering ends.

Sound	*Representation*	*Sound*	*Representation*
[f] ——————→	f, ph, gh	na	な
[f] [v] ‒ ‒ ‒		ni	に
[f] or silent ‒ ‒		nu	ぬ
[n] ———————	n, kn, gn	ne	ね
[ai] ———————	ais, ay, aye, ei, eigh, eye, i, ie, igh, y, ye	no	の

Direct link of two or more consonants.	No direct link of consonants. Consonants are always linked through a vowel or vowels.

Unstable script-phonetic relationship: every sound *is not* represented by corresponding specific letter.	Stable script-phonetic relationship: every sound *is* represented by corresponding specific letter (like in i.t.a.).

Figure 10–3
This chart describes the differences between our alphabet and the Japanese *kana* **script with respect to phonetic stability. Unlike our alphabet, the** *kana* **script has one specific symbol for every sound. (After Makita, 1968)**

Relatively few of the children with reading problems have trouble with kana, and almost none have difficulty after the third grade. Since reading kana, like English, is based on decoding visual forms that represent the sounds that make up words, it is tantalizing to speculate on the reasons for the discrepancy between a national reading failure of 10 percent in the United States and only 1 percent in Japan.

There are three differences between kana and the English alphabet. First, kana has no symbols that are mirror images of each other (we have d and b, p and q). Japanese children may initially draw a symbol the wrong way, but they overcome that tendency early. They learn to see the reverse of a symbol as an error and not as a form that is sometimes correct. Second, most kana symbols stand for a whole syllable—a consonant plus a vowel sound (such as *na, ni,* or *nu,* not *n* or *a* alone). Third, and perhaps most important, each of the forty-eight symbols in kana stands for only one sound, whereas in the English alphabet, one letter can stand for several sounds (*c* is both hard and soft, *a* is both long and short, and a letter such as *o* can make a variety of sounds: *bow, book, lot, for*). Hence, it seems likely that kana script is easier to master than English because the relation between sound and symbol is more stable and consistent, as is shown in Figure 10–3 (Makita, 1968).

Learning to Read English

Unquestionably, our writing system is a challenge. Any language that pronounces *caught* and *fought* similarly but spells them differently should be expected to generate more learning problems than a writing system such as the Japanese kana.

What, exactly, is involved when a child begins to learn how to read? There are some specific requirements that must be met if the child is to decipher the simplest of words.

Recognizing word boundaries. First, elemental as it may seem, children need to know what a word is. Adults can recognize the difficulty from their own experience in hearing an unfamiliar language. In the apparently uninterrupted flow of sound, it is difficult to tell where one word ends and the next one begins. To young children, their own language may seem like a continual river of sound, and the short momentary breaks that they may hear may not correspond to the words themselves. Many normal preschool and kindergarten children who do not read do not appreciate what a word is. One investigator read sentences to children from four-and-a-half to seven-and-a-half years old. After each one the child was asked to repeat the sentence, tapping on the table for each word he heard. Younger nonreaders performed less well than the older children who could read. The younger children regarded *red ball* or *the cat* as one rather than two words (Ehri, 1975).

In a similar study five-year-olds were asked to tap on the table each time that they heard the teacher say a word (a sentence such as "John has enough money" should be signaled by four taps). Then the children had to look at a card with the words typed in primer print and say whether or not the card had the same number of words as the spoken sentence. Many children tended to divide the spoken utterances into units that did not correspond to the printed words (Holden and MacGinitie, 1972). Children need to acquire a concept of *word* as an entity and recognize that there are word boundaries in the speech they hear as well as in print.

Why is reading in an alphabet system difficult? The history of writing systems offers some clues. The first writing systems were simply *pictographs*: pictures that told the story of a sentence. A pictograph sentence depended on exact representations of objects or events. Consider the sentence "The lion ate the small zebra." In pictures, it may be:

lion   ate   small zebra

Historically, the next step was to establish a set of standard designs to symbolize certain meanings. Though highly stylized, these signs still evoked the original objects and events—they were called *logograms*. For the sentence above, a logogram may be:

lion   ate   small   zebra

Note that in the logogram there is a more arbitrary and less obvious relation between the symbol and its meaning than in the pictogram.

The next step was the most important: instead of standing for the meaning of the entire word, symbols came to stand for the sound of individual syllables in words. These signs made up a *syllabary*. In syllabary form, the sentence may read:

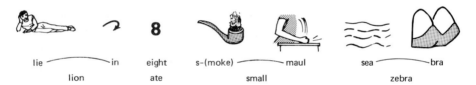

lie ——— in   eight   s–(moke) ——— maul   sea ——— bra

lion   ate   small   zebra

In this system the reader must remember the sound intended by the symbol and then integrate the word. *Kana,* the Japanese script, uses a syllabary.

The last step was the invention of the alphabet (about five thousand years ago). It is believed that the alphabet was only invented once, while syllabaries were invented many times. Our alphabet has the advantage of containing only twenty-six symbols, but it has a disadvantage as well: each symbol has many different sounds that change depending on the other letters that combine with it. Furthermore, it is not possible to isolate a pure sound that goes with each letter of the alphabet—x, m, and g do not stand for simple pure sounds. Since the beginning reader in America must realize that the symbols he sees on the page stand for different sounds in the words he hears spoken, learning to read by an alphabet is far more difficult for him than it is for the Japanese child who learns to read Kana by a syllabary.

Coordinating symbols and sounds. Consider the task of the child who already knows the names of all the letters of the alphabet. She must analyze and combine those letters into a sound she knows. Suppose the word is *dog*. If she analyzes the sound of each letter, she will come out with *du-uh-gu,* which is a three-syllable word bearing little relation to the word *dog.* She can say *du-uh-gu* rapidly over and over again and still fail to recognize the word on the page. Since she knows the letters, the problem is not one of visual perception. Since she can repeat the word if her teacher says it and asks her to repeat it, the problem is not auditory perception either. She faces a complex cognitive problem involving, at a minimum, (1) realizing that the printed word stands for a familiar sound she knows and has heard in her language, (2) remembering how *o* sounds when it is paired with *d* and *g* in contrast to how it sounds when it is paired with *b* and *w* as in *b-o-w* or with *c* and *w* as in *c-o-w,* and (3) continuing to match the sounds (made while attempting to read the word) to the sounds of the words she knows. Notice that all three requirements are profoundly cognitive (Liberman, 1971, 1973).

Eleanor J. Gibson and Harry Levin have written an important review of our knowledge of the reading process (Gibson and Levin, 1975). They point out that in learning to read the child must unconsciously acquire two sets of rules. One set is composed of rules for letter combinations in words; the other is composed of rules for word combinations that occur in sentences. The young reader must learn that *mat* is rarely followed by a final consonant and is usually followed by a vowel, often *e.* He must also learn that the two words *the dog* are never followed by a word that describes the dog and are usually followed by a verb. Since the child is first and foremost reading for meaning, a first-grade child who sees the sentence "The dog whined" and knows the rule that adjectives must occur before the nouns they modify will unconsciously

---

Mairzy Doats and dozy doats
And liddle lamzy divey
A kiddley divey too
Wood'n you?

The lyrics of "Mairzy Doats," a popular song of the 1940s, were based on a joke: when properly enunciated, the words actually were:

Mares eat oats and does eat oats
And little lambs eat ivy.
A kid will eat ivy, too.
Wouldn't you?

While six-year-old schoolchildren might never have heard the song, their ears sometimes play the same tricks. Children may not recognize the correct boundaries of distinct words, just as song lovers of the forties heard "mairzy doats" instead of "mares eat oats." They may not know the meaning of a word being used (encountered in a story, the word *doe* to describe a female deer may be an unknown concept). Or they may pronounce the word incorrectly. If a child is used to saying "lil" instead of "little" (and used to hearing it all around her, as she may in many parts of America), she will have a hard time remembering that she must put in two *t*'s when she writes the word. In school, misunderstandings such as these are no joke: any one of them can slow down a child learning to read.

eliminate the hypothesis that *whined* may be *white*. He will try instead to guess at a verb. If he has difficulty figuring out how to pronounce *whined,* he may guess *walked* or *went.* Almost 90 percent of all errors beginning readers make are substitutions for the word in the text. The child substitutes a word that makes sense to him, given the other words in the sentence (Weber, 1968).

Recognizing individual words. Learning to read individual words, not just identifying separate letters, is the most common problem for beginning readers. Children can learn to read words two ways. One is by analyzing the individual sounds of the word. A second way is by learning to recognize the whole word, that is, the entire pattern of its letters. Chinese children learn Chinese characters through recognition of the whole symbol. In America first-grade teachers sometimes use this method for the seven days of the week or the names of the children in the classroom.

But it appears that children learn to read faster when they analyze and integrate the sounds of separate letters or groups of letters than when they try to recognize the whole word. This conclusion was verified in a study in which children learned to read unfamiliar words

---

It appears that young children (preschool through second grade) can detect the number of syllables in a spoken word more easily than they can detect the number of distinct phonemic sounds. One group of children was asked to tap out the number of sounds in spoken utterances such as *is, my,* and *toy,* while another was asked to tap out the number of syllables in words such as *popsicle, dinner,* and *valentine.* Although all children improved with age, they could all distinguish the number of syllables in words better than they could the number of sounds. This suggests that it is easier for children to match the syllables of printed words to the language they know. If that is true, perhaps they should first be taught syllables (as in the Japanese script *kana*) before they learn the sound of individual letters.

Two psychologists at the University of Pennsylvania have tried to teach a sylla-bary to kindergarten children who did not know how to read (Gleitman and Rozin, 1973). The children were taught a system of signs that stood for syllables rather than for phonemes, and soon they were reading sentences and phrases such as "Before I open the candy"

after being instructed for only five hours. These psychologists have suggested that a syllabary may be a good introduction to reading for those children who may have trouble or who are not initially highly motivated to read. The syllabary should not be regarded as a substitute for phonics—the use of elementary speech sounds in teaching beginners to read. However, it can get children excited about reading and help them to appreciate that the funny designs printed on the page stand for the different sounds in familiar words.

Training words	Phonetic symbols	Transfer words	Phonetic symbols
و ر ا ڧ	fa:ru:	ى ر ى م	mi:ri:
ى د ا ڧ	fa:di:	و ت و م	mu:tu:
ا ڧ ى ت	ti:fa:	ا ش و ك	ko:ša:
ى ڧ ـوت	tu:ni:	ى ا ڧ ك	ka:fi:
ا ش ى ش	ši:ša:	ا ڧ ى ن	ni:fa:
ى م ى ش	ši:mi:	ى ا د ن	na:di:
ى ڧ ا د	da:fi:	ا ش ى ر	ri:ša:
و ك و د	do:ko:	ى ڧ ى ر	ri:fi:

Figure 10-4
Unfamiliar Arabic words were used to test whether children could master words better by analyzing their components or by whole-word recognition. The children who analyzed the words did best. (After Bishop, 1964)

written in Arabic (see Figure 10-4). Some were taught to decipher these Arabic words by analyzing the components of the written word and some through the whole-word method. Later, each group was tested on both letter and word recognition (Bishop, 1964). Children who had learned to recognize the words by first analyzing the letters and synthesizing them into the unfamiliar word were then better able to read a new list of words.

Although it used to be believed that children with reading problems *misperceived* the letters and words, it now appears that the errors made by poor readers are not primarily perceptual. Most poor readers can name the letters of the alphabet, visually discriminate among different letters that look alike, and detect individual letters in long strings of words. One experiment with fifteen poor readers found that the highest error rate for letter reversal (reading *b* for *p* or *d* for *b*) was only 20 percent (Sidman and Kirk, 1974). And reversal errors declined by half as the experimental testing continued. With a little practice the children became adept at discerning *b* from *d*. Toward the end of the experiment the children made almost no errors in writing or naming a *d*, when a *d* was shown (see Figure 10-5).

Even when the task is made difficult and children have to search for a single letter in a display containing twenty-five different groups of letters—some real words and some nonsense—sixth-grade children who

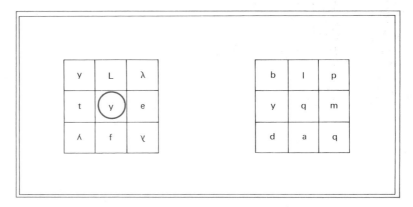

Figure 10–5
"Matrix displays" such as these were used to test children's ability to match figures to the sample. First, a sample letter was projected onto the center window of the matrix; when the child pressed the center window, other figures appeared in the outer windows. If the child pressed the correct matching outer window, chimes rang and a penny was delivered. The low incidence of reversal errors suggests that problems other than those of perception are the cause of reading failure. (After Sidman and Kirk, 1974)

are good readers do not perform significantly better than poor readers; in one study the error rate was 8 percent for good readers and 9 percent for poor readers (Mason, 1975).

Moreover, poor readers make very few errors when asked to copy designs of letters or words. But they cannot *read* the letters in words. A poor reader who correctly copies the word *cod* on paper is apt to pronounce it *cop*. But the fact that he copies the three letters correctly suggests that he perceived the *d* correctly and does not have a perceptual deficit. He sees the letters and word accurately but apparently cannot retrieve the auditory sound for the word (Vellutino, Steger, and Kandel, 1972).

Final consonants, vowels, diphthongs, and double consonants. Children tend to make more errors on the final consonants of words than on initial consonants (Shankweiler and Liberman, 1972). Printed vowels constitute a major problem, though vowel sounds are easily detected when heard in speech. When children were asked to repeat words they heard on a tape, they made fewer errors in repeating vowels than consonants (Shankweiler and Liberman, 1972). This is because vowel sounds are more intense and last longer than consonants. Vowels seem to persist longer in memory as echoes than do consonants. But when printed, vowels lose the distinctiveness they have as sounds.

In addition, the vowels change rules of pronunciation in a way that children must find capricious. The less stable the vowel, the more trouble children have with it. There is a lower rate of error for the short *i* sound, which is almost always represented by the letter *i*, than for the short *u* sound, which can be represented by a variety of letters or combinations: *u, oo, ou.*

Children have great difficulty with diphthongs (pairs of vowels), such as *oo, ee, oy, eu, ou, ai, ei.* In diphthong combinations two vowels together make one sound, as *oi* in *soil.* But often the child does not know if the *o* in *soil* should go with the *s* and be pronounced *so-il* or with the *i* and be pronounced *s-oil.*

Similarly, children with reading problems have difficulty with specific pairs of consonants such as *fl, lk, ch,* and *ph.* When faced with the word *witch* for example, the child is not sure whether the *c* should be paired with the *t* or with the *h,* or pronounced separately.

The Initial Teaching Alphabet can be an aid toward mastering the irregularities of the vowels and double consonants (see boxed insert page 422). It includes different symbols for sixteen possible vowel sounds. Children of average intelligence master it easily. When the time comes to change over to the standard alphabet, after some initial difficulties they show a slight edge in performance over children who use the standard alphabet from the beginning (Downing, 1971).

Familiarity with words. Even if the child does not know how to spell a word, if he is familiar with its sound and meaning, he will have an easier time blending the separate syllables and letters into the correct sound than if he has not heard the word before or does not know its

meaning. If children hear the separate syllables of two-, three-, and four-syllable words with a delay between each syllable (like *po-ta-to*), they have no trouble recognizing the word, even if there is a seven-second delay between the syllables. But this is true only if the word is familiar. If it is a word they do not know (either a nonsense word, such as *ilgup,* or a new word they have never heard, such as *national*), they have great difficulty recognizing the word that the syllables formed (Engle, 1975). Hence, a child's prior familiarity with the words in any reading exercise is a critical factor determining how well he will be able to read them.

The better the child's knowledge of a word, the faster he will be able to recognize it. In one experiment (Doehring, 1976) the word *boat* appeared in the lower part of a rectangle and one identical and two similar words—*boat, baot,* and *boad*—appeared in windows above it. The child was asked to press one of the three top windows when he recognized which of the words was identical with *boat*. The child who knew that *boat* was a word performed faster. Similarly, in reading paragraphs, the child read the word *boat* faster in a meaningful sentence ("The big black boat was on the water") than in a nonsense phrase ("The fish ate boat in time"). Unfamiliarity with words is apt to be more characteristic of lower-class children with language retardation and of children from homes where black English, nonstandard English, or a foreign language is spoken.

The role of memory. In some cases poor reading may be due to a memory deficit, which is a more serious problem in cognitive functioning than unfamiliarity with words. By the time the child reads "The big black boat" he may have forgotten the context of the paragraph. In one study of twelve-year-old boys, those with reading problems were more apt to forget an event seen briefly than the boys who were adequate readers. The children were shown a circle of eight letters or eight designs, which disappeared from the circle after 150 milliseconds. Sometime within 2 seconds later a teardrop indicator appeared at one location on the circle where a letter or a design had been shown. The child had to point, on another card containing all eight images, to the one that had been in the place of the teardrop. If the teardrop appeared within 200 milliseconds of the disappearance of the image, reading-disabled and normal children performed equally well. But if the delay was greater than 200 milliseconds, the reading-disabled boys made more errors, suggesting that the memory of the original image had faded (Morrison, Giordani, and Nagy, 1977).

Finally, a child may be a slow reader because he does not activate the cognitive units (described in Chapter 4) that he possesses.

In sum, the main problem for most children is not an inability to discriminate perceptually among the letters nor an inability to learn the names of the individual arbitrary symbols we call letters. The problem is more likely to be a cognitive one—difficulty in knowing how a letter or combination of letters should sound when it is part of a word or in remembering the words that were recognized. Familiarity with the letters and their sounds is the best predictor of a child's rate of reading progress. One team of investigators gave a large battery of tests to

"The addition is easy—but I tend to be nonverbal, and the apples throw me."

"Catch-5"

The greatest difficulty for beginning readers concerns the mastery of vowels. Salient when spoken, vowel sounds are undistinguished when written down. Furthermore, the messages they send are confusing to young readers, as they are to anyone learning English as a second language.

The five alphabet letters used to transcribe vowel sounds—*a, e, i, o, u*— group and regroup to form a large number of subtly varying sounds. (The Initial Teaching Alphabet, printed below, includes sixteen possible vowel sounds.) At sea in a confusion of vowels, where the rules are complicated and the exceptions numerous, children need special help to work their way out of "Catch-5"—it is a challenge to teachers' ingenuity.

a	ɑ	æ	au	b	c	çh
apple	f**a**ther	r**a**te	t**au**t	**b**ig	**c**at	**ch**ick
d	ɛɛ	e	f	g	h	ie
dog	m**ea**t	**e**gg	**f**ill	**g**un	**h**at	t**ie**
i	j	k	l	m	n	p
d**i**p	**j**ig	**k**it	**l**amp	**m**an	**n**et	**p**ig
œ	o	ω	ꞷ	ou	oi	þh
t**oe**	h**o**t	b**oo**k	m**oo**n	v**ow**	**oi**l	**th**in
r	ɼ	s	ʃh	ŋ	ʒ	t
run	b**ir**d	**s**ad	**sh**ip	si**ng**	vi**si**on	**t**ap
y	þh	ue	u	v	w	wh
yell	**then**	d**ue**	**u**gly	**v**an	**w**ill	**wh**en
z	ʃ					
zoo	ro**se**					

five-year-olds the summer before they entered kindergarten and then assessed how well the children were reading when they reached the third grade. The best predictor of reading skill was knowledge of the alphabet in the months before kindergarten (Stevenson et al., 1976). This study suggests that familiarity with the elements of words is the best preparation for learning to read.

The Effects of Language Environment

Another source of reading difficulty has been attributed to the child's language environment at home, since a large number of American children who cannot read come from homes where a foreign language or a nonstandard English dialect (usually a black dialect) is spoken.

It is possible that a child who hears the English word *fire* pronounced like *fur* at home and hears some words pronounced without standard endings ("Come here quick" instead of "Come here quickly") may have some trouble understanding the teacher's instructions and recognizing written words. Reasonable as this idea appears, research suggests we cannot put too much of the blame for reading failure on this kind of linguistic interference. In one study (Genshaft and Hirt, 1974) black and white fifth-grade children of average intelligence and similar social class listened to a tape recording of fifteen English words (such as *solid, bust, sister, wheels, dig, blood*) that had special meanings in black English (for example, *blood* means *brother*). The words were spoken in black dialect. The children had to listen to the words and then try to recall as many of them as possible. Both black and white children recalled the same number of words! In addition, the same fifteen words were used in two sets of sentences. One set of sentences was spoken in standard English ("When my father is very ill, he usually has my mother call his *boss*"). The other set was spoken in black dialect ("Dat cat, he sho' nuff wear some *boss* clothes evera time he makes da scene"). The children had to repeat each sentence immediately after hearing it. Black and white children performed equally well on the standard English sentences. The black children, in fact, recalled them better than they did the sentences in black dialect. But the black children performed much better on the black-dialect sentences than did the white children (see Figure 10–6). This study suggests that black children, rather than suffering from a deficient language system, are really bilingual and that linguistic

Figure 10–6
Black and white fifth-grade children were compared to see how well they remembered sentences read aloud in standard English and black dialect. On standard English sentences the performance of the groups was very similar, but on black-dialect sentences the white students did not perform as well. (After Genshaft and Hirt, 1974)

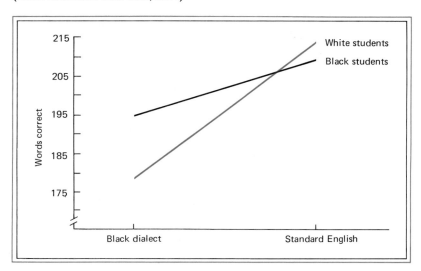

interference from a dialect may not be a major cause of reading failure after all.

An experiment in reading, rather than listening, yielded the same finding (Marwit and Neumann, 1974). Black and white second-grade children were given a reading comprehension test. Some of the sentences were in standard English ("Roy plays with the cow; the cow's name is Spotty"); others were in black dialect ("Roy, he play with the cow, the cow name Spotty"). Again, all the children did better reading standard English than nonstandard English. Therefore, the fact that black children grow up exposed to black dialect does not seem to be important in explaining why poor black children have more trouble learning to read than middle-class white children.

Since existing scientific information suggests that neither brain damage, visual discrimination problems, nor dialect can account for the majority of reading failures in America (although they do account for some), we are left with the frustration of not understanding why almost a million American children have inordinate difficulty learning to read during the first years of school. Many psychologists assume that the motives, fears, and emotions of the children, discussed in Chapter 7, are partly responsible for the difficulty. But whatever the initial reasons for difficulty, the experience of failing makes children afraid of another failure and leads them to be increasingly wary of school tasks and to gradually withdraw their effort as they become convinced they cannot do what is expected. Thus, independent of the many different forces that lead to original learning difficulty, the child develops two new problems—fear of the task and low expectancy of success.

Implications for Teaching: Strategies and Curricula

Let us consider, finally, the possible contribution of the teacher's techniques. Perhaps some ways of teaching reading are better than others. We shall focus on the children who do not have serious neurological, muscular, or sensory handicaps but who nevertheless have specific problems mastering reading. Although the discussion thus far has concentrated on the first phase of reading, namely recognizing words, reading comprehension and reading speed are quite separate problems. Some children can read words accurately but have little or no idea of what they have read. Some older children who can read and comprehend words and sentences do so very slowly, and their inefficiency is a serious handicap in high school and college. Problems with comprehension and speed are probably not related to the nature of the printed English language or dialect problems but are due, in part, to motivation and conflict. The main point is that the strategies to use will depend on the age of the child and whether analyzing, comprehension, or speed is the central difficulty.

Planning Curricula That Work

Reading programs for children should address several levels at once: letters, syllables, words, and sentences. Gibson and Levin (1975) suggest three guiding principles for curricula. First, the material to be read must make sense to the child for she is *always reading for meaning.* Beginning reading should involve sentences, albeit simple ones. They should be written in a style that matches the speech the child is accustomed to hearing. Second, the words in sentences should be familiar so that they can be mastered easily to prevent disappointment and fear of failure. Third, since the major task in reading is to learn the *rules* for letter and word combinations, lessons should be planned in order to present a particular rule in a variety of contexts. If the task is teaching that *lk* sounds like *k* in many words, such as *walk* and *talk,* this letter unit (*lk*) should be presented in all the words in which it has that sound. Similarly, if the child is to learn what the diphthong *oo* in

the middle of the word sounds like, the double *oo* should be presented in all relevant contexts, such as *soon, moon, boon,* and *loon.* In a separate context, the child can be given *book, look, brook,* and *cook.*

Gibson and Levin do not believe anyone has discovered the panacea for reading failure. After describing their own curriculum for learning to read, they conclude:

> Is this better than other programs? Frankly, we do not know ... and even if it were we would be hard put to choose the appropriate control groups. We are left with the modest claim that children learn to read and that there are a host of methods and materials which teachers may exploit any way they see fit. For our purposes we would be most pleased to see teachers be aware of the nature of reading and choose those methods and materials that make sense to them rather than be tyrannized by some prescription about how reading must be taught. (1975, pp. 331–32)

Phonics Drill Cards

Young children with reading problems benefit from materials that give them steady, consistent practice with the symbols, the troublesome vowel and consonant pairs, and the "outlaw" words that do not conform to the usual rules. For instance, the widely used Gillingham method uses drill cards as a basic tool (see Figure 10–7). On the front of some cards is a combination of letters: *wh, igh, sh,* and so forth. As the

Figure 10–7
Drill cards help children master the rules of phonics. Here, the front of the card shows a long u symbol. On the back are listed all the possible vowel combinations that can be used to symbolize the long u sound. (Gillingham and Stillman, 1960)

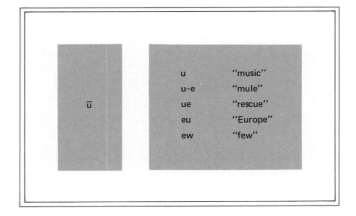

teacher holds up one card at a time, the student names the letters, makes the sound they symbolize, and gives an example of a word that uses the sound: "sh says *sshh* as in *wish*." Other cards have a phonetic symbol for a vowel *sound* on the front, such as $\bar{u}$ and on the back, list all the *symbols* that make that sound, plus a key word for each one: $\bar{u}$, *music; u-e, mule; ue, rescue; eu, Europe; ew, few* (Gillingham and Stillman, 1960).

Gradually, each child builds up a "collection" of familiar sounds. Teachers assign reading materials using only words made up of familiar sounds. If a few unfamiliar sounding words must be included, the teacher presents them on a separate list and tells the child how they are pronounced. In that way the child is not left guessing: she is sure the words *will be made of sounds she knows.*

Words are learned according to a system. Children may learn all the *-ough* words that say *uff* (as in *rough* and *tough*) at one time. When they know them, they no longer need to worry that an unfamiliar one will suddenly appear in the reading.

| a = apple | ie = tie | oe = toe |
| æ = ræte | ɛɛ = mɛet | ue = due |

Figure 10–8
Using original symbols to distinguish among different sounds (*a* as in *apple*, but *ae* as in *rate*), the Initial Teaching Alphabet can help children untangle the correspondence between sound and symbol in the English language. (Downing, 1967)

Initial Teaching Alphabet

The Initial Teaching Alphabet (i.t.a.) is another useful tool (see Figure 10–8). It consists of a set of forty-four symbols, each symbol having an exact correspondence to the sound it represents, like Japanese *kana* script. While the use of i.t.a. involves two learning steps (first the child must master the symbols of i.t.a. and later he must transfer what he knows to the traditional twenty-six-letter alphabet), it has proven advantageous for many children who have a difficult time in the early years of reading. The use of color phonics is also a technique to aid reading. Instead of being printed uniformly in black, reading material is printed in various colored inks, so that sounds are differentiated by color. The long *e* in *team* may be red, the silent *e* in *mule* yellow, and the short *e* in *head* blue.

What about Perceptual Training?

Since a few children persist in confusing letters with similar shapes (such as *b, p, d,* and *q*), many teachers and psychologists have assumed that a possible reason for this failure is perceptual impairment—some difficulty in discriminating *p* from *b*, for example. A number of tests have been devised to measure a child's perceptual ability, such as the Frostig Figure Ground Test. Children who score low on these tests have often been treated to intensive exercises with blocks, squares, diamonds, textures, beads, and puzzles. When their reading skills subsequently improve, perceptual training gets the credit.

But critics of this view regard the results differently. First, as we indicated earlier, confusion of letters is not an important source of error in reading, even among children with reading problems. Second, the critics say that the reason these activities help is that any positive, individual effort mobilizes the child's attention, motivation, and ability to orient to the task at hand. The chief advantage of "perceptual training" activities is that they allow the child (and indirectly, parents and teachers) to focus on a specific task that is easy rather than on the difficult and emotionally more distressing one of reading.

Providing a Better Self-Image

It is not surprising that after seven or eight futile years of school, children who are "learning disabled" or "retarded" in reading are likely to drop out and turn up in juvenile court. They vent their frustration at failing, their anger at the schools that failed them, and their despair about learning skills in a variety of ways—most of them detrimental to themselves and to society.

The child sees a reflection of himself on many sides: in the teacher's attitude towards him (whether she hurries him along or encourages him to take the time he needs to answer a question, seems pleased with him or discouraged); in how his classmates treat him; in how quickly—or slowly—he masters new material compared to other children. And he is aware of the labels he—or his class—is given: "retarded," "culturally disadvantaged," "slow," are hardly badges of distinction. A major task of the school is to hold up a better mirror so that the child he sees reflected there is a child he can respect.

In order to prevent the downward spiral of initial failure/fear of failing/future failure, some schools attempt to identify "high-risk" children in the first grade or earlier. In some cases, it may be useful to postpone a child's entrance into first grade until he seems emotionally and cognitively prepared for school. While a starting age of five-and-one-half years is fine for many children, it can sometimes trigger learning problems that could be avoided if the child waited an extra year before beginning formal instruction in reading and arithmetic.

Special attention, both academic and personal, may be able to break the downward spiral. Rather than removing high-risk pupils from the regular classroom and putting them in special classes, early intervention programs try to increase their skills by providing additional tutoring, in small groups or in a one-to-one relationship with a teacher. Many schools are experimenting with a plan that uses parents and high-school students to tutor younger children with reading problems, and this strategy seems to be successful. By encouraging the children, showing them that they can succeed, and strengthening their reading skills, early intervention programs can change a child's status in school and improve—if not always ensure—his chances of proceeding at a more average rate.

For older children who already have a long history of failure and feel discouraged about and hostile toward school, teachers must create an accepting atmosphere. The principal's attitude toward failing children sets a tone for the school, either positive or negative. And naturally, the attitudes of the other children are critical. But usually, it is the classroom teacher who is the key to the success or the failure of special programs. Even children who may be inclined to taunt and belittle a slower classmate will take their cue from a teacher who makes it clear that all the students need help and that none of them should be ridiculed.

Arranging the School Day

In addition to creating an atmosphere of acceptance, it is necessary to organize the child's academic experience so that he achieves some success every day.

Special classes have existed in public schools for a long time because of the belief that some children share learning problems and can make greater progress if they are kept together under the supervision of a specially trained teacher. Actually, the evidence rationalizing this strategy is equivocal. One study showed that these children seemed to achieve more when they were in regular classes but had a better self-image when they were in special classes, presumably because they were competing more realistically against children whose abilities did not outstrip their own (Cassidy and Stanton, 1959).

A serious problem is the tendency to create special classes on the single criterion of similar I.Q. score. Children have been grouped together in the belief that if they have similar I.Q. scores, they need similar instruction. But in fact, children with the same I.Q. scores often have very different patterns of skill development, experiences, and needs. Special classes often contain children of radically different abilities, even ranging from nonreaders to those who can read at a sixth-grade level (Bruininks and Rynders, 1971).

There is still a place for special classes in the public school system, where particular programs can help the child who has difficulty making progress in a regular class. but "mainstreaming" has become a prominent strategy, and there is an increasing amount of integration between special and regular classes (see Figure 10-9). Flexible plans allow slower children to spend some time with their classmates in activities in which they can participate: libraries, music or art classes, discussion groups concerning problem solving or values, news presentations, movie showings, science walks. These activities can be a step toward moving into the regular classes more permanently.

For many children who have difficulty concentrating—whether the causes are organic or environmental—it is helpful to create a classroom setting that reduces distractions to a minimum: pale and restful colors, few pictures or maps on the walls, materials and games kept in cupboards instead of openly displayed around the room to tempt the child's attention (Cruickshank and Johnson, 1967).

Residential school with program geared to group characteristics (deaf, blind, etc.).

Special classes in a special day school with programs geared to group characteristics (deaf, mentally retarded, blind).

Special class in regular schools with limited or no structured contact with children enrolled in the regular class.

Special class in regular schools with structured contact with pupils enrolled in regular class in nonacademic situations.

Special class in regular school with structured contact with pupils enrolled in regular class in both academic and nonacademic situations.

Pupils enrolled in regular class with intensive individual or group tutoring. Program and time determined by individual needs.

Pupils enrolled in regular class with intensive individual or group tutoring with program determined by individual needs. Resource help to classroom teachers in adaptation of curriculum and tasks to individual needs.

Pupils enrolled in regular class after short-term tutoring for purposes of diagnosis and program planning. Resource help and aid to teacher in program adaptation. Inservice training to regular class teachers.

Regular class enrollment with resource help to classroom teacher. Diagnosis and behavior observation is the responsibility of the classroom teacher. Inservice training to regular teacher.

Figure 10–9
This diagram outlines one way of looking at the needs of children and arranging appropriate educational settings for them. It suggests that only a small proportion of children with special needs require self-contained classrooms and that others can benefit from staying in the main school system if the right provisions are made. (Willenberg, 1970, p. 123)

Teachers often find that they must schedule much shorter sessions than they anticipated. Instead of planning a reading or art activity for forty minutes, they need to plan two or even three periods of ten to fifteen minutes each. As the year progresses, the teachers find that they can lengthen the activities, so that by the end of the year most of the class can spend thirty minutes reading, whereas in September the average child's focus of attention lasted only ten or fifteen minutes.

Another procedure places all the students in the regular classroom and provides supportive services for the teacher. These services take different forms. The resource room, furnished and arranged for small

groups, allows teachers to instruct children at a more individualized pace. It may have special instructional materials, such as closed-circuit television, programed instruction, a controlled reader that projects type onto a screen at an adjustable rate, film strips, projectors, and tape recorders, all useful in helping children who cannot read easily. Since the equipment tends to be expensive and difficult to move, it is easier to keep it in a central resource room and bring the children to it.

A child may spend most of his time working in the resource room at the beginning of the year, but as the year progresses and he is able to do more work at grade level, he spends more time in the regular classroom. In some cases, the resource rooms are also available to students without learning problems. By scheduling "open hours," teachers may use visits to the resource room as a privilege, earned after good behavior or performance. The practice of open hours can help remove the stigma from children who regularly go to the room for their schoolwork. It is even possible to promote the room as an especially desirable privilege by arranging to have some students, known for their leadership and school success, "referred" to the resource room for visits (Prouty and McGarry).

Another alternative is to use the roving teacher—a specialist in learning problems who moves from classroom to classroom and provides tutoring sessions with small groups. Some kind of team teaching, where more than one teacher is responsible for a classroom, is almost a prerequisite for classes that integrate students of varying abilities.

Encouraging a Reflective Attitude

A reflective attitude is an important and useful trait in reading. Although speed reading is admirable in more mature students, it should not be emphasized in the first grade. The need for time to think was corroborated by a study with beginning students: pairs of four-letter words were projected onto a screen. Sometimes both words were the same (*suit/suit*) and sometimes a letter or two was interchanged (*suit/siut*). The children were asked to say whether or not both words were the same. The slides were left on the screen for one-half second, one second, or three seconds: the faster the exposure, the more errors were made, especially by poorer readers. But if the words were left on the screen long enough, everyone did better, and *there were no differences between good and poor readers* (Bonsall and Dornbush, 1969).

Using Relevant Reading Texts

High-interest low-level reading books are a fairly recent innovation and have produced good results with older students. Obviously, a thirteen-year-old boy will be resistant if he is asked to read a second- or a third-grade book, since the stories it contains are unrelated to his interests and have overtones of "childishness." High-interest low-level readers are short but exciting. Printed in a clear, large type, they use

carefully controlled vocabulary. But the stories—they may concern a teenager who runs away from home or a drug bust—deal with age-relevant topics, feelings, and ideas.

Capacity for Recovery

If proper, consistent tutoring and rehabilitation are instituted for children with reading disabilities and the home and neighborhood environment support the value of school success, there is good reason to believe that the majority of children with serious reading problems can learn to read and go on to successful life careers. Elementary-school children who had severe reading problems were followed up eight to ten years after they had been referred to reading clinics. Of forty-four children aged eight to fourteen seen at the University of Chicago Reading Clinic, forty-one had completed high school, twenty-seven of whom had also completed college and one of whom had completed medical school—a range of educational progress that parallels a random sample of children from the same social class (Robinson and Smith, 1962).

A similar follow-up study investigated fifty children seen at the reading clinic at the University of Pennsylvania. The proportion of adolescents and young adults in this group who were attending high school and college was not smaller than the proportion in the general population (Preston and Yarington, 1967).

In a third study, fifty-six boys from middle-class families attending a private school in Pennsylvania during the years from 1930 to 1947 were followed up in 1964 and 1965 when they were adults in their thirties. The boys who had been the poorest in their class in language and reading skills in elementary school had, as adults, attained the same high level of education as the boys who had progressed normatively. Indeed, they had graduated from colleges such as Brown, Yale, Swarthmore, and Oberlin: two were doctors, two were professors, and two were scientists. Thus, when a child has a supportive middle-class environment, attends good schools, and receives rehabilitative therapy of good quality, academic retardation and serious reading disability do not doom that child to life failure (Rawson, 1968).

Recovery is less common among poor readers from families living in poverty because less effort is made to help them. Low-income families are preoccupied with maintaining a minimal living standard. Moreover, peers and neighborhood adults may place less value on education, be less ashamed about school failure, and be less confident that rehabilitation will work. Under these circumstances, reading problems are apt to persist, or worsen, severely handicapping the adolescent and the adult. But the three studies outlined above demonstrate that adult failure is not inevitable for children with serious reading problems.

We have seen that there are different reasons children fail in school and have suggested that many can be helped to master reading and arithmetic if certain conditions are met. In Scandinavia a "normalization process" concentrates on giving children with special needs the training, experience, and skills they will need to lead normal lives. American schools are moving in the same direction for students who are having special difficulties, whether for biological or nonbiological reasons. This is not to say that all children are capable of achieving at an equally high level any more than all will grow up able to run the four-minute mile. But clearly the schools can confront the problems of children with special needs in a more vigorous and effective way.

Summary

There are a number of different reasons children fail in school. A small group have sensory impairments: they are blind or partially sighted, deaf or hard of hearing. While these handicaps are unquestionable obstacles to learning, they need not prevent children from mastering school skills, some in a public-school setting. Injuries to the central nervous system can produce delayed or deficient motor coordination, or interfere in subtle and unknown ways with a child's learning, even if he attains average scores on an intelligence test. Physical, sensory, and neurological problems require special kinds of instruction, often in special schools. However, they do not seem to be the primary cause of school failure for the majority of children. It is estimated that no more than one quarter of school failures are due to biological impairment of the brain.

Some children do not merely learn things at a slower pace than average—they will never master some skills at all, because of damage to the brain due to genetic factors, maternal illness during pregnancy, or childhood infection. While these children may be in the public school system, they are usually in special classes and unlikely to be incorporated into the regular classes.

The majority of children doing poorly in school—those who are in the lowest 10 percent of the average class and are discouraged and often disruptive—do not suffer from serious sensory, physical, or neurological impairments. Labels for this group include culturally retarded, learning disabled, and slow learning. These children have greater trouble learning and, most critically, have a difficult time learning to read. There are a number of possible explanations for their failure—some biological and some experiential. Delayed cerebral maturity and minimal brain damage have been suggested as potential causative factors, but it is difficult to determine the presence of these biological conditions in a particular child. Possible nonbiological causes include the difficulty of our writing system, the child's motivation (discussed in Chapter 7), the curricula, and the teachers' strategies. While our writing system includes an unstable correspondence between sound and symbol, it is likely that the students' motivation and the teachers' strategies play an important role.

Whatever the initial reasons for academic failure, once children are convinced that they cannot do schoolwork well, they become afraid of the next task and develop a low expectancy of success.

In order to prevent the downward spiral that results from failure, schools need to allow some success from the start. Some programs identify high-risk students in kindergarten and first grade, then provide extra tutoring that may keep them from falling far behind. For older children with entrenched expectations of failing, the school needs to create an environment in which they feel safe in making new efforts and in which success can be achieved and is rewarded. This requires making adjustments in schedules and classroom arrangements and choosing curricula that more directly confront the language of symbols used in writing and mathematics.

Projects

1 Find out what hearing and vision tests are administered in the school system where you live or attend college. How old are the children when the tests are administered? What do the schools do to help students whose tests indicate sensory impairments?

2 "Three times as many boys as girls fail to learn in school." Quote this statistic to several people and ask them to speculate about the reasons for this.

3 You are a specialist in a school system that wants to test all students at age five in order to diagnose learning disorders. You have arranged a meeting with the parents to explain this procedure and to secure written permission to administer a battery of tests (vision, hearing, Wechsler Preschool and Primary Scale of Intelligence) to each child. Using classmates to play the parents, role-play the meeting. Then discuss the attitudes that surfaced concerning learning disabilities.

4 Suppose that you and a classmate are team teaching in an elementary school and will have special needs children in your class for the first time. You are anxious to foster humanistic attitudes among your students and prevent humiliation of the special needs students. How will you go about doing this?

5 In this year's issues of *Child Development* and *Exceptional Children*, read the articles about learning disabled pupils. Does the same pattern of difficulties emerge in the two journals? How similar are the educational prescriptions? Next, read the articles in these journals on the same topic from eight years ago. Note the similar and dissimilar points made and write a short report on the changing views of learning disabilities.

6 If you could have a hand in establishing a small community that would enable children who had previously failed in school to learn and later work, how would you structure it? What skills would be most important? How would you group the students, if at all? What techniques would you emphasize?

Recommended Reading

Birch, H. G., and Gussow, J. D. *Disadvantaged children: Health, nutrition and school failure.* New York: Harcourt Brace Jovanovich, 1970. Summarizes the health and intellectual characteristics of children who are born in poverty and makes the case that these children begin life with a serious disadvantage.

Gibson, E. J., and Levin, H. *The psychology of reading.* Cambridge, Mass.: M.I.T. Press, 1975. The most scholarly summary of our knowledge about the reading process and how it goes wrong.

Kavanagh, J. F., and Mattingly, I. G. (Eds.). *Language by ear and eye: The relationship between speech and reading.* Cambridge, Mass.: M.I.T. Press, 1972. A series of essays on the reading process and the causes of reading difficulty.

classroom atmosphere and management

11

Since most American schools share the same primary missions—to transmit basic academic skills and to help mold the character and personality traits our society values—it is not surprising that classrooms throughout America appear very similar. Traveling from school to school in different parts of the country, an observer will note strong parallels in the way the school day is organized, what subjects are required, and how they are taught. What differences exist are due, first, to variation in motives, attitudes, and abilities of the students and, second, to the way those characteristics interact with the philosophies, personalities, and talents of the teachers. It is this interaction between students and teachers that determines the atmosphere of the classroom. Nevertheless, since the teacher does have some freedom to organize classroom activities according to personal preference, it is useful to discuss the teacher's values, especially those that influence the academic progress of the students.

Most teachers have three primary goals—to instill a motivation for learning, to prepare children to be more effective citizens in society, and to teach them academic skills. In the minds of most teachers the first two are as important as the last. A first-grade teacher comments to an interviewer, "What am I trying to do most of all? Well, in the first grade, I'm trying to teach the child to read and want to read. But what I suppose I'm really doing is trying to get that child ready to live in society, to take care of himself, and to become the proper kind of member of that society" (Lortie, 1975 p. 112). Teachers feel they have had a good day when students cooperate, behave themselves, and demonstrate positive feelings; when they show that they want to learn and enjoy instruction (Lortie, 1975).

The average teacher likes to see himself or herself as the captain of a ship of thirty children—isolated from the mainland, with no intrusions from other teachers or from principals. A teacher comments, "A good day for me . . . is a smooth day. A day when you can close the doors and do nothing but teach. When you don't have to collect picture money or find out how many want pizza for lunch or how many want baked macaroni or how many want to subscribe to a magazine. If you

can have a day without those extra duties that would be a good day"
(Lortie, 1975, p. 165).

Another teacher says, "I think to me a day is good without
interruption. . . . There is no gym, no TV, no program to take the
children out of the room, but those days are getting less all the time"
(Lortie, 1975, p. 169). In the view of most teachers there should be a
continuous productive exchange between the teacher and the children.
Other people only get in the way by taking the teacher's energy and
attention away from the primary setting, the classroom.

Philosophical Choices Teachers Make

Whether they realize it or not, teachers face four major decisions in the
classroom, and their personal philosophies, often unexamined,
influence their decisions. Since they are mainly ethical decisions,
teachers should be acutely conscious of the choices they make and the
reasons they have selected one over another, so that they can evaluate
the usefulness of those decisions. The four decisions concern the
teacher's attitude toward disruptive behavior, autonomy in academic
pursuits, the balance between competition and cooperation, and the
exercise of authority in the classroom.

Attitude toward Disruptive Behavior: Rigid or Flexible?

Every social situation has certain prescribed rules. In the theater the whispers of one member of the audience should not disturb another; at a football game one spectator should not block the view of another. The classroom, too, has certain rules that must be followed if the work is to proceed constructively. Excessive aggression, disobedience, and noise must be controlled. All teachers agree that they need to prevent the classroom from becoming unruly, but they differ in how permissive or rigid they should be toward minor or occasional violations of reasonable rules of conduct. Some teachers brook little or no opposition to the rules they adopt; they are like teachers in contemporary rural China who require conformity to a fixed set of standards. Those who take a more permissive posture weigh the intention of the child and the context within which he misbehaves; they tend to tolerate occasional pranks, noise, and misdemeanors. Teachers usually interpret the mood of the classroom according to their own values. One teacher observing a classroom full of activity and noise sees initiative, interest, and enthusiasm, whereas another teacher viewing the same classroom sees insolence, immaturity, and aggression.

Academic Work: Self-directed or Structured by the Teacher?

A second important choice the teacher must make concerns the degree of autonomy given each child in pursuing his work. Some teachers want to direct the curriculum and decide what the child will be working on. Some want all the children to work together at the same rate on the same material. Others prefer to have each child set his own individual pace. Although this decision reflects the teacher' philosophy of education, she cannot, of course, make the decision independent of school policy, the principal's views, and the preferences of the community. Highly motivated and responsible children can more easily be permitted to pace themselves, if that is the teacher' preference. But children who are not highly motivated or who are accustomed to being told what to study may not be ready to initiate their own plans. Teachers who want to see them move toward greater autonomy should gradually give them chances to learn self-direction rather than insist that they take all responsibility for their work.

Some provocative conclusions about the effect of structured versus self-directed conditions came from a study of ten-year-old boys making model airplanes in a club project. The children were divided into three groups, each having an adult leader. A hidden observer reported the percentage of time the children spent in effective work (see Figure

11–1). In the first group, where the adult made no attempt to direct the activities, the boys spent little time on the project. In the second group, which worked out a system of cooperative leadership with the help of the adult, the boys used their time more constructively. In the third group, which was dominated by the adult, some boys resisted the tight supervision; others accepted it and spent a good deal of time on the project, and they were the most productive of all, as long as the leader remained in the room. When the leader left the room, however, only the cooperative group maintained the same work level: the level of both the resistant and accepting boys in the leader-dominated group dropped substantially. But both the groups that had direction of some sort were more productive than the group that had none (White and Lippitt, 1960).

The results raise an important value question: should teachers strive to elicit the greatest amount of work from their students, or should they attempt to increase each student's personal responsibility for his own progress? A teacher choosing the latter course risks widening the range of student performance, so that some students sprint ahead while others remain behind. Since wide variation in levels of performance can

Figure 11–1
When ten-year-old boys were observed in club activities, the percentage of time spent on work projects varied depending on the degree of leadership. One group was completely undirected and spent little time working. A second group worked out a system of cooperative leadership and spent its time more productively. In the third group, which was leader-dominated, the boys who were resistant to the adult supervision did less work than the boys who accepted it. But all the boys who had some form of leadership were more productive than those who had none. (Adapted from White and Lippitt, 1960)

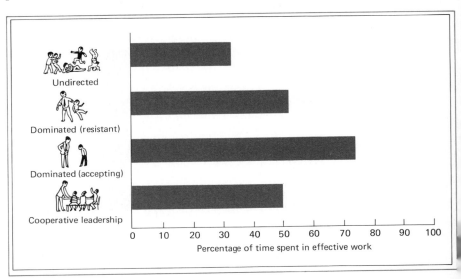

complicate the teacher's task, many teachers prefer to supervise the students' progress closely, holding back very able students and coaching slower ones in order to consolidate the group.

Classroom Mode: Competitive or Cooperative?

Some teachers believe a competitive atmosphere in the classroom is valuable, while others prefer to encourage children to help one another work and to reduce individual competition. The competitive spirit has been popular in American schools (reflecting the strong value placed on competition in our culture), but recent changes in values among American youth have increased the emphasis on cooperation in some schools.

One investigator wanted to determine whether students in a programed physics course in a Pittsburgh high school would perform better working alone or with other classmates. The experimental lesson was a 660-frame linear program on atomic physics. One hundred and sixty-six students were assigned to work either individually or in groups of four. The groups (some homogeneous in ability, some mixed) were characterized by three kinds of social interaction: *group pacing,* where each group worked at a pace set by the last member to complete each frame; *public discussion* of how each member responded to the frame; and *group discussion,* where members were permitted to discuss the material of each frame after all had completed it. All the students were given a criterion-referenced test at the end of the period of study, and all learned some atomic physics. Social interaction neither helped nor hindered level of mastery of the primary material. It did, however, slow down the lesson so that efficiency was greater for the students working individually. In the mixed groups social interaction helped the slower students but slowed down the more capable ones (Kress, 1969). The experiment emphasizes the value judgment inherent in a teacher's decision to have children work alone or in groups. If the goal is to maximize each child's progress, the teacher should promote individual work so that no student is held back by another. If the goal is to equalize the group's progress, she should rely more on social interaction to permit better students to help less capable ones. Science cannot tell the teacher which choice is best; it is a matter of the personal philosophy of the teacher and the values of the parents in the community.

Running the Classroom: Teacher Control or Student Participation?

Teachers also make a choice concerning the degree of control and authority they will exercise. The teacher-dominated class is a natural outcome of the almost universal belief that children should be obedient to adults, and as a result, this model has been the most common in American schools. Typically, teachers choose the material, method of presentation, and assignments and respond to the student's work and conduct with evaluative grades and informal comments. They determine the rules by which the classroom runs and are the sole judges in arbitrating disputes. In a teacher dominated classroom the

teacher lectures, gives directions, criticizes, and justifies authority (Withall, 1949).

A classroom in which children make a contribution to establishing the rules is a relatively new notion in educational philosophy, reflecting our changing view of the role of the child. It is a logical extension of the increasing egalitarianism in American culture. Although young and still emerging as individuals, children are viewed as capable of rational opinions and valid feelings that should be acknowledged rather than ignored. In this context, teachers do not abandon their responsibility as guides but help the students participate in planning and implementing rules. In allowing them the opportunity to exercise greater personal choice, teachers hope that the students will become more responsible. Students are encouraged to use democratic procedures in establishing class goals and to work with the teacher in planning the classroom's activities. A group-controlled classroom permits children to set and enforce regulations for acceptable behavior, welcomes questions, and encourages expression of many points of view. Most important, it takes into account the students' feelings about their performance (Heil, 1960).

Results of Major Choices

How much autonomy does each child have for selecting and pacing work, and how permissive is the teacher toward disruptive behavior? The teacher's decisions on these two dimensions are major determinants of classroom atmosphere and can produce four different kinds of classrooms. A classroom in which the teacher gives children high autonomy for schoolwork and is permissive regarding disruptive behavior is least common and is represented by very permissive private schools such as Summerhill, the well-known English school founded by A. S. Neill. A class with high autonomy for work but low permissiveness for disruptive behavior is characteristic of many small, private schools for middle-class students. Low autonomy for work and low permissiveness for disruption typify most traditional American classrooms, while low autonomy and high permissiveness are most often found in ghetto schools, where the teacher finds it difficult to change the behavioral patterns that were acquired during the preschool years.

Is There a Correct Choice? There is no general prescription that tells a teacher what choices he should make, independent of the types of students in a particular classroom. If the teacher has a strong personality he can, to some degree, persuade students to subscribe to his values. But he may also arouse feelings of opposition in students whose values do not concur with his. *Harmony in the classroom depends on the match between the* *values, the temperaments, and the personalities of the students and those of the teacher.*

Imagine a teacher who demands order and neatness, gives highly structured lessons, and is assigned to a school in a small upper-middle-class suburb where the majority of students come from families who encourage high standards of mastery and autonomy but set a permissive standard regarding neatness, politeness, and emotional spontaneity. The teacher will generate tensions in that class. Her students will resent being told exactly what to do and will chafe at restrictions that prevent them from exploring material on their own. Their skepticism about her omniscience may even make the teacher uncertain. If she interprets their behavior as disrespect, she is likely to tighten her rules and demands, increasing the misunderstanding between herself and the students.

But if the same teacher is assigned to a rural township with children from families who encourage respect, politeness, and obedience to authority and have a passive attitude toward the mastery of new material, she will find it fairly easy to achieve a harmonious atmosphere. The students will be prepared to adopt a polite and obedient posture toward her and accept her rules. The teacher, prepared to give highly structured lessons, will find students who expect to be told what and how to study. Since the students and the teacher meet each other's expectations, there will be less opportunity for misunderstanding and tension.

A number of studies confirm the view that the match between student characteristics and teacher attitudes is the most important factor influencing the atmosphere of the class. In one study, boys in grades eight and nine from twelve different social studies classes taught by men took a personality scale that revealed the degree to which they preferred authoritarian adults, as well as the students' attitudes toward flexibility and compulsiveness in their own work. Boys who were compulsive tended to perceive their social studies teacher as less authoritarian than those in the same class who were much less compulsive. Compulsive students did less work when they felt their teacher was not authoritarian, while less compulsive students did more work when they saw the teacher as nonauthoritarian (Goldberg, 1968). Students who prefer authoritarian teachers view them positively and do more work for them. This is a good example of the importance of the match between teacher and pupil.

Moreover, if a student is relatively free from anxiety over mastery, he tends to perform better in student-centered courses than in teacher-dominated courses. But if a student is anxious about his ability to perform well, he tends to perform better in a teacher-dominated version of a course, as is shown in Figure 11–2 (Dowaliby and Schumer, 1973).

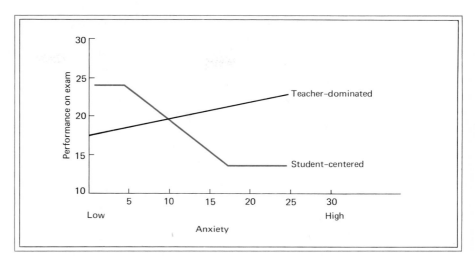

Figure 11–2
As shown on this graph, students relatively free from anxiety about mastery tended to perform better in student-centered courses than in teacher-dominated courses, but students anxious about their ability to achieve tended to perform better in the teacher-dominated version of the course. (Adapted from Dowaliby and Schumer, 1973)

The importance of the match has other scientific support. In any group of students motivated to master school material, some are most highly motivated to achieve under the teacher's close supervision. Others are most highly motivated to work toward goals that they have helped to determine. One hundred college freshmen were given tests to measure whether their motive for achievement was best gratified through conformity to authority or through independent and autonomous behavior. Then the two types of students were assigned to four introductory psychology sections. All the classes were taught by the same instructor, but he adopted different attitudes. In two of the classes he emphasized conformity, lectures, factual knowledge, and required attendance. In the other two classes he permitted more autonomy. Students participated in class discussions and were encouraged to generate ideas rather than memorize facts. All students took an identical examination of multiple-choice and essay questions at the end of the semester. Students who were motivated to achieve in a conforming atmosphere did better in a structured class than those who desired autonomy. Conversely, in the autonomous sections students whose motive for achievement was gratified best in a more independent setting did better than those who had a conforming posture (Domino, 1971). These findings suggest that rather than seeking the best way to

teach all students, it is better to seek the best match between the teacher's strategies and the students' needs, personalities, and past habits.

Distin-
guishing
between
Two Goals:
Favorable
Attitudes
versus
Academic
Progress It is important to distinguish between two goals: improving academic performance and fostering desirable attitudes and behavior. It is possible, for example, to obtain a harmonious match between highly directive teachers and docile students. In such a match, the students will be likely to master academic material. But does that mean that the class will be an unqualified success?

If everyone in the society agreed on the ideal of conforming students, the class would have to be judged a success. In this country, however, there is a lack of consensus on what kind of students parents want to see the schools develop. Some teachers prefer docile, conforming students (Feshbach, 1969). But individual parents often dissent, hoping instead that the school will promote more initiative and self-reliance in the children than the family has been able to or, on the other hand, wishing the school to affirm their own training and encourage questioning students. Sometimes the students themselves disagree about the value of the docile student, so that high-school students agitate for programs in which they have more opportunity to exercise their autonomy, develop self-reliance, and be responsible for their own conduct and academic progress.

What about the claims made for experimental curricula? Some that add variety and richness to the classroom do not, in fact, affect academic achievement. Eighty-eight fifth- and sixth-graders were part of a social studies unit on adaptation, focusing on the Iban tribe of Borneo and the Eskimo of northern Alaska. They were assigned to two kinds of classes. Members of the *competitive* group worked individually in their workbooks. After each five-lesson period posters were awarded to the six individuals with the best workbooks. Members of the *cooperative* group were assigned to subgroups, each of which had six students and worked as a unit to complete various inquiry activities. They divided the tasks among themselves, assessing the information on adaptation and making group decisions about which evidence to include in their workbook. After each five-lesson period the members of the subgroup judged to have the best workbook were each given a poster as a reward. When the unit was over, all the students were given an achievement test on the material and an attitude scale to assess their feelings about the material and about the cooperative or competitive teaching method. The results indicated, first, that the cooperative members liked sharing information, working together, talking with one another, and receiving group grades and, second, that the cooperative students liked social studies more than the competitive students did (though both had been exposed to the same material). The cooperative method clearly enhanced the students' enthusiasm about the course. But it did not affect achievement: there was little difference in the scores of the two groups on the final achievement test (Wheeler and Ryan, 1973).

Two Los Angeles elementary schools—one with team teaching and one without—evaluated achievement in reading, spelling, and arithmetic. Although teachers in the school with team teaching liked their jobs better, and the parents were more favorable in their opinion of the school's effectiveness, there was no difference in achievement scores between the two schools. In fact, the reading level was a little lower in the team teaching school (Rhodes, 1971). Both studies support the thesis that changes in teaching style often promote more desirable attitudes in children, but the changed attitude does not necessarily lead to better academic performance.

The Characteristics of the Teacher

A large group of teachers was asked whether or not it agreed that, in general, the personality characteristics of a teacher are more important than any particular knowledge or set of skills that the teacher possesses in determining success in teaching. Three out of every four teachers said they agreed (Marram, 1971). Other studies verify this common belief. Although personality traits are not easily modified (and even more difficult to measure), it is reassuring to know that certain teacher characteristics can have a positive influence on student behavior. Three major traits are warmth, a sense of justice, and attitude toward error. A fourth important characteristic—one that can be modified and measured—is competence. Let us consider each in turn.

Warmth: Do Students Perceive They Are Valued?

Warmth need not be effusive: teachers who genuinely like and respect students will convey their interest, even if their manner is low-keyed or reserved. The degree of warmth manifested by the teacher is an important quality, determining whether or not the student feels the teacher values her as an individual. In the early elementary grades teachers can make an effort to get close to children with gestures, as well as friendly words, bending down to talk to them, resting a hand on their shoulders for a minute. Junior-high or high-school students may think physical contact is overfamiliar or intrusive, but in those grades teachers can indicate interest by individual and informal contacts, outside the classroom as well as in the school (Good and Brophy, 1973).

Perceived teacher warmth correlates strongly with favorable student ratings of teachers (Baird, 1973). Unfortunately, warmth is not a quality that anyone can deliberately adopt with ease. But teachers who

naturally like children display a spontaneous acceptance that the children sense and appreciate. Such a teacher can be firm, even authoritarian, for she has already persuaded the children that she values them.

Justice: Do Students Believe They Are Treated Fairly?

Consistency in enforcing rules and dealing with misdemeanors engenders student respect. Children are more willing to accept both punishment and difficult work assignments if they believe the teacher treats all students equally. A teacher who dispenses justice with an uneven hand, or punishes more severely than the situation warrants, can create hostility and resentment. If teachers allow difficult work and actual punishments to become interrelated in children's minds, the children may suspect that they are being punished when they are given challenging assignments.

Attitude toward Error

As we saw in Chapter 4, many children have a tendency to be either reflective and concerned with error, or impulsive and less concerned. These tendencies can be modified, however. A child who deliberates

too long over each problem can be encouraged to be less fearful of error and take a chance. Children who make many errors because they answer too quickly can be taught to pause and mentally eliminate potentially incorrect answers before they speak or write them on paper.

Teachers differ in how permissive they are toward both their pupils' errors and their own. Teachers who believe that children should not make mistakes penalize incorrect answers; often they are the same teachers who do not like to be wrong themselves. Other teachers are more tolerant of error, believing that a child who is too concerned about making mistakes will be inhibited and too frightened to be creative in the classroom. In the words of one experienced teacher, "I don't want the children in my room to feel nervous about their work; I don't want the nerves in the backs of their necks to become tense" (Jackson, 1968, p. 128).

Although an overly reflective teacher may be troublesome for an impulsive student (and vice versa), she may also moderate the child's tendency by modeling an alternative pace in dealing with academic work. (This is one of the times when a teacher who possesses a trait different from the child's may help him.) A large group of first-grade teachers and a random sample of their students were measured at the beginning of the school year to see if they were reflective or impulsive. At the end of the year the children were measured again. Impulsive children—especially boys—who had spent the year with older, experienced, and reflective teachers had grown more reflective (Yando and Kagan, 1968).

Competence

The teacher's competence at the skill he is teaching has an important effect on children's schoolwork and can be deliberately improved. Familiarity with and mastery of the material depends on the teacher's knowledge of the subject, wisdom about its use, judgment in choosing the appropriate level, and strategies for presenting it. Competence also involves careful planning before class, organizing materials, displaying diagrams or outlines on the blackboard, and providing backup plans for students who finish assignments early, to ensure that the class hour proceeds without unnecessary delays and interruptions. "Bear in mind that when students are asked to wait with nothing to do, four things can happen and three of them are bad: the student may remain interested and attentive; he may become bored or fatigued . . . he may become distracted or start daydreaming, or he may actively misbehave" (Good and Brophy, 1973, pp. 174–75).

A teacher who is not in command of his material conveys uncertainty: worse, he allows the students to question the basic worth of the lesson. Competent handling of a lesson, on the other hand, reassures students and affects how well they master the material. In New York City fourteen first-grade teachers were observed while they taught reading, then questioned about their preferences for the phonics or whole-word approach. The children were tested before and after instruction to see which ones had gained the most. Naturally, the children who had come to school best prepared improved the most in reading. But aside from the children's initial reading ability, the most important factor associated with improvement was the observer's rating of the teacher's competence: her skill in choosing material at the appropriate level for each child and her choice of the phonics approach (Chall and Feldmann, 1966).

Identifying Problems in Classroom Control

When asked about the behaviors that distress them, teachers appear most concerned about disruptive conduct that interferes with class work—noise, dishonesty, impertinence, disobedience, low motivation, aggression, and rudeness. Clinical psychologists, however, identify a different constellation of behaviors that signal serious problems in students. In one study that examined problem behavior the teachers turned out to be most concerned about aggressive, disobedient, and antisocial behavior that frustrated *their* goals, while the psychologists were more troubled by behaviors—shyness, suspicion, oversensitivity, and daydreaming—that blocked *the child's* goals. Although not

Note etched on a high-school desk:

Dear Desk Reader,

How are you? I sit here in C block. What are you doing? I'm bored. Who are you, desk reader? Identify yourself immediately. I will identify me. My name is Chippy. Do you know the wrestling team is 5–0? There is a match this afternoon. Wish them luck.

Although teachers are most likely to identify aggressive, antisocial, and disruptive conduct as problem behaviors in the classroom, a second constellation is often overlooked: shyness, suspicion, oversensitivity, and daydreaming also characterize uninvolved students, but their problems may be ignored because they do not draw attention to themselves by conspicuous actions.

disruptive to the other students or the teacher, these behaviors interfere with the child's attaining important educational objectives (Tolor, Scarpetti, and Lane, 1967).

Teachers and psychologists rank the seriousness of behaviors somewhat differently; nevertheless, both asocial behavior and excessive withdrawal are associated with poor academic achievement. Investigators studied 809 children in grades one through seven in thirteen schools in a large city. According to evaluations of the thirty-two teachers involved, about half the children in each class were performing adequately. But about 30 percent of the students were "at risk" academically. These children were categorized as being overly dependent on the teacher, impulsive, disruptive, defiant, inattentive, or unable to comprehend the material (Spivack, Swift, and Prewitt, 1971).

Marshall Swift and George Spivack (1975), two sensitive observers who have spent many years studying children in classrooms, contend that conventional wisdom underestimates the extent of personal disturbance among children and suggest that perhaps from 25 to 30 percent of the children in a typical classroom display some kind of problem behavior. Curious about the precise dimensions of the problems, Swift and Spivack have tried to pinpoint the specific classroom behaviors that signal adaptive difficulties in students and have constructed a list of ten problems that recur in most classrooms.

These behavior problems are:

1 Inattentiveness, apathy, and withdrawal from class activities.
2 Overreliance on the teacher and other children to a point where the child is unable or unwilling to make decisions or attempt academic tasks on his own.
3 Poor rapport with the teacher; the child is suspicious, afraid, or distrustful of the teacher.
4 Impatience and impulsiveness, which interfere with the ability to plan and lead to errors on many school tasks. The child's need to respond quickly can be due to the fact that he cannot tolerate the uncertainty of an unfinished task or does not care about the quality of his work.
5 Low personal motivation, initiative, and involvement, which are reflected in minimal participation in the work of the classroom and a reluctance to share and explore ideas with the teachers or classmates.
6 Irrelevant answers and a talkativeness that interrupts class activity, often characterizing a child who wants attention or one who grasps only inconsequential aspects of the class discussion. (One child was asked, "What year did Washington cross the Delaware?" and replied, "It was very cold at Valley Forge.") Some children persist in talking, making wild guesses, losing their train of thought, or talking about their personal concerns.
7 Hostility, defiance, and negative feelings and actions. These attitudes take many forms, from belittling the lesson ("I have more important things to do than this stupid math") to calling a teacher names or destroying class property. But all acts aim to reduce the importance of academic tasks and discredit everyone involved in them.
8 Anxiety over achievement and failure, which underlies the behavior of children who are ill at ease when questioned, react to any criticism of their work as if they were being attacked personally, and chronically fear that their work will be judged inadequate.
9 Restless and hyperactive behavior, which differs from impulsiveness, for it suggests a need to interact with other children. Restless children talk, clown, tease, and bump into others. If there is any other activity in the room, they must join in. Although not necessarily hostile, restless behavior can be based on a need for attention or an irrepressible level of physical energy.
10 Minimal faith in the self's ability to gain success or control reactions of others. This trait is characteristic of a child who blames his failure on outside circumstances, teacher indifference, or a test that is "too hard."

Some of these problem behaviors are correlated (for example, impatient, impulsive children are often restless; children who have poor rapport with the teacher are likely to be withdrawn from class activities). Although we considered some actions teachers may take to deal with these situations earlier in the book, especially in Chapter 7, we will summarize in the next section the suggestions of Swift and Spivack for dealing with these problems, for their recommendations are specific and potentially useful.

Implications for Teaching

In managing the classroom and creating a constructive atmosphere, teachers must draw on all their knowledge—from common sense to specific strategies suggested by psychologists. Some of Swift and Spivack's suggestions reflect the wisdom of experienced teachers:

1 Be friendly, humane, and warm to the children.
2 Do not require a child to do something she is unable to do.
3 Do not punish a child in front of other classmates.
4 Try to arrange conditions so that the child experiences success rather than failure.
5 Do not reward maladaptive behavior you want to extinguish (for example, avoid saying, "Louise, are you running in the aisles *again?*").
6 Reward the child when she behaves appropriately.

In addition, Swift and Spivack suggest particular strategies to deal with the behaviors outlined earlier.

Some Specific Strategies

Teachers sometimes assume they know why a child is *inattentive* but they may be mistaken: an accurate diagnosis is difficult. Inattentive children may be bored, or they may be anxious. Teachers should explore the issue by talking to the children, perhaps approach them by saying, "Sometimes things happen that are so important to us, it is hard to think of anything else; what are some important things that have happened to you?" Discovering the reasons for inattention may enable teachers to help redirect the students' concentration. In order to hold students' attention, teachers can make the effort to call on them in random order rather than in predictable patterns alphabetically or along one row of desks. They can also interject a question ("What do you think is going to happen in the story next, Mary?") to a child whose attention is wandering; move closer to a child; or signal, with a gesture or a glance, that he, too, should listen to another child reading aloud.

Shorter work spans can also improve concentration; children who are unable to focus on a task for forty minutes may be willing to attend for fifteen or twenty (gradually, as the year goes by, the allotted time can be increased). Attempting to draw out the child about his thoughts and feelings and relating them to the subject at hand helps a child commit his own thoughts to the project. Finally, generating uncertainty by introducing surprises—such as a sneak quiz or an unplanned trip to the auditorium to see a movie—increases student attention during the day's activities. Novelty, as we saw in Chapter 7, is an important ingredient in maintaining classroom interest.

To increase children's *independence*, teachers should try to make them feel more secure in the classroom by making assignments clear, simple, and manageable and breaking down tasks into separate parts. When one part is successfully completed (and the child's success has been recognized), the child can proceed to the next component with more confidence. Individualized instruction is useful for children lacking self-esteem, since they can proceed at their own rate without worrying that they will fall behind the rest of the class. It is helpful, too, to allow children chances to make some choices of their own, such as working on the assignments for math, spelling, and reading in any order they choose, or deciding how to spend their free time.

As previously discussed, in order to encourage greater reflectivity in children who are *overly impulsive*, teachers can convey to them that accuracy, not speed, is important. The impulsive child often believes that finishing the task, rather than doing it correctly, is paramount. The teacher can encourage him to plan ahead, meeting with the student at the beginning of a project to draw up a series of steps he should pursue, checking with him later to see how the project is progressing, and finally, having a review session that focuses not only on the quality of the end product, but on how well the project proceeded according to the planning strategies. In a variety of ways, the teacher says, "Success is getting the directions straight, success is following all the directions correctly; success is going slowly to be sure" (Swift and Spivack, 1975, p. 76).

To increase the initiative and participation of *uninvolved students*, the teacher should consider talking with their parents. The parents' lack of interest, or overriding concern that their children be obedient in school, may be contributing to the students' detachment. If possible, the teacher should find out about the child's interests so they can be tied to the work in school. It helps to invite children to verbalize their thoughts (for instance, by showing a picture and asking them to think of all the ideas they can about what is going on in the picture, or by having them make up segments of stories in a group). This strategy must be used in a way that encourages rather than intimidates the child.

Children who *speak irrelevantly and intrusively* are often unaware that their answers are not to the point (as in the case of the "Valley Forge" answer). Some children offer such answers to gain attention; others have had little experience in the social give-and-take necessary in the classroom. In rare cases the child is seriously disturbed. The teacher should ensure that the child receives enough attention so that his need for recognition is partially satisfied. Praising a child for controlling the urge to interrupt or channeling it (by having him raise his hand and wait until he is called on) are other useful techniques. Helping the child to perceive the relationship between a question and a relevant answer is often necessary. The teacher should give attention to relevant and appropriate answers but ignore inappropriate ones so the child learns to discriminate between the two. Teachers can help the students develop awareness of social skills by pointing out techniques to the child who lacks them: "Whenever people get together and talk, they follow certain rules: they listen to others, they wait for another person to finish before they start talking" (Swift and Spivack, 1975, p. 100).

One of the most threatening problems to teachers is posed by the child who is openly *hostile, aggressive, and defiant*. Certainly, the teacher should define and clarify the limits and insist on them equally for all students. But at the same time, the teacher should allow rebellious children to feel that they have some choices on more negotiable tasks. (If the child must work on arithmetic, permit her to choose which problems she will do, or when she will do them.) Sometimes role-playing in small groups, with the teacher taking the part of the defiant child, can bring about a change in the student's perceptions of her own behavior. (Aggression will be discussed further at the end of this chapter.)

A better sense of self-esteem must be fostered in children who are unusually *fearful of failure*. As with overly dependent children, providing tasks at which the child can be successful and an environment that reduces competitive pressures permits a child to gain confidence. In addition, the teacher should help him learn to tolerate some anxiety.

Legitimizing the opportunity to let off steam is an important strategy in dealing with *restless students*. It is obviously less of a problem for classes in which a certain amount of physical activity is incorporated in the plan for the lesson. The teacher should try to increase the child's self-control, rather than punishing his restlessness.

When the child *blames others for his poor performance*, the teacher should first check on the validity of his claims. (Is she helping him enough, or did she inadvertently let him down? Does she give him work that is too difficult?) To help children overcome a sense of helplessness, teachers should give them more opportunities to plan their own work, letting them contract to do a particular assignment, or allow them greater freedom in choosing a topic to pursue. Furthermore, the teacher should take pains to review the work with them, point out where the student was successful and when he achieved what he intended (perhaps by encouraging the child to tell, in his own words, the steps he followed to solve a problem).

These strategies can increase the teacher's competence in managing the classroom. In addition, a more specific set of techniques, called behavior modification, has recently been applied to classrooms and in many cases has instilled more confidence in teachers. Let us examine how, and how well, these techniques work.

Behavior Modification: One Form of Classroom Management

Behavior modification is a set of practices that uses the consequences of behavior to strengthen or weaken future behavior. On the assumption that most human actions are learned, four basic models suggest ways that undesirable behaviors can be eliminated and new, more desirable ones substituted in their place.

The *classical conditioning model* substitutes a new response to old stimuli. If a child has a response of fear to a large dog, for example, a therapist will try to substitute relaxation for fear as a response to the sight of the dog. The *observational learning model* produces change by having the child observe the new behaviors in someone else and then practice them himself. The *self-regulation model* has the person change his own behavior through monitoring, assessing, and comparing his own actions to those of some new standard he has set for himself. Finally, the *operant conditioning model* (described in Chapter 3) emphasizes the receipt of specific reinforcements for the person's new, more desirable behaviors (Kanfer, 1973).

The operant conditioning model is the one most frequently used in changing classroom behavior. The techniques are based on the principles of operant conditioning: positive and negative reinforcement, shaping, schedule of reinforcement, satiation, and extinction. In simplest terms, here is how these principles work.

Principles of Behavior Modification

Reinforcement. A student initiates a behavior and the teacher responds. If the teacher's reaction is one the student desires (what is called positive reinforcement), the student is likely to repeat the original behavior. Since a positive reinforcement is any event following a particular action that increases the chance of that action recurring, there are a variety of events that can function as positive reinforcements. One systematic use of positive reinforcements has come to be called a *token economy*. In a token economy the students who engage in appropriate behavior receive tokens (such as chips or slips of paper), which they can exchange later for a variety of desirable objects, including money and gifts (Brown et al., 1975).

Shaping. This strategy seeks to bring about a single behavior rather than attempting to change the entire constellation of actions at once. Changing several individual behaviors, one after another, may cumulatively achieve the larger change. Thus a teacher who wants a boy to stop yelling and hitting and to pay attention to her begins by curtailing the yelling. She works slowly on each behavior that comprises the total complex she is trying to achieve.

Schedule of reinforcement. An unpredictable schedule of reinforcement seems to be more effective in maintaining new behaviors than a schedule in which the child is rewarded every time. Rewards that are given 50 percent or 75 percent of the time are more influential than rewards that are given every time (or rarely). Unpredictable schedules put the student in a state of mild uncertainty. She is not disappointed if a reward is not forthcoming, nor is she bored because it is presented every time.

Satiation. After a time a reward may lose its effectiveness, and the student will no longer respond to its incentive power. At this point, the

"Getting an 'A' or a star is all right, but I'd like some sort of profit-sharing plan around here."

teacher needs to introduce a new reward that will propel the student to renewed efforts.

Extinction. If a behavior receives no reward over a long period of time, it is likely to be discontinued (extinguished). A student who interrupts the class by snapping his chewing gum will tend to continue the behavior as long as he attracts the teacher's attention (even her disapproval) and his classmates' approving laughter. If the class agrees to ignore these sounds, he may discontinue them, as the reward was not in making noises but the reactions they produced.

These are the major principles behind behavior modification. But their systematic application is often difficult to achieve. In order to modify behavior successfully (and that also means predictably; the goal is pinpointed change, not random improvement), the principles must be applied in a methodical way. First, the goals must be established clearly. There may be a greater chance of enlisting student cooperation if the pupils have helped to set the goals. But however they have been established, the class must understand them: children cannot meet classroom standards if they are unsure about what is expected of them. Second, the goals must be focused: the technique works best when the teacher is not trying to change many different behaviors at once.

Clearly, teachers should be certain that the students have the ability and the skill to meet the goals. For instance, a student may understand that the objective is to solve ten geometry problems, but if she does not know that the sum of the angles of a triangle is always 180 degrees, she will not be able to solve the problems.

After systematically outlining the goals, the teacher needs to have the classroom procedures systematically monitored. Keeping records is an integral part of behavior modification. Teachers need accurate statements of what took place at each stage in order to verify the effects of the strategy. Since it is almost impossible to record the relevant events in a room full of students and teach at the same time, a successful recording depends on the presence of a second person in the class who observes and takes notes on the average level of the behavior before intervention and the schedule of reinforcement.

A case of increased study behavior

Mrs. Adams wants to modify study behavior during the seventh-grade mathematics class. She draws up a chart that will record the study behavior of students during a particular time interval. Study behavior is characterized by paying attention to the book or paper, writing out problems, reviewing old work. Nonstudy behavior is talking to another student, being out of the chair, calling across the room, and so forth. In the first interval the observer records the percentage of time each student spends in study behavior (he may observe for a week or more to obtain a realistic average). The average time spent in study behavior during this period is the *baseline*.

Next, Mrs. Adams begins the reinforcement phase. During this period (which may extend over several days or weeks) she rewards students when they are engaged in study behavior. She may say to one, "That's good work, Jeffrey," to another, "You really have written out the steps in the problems in a clear way, Lisa," or with a third, merely stand beside the desk and nod reassuringly. The observer notes the changes in the students' behavior on his chart.

The third stage is the period of reversal. Now Mrs. Adams refrains from praising or encouraging the students as she has been; the strategy results in a drop in study behavior.

Finally, there is a second period of reinforcement: she resumes the rewards, and the observer records an increase in study behavior.

Praise or Ignore

One characteristic of behavior modification as it is used in schools is the practice of relying more on positive rewards than on punishment. This strategy differs from an intuition many teachers have. They find it easy to praise the behavior they want to encourage ("Such a neat paper, Phyllis") but are equally ready to reprimand or belittle behavior they want to discourage ("Terry, stop running around the room; no wonder you never get any spelling done, since you're never in your seat"). Behavior modification's catechism is: "Praise. If you can't praise, ignore."

This feature of behavior modification depends on a deliberate and resolute determination by the teacher, for it runs counter to the teacher's spontaneous tendency to criticize behavior that should be discouraged. This rule evolved from two principles of operant conditioning: reinforcement and extinction. Although intended to have a negative effect, certain events planned as punishments have an unforeseen but positive reinforcing effect. "Stop running around the room," the teacher says in a stern voice. But this remark may be gratefully received by a child who does not mind being disparaged nearly as much as he minds being ignored and is secretly delighted to be singled out.

Instead of expecting negative comments to discourage a child's misconduct, psychologists focus on another phase of operant conditioning: extinction. Since an *unrewarded* behavior is likely to be extinguished after a period of time, perhaps a specific behavior can best be discouraged by ignoring it.

The other half of the strategy—praising the child—depends on "catching the children being good." Since the strategy is being applied precisely because certain students are not behaving in an appropriate way, teachers may protest that they will never have the chance. Practitioners of behavior modification have two replies. First, an observer in the classroom can almost always report instances of desired behavior that the teacher overlooked—either because her attention was focused somewhere else at the time or because she takes good behavior for granted and only notices the child's behavior when it is inappropriate. Second, it is not necessary to wait until the desired behavior is displayed perfectly in order to offer positive reinforcement. Consider the child who cannot stay in his seat during the time set aside for individual work in mathematics. The teacher's ultimate goal is to have him seated and working for the entire time. But following the principle of shaping, she can set a short-term objective: to reduce the number of times he leaves his seat. Even though he has left his seat several times during the period, the teacher may praise him for staying in his place more of the time than he had previously. She can make a simple chart and tape it to his desk, then put a check on it each time he feels compelled to jump up. When the chart shows that he jumped up fewer times than he had the day before, she can honestly commend him; furthermore, he can see for himself that he has made progress.

There is the danger that the teacher's behavior—rewarding and ignoring—will be extinguished before the students' unwanted behavior. After they have initiated a strategy of praise or ignore, teachers sometimes discover that there is an increase in undesired behavior. As a result, they grow discouraged and may discontinue the attempt. Experience suggests that they should keep trying, even if the early results are disappointing.

A case of increased participation in French class

Miss Ziller was teaching French, using the Aural-Oral method which requires class members to speak in French in response to her speaking in French. Sam would never speak. No matter what she said he remained silent. Miss Ziller described what happened:

"I did not penalize Sam for his silence. I continued the drills, passing on to the next student without interrupting the work or embarrassing Sam. One day Sam muttered some words while covering his mouth with his hand. I acknowledged Sam's response with a smile and a nod and continued the drill as if Sam had given the correct answer. Actually at that point I had not understood what he had said. I acknowledged each effort that Sam made to respond even though his pronunciation was not flawless. Gradually, he began to speak more distinctly, no longer covering his mouth with his hand. He seemed much less embarrassed by the inevitable errors one makes in the process of learning to speak a foreign language." (Krumboltz and Krumboltz, 1972, p. 40)

Choosing Appropriate Reinforcements

The individualization of reinforcements improves the chance for a successful outcome. Since children's personalities vary so much, it is understandable that a reward that appeals to one child may hold little attraction for another. To a large extent, the success or failure of the procedure depends on finding rewards to fit the student or, even better, giving the child a chance to select from a large assortment of reinforcers (such as the rewards suggested in the boxed insert on page 465).

A case of reading improvement

Mary was a poor reader. The teacher recorded Mary's efforts, noting the correct responses as well as the number and type of errors. At the end of a week she tallied the record and found that Mary averaged sixteen words a minute read out loud, with three errors. Having established a baseline, she began efforts to reinforce Mary's reading. However, Mary was so shy that the teacher's praise seemed to embarrass her more than please her. Then the teacher noticed that Mary often turned to look at the hamster's cage. "Would you like to hold the hamster?" she asked. Mary nodded.

The teacher suggested that Mary earn reading points that could be redeemed for time spent holding the hamster, and Mary agreed. At the end of the week, Mary's reading rate had increased from sixteen correct words a minute to twenty-five, and the errors had decreased from three to one or two per minute. (Sarason, Glazer, and Fargo, 1972, p. 26)

In addition to the normal array of rewards in school, teachers may draw on the approval or cooperation of other classmates. If Tony is having a difficult time settling down, the teacher may turn to two other students and say, "Don and Cathy, I think Tony would like to work on those maps with you." The teacher can also enlist the cooperation of parents. It may be as simple as sending a note home telling about a child's former difficulty, noting the improvement, and asking parents to say an encouraging word to the child. Or it may be a direct appeal for help. Teachers and parents can work together on changing a child's behavior if they have a mutual understanding about the goals of the experiment.

A case of reducing aggression

In the teacher's lounge one day, Dick Phillips told his colleagues about the unexpected trouble he'd had with LeRoy, his playground fighter.

"Behavior modification sounds simple until you really try it. I figured the thing to do with LeRoy was to send him home when he got into fights. I had a conference with him and his parents. They are very cooperative people, too cooperative, as it turned out. We all agreed,

A Choice of Rewards

Activities

FOR THE INDIVIDUAL:

Paper folding (origami)

Making poster for upcoming school event

Reaching into a "surprise sack" for a token gift

Choosing one's own seat in the room

Reading a book or magazine

Rocking in the rocking chair

Painting or drawing pictures

Daydreaming

Doing crossword or jigsaw puzzles

Listening to tape recorder on earphones

Playing with a toy instead of resting at nap time

Sharpening pencils

Being in charge of raising or lowering window shades

Cleaning erasers, blackboard

Watering plants

Feeding the fish or gerbils

Putting the shelves in order

Running errands for the teacher

Being the teacher's "assistant for the day"

FOR A GROUP OR THE CLASS:

Playing cards, chess, or board games

Having a general gripe session

Having a box-lunch auction

Having a spelling bee

Holding a panel discussion on topic of students' choice

Putting on a talent show

Going on a field trip to the zoo, museum, park, local newspaper office

Having a Hobby Day, where children show their hobbies.

Having a Let's Exchange Day, where students trade books or toys

Holding class out of doors

Dancing to records brought in by students

Having a white elephant sale (nothing over five cents)

Tangible rewards

Balloons

Toys from the 5 & 10 (bubble blowers, marbles)

Stars, stickers

Points, checkmarks on a bulletin-board chart

Raisins, popcorn, apples, milk, marshmallows

Baseball cards

Use of teacher's supplies, such as stapler, paper punch

Buttons with current sayings on them

Blue-ribbon awards ("The Christopher Robin Work Award")

Comic books

Secondhand magazines

Magic markers, multicolored pen

Picture postcards

(Adapted from Clarizio, 1971)

LeRoy included, that LeRoy simply couldn't continue fighting at school, and I thought things were under control.

"The first day or two, LeRoy stuck with the contract he'd made, but before the week was over he was back to slugging it out with anyone he could find. So I promptly sent him home, as we'd planned. The next day, LeRoy was fighting again, and I sent him home again. His attitude seemed kind of smug."

"He'd out-maneuvered you," Cecelia Moore said, "getting out of going to school."

"I thought he would be at home with no one to play with. I was sure isolation would work, but there was one thing I didn't know about. His father is a plumbing contractor, and whenever LeRoy went home, his father, not wanting him to be running loose or restless, took him out with him on his jobs. LeRoy loved it. No wonder he didn't care if he were sent home from school. He was being positively reinforced for fighting on the playground!"

Cecelia shook her head.

"Actually, it's turning out okay," Dick said. "I blame myself for not making it clear when I met with his parents just what we were trying to achieve. I've talked with his family again, and his father has stopped rewarding LeRoy for getting into trouble at school—something he'd had no intention of doing, of course. Furthermore, LeRoy's father has come up with a positive reward by permitting his son to help him after school if he didn't get into fights. And I began reinforcing LeRoy after recesses in which he didn't get into trouble, like asking him to carry out a special chore for me. I don't know whether it was because of the change in his father's behavior or the change in my behavior, but LeRoy hasn't had a fight in three weeks now and seems more interested in what is going on in class. One of the things I've learned from this was that I had overfocused on sending LeRoy home when he violated the contract and had underfocused on the need to give him positive reinforcements the first day or two when he actually had stopped fighting. Now, instead of taking such initial improvement for granted I'm more alert to providing positive reinforcement as soon as the desired behavior occurs, so that this behavior can be strengthened." (Sarason, Glazer, and Fargo, 1972, p. 27)

Negotiating a Contract

In order to define the results of a bargaining session, teachers and students sometimes draw up a contract specifying the work the student will do and the rewards he will receive when it is completed. A contract puts the agreement on paper so that there is less chance that the teacher or student will forget or misunderstand the terms.

The teacher may initiate the contract, stating the terms, the work required, and the deadlines, and suggest the reward. Older or more responsible students may present their own contracts based on the work they plan to do and the rewards they want to receive. The teacher simply reads and approves the plans they have initiated. The most common contract falls between these two extremes. Together, the teacher and the individual student come to terms (perhaps the teacher insists on choosing the reward). In any case, the understanding exists that if the contract's work requirements are met, the student receives the designated reward; otherwise, he does not.

This is an example of a contract drawn up by a teacher and a sixteen-year-old student in a social studies class (adapted from Clarizio, 1971):

Between Karen Colby and Ms. Sand

Karen agrees to:
1 Complete assigned reading on the Sioux and write a two-page report. (5 points)
2 Hand in assignment on date due.

Teacher agrees to:
1 Check homework.
2 Not reprimand or comment when home-work is not completed or handed in.

Karen can exchange her points for:
1 Free period time during class (5 points per 5 minutes)
2 An exemption from the social studies quiz (20 accumulated points)

Signed _____
                    Student
Signed _____
                    Teacher

Effective-ness of Token Reinforce-ment Systems

Token reinforcements substantially improved the reading skills of a group of low-achieving fifth- and sixth-graders from a poor urban area. The children in this experiment had scored at least two years below the norm for their grade level on the reading section of the Stanford Achievement Test. The experimental group attended a remedial education program during one summer, through the next school year and the following summer (they met for an hour a day in the winter, and three hours a day in the summer). Standard remedial material in reading and arithmetic was used, and during the school year they were also given work related to what they were studying in other classes.

The token reinforcement system worked like a trading-stamp plan. Each child was given a folder containing four groups of different-colored pages, each marked off into little squares. After a child completed an assignment correctly, he was given points by the teacher, who marked the squares of the colored pages with a felt pen. Filled pages of points were redeemable, according to their color, for a variety of goods and events. Blue pages were worth weekly field trips to the circus, swimming pools, the zoo, sporting events, and so forth; green pages could be redeemed for a daily snack of a sandwich, milk, fruit, and a cookie; pink pages for money and items available in "the store" set up for the experiment: candy, toiletries, novelties, and clothing. The yellow pages were for long-range goals that might have taken several weeks or months to obtain, such as clothes, inexpensive watches, and secondhand bicycles.

By the end of the second summer the students had gained, on the average, a full year in achievement level. A control group (not on the token plan) made only half the gain of the experimental group (though some individuals in the control group achieved significant gains). Furthermore, while some children in the control group scored even lower than they had the year before, none of the experimental children showed any regression (Wolf, Giles, and Hall, 1968).

Another token reinforcement project concentrated on changes in classroom behavior. A group of junior-high-school students were several grade levels behind in achievement, had reading deficiencies, and were disruptive (cursing the teacher, refusing to obey requests or do assignments, throwing pencils, fighting, and chasing about the room). When the class was first observed, the group was actually studying an average of 29 percent of the time. In the first phase of the experiment the teacher provided social reinforcement for eleven days: she went to students who were studying quietly and praised them, called only on students who raised their hands, and complimented the entire group when all were studying quietly. This increased the average study rate to 57 percent. In the next phase a kitchen timer was set to go off at random intervals. Pupils who were in their seats and quiet when the timer sounded were given a mark on a card; each mark allowed them to leave one minute earlier for lunch. There was an immediate increase in study behavior (74 percent). Finally, a point system was instituted, with points redeemable for rewards suggested by the pupils themselves when they were asked, "What would you like to do if you had one free period?" "Earn points" were given for good behavior, "minus points" for poor behavior. The results of the point system were apparent on the first day; the average study rate rose to 83 percent (Broden et al., 1970).

Pros and Cons of Behavior Modification

Most parents and teachers have few philosophical objections to this procedure's reliance on positive rewards, since it is human nature to praise actions we want to encourage in children. Nevertheless, its systematic application in the classroom has raised objections.

Some critics question how well the strategy works in practice. One important determinant of its effectiveness is whether a student has a positive attitude toward the teacher and therefore wants to change his behavior for her. Two hundred and fifty-six students in the eighth grade were given a twenty-item questionnaire and asked to choose the statement that would best describe their own reactions to a teacher's reward or punishment. Their responses varied according to whether

"This should give them something to think about."

they were responding to a teacher they liked or disliked. The items described a common classroom episode illustrating a sequence of student behavior and teacher reinforcement. Both positive and negative reinforcements were included. When students responded to the questionnaire with reference to a hypothetical "liked" teacher, the reinforcement apparently had value. But if the student was responding to a hypothetical "disliked" teacher, the value of the reward was diminished (Davison, 1972).

Not all psychologists concur that exclusive reliance on positive rewards is the most effective way to change a child's behavior. As one psychologist put it, "It is impossible for children to learn what is *not* approved and tolerated simply by generalizing in reverse from the approval they receive for the behavior that *is* acceptable" (Ausubel, 1968, p. 461). These objections suggest that although behavior modification is productive, it is not a complete strategy.

On ethical grounds, the main reservation concerns the possible effects of widespread character manipulation. While extinguishing a child's tendency to fight in the classroom appears to be an appropriate goal, one may ask whether next year the teacher will attempt to extinguish his tendency to ask awkward questions in class. Many fear that a tool as potentially effective as this one can also be dangerous if one group of people (a handful of teachers or a group of neighborhood parents) became determined to alter the behavior of individuals in a serious way.

On many practical grounds, some psychologists maintain that behavior modification is effective only as long as the child wants it to work. They contend that it is an illusion to believe that the child is in the grip of the teacher's schedule of rewards and cannot escape (Brown et al., 1975). The child decides whether he wishes to go along with the teacher's modification schedule. If he does, he may alter his behavior. But the child can decide to stop cooperating at any moment. Hence, the fear that behavior modification is overly manipulative and will make robots of children exaggerates children's helplessness and passivity. At the same time, however, it is a serious distortion of the facts to contend that consistent application of behavioral modification principles will give the teacher permanent control of the classroom.

Indeed, it is likely that many children will believe they have some control of the teacher! One first-grader was in a class with a teacher who had all the children on a chip system. On the day of the class tea the boy said to his mother as he left for school, "I think I'll lose a chip today so I'll have to stay after school. That way, I'll already be in the room when you come for the tea." The child is aware of the reinforcing schedule, and if he wants chips, stamps, rewards, or a pat on the back, he simply issues the behavior he knows will ensure their delivery. Therefore, it is not clear who is being manipulated. Both teacher and student feel they are in control—and, indeed, both are—for each is free to withdraw from the contract at any time.

Some critics object to the technique for other reasons, believing that there is a high price attached to the success of these strategies. Although rewards of one kind or another have been inextricably part of schoolwork, there is some concern that the strategy of behavior modification sends a subtle message to the child that his efforts are worthwhile only because an extra reward has been guaranteed. Closed systems of reward may prevent the students from realizing the inherent excitement and satisfaction in mastering new material for its own sake and developing social skills that allow individuals to work together in groups.

Behavior modification, however, has advantages for both teachers and students. Its greatest strength, perhaps, is in giving inexperienced teachers a set of rituals to rely on in the classroom. Many teachers are apprehensive about their ability to handle aggressive and inattentive students. By learning behavior modification principles, they gain confidence that they can apply particular strategies when problems arise. Experienced teachers often use the principles unconsciously, but explicit knowledge of the principles may make their application more efficient.

Behavior modification also gives some students a rationale for obedience and studiousness. Some students, especially those in junior high and high school, feel that conforming to the teacher's authority is childish, regressive, or ill-suited to their sex-role identity. If the teacher offers rewards, students who want to master school tasks and behave civilly may find it easier to accept the teacher's demands. They can save face by saying to themselves, "I would like more recess time, or to have that prize, so I may as well go along with those silly requests."

In the end, the key element is the social contract between the child and the teacher. The child's willingness to enter into that agreement is essential. If he does not like or respect the teacher, no amount of behavior modification will work. It is important to recognize that behavior modification is not a magic technique that will turn all classrooms into models of harmony, motivation, and accomplishment.

If behavior modification techniques are not a panacea, one may ask why they have become so popular and why so many psychologists and teachers celebrate their effectiveness—as if rewarding children for desirable actions is a new idea rather than one of the oldest. There are several reasons. First, teachers face a difficult problem in controlling a classroom of thirty children—unrelated and previously unknown to the teacher. Young teachers have good reason to lack confidence in their ability to maintain control. In practice, they have only a few strategies they can count on:

1 Punishing the child through exclusion from the class, withdrawal of privileges, poor grades, or corporal punishment.
2 Consulting directly with the family to enlist its cooperation.
3 Appealing to the child's conscience and his desire to maintain an accepting and cooperative relation with the teacher.
4 Giving positive rewards for desirable behavior—namely, behavior modification.

In the past, teachers mainly used punishment and appeal to the child's conscience. But secular changes in our society have limited the teacher's ability to use these strategies. As a result of the psychological theories of the last twenty or thirty years, our society has been persuaded that a child should not be afraid of the teacher or of punishment—punishment is regarded as psychologically unhealthy for children. There is, of course, no firm proof for that belief: one cannot know how a child interprets a particular action (such as staying after school) that is called a punishment. Nevertheless, the belief prevails that punishment should be avoided because of its potential ability to create anxiety. Indeed, the 1975 Supreme Court ruling that permitted states to decide if their teachers could physically punish children in school came as a surprise to many Americans.

There is increasing heterogeneity between the background of the teacher and the backgrounds of the thirty pupils in her class, especially in large urban areas. It is more difficult for the teacher to assume that she and the students, as well as their families, have a sympathetic relationship and common values and share an understanding—that instruction is a team effort involving child, family, and teacher and that all must cooperate to accomplish that mission.

During the last twenty years school and family have become increasingly divided. Teachers unionized and went on strikes; parents regarded them as selfish and more concerned with their salaries, promotions, and job perquisites than with the task of education. Families have increasingly blamed the schools, rather than accepted responsibility themselves, for children's misbehavior and lack of academic progress. Thus family and teacher are somewhat suspicious of one another, lowering the teacher's confidence that she can use the family collaboratively when a child is in trouble. Simple, obviously helpful techniques are not exploited. For example, the teacher in modern America would rarely call a parent on the telephone after school was dismissed to inquire about a child who seemed ill at ease, tired, or frightened that afternoon. Parents rarely feel that it is proper to call the teacher at home in the evening, as they may a physician, if they are troubled by the child's inability to do his homework or if he seems worried about school. Moreover, this mutual suspicion is communicated to the child, limiting the teacher's ability to appeal to the child's affection for her or to his conscience.

Thus the average teacher is left with only one technique— manipulation of positive reinforcements. It is a little like putting an artist in a studio with neither paints nor easel, but only a small brush. The new teacher recognizes the limitations on her power and persuasiveness, feels the enormous responsibility of her job, and is justifiably uncertain. She will seize any set of techniques that seems—as behavior modification does—to promise her a way of maintaining control. And this is one reason behavior modification has become so popular. It is a set of rituals that the teacher can use to buffer anxiety.

The lack of other options, then, and the uncertainty of new teachers are two major reasons for the popularity of behavior modification. A third stems from its association with scientific methodology. We live in an age that celebrates the power of science. Hence, suggestions for managing classrooms that seem to be based on scientific principles and data appear more glamorous and efficacious and tempt the teacher to see her profession as a scientific occupation. This lends increased status to the educational enterprise.

These are not reasons for rejecting the use of behavior modification. As we indicated, systematic reward for those behaviors the teacher wants to promote can, on occasion, have beneficial effects and should be used as part of the teacher's total strategy.

How To Prevent Disturbance

In managing the classroom, the teacher's most important task is to use good judgment and discrimination in gauging how strongly to react to misconduct or disruption. Some kinds of behavior can be more profitably ignored than reprimanded; by reacting immediately to an incident that was really minor, the teacher may provoke, rather than quell, the disruption she wanted to avoid. If a student discovers that the teacher can be drawn into an open confrontation by such small gestures as slamming a desk top or whispering to a neighbor, he will realize that he has stumbled onto powerful artillery that can be used to delay and distract the class from the lesson over and over again. Or a teacher may properly choose to ignore a disruption because it was an isolated incident (such as one student burping loudly as she is reading) and not representative of a pattern of behavior that needs to be modified.

On the other hand, a teacher needs to deal with a budding disturbance before it grows into a serious disruption. Investigators Jacob Kounin and Paul Gump (1958) describe the "ripple" effect that occurs when an originally small interchange between two students is allowed to escalate without intervention from the teacher. Once past a certain "tipping" point, like a small fire that is suddenly out of hand, the students' attention is captured by the disturbance, their resistance to it weakens, and most of the class is involved. Substantial effort will be needed to turn the class around again. It is a great deal easier to halt the disturbance by firm (not threatening) means before it reaches the tipping point.

How can a teacher know when it is time to intervene and how strongly to react? An experienced teacher monitors the classroom closely. By scanning the room and catching the eye of all the students from time to time, he indicates that he is aware of everything that transpires in the room (Kounin, 1970). This stance gives him two advantages. He appears to the students to know what is going on, and this inhibits disruptions. And by keeping in close touch with each student, like a symphony conductor who knows that when he turns to the strings they will be waiting for his signal, he is in a position to send some signal to the student whose attention has wandered.

Psychologists Thomas L. Good and Jere E. Brophy (1973) describe interventions that can be used in succession. The mildest is catching the student's eye and holding his gaze for a few extra seconds so that he knows the teacher knows something is going on. (Obviously, this can be implemented faster if the teacher has been scanning the room, and the student expects it.) Sometimes the effect can be stronger if the teacher shakes his head slightly at the student, or stops speaking for a few seconds; an unexpected silence in the teacher's conversation draws attention.

If the teacher is moving around the room as the lesson is in progress, simply moving nearer to the child who is misbehaving may quiet him; touching the student lightly to indicate restraint is useful with elementary-school children (though high-school students are likely to resent it). The advantage of these devices is that they do not cause an open break in the lesson.

Another device to catch a student's wandering attention is to call on him: it demands that he focus on the lesson, without mentioning his misbehavior. Good and Brophy draw a fine line between useful and counterproductive ways to do this:

> The questions asked in these situations must be ones that the student can answer, or at least can make a reasonable response to. If there is no way that the student can meaningfully respond to the question because he was not paying attention to the previous one, the question should not be asked. To do so would only embarrass the student and force him to admit that he was not paying attention (thereby violating an important principle, by focusing on the *misbehavior* instead of the lesson). (Good and Brophy, 1973, p. 200)

Many classroom signals, commonly sent as negative commands, can be more constructively phrased in a positive way (see boxed insert on page 475).

Handling Disruption When It Occurs

Sometimes teachers must restore order to a uniformly loud class. Quieting techniques vary from a loud "Now students . . ." or a quick

Positive Language	Negative Language
Close the door quietly.	Don't slam the door.
Try to work these out on your own without help.	Don't cheat by copying your neighbor.
Quiet down—you're getting too loud.	Don't make so much noise.
Sharpen your pencil like this (demonstration).	That's not how you use a pencil sharpener.
Carry your chair like this (demonstrate).	Don't make so much noise with your chair.
Sit up straight.	Don't slouch in your chair.
Raise your hand if you think you know the answer.	Don't yell out the answer.
When you finish, put the scissors back in the box and put the bits of paper on the floor into the wastebasket.	Don't leave a mess.
These crayons are for you to share—use one color at a time and put it back when you're finished so others can use it too.	Stop fighting over those crayons.
Your understanding is important here, so use your own ideas. When you do borrow ideas from another author, be sure to acknowledge them. Even here, though, try to put them in your own words.	Don't plagiarize.

(Good and Brophy, 1973, p. 179)

clap of the hands to a private signal: the teacher may raise her hand and wait while students, spotting her signal, become silent and raise their hands as a signal to other students. An elementary-school teacher may simply walk to the wall switch and click off the lights. One high-school instructor approaches groups of students in turn, bends forward with his finger to his lips, and says "Sshh" until the room is quiet; his success apparently results from each small group feeling that it has been personally approached and appealed to.

Keeping the proper focus can help teachers decide what strategy to use when they must intervene. Whatever actions they take or words they use, they should make clear that they are displeased with the behavior, not with the child. Inevitably, active intervention is personal (since the teacher is finally forced to focus on the child or children causing the disturbance). But the less personal the intervention, the more effective it is in restoring order to the room.

The Effective Use of Punishment

Punishment should not embarrass or demoralize the student. Properly used, it restrains the unwanted behavior so that the desirable behavior has a chance to emerge. One analogy compares the struggle to that of a long-distance runner:

> With a child who is having problems, it is as if you had a strong runner (undesirable behavior) and a weak runner (desirable behavior) racing for a prize. The strong runner is used to winning, so you hold him back (punishment) and let the weak runner win the race and get the prize (positive reinforcement). You keep on doing this until the weak runner has had so much practice his legs are getting very strong and he enjoys running for the prize. When you think he has practiced enough that he can beat the strong runner, you let go of the formerly strong runner you have been holding back (remove punishment) so they can both race. As the previously weak runner (desirable behavior) keeps on winning (positive reinforcement), the formerly strong runner (undesirable behavior) gives up (is extinguished) because he never wins anything (no reinforcement). He won't give up as long as he is held back, but if he keeps on losing (no reinforcement) he will.
> (Hunter, 1967; quoted in Clarizo, 1971, p. 121)

It is easier to list the kinds of punishment that are ineffective and inappropriate than to specify the kinds that are constructive. Assigning a task such as writing "I will not interrupt in class" a hundred times is not effective, since it tends to stiffen the student's resentment and, furthermore, persuades him that other schoolwork may actually be as pointless as this exercise. Under some circumstances, it can prove useful to have the student write a short essay describing how he feels in class and why he does not attend to the lesson.

Withdrawing privileges is one form of punishment that can be used effectively. It should not be announced as a decree from the teacher but explained (preferably in a private session) so the student knows why he is being punished and what he can do to regain his standing. It is important that the teacher maintain an objective manner and not be lured into an explosive denunciation of the student's shortcomings, thereby focusing on his character rather than on his misconduct. For the same reason, the punishment should be reasonable and moderate; it should not suggest that the teacher is out of control and overreacting.

Isolation from the group is a more severe punishment (with very young children it may seem extremely severe and should be used cautiously). To be effective, the isolation should function as a negative reinforcement and not inadvertently turn into a pleasurable experience for the student. (She may prefer being sent to the library—or even out into the hall—to staying in a class she finds boring.) Since both withdrawing privileges and isolation have more impact the first times they are used than after repeated usage, it is obvious that they should be resorted to only when other attempts at control have been exhausted.

Other Alternatives

When a child appears to present a serious behavior problem, it may help to ask the parents in for a consultation. Sometimes a meeting between parents and teachers clears up a misunderstanding and explains more about the causes of a child's actions; often it marks the start of a more united front between home and school, so that a child no longer feels he can manipulate both sets of authorities by playing one off against the other.

If the teacher finds that she cannot manage a student by any resources or strategies within her reach, she may need to consult with the school psychologist. Occasionally, specific disruptive behavior reflects the bad "chemistry" between a teacher and student that has been exacerbated by his misconduct and the teacher's continuing inability to change it. For that reason, reassigning a student to a different teacher is sometimes useful. A fresh environment, less scarred by months of familiar battles, may enable a student to make a new start and improve his behavior. Whenever a student is transferred, it is important to minimize the sense of failure on the part of teacher or student—and also any sense of victory.

A sense of victory, or at least of satisfaction, is justified, though, for the teacher who succeeds in establishing and maintaining a classroom atmosphere that is neither repressive nor chaotic, but constructive and harmonious. While it requires steady monitoring and frequent regulating, it reflects—and in turn, nurtures—the active participation of the students and their interaction with the teacher and the school tasks.

The Structure of American Schools

Certain psychological consequences are products of the way our schools are structured, the way a callus on a small toe is created by a tight shoe. The callus would never have appeared had not the shoe been tight. Let us consider some aspects of the structure of our schools and their effects.

The peer group. In typical agricultural villages that exist in all parts of the nonmodern world, an eight-year-old spends most of the day with one or two children his own age and half a dozen more children ranging in age from infancy to adolescence. He understands that a child much younger or much older than he naturally has a different level of ability, and he does not feel terribly uneasy about not being as competent as a thirteen-year-old. He knows his time is coming.

But American schools place each child in a situation with a large number of other children the same age. This arrangement makes each child concerned with his relative ability, forcing him to evaluate himself in comparison with a large group of his contemporaries. Even outside of the classroom the typical child plays with a group of peers, for after-school activities are also sharply age-graded. In this situation small differences in ability are exaggerated. The child who is of average ability in reading or baseball cannot effectively rationalize the fact that he does not read or play baseball as well as a particular classmate. Differences in ability among ten-year-olds, quite small when compared with differences between an eight-year-old and a thirteen-year-old, are distorted out of proportion to the "true" difference. Grouping children by age sharpens expectancy of success or failure for those who are more or less talented and leads to a competitive attitude with peers.

The work assigned. In most nonmodern societies the tasks assigned to children are well within their ability. The average ten-year-old can chop wood, carry water, irrigate crops, and carry a baby around in a cloth. Moreover, parents in these societies are sensitive to their children's competence and refrain from assigning chores until they feel the child is able to carry them out efficiently. Parents do not use a child's age as the criterion for deciding when he is ready for certain tasks, but rather they watch his emerging behavior and judge when he has acquired the proper thoughtfulness, understanding, and sense of responsibility necessary for the work.

Our educational system, however, assigns schoolwork primarily on the basis of age, not individual competence. True, we give reading readiness tests, but the more subtle qualities of attentiveness, motivation, persistence, and responsibility, and the abilities of the executive discussed in Chapter 5, are rarely assessed. Hence, for some children the tasks assigned are not within their sphere of competence, and as a result, some American seven-year-olds begin their primary chore (reading) with desperate tension, while their counterparts in an agricultural village are beginning their first chores with confidence.

Streaming by ability. The ten-year-old in the nonmodern village is given the task of chopping wood or carrying water. The criterion for adequate functioning is clear, and if he carries out the task well, he has a sense of mastery. Few adults are comparing his talent for carrying water with that of other children. Adults do recognize differences among children in health, vitality, sense of responsibility, conduct, and ability to understand what they are told, and these judgments are correlated to some degree with the child's ability on tests of memory (Klein, Freeman, and Millet, 1973). But despite these real differences in psychological and physical components of competence, the variability in carrying out the chores is minimal.

By contrast, American schools, faced with extraordinarily diverse abilities to meet the school's demands, are forced to stream children by ability. Most of the time they are grouped within the classroom in A, B, or C reading groups; sometimes they are grouped in different classrooms. But the children always know they have been classified. The practice produces a social structure in which some children feel more competent and some less competent. The former try to maintain their standing and work harder so that they will not lose their position of privilege, while the latter develop feelings of discouragement that become more entrenched with time. It is an inevitable result of including, in the same room, thirty children of the same age but of varying degrees of readiness for academic work. Although it is pure fantasy in our society, if all thirty children were of equal ability or if each child had an individual tutor and there were no classrooms, these attitudes would not develop so strongly. This is what we mean when we say that the structure of the classroom has a profound effect on the child. If the structure did not exist, the consequences described would not occur or they would be attenuated.

Changing teachers every year. Assigning different teachers for each grade may prevent child and teacher from developing any serious affective involvement with each other, for each knows that the relation lasts for only ten months. Consider the advantages of having the same teacher for kindergarten through grade four. The teacher would get to know each child very well. Actual identification of teacher with child and child with teacher would increase. With time the teacher would be better able to help the child, and the child who was initially defensive with the unfamiliar kindergarten teacher might gradually come to trust her. Children would not have to waste energy each year sizing up a new teacher and testing her limits. We retain our system of one teacher each year because we see school as a place that teaches skills, and each teacher is presumably maximally competent with one particular grade or age. Our present system is also maintained to avoid the halo effect: if a teacher acquired a negative halo for a particular child, it would obstruct progress. Children should have a chance to begin fresh with a new teacher if they made a bad impression initially. But that complaint could easily be avoided by having the child change teachers if the family requested it.

Separation of school and home. Perhaps the saddest aspect of the structure of American schools is the implicit understanding that when the child leaves school at 3:30, he crosses a boundary of sovereignty. The teacher knows that from that time until the following morning she does not have to be concerned with this child; indeed, she is not to intervene in the family. This contract is due in part to a need to respect family values. Most families see the teacher as the child's hired tutor, who is supposed to do her job and not ask questions. This social contract has serious disadvantages when the family needs help. The school is an appropriate agency to give that help, and teachers could be trained to see themselves as professional counselors and friends as well as educators. They would not turn off their concern and responsibility after children were dismissed from school. They could call parents in the evening if a child was upset during the day. They might drop in on a birthday! They would be concerned with each child, and both child and family would know that. Perhaps then we would be able to restore the trust between school and home that has eroded over the last twenty years.

Power and responsibility. One of the problems in modern schools stems from a division of power and responsibility. During the medieval ages, parents hired a tutor to teach their particular child basic skills. If the child failed, it was the tutor's responsibility. But the tutor had the power to change his tactics and to determine the course of study. Both power and responsibility were vested in the same person. Modern schools, by contrast, have taken the power from the teacher yet left her with the responsibility. The teacher is faulted if the child fails to learn, but the plan for the school day, the time a teacher can devote to each skill, and the curriculum she may use are usually decisions made by others. She has little power to make the choices for which she is responsible. In some large school systems no single person has either the power or the responsibility. An unwieldy bureaucratic structure dilutes power and responsibility, weakening the teacher's active involvement and concern with her task. It is not surprising that a teacher often aims to please the authority figures immediately above her rather than the families of the children she is supposed to serve. The movement toward more parental involvement in school and parental control is one response to this aspect of American school structure. It is to be hoped that this trend will bring salutary effects.

Summary

Teachers face four major decisions: whether their attitude toward disruptive behavior will be rigid or flexible, whether academic work is to be self-directed or structured by the teacher; whether the classroom ethic is to be competitive or cooperative; and whether the classroom will be teacher-dominated or student-centered. The first two choices are major determinants of classroom atmosphere and intersect to produce four different kinds of classrooms, typically represented by a private permissive school such as Summerhill, a private middle-class school, a traditional public school, and a ghetto school.

Harmony in the classroom depends on the match between the values, the temperaments, and the personalities of the students and those of the teacher. Therefore, it is impossible to prescribe the correct choices to be made independent of the types of students in a particular class. Several studies verify the importance of this match: one compared the achievements of compulsive and less compulsive students with regard to their perception of the teacher as authoritarian or nonauthoritarian. Another compared the performances of more anxious and less anxious students (with regard to mastery) in teacher-dominated or student-centered classes.

Since schools are charged with two tasks—teaching necessary skills and fostering desirable attitudes—it is important to distinguish between these goals in assessing the success of any classroom's approach. A number of experimental teaching methods may contribute to variety in the class and a sense of richness and personal satisfaction among the students and the teachers (and hence, be worthwhile for those reasons) but fail to improve academic performance.

In addition to making conscious choices, the teacher's personality affects classroom atmosphere. In particular, four characteristics can have a positive influence on student behavior: warmth (do students perceive they are valued?); justice (do students believe they are treated fairly?); the teacher's attitude toward error; and the teacher's competence.

In identifying problems in classroom behavior, it becomes apparent that aggressive, disobedient, and antisocial behaviors are conspicuous to the teacher; but another constellation of shy, suspicious, and withdrawn behaviors, while not disruptive, also indicates that a child is having trouble attaining his educational objectives. Both sets of behavior are associated with poor academic performance. Some biological injury to the nervous system is likely to be a cause in a small percentage of cases; in the remainder, psychological factors appear to be responsible.

Classroom management, in recent years, has often involved a set of practices called behavior modification, based on the principles of operant conditioning; reinforcement, shaping, schedule of reinforcement, satiation, and extinction. Systematically applied, these principles often prove effective, especially as they usually dwell on the positive aspects of a child's behavior ("praise or ignore") rather than on the negative ones—the behaviors that the strategy is attempting to change. Use of desirable and appropriate rewards and individual contracts frequently contribute to the strategy's success. Although it is effective, behavior modification has its critics. While some critics object to the use of rewards, others are concerned with the degree of manipulation involved. In practice, it is likely that the strategy works as long as the children want it to (in other words, they deliberately respond in order to receive the benefits being offered) and is uneffective if children refuse to go along with it.

To prevent classroom disturbance, teachers need to know when to intervene, how strongly to react, and how to focus wandering attention. They also must be able to handle it when it arises by using various quieting techniques or employing punishment properly so as to allow the desirable behavior to emerge.

Five particular aspects of the structure of American schools contribute to children's problems. They are the peer group, the work assigned, streaming by ability, changing teachers every year, and the separation of school and home.

Projects

1 In a subject area of your choice, plan a high-school lesson in three different ways: one leader dominated; another leaderless; and a third a cooperative group activity.

2 With a number of classmates (at least eleven) role-play an elementary-school class in which the players portray the ten problem behaviors identified on page 455. If possible, videotape the role-playing so that participants can later observe. Alternatively, ask other members of the class to observe and later discuss the problem behaviors and how they affected the dynamics of the class.

3 With a classmate, design for one another and implement a behavior modification program (positive reinforcement) to help each of you overcome a problem interfering with your academic progress (for example, cutting classes, being unprepared for tests, procrastinating on term papers).

4 With a group of students, discuss and write a definition of discipline that examines what behaviors should be disciplined and by what means.

5 Review articles on classroom management in the current year's issues of three of the following journals: *Merrill-Palmer Quarterly of Behavior and Development, Journal of Experimental Education, Journal of Educational Research, Developmental Psychology, and Journal of Educational Psychology*. What proportion are on behavior modification? What other aspects of classroom management are considered? Outline an article of your own on another dimension of classroom atmosphere and management for one of the journals.

6 Visit an alternative school or classroom in which rules are made and enforced cooperatively. Observe classroom behavior. Interview the students to ascertain their roles in the system and their commitment to it. In your estimation, does this method work better than the more traditional methods you have experienced or observed?

Recommended Reading

Clarizio, H. F. *Toward positive classroom discipline.* New York: John Wiley, 1971. A summary of how the teacher may create a classroom that is controlled and orderly and yet has a positive, constructive atmosphere.

Good, T. L., and Brophy, J. E. *Looking in classrooms.* New York: Harper & Row, 1973. Indicates how the teacher may be more sensitive to the meaning of the behavior of his or her children.

Jackson, P. W. *Life in classrooms*. New York: Holt, Rinehart and Winston, 1968. A realistic summary of what classrooms are like in American schools.

Lortie, D. C. *Schoolteacher: A sociological study*. Chicago: University of Chicago Press, 1975. Summarizes the results of interviews with teachers and reports their attitudes toward their job.

Sarason, S. B., Davidson, K., and Blatt, B. *The preparation of teachers*. New York: John Wiley, 1962. An interesting and well-written brief book on the role of the teacher in the classroom and how he or she can be better trained to create a more positive classroom atmosphere.

current problems and
tentative solutions

four

social class and ethnicity

12

Suppose you were a visitor from a far-off planet trying to make sense of the behavior of the people and of the structure of the institutions in the United States. Your first task would be to look for regularities that might lead you to some understanding of the society. If you happened to spend your early weeks observing the schools of Birmingham, Alabama, you would note that more black than white schoolchildren obtain low scores on achievement tests for reading and arithmetic. You have discovered a difference, but you do not know the reason for it. The difference in school achievement could be due to skin color or to some other factor associated with skin color, for you also notice that black children live in poorer neighborhoods and in more crowded and less comfortable homes than do white youngsters.

Your next stop is a school in New York City. Here you see that not only black children but also Puerto Ricans perform less well than whites. Several months later, in Texas, you discover that Mexican-American children do less well in school than their white classmates. Now it seems unlikely that poor performance in school is a simple function of skin color. But what about ethnicity?

It is true that membership in certain ethnic minorities also relates to poor school performance. Many students are new arrivals in America, hear a new language at school, and feel set apart from their English-speaking classmates. American Indians, whose families have lived here for generations, also feel excluded. They have been a less visible problem in the schools than blacks, yet two-thirds of American Indian children do not go beyond elementary school (Mondale, 1973). The theory that outsiders have difficulty adjusting to school gains credibility as we learn that sixty years ago immigrant Irish and Italian children in Boston were having the same kind of difficulty in school that the Puerto Ricans now have in New York City. Yet in all three groups that you observed in school—black, Mexican-American, and Puerto Rican—some children are doing very well.

You return to New York City to think about the problem, spend a day visiting Manhattan schools that have Chinese, blacks, Jews, and Puerto Ricans, and make a new discovery. Six- and seven-year-old children are given tests that assess their language and arithmetic knowledge as well as their ability to reason with words and with

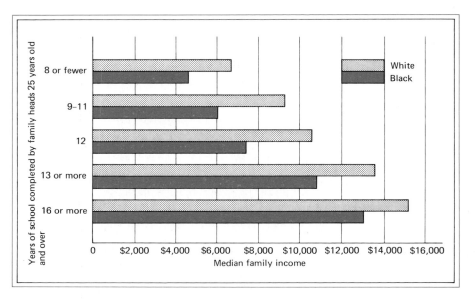

Figure 12-1
This graph shows median family income (a four-year average) by education and race of family head. The family income of both blacks and whites increases in proportion to the number of school years completed by the head of the family; for example, a white family whose head has eight or fewer years of school earns just under $7,000, while a white family whose head has completed sixteen or more years of school earns about $15,000. (Adapted from *Social Indicators*, 1973)

geometric shapes. In all four ethnic groups the middle-class children perform better than the lower-class children (Lesser, Fifer, and Clark, 1965).

Apparently, then, poor school performance is not a simple function either of race or ethnicity. Corroborating that conclusion is the fact that when intelligence tests are given to black children and white children from both middle-class and upper-middle-class families, there are no important differences in I.Q. between blacks and whites of the same social class. However, significant differences in I.Q. are found between poor and middle-class children regardless of skin color (Burnes, 1970).

It would seem reasonable, then, to hypothesize that rather than skin color or ethnicity, the child's socioeconomic class is the primary determinant of school performance. (By *socioeconomic class* we mean a combination of income, education, and occupation, which are usually correlated, although not perfectly. See Figure 12-1.) This hypothesis is, in fact, borne out by many studies. When groups of failing children are closely examined, poverty emerges as the most salient common characteristic, not only in the United States, but over the world. In England, Israel, Guatemala, and Japan, poor children do less well in school than the more affluent. In America the difference in reading achievement between white and black children is closely related to differences in the educational level and income of parents, too. The main reason that membership in some ethnic minority groups is correlated with academic deficiency is that these groups are among the nation's poorest.

The Impact of Poverty on Learning

The United States Office of Education's massive study, *Equality of Educational Opportunity* (1966)—called the Coleman Report after its director, James S. Coleman—came to the following conclusions:

1 Poor children were doing more poorly in their schools than middle-class children were doing in theirs.
2 Schools were still very segregated.
3 Minority children tended to perform better if they found themselves in a classroom with a majority of middle-class children, and in that case, their achievement rose, but not at the expense of the middle-class children's performance.

The strong relation between family income and school performance tempts one to suggest that the solution may be to supplement the income of poor families, bringing it up to a nonpoverty level. However, this will not change their position relative to the rest of society. They will still be poor in comparison to others, and their status will continue to be lower than that of the more affluent. Relative poverty, rather than any particular level of yearly income, seems to be the significant factor in affecting a child's academic progress.

Consider the situation in isolated agricultural villages in eastern Guatemala, where everyone lives in huts with no sanitation or electricity. Although everyone is poor by American standards, annual incomes still cover a range—from $50 to $500—and the relation between income and performance on intellectual tasks parallels the pattern in the United States. In one study children from these villages were given tests of vocabulary, memory, perceptual analysis, evaluation, and conservation of area. The size of the child's vocabulary was related to two indexes of economic status in the villages—the size and quality of the family's house and the availability of books and toys in the home. (The correlation between the family's economic status and the child's score was approximately .30 for the seven-year-old children.) And children with higher vocabulary scores were more likely to be promoted at the end of the first year of school and to obtain higher scores on national achievement tests for mathematics and language administered by the Guatemalan government (again, the correlation was about .30). However, the relation of the family's social class to the child's memory and conservation scores was much lower and generally not significant. Thus, as in modern America, *verbal skills* are more highly developed among children from families who have a little more status than their neighbors, but the competences involved in memory and conservation develop more evenly in children of both poor and better-off families. One reasonable explanation of this difference is that the families with slightly more status and wealth appreciate the importance of verbal skills and so encourage them more consistently in their children (Klein, 1975).

Thus in one region of a country the range in annual income between economically secure and poor people may amount to $400 and in another it may be $15,000, but the effect is similar. Even in a community where everyone is relatively poor by American standards, the very poor seem to be less able intellectually than the ordinary poor.

Why Are Poor Children Less Able Students?

Poor families, in addition to lacking money for adequate food and medical care, frequently lack the hope that they can better their lives, and they communicate that message to their children. It matters, of

course, if a child can understand the language the teacher speaks and if
he has eaten breakfast that morning. But psychological factors also
exert a decisive influence on degree of intellectual mastery. Families
that see themselves as having less money, status, and resources than
their neighbors hold attitudes and encourage values in their children
that seem to obstruct the child's school progress.

Differences in the psychological development of children from
different social classes are seen during the first year of life. For
example, middle-class parents talk more often to their ten-month-old
infants than lower-class parents (Tulkin and Kagan, 1972). By age two, a
child in an intact lower-class family spends his day with a mother who
is more intrusive and prohibitive and plays with him less than does a
child in an economically more secure family, in which the mother plays
more and says "Stop that!" less often. The possible results of this
difference in parent-child experience are greater verbal skills and a less
fearful view of authority for middle-class children (Minton, Kagan, and
Levine, 1971).

The tendency for middle-class parents to be less intrusive and more
verbal with their children also leads their children to gain more from
watching educational television programs such as "Sesame Street."
Among children who watched "Sesame Street" often, the rate of gain in
learning letters was the same whether children were poor or affluent.
However, while the scores of both groups had risen by the end of the
first year, the more affluent children—who had scored higher in the

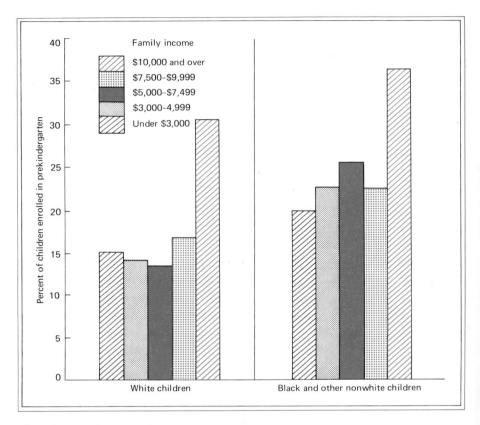

Figure 12–2
Among both white and nonwhite children, substantially higher numbers of prekindergarten enrollments occur in families with incomes of over $10,000 a year. Since preschool experience may contribute to later school success, children from affluent families have an advantage over those from poor families with respect to readiness for school skills. (Adapted from *Social Indicators*, 1973)

beginning—still outpaced poor children because they were initially more familiar with letters, they watched the program more often, and their parents talked with them more frequently about the material (Ball and Bogatz, 1970). Similarly, the more affluent the parents, the more likely they are to enroll their children in prekindergarten programs (see Figure 12–2).

As the child grows older, he develops fears and anxieties. They are such a common part of childhood that adults too easily dismiss them as an inevitable part of growing up. Nevertheless, children from poor families have realistic fears that are an indication of how they live, rather than just a reflection of the passing stages of childhood (though they are not immune from those fears, either). A middle-class child may fear ghosts, but his parents, while respecting his worry, can reassure him that no ghost will appear in his hallway. Ghetto children, on the other hand, report more fears of rats and roaches, which their parents cannot dismiss as fantasy (Nalven, 1970).

How Children See Their Futures

When poor children first enter school, they are not yet aware of their intellectual inadequacies compared to the middle-class children, and as a result they tend to overestimate their abilities. Groups of kindergarten and first-grade children from both poor and middle-class families were given a set of problems to solve and asked before they started how well they thought they would do on each test. Besides scoring higher, the middle-class children also guessed more accurately what their actual scores would be. The poor children overestimated how well they could do (Milgram et al., 1970). However, continued exposure to more competent children gradually had a sobering effect. By the tenth grade, the wishful thinking has vanished and many less able students have adjusted their hopes downward, while successful students continue to have high aspirations. Middle-class high-school students want more education and expect better vocational positions than do lower-class students (Harrison, 1969).

Black students and white students have different expectations about their future jobs. Poor black students express less feeling of personal control over job choices and more pessimism about enjoying their work or succeeding at it. Statements such as the following were presented to groups of both black and white students: "You get into an occupation mostly by chance," "Whether you're interested in a particular kind of work is not as important as whether you can do it," and "Choose a job in which you can be famous" (Greenberger and Marini, 1972, p. 7). More black than white students endorsed these statements. Aware that their opportunities are more limited, black students seem to be less interested in long-term occupational advancement that may require years of preparation and work than in opportunities that provide immediate financial success.

Conflicting Value Systems

In addition to class values and experiences widely shared by poor families, other specific values are common to people who share particular customs and ways of life. These values do not always coincide with prevailing American attitudes and can have an adverse effect on how fast their children learn school skills.

Competition versus cooperation. The American stress on competition is not necessarily shared by all communities. Mexican children in small, rural villages, for example, grow up in a culture that encourages cooperation. In games that involve rivalry, Mexicans are the most cooperative and Anglo-Americans the most competitive, while Mexican-Americans fall in between the two extremes (Kagan and Madsen, 1971). Since most schools in America tend to promote competition rather than cooperation, American schools are more responsive to the attitudes of middle-class white children than to those of Mexican-Americans, which may be one reason Mexican-American children, especially those from rural backgrounds, perform less well in school. Urban children from Mexico City, however, behave much the same as the competitive groups in the United States, suggesting that the cooperative behavior of Mexican village children represents the value of a specific subculture rather than a broad national characteristic (Madsen and Shapira, 1970). Children who have grown up in rural areas, therefore, seem likely to be handicapped in schools that stress competitive behavior.

Assertiveness versus submissiveness. Some communities engender a submissive attitude on the part of children and discourage assertiveness. Whether a child has learned to act one way or another affects his tendency to speak up in class. Among Mexican-American children, the most shy and inhibited have lower language achievement scores than less timid, more extroverted children, probably because they are the least likely to speak up in class, to answer questions, and to seek out contacts with their classmates and adults (Stedman and Adams, 1972).

If children raised in a rural village are predisposed to inhibit competitive and assertive behavior in class, children from another subculture—migrant workers—also have great difficulty in acclimating to school well enough to take an active part. Migrant workers not only receive less education and earn lower wages than any other occupational group in the country, they also move constantly and their children learn early that they are outcasts in school: " 'The schools, when you go to them, they don't seem to want you, and they'll say that you're only going to be there a few weeks, so what's the use?' said one ten-year-old boy" (Coles and Huge, 1969, p. 18).

A study of Florida migrant workers describes the central problem, which once again is psychological:

> Except for migrant children, every child learns to cope with the caste system of his peers. He learns that there is mobility in this system, that yesterday's clown can be tomorrow's hero. The migrant child does not have this chance when in school he confronts the rest of the world for the first time. . . . So the greatest single effect the school could have upon migrant children is lost the first year it deals with them. (Kleinert, 1969, p. 92)

The children of migrant workers are not drawn from a single ethnic group, but they are transient visitors to the class and never have the time or opportunity to feel at home in the school. Like the child from a rural village, they feel out of place and unable to adapt quickly to the school's values; as a result, their performance suffers.

School Factors Affecting Performance

Psychological factors and environmental conditions put poor children at a disadvantage from the day they enter school. But instead of alleviating their problems, the situation in school may add to them. The two most important influences on how a child performs are the opinion of the teacher concerning the poor student's capabilities and the values and educational backgrounds of her classmates.

How Teachers Regard Their Students

Teacher expectations. The values of the teachers—who are usually from middle-class backgrounds—are different from the values learned by children from poor neighborhoods and families. Some school values

> "... the difference between a lady and a flower girl is not how she behaves, but how she's treated." George Bernard Shaw's play *Pygmalion*, the story of a flower girl's transformation into a proper lady, goes back to classical Greek mythology and is still relevant today, a poignant reminder that people live up to the expectations others have of them—or they live down to them.

seem irrelevant to lower-class children and, therefore, cannot engage their motivation. As a result, they may not succeed initially at school tasks and acquire a lower expectancy of success that, in turn, contributes to continued poor performance. The child's view of his future is shared by his parents and neighbors and does not stop at the school door. As far as the child's education is concerned, a major problem is that the teacher tends to share the same view of the child that the larger community holds.

Teachers believe that the lower-class child is more likely to be "mentally retarded" than the middle-class child. A group of 288 teachers from sixteen states were sent nine hypothetical, but realistic, profiles of male students (Smith and Greenberg, 1975). Each profile described the child's socioeconomic class, school performance (including I.Q. and achievement scores), and behavior outside of school. In all the profiles, the achievement scores and school performance were identical, and every child was described as having an I.Q. between 68 and 81 (traditionally considered the range of borderline retardation). A sample profile follows:

Johnny's most obvious difficulty in school is in communicating with others. He has trouble in getting his own ideas across and in understanding the ideas of others. In both his written and oral work he makes many grammatical errors. Johnny rarely completes his school assignments without assistance. Although he typically makes attempts to do his homework, his efforts demonstrate a lack of comprehending either the directions or the content of the assignment. This tends to be more true of his verbal than his quantitative work. Johnny also does better in rote learning than in interpreting material of a more complex nature. Johnny is not a discipline problem, nor does he have any difficulty in following rules and regulations established by the school. However, when he makes mistakes, he does tend to become frustrated and has been known to rip up his papers in disgust. In school, he has been tested three times over a period of six years. On standard intelligence tests he obtained scores between 68 and 81, and on achievement tests typically performed at a level two to four grades below the national norms. (p. 320)

In varying cases, the above profile was ascribed to an upper-middle-class child, a lower-middle-class child, or a lower-class child. For each category, one of the following descriptions was added to the profile.

Upper-middle class

Johnny Jones lives with his parents in an eight-room home, purchased directly after his father was promoted to a middle management position in a rather large company. Johnny's mother, a housewife, frequently attends Parent-Teacher conferences at the school in order to discuss his problems with his teachers.

Lower-middle class

Johnny Jones lives with his mother, father, and two younger brothers in a small, four-room house close to the factory where Mr. Jones is employed as a semi-skilled worker. Mrs. Jones irregularly attends Parent-Teacher conferences to discuss Johnny's problems with his teachers.

Lower class

Johnny Jones lives with his mother and three younger brothers in a one-bedroom apartment in an older multiple-family dwelling. Since Johnny's mother is unskilled and unemployed, support for the family is provided by the welfare program. Due to the presence of the young children at home and the lack of child-care facilities, the mother is unable to respond to requests from teachers inviting her to attend the Parent-Teacher conferences in order to discuss Johnny's problems. (p. 320)

In addition, one of three types of behavior outside of school was described in each profile: competent nondeviant, competent deviant, or incompetent nondeviant.

The teachers were asked to read the profiles and decide on proper class placement, curricula, expectations for the future, and appropriateness of the label "mentally retarded." The results reveal that the lower the socioeconomic class of the child, the more likely the teacher was to regard the label "mentally retarded" appropriate.

Teacher misapprehensions. Teachers not only have lower expectations of the intellectual abilities of poor children, they also have more erroneous ones. In one study, statements were given to fourth- and fifth-grade students from poor families that included the following: "I wish I could go to more movies," "I am too careless," "I want to learn how our national government works," and "I want to learn how to read better." The students were to say whether they thought each was an important or an unimportant problem, while their teachers were to indicate what they thought the students would say. Nearly one-fourth more teachers than students checked items such as "I want to learn how to dress neatly," "I wish I could watch more programs on TV," and "I wish I could go to more movies," which suggests that middle-class teachers believe that lower-class students are more concerned with television and appearance than the students actually are. On the other hand, three times as many students as teachers checked the questions "I want to learn how our city government works," and "I want to learn how our national government works," suggesting that teachers underestimate the political interests of lower-class students (Howard, 1968).

Teacher preferences in student personalities. Judging from the way two hundred student teachers responded to hypothetical story situations depicting boys and girls with different personality traits, young teachers feel more positive toward conforming, tidy children than they do toward nonconforming, untidy children. Since more middle-class children are apt to fall into the first category and more lower-class children into the second, it is likely that the average teacher harbors more negative attitudes toward poor children (Feshbach, 1969).

What Children Learn from Their Classmates

The Coleman Report came to a conclusion that was somewhat surprising at the time it was written. When a child goes to school, the report suggested, the factor that will most greatly influence what and how much he learns is not a well-endowed science room or even the teachers he meets, though clearly they are important. The most important factor in his schooling—other than his socioeconomic background—will be the children in his classroom:

> The most important predictor of how well a child would do in school was his socioeconomic background and who his classmates were. . . . It appears that a pupil's achievement is strongly related to the educational backgrounds and aspirations of the other students in the school . . . if a minority pupil from a home without much educational strength is put with classmates with strong educational backgrounds, his achievements are likely to increase. (Coleman, 1966, p. 22)

A schoolchild spends six hours a day with his classmates, who offer him companionship, loyalty, and prejudices. They pass around, in addition to jokes, gum, and notes, their view of the world. Student attitudes do not need to be stated as explicit opinions; they are conveyed implicitly in what the students approve of and what they belittle. A child living in a poor neighborhood is likely to play with friends who have strong ideas about what is worthwhile (such as physical strength and attractiveness) and what is laughable (such as

Leon's mother says:

"He don't listen, I know it. I tell him, you shut up and be a good boy and do just what your teacher tell you, hear? His pappa, when he was home, he used to say the same thing. He say he gonna beat him if he don't behave in school. But I can't do nothing with him."

Leon's teacher says:

"Sometimes he's wild, just asking to be yelled at. We can't let these kids get the jump on us, you know, or we're really in trouble. He knows how it is, if he carries on too much he'll get yelled at or hustled into this seat. Won't be able to do that in a couple of years, though, look how big he's getting. But more often, he just goes into a corner and sits and stares. Like he doesn't hear anything that's going on. I turn to him and say something simple, you know, ask him a simple arithmetic problem maybe. He just stares back. Like he's listening to something going on in his head, and he isn't really there at all."

Leon says:

"My teacher? I don't mind him. Not like the teacher I had last year, she couldn't get me to do *nothin'*. Just like my mother. She's always tellin' me to do something. She say, quit bouncin' that ball in here, you drivin' me crazy, then when I head for the door, she say, you goin' out there? Don't go out in the street, you stay in here. Now I don't pay any attention. I got my own keys, I do what I want. Man, I'm on my own. I don't care what anybody say."

Leon's chances?

zealous intellectual curiosity). Since all children need friends, poor children are reluctant to display an enthusiastic attitude toward school, for that would cut them off from their friends.

Children are also likely to influence one another's attitudes about where to put the blame for their failure or the credit for their success. As we saw in Chapter 7, there seems to be a relation between believing that your behavior is the reason for your success or failure and eventually succeeding or failing. Lower-class black children are more likely to credit events in their lives to outside forces, such as chance and the behavior of powerful adults; white children and middle-class black children are more apt to see these events as the results of their own efforts and skills (Battle and Rotter, 1963). Among poor, black eighth-grade students, those who were achieving in school were more likely to believe they controlled events in their lives (Buck and Austrin, 1971).

The Language of Minority-Group Children

As we have seen, there are *no* important differences in I.Q. between black and white middle-class children, but significant differences do exist between poor and privileged children, with children from poor families scoring lowest. What is interesting, moreover, is the pattern of subtest scores on the I.Q. test (see Figure 12–3). On tests for memory and puzzle solving, which require thought and concentration, social-class differences are smaller than they are for tests involving knowledge of words and information, which do not require much thought or concentration. This fact suggests that the poor child's lower I.Q. is partly due to his unfamiliarity with the language, information, and sentence style promoted by middle-class families and schools (Burnes, 1970).

Figure 12–3
Subtest scores on the Wechsler Intelligence Scale for Children show that the significant differences among groups of children are determined by class, not race. The sharpest differentiations occur in the vocabulary subtest. (After Burnes, 1970)

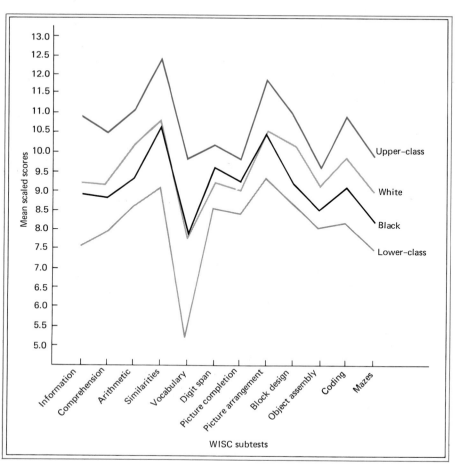

Many poor children speak a nonstandard English dialect that nevertheless has its own internal rules and idioms. Many black pupils are not linguistically deficient, merely linguistically different. Both black and white children were asked to repeat sentences in both standard and nonstandard English (Baratz, 1969, p. 893):

1 "Does Deborah like to play with that girl that sits next to her in school?"
2 "I asked Tom if he wanted to go to the picture that was playing at the Howard."
3 "Do Deborah like ta play wid da girl that sit next to her at school?"
4 "I aks Tom do he wanna go ta the picture that be playin' at the Howard."

White children repeated the standard sentences more accurately than black children. However, the black children made consistent mistakes. Instead of "I asked Tom *if he wanted* . . . ," 97 percent of the black children answered with "I aks Tom *did he wanna* . . ." But black children were more accurate than white children in repeating the nonstandard sentences.

If black children learn a well-ordered but different language from white children, they will be at a disadvantage in reading and spelling classes that use standard English. For that reason, schools are justified in testing black children to find out how well they speak standard English. But more often schools test them to assess how well they have developed language, not realizing that a test given in standard English fails to ascertain their agility with the language they know best.

One investigator invented a test, intended to be culture-fair, that used street slang. It included argot about drugs (*horse, to shoot up*), gang fighting (*stomping, ratpacking*), and law enforcement (*bulls, busted, the P.O.*). The test was given to a large group of boys, including some in institutions for delinquents. The poorer a child's grades in school, the higher he scored on the slang test (Kulik, Sarbin, and Stein, 1971). If the slang words constituted the vocabulary test commonly used to measure I.Q., young middle-class boys would have lower scores because they think "bulls" live in meadows.

Apart from not knowing the right words, some children's unfamiliarity with linguistic concepts can prevent efficient conceptual reasoning. Urban and rural children in Kenya were asked to group seventeen pictures of animals into conceptually similar classes. Unschooled rural children grouped the animals into two categories—*wild* and *domestic*. Urban children sorted them according to *color* and *shape*—concepts that many teachers regard as less "mature" than *wild* and *domestic* because they are less abstract (Fjellman, 1971). Though unschooled, the rural children used more mature concepts than the urban children because they were more familiar with the concepts of *wild* and *domestic*.

Figure 12-4
**This is an example of one of the cards used in teaching the principles of
conjunctive, disjunctive, and relational concepts. It correctly illustrates the
conjunctive concept *smiling or frowning* and *adult or child*, the disjunctive
concept *adult or child*, and the relational concept *more men than women*.
When poor children are given the chance to become familiar with the cards
and related material, they learn the three types of concepts as easily as
middle-class children. (After Securro and Walls, 1971)**

Proper preparation for learning a new concept can improve a child's
performance on mental tasks. A group of children was asked to learn
three different kinds of concepts—conjunctive, disjunctive, and
relational—working with cards that showed from one to six, happy or
sad faces of adults or children (see Figure 12-4). A conjunctive concept
takes into account two dimensions (for example, three faces and all
smiling). A disjunctive concept involves one of two attributes being
correct (for example, child faces or sad faces). A relational concept
involves a quantitative relation between two dimensions (for example,
more smiling faces than sad faces). When lower-class children were
given an opportunity to become familiar with the cards and lifelike
stimuli to work with before the task began, they learned the three kinds
of concepts as easily as middle-class children—indicating that lower-
and middle-class children may be equally competent if the former first
gains familiarity with the requirements of the task (Securro and Walls,
1971).

Optimal conditions of testing and increased familiarity with

materials are among the most important factors affecting good
performance on tests. In a recent study isolated Indian children from
six to twelve years of age, living in poor agricultural villages in
Guatemala, were administered a complicated memory task. The
examiner presented two pictures of a house and a dog, for example,
and the child had to remember the order of the two pictures. The
examiner then added a third picture (house, dog, glass), and the child
had to remember the order of the three. The process continued until the
child either reached twelve pictures or failed. Most American children
can remember twelve pictures by age nine or ten, while the Indian
ten-year-olds were able to remember only five or six. But the examiner
returned several months later and readministered the same test to the
Indian children under more optimal conditions. This time each test
session lasted only ten or fifteen minutes so that motivation remained
high throughout and attention never lagged. Under these conditions
many, though not all, of the ten-year-old children who previously had
remembered only five or six pictures could now remember all twelve.
The patience of the examiner and the slower pace of testing revealed
the competence that did not appear when the testing sessions were
longer and the materials less familiar (Kagan et al., unpublished).

Of course, there are different levels of competence at a task. The
child may be able to perform a task correctly but be unable to explain
the task to another child. Groups of middle- and lower-class
fifth-graders were asked to carry out a set of instructions such as
"When I put a white circle in the middle of the board, you put a penny

on the red circle" and then to explain the instructions to someone else. Both groups could do the task. But the lower-class children, who were good as listeners and performers, were less able as communicators (Pozner and Saltz, 1972).

Difficulties in Motivating Children from Poor Families

Poor children are less familiar with the questions on school tests and often do not understand the tasks. They are less highly motivated to show what they know and less seduced by the rewards that tempt middle-class children. Part of a child's eagerness to master a new skill rests on her enthusiasm for the reward she receives when she performs well. A child is likely to work hard to learn a skill if it brings satisfaction and avoids punishment. In the classroom the reward for success in mastering a new step is not a superficial luxury; it can be a key part of the learning.

But reinforcements that traditionally work with middle-class children are often less enticing for poor children. Middle-class children are apt to be satisfied with impersonal rewards, such as good grades. Children from poor families are less impressed by grades; they prefer personal expressions of praise and hugging, or more tangible rewards, such as a piece of candy for a right answer (Zigler and Kanzer, 1962).

Economically privileged children, furthermore, have had more experience with postponed rewards. For example, having been told that by going to bed early one night they can stay up later the next night to go to a movie and having, in fact, experienced that promise being kept, they are more ready to believe that a reward in school can be promised, postponed, and still delivered. A child living in poverty does not arrive at school with the same confidence that a promise is a promise. In her world, a child takes what she can when she has the chance—she does not pass it up now and expect to see it offered a second time. Hence, many rewards offered in school are of less significance to lower-class children.

What Can Go Wrong in a Ghetto School

The school is in a gray neighborhood that has two- and three-family houses with paint peeling from the porch rails and, occasionally, an empty house whose windows are closed with wooden boards. But there is an unmistakable sign that something more ominous than peeling paint is around the neighborhood: the corner supermarket has wire netting over its big front windows.

The school, uninspired when it was designed fifty years ago, also has wire netting over its windows, and a name is chiseled in stone over the door: *Michael Joseph O'Leary.* Young black children, many on welfare, start each school day with a reminder that the school was built for children other than themselves.

The school door is made of steel. "Even so," one teacher says, "the kids can get through somehow. Probably because the locks have been smashed so many times that they can't hold anymore. We can't leave anything in the school overnight; it disappears. If we want to use anything like a tape recorder or a movie projector, we bring it in the morning and take it home in the afternoon. As a result, there isn't much we use, since the teachers get tired of lugging stuff back and forth."

Half the second-grade children are out of the room, reading with an outside aide (whose funding is expected to stop at the end of the year). Even with only ten children left, the classroom atmosphere is hectic: cupboard doors and desk drawers hang open, the floor is littered with papers and nails from the hammering table, three girls loll across the desk tops, a boy sits on an overturned chair. Jostled by children who are running or shuffling, one little boy stands with a book and reads; he takes a step or two out of the way, but his eyes never leave the page. In the corner, a boy talks into a tape recorder and plays back his voice. Three children are wearing their coats: it turns out that all three also have great difficulty with schoolwork.

During the morning there are extremes of chaos and quiet. At recess there is a sudden inundation of children returning from reading; the noise rises from two tape recorders, a cassette television, hammering, twenty-one children, games of tag, and an argument ("You don't know nothin', you bad, black boy!") that turns into fisticuffs.

"That's just a little fight. No real violence this morning," says the teacher. "Sometimes I go home at the end of the day frightened. I've had two stabbings, both by that quiet little girl in the purple overcoat." There are the overcoats again: meager comfort for unhappy children.

Not everyone is running around. James, who was reading in the middle of the commotion before, is now intently playing with a box of anagram blocks. Leon sits on the floor, involved in nothing, watching everything. And Arlen, quiet, sad, frustrated, wanders from place to place, occasionally exchanging a word with someone, but his mind is elsewhere. "He's headed for serious trouble," says the teacher. "He's nine, and he doesn't yet have a five-year-old's skills. Most of the stimulation in the room comes from words, so if he's here six hours a day, four are pure frustration for him. Retarded? I don't think so. Of course, there's no one here to test him. It's too late for him already. In another situation he might catch up. But the policy here is that we only keep a child back one year and then we move him on. There are no special classes and no personnel. It's politics: the money comes to the district, not the school, and another school a few blocks away, with

more white kids and fewer welfare families, gets goodies like reading specialists. We get nothing."

The children, lolling, hugging, fighting, not only touch each other a lot, they are also very aware of one another's electricity. They are always ready and waiting for the next explosion—for an outburst of laughter as much as a shout or a fight. It is as if most of their energy is invested in paying attention to one another, watching and watching out; schoolwork by comparison seems pale and bland.

It is not all bad. The teacher is firm, but sympathetic, and willing to experiment. He encourages games and lets the children have turns with the tape recorder as rewards for doing a piece of work. Both with the tape recorder and a game with toothpicks and glue, children seem interested and curious. During the phonics lesson all twenty-one children sit down and underline consonant blends on a work sheet (except Arlen, who does not even bother to get a piece of paper). The teacher puts the answers on the board, and some children copy them ("It's too demoralizing for them not to have a paper to hand in," the teacher says), while others bend over their papers and circle the answers on their own. "At first I was permissive, and they walked over me as if I were loud furniture," says the teacher. "Now I tell them we're going to do a piece of work, and by golly, they do it."

Many good suburban schools are struggling away from structured classes. But the view looks different from the Michael Joseph O'Leary School. Although the most striking aspect of this classroom is the lack of concentration, the children do not appear unintelligent. And they are for the most part aware and friendly. During recess they offer a visitor bites of their potato chips from home, and when one boy, irritated by his friend, says, "What the _____!" he stops, glances her way, shrugs, and says to his friend, "Listen, don't make me swear in front of a lady." But except for fifteen minutes during the phonics lesson there is no sitting still and little focus. The noise is continuous and the children move around constantly. They do not respond to planned, specific stimulation unless it seems extraordinary. If the children are not prepared to take what the school offers, neither does the school appear to offer much that entices these children.

Implications for Teaching

The Case for Improving Schools in Poor Neighborhoods

Fewer material possessions and less status and power lead the poor to feel less potent than they would if all families had similar resources. Consciousness of this lack is the critical information that leads economically less-advantaged parents to develop a sense of futility, which they communicate to their children. Since the perception of being relatively disadvantaged is important in producing the attitudes and child-rearing practices of poor families, it is reasonable to suggest that education alone will not completely eliminate the differences in performance between lower- and middle-class children. Moreover, since the middle class does not stop gaining in income if more adolescents from poor families obtain more education, education alone may not close the income gap in a serious way.

Before the publication of the Coleman Report many middle-class Americans believed that if children received a good education, they would be able to find well-paid jobs as adults. We now realize that children who most need the extra advantage are least likely to receive a good education. Even though the attainment of good jobs does not depend solely on education (wider economic forces need to be confronted in order to approach that goal), the child who graduates from high school is much more likely to get a better job than one who drops out. Nonetheless, Christopher Jencks, in his book *Inequality*

Integrated Schools

It is not possible to make any simple statement about the effect of busing to achieve integration in schools. Planned integration is a potential tool for improving school as a place both to learn skills and to meet new values. Academically it may, in some circumstances, improve the intellectual growth of some children by enriching the social mix in the classroom: more poor children may sit beside privileged children and benefit from the association. In other circumstances, busing may lead to healthier attitudes between white and black children, although it may not have any influence on reading levels.

But the effect of any reform that produces integrated schools will depend, in a serious way, on the attitudes of the families involved and on the size, the racial profile, and the mood of the community and the schools.

For example, a child who is being bused to a community against her family's wishes and who hears each night at dinner the bitterness and anger her parents feel over this coercion will certainly profit less from busing than a child whose parents are enthusiastic about the school she is now attending.

Although the benefits of integration and busing are publicly endorsed in terms of academic gain and measured in terms of test performance, it is likely that privately many people believe that the important rationale for busing is not academic: they hope, rather, that a more widespread association between young black and white children may lessen the injurious suspicion generated by segregation, regardless of gains in reading and arithmetic. Attempts to measure the effect of integration by busing should never look only at test scores. In addition, they must also assess the attitudes of the children and their families to see if salutory gains have been achieved.

(1972), suggests that decreasing educational disparities will not make all American adults economically more equal.

This position has bothered many Americans who want to believe that education will solve our social problems, raise everyone's standard of living, and make all Americans feel a sense of participation in and responsibility for the national mission. To some degree this wish has a basis in reality. As indicated earlier, both the educational attainment and the average income of American blacks are lower than those of white wage earners. National averages, however, can conceal advances that occur among specific segments of the population. An important study reveals an additional part of the picture. In 1968, among intact black families living outside the South, a family headed by a person between twenty-four and thirty-five years old with one to three years of college had a median income 111.1 percent higher than one headed by a person with only one to three years of high school. Hence, for certain regions of the country and for certain age groups additional education does seem to be associated with higher income (Moynihan, 1972).

Diversity of Skills

In Chapter 10 we discussed at some length the differences in individual pace among students (we will return to that question again in Chapter 13). Significant differences in individual strengths also occur among students.

Even within socioeconomic classes there are differences among children of different ethnic groups in the profile of intellectual talents. In the beginning of this chapter we mentioned a Manhattan school that had Chinese, black, Puerto Rican, and Jewish students. Statistical analysis showed that each ethnic group had a specific profile of abilities (see Figure 12–5). Chinese children were better on spatial tests than

Figure 12–5
Chinese, Jewish, black, and Puerto Rican students were given tests that measured ability with words, reasoning, number, and spatial forms. Although there were variations in ability within the four ethnic groups, taken as a whole each one showed a particular profile of intellectual talents. (After Lesser, Fifer, and Clark, 1965)

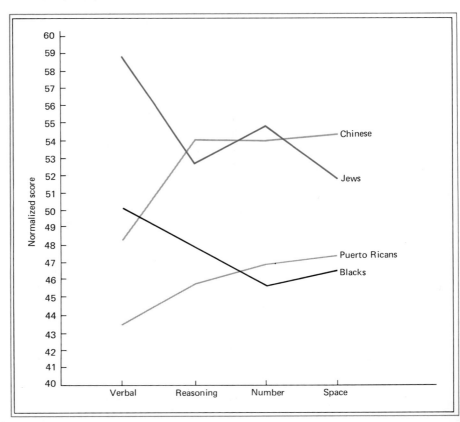

they were on language tests, while Jewish children had the opposite profile (Lesser, Fifer, and Clark, 1965). Obviously, we want to nourish this kind of diversity whether in groups or individuals and not subvert it by insisting that the Chinese students try to bring their vocabulary scores into line with those of the most verbal Jewish students in the classroom.

Let us now consider some practical steps that can be taken to improve education for children from poor families.

Strategies To Aid the Performance of Poor Children

Several educators have suggested that useful study techniques are often poorly developed in children from low-income families. Efforts to teach the children these strategies have produced some surprisingly positive results. We have already discussed the importance of rehearsal. The teacher can show a child how he can help himself remember the numbers in a digit span or the objects in a picture by saying the names to himself as he focuses on them. Whispering "four, seventeen, nine, and twelve" helps him to "lock" the numbers into his memory.

Psychologists have suggested that for most tasks in school, children must engage in conceptual activity that depends on rehearsal and transformation. It appears that children from middle-class families tend to do this more regularly and more automatically than children from poor families. One psychologist devised a procedure to help the schools deliberately train children to use these techniques (Rohwer, 1972). There were three groups of second-grade children, each composed of poor black children and middle-class white children. All the children were given two forms of a memory test, one as a pretest and one as a posttest. (For instance, shown a picture of a dog and a gate, the children had to learn that the dog went with the gate and remember that association for the posttest.) The control group was simply administered the tests, with no help or instructions between pretest and posttest. The training group was deliberately instructed. The children were reminded to visualize the objects they were shown, to name them (saying "dog," "gate"), to make up sentences describing what was happening ("The dog is opening the gate"), and to create a mental picture of that action. This group was trained twenty minutes a day for five days. The third group of children—the practice group—was also seen twenty minutes a day for five days, but it was not given any instructions; the children simply practiced taking the tests over and over. The middle-class children in both the training group and the practice group showed more improvement than those in the control group, who only took the pair of tests. However, the children from poor families received virtually no benefit from just practicing but did improve when they were *trained*. The study suggests that children from poor families can be trained to learn new information more efficiently and that deliberate, specific training in relevant skills is more effective than just exposure to and practice with tests.

Two other experiments also focused on methods of tutoring to improve the study habits of children. In one, two groups of five-year-olds from poor families (white, black, and Puerto Rican) were selected on the basis of relatively low scores on tests of cognitive performance and placed in tutorial programs (Blank, Koltuv, and Wood, 1972). In both groups, the children met with teachers in a one-to-one context for fifteen-minute sessions, working with the toys and equipment commonly found in nursery schools. One group used the *traditional tutorial program,* which stressed giving the children many different kinds of stimulation—toys, sounds to make, colors, shapes and textures to manipulate—in order to broaden their experience and stimulate their curiosity. The other group used the *structured tutorial program,* which was less concerned with the enriching qualities of material than with diagnosing and correcting the child's mistakes. A third group was given no special tutoring and acted as a control group. This program was based on the assumption that a child who shows impaired cognitive performance is afraid and has inefficient habits, both of which cause errors in performance. It did not just allow children the "freedom to make mistakes" but used their reactions as opportunities for further exploration. For example, if the child pulled his hand away from a piece of steel wool, the teacher asked, "Why?" If the child answered, "I don't know," the teacher would help the child focus on relevant features, perhaps by saying, "Well, how does that steel wool feel?" If he still said, "I don't know," she would offer him a piece of velvet to touch, so that the contrast between softness and roughness would become apparent to him. When the child answered correctly that the steel wool felt rough, she would repeat the initial question "Why?" so that he would pay attention to the material that made the object feel "rough." In this way, the children were required to focus on and examine the elements involved in a problem. After four and one-half months of sessions four days a week, the children in the structured tutorial program had gained 15 points on the full-scale WISC, while the children in the traditional tutorial program had gained only about 8 points, and those exposed to no special program gained about 5 points (see Figure 12–6). Children who are fearful of making mistakes constantly say "I don't know" to questions. By diagnosing and correcting error patterns, teachers can help these children handle the elements of a problem and, as a result, reduce their fear.

Another experiment compared black elementary- and junior-high-school students from a public school in a poverty area, all of whom were a year and one-half or more behind in basic school skills, with middle-class white students enrolled in a school for learning disorders. Both black and white students were divided into three groups. The control group received no remediation. The second group

WISC SCORES FOR THREE GROUPS OF KINDERGARTEN CHILDREN

I.Q.	TIME	STRUCTURED TUTORIAL GROUP	TRADITIONAL TUTORIAL GROUP	CLASSROOM CONTROL GROUP
Full scale	Pretest	83.3	82.9	85.4
	Posttest	98.3	91.0	90.9
Verbal	Pretest	78.3	78.9	81.5
	Posttest	90.1	82.6	81.9
Performance	Pretest	92.1	90.4	92.4
	Posttest	107.5	101.7	102.7

Figure 12–6
In a comparison of tutoring methods used to improve the intellectual skills of kindergarten children from poor families, the greatest gains were achieved by children in a structured tutorial program, which concentrated on diagnosing the errors made by children and helping them to understand the separate steps involved in solving the problem. (Adapted from Blank, Koltuv, and Wood, 1972, p. 215)

attended a public-school enrichment program that used some individualized procedures and focused on reading and language skills. The third group attended a private program with individualized instruction, extra classroom support, an atmosphere of experimentation and positive reinforcement, and a low pupil-teacher ratio. The children in the third group, both the middle-class and the disadvantaged, made the greatest gains on the California Achievement Test—about one year and one month—while the children in the enrichment program did not make significantly greater gains than the control group (Feshbach and Adelman, 1974).

In addition to learning strategies, students benefit from more help in the classroom. There are an increasing number of teacher's aides in the schools, and the presence of these paraprofessionals is having an impact on how children learn, since the indications are that children in classrooms with aides make greater gains in reading than those in classrooms without aides (Riessman and Gartner, 1969). An aide allows the teacher more time to give individual attention to children and does some tutoring herself. The aide in the classroom may also be a mother in the neighborhood. By drawing mothers from the immediate community, rather than from a distant and possibly richer one, a teacher's aide program brings parents closer to their children's schools and schooling and gives principals and teachers a chance to hear another voice besides their own.

A major step in improving schools has been the design of

"compensatory education" programs, whose specific aim is to increase the knowledge and the cognitive skills of young children who are likely to have serious difficulty in school. We will discuss these programs in detail in Chapter 13. Unquestionably, improving the academic strengths of children early in their school careers is essential in narrowing the gap between the educational opportunities of poor and middle-class students.

Finally, we can try to make the school a positive, productive place for poor children by widening our expectations of what they will learn and do there. A child's cognitive maturation is only one factor in his growth: the school can extend its interest to other facets of his development. Furthermore, his cognitive growth is less likely to proceed at an optimum pace as long as he feels antagonistic, unwelcome, or unfamiliar in his classroom. By encouraging abilities in art, athletics, and music, as well as in reading and arithmetic, schools have a chance to engage a child's motivation, widen his scope of activity, and improve his academic performance.

A Ghetto School That Works

In a large American city the Lincoln elementary school stands downtown near a university and several low-income housing projects.

In the past, when the neighborhood was largely white and middle-class, Lincoln was a training school for university students. Today, the school population is almost entirely black and poor. Lincoln's tradition as a training school is operative in a new way, however: several approaches to teaching children from poor families are being tried and may prove useful examples for other schools to follow.

In Mrs. Raphael's third-grade room, good light comes in from a wall of windows. Desk and chair units are arranged in small groups. Along one wall are carrels equipped with tape recorders and earphones. The walls are not cluttered, but there are some cutout magazine pictures of black people working and playing, a map of the state, a few samples of drawings, and a chart showing the reading progress of each pupil. On tables in the back of the room stand scenes in shoeboxes that the children are making for social studies. Constructed of clay, paint, and paper, they show aspects of the city's life. One label reads, "i am going to make Truman Stadium, and when i get time i will show you each how i am going to make it out of paper and then i will show you and the teacher. i might stand up in front of the class and i might pass it around. pass it back to me."

The first thing that a visitor notices is that everyone is busy. In a class of twenty children, some are working in groups and some alone, but everyone is working. Two teachers consult with the children. But even when they are not under the teachers' immediate supervision, the children go right on working. One boy has a mathematics workbook and a ditto sheet. Two boys sit side by side in a carrel, reading two copies of the same book. They take turns reading out loud and occasionally read in unison. A number of pupils sit in a group and read to themselves, and several more sit alone, studying reading workbooks. One girl gets up to look for the answer card for her workbook so that she can check her own spelling.

One group of children has finished all the work and is making sit-upons out of woven strips of newspaper for the class picnic the next day. For five or ten minutes, everyone concentrates. Then a little boy gets up, puts away his workbook, and sits down, staring into space; he gets up again and moves around the room.

"Robert," calls Mrs. Raphael, "you have not yet begun to read. Get a book. No, get a hardbacked reader under the readers—level ten. Not that one, it's too low for you. That's a good one." The boy sits down. There is some more scuffling of feet and a long look from Mrs. Raphael, and then he, too, is reading.

"He hasn't gone as far as most of the children," she explains quietly. "But he came to me this year in low books, and when you think of where he began, he's made as much progress as the others."

Another child goes over to a carrel, picks out a book and a tape to go with it, plugs it into the recorder, and settles down. This is a read-along—a standard reading book with tapes added—that allows a child to take in the words through his eyes and ears simultaneously.

The tape omits a phrase here and there so that the child receives that phrase visually.

A little girl goes to the shelf under the windows where cartons contain folders with math examples and problems, arranged in sequence of complexity. Earlier she had taken a pretest to determine what material she already knew and where in the sequence her ability stopped. Now she goes to a cardboard box marked for her level and finds some materials to help her learn the skills involved in a problem such as this one:

$17 - 6 = 11$
Does $17 - 11 = 6$?
Does $11 + 6 = 17$?

The teachers have put materials in the box—in this case, paper cutouts of fish—to help the pupils visualize addition and subtraction. The pupils use the folders and the materials in the boxes, as well as the teachers' help, to move along the sequence of steps necessary to master this stage of mathematics.

A boy leaves his earphones in the carrel and comes up to Mrs. Raphael to have his dictation corrected. Every word is right except *haul.*

"Say this word, Peter," says the teacher.

"How."

"I think you should go back and listen to the tape again. Listen for that word." She circles it with a pencil. He is back in a few minutes with *haul* printed on his paper.

"That's right. But Peter, do you know what it means?"

"Like shouting."

"No, not *holler—haul.* 'My father hauls the garbage in his truck.' " Peter nods.

What is going on at Lincoln? It is not hard to see and feel what the school accomplishes. How it is done is less easy to decipher. It appears that three elements work together: individualized instruction, the pupils' real interest in the work and legitimate sense of accomplishment, and the teachers' high expectations for performance and low tolerance for aimlessness or disruptive behavior in the classroom.

The nearby university has provided a curriculum of individualized instruction for the first five grades. The curriculum is based on two notions: first, that the school must be willing to adapt to the child and begin where he begins and, second, that a sense of mastery is critical in a child's motivation. If he is to feel an honest sense of accomplishment, he must work with material that is not already known but not too far out of his reach—only a little. Read-along books and tapes, self-checking workbooks, and sequential mathematics boxes are aspects of a curriculum designed to help each child start at his level, proceed at his own pace, and be proud of his individual progress.

Mrs. Raphael's character as a teacher is an important part of the classroom atmosphere. Her manner is firm, authoritative, and very businesslike. Her warmth is apparent. But one senses that she is there to do a job and that she is very sure of herself. She is not easily agitated. That Ms. Massalsky, the roving teacher who worked with her that morning, shared the same qualities of confidence and firmness was evident in an exchange that took place over two children who fell into a scuffle that might have escalated into a fistfight. Ms. Massalsky stood over them and spoke in a low, firm voice.

After a minute or two Mrs. Raphael said, "Would you like me to settle it?"

Equally quietly, Ms. Massalsky answered, "No, I want Roger and Elena to sit down and open their books."

After another minute or so of sulky faces, they both did just that.

While a few other schools around the country have enjoyed considerable success in teaching values and skills to children from poor families, it is a mistake to idealize such schools. Viewed closely, they prove to have their own share of unresolved problems and are struggling to achieve greater progress. Nevertheless, it is worthwhile to examine such a school to see what combination of factors has produced a situation in which the children are actively, even enthusiastically, engaged in mastering specific cognitive skills. While a good deal of research, money, and administrative effort have gone into Lincoln, the realities of individualized instruction, pupil interest and satisfaction, and high teacher expectations are not rare commodities that can only flourish in this school. They represent a goal to be attained in other inner-city schools.

A Rising Tide To Raise All Boats

When we design programs that make school seem like a worthwhile place for poor children and when we measure the effect of these programs, it seems useful to widen our vision. There are no absolute decrees about what children should learn. In the schools of ancient Sparta children were ranked according to their athletic ability; we rank children by their skills in reading and arithmetic. All children must learn these skills. But just as teachers who sacrifice warmth and friendliness toward their pupils for the goal of better cognitive performance often achieve the opposite effect from the one they intended, schools that focus only on a child's cognitive talent without regard for his sense of confidence and curiosity may hamper his future accomplishment, sense of mastery, and confidence. We should expand the number of talents that we applaud during the early school years and reward any talent that the child shows. We should arrange conditions so that the poor child does not become frightened and depressed about his performance in school before he has had a chance to gain the competence the school expects. Perhaps the most important task is to show that school is a friendly place. The honest reward of praise for a variety of attitudes will encourage diversity and will help many children who enter school less well-prepared and less highly motivated for reading and arithmetic than other children.

Summary

Children from economically disadvantaged families are apt to be poorer students than children from middle-class families, a phenomenon that has troubled and perplexed Americans for some time. The evidence shows that race or ethnicity alone is not a factor. Although many children from minority families do have difficulty in school, it appears that their poverty, not their ethnicity, hampers academic performance. Nor is this a uniquely American situation: in any country, even a country where most people are poor, the very poor children have the greatest difficulty in school. It is likely, therefore, that the psychological conditions and attitudes associated with poverty handicap the child's progress. Children from poor families are more likely than middle-class children to believe that events governing their lives and choices are outside of their control. Lower-class children come to school less well prepared for schoolwork, it is true. But in

addition, they assimilate a set of values at home and on the street that leads them to be discouraged about their futures, predisposed to be hostile to teachers, uninterested in unfamiliar school material that seems irrelevant, and less motivated to achieve.

To compound the problem, teachers signal their low expectations for these children. Their low opinion of the students' capacity to perform school tasks is often erroneous and is based on misunderstanding, prejudice, or lack of knowledge. (A Puerto Rican child who cannot spell English words, for instance, may not be "slow"—only unfamiliar with English sounds and symbols.)

A child's classmates exert a strong influence on his expectations and actual performance. One of the significant and, at the time, surprising findings of the Coleman Report was that aside from socioeconomic background, the strongest predictor of how well a child would learn in school was who his classmates were: middle-class children, who have higher expectations, as well as better intellectual preparation, can help to improve the school performance of children from less economically secure backgrounds.

Discovering why children perform poorly in school has been a puzzle. Even more challenging than explaining their failure is developing school structures and teaching strategies that can make school a more productive place for poor children. One strategy involves giving children a chance to practice intellectual activities that their classmates may have already tried out before school, such as exercises that train the technique of rehearsal or that teach children to visualize a new word or concept as it is introduced symbolically. Compensatory education programs, designed to increase conceptual activity and allow adequate time for practice, have yielded positive results. Schools often maintain a narrow, academic emphasis: celebrating skills or talents in music, the arts, sports, and group activities gives students a chance to acknowledge their competence and success in other areas. Changing, or at least widening, the official view of what school should do is one way to attract the attention and increase the motivation of students who would otherwise find it irrelevant. In the past, teachers with middle-class attitudes have found themselves in conflict with poor children because of differences in their assumptions and values. Clearly, teachers who are better prepared to understand their pupils and to approve of them will have greater success in teaching academic skills.

Projects

1 Suppose that you have decided to spend a year working on possible solutions to the problem of poor education among migrant children, either as a teacher, a tutor, or a researcher. You have discovered that the Ford Foundation is likely to provide financial support for such a project if it is well conceived. Write a preliminary proposal that you would send to the director of the foundation.

2 Research parent-involvement programs in several educational journals. Meet with some classmates and discuss ideas that may increase parent participation, bearing in mind the problems of working parents, day-care difficulties, disinterested parents, and single parents. In a report to the class, theorize on why such programs may or may not be successful with students and parents from poor families.

3 Find a recent study on self-esteem and its importance in school success. Relate that knowledge to the information in this chapter and give a report on the relationship to the class.

4 Plan a lesson or an activity for an elementary-school social studies class that will help the students understand the concept *prejudice*.

5 Observe a class in a school in a poor neighborhood. Pretending that you are an authority on motivation and have been engaged as a consultant to the school, compose a set of recommendations that you would make to the teacher of the class.

6 The children's television program "Sesame Street" is designed to foster readiness in preschool children. Watch several episodes and judge whether or not they achieve this goal. Support your decision with examples.

Recommended Reading

Jencks, C. *Inequality*. New York: Basic Books, 1972. Summarizes an investigation on the relation between amount of education and amount of income and concludes that changes in education cannot themselves overcome economic inequality in the United States.

Lesser, G. S., Fifer, G., and Clark, D. H. Mental abilities of children from different social class and cultural groups. *Monographs of the Society for Research in Child Development,* 1965, *30* (4, Serial No. 102). Summarizes research on different ethnic groups in New York City and shows that the profile of cognitive talents differs among them.

tomorrow's 13 education: meeting individual needs

America continues to grow in size and diversity. Faced with children of widely heterogeneous abilities, values, and personalities, educators can no longer assume that one strategy of teaching or one curriculum will best serve the majority of students. Educational procedures are beginning to accommodate to the individual child. In this last chapter we shall consider some ideas developed during the last ten to fifteen years—and some emerging now—that are likely to grow in importance during the coming decade.

Compensatory Education

As indicated in Chapter 12, average first-grade children from poor families are less well prepared than their middle-class counterparts to profit from instruction in reading and arithmetic. Once educators became sensitive to this problem, they tried to help these children.

Their help, which came to be called compensatory education, has generated both confusion and controversy. What does the phrase mean and how—and how well—does the concept work in practice?

Compensatory education is the intervention in the lives of children who are likely to encounter serious difficulty in school in order to improve their chances for academic success. Historically, compensatory education began by concentrating on the preschool years. Since the middle 1960s, however, it has extended upward into programs designed for the primary grades and downward into programs for infants.

It is difficult to identify the goals of compensatory education programs and to evaluate their success because the pluralistic nature of American society resists a consensus on what the goals should be. It would certainly simplify the challenge if we could say, "These are the aims of compensatory education" and design programs accordingly. Although conceivable in some societies, this approach is out of the question in our own. In surveying a small proportion of existing programs, it is important to remember that since there will always be a variety of goals, we must expect a variety of solutions as well.

Programs for Preschool Children

When the public demand for early education surfaced, there were few established programs that could fill the need and little professional lore about the special requirements of preschool children from poor or minority families. Yet almost everyone agreed that preschool education should be based on a firm understanding of how young children develop. It was natural that psychologists already interested in child development would be drawn to the challenge of formulating programs to meet the new demand. A number of them articulated the rationale for compensatory education.

Among the many arguments proposed, perhaps the most important single theme was presented by Joseph McVicker Hunt (1961). After reviewing evidence drawn from various fields of psychological research, he suggested that the old conception of intelligence as something fixed by genetic endowment was no longer useful. Instead, he proposed that intelligence should be viewed as "plastic," subject to environmental influence—especially during the early years. Hence, Hunt argued, a major emphasis should be placed on education during the first five years. He called his guiding principle "the problem of the match" and stated that, in devising preschool programs, one should choose intellectual and emotional demands that slightly exceed the child's competence. Like Piaget, Hunt believed that children are naturally motivated when their curiosity is aroused. To accomplish this, teaching situations need to be structured to match children's knowledge and intellectual capabilities.

During the same decade another psychologist also advanced a brief for early education. Benjamin Bloom (1964) argued that since a person's I.Q. at age seventeen could be more accurately predicted by intelligence test scores obtained when he was between the ages of six and ten than by his scores during the first three years of life, it seemed reasonable to conclude that I.Q.'s can be most easily influenced during the preschool years. Bloom implied that educational interventions in those early years may have a significant effect, but it was not clear what the design of such intervention programs should be.

Identifying Goals of Preschool Education

Before 1960 most nursery schools served the children of middle-class families, and Freudian-based theories of emotional and social development dominated the thinking of psychologists. As a result, preschools focused almost entirely on children's psychosocial development. But since that time, preschool programs—many serving children who are not expected to perform well academically—have explicitly taken on a new role: preparing children for elementary-school work. The preschool emphasis on intellectual development does not necessarily imply a lack of concern for other aspects of the child's growth. Although some psychologists and educators believe that social and emotional development will take care of themselves, others believe that intellectual growth will only proceed optimally if children's social, emotional, and physical health needs are met at the same time. Most psychologists probably walk a middle road on this issue; they focus their efforts on intellectual growth because the academic problems of children from poor families appear to be primarily cognitive. Moreover, it is easier to construct and evaluate curricula for intellectual competences than for social and emotional development.

But we are still left with the question, What competences should the preschooler develop? Different answers to this question have led to different programs. Whereas some program designers established a pattern of direct instruction in order to improve specific school-related skills and knowledge, others preferred to create a classroom environment that encouraged the children's active initiative and participation in order to nourish general cognitive processes. The following section tries to convey a sense of this variety.

Three Types of Programs

General enrichment programs. Initially, programs for children from poor families—such as Project Head Start—were based on the assumption that these children lacked variety in experience and intellectual challenge. Preschools tried to offset this apparent deficit. Children were given toys and games that stimulated their senses and encouraged their reasoning skills. Carved wooden blocks to fit into holes of the same shapes; felt boards with cutout figures, animals, trees, and houses to arrange into patterns; sand tables on which to use pans and molds to make shapes from wet sand; colored beads to string; and musical instruments, such as homemade tambourines, triangles, and drums, were all common preschool toys. Children were also taken on field trips to neighborhood shops, or to a museum or a firehouse. There was no formal teaching of academic skills. Teachers assumed that exposure to a variety of experiences would produce intellectual advances and enhanced motivation.

One reason educators used a general enrichment approach in early Head Start programs was that they were accustomed to this format in middle-class nursery schools. But over time, as they came to realize that the approach was too indirect to meet the needs of children from poor families, many of the programs changed. In order to catch up, these children required a more explicit intellectual content.

Programs with direct cognitive emphasis. As preschool programs shifted their focus to more specific cognitive goals, designers developed curricula that emphasized both academic achievement and improved attitudes toward schoolwork. A good deal of the emphasis was linguistic: the programs concentrated on teaching vocabulary and on verbal interaction among the children and the teachers. They also taught concepts directly, in the belief that understanding what a concept is, as well as familiarity with common concepts, was an important prerequisite to academic success. Packs of cards, lotto games, dominoes, toy animals, and pictures of household articles were used to

teach fundamental principles of sorting, matching, and classifying. Children used cards or dominoes for counting, or arranged pictures of household articles into sets by use: cleaning, cooking, clothes, tools. Manipulating simple objects such as poker chips, masonite shapes, pegboards and elastics, hard candies, and bottle caps, instead of simply looking at pictures, helped the children master concepts. Placing all the red poker chips in one box, for instance, or making a set of objects that was both *red* and *small* gave them practice in classifying.

Often the children built up their vocabulary and grammatical skills simultaneously, learning words and concepts to describe objects, people, functions, and relations. Handling a small toy dog and a block, the child could master the distinction between "The dog is on the block" and "The dog is behind the block."

Programs varied in procedure. In one, three-year-old children attended the program for a few hours a day over a period of seven months in order to become acquainted with the tasks of first grade. They worked on language and mathematical concepts, read books and described what they saw happening in the pictures, began to think about story continuity, and expanded their vocabulary (Karnes et al., 1964). Other programs worked with children for a year or two (Gray and Klaus, 1970; Weikart, 1971).

Language is central to cognitive functioning and poor and middle-class children differ in language skills and in performance on I.Q. tests, which emphasize language ability. Therefore, many planners viewed improved language development as the principal sign of a program's success. While the programs just described deliberately taught new vocabulary and verbal concepts, others concentrated exclusively on language, attempting to teach children to speak the standard English believed necessary for school success. We will describe two of them.

One approach, developed by Carl Bereiter and Siegfried Engelmann (1966), was concerned with language as it is used in a typical school, on the assumption that the characteristics of nonstandard English interfere first with children's speech and later with their ability to read. The program directly instructed children in standard English just as they would have been taught any new skill or, most particularly, a foreign language.

What are some common speech errors made by a child from a poor family?

(a) He omits articles, prepositions, conjuctions, and short verbs from statements. For 'This is a ball" he will say, "Dis' ball."

(b) He does not understand the function of *not* in a sentence. An example: a child is presented with three objects and is asked to point to the cup, the spoon, and the block. He does this and is then asked to point to "something that is not a cup." He points to the cup.

(c) He cannot produce plural statements correctly and cannot perform the actions implied by plural statements. "These are balls" becomes "D'ese ball" or "These is balls."

Whether these language characteristics represent a language that is a valid but different language from standard English or whether they represent a substandard English dialect, incapable of being used for serious cognition, need not be argued here. What is evident is that such characteristics are not those of the language used in the public school. (Osborn, 1968, p. 37)

To change the child's patterns of speech, teachers used a highly structured approach and relied on a stylized pattern of drill. For instance:

On the first day of school, the children begin learning the basic pointing-out or identifying statement. Since the object of the lesson is to teach the statement form, and not new object names, familiar objects are used. The teacher has several of these in a box on her lap. She holds up one and says, "This is a cup. Let's say it." She says slowly and rhythmically with the children, "This is a cup." The teacher says, "Let's say it again. This is a what?" The teacher says with the children at a little faster pace, "This is a cup."

Several more group responses follow. Then the teacher calls on one child. "Danny, what is this?" The criterion for successful performance of the task is to say all four words in the proper order. Perfect pronunciation of each word is not an expectation. If, as is common, a child leaves out an *a* or *is* and *a,* the teacher will repeat the sentence, clapping her hands and saying the words that have been left out. She will have the children saying the same words as they repeat the sentence.

When the children are able to make a reasonable rendition of the identity statement, they are taught the *not* statement. The teacher points to and identifies three objects on a tray in her lap, "This is a cup; this is a comb; this is a block." She then points to the cup and says, "This is not a comb; is this a comb?" She makes the statement with the children, "This is not a comb." If a child says, "This is a cup," the teacher assures him that he is correct but that she is asking about a comb. She repeats the question, "is this a comb?" to which the answer is, "No, this is not a comb." The children repeat, together and separately, alternating affirmative and negative statements about objects on the tray and things in the room. (Osborn, 1968, pp. 41–42)

Two other program designers, Marion Blank and Frances Solomon (1969), also focused on exactness of expression and reasoning. But they did not use patterned drills, nor did they insist that children speak perfect standard English. Instead, they held semistructured conversations with each child, proceeding from the child's interests at that moment.

In the sample conversation below, notice that the child is confronted with a situation in which the teacher uses no gestures: the child must understand and use language as the means of communication. The righthand column represents an interpretation of the rationale for the teacher's particular reactions (Blank and Solomon, 1969, p. 49):

Dialogue	Interpretation
TEACHER: I'm going to draw a picture, and then you're going to make one just like it. I'll give you a paper. What color crayon would you like to use? JULIE: Yellow. (Child chooses correctly, immediately starts drawing in usual impulsive manner.)	Teacher's statements are designed to (1) tune child in to intended activity; (2) have her make a specific verbal choice which will determine her next action. Had child's choice not been consistent with verbalization, teacher would have initiated interchange to correct child.
TEACHER: *Wait.* Don't draw anything yet. JULIE: (Halts and focuses.)	Teacher attempts to delay impulsiveness.
TEACHER: (Draws a circle.) What did I draw? JULIE: A ball.	Teacher is not concerned with a label per se, but rather with posing a question so as to keep the child's attention.
TEACHER: Could you make that ball? Make one just like mine. JULIE: (Succeeds.)	Using child's word, teacher utilizes imitation as a means of getting child to complete a simple task.

Since the Blank and Solomon program involved spontaneous conversation between one teacher and one child, it could not be highly sequenced and structured ahead of time. The teacher had to follow where the child led, keeping in mind the aims of the program and making a moment-to-moment assessment of the child's capabilities. This program called for a highly trained teacher, sensitive to the child's abilities. And since it required one teacher for one child, it was more expensive to implement than the Bereiter-Engelmann plan and therefore was used less widely.

Programs based on Piagetian theory. Piaget's work sensitized psychologists and educators to the preschool child's potential for intellectual development, and it is not surprising that many have mined Piaget's writings to find implications for preschool programs. One of the best examples was developed by Constance Kamii and Rheta DeVries (1977).

Unlike many programs that claim Piagetian inspiration, this one did not try to teach the child to solve Piagetian problems such as the conservation of water or the class-inclusion problem of brown and wooden beads. Rather, these tasks were used only to ascertain the child's level of cognitive development. They were not regarded as inherently important cognitive accomplishments.

Kamii and DeVries wanted to encourage the processes of thinking and the classes of knowledge central to Piaget's view of intelligence. In contrast to the two language programs just described, their program focused on the reasoning and the knowledge that is expressed in language rather than on the development of a larger vocabulary and a more standard form of English.

The children chose rather freely among the traditional activities of nursery school (block building, art, pretend play, stories, sand and water play, puzzles, and so forth). The heart of the curriculum was based on the way the teacher directed the children's attention to certain features of objects or to relations among them and posed problems that stretched their thinking. Here is one example: the teacher put out a collection of wooden rods of different diameters, some flat wooden boards, and a few cardboard cartons. Her objective was to have the children use the rods to transport the boards or boxes. She began by asking the children what they might do with these objects. At first there was a good deal of experimenting: the children used the rods as drumsticks and swords, among other things; but then some children began to make a track out of the rods. More advanced four-year-olds selected rods of the same diameter, then took turns pushing themselves or their friends along the rods in a box or on a board (see Figure 13–1A). Younger pupils, however, made a track of rods of different sizes, as if the important goal were to fill up the space underneath a board (see Figure 13–1B). They did not realize that in order to achieve a smooth ride the board or box must slide over rods of the same diameter (Kamii and DeVries, 1977). In playing with this simple equipment, the children explored some logical and mathematical principles (the size of the rods, the necessity of similar diameters), examined questions of

Figure 13–1
In arranging rods to make a track so that a board could ride smoothly along, older preschool children grasped the idea that the rods needed to be of the same diameter and spaced regularly (A). Younger children in the group did not realize the spatial necessities involved in making a track. They used rods of different diameters and erroneously thought it was important to fill up all the space underneath the board (B).

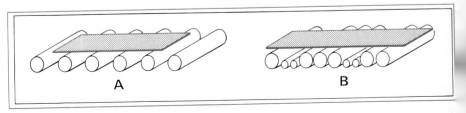

A

B

time and space (the relation between the spatial length of the track and the temporal length of the ride), and enriched their understanding of the physical world.

Observers often find it difficult to distinguish between a Piagetian preschool program and a more traditional nursery school because, on the surface, the activities are similar. The distinguishing feature of the Piagetian program is the teacher's continuing attempts to determine the child's thought processes and to act in accord with the child's level of logical and conceptual thought.

Elementary School: Project Follow-Through

As children from Head Start programs entered elementary school, many lost the advantages that they had secured while in the program, partly because schools made no effort to accommodate to their special needs. In order to consolidate the progress achieved by children while in Head Start programs, compensaory education widened its scope and experimented with a variety of programs in primary grades. We will concentrate here on a national compensatory program called Project Follow-Through. In Project Follow-Through, each school chose a program whose ideas seemed sympathetic and appropriate to the community's needs. Each educational program was adopted and used in a dozen or so schools in various parts of the country; parents and community leaders were involved in the program. It provided an unusual opportunity to assess contrasting programs in a variety of locations and involving a number of ethnic groups.

Project Follow-Through operated in kindergarten through third grade, and in its peak years included some eighty-two thousand children enrolled in schools in 172 locations. Let us look first at the kinds of programs that were offered and then try to evaluate them.

Individual programs in Project Follow-Through can be differentiated by a number of distinct features; nevertheless, all can be grouped into two primary types: *highly structured* (by the teacher) or *child-oriented*. One of the highly structured programs, modeled after the principles of Engelmann and Bereiter, tried to teach the academic skills that children require in school, using the direct drill methods described earlier in the preschool language program (Engelmann-Becker Follow-Through Model, University of Oregon). Another highly structured program, based on behavior modification principles, used tokens and systematic reinforcement to reward the children's progress in reading, language, writing, mathematics, and social behavior, in an approach similar to the one outlined in Chapter 11 (Behavior Analysis Approach, University of Kansas).

The child-oriented programs relied on the children's interests and initiative. The teachers set up a planned environment in which the curricula and materials, rather than the teacher's instructions, directed each child's attention to activities that would facilitate cognitive development. While each of the child-oriented programs has some particularly worthwhile features, the Responsive Education Program (Far West Laboratory, San Francisco) provides an especially good example of this approach. Successfully integrating concern for the child's attitudes and initiative with an emphasis on intellectual skills, it struck a balance between the teacher's direction and the student's initiative.

Close-up of a child-oriented program. The Responsive Education Program relied on creating a rich learning environment for the students rather than presenting subject matter in structured lessons. Initially the classrooms were organized into learning centers (called booths) for reading, mathematics, tape listening, science, and art. The children chose the activities that interested them and stayed with an activity as long as they wished; in this respect, the program was quite flexible. Booth attendants answered questions and let the children know immediately how well they had solved a particular problem. Over time these centers evolved into concept areas that transcended the original boundaries: for instance, a child reading about a girl making a paper boat, coating it with candle wax, and floating it in a pond would be encouraged to move to the science booth and try making a boat of her own to float in a pan of water.

The pace was directed by the child, while the materials were designed to provide definite direction in the studies. Some commercial teaching materials were used, but the program also tested some new learning tools, many in the form of games. The program emphasized problem solving as a means of developing the children's self-concept and intellectual skills, and the tools encouraged them to work out solutions that the teachers then verified or helped to modify.

The program did not concentrate on the deficiencies of children from poor and minority families, subtly urging them to behave more like middle-class students. Instead, it celebrated cultural differences in some of the teaching materials used, as well as through explicit directives to the teachers in booklets such as *Responding to Black Children* and *Mexican-Americans: A Handbook for Educators.*

Infancy Programs

Since compensatory preschool programs were only partially successful, some psychologists turned their attention to children in the earliest years of life, believing that intervention during infancy and very early childhood might prevent some of the difficulties that later hindered four-year-olds.

Infancy programs are based on a general theory of stimulation: colors, shapes, sounds, and motions are used to accelerate the children's development at several levels. Tutors provide increased tactile stimulation for infants under a year by rocking and jouncing the babies in a friendly way. They provide visual and auditory stimulation by hanging bright mobiles over their cribs or attaching music boxes with a pull-string that the infant can reach. One project put striped mittens on infants a few months old so that they would "discover" their hands ahead of schedule (White, 1971).

As the children grow older, tutors take them in strollers for walks to the grocery store, the zoo, or the library, where they look at picture books. Children from one to three years of age have participated in some of the activities that characterize preschool programs for three- and four-year-olds: singing songs, reciting nursery rhymes, listening to records, playing with puzzles, blocks, finger painting, stringing beads, handling clay, sorting buttons; and identifying pictures of animals. And from the earliest age language stimulation has been an important aspect of infant programs: the tutors talk to the children (even before they are old enough to answer), taking care to use names of objects and actions as the child experiences them.

In some cases tutors work in the home setting (Gordon, Guinagh, and Jester, 1977; Schaefer and Aaronson, 1977). Others work with children who attend day-care centers (Lally and Honig, 1977).

Frequently tutors work with parents to help them learn more constructive ways of stimulating their children cognitively. Increasingly, programs have included parent support in addition to parent education. One long-range project now underway in Massachusetts, the Brookline Early Education Project, is examining the effects of a planned support system for families. The staff acts as a resource for families. They make weekly or monthly visits to homes, and the families visit the center with their infants, although there is no direct tutoring of children (Pierson, 1974).

These programs are designed to produce long-term, rather than immediate, effects of intervention. Most significantly, they extend the notion of education to very young children.

Evaluating Intervention Programs

How should we evaluate programs that attempt to improve a child's chance of academic success? The I.Q. score is one obvious index. Although it is a fallible guide to all aspects of competence, it is nevertheless useful in predicting the likelihood that a child will perform well on academic tasks. Standardized achievement tests are another objective measure for children already in school. Motivation, interest, and expectancy of success are less amenable to precise measurement but should nevertheless be considered in an evaluation.

Most often, evaluations of effectiveness are made by the people who are implementing their own programs; comparisons among different programs by more impartial investigators are less frequent. Two exceptions are seen in studies of compensatory preschool programs and of Project Follow-Through.

One study compared preschool children from four different types of Head Start programs and followed them for three years afterwards, through the second grade. All the children were from economically deprived families in Louisville, Kentucky. Two classes participated in programs based on the theories of educator Maria Montessori, emphasizing development of the senses, conceptual development, competence in daily activity, character development, and self-direction, all in a quiet and orderly atmosphere. Four classes were characterized by traditional enrichment, four used Bereiter-Engelmann programs, and four more took part in a program called Darcee, which, like Bereiter-Engelmann, focused on language and conceptual improvements and tried to develop attitudes conducive to academic achievement in a structured atmosphere. In addition to these fourteen classes, a control group of children not participating in a preschool program was also evaluated.

The findings showed that the two structured programs, Darcee and Bereiter-Engelmann, produced greater gains on the Stanford-Binet I.Q. test than either the Montessori or general enrichment programs. Over the next three years, however, after the programs had ended, there was a steady decline in I.Q. for the children in all the groups; the sharpest decline was for those who had been in Bereiter-Engelmann classes. In general, the I.Q. gains of the children in the Head Start programs had disappeared by the time they were in the second grade (Miller and Dyer, 1975).

An evaluation of seven programs in Project Follow-Through found that different goals and methods apparently produce different results. The two highly structured and academically oriented programs generally produced higher reading and mathematics scores than did the five more flexible programs. The more time spent in such instruction (in either direct drill or behavior modification programs), the higher the achievement test performance, suggesting that a highly structured program aimed at specific academic skills is the best choice if improvement in those skills is the primary goal.

More flexible classrooms, on the other hand, produced lower absence rates, more initiation of conversation on the part of the children, and more independent activity (both academic and nonacademic) than did the structured classrooms. This effect was in accord with the aims of these flexible, child-oriented programs, whose sponsors believed that greater responsibility and more independent

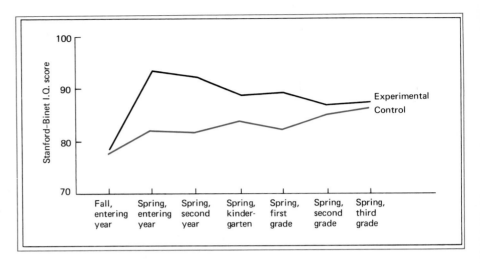

Figure 13–2
Children who participated in a preschool program with cognitive emphasis obtained significantly higher scores on the Stanford-Binet I.Q. test than children in a control group. This superior functioning, however, disappeared by the third grade. (After Weikart, 1971)

activity in the earlier grades would, in the long run, produce better school performance later. It should be pointed out, however, that the study had no way of ascertaining whether children in these five programs would continue their independent and self-initiating styles in later years and in other circumstances. In short, although discussion will continue regarding the most important gains to effect in children who are likely to fail, this study suggests that some correspondence can be expected between a particular method and a particular outcome (Stallings, 1975).

Moreover, the two studies cited confirm that what happens in classrooms seems to make a difference. In recent years several investigations have suggested that schooling does not matter very much—that a child's family and socioeconomic background are the only irrevocably decisive factors determining his future. These reports, by contrast, imply that school experience can have an important impact on the child, even if the family's influence is primary.

To sum up, programs that focus primarily on raising I.Q. scores of preschool children are successful in improving cognitive abilities of young children while they are in the program (see Figure 13–2) and tend to produce gains in linguistic skills and higher scores on achievement tests when the children enter the first grade. But unfortunately, after children graduate from the program and spend a few years in elementary school, their test scores decline, while those of middle-class children rise. By the fourth or fifth grade, their scores are not very different from those of children from the same social class and ethnic group who did not participate in the compensatory program.

We can infer that these programs primarily familiarized the child with some of the information being asked on I.Q. test questions, enabled him to establish rapport with strange adults, and temporarily increased his motivation to do well on tests—but did not produce a fundamental change in cognitive capacity. A good program may owe some of its success to its ability to reduce a child's anxieties. When the teacher stays with the group all the time, the children get a chance to know her and feel comfortable with her. Even children who attend a nursery school that has no special program learn to feel at ease with a teacher and other children, become familiar with tests and games, and often display higher I.Q.'s than comparable children who do not attend nursery school (Zigler and Butterfield, 1968).

But intellectual abilities are dynamic, not static, and must be consistently nurtured and stimulated. Hence, the findings can also be interpreted to mean that the programs temporarily improved some of the cognitive competences of children, but not permanently: when the programs stopped, the rate of growth in these talents slowed. This is not an unreasonable conclusion. Consider this analogy: a child needs a certain number of calories to grow optimally. If the child who has been malnourished for two years is put on an improved diet, she begins to gain weight and to grow taller. But if the extra nutrition is withdrawn and she is returned to her old diet, her rate of growth will slow significantly. Thus a conscientious and informed preschool program may indeed improve some cognitive abilities, but a two- to three-year part-time program cannot be expected to have a permanent effect.

Moreover, while intervention programs may or may not improve a child's cognitive abilities, that is not their only function. Some claim that it is not even the most important one. Head Start tacitly subscribed to other aims: improving health care, bringing black and white children into contact, and drawing parents closer to the classroom by using them as teacher's aides. Unfortunately, these less tangible goals are difficult to measure, and it is not known how well they were achieved. But if Head Start was even partially successful in these areas, the effort would seem to have been worthwhile.

Children from poor families are not alone in needing special help in school. Any group of children is characterized by a wide range of abilities, academic strengths, motivations, preferred methods of solving problems, and rates of progress. As educators have realized just how many fine distinctions exist among children, the line between the average child and the one with special needs has become less distinct. Each child has a special profile of strengths and weaknesses. Schools continue to struggle with an issue raised in Chapter 1: how to provide optimal education for each child. How can education be tailored to meet individual needs?

Adapting Education to Individual Differences

Before education can be adapted to individual differences, it is obviously necessary to identify the ways in which children vary. One variation involves *aptitude*—the degree to which a child is prepared to learn a new skill. Presumably, different forms of instruction can be "matched" to children with different aptitudes, but so far extensive attempts to achieve this kind of matching have not turned up many useful suggestions (Bracht, 1970; Cronbach and Snow, 1969).

Children also vary in their motivation. Can the teacher, or the instructional materials, improve motivation in a child? Behavior modification programs, described in Chapter 11, attempt to change motivation through a systematic use of rewards; and as discussed in Chapter 7, teachers increase the chances of focusing a child's attention on the work when they are able to identify and teach to his individual hierarchy of motives.

One of the most clearly observable differences among children is the rate at which they learn school skills. In a traditional classroom the teacher wants to be sure that most of the students have mastered a step before moving on to the next one. But in every class two groups are likely to suffer from this procedure: students who need more time to master what is being taught and students who master it quickly and are eager to move ahead. Rate of learning is not an entirely independent factor; for any child, it seems to be a function of how much time the child is *willing to spend* working (which is another way of describing motivation) and how much time the child *actually needs* in order to learn the task (which is an index of aptitude).

Nevertheless, one way to adapt to individual differences is to directly address the characteristic learning rate—without inquiring too deeply into how the child's motivation may be improved or aptitudes modified. Under the name *mastery learning*, this approach is being used with promising results.

The Theory behind Mastery Learning

Let us assume that the material to be learned in a particular unit is inherently structured into a hierarchy. To give some simple examples: in order to count to one hundred, children must first be able to count to ten; in order to spell words, they must first know how to write individual letters. In Chapter 8, you will recall, we described Gagné's concept of chain learning, in which one concept depends on the mastery of a previous one, or an item of knowledge requires some previous knowledge. In other words, learning more complex tasks depends upon first learning some simple tasks that are components of the larger unit.

Research can suggest whether or not a particular body of material has a hierarchical organization. Suppose you give a group of people a test on tasks taken from what you presume to be different positions in the hierarchy (some complex, some less complex, some simple). Anyone who passes a task of intermediate complexity will also pass all the tasks that come before it; that is, all the tasks that are "simple." On the other hand, once a person begins to fail tasks at a particular point in the hierarchy, he will not be able to pass more difficult tasks. Another strategy is to teach a presumably simple task, and test to see if the student later transfers that learning to a more complicated task.

In developing a mastery learning program, the specific material to be learned is first analyzed carefully to see what relations exist among the tasks and which steps are prerequisite to others. Then, wherever possible, the material is ordered into a hierarchical sequence where the simplest and most fundamental steps appear first and lead to more complex ones. Obviously, some academic materials are highly conducive to this kind of ordering, others are not. Mathematics, for instance, can be far more easily and honestly arranged sequentially than can social studies or art appreciation. Once the material has been analyzed systematically and arranged sequentially, a method must be developed for assessing at what point each student should appropriately enter the sequence, so that instruction can begin at the level above those steps that have been mastered. This placement permits children to receive credit for material they know and to progress, without wasting time on familiar tasks, to new material. Then, instruction should be arranged so that children can work either alone or in small groups, allowing members of the class to work at many different levels simultaneously and permitting most children to proceed independently with their work while the teacher is occupied with a small group. In addition to sequenced learning steps, therefore, the design requires materials that the children can work on without moment-to-moment guidance from the teacher.

Finally, just as diagnosis of the appropriate point for entering the instructional sequence is required, some form of assessment is necessary to determine when a student is ready to move on from one level of the sequence to the next.

A number of attempts have been made to apply these theoretical principles to practical elementary-school curricula. Individually Prescribed Instruction, or IPI (Lindvall and Bolvin, 1967), and Primary Education Project, or PEP (Resnick, Wang, and Rosner, 1977), both developed at the University of Pittsburg, use a series of pretests and posttests to ascertain where children should begin in the instructional sequence and when they are ready to move on. Teaching tools include some commercial materials in adapted forms but also many items specifically designed to fit into the sequence and instruct on particular tasks. Although PEP and IPI differ in some details of emphasis, they share important features. Let us examine the details of PEP to see a mastery program in practice.

PEP: A Mastery Approach to Primary Skills

For the sake of convenience, students in PEP programs are grouped roughly according to age: five- and six-year-olds, seven- and eight-year-olds, nine- and ten-year-olds. At the end of every school year, some children can be expected to move on to the next group. But this chronological boundary does not imply boundaries in schoolwork. In traditional classrooms it is assumed that certain skills and topics will be covered in the first grade, others in the second, and so forth. Accordingly, the closing days in June find most teachers preoccupied with which students have reached the finish line and which have lagged behind (to say nothing of those who had finished a month before). Since a major feature of the mastery approach is an insistence on an individual rate of progress, as opposed to an average group rate, PEP curriculum sequences reflect long-term development and ignore grade lines. Thus an extremely bright six-year-old pupil may master all the skills and content traditionally taught during the first three years of school in one year, while a slow student may take two or three years to acquire the abilities mastered by the "average" child in one year.

Let us look at a *quantification curriculum* (see Figure 13–3) to see how an actual sequence planned for primary-grade children looks. This

OBJECTIVES OF THE QUANTIFICATION CURRICULUM

	Given:	The child can:
Units 1 and 2 Counting and One-to-One Correspondence	A. Sets of up to 5 objects or up to 10 objects B. Set of moveable objects C. Fixed ordered set of objects D. Fixed unordered set of objects E. A numeral stated and a set of objects F. A numeral stated and several sets of fixed objects G. Two sets of objects H. Two unequal sets of objects I. Two unequal sets of objects	A. Recite the numerals in order B. Count the objects moving them out of the set as he counts C. Count the objects D. Count the objects E. Count out a subset of stated size F. Select a set of size indicated by numeral G. Pair objects and state whether the sets are equivalent H. Pair objects and state which set has more I. Pair objects and state which set has less

	Given	The child can:
Units 3 and 4 Numerals	A. Two sets of numerals B. A numeral stated, and a set of printed numerals C. A numeral (written) D. Several sets of objects and several numerals E. Two numerals (written) F. A set of numerals G. Numerals stated	A. Match the numerals B. Select the stated numeral C. Read the numeral D. Match numerals with appropriate sets E. State which shows more (less) F. Place them in order G. Write the numeral
Unit 5 Comparison of Sets	A. Two sets of objects B. Two sets of objects C. A set of objects and a numeral D. A numeral and several sets of objects A set of objects and several numerals E. Two rows of objects (not paired) F. Three sets of objects	A. Count sets and state which has more objects or that sets have same number B. Count sets and state which has less objects C. State which shows more (less) D. Select sets which are more (less) the the numeral Select numerals which show more (less) than the set of objects E. State which row has more regardless of arrangement F. Count sets and state which has most (least)
Unit 6 Seriation and Ordinal Position	A. Three objects of different sizes B. Objects of graduated sizes C. Several sets of objects D. Ordered set of objects	A. Select the largest (smallest) B. Seriate according to size C. Seriate the sets according to size of objects D. Name the ordinal position of the objects
Unit 7 Addition and Subtraction (sums to 10)	A. Two numbers stated, set of objects, and directions to add B. Two numbers stated, set of objects, and directions to subtract C. Two numbers stated, number line, and directions to add D. Two numbers stated, number line, and directions to subtract E. Addition and subtraction word problems F. Written addition and subtraction problems in the form: x or x $$\underline{+y} \quad \underline{-y}$$ G. Addition and subtraction problems in the form: $x + y =$ or $x - y =$	A. Add the numbers by counting out two subsets then combining and stating combined number as sum B. Count out smaller subset from larger and state remainder C. Use the number line to determine sum D. Use number line to subtract E. Solve the problems F. Complete the problems G. Complete the equations

Figure 13–3
In this section of a quantification curriculum, each unit is divided into a series of objectives. The center column states components of the objective, while the righthand column describes, in terms of behavior, what the child who has mastered the objective can do. Some tasks are prerequisite to others (reciting numerals in order up to ten is a prerequisite to counting objects up to ten), but in some cases steps may be skipped and students may take different paths to reach the same objective. (Adapted from Resnick, Wang, and Rosner, 1977, pp. 224–25)

part of the plan is divided into seven component units. Each step of mastery is stated in terms of behavior: what the child will be able to *do*.

Some tasks are prerequisite to others, as you will notice if you study units 1 and 2 in the chart in Figure 13–3: A (recite up to 10) is prerequisite to B (count objects). But the tasks are not strictly linear. After mastering the first two steps, the pupil may proceed to C (count a fixed ordered set of objects) and then to D (count a fixed unordered set of objects), or she may skip C and D and go to E (count out a subset of a stated size). Either the A-B-C-D path or the A-B-E one will permit the pupil to master F (select a set of the size indicated by a stated numeral).

PEP classrooms are not "open" in the sense that the children are completely free to choose what to work on. But the process operates according to a series of contracts arranged between teacher and student. At the beginning of each session, children receive assignments (they may also help to establish them) that they must complete in a specified time, to be negotiated with the teacher. They can choose which assignments to work on first, however, and what order to work on them. When the work is completed, the children are free to choose another activity. Along with individualized instruction, self-scheduling permits greater flexibility in managing work, and as a result, fewer behaviors are seen as problems. Two children can talk quietly about a movie they saw over the weekend before they begin working without disturbing a group session. Self-scheduling satisfies most pupils. When occasionally a child flounders within this plan, teachers act to provide more structured direction. Self-scheduling also satisfies teachers and, especially, two types of parents: those who had thought their children were not learning enough and now see an increase in skills mastered, and those who had thought school was too rigid and now see their children in charge of managing much of their own work.

PEP is successful in teaching the stated skills, although, naturally, children display different profiles and do not all progress uniformly. Figure 13–4 shows the profile of one child, Roy, as he progressed through a quantification curriculum.

Some Limits to Mastery Learning

The mastery learning approach was developed to adapt to different rates of learning among individual students. Measured against that criterion, it has proven successful.

Furthermore, in permitting the child considerable freedom both in pace and in choice of material and in helping the child to feel an increasing sense of confidence, this approach achieves highly desirable benefits of another kind: the classroom atmosphere tends to be harmonious and constructive.

Nevertheless, there are limits to this approach. First, as we have indicated, mastery learning programs have been most successful in subject areas that have an inherently hierarchical pattern. In PEP, one

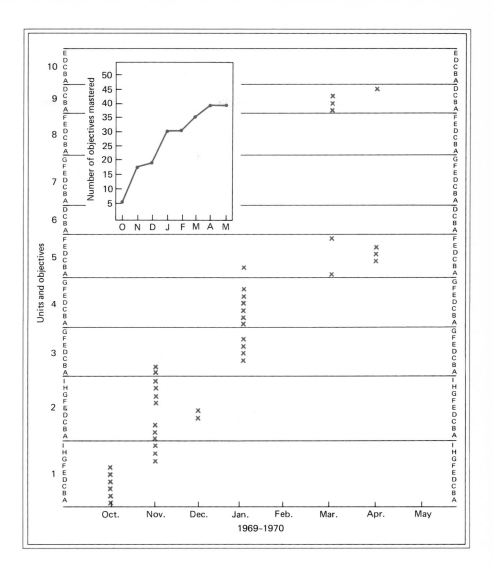

Figure 13–4
The large chart shows the profile of one child, Roy, as he mastered particular tasks in a quantification curriculum. (The inset graph shows Roy's general rate of progress in the same period.) In October he began unit 1 and mastered tasks A through F by the end of the month. In November he mastered G, H, and I, completing unit 1, and began unit 2. He mastered A, B, and C and had a difficult time with D and E, which he did not finish until December, but in the meantime he completed F, G, H, and I and went on to begin unit 3. Notice that he never mastered 3G or 4G, both of which ask the child to write numerals, indicating that he probably had difficulty with motor control (earlier tasks show that he knew the numbers). In that case, he need not be slowed down; he could go to a box with numeral cards or rubber stamps, pick out the right one, and use it to answer. Unit 5 apparently also presented some difficulty, as February and March passed before he completed all the tasks. But in the meantime he jumped to unit 9 (units 7 and 8 were suspended in this class). (After Resnick, Wang, and Kaplan, 1973)

instructional sequence involves mathematics skills. Another concerns an early reading sequence that uses a workbook and readers, tapes, letter cards, group storybooks, games, and special activities with a teacher. Not all academic material is so amenable to sequenced instruction. Literature and social studies, for example, are difficult to arrange into a hierarchy, as are advanced reading comprehension abilities. Although a hierarchy might conceivably be imposed on these areas, it would force the content into arbitrary patterns and reduce much of the subtlety that enriches less easily organized material.

Second, since mastery learning programs utilize individual work and self-instruction for most of the teaching, they are, again, more suitable for some subjects than for others. In a subject that depends on teacher-guided interaction in a group (social studies might be an example), mastery procedures would be more difficult to arrange.

Computer-assisted Instruction

In certain instances, the use of machines can significantly enhance the efficiency of instruction. The computer is one of the most promising examples of "hardware technology" with a potential for improving education.

Computers have a number of capabilities that make them suitable as educational tools, To illustrate, let us consider a student participating in a computer-assisted instruction (CAI) program in mathematics. The

student—imagine a nine- or ten-year-old girl—sits down in front of a computer console, which is likely to look something like a television screen with a typewriter keyboard attached (although a number of other kinds of consoles may be used). She types in her name and perhaps an identifying number that she regularly uses when working on CAI. With this information the computer is able to locate her "file"—that is, all the information on how she has performed previously, whether during instructional sessions or on tests. On the basis of this past history, the computer selects and presents a lesson, perhaps in multiplication. A problem is displayed on the screen along with a demonstration of how to solve it. A new problem is then presented, and the child must respond. She types in her answer, which is correct. The computer responds with a typed message that says something like "Great! You got that one!" Then it selects another problem, probably a little more difficult, since the previous answer was correct. This time the girl makes an error. The computer recognizes the error, types out a message that tells her she is wrong, suggests where the difficulty may lie, and asks her to try again. On the next attempt she is correct, and after another "that's right" message, the computer goes on to select a third problem—but probably *not* one of greater difficulty, in light of the error the girl just made.

Several important things are happening during this exchange. First, the computer responds to the girl's answers item by item—she does not practice on a set of problems, turn them in, and then wait a day or two to find out how she did. As a result, she is less likely to persist in an incorrect solution pattern. Second, the computer responds quickly—a good way to maintain her interest. Third, the computer adapts its performance demands at several levels. The difficulty level of the lesson as a whole is chosen according to the child's past performance. In addition, within the lesson specific items are selected according to her present performance, so that harder problems appear as the girl demonstrates that she can do easier ones, and easier ones are selected when she is having a difficult time. Finally, the computer continually reviews items or classes of items that perplex the child and drops out of the review set any items that are well learned. These are accommodations that a teacher would not be able to achieve while working with a class. Even when working alone with a child, a teacher has difficulty keeping track of responses in as much detail as the computer can. Still, a teacher compensates in other ways—probing for the reasons for the girl's response, providing personal encouragement, perhaps reminding her of a similar problem yesterday. Thus, when planning where to use computers in an instructional program, teachers must take into account the emotional needs of the child as well as the academic goals.

Some people who work in CAI (for example, Atkinson, 1968; Suppes and Morningstar, 1972) distinguish between *drill programs* and *tutorial programs.* Drill programs assume that a teacher handles the conceptual teaching of a new topic, while the computer provides the opportunity for drill and practice. In tutorial programs the computer provides the basic introduction to a topic as well as the practice sessions.

The Stanford CAI arithmetic programs—among the best-developed and most widely used drill programs—arose out of a project at Stanford University that used computer facilities as the basis for providing individual practice on the computational skills customarily taught in grades one through six (Suppes, Jerman, and Brian, 1968; Suppes and Morningstar, 1972). The designers presupposed that practice in basic addition, subtraction, multiplication, and division, as well as in the more complex operations that used these skills in combination, was essential if children were to become competent in performing computational tasks. The designers also assumed that drill should proceed from easier to more difficult problems, include an element of speed, and strive for a high and lasting degree of accuracy.

The Stanford programs, like most standard school mathematics curricula, included practice in all the basic arithmetic skills at levels of difficulty appropriate to different age groups. But because they used the computer as a medium for practice, they provided a unique opportunity to study drill at its most effective.

To give an idea of the way a computer can maximize the effectiveness of a drill exercise, let us describe briefly how the programs worked, from the point of view of the child and the teacher. One or more computer terminals was made available to students in or near each participating classroom. Each child was scheduled to go to the terminal once a day to spend from five to fifteen minutes solving problems presented by the computer. The drill materials were organized into *concept blocks,* each designed to be completed in three to twelve days, that supplemented similar content taught in a textbook series. Within each concept block the computer was able to present problems at five levels of difficulty; it could make a decision based on an individual child's performance on his pretest score. On succeeding days the level of difficulty was adjusted according to the child's practice score on the previous day. Children who scored between 60 and 79 percent remained at the same level; those who scored 80 percent or above moved to the next hardest level; and those who scored below 60 percent were given easier problems. Review drills were chosen by the computer so that all children had extra practice on the material with which they were having greatest difficulty.

This CAI form of arithmetic drill contrasts with traditional paper-and-pencil drill in several important ways. First, as we saw with the girl at the console, the computer gives immediate feedback on every response a child makes. Not only does it store information on errors in order to make a decision for tomorrow's work and for future review lessons, it also tells the child how well he is doing today. If an answer is correct, the computer prints out a message that says so; if a child gives the wrong answer, the computer tells him so, lets the child try again, and after a certain number of tries prints out the correct answer. The computer's immediate responsiveness is one of its assets. Further, if a child is taking too long to solve a particular problem, the computer gives a "time is up" signal to encourage the child to work at a faster pace.

A second advantage of computerized drill is that it allows practice to be precisely individualized. Even though all children in a class work on the same general set of concepts, the specific problems presented to children are adjusted daily to their own performance levels. This individualization means that students are neither overwhelmed with problems that are too hard, nor bored with problems that are too easy.

Third, all drill is private; the student at the computer cannot become the butt of jokes and comments by classmates who think him "slow" or "dumb."

A fourth advantage concerns time. Children spend only a few minutes a day at the computerized drill program, much less than they may spend in comparable classroom-style paper-and-pencil drill. For the teacher the saving in time is even greater, since there is no need to correct endless drill papers. Yet the information about student progress that the teacher needs for planning classroom and individual instruction is available, collected and tabulated by the computer, and it is extensive. This information is also a rich source of data for investigators who want to understand what features of arithmetic problems make them harder or easier to solve and what processes children use as they solve computational problems of various kinds.

Evaluating Computer Programs

The Stanford programs sought to provide maximally effective drill and practice. How successful were they in this effort? Data gathered during the most intensive period of study were used to analyze the performance of almost four thousand children in grades one through six from selected sites in four different states. Comparisons were made of the Stanford Achievement Test (SAT) scores of children who had participated in the CAI program and control groups who simply received standard classroom instruction. On most sections of the SAT test and in most grades, the CAI children improved significantly more than did the control children. This was true even for tests that stressed concepts and applications rather than strictly computational skills (Suppes and Morningstar, 1972). And this effect was obtained with only eight months of work and only five to eight minutes per day at the computer.

But what if the control classes had had supplementary paper-and-pencil drill? Through an unforeseen set of events, the study of the Stanford programs was able to provide an answer to this question as well. In the course of the evaluation, one of the control schools was so dismayed by its low pretest scores that it initiated its own paper-and-pencil drill sessions. *Children who had this extra work for eight months actually did better on the posttest than the CAI children.* Other more recent, deliberately planned evaluations of CAI versus paper-and-pencil drill programs corroborate that finding (Jacobson, 1975). However, these control children had to put in twenty-five minutes per day of extra work, compared to the five-to-eight minute computer sessions, and the teacher had to spend extra time grading their papers. Nevertheless, these results suggest that it was practice in general, not necessarily practice on a computer terminal, that led to improved performance. The computer can make drill and practice easier and more palatable to both children and teachers. But many of the benefits of drill can be made available without technological devices.

The Stanford group also designed a program in early reading instruction that has been used in a number of schools. The program is tutorial in that it provides the initial instruction as well as drill, and it teaches both decoding and comprehension skills. Children spend about half an hour a day on the program and seem to make progress comparable to normal school progress—but they require less instructional time. An especially interesting feature is that the program appears to help boys perform as well as girls on early reading, despite the fact that with most conventional instruction, boys perform less well. Apparently, the idea of using a machine motivates the boys more than standard classroom work does (Fletcher, in press).

Although programs such as these have already seen actual school use and evaluation, computer-assisted instruction on a wide scale is still a promise for the future rather than a present reality. As computers become less expensive and cumbersome and as computer programing techlology becomes even more sophisticated, we can probably expect to see CAI play an increasingly prominent role in the educational system.

The Gifted Child

When we say a child is *gifted*, what do we mean? The word suffers from the same ambiguity as the word *retarded*, and defining it involves the same problems noted in our discussion of absolute versus relative retardation in Chapter 10. If we let the score on the I.Q. test be the criterion for identifying gifted children (and this is typically the case), then we are using a relative standard. Some children attain very high I.Q. scores—in the top 1 percent—without showing a qualitatively

unique talent in any special area. They have a larger vocabulary, read faster, and learn arithmetic more easily than their classmates, but the differences between them and the average child seem to be a matter of degree, not quality. On the other hand, a very small group of children possess a special talent, or even talents, that are of a substantially different quality from those of their peers. Some have rare artistic ability. Others display remarkable skill in music, mathematics, or science. Sometimes these children also have very high I.Q.'s, but not always. Moreover, it is more common to find a child with a special talent in one area, or perhaps two, than to find one who is gifted in several areas.

Changing Attitudes toward Gifted Children

The second quarter of this century saw a rising concern about children who had superior intellectual ability, and educators made efforts to provide special programs for them. Children were diagnosed as gifted on the basis of a very high I.Q. score (usually above 130, which placed them in the top 1 percent of all children their age) or a conspicuous talent or talents in art, mathematics, science, music, poetry, or composition. Parents and teachers recognized that such exceptional talent was rare and agreed that special educational experiences should be provided for these children. Either they were given supplementary work and opportunities to enrich their curriculum in a regular classroom or else they were segregated in a special school or classroom. One of the most famous schools for gifted children was Hunter Elementary School in New York City, where admission was restricted to children with very high I.Q.'s.

A famous longitudinal study of gifted children was begun in the early 1900s by Lewis Terman. You will remember him as one of the designers of the American version of the Binet intelligence tests. Elementary-school children from California whose I.Q.'s were above 140 were followed through middle age (Terman, 1930). It was found that, contrary to some myths, these talented children were not more neurotic, disturbed, or unhappy than average children. In fact, they were psychologically healthier. They led active social lives and went to college, where they typically attained B averages. Compared to the rest of the population, they were more successful in their careers and had happier marriages. These findings supported America's general admiration for talented people. Communities were willing to invest time and money to guarantee that gifted children could actualize their talents to the fullest.

Then a strange thing began to happen as the mood in the nation changed. America became self-conscious about the academic problems of the children of poor and ethnic minorities. Many citizens began to feel guilty about spending money for a few middle-class children with high I.Q. scores, while several million lower-class children with low I.Q. scores were doing poorly in school. During the 1960s, when the trend against privilege and elitism increased, the skepticism about programs for gifted children deepened. The celebration of egalitarianism generated a resistance to institutional practices that enhanced the status of a few. Gradually, the earlier interest in gifted children was diluted, and communities disbanded classes for them. By 1970 it had become increasingly difficult to find programs for intellectually talented children.

Philosophically, there need not be an inconsistency between providing equal educational opportunities for all children and special opportunities for gifted children. After all, it is widely accepted that if poor children start school at a disadvantage, every effort should be made—and special programs provided, extra cost notwithstanding—to help them catch up. Furthermore, if these children prove to be exceptionally able, they should be given the chance to excel. One would not ask them to arrest their progress just because they reached an "average" level. Nor should we ask the child who enters school with an exceptional talent to suppress it in order to conform to the performance of his peers. Ideally, each child should be enabled to reach as high as he or she can. That is the true meaning of "equal opportunity."

In practice, of course, we do not always adhere to the principles of egalitarianism. Indeed, if we did, we would have to disband athletic scholarships and the football games on New Year's Day because the talented athletes who participate in these activities, like students with exceptional mathematical skills, are given special privileges. Probably we have resisted that step toward "equality" because athletes are more likely to come from lower- and middle-class families, while the intellectually talented are more likely to come from upper-middle-class families. Since as a nation we have been trying to reduce the gap in power, wealth, and status between the social classes, people have been more receptive to abandoning educational advantages for gifted students.

There is more to a talented child than potential status and power as an adult, however. Neglecting gifted children has two disadvantages. It prevents these children from perfecting their abilities, thus depriving them and their families of the gratification that comes from creative intellectual work. More important, it deprives society of the full realization of talents that may create great music, art, medical discoveries, and technical inventions. In short, our society cannot afford to waste or lose its human resources any more than it can afford to lose its natural resources.

Fortunately, attitudes are changing. The federal government has set up the Office of the Gifted and Talented, which has sponsored a series of leadership training seminars in forty-eight states and allocated funds to states and local school districts to use in programs for gifted children.

Traditionally, there have been two kinds of programs: *enrichment* and *acceleration*. Enrichment programs augment course material by providing extra reading; exposure to filmstrips and video tapes; encounters with professionals from particular fields, who come to the

---

The funding difficulties of programs for exceptionally talented children, which reflect the country's skepticism about promoting efforts for an elite group, are illustrated in the story told by Dr. James J. Gallagher, director of the Frank Porter Graham Child Development Center of the University of North Carolina. A school board was confronted with a request for extra money for expensive equipment, extensive transportation, and special teachers for a select group of students. The students were to be released from part of the school day to pursue their particular area of interest. It was just the kind of request that runs into resistance, and the school board was inclined to turn it down as doing too much for one group until it found out which group of "gifted" students was to benefit: the varsity football team (Maeroff, 1976).

school; and independent study projects. Often children are taken out of their regular classes and brought together with other gifted children for a part of the school day or during the weekend. The Talcott Mountain Science Center, for instance, located on a mountain top outside Hartford, Connecticut, is a Saturday enrichment program that draws students from all over the state. The center screens students nominated by their schools and offers instruction in astronomy, meteorology, geology, and computer mathematics.

Radical Acceleration

Although enrichment programs may fulfill the intellectual needs of most bright students, they may fail to challenge a few, extremely able ones. For those whose precocity is demonstrated in mathematics and physical science, acceleration may be a preferred choice.

Strategies for optimizing educational challenges for such students are outlined in a study of several junior-high-school boys who skipped high school and entered Johns Hopkins University (Stanley, 1974). In 1969 a professor at the university, Julian C. Stanley, learned about an eighth-grade boy, "David," who showed a remarkable knowledge of computers. When tested, his scores on some standard verbal and mathematics aptitude tests compared favorably with scores of freshmen entering John Hopkins, while his scores on more difficult tests exceeded those of most entering freshmen. Although a perceptive math teacher had helped him to complete a two-semester course in college algebra, trigonometry, analytic geometry, and some calculus (David had studied at night, without credit, at a nearby state college), the local high schools, both public and private, were not flexible enough to consider letting him take advanced senior math, chemistry, or physics.

Consulting with David's parents, Stanley considered the problems that might arise from enrolling David at the university. Would the college atmosphere prove too demanding or frustrating for a shy boy? Would the work habits of an eight-grader be able to sustain the workload of a college freshman? With no other alternative available, however, David entered Johns Hopkins in September, 1969, taking only subjects in which he was most interested and most competent: honors calculus, sophomore general physics, and basic computer science. He continued to take difficult courses as he went through college, but he felt he was enjoying the best of both worlds—a home community and a selective university—and was graduated with a 3.4 grade-point average.

David had been a conscientious, studious eighth-grader. "Bill," a second candidate for radical acceleration, had begun to rebel against work that he correctly saw as unprofitable and was alienated from other boys his age who resented his long hair and intellectual conversation. Proceeding cautiously, Stanley wrote to the high-school principal describing Bill's unusual abilities in math and science and suggesting that he be allowed to take advanced courses when he entered the ninth grade. After the principal rejected most of the suggestions. Bill entered Johns Hopkins at age thirteen, taking honors calculus, physics, and computer science. His average for the first semester was 3.75. Bill's social maladjustment in junior high school proved to have been situational. He made friends on campus and in the Sierra Club, where he found students who shared his interest in hiking and mountain climbing.

A related Johns Hopkins program has searched out unusually able students throughout the state of Maryland. Standardized tests were administered to 954 seventh- and eighth-graders in the upper 2 percent of their grades, and the top scorers—about 6 percent of the group—were invited to Johns Hopkins for further testing. While college-level tests for junior-high-school students would devastate many, it is important to bear in mind that these are not merely "bright" students, but a handful of highly exceptional ones. Only very difficult tests can differentiate their abilities. Typical grade-level tests do not provide a high enough ceiling for such students, who may find themselves grouped with other able but less exceptional classmates in the 99th percentile and still find their schoolwork insufficiently challenging.

Problems arise when young, highly precocious adolescents are confined to a traditional school setting. Not all of them can be advantageously enrolled in college, for some are not able to make the adjustment at their age. This factor cannot be ignored; but if the student is mature, he will benefit from the challenge of advanced work in a more adult setting. Although some research is under way at Johns Hopkins to study verbally precocious students, advanced study in the humanities may require the deepening social awarenes that comes with age and experience. So far, acceleration appears to be most appropriate for students gifted in mathematics and science.

Creativity

Although interest in gifted children goes back at least half a century, interest in the creative child is more recent and has a different flavor. After 1960 our beliefs began to turn against close conformity to convention, acquiescience to authority, and control of emotional expression, adopting a more permissive attitude toward harmless disobedience and encouraging a freer expression of feeling. As nonconformity in daily behavior became acceptable, so did nonconformity in intellectual products. Educators, along with parents, began to regard novel intellectual work as desirable. Gradually, novelty became equated with creativity, and a six-year-old who drew a man with four legs rather than two or painted a broken toy when asked to draw a Christmas scene was regarded as creative. These shifting attitudes in the school, of course, reflected a change in society, where artists were often labeled creative simply because their work was novel.

Components of Creativity

While producing a more liberated atmosphere, these developments were not entirely fortunate, for although novelty is one characteristic of a creative product, it is not the only—nor the most important—quality. A creative intellectual product has at least two other attributes. First, it is a constructive and appropriate solution to a problem. Many novel ideas are not constructive solutions: a lecturer with laryngitis standing in front of a large assembly can dismiss the audience and go home—certainly a novel action, but not very constructive or appropriate. As an alternative, he may invite someone in the audience to read his prepared speech; that response has a creative flavor.

Second, a creative product fuses known elements and facts into a new and coherent synthesis. The rearrangement of known facts into a new pattern satisfies aesthetically because it is simpler and more efficient. Packing a piece of luggage can be a useful metaphor. The person has arranged the contents in such a way that the bag will not close easily. The creative idea rearranges the "items" (the facts) so that they fit together in a more pleasing way and allows the bag to close easily. To choose an example from science: we regard the current theory of oxygen as a creative idea because it explains why substances lose weight after they burn and also why a lighted match soon goes out if it is placed in a closed chamber, two phenomena that older theories could not easily explain. The creative idea synthesized both facts into a coherent and satisfying principle.

Or consider an example from literature: Herman Hesse's novels, such as *Siddartha* and *Narcissus and Goldmund,* are regarded as creative because they unite two conflicting ideas of twentieth-century Western culture—man's wish for a civilized life of order, reason, and social control and the wish for a freer and more sensual state closer to nature—into one story.

Most of us have little trouble recognizing a creative idea, even though we may not be able to produce one ourselves. Unfortunately, the research on creativity in schoolchildren tends to concentrate on the novelty of a product and to ignore its appropriateness to a problem and the coherent integration of known elements into a new idea. As we have explained the term, young children are not likely to be very creative, simply because they lack sufficient knowledge and are rarely faced with problems that demand an original solution. We should not belittle originality in young children, but we should not confuse it with creativity. Driving past an abandoned factory in a city, a three-year-old may say, "I don't like those rusty buildings." To the adults in the car, "rusty buildings" may seem a creative image, conveying a sense of corrosion, obsolescence, and decay. While the image is certainly evocative and would have done credit to a poet over the age of ten, it is important to realize that the three-year-old's intention was not to create a colorful image, but only to describe old buildings with concepts familiar to her: the disused and rusty pails and shovels she had seen discarded in back of her grandfather's country barn.

A creative product is characterized by mental discipline as well as originality. The creator adheres to rules and accommodates to known facts, as in the case of a chess player making a brilliant move or a young mechanic suddenly seeing how a carburetor can be fixed when the proper parts are not available. Creativity, in spite of some mystique, is not an unconstrained expression of ideas that acknowledges no boundaries and addresses itself to no special problem.

Characteristics of Creative People

Some research has attempted to determine the personal characteristics of creative children and adults. One of the most important studies was done by a team of California psychologists led by Dr. Donald MacKinnon (1965). MacKinnon asked a large number of people who were knowledgeable about architecture to nominate the most creative architects in the country. Forty of these creative architects were carefully assessed and compared with other architects who were judged very successful but not highly creative. There were many differences between the groups, but three were most important: creative architects placed a premium on imagination and original ideas; they liked being alone, did not like socializing, and enjoyed independence and solitary work; and they were less concerned with what others thought of them or their work. Differences between the most and the least creative architects did not involve their intellectual abilities as much as their motivations and conflicts. It is not a coincidence that the creative architects valued the originality of their products more than the efficiency of their designs. Creative people consciously set out to search for an original solution, even if it proves unpopular or is rejected because it is unconventional. They do so because *they* want to be creative! Less creative though intellectually able and successful adults turn to their peers and to society for standards; knowing what the society values, they try to keep within those boundaries.

Two other psychologists studied creativity among children (Wallach and Kogan, 1965). The children were asked questions such as "How

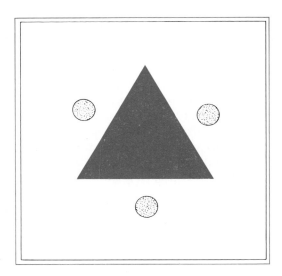

Figure 13–5
What can this drawing be? When two psychologists studied children to find out which ones were good at generating original ideas, they considered "three mice nibbling at some cheese" a creative response, whereas "three people sitting at a table" was not judged creative because it was more obvious. (After Wallach and Kogan, 1965)

many ways can we use a newspaper?" or to name all the things a particular geometric drawing might represent. For example, they were shown a triangle with a little circle next to each side (see Figure 13–5). "Three mice nibbling some cheese" was considered an original answer, while the response "three people at a table" was not judged creative because it was more obvious. The ability to generate original and unique ideas was the measure of creativity. The children were also given intelligence tests; there was no strong relation between creativity scores and intelligence scores. Children who were highly creative and highly intelligent were also confident, liked to socialize, and had many friends. That personality profile is, of course, inconsistent with the one that emerged in MacKinnon's study of creative architects, probably because the tests given to children primarily measured originality, without taking into account the two other factors of creativity: appropriateness to the problem and coherent synthesis. Children who displayed low creativity but high intelligence, by contrast, were cautious and afraid of error and rejection. This finding is in accord with the suggestion made in Chapter 4: people who are overly anxious about making mistakes will not produce original ideas.

Since creativity requires a large corpus of knowledge, children with high I.Q.'s are more apt to be creative, for the I.Q. test is a good measure of how much a child knows. Furthermore, as we have seen, creative adolescents and adults *want* to be creative. They value imagination and are less concerned with conforming to the opinions of others, traits that are more consistently encouraged in upper-middle-class than lower-middle-class homes. Hence, creative adolescents and adults are more likely to come from homes of well-educated families than from those in which parents have not gone to college, in part because the upper-middle-class home fosters the motives and the acquisition of knowledge necessary for adult creativity. One psychologist studied ten exceptionally creative adolescent girls, sixteen to seventeen years of age, who came from the New York metropolitan area and were selected from a large pool of several thousand highly intelligent students. These ten girls all came from upper-middle-class families who valued intellectual effort; they were less restricted by their parents than the average adolescent their age, and learned to read early, and prodigiously. Their elementary-school teachers had taken an interest in them. They had had highly creative hobbies as children, and like the architects, they described themselves as *imaginative* (Schaefer, 1970).

By the time children reach school age, their particular predispositions toward creativity—like many other aptitudes useful in school—have already taken shape to some extent. As with other academic abilities, potential for creativity differs from child to child. Nevertheless, schools can make efforts to offset obstacles to creative thinking.

Richard Crutchfield (1973), a psychologist at the University of California, suggests five obstacles: (1) inability to define the problem clearly or correctly; (2) insufficient knowledge; (3) rigidity and inability to put aside popular assumptions; (4) lack of a period of incubation (the problem has to sit in the mind for a while); and (5) fear of error for an unconventional idea.

Creativity has been increasingly emphasized in the schools. When the aim is to help children formulate intellectual responses that are constructive and appropriate as well as original, the schools' efforts are worthwhile. But there is another reason for fostering creativity—and that is to change the child's attitude toward error. Encouraging creative solutions to problems can reduce some children's anxiety over failure and promote greater emotional spontaneity. Thus curricula encouraging creativity have a hidden mission: to influence emotional qualities in the child.

Encouraging Creative Thinking in School

If schools wish to encourage creativity, they can do it best by setting up problems to be solved within a specific context. For instance, a child can be asked to paint a scene on a piece of paper three inches square

with only two colors (rather than told to do what she wants with a twelve-inch square page and a dozen bottles of paint). Modern China goes to an extreme in stifling originality, for in the typical art class all fifty children are given a model and told to copy it. America may to go another extreme in placing too few constraints on the intellectual work of children.

Science classes can stimulate creativity by setting up real problems, both verbal and practical. How can we get rid of nuclear wastes safely and economically? How can we diagnose earthquakes or obtain heat from the sun? Teachers may pose problems that earlier scientists faced, such as how to measure the speed of a falling body, how to find out if weight and size are inherited in mice, how to build an edifice of wood without nails, how to determine the humidity in the air or the average rainfall in September. In each of these exercises the teacher invites the child to think originally, to be unafraid of error and to let his imagination soar, but to keep in mind that there is a goal—or standard—against which to evaluate each idea. But if a problem is not set, the child has no way to gauge how constructive his ideas are. If all he can assess is novelty, then originality for its own sake is promoted.

A major source of creative ideas is the metaphor—a symbolic translation of a phenomenon, usually in words. Water flowing in a pipe is a metaphor for electricity. Twilight is a metaphor for old age. Metaphors can also be visual, such as in a film in which the end of the day conveys the dying of an old man. Sergei Prokofiev used musical metaphors in *Peter and the Wolf*, where the ominous presence of the wolf is signaled by the horns, the carefree wanderings of the young boy by the strings, the duck by the oboe, and the bird by the flute. Children can be encouraged to view a particular problem in terms of another model or a metaphor. The model usually provides a hint or a clue to solving the problem at hand. For example, Freud used the nineteenth-century theory of physical energy as a metaphor for psychological energy, which he called libido. Since physical laws stated that all energy was conserved—none was lost or gained—Freud assumed that each person had a fixed amount of libidinal energy that was concentrated in different parts of his body during different ages.

Consider some topics for which metaphors may be helpful. High-school students discussing the problem of increasing population density and psychological isolation in our cities can be asked to generate metaphors for society, such as a colony of bees or a flock of birds. Each model has different implications, for each social group of animals provides a different metaphor for humans. Birds mate in pairs; bees do not. Bees are hierarchically organized, and some of the colony does not reproduce. Birds are not hierarchically organized, and all are capable of reproduction. The teacher may ask students to think of ways to promote a positive change in our society, using animal evolution as the metaphor. In evolution, contact between related species that are reproductively compatible encourages new forms.

A small number of children are extraordinarily creative or highly gifted. But they are by no means the only children whose talents and insights should be developed. The pleasure of making new objects or seeing ideas in a new way is one of the joys of life, whether it becomes the basis for professional work or the sustaining thread of a private hobby. Meeting each child's individual needs, perhaps the most important challenge in American education, requires that schools begin where each student begins, and go with him as far as he can go. The span of that journey relative to the group's is not insignificant. But each child's relative position must not blind us to the significance of each child's journey. In surveying their own progress, children need their teachers' help in looking in both directions, in seeing, and in saying, not only "Look how far I still have to go," but also "Look how far I have come."

Summary

American education faces the challenge of meeting individual needs. In this chapter, we have considered five major avenues of development.

Compensatory education—intervening in the lives of children who are likely to encounter serious difficulty in school in order to improve their chances for academic success—began in the mid-1960s by focusing on the preschool years. Based on the belief that intellectual talents can be influenced in the early years by enriching the children's environment, programs provided sensory stimulation and a wide variety of experiences but little formal intellectual content. Over time, many preschool educators concluded that this approach was too indirect and shifted to programs that had a more direct effect on cognitive skills. Most programs specifically tried to improve language. Some taught vocabulary and concepts, others concentrated on drilling standard English or extending language use. And some programs, based on Piagetian theory, tried to foster development of thinking and classes of knowledge central to Piaget's view of intelligence, rather than specific vocabulary. Children enrolled in preschool programs made gains that were impressive, but impermanent. Once in elementary school, they soon lost any academic advantage that they had achieved. To consolidate these gains, compensatory education experimented with a variety of programs in primary grades. Project Follow-Through, for instance, was implemented nationally but in different forms—some programs were highly structured and others child-oriented. Besides reaching thousands of children, it provided the opportunity to compare the results of a variety of methods. Other investigators turned to infancy and developed programs based on sensory stimulation at an early age. Evaluating compensatory programs is difficult: gains in achievement or I.Q. are comparatively simple to measure, but equally significant improvements in motivation, interest, or expectancy of success are less amenable to precise measurement. Generally, intervention programs can make a difference, but different designs yield different results: highly structured programs were most successful in producing higher reading and mathematics scores, whereas more flexible and child-oriented programs produced lower absence rates and more independent activity.

Adapting education to individual differences has produced some promising results. Mastery learning attempts to organize a body of knowledge into small tasks, sequentially ordered so that one task is prerequisite to another and more complex tasks are composed of simpler ones. When material is arranged in a hierarchy of this kind each child can proceed at his or her own rate. Mastery learning has limitations, however, since some material cannot be easily arranged sequentially.

Computer-assisted instruction has the advantages of individualizing instruction and permitting children to work at their own pace. It can provide both tutorial and drill programs, accommodate to a child's level of performance, give immediate feedback, and store an entire "file" on each child's progress. Studies suggest that the increase in practice, rather than the computers themselves, may account for students' improvement. But CAI will probably play a wider role in education in the future.

Gifted children—those with unusually high I.Q. scores or a remarkable talent in a particular area or both—also have special needs, but in recent years America has been less willing to acknowledge their needs than those of disadvantaged students. Enrichment programs, the most common effort made on behalf of gifted children, augment regular courses by providing extra reading, study opportunities, and independent study projects. Acceleration—allowing a young student to participate in higher education programs—is an alternative that is occasionally appropriate for highly skilled students.

Creativity, for all the misunderstandings about its dimensions, is a quality to be nourished. It is not to be confused with novelty or with unconstrained expression of ideas. Creative ideas are characterized by mental discipline as well as by originality. Research suggests that creative people place a premium on imagination, enjoy independence and solitary work, and are less concerned with the opinions of people around them. Schools that want to foster creative thinking in all students can best accomplish it by setting up problems to be solved within a specific context and by encouraging metaphorical thinking as a means to discovering new connections among familiar ideas.

Projects

1 Convene a group of classmates to discuss how well past schooling met individual needs. Was anyone enrolled in CAI, mastery learning, Montessori, or Head Start programs? If so, how did she react to them? How well, if at all, are the individual needs of members of the group being met in college? Has anyone in the group ever undertaken an independent study project? Before adjourning the group, compose a list of members' ideas that would help teachers meet the individual needs of their students.

2 Write to the U.S. Department of Health, Education and Welfare, or to the State Office of Education, for information on funding currently available to support the education of gifted children. Concurrently, research programs in progress for these children available in the state where you live or attend college. Report your findings to the class.

3 Obtain from Synectics Education Systems, 121 Brattle Street, Cambridge, Massachusetts 02138, a sample of the metaphorical approach to learning that can be demonstrated in a class. Try this approach in your class and discuss its impact as well as its applicability to schools in which your classmates may be teaching.

4 Visit the following types of day-care centers: one operated by a manufacturing company for employees' children; one serving the children of a university's staff; an urban neighborhood day-care center; and a suburban day-care center. Decide ahead of time what aspect you will focus on (some suggestions are curriculum, schedules, space, grouping, materials and equipment, fees and/or tuition, staffing). From your observations, write what you perceive to be the educational goals of each of these centers.

5 An evaluation of Project Follow-Through found that highly structured and academically oriented programs generally produced higher reading and math scores, while more flexible programs produced lower absence rates and more independent activity. Poll ten teachers to find out which approach they would favor in their own classes.

6 Read articles on creativity in issues of the publications listed below. Outline the major points of each in preparation for a research paper on creativity. State the major theme of your paper, drawing on the information in the articles. The publications are: *Developmental Psychology, Exceptional Children, American Education Research Journal, Journal of Educational Psychology, Journal of Experimental Psychology, Psychology in the Schools, Childhood Education, School Review, Educational Forum, Instructor, Grade Teacher,* and *Learning.*

Recommended Reading

Bereiter, C., and Engelmann, S. *Teaching disadvantaged children in the preschool.* Englewood Cliffs, N.J.: Prentice-Hall, 1966. A summary of a special program for intervening in the cognitive development of disadvantaged children prior to school entrance.

Day, M. C., and Parker, R. K. (Eds.). *The preschool in action: Exploring early childhood programs* (2nd ed.). Boston: Allyn & Bacon, 1977. Contains a series of chapters describing early childhood programs for preschool children.

Stallings, J. Implementation and child effects of teaching practices in follow-through classrooms. *Monographs of the Society for Research in Child Development,* 1975, 40 (7–8, Serial No. 175). A summary of research evaluating the later progress of school-age children who had been in Head Start and are now in school programs that are attempting to maintain the gains accomplished during the preschool program.

Stanley, J. C., Keating, D. P., and Fox, L. H. (Eds.). *Mathematical talent: Discovery, description and development.* Baltimore: Johns Hopkins University Press, 1974. Summarizes an important project on discovery of and curricula for children who have unusual mathematical ability.

Terman, L. M. *Genetic studies of genius* (Vol. 3). Stanford, Calif.: Stanford University Press, 1930. One in a series of volumes that summarize the famous study of extremely intelligent children who were followed from school age through adulthood by the author.

epilogue on education

The education of children has always been one of society's central tasks, for each new generation must learn the skills necessary for economic survival, the values and styles of interaction that keep a social group in harmony with itself and nature, and the knowledge necessary to buffer uncertainty. Through most of history children were educated primarily by the family; parents, older siblings, grandparents, and to some degree peers taught them to herd, hunt, plant, reap, and weave. Only after thousands of years did this form of tutoring change. Social and economic changes required the learning of new technical skills that parents did not know and children could not easily learn through observation or apprenticeship. Now adults outside the family were needed as teachers.

Competence in subject matter and character traits that make the teacher an admired role model—the same qualities that made a good tutor in fifth-century Athens or fifteenth-century France—are the ones that make a good teacher today. In many ways, education is an art. One serious misconception of modern educational psychology is that somewhere a perfect prescription exists for teaching a subject, like a formula for synthesizing a drug or a recipe for making a soufflé. But teachers are neither chemists nor chefs, and children are not mindless objects. Students can—and do—decide whether or not they are willing to be influenced by the teacher. Furthermore, educational psychology is not yet mature enough to write elegant prescriptions. Only when we know more about children and how they interact with their social environment will we be able to offer workable suggestions that are both powerful and applicable to specific students.

Nevertheless, the introductory course in educational pychology has often been regarded as primarily practical, rather than scientific or philosophical, aiming to give the teacher recipes that will make the job easier and resolve personal apprehension. That may be one reason American teachers have always been overly eager to depend on the advice of experts and reluctant to engage in reflective thought. They have not been trained to see themselves as professionals who must make difficult decisions about behavior in their classrooms.

But we believe that a deep understanding of what is known about schoolchildren is a better preparation for teaching than is a facile reliance on procedures that are easy to carry out but of unproven validity. Thus, although this book does give advice, its major aim is to present knowledge, frail as it is, about the development and behavior of children and how they perform in the classroom. We have included a great deal of theory and experimental data that do not, on the surface, seem to have immediate practical implications. We have talked at length about historical developments in education, traditions in other cultures, cognitive processes, motives and emotions—but rather little about how to teach fractions or what to do when a child misbehaves. There is simply no single or best way to deal with these problems. On the other hand, teachers who are equipped with the most recent and respected knowledge will be able to use it, with their own wisdom and at their discretion, in deciding what to do in class. They will have the tools they need to discriminate carefully between ideas and procedures that are useful and those that have no basis in fact or are inconsistent with what is known about children.

Psychotherapy has been likened to education. In some senses, education can be considered psychotherapy. Children can be regarded as patients, for they do not yet possess the attributes that will permit successful adaptation to their society; the school is there to help them. As in therapy, the child in school must *want* to change in the direction the teacher intends or he will make little progress. The teacher has some power to enhance motivation, but if the child has no desire to learn academic skills, the teacher's power is limited.

A second important principle in therapy states that patient and therapist must concur that particular rituals will cure a particular problem. They must subscribe to the same beliefs. A person who believes firmly in psychoanalytic theory is unlikely to be helped by a therapist who uses behavior modification techniques. A rural Guatemalan Indian who believes in the dances and white powders of a shaman will feel better after a session with the native doctor but not after one with a psychoanalyst. So, too, with education. The child has to believe that learning to read, write, and spell; performing experiments in chemistry; and understanding social studies, Shakespeare's plays, and the causes of the Revolutionary War are useful. Most American children do believe in the value of schoolwork because of their socialization at home. But in some cases, family and peer-group values produce a child who does not believe in the worth of the school's rituals. Such a child, resisting the teacher, will not gain much from the classroom. Exposure to information and skills is not enough. A recent experiment on the effect of educational television on rural Mexican children underscored this point dramatically. One group of poor Mexican four-year-old children living in rural hamlets outside Mexico City saw a Spanish edition of "Sesame Street" regularly over a six-month period, while a comparable group of children did not. At the end of the period, there was no difference in knowledge of letters or reading skills between the children who watched the program and those who did not (Diaz-Guerrero and Holtzman, 1974).

American families place a high value on acquisition of intellectual skills; mothers talk to their children about the television program and encourage and support the skills being taught. Hence, the typical American child benefits from watching "Sesame Street." But rural Mexican mothers, busy with their chores, neither sit with their children while they watch the program nor talk with them about it. Exposure alone is not enough.

A third ingredient in successful psychotherapy involves the patient's perception of the therapist. The patient, investing the therapist with a special kind of power, must believe the therapist has skills he himself lacks and that the therapist cares for him and his welfare. The same investiture is useful in education. A teacher must be perceived as a person with status and competence who is concerned about students, not as just another person in the labor market doing his job. Unfortunately, recent developments in the educational profession are diminishing the aura. Teachers, voluntarily banding together in unions, emphasize their technical skills rather than their human qualities. The trend may seriously impair their ability to educate effectively, for when parents decide that teachers are no different from electricians or plumbers, they will communicate that attitude to their children. Teachers will lose their special legitimacy, and as a result, what they do will lose its most serious, almost spiritual connotation.

Education in America may be a little too preoccupied with ends and not enough with means. During the fourteenth and fifteenth centuries in Europe the church became increasingly corrupt. Priests sold

Schools Could Celebrate More Talents Than They Do Presently

indulgences to members of the church, and for a fee a person could absolve his monthly sins and feel momentarily virtuous, as one purchases a meal at a restaurant to assuage hunger temporarily. Soon, citizens came to view priests as selfish, and the church and the priests lost their special power. Martin Luther sparked the Reformation by protesting these practices and attacking the power of the established church and the priests.

Our schools are becoming places where certificates are awarded that permit a person to move to a higher position of status, not unlike the indulgences sold in the fifteenth century certifying that a person was free from sin. We may soon see a reformation in education. Indeed, there are straws in the wind: in some urban areas parents who are unhappy with the public schools are withdrawing their children and establishing their own educational programs in homes or in the basements of churches.

Many changes can be suggested that will help the educational institution serve society better. However, we regard four as being especially pertinent and beneficial.

Create Smaller Groups

American schools have grown too large, producing a situation in which many students in big junior and senior high schools feel themselves to be an anonymous group. When colonial Americans first discussed establishing schools, they were aware of the consequences of large school populations and many suggested limiting schools to no more than several hundred students. As described earlier, Roger Barker and Paul Gump (1964) have shown that more students participate in school activities in a small school than in a large one. It is probably not a coincidence that a large number (greater than chance would determine) of our eminent citizens—scientists, astronauts, politicians—grew up in towns and cities with under one hundred thousand people and attended small schools. Despite the fact that large regional and urban schools have better facilities, such as laboratories and gymnasiums, as well as access to museums and zoos, they produce fewer highly successful and achieving adults than one would expect, while the smaller schools with fewer advantages produce more. As we indicated in Chapter 7, the child's expectancy of success is a vital determinant of her motivation and progress. Imagine a girl of slightly better than average intelligence and academic ability. In a typical large high school in a big city she will know many more girls her age whom she believes outpace her than if she lived in a small town and attended a small school. The fewer her rivals, the more likely she is to develop a high expectancy of success.

We cannot change the size of our cities or tear down our large schools, but organizational changes can be made to simulate a small school. Consider a regional high school with 6,000 students in grades ten through twelve. The school functions as one unit: there is one varsity athletic team in each sport, one debating team, one valedictorian, one yearbook, one class play. Suppose the school was administratively made into six high schools of 1,000 students each. We would have increased by a factor of six the number of adolescents who can participate in the vital activities of the school. There would be six athletic teams in each sport, six valedictorians, six yearbook staffs. Each student would have a smaller referent group with which to compare himself. Instead of 2,000 students in a regular American history course, all competing for the school's history achievement award, there would be only 330 students. Such conditions would help decrease feelings of anonymity and increase the students' affective involvement with the school.

Celebrate a Plurality of Talents A second beneficial change involves broadening the list of talents that we reward. The typical American school places a high value on academic activities: language, mathematics, science, English, history, and social studies. Although art and music are taught, they are regarded as *avocations*—hobbies or spare-time activities available after the academic material has been mastered. A great many children have special talents in nonacademic areas, but they do not feel that these are worth as much. The school could enhance confidence and self-esteem in many students by seriously and honestly celebrating these talents. Students gifted in auto mechanics or photography would have access to prizes and rewards on a par with those given for language, mathematics, science, and sports. If one function of education is to increase a sense of mastery and expectation of success, then such a change in the values of the school could benefit many.

Use Para-profes-sionals The primary-grade teacher with thirty pupils of widely varying abilities has a difficult job and needs help. During the early grades many children need individualized attention, but the classroom teacher does not have time to spend a quiet hour every day with each of six children who need special help. Yet many parents and older retired people in the neighborhood, as well as high-school students, would welcome the opportunity to work with a child one hour a day. The high school could establish an elective course in which students went to a nearby elementary school several hours a week and worked individually with a child who needed help in reading or arithmetic. Classroom teachers would, of course, supervise these paraprofessionals. This plan is being implemented in many places in the country with such positive reactions that it should be adopted more extensively.

Unlock the Link between Academic Success and Elitism

A recent development in our society, as we discussed earlier, has unfortunate consequences for very gifted students. We used to respect and honor superior talent; now we are ambivalent, even embarrassed, about it. As egalitarianism has become America's central mission, any practice that implies one person's superiority to another has acquired a negative connotation. Students, as well as teachers, sense the school's subtle reluctance to allow a talented student to move too far ahead of the others or to award special privileges to students with excellent grades and high motivation. This practice not only frustrates the student who enjoys mastery—it also deprives society of a potentially creative adult. Egalitarianism means equal opportunities to succeed, and equal justice before the law: students who are highly gifted in mathematics have no more dignity nor are they entitled to different justice than those who are less talented. But we must break the illogical association between an individual's talent and the class action suit Americans have brought against elitism. Talent is a thing of beauty, to be encouraged and valued; it is not a blemish to be hidden from view.

reference list

Chapter 1

Abbott, J. *The way to do good: Or the Christian character mature.* Boston, 1836.

Baxter, R. *A Christian directory* (Vol. 3, No. 50). London, 1825. Originally published in 1673.

Bentwich, J. S. *Education in Israel.* Philadelphia: Jewish Publishing Society of America, 1965.

Broudy, H. S. *The real world of the public schools.* New York: Harcourt Brace Jovanovich, 1972.

Butts, R. F. The public school: Assaults on a great idea. *The Nation,* April 30, 1973, pp. 553–560.

Carcopino, J. *Daily life in ancient Rome.* New Haven, Conn.: Yale University Press, 1940.

Castle, E. B. *Ancient education and today.* Harmondsworth: Penguin Books, 1961.

Cremin, L. A. *American education: The colonial experience, 1607–1783.* New York: Harper & Row, 1970.

Department for Aliya and Absorption. *The educational system in Israel, a guide for olim.* Information and Publication Division, State of Israel, Ministry of Immigrant Absorption, 1972.

Dollar, B. Child care in China. *Saturday Review of Education,* May 1973, pp. 29–33.

Enlivening studies and accentuating student initiative. *Peking Review,* February 23, 1973, pp. 10–13.

Fun in the garden. Peking: Foreign Languages Press, 1965.

Jencks, C. *Inequality: A reassessment of the effect of family and schooling in America.* New York: Basic Books, 1972.

Jenga Twelve. Tanzania, 1972, pp. 14–19.

Katz, M. B. *The irony of early school reform.* Boston: Beacon Press, 1968.

Kessen, W. *Childhood in China.* New Haven, Conn.: Yale University Press, 1975.

Kitto, H. D. F. *The Greeks.* Baltimore: Penguin Books, 1965.

Mehnert, K. *China returns.* New York: E. P. Dutton, 1972.

Schools with a difference. *Newsweek,* April 23, 1973, pp. 113–116.

Sidel, R. *Women and child care in China.* New York: Hill & Wang, 1972.

Talmon, Y. *Family and community in the kibbutz.* Cambridge, Mass.: Harvard University Press, 1972.

Vacation activities for children. *China Reconstructs,* May 1973, pp. 46–48.

Viscusi, M. *Literacy for working: Functional literacy in rural Tanzania.* Paris: Workshops of UNESCO, 1971.

White, D. Students get back to ethnic roots. *Boston Globe,* June 20, 1973, p. 41.

Wishy, B. *The child and the republic.* Philadelphia: University of Pennsylvania Press, 1968.

Wolins, M., and Gottesmann, M. (Eds.). *Group care: An Israeli approach, the educational path of youth aliyah.* New York and London: Gordon and Breach, 1971.

Chapter 2

Astin, H. S. Stability and change in the career plans of ninth-grade girls. *Personnel and Guidance Journal,* 1968, *46,* 961–966.

Berk, L. E., Rose, M. H., and Stewart, D. Attitudes of English and American children toward their school experience. *Journal of Educational Psychology,* 1970, *61,* 33–40.

Blom, G. E. Motivational and attitudinal content of first-grade reading textbooks. *Journal of the Academy of Child Psychiatry,* 1971, *10,* 191–203.

Bouwsma, W. J. Models of the educated man. *The American Scholar,* Spring 1975, p. 21.

Castle, E. B. *Ancient education and today.* Harmondsworth: Penguin Books, 1961.

Clifford, M. M. Effects of competition as a motivational technique in the classroom. *American Educational Research Journal,* 1972, *9,* 123–137.

Clifford, M. M., Cleary, T. A., and Walster, G. W. Effects of emphasizing competition in classroom testing procedures. *Journal of Educational Research,* 1972, *65,* 234–238.

Davison, D. C. Perceived reward value of teacher reinforcement and attitude toward teacher: An application of Newcomb's balance theory. *Journal of Educational Psychology,* 1972, *63,* 418–422.

deCharms, R., and Moeller, G. H. Values expressed in American children's readers, 1800–1950. *Journal of Abnormal and Social Psychology,* 1962, *64,* 136–142.

Dick and Jane as victims: Sex stereotyping in children's readers. Princeton, N.J.: Women on Words and Images, 1972.

Feshbach, N. D. Student teacher preferences for elementary school pupils varying in personality characteristics. *Journal of Educational Psychology,* 1969, *60,* 126–132.

Girls lag on tests: Unequal education? *U.S. News and World Report,* October 20, 1975, p. 54.

Good, T. L., and Brophy, J. E. Behavioral expression of teacher attitudes. *Journal of Educational Psychology,* 1972, *63,* 617–624.

Harris, T. L., Creekmore, M., Greenman, M. H., and Allen, H. B. *Zip! pop! go!* Oklahoma City: The Economy Company, 1972.

Hoffman, B. *Albert Einstein: Creator and rebel.* New York: Viking Press, 1972.

Jencks, C. *Inequality: A reassessment of the effect of family and schooling in America.* New York: Basic Books, 1972.

Johnson, C. *Old time schools and school books.* New York: Macmillan, 1904.

Kagan, J. The child's sex role classification of school objects. *Child Development,* 1964, *35,* 1051–1056.

Kagan, J., and Moss, H. A. *Birth to maturity.* New York: John Wiley, 1962.

Karnovsky, A. *Sex differences in spatial ability: A developmental study.* Unpublished thesis, Harvard University, 1973.

Kohlberg, L. Stage and sequence: The cognitive developmental approach to socialization. In D. A. Goslin (Ed.), *Handbook of socialization theory and research.* Chicago: Rand McNally, 1969.

Kohlberg, L., and Gilligan, C. The adolescent as a philosopher: The discovery of the self in a postconventional world. In J. Kagan and R. Coles (Eds.), *Twelve to sixteen: Early adolescence.* New York: Norton, 1972.

Landsmann, L. So what if the butterfly dies? *Instructor,* August/September 1973, pp. 92–94.

Litcher, J. H., and Johnson, D. W. Changes in attitudes toward Negroes of white elementary-school students after use of multiethnic readers. *Journal of Educational Psychology,* 1969, *60,* 148–152.

Maccoby, E. E., and Jacklin, C. W. *The psychology of sex differences.* Stanford, Calif.: Stanford University Press, 1974.

McCracken, G., Walcutt, C. C., Bond, M. F., and Faircloth, E. *Basic reading, reader 2–1.* Philadelphia: J. B. Lippincott, 1964.

Michelak, J. City life in primers. *The Herald Tribune,* January 26, 1965.

Mussen, P. H., Conger, J. J., and Kagan, J. *Child development and personality* (4th ed.). New York: Harper & Row, 1974.

Parsley, K. H. Jr., Powell, M., O'Connor, H. A., and Deutsch, M. Are there really sex differences in achievement? *Journal of Educational Research,* 1963, *57,* 210–212.

Richmond, B. O., and Weiner, G. Cooperation and competition among young children as a function of ethnic grouping, grade, sex, and reward condition. *Journal of Educational Psychology,* 1973, *64,* 329–334.

Rosen, B. C. Social change, migration, and family interaction in Brazil. *American Sociological Review*, 1973, *38*, 198–212.

Saunders, C. W. The busy bees. *Union Reader No. 2*, 1861.

Sechrest, L. B. The motivation in school of young children: Some interview data. *Journal of Experimental Education*, 1962, *30*, 327–335.

Stainback, W. C., and Stainback, S. B. A close look at a variety of reinforcers. *Training School Bulletin*, 1972, *69*, 131–135.

Storm, T., Anthony, W. S., and Porsolt, R. D. Ethnic and social class differences in performance for material and nonmaterial rewards: New Zealand children. *Journal of Personality and Social Psychology*, 1965, *2*, 759–762.

Taylor, J. O. *The district school*. New York: Harper & Bros., 1834.

Taylor, P. H. Children's evaluations of the characteristics of the good teacher. *British Journal of Educational Psychology*, 1962, *32*, 258–266.

Tolor, A., Scarpetti, W. L., and Lane, P. A. Teachers' attitudes toward children's behavior revisited. *Journal of Educational Psychology*, 1967, *58*, 175–180.

Tulkin, S. R., Muller, J. P., and Conn, L. K. Need for approval and popularity: Sex differences in elementary-school students. *Journal of Consulting and Clinical Psychology*, 1969, *33*, 35–39.

Walker, J. *The teacher's assistant in English composition*. Boston: J. T. Buckingham, 1810.

Wasserman, S. A. Values of Mexican-American, Negro, and Anglo blue-collar and white-collar children. *Child Development*, 1971, *42*, 1624–1628.

Whyte, W. H. Jr. *The organization man*. New York: Simon & Schuster, 1956.

Wishy, B. *The child and the republic*. Philadelphia: University of Pennsylvania Press, 1968.

Yudkin, M. *The character builders*. Unpublished paper, Harvard University, 1971.

Chapter 3

Bolles, R. C. Reinforcement expectancy and learning. *Psychological Review*, 1972, *79*, 394–409.

Brown, R. W., and Herrnstein, R. J. *Psychology*. Boston: Little, Brown, 1975.

Elkind, D. Giant in the nursery—Jean Piaget. *New York Times Magazine*, May 26, 1968, pp. 25–80.

Farnham-Diggory, S. *Cognitive processes in education: A psychological preparation for teaching and curriculum development*. New York: Harper & Row, 1972.

Gagné, R. M. *The conditions of learning*. New York: Holt, Rinehart and Winston, 1965.

Ginsburg, H., and Opper, S. *Piaget's theory of intellectual development: An introduction*. Englewood Cliffs, N.J.: Prentice-Hall, 1969.

Inhelder, B., and Piaget, J. *The growth of logical thinking from childhood to adolescence*. New York: Basic Books, 1958.

John, E. R., Chesler, P., Bartlett, F., and Victor, I. Observational learning in cats. *Science*, 1968, *159*, 1489–1491.

Kagan, J. *Change and continuity in infancy*. New York: John Wiley, 1971.

Locke, J. *Essay concerning human understanding* (Rev. ed., Vol. 1, J. W. Yolton, Ed.). London: Dent, 1965.

Pavlov, I. *Conditioned reflexes: An investigation of the physiological activity of the cerebral cortex* (G. V. Anrep, Ed. and trans.). Oxford: Oxford University Press, 1927.

Penfield, W. The uncommitted cortex. *Atlantic Monthly,* July 1964.

Piaget, J. *The origins of intelligence in children.* New York: International Universities Press, 1952.

Skinner, B. F. *The behavior of organisms.* New York: Appleton-Century-Crofts, 1938.

Chapter 4

Doob, L. W. Eidetic images among the Ibo. *Ethnology,* 1964, *3,* 357–362.

Farnham-Diggory, S. *Cognitive processes in education: A psychological preparation for teaching and curriculum development.* New York: Harper & Row, 1972.

Flavell, J. H., Beach, D. R., and Chinsky, J. M. Spontaneous verbal rehearsal in a memory task as a function of age. *Child Development,* 1966, *37,* 284–299.

Frender, R. *The development of conceptual organization in the free recall of bilingually educated children.* Unpublished doctoral dissertation, Harvard University, 1975.

Gibson, E. J. *Principles of perceptual learning and development.* New York: Appleton-Century-Crofts, 1969.

Gotkin, L. G. A calendar curriculum for disadvantaged kindergarten children. *Teaching College Record,* 1967, *68,* 406–416.

Gregory, R. L. Choosing a paradigm for perception. In E. O. Carterette and M. P. Freedman (Eds.), *Handbook of perception* (Vol. 1). New York: Academic Press, 1974.

Guilford, J. P. Three faces of intellect. *American Psychologist,* 1959, *14,* 469–479.

Hagen, J. W., Jongeward, R. H., and Kail, R. V. Cognitive perspectives on developmental memory. In H. W. Reese (Ed.), *Advances in child development and behavior.* New York: Academic Press, 1975.

Harris, G. J., and Burke, D. The effects of grouping on short-term serial recall of digits by children: Developmental trends. *Child Development,* 1972, *43,* 710–716.

Kagan, J. *Change and continuity in infancy.* New York: John Wiley, 1971.

Kagan, J. *Cognitive development,* in press.

Kagan, J., Kearsley, R., Zelazo, P. *The effect of day care on development,* in press.

Kagan, J., Klein, R. E., Finley, G., Rogoff, B., and Nolan, E. *A cross-cultural study of cognitive development,* unpublished.

Kagan, J., and Kogan, N. Individual variation in cognitive processes. In P. H. Mussen (Ed.), *Carmichael's manual of child psychology* (3rd ed., Vol. 1). New York: John Wiley, 1970.

Kopp, C. B., and Shaperman, J. Cognitive development in the absence of object manipulation during infancy. *Developmental Psychology,* 1973, *9,* 430.

Kreutzer, M. A., Leonard, C., and Flavell, J. H. *An interview study of children's knowledge about memory.* Unpublished manuscript, 1974.

Moely, B. E., Olson, F. A., Halwes, T. G., and Flavell, J. H. Production deficiency in young children's clustered recall. *Development Psychology*, 1969, *1*, 26–34.

Morrison, F. J. *A developmental study on the effect of familiarity on short-term visual memory.* Unpublished doctoral dissertation, Harvard University, 1971.

Mussen, P. H., Conger, J. J., and Kagan, J. *Child development and personality* (4th ed.). New York: Harper & Row, 1974.

Neisser, U. *Cognitive psychology.* New York: Appleton-Century-Crofts, 1967.

Rosch, E. G. Universals and cultural specifics in human categorization. In R. Breslin, S. Bochner, W. Lonner (Eds.), *Cross-cultural perspectives in learning.* New York: Halsted Press, 1975.

Siipola, E. M., and Hayden, S. D. Scoring eidetic imagery among the retarded. *Perceptual and Motor Skills*, 1965, *21*, 275–286.

Super, C. M. *Long-term memory in early infancy.* Unpublished doctoral dissertation, Harvard University, 1972.

Wallach, M. A., and Kogan, N. *Modes of thinking in young children.* New York: Holt, Rinehart and Winston, 1965.

Yando, R. M., and Kagan, J. The effect of teacher tempo on the child. *Child Development*, 1968, *39*, 27–34.

Yates, F. A. *The art of memory.* Chicago: University of Chicago Press, 1966.

Zaslavsky, C. *Africa counts: Number and pattern in African culture.* Boston: Prindle, Weber & Schmidt, 1973.

Chapter 5

Brainerd, C. J. Inducing ordinal and cardinal representations of the first five natural numbers. *Journal of Experimental Child Psychology*, 1974, *18*, 520–534.

Brainerd, C. J., and Fraser, M. A further test of the ordinal theory of number development. *Journal of Genetic Psychology*, 1975, *127*, 23–33.

Bruner, J. S. *The process of education.* Cambridge, Mass.: Harvard University Press, 1960.

Flavell, J. H., Friedrichs, A. G., and Hoyt, J. D. Developmental changes in memorization processes. *Cognitive Psychology*, 1970, *1*, 324–340.

Gelman, R., and Tucker, M. F. Further investigations of the young child's conception of numbers. *Child Development*, 1975, *46*, 167–175.

Kagan, J., Klein, R. E., Finley, G., Rogoff, B., and Nolan, E. *A cross-cultural study of cognitive development,* unpublished.

MacNamara, J. A note on Piaget and number. *Child Development*, 1975, *46*, 424–429.

Rogoff, B., Newcombe, N., and Kagan, J. Planfulness and recognition memory. *Child Development*, 1974, *45*, 972–997.

Schachter, F. F., Krishner, K., Klips, B., Friedricks, M., and Sanders, K. Everyday preschool interpersonal speech usage: Methodological, developmental, and sociolinguistic studies. *Monographs of the Society for Research in Child Development*, 1974, *39* (3, Serial No. 156).

Warshauer, T. Second-grade arithmetic lesson. Beverly School System, Beverly, Mass., 1975.

Winer, G. A. Conservation of different quantities among preschool children. *Child Development,* 1974, *45,* 839–842.

Winkelmann, W. Factorial analysis of children's conservation task performance. *Child Development,* 1974, *45,* 843–848.

Zaslavsky, C. *Africa counts: Number and pattern in African culture.* Boston: Prindle, Weber & Schmidt, 1973.

Chapter 6   Borke, H. Interpersonal perception of young children: Egocentrism or empathy. *Developmental Psychology,* 1971, *5,* 263–269.

Darwin, C. *The expression of the emotions in man and animals.* New York: Appleton, 1892.

Demos, E. V. *Children's understanding and use of affect terms.* Unpublished doctoral dissertation, Harvard University, 1974.

Izard, C. E. *The face of emotion.* New York: Appleton-Century-Crofts, 1971.

Kagan, J. *Change and continuity in infancy.* New York: John Wiley, 1971.

Kagan, J., Hosken, B., and Watson, S. Child's symbolic conceptualization of parents. *Child Development,* 1961, *32,* 625–636.

Lewis, W., Wolman, R., and King, M. Development of the language of emotions. *American Journal of Psychiatry,* 1971, *127,* 1491–1497.

Maslow, A. H. *Toward a psychology of being* (2nd ed.). New York: Van Nostrand Reinhold, 1968.

Novey, M. S. *The development of knowledge of others' ability to see.* Unpublished doctoral dissertation, Harvard University, 1975.

Osgood, C. E., Suci, G. J., and Tannenbaum, P. *Measurement of meaning.* Urbana: University of Illinois Press, 1957.

Scarr, S., and Salapatek, S. Patterns of fear development during infancy. *Merril-Palmer Quarterly,* 1970, *16,* 53–90.

Tompkins, S. S. *Affect, imagery, consciousness* (2 vols.). New York: Springer Publications, 1962–1963.

Chapter 7   Alschuler, A. S., Tabor, D., and McIntyre, J. *Teaching achievement motivation.* Middletown, Conn.: Education Ventures, 1970.

Ardrey, R. *The territorial imperative.* New York: Atheneum, 1966.

Ashton-Warner, S. *Spinster,* New York: Simon & Schuster, 1958.

Barker, R. G., and Gump, P. V. *Big school, small school: High school size and student behavior.* Stanford, Calif.: Stanford University Press, 1964.

Barton, K., Dielman, T. E., and Cattell, R. B. Personality and I.Q. measures as predictors of school achievement. *Journal of Educational Psychology,* 1972, *63,* 398–404.

Battle, E. S. Motivational determinants of academic competence. *Journal of Personality and Social Psychology,* 1966, *4,* 634–642.

Chang, B. *The relation between identification with a model and attentiveness to verbal information from the model.* Honors thesis, Radcliffe College, 1965.

Clifford, M. M., and Cleary, T. A. The relationship between children's academic performance and achievement accountability. *Child Development*, 1972, 43, 647–655.

deVaron, T. Growing up. In J. Kagan and R. Coles, *Twelve to sixteen: Early adolescence.* New York: W. W. Norton, 1972.

Dweck, C. S., and Reppucci, N. D. Learned helplessness and reinforcement responsibility in children. *Journal of Personality and Social Psychology*, 1973, 25, 109–116.

Education: Learn all about it. *Newsweek*, January 7, 1974, p. 42.

Jordan, J. V. *The relationship of sex-role orientation to competitive and noncompetitive achievement behavior.* Unpublished doctoral dissertation, Harvard University, 1973.

Kolesnik, W. B. *Educational psychology* (2nd ed.). New York: McGraw-Hill, 1963.

Korda, M. Time as money, power, and sex. *New York Magazine*, January 14, 1974.

Lerner, L., and Weiss, R. L. Role of value of reward and model affective response in vicarious reinforcement. *Journal of Personality and Social Psychology*, 1972, 21, 93–100.

McClelland, D. C. Toward a theory of motive acquisition. *American Psychologist*, 1965, 20, 321–333.

Morrison, E. Underachievement among preadolescent boys considered in relationship to passive aggressive. *Journal of Educational Psychology*, 1969, 60, 168–173.

Preston, R. Reading achievement of German and American children. *School and Society*, 1962, 90, 350–354.

Roethlisberger, F. J., and Dickson, W. J. *Management and the worker.* Cambridge, Mass.: Harvard University Press, 1939.

Rosenkrans, M. A. Imitation in children as a function of perceived similarity to a social model and vicarious reinforcement. *Journal of Personality and Social Psychology*, 1967, 7, 307–315.

Samuels, S. J., and Turnure, J. E. Attention and reading achievement in first-grade boys and girls. *Journal of Educational Psychology*, 1974, 66, 29–32.

Seaver, W. B. Effects of naturally induced teacher expectancies. *Journal of Personality and Social Psychology*, 1973, 28, 333–342.

Stein, A. H., Pohly, S. R., and Mueller, E. The influence of masculine, feminine, and neutral tasks on children's achievement behavior, expectancies of success, and attainment values. *Child Development*, 1971, 42, 195–207.

Watson, J. D. *The double helix: A personal account of the discovery of the structure of DNA.* New York: Atheneum, 1969.

Wattenberg, W. W., and Clifford, C. Relation of self concepts to beginning achievement in reading. *Child Development*, 1964, 35, 461–467.

Weiner, B., Heckhausen, H., Meyer, W. U., and Cook, R. E. Causal ascriptions and achievement behavior: A conceptual analysis of effort and reanalysis of locus of control. *Journal of Personality and Social Psychology*, 1972, 21, 239–248.

Zaslavsky, C. *Africa counts: Number and pattern in African culture.* Boston: Prindle, Weber & Schmidt, 1973.

Zigler, E., Abelson, W. D., and Seitz, V. Motivational factors in the performance of economically disadvantaged children on the Peabody Picture Vocabulary Test. *Child Development*, 1973, *44*, 294–303.

Chapter 8 Broman, S. H., Nichols, P. L., and Kennedy, W. A. *Preschool I.Q.: Prenatal and early development correlates.* New York: John Wiley, 1975.

Chavasse, P. H. *Advice to mothers on management of children.* Philadelphia: J. B. Lippincott, 1869.

Guilford, J. P. *The nature of human intelligence.* New York: McGraw-Hill, 1967.

Haggard, E. A. Social status and intelligence. *Genetic Psychology Monographs*, 1954, *49*, 141–186.

Holtzman, W. H., Díaz-Guerrero, R., and Swartz, J. D. *Personality development in two cultures.* Austin: University of Texas Press, 1975.

Howland, Mrs. *The infant school manual* (9th ed.). Worcester, Mass.: Dorr, Howland and Co., 1839.

Jensen, A. R. How much can we boost I.Q. and scholastic achievement? *Harvard Educational Review*, 1969, *39*, 449–483.

Kagan, J., Klein, R. E., Finley, G., Rogoff, B., and Nolan, E. *A cross-cultural study of cognitive development,* unpublished.

Katz, M. B. *The irony of early school reform.* Boston: Beacon Press, 1968.

Kimble, G. A., Garmezy, N., and Zigler, E. *Principles of general psychology* (4th ed.). New York: Ronald Press, 1974.

Lewontin, R. Address at Massachusetts Institute of Technology, April 1975.

Piaget, J. *The origins of intelligence in children.* New York: International Universities Press, 1952.

Scarr, S., and Weinberg, R. A. I.Q. test performance of black children adopted by white families. *American Psychologist*, 1976, *31*, 726–739.

Shields, J. *Monozygotic twins.* London: Oxford University Press, 1962.

Shimberg, M. E. *An investigation into the validity of norms with special reference to urban and rural groups.* Archives of psychology, No. 104, Columbia University, 1929.

Smith, M. W. Alfred Binet's remarkable questions: A cross-national and cross-temporal analysis of the cultural biases built into the Stanford-Binet Intelligence Scale and other Binet tests. *Genetic Psychology Monographs*, 1974, *89*, 307–334.

Smith, R. T. A comparison of socioenvironmental factors in monozygotic and dizygotic twins, testing an assumption. In S. G. Vandenberg (Ed.), *Methods and goals in human behavior genetics.* New York: Academic Press, 1965.

Sontag, L. W., Baker, C. T., and Nelson, V. L. Mental growth and personality. *Monographs of the Society for Research in Child Development*, 1958, *23*(2, Serial No. 68).

Terman, L. M., and Merrill, M. A. *Measuring intelligence: A guide to the administration of the new revised Stanford-Binet tests of intelligence.* Boston: Houghton Mifflin, 1937.

Wallach, M. A. Tests tell us little about talent. *American Scientist*, 1976, *64*, 57–63.

Wechsler, D. Intelligence defined and undefined. *American Psychologist,* 1975, *30,* 135–139.

White, S. H. Social implications of I.Q. *Principal,* 1975, *54,* 4–14.

Williams, R. L. Black intelligence test of cultural homogeneity. *Newsweek,* December 19, 1973, p. 109.

Wilson, R. S. Twins: Pattern of cognitive development as measured on the Wechsler Preschool and Primary Scale of Intelligence. *Developmental Psychology,* 1975, *11,* 126–134.

Chapter 9

Air Training Command. *Improvement of grading practices for Air Training Command schools.* ATRC Manual 50–900–9. Scott Air Force Base, Ill.: Headquarters, Air Training Command, 1952.

Baker, A. O., and Mills, L. H. Biology workbook to accompany *Dynamic biology today.* Chicago: Rand McNally, 1943.

Bloom, B. S., Engelhart, M. D., Furst, G. J., Hill, W. H., and Krathwohl, D. R. *Taxonomy of educational objectives: The classification of educational goals. Handbook I: The cognitive domain.* New York: David McKay, 1956.

Doyle, K. O. Theory and practice of ability training in ancient Greece. *Journal of the History of the Behavioral Sciences,* 1974, *10,* 202–212.

Ebel, R. L. Measurement and the teacher. *Educational Leadership,* 1962, *20,* 20–24.

Ebel, R. L. *Essentials of educational measurement.* Englewood Cliffs, N.J.: Prentice-Hall, 1972.

Gage, N. L., and Berliner, D. C. *Educational psychology.* Chicago: Rand McNally, 1975.

Hawkes, H. E., Lindquist, E. F., and Mann, C. R. *The construction and use of achievement examinations.* Boston: Houghton Mifflin, 1936.

Hofstadter, R., Miller, W., and Aaron, D. *The American republic* (Vol. 2). Englewood Cliffs, N.J.: Prentice-Hall, 1959.

Kurfman, D. G. Teacher-made tests in the social studies. *Educational Leadership,* 1962, *20,* 16–19.

Madden, R. Gardner, E. F., Rudman, H. C., Karlsen, B., and Merwin, J. C. *Stanford achievement test, primary level II, form A.* New York: Harcourt Brace Jovanovich, 1972.

Page, E. B. The imminence of grading essays by computer. *Phi Delta Kappan,* 1966, *47,* 238–243.

Stanley, J. C., and Hopkins, K. D. *Educational and psychological measurement and evaluation.* Englewood Cliffs, N.J.: Prentice-Hall, 1972.

Starch, D., and Elliott, E. C. Reliability of grading high-school work in English. *Scholastic Review,* 1912, *20,* 442–457.

Steinberg, M. *Boston Globe,* October 21, 1974.

Teigs, E. W. *Educational diagnosis* (Educational Bulletin No. 18). Monterey: California Test Bureau, 1952.

Test Service Bulletin No. 48. New York: The Psychological Corporation, 1954–1955.

Tuckman, B. W. *Measuring educational outcomes: Fundamentals of testing.* New York: Harcourt Brace Jovanovich, 1975.

Chapter 10

Balow, I. H. Sex differences in first-grade reading. *Elementary English,* 1963, *40,* 303–320.

Benton, A. L. Minimal brain dysfunction from a neuropsychological point of view. In F. F. de la Cruz, B. H. Fox, and R. H. Roberts (Eds.), *Minimal brain dysfunction.* Annals of the New York Academy of Science (Vol. 205), 1973.

Birch, H. G., and Gussow, J. D. *Disadvantaged children: Health, nutrition, and school failure.* New York: Harcourt Brace Jovanovich, 1970.

Bishop, C. H. Transfer effects of word and letter training in reading. *Journal of Verbal Learning and Verbal Behavior,* 1964, *3,* 215–221.

Bonsall, C., and Dornbush, R. L. Visual perception and reading ability. *Journal of Educational Psychology,* 1969, *60,* 294–299.

Bortner, M., Hertzig, M. E., and Birch, H. G. Neurological signs and intelligence in brain damaged children. *Journal of Special Education,* 1972, *6,* 325–333.

Bruininks, R. H., and Rynders, J. E. Alternatives to special class placement for educable mentally retarded children. *Focus on Exceptional Children,* 1971, *3,* 1–12.

Cassidy, V. M., and Stanton, J. E. *An investigation of factors involved in the educational placement of mentally retarded children: A study of differences between children in special and regular classes in Ohio* (Cooperative Research Project No. 043). Columbus: Ohio State University, 1959.

Chess, S. Neurological dysfunction and childhood behavioral pathology. *Journal of Autism and Childhood Schizophrenia,* 1972, *2,* 299–311.

Clark, M. Hearing: A link to I.Q.? *Newsweek,* June 14, 1976, p. 97.

Critchley, M. *Developmental dyslexia.* London: Heineman, 1964.

Cruickshank, W. M., and Johnson, G. O. (Eds.). *Education of exceptional children and youth* (2nd ed.). Englewood Cliffs, N.J.: Prentice-Hall, 1967.

Crump, E. P., Horton, C. P., Masuoka, J., and Ryan, D. Growth and development. I. Relation of birth weight in Negro infants to sex, maternal age, parity, prenatal care, and socioeconomic status. *Journal of Pediatrics,* 1959, *51,* 678–697.

Doehring, D. G. Acquisition of rapid reading responses. *Monographs of the Society for Research in Child Development,* 1976, *41*(2, Serial No. 165).

Downing, J. A. *Evaluating the initial teaching alphabet.* London: Cassell and Co., 1967.

Downing, J. A. Initial teaching alphabet. In L. C. Deighton (Ed.), *The encyclopedia of education* (Vol. 5). New York: Macmillan, 1971.

Dunn, L. M. Special education for the mildly retarded: Is much of it justifiable? *Exceptional Children,* 1968, *35,* 5–22.

Dykstra, R., and Tinney, S. Sex differences and reading readiness, first-grade achievement and second-grade achievement. *Reading and Realism: Proceedings of the International Reading Association,* 1969, *13,* 623–628.

Ehri, L. C. Word consciousness in readers and prereaders. *Journal of Educational Psychology,* 1975, *67,* 204–212.

Eisenberg, L. In G. Schiffman, *Dyslexia*. Washington, D.C.: National Reading Center, 1976.

Engle, P. Unpublished manuscript. Guatemala City, Guatemala: Institute for Nutrition of Central America and Panama, 1975.

Genshaft, J. L., and Hirt, M. Language differences between black children and white children. *Developmental Psychology*, 1974, *10*, 451–456.

Gibson, E. J., and Levin, H. *The psychology of reading*. Cambridge, Mass.: M.I.T. Press, 1975.

Gillingham, A., and Stillman, B. W. *Remedial training for children with specific disability in reading, spelling, and penmanship* (7th ed.). Boston: Educators Publishing Service, 1960.

Gleitman, L. R., and Rozin, P. Teaching reading by use of a syllabary. *Reading Research Quarterly*, 1973, *8*, 447–501.

Hammill, D. Learning disabilities: A problem in definition. *CEC Division for Children with Learning Disabilities Newsletter*, Spring 1974, pp. 28–31.

Hobbs, N. *The future of children*. San Francisco: Jossey-Bass, 1975.

Holden, M. H., and MacGinitie, W. H. Children's conceptions of word boundaries in speech and print. *Journal of Educational Psychology*, 1972, *63*, 551–557.

Johnson, G. O. The education of mentally retarded children. In W. M. Cruickshank and G. O. Johnson (Eds.), *Education of exceptional children and youth* (2nd ed.). Englewood Cliffs, N.J.: Prentice-Hall, 1967.

Jones, J. W., and Collins, A. P. *Educational programs for visually handicapped children* (Office of Education Bulletin No. 6). Washington, D.C.: U.S. Government Printing Office, 1966.

Kalverboer, A. F., Touwen, B. D. L., and Prechtel, H. F. R. Follow-up of infants at risk of minor brain dysfunction. In F. F. de la Cruz, B. H. Fox, and R. H. Roberts (Eds.), *Minimal brain dysfunction*. Annals of the New York Academy of Science (Vol. 205), 1973.

Kenney, T. J., Clemmens, R. L., Hudson, B. W., Lentz, G. A., Cicci, R., and Nair, P. Characteristics of children referred because of hyperactivity. *Journal of Pediatrics*, 1971, *79*, 618–622.

Liberman, I. Y. Speech and lateralization of language. *Bulletin of the Orton Society*, 1971, *21*, 71–87.

Liberman, I. Y. Segmentation of the spoken word and reading acquisition. *Bulletin of the Orton Society*, 1973, *23*, 65–77.

Makita, K. The rarity of reading disability in Japanese children. *American Journal of Orthopsychiatry*, 1968, *38*, 599–614.

Marwit, S. J., and Neumann, G. Black and white children's comprehension of standard and nonstandard English passages. *Journal of Educational Psychology*, 1974, *66*, 329–332.

Mason, M. Reading ability and letter search time. *Journal of Experimental Psychology*, 1975, *104*, 146–168.

Mattis, S., French, J. H., and Rapin, I. Dyslexia in children and young adults: Three independent neuropsychological syndromes. *Developmental Medicine and Child Neurology*, 1975, *17*, 150–163.

Morrison, F. J., Giordani, B., and Nagy, J. Reading disability: An information processing analysis. *Science, 1977, 196,* 77–78.

Owen, F. W., Adams, P. A., Forrest, T., Stoltz, L. M., and Fisher, S. Learning disorders in children. *Monographs of the Society for Research in Child Development, 1971, 36*(4, Serial No. 144).

Preston, R. C. Reading achievement of German and American children. *School and Society, 1962, 90,* 350–354.

Preston, R. C., and Yarington, D. J. Status of fifty retarded readers eight years after reading clinic diagnosis. *Journal of Reading, 1967, 11,* 122–129.

Prouty, R. W., and McGarry, F. N. The diagnostic/prescriptive teacher. In The Council for Exceptional Children, *Principals training program book of readings.* Austin, Texas: Educational Service Center.

Rawson, M. B. *Developmental language disability.* Baltimore: Johns Hopkins Press, 1968.

Reitan, R. M., and Boll, T. J. Neuropsychological correlates of minimal brain dysfunction. In F. F. de la Cruz, B. H. Fox, and R. H. Roberts (Eds.), *Minimal brain dysfunction.* Annals of the New York Academy of Science (Vol. 205), 1973.

Robinson, H. M., and Smith, H. K. Reading-clinic patients ten years after. *Elementary School Journal, 1962, 63,* 22–27.

Robinson, N. B., and Robinson, N. M. *The mentally retarded child.* New York: McGraw-Hill, 1965.

Rushford, G. Glossary of terms relating to children with hearing problems. *Volta Review, 1964, 66,* 750–753.

Satz, P., Freil, J., and Rudegair, F. *Some predictive antecedents of specific reading disability.* Unpublished paper, University of Florida, 1974.

Satz, P., and van Nostrand, G. K. Developmental dyslexia: An evaluation of the theory. In P. Satz and J. Ross (Eds.), *The disabled learner: Early detection and intervention.* Rotterdam, The Netherlands: University of Rotterdam Press, 1972.

Scholl, G. T. The education of children with visual impairments. In W. M. Cruickshank and G. O. Johnson (Eds.), *Education of exceptional children and youth* (2nd ed.). Englewood Cliffs, N.J.: Prentice-Hall, 1967.

Shankweiler, D., and Liberman, I. Y. Misreading: A search for clues. In J. F. Kavanagh and I. G. Mattingly (Eds.), *Language by ear and by eye: The relationship between speech and reading.* Cambridge, Mass.: M.I.T. Press, 1972.

Sidman, M., and Kirk, B. Letter reversals in naming, writing, and matching to sample. *Child Development, 1974, 45,* 616–625.

Silverman, L. J., and Metz, A. S. Number of pupils with specific learning disabilities in local public schools in the United States: Spring, 1970. In F. F. de la Cruz, B. H. Fox, and R. H. Roberts (Eds.), *Minimal brain dysfunction.* Annals of the New York Academy of Science (Vol. 205), 1973.

Silverman, S. R. Deaf children. In H. Davis and S. R. Silverman (Eds.), *Hearing and deafness* (Rev. ed.). New York: Holt, Rinehart and Winston, 1960.

Smith, A., and Sugar, O. Development of above normal language and intelligence twenty-one years after left hemispherectomy. *Neurology, 1975, 25,* 813–818.

Sommers, R. K., and Taylor, M. L. Cerebral speech dominance in language disordered and normal children. *Cortex, 1972, 8,* 224–232.

Stein, D. G., Rosen, J. J., and Butters, N. *Plasticity and recovery of function of the central nervous system.* New York: Academic Press, 1974.

Stevenson, H. W., Parker, T., Wilkinson, A., Hegion, A., Fish, E. A longitudinal study of individual differences in cognitive development and scholastic achievement. *Journal of Educational Psychology,* 1976, *68,* 377–400.

Vellutino, F. R., Steger, J. A., and Kandel, G. Reading disability: Investigation of the perceptual deficit hypothesis. *Cortex,* 1972, *8,* 106–118.

Weber, R. M. The study of oral reading errors. *Reading Research Quarterly,* 1968, *4,* 96–119.

Wender, P. H. Some speculations concerning the possible biochemical basis of minimal brain dysfunction. In F. F. de la Cruz, B. H. Fox, and R. H. Roberts (Eds.), *Minimal brain dysfunction.* Annals of the New York Academy of Science (Vol. 205), 1973.

Willenberg, E. P. Levels of instructional intervention within public-school special education programs. In C. H. Meisgier and J. O. King (Eds.), *The process of special education administration.* Scranton, Penn.: Intext Educational Publishers, 1970.

Willerman, L. Social aspects of minimal brain dysfunction. In F. F. de la Cruz, B. H. Fox, and R. H. Roberts (Eds.), *Minimal brain dysfunction.* Annals of the New York Academy of Science (Vol. 205), 1973.

Chapter 11   Ausubel, D. P. *Educational psychology: A cognitive view.* New York: Holt, Rinehart and Winston, 1968.

Baird, L. L. Teaching styles: An exploratory study of dimensions and effects. *Journal of Educational Psychology,* 1973, *64,* 15–21.

Broden, M., Hall, R. V., Dunlap, A., and Clark, R. Effects of teacher attention and a token reinforcement system in a junior-high-school special education class. *Exceptional Children,* 1970, *36,* 341–349.

Brown, B., Stolz, S., Wienckowski, L., and Parloff, M. *Behavior modification: Perspective on a current issue.* Washington, D.C.: National Institute of Mental Health, January 1975.

Chall, J., and Feldmann, S. First-grade reading: An analysis of the interactions of professed methods, teacher implementation, and child background. *The Reading Teacher,* 1966, *19,* 569–575.

Clarizio, H. F. *Toward positive classroom discipline.* New York: John Wiley, 1971.

Davison, D. C. Perceived reward value of teacher reinforcement and attitude toward the teacher. *Journal of Educational Psychology,* 1972, *63,* 418–422.

Domino, G. Interactive effects of achievement orientation and teaching style on academic achievement. *Journal of Educational Psychology,* 1971, *62,* 427–431.

Dowaliby, F. J., and Schumer, H. Teacher-centered versus student-centered mode of college classroom instruction as related to manifest anxiety. *Journal of Educational Psychology,* 1973, *64,* 25–132.

Feshbach, N. D. Student teacher preferences for elementary-school pupils varying in personality characteristics. *Journal of Educational Psychology,* 1969, *60,* 126–132.

Goldberg, J. B. Influence of pupils' attitudes on perception of teachers' behaviors and on consequent schoolwork. *Journal of Educational Psychology*, 1968, *59*, 1–5.

Good, T. L., and Brophy, J. E. *Looking in classrooms*. New York: Harper & Row, 1973.

Heil, L. M. *Characteristics of teacher behavior related to the achievement of children in several elementary grades* (Cooperative Research Project No. 352). Mimeographed, Brooklyn College, 1960.

Hunter, M. *Reinforcement*. El Segundo, Calif.: TIP Publications, 1967.

Jackson, P. W. *Life in classrooms*. New York: Holt, Rinehart and Winston, 1968.

Kanfer, F. H. Behavior modification—an overview. In C. E. Thoreson (Ed.), *Behavior modification in education* (The 72nd Yearbook of the National Society for the Study of Education). Chicago: University of Chicago Press, 1973.

Klein, R. E., Freeman, H. E., and Millet, R. Psychological test performance and indigenous conceptions of intelligence. *Journal of Psychology*, 1973, *84*, 219–222.

Kounin, J. S. *Discipline and group management in classrooms*. New York: Holt, Rinehart and Winston, 1970.

Kounin, J. S., and Gump, P. V. The ripple effect in discipline. *Elementary School Journal*, 1958, *62*, 158–162.

Kress, G. C. A study of the effects of administering programmed instruction to interacting groups. *Journal of Educational Psychology*, 1969, *60*, 333–338.

Krumboltz, J. D., and Krumboltz, H. B. *Changing children's behavior*. Englewood Cliffs, N.J.: Prentice-Hall, 1972.

Lortie, D. C. *Schoolteacher: A sociological study*. Chicago: University of Chicago Press, 1975.

Marram, G. *Visibility of work in the education process: Evaluation and authority for nurses in hospitals and teachers in open and closed schools*. Unpublished doctoral dissertation, Stanford University, 1971.

Rhodes, F. Team teaching compared with traditional instruction in grades kindergarten through six. *Journal of Educational Psychology*, 1971, *62*, 110–116.

Sarason, I. G. Glazer, E. M., and Fargo, G. A. *Reinforcing productive classroom behavior*. New York: Human Sciences Press, 1972.

Spivack, G., Swift, M., and Prewitt, M. A. Syndromes of disturbed classroom behavior. *Journal of Special Education*, 1971, *5*, 269–292.

Swift, M., and Spivack, G. *Alternative teaching strategies: Helping behaviorally troubled children achieve: A guide for teachers and psychologists*. Champaign, Ill.: Research Press, 1975.

Tolor, A., Scarpetti, W. L., and Lane, P. A. Teachers' attitudes toward children's behavior revisited. *Journal of Educational Psychology*, 1967, *58*, 175–180.

Wheeler, R., and Ryan, F. L. Effects of cooperative and competitive classroom environments on the attitudes and achievements of elementary-school students engaged in social studies inquiry activities. *Journal of Educational Psychology*, 1973, *65*, 402–407.

White, R., and Lippitt, R. Leader behavior and member reaction in three "social climates." In D. Cartwright and A. Zander (Eds.), *Group dynamics*. Evanston, Ill.: Row-Peterson, 1960.

Withall, J. The development of a technique for the measurement of social-emotional climate in classrooms. *Journal of Exceptional Education*, 1949, *17*, 347–361.

Wolf, M. M., Giles, D. K., and Hall, R. V. Experiments with token reinforcement in a remedial classroom. *Behavioral Research and Therapy*, 1968, *6*, 51–64.

Yando, R. M., and Kagan, J. The effect of teacher tempo on the child. *Child Development*, 1968, *39*, 27–34.

Chapter 12   Ball, S., and Bogatz, G. A. *The first year of Sesame Street: An evaluation*. Princeton, N.J.: Princeton Testing Service, 1970.

Baratz, J. C. A bi-dialectical task for determining language proficiency in economically disadvantaged Negro children. *Child Development*, 1969, *40*, 889–901.

Battle, E. S., and Rotter, J. B. Children's feelings of personal control as related to social class and ethnic group. *Journal of Personality*, 1963, *31*, 482–490.

Blank, M., Koltuv, M., and Wood, M. Individual teaching for disadvantaged kindergarten children: A comparison of two methods. *Journal of Special Education*, 1972, *6*, 207–219.

Buck, M. R., and Austrin, H. R. Factors related to school achievement in an economically disadvantaged group. *Child Development*, 1971, *42*, 1813–1826.

Burnes, K. Patterns of WISC scores for children of two socioeconomic classes and races. *Child Development*, 1970, *41*, 493–499.

Coleman, J. S. *Equality of educational opportunity*. Washington, D.C.: U.S. Office of Education, 1966.

Coles, R., and Huge, H. Peonage in Florida. *New Republic*, July 26, 1969, pp. 17–21.

Feshbach, N.D. Student teacher preferences for elementary-school pupils varying in personality characteristics. *Journal of Educational Psychology*, 1969, *60*, 126–132.

Feshbach, S., and Adelman, H. Remediation of learning problems among the disadvantaged. *Journal of Educational Psychology*, 1974, *66*, 16–28.

Fjellman, J. *The myth of primitive mentality: A study of semantic acquisition and modes of categorization in Akamba children of south central Kenya*. Unpublished doctoral dissertation, Stanford University, 1971.

Greenberger, E., and Marini, M. M. *Black-white differences in psychosocial maturity: A further analysis* (Report No. 136). Baltimore, Md.: Center for Social Organization of Schools, Johns Hopkins University, 1972.

Harrison, F. Aspirations as related to school performance and socioeconomic status. *Sociometry*, 1969, *32*, 70–79.

Howard, D. P. The needs and problems of socially disadvantaged children as perceived by students and teachers. *Exceptional Children*, 1968, *34*, 327–335.

Klein, R. E. *The cognitive development of Guatemalan children*. Guatemala City, Guatemala: Institute for Nutrition of Central America and Panama, Report for AID, December 1975.

Jencks, C. *Inequality: A reassessment of the effect of family and schooling in America*. New York: Basic Books, 1972.

Kagan, J., Klein, R. E., Finley, G., Rogoff, B., and Nolan, E. *A cross-cultural study of cognitive development*, unpublished.

Kagan, S., and Madsen, M. C. Cooperation and competition of Mexican, Mexican-American, and Anglo-American children of two ages under four instructional sets. *Developmental Psychology*, 1971, 5, 32–39.

Kleinert, E. J. The Florida migrant. *Phi Delta Kappan*, October 1969, pp. 90–93.

Kulik, J. A., Sarbin, T. R., and Stein, K. B. Language, socialization, and delinquency. *Developmental Psychology*, 1971, 4, 434–439.

Lesser, G. S., Fifer, G., and Clark, D. H. Mental abilities of children from different social class and cultural groups. *Monographs of the Society for Research in Child Development*, 1965, 30(4, Serial No. 102).

Madsen, M. C., and Shapira, A. Cooperative and competitive behavior of urban Afro-American, Anglo-American, Mexican-American, and Mexican village children. *Developmental Psychology*, 1970, 3, 16–20.

Milgram, N. A., Shores, M. F., Riedel, W. W., and Malasky, C. Level of aspiration and locus of control in disadvantaged children. *Psychological Reports*, 1970, 27, 343–350.

Minton, C., Kagan, J., and Levine, J. Maternal control and obedience in the two-year-old. *Child Development*, 1971, 42, 1873–1894.

Mondale, W. F. United States Senate Committee on Equal Educational Opportunity Report, 1973.

Moynihan, D. P. The schism in black America. *The Public Interest*, No. 27, Spring 1972.

Nalven, F. B. Manifest fears and worries of ghetto vs. middle-class suburban children. *Psychological Reports*, 1970, 27, 285–286.

Pozner, J., and Saltz, E. *Social class, conditional communication, and egocentric speech* (Report No. 2). Detroit, Mich.: Center for the Study of Cognitive Processes, Wayne State University, 1972.

Riessman, F., and Gartner, A. New careers and pupil learning. *California Teachers Association Journal*, 1969, 65(2), 6–9.

Rohwer, W. D. Learning, race, and school success. In S. Chess and A. Thomas (Eds.), *Annual progress in child psychiatry and child development*. New York: Brunner/Mazel, 1972.

Securro, S., and Walls, R. T. Concept achievement of culturally advantaged and disadvantaged children utilizing artificial and lifelike stimulus tasks. *Journal of Educational Psychology*, 1971, 62, 531–538.

Smith, I. L., and Greenberg, S. Teacher attitudes and the labeling process. *Exceptional Children*, 1975, 41, 319–324.

Social Indicators, 1973. Washington, D.C.: Office of Management and Budget, U.S. Department of Commerce, Executive Office of the President.

Stedman, J. S., and Adams, R. L. Achievement as a function of language competence, behavior adjustment, and sex in young, disadvantaged Mexican-American children. *Journal of Educational Psychology*, 1972, 63, 411–417.

Tulkin, S. R., and Kagan, J. Mother-child interaction in the first year of life. *Child Development*, 1972, 43, 31–41.

Zigler, E., and Kanzer, P. The effectiveness of two classes of verbal reinforcers on the performance of middle and lower class children. *Journal of Personality*, 1962, 30, 157–163.

Chapter 13   Atkinson, R. C. Computerized instruction and the learning process. *American Psychologist*, 1968, *23*, 225–239.

Bereiter, C., and Engelmann, S. *Teaching disadvantaged children in the preschool.* Englewood Cliffs, N.J.: Prentice-Hall, 1966.

Blank, M., and Solomon, F. How shall the disadvantaged child be taught? *Child Development*, 1969, *40*, 47–61.

Bloom, B. S. *Stability and change in human characteristics.* New York: John Wiley, 1964.

Bracht, G. H. Experimental factors related to aptitude-treatment interactions. *Review of Educational Research*, 1970, *40*, 627–645.

Cronbach, L. J., and Snow, R. E. *Individual differences in learning ability as a function of instructional variables* (Final report, School of Education, Stanford University. Contract No. DEC 4-6-061269-1217). Washington, D.C.: U.S. Office of Education, 1969.

Crutchfield, R. The creative process. In M. Bloomberg (Ed.), *Creativity.* New Haven, Conn.: College and University Press, 1973.

Fletcher, J. O. The design of computer-assisted instruction in initial reading: The Stanford projects. In L. B. Resnick and P. Weaver (Eds.), *Theory and practice of early reading.* Hillside, N.J.: Lawrence Erlbaum Associates, in press.

Gordon, I. J., Guinagh, B., and Jester, R. E. The Florida parent education, infant and toddler programs. In M. C. Day and R. K. Parker (Eds.), *The preschool in action: Exploring early childhood programs* (2nd ed.). Boston: Allyn & Bacon, 1977.

Gray, S. W., and Klaus, R. A. The Early Training Project: A Seventh-year report. *Child Development*, 1970, *41*, 909–924.

Hunt, J. M. *Intelligence and experience.* New York: Ronald Press, 1961.

Jacobson, E. *The effect of different modes of practice on number facts and computational abilities.* Unpublished manuscript, Learning Research and Development Center, University of Pittsburgh, 1975.

Kamii, C., and DeVries, R. Piaget for early education. In M. C. Day and R. K. Parker (Eds.), *The preschool in action: Exploring early childhood programs* (2nd ed.). Boston: Allyn & Bacon, 1977.

Karnes, M. B., Hodgins, A. S., Stoneburner, R. L., Studley, W. M., and Teska, J. A. Effects of a highly structured program of language development on intellectual functioning and psycholinguistic development of culturally disadvantaged three-year-olds. *Journal of Special Education*, 1964, *2*, 405–412.

Lally, J. R., and Honig, A. S. The family development research program. In M. C. Day and R. K. Parker (Eds.), *The preschool in action: Exploring early childhood programs* (2nd ed.). Boston: Allyn & Bacon, 1977.

Lindvall, C. M., and Bolvin, J. O. *Programmed instruction in the schools: An application of programming principles in "individually prescribed instruction."* Sixty-sixth Yearbook of the National Society for the Study of Education, Part II. Chicago: 1967.

MacKinnon, D. W. Personality and the realization of creative potential. *American Psychologist*, 1965, *20*, 273–281.

Maeroff, G. I. A new day for the gifted. New York Times, April 25, 1976, p. 1.

Miller, L. B., and Dyer, J. L. Four preschool programs: Their dimensions and effects. *Monographs of the Society for Research in Child Development,* 1975, 40(5–6, Serial No. 162).

Osborn, J. Teaching a teaching language to disadvantaged children. In M. A. Brottman (Ed.), *Language remediation for the disadvantaged preschool child. Monographs of the Society for Research in Child Development,* 1968, 33(8, Serial No. 124).

Pierson, D. E. Brookline Early Education Project: One model for an early start. *Top of the News,* November 1974.

Resnick, L. B., Wang, M. C., and Kaplan, J. Task analysis in curriculum design: A hierarchically sequenced introductory mathematics curriculum. *Journal of Applied Behavior Analysis,* 1973, 6, 679–710.

Resnick, L. B., Wang, M. C., and Rosner, J. Adaptive education for young children: The Primary Education Project. In M. C. Day and R. K. Parker (Eds.), *The preschool in action: Exploring early childhood programs* (2nd ed.). Boston: Allyn & Bacon, 1977.

Schaefer, C. E. A psychological study of ten exceptionally creative adolescent girls. *Exceptional Children,* 1970, 36, 431–441.

Schaefer, E., and Aaronson, M. Infant education research project: Implementation and implications of a home tutoring program. In M. C. Day and R. K. Parker (Eds.), *The preschool in action: Exploring early childhood programs* (2nd ed.). Boston: Allyn & Bacon, 1977.

Stallings, J. Implementation and child effects of teaching practices in follow-through classrooms. *Monographs of the Society for Research in Child Development,* 1975, 40(7–8, Serial No. 175).

Stanley, J. C. Intellectual precocity. In J. C. Stanley, D. P. Keating, and L. H. Fox (Eds.), *Mathematical talent: Discovery, description, and development.* Baltimore, Md.: Johns Hopkins University Press, 1974.

Suppes, P., Jerman, M., and Brian, D. *Computer-assisted instruction: Stanford's 1965–66 arithmetic program.* New York: Academic Press, 1968.

Suppes, P., and Morningstar, M. *Computer-assisted instruction at Stanford, 1966–68: Data, models, and evaluation of the arithmetic programs.* New York: Academic Press, 1972.

Terman, L. M. *Genetic studies of genius* (Vol. 3). Stanford, Calif.: Stanford University Press, 1930.

Wallach, M.A., and Kogan, N. *Modes of thinking in young children.* New York: Holt, Rinehart and Winston, 1965.

Weikart, D. P. *Early childhood special education for intellectually subnormal and/or culturally different children.* Washington, D.C.: National Leadership Institute in Early Childhood Development, October 1971.

White, B. L. *Human infants: Experience and psychological development.* Englewood Cliffs, N.J.: Prentice-Hall, 1971.

Zigler, E., and Butterfield, E. C. Motivational aspects of changes in I.Q. test performance of culturally deprived nursery school children. *Child Development,* 1968, 39, 1–13.

Epilogue   Barker, R. G. and Gump, P. V. *Big school, small school: High school size and student behavior.* Stanford, Calif.: Stanford University Press, 1964.

Díaz-Guerrero, R., and Holtzman, W. H. Plaza Sesamo. *Journal of Educational Psychology,* 1974, 66, 632–643.

glossary

accessibility of concept: The degree to which a concept can be described and talked about.

accommodation: The process by which knowledge is changed in accord with new experiences; a Piagetian concept.

achievement motivation: Desire to improve one's talents for their own sake.

affect: A word used to describe certain changes in feeling state; synonymous with emotion.

affiliation: A close relation with a group or an individual; a primary value in the contemporary United States. (See *group affiliation*)

aptitude: The degree to which a person is prepared to learn a new skill.

assimilation: The process of incorporating a new object or idea into existing knowledge; one of Piaget's main concepts.

association: The process of relating a new object or event to prior knowledge.

attention: Concentration on the aspects of one's environment.

autonomy: Independent and individual action; a primary value in the contemporary United States.

baseline: In behavior modification technique, the occurrence of a particular behavior before reinforcement begins.

behavior modification: A set of practices that uses the consequences of behavior to strengthen or weaken future behavior; it is frequently used in changing classroom behavior.

bell-shaped curve: See *normal probability curve*

CAI: See *computer-assisted instruction*

cardinal: A numerical concept applied to a set of objects; a property of that set that does not change even if the specific objects or their arrangement changes. (Compare *ordinal*)

central dimensions: The primary descriptive or functional characteristics that convey the essence of a concept.

chaining: Gagné's third learning type; chaining involves the linking of a stimulus and a response before reinforcement occurs.

class: A category or a concept that nests into others in a hierarchical manner.

classical conditioning (also called respondent conditioning): The repeated pairing of an unconditioned stimulus with a conditioned stimulus so that by association the conditioned stimulus evokes the same response as the unconditioned stimulus.

class inclusion: Consideration of a whole and a part of a whole simultaneously; one of the operations of the concrete operational stage.

cognition: The process of acquiring, storing, transforming, creating, using, and evaluating knowledge.

cognitive competence: The potential capacity to apply certain intellectual processes to problems.

compensatory education: Instruction for children who are likely to encounter serious difficulty in school in order to improve their chances for academic success.

competence: A potential ability; a capacity for a task.

competition: The striving for a goal in which one person tries to attain the goal ahead of others; a primary value in the contemporary United States.

computer-assisted instruction (CAI): A method of programed teaching in which a child interacts with a computer.

concept: A mental representation of a set of attributes shared by a group of related objects, events, or experiences.

concrete operational stage: The third stage of Piaget's theory of cognitive development, occurring generally between the ages of seven and eleven; characterized by certain abilities such as conservation.

conditioned response: A learned response to a stimulus that did not previously elicit that response.

conditioned stimulus: An object or event that elicits a response that prior to conditioning did not elicit that response.

conservation: According to Piaget, the rule that qualities such as quantity, volume, and weight of an object do not change with alterations in the physical appearance of that object.

conservation of number: The rule that number is a property of a particular set of objects and does not change even if the objects or their arrangement changes.

correlation coefficient: A statistic that represents the degree of relation or association between two sets of events.

creativity: Problem-solving behavior that is original, constructive, and appropriate, as a result of using known elements and facts to form a new idea.

criterion-referenced test: A test that measures how well a person meets a particular, preestablished level of performance. (Compare *norm-referenced test*)

differentiation: The number of different but related examples of a particular concept.

diphthong: A pair of vowels.

directed cognition: Thought aimed at a particular goal. (Compare *undirected cognition*)

discrimination: The process by which an organism responds one way to one stimulus and in a different way to another, similar stimulus.

discrimination learning: Gagné's fifth learning type; it involves, first, perceptually differentiating among events and, second, attaching the proper labels to each of them.

dyslexia: Serious inability to read with normal proficiency in spite of average intelligence, adequate instruction, and suitable environmental support.

egalitarianism: The belief that all people should have equal legal, economic, social, and political rights, and be judged by their talents and products, not by their sex, race, ethnicity, or religion.

egocentric: The state of being unable to take the viewpoint of another person.

eidetic imagery: Ability to maintain mentally and to describe in detail an object or event that has been removed from sight.

equilibration: The resolution of the tension between assimilation and accommodation; one of Piaget's main concepts.

evaluation: The consideration or assessment of the validity of one's intellectual products and solutions generated.

executive processes: A set of cognitive functions that organizes the units and processes of cognition, keeps track of what the mind has learned, and recognizes when a problem has been solved.

expectancy: The anticipation of how one will perform a task; it influences how much effort is expended on a task and how well the task is actually performed.

externalizer: One who attributes success or failure to forces and conditions outside of his control. (Compare *internalizer*)

extinction: In behavior modification, the discontinuation of a behavior due to the absence of a reward for that behavior.

formal operational stage: Piaget's fourth stage of cognitive development, which begins at about age twelve, in which a child transcends concrete reality; starts to reason about properties, facts, propositions, and relationships; assumes hypothetical conditions; and generates implications.

formative evaluation: Testing that provides feedback as to how well students are mastering a particular subject matter as they go along and what problems are being encountered; helps focus on particular skills necessary for movement toward final mastery. (Compare *summative evaluation*)

generalization: The tendency of an organism to respond in the same way to two or more similar stimuli.

genotype: A particular set of genes.

gifted child: A child who has a very high I.Q. (usually above 130) or a unique talent, or talents, in a particular area.

grade-equivalent score: A test score expressed in relation to age or school grade.

group affiliation: A close, personal association with a group; a primary value in the contemporary United States. (See *affiliation*)

grouping: According to Piaget, a logical structure that characterizes the concrete operational stage of thought.

halo effect: A term that refers to a teacher's allowing previous impressions of a student's performance to interfere with the assessment of the student's current performance.

hard sign: A neurological term referring to a symptom that is highly likely to indicate brain damage; hard signs include motor tremors, paralysis, serious irregularities in brain wave patterns, and delayed or absent speech. (Compare *soft sign*)

Hawthorne effect: A term used to describe an effect achieved primarily by a change in circumstance.

hypothesis: A mental idea of possible ways to solve a problem.

identification: A process in which a child believes a similarity exists between himself and another person and thereby shares vicariously in the person's emotional state.

image: A detailed mental representation of an object or an event, created from a schema.

imitation: The expression in action of a behavior observed in another.

impulsive: A term used to describe children who only briefly consider the appropriateness or accuracy of their solution to a problem before accepting and reporting it. (Compare *reflective*)

Initial Teaching Alphabet (i.t.a.): An alphabet of forty-four characters with a single sound for each character, used for teaching beginners to read English.

intelligence: A term used to connote generalized mental ability.

intelligence quotient (I.Q.): A score obtained from taking an intelligence test, which compares one's performance with that of others of the same age.

internalizer: One who attributes success or failure to his own effort or ability. (Compare *externalizer*)

interpreted feeling state: A detected and interpreted change in internal bodily state.

I.Q.: See *intelligence quotient*

i.t.a.: See *Initial Teaching Alphabet*

kana: A form of Japanese script consisting of forty-eight forms, each of which stands for a different sounding syllable. (Compare *kanji*)

kanji: A kind of Japanese script in which each visual form stands for a whole object or idea, not simply a phonetic sound. (Compare *kana*)

learning: A change in behavior, knowledge, cognitive skills, or emotional feelings in an organism that lasts longer than a few moments.

logogram: A written symbol used to represent a whole idea. (Compare *pictograph, syllabary*)

long-term memory: A memory system that potentially retains information for a long time. (Compare *sensory memory, short-term memory*)

mastery learning: An approach to learning hierarchically organized subjects in which learning complex tasks depends on first learning simpler tasks that are components of the larger one.

maturation: The gradual and inevitable changes in size, physiology, and psychological functioning that normally occur in all individuals from birth through adulthood as a result of inherited processes operating in a reasonably normal environment.

mean: The average score on a test.

median: The score that separates the lower half of a group of scores from the upper half.

mnemonic device: A memory aid that helps to register new information.

mode: The score obtained by the largest number of people taking a test.

motive: A cognitive representation of a desired future goal, associated with the tension between an unsatisfactory present reality and a presumably more satisfying future state.

nonstandard English: A form of English that deviates from normally accepted standards of the English language, with its own internal rules and idioms; usually applied to black dialects in the United States.

norm: The average score obtained on a test by a large group of a particular age or grade level.

normal probability curve (also called bell-shaped curve): An idealized mathematical concept in which the mean, mode, and median are the same; it takes the form of a bell-shaped curve, which is divided in half by the mean, mode, and median.

norm of reaction: A term used to describe the fact that a particular set of genes can have different outcomes in different environments.

norm-referenced test: A test that measures how well a person performs on a particular test in comparison to people of the same age who are taking the test. (Compare *criterion-referenced test*)

observation: A mode of learning whereby children gain knowledge through listening, watching, noticing, or reading. (Compare *reflective thought*)

operant conditioning: Learning process by which a subject learns to perform a particular operation as a result of receiving a reward.

operation: A special mental rule whose chief characteristic is that it is reversible; a major concept in Piaget's theory. For example, the knowledge that one can break a ball of clay into two pieces and then reverse that action and put the pieces together to restore the original piece is an operation.

ordinal: A numerical quality assigned to an object that emphasizes the magnitude relation of a set of numbers. (Compare *cardinal*)

peer group: A group of equals (usually based on age for children) to which a person belongs; a major influence in the child's socialization process.

percentile rank: A statistic that indicates an individual's standing relative to a group; it indicates what percent of the group's scores was lower than the individual's.

perceptual training: Individual exercises to help children who have trouble reading learn to distinguish between letters with similar shapes, for example, *p* and *b*.

perception: The extraction of information from sensory stimulation.

performance: Overt problem-solving behavior; what people show they can do.

perseveration: The repetition of words, gestures, or questions; a soft sign of brain damage.

phonics: A method of teaching beginners to read using elementary speech sounds.

pictograph: A picture used to convey an idea. (Compare *logogram, syllabary*)

predictive validity: The degree to which a test predicts future performance in a subject area.

preoperational stage: Piaget's second stage of cognitive development, occurring generally in the years from one and a half to seven; during this period children learn to use language and other symbols, but they do not possess the groupings of conservation or class inclusion, or other operations of the concrete operational stage.

process: A cognitive method used to manipulate units in directed mental activity, according to certain rules. Perception, memory, generating possible solutions, evaluation, and implementing appropriate solutions are processes.

rate of development: The speed at which a competence grows.

raw score: A test score given in terms of the number of questions answered correctly.

readiness: The level of preparedness and ability needed to undertake a new skill; it is a function of the interplay of maturation and experience.

recall: A way to measure what is remembered by asking a person to retrieve all the necessary information from his memory; essay questions use recall. (Compare *recognition*)

recognition: A way to measure what is remembered by asking a person to demonstrate that he recognizes what he has learned; true-false questions use recognition. (Compare *recall*)

reflective thought: A mode of learning whereby children gain knowledge through mentally working on experiences they observe and reinforcements they receive. (Compare *observation*)

reflective: A term used to describe children who spend a long time considering the appropriateness and accuracy of their solution to a problem and rejecting the ones that seem incorrect before accepting and reporting it. (Compare *impulsive*)

rehearsal: Mental or verbal recitation of information that has been perceived, in order to facilitate its storage and recall.

reinforcement: An event following a particular action that increases the likelihood of that action occurring again.

relational term: A word used to describe a comparative quality, for example, *bigger*, *lighter*, *thinner*.

reliability: An important criterion for a good test; a test has reliability if it consistently measures what it is supposed to measure.

respondent conditioning: See *classical conditioning*

response: A reaction to a stimulus.

retardation: A term applied to those persons whose functioning is less competent than the average person of that age.

role: Behavior expected of someone in a particular position in society.

role model: A person whom a child admires and therefore may want to imitate.

rule: A statement that relates two or more concepts; it may describe either static or dynamic relations, or formal or informal relations.

salience: The intensity and attention-getting quality of a particular set of feelings.

satiation: The point in behavior modification at which a reward loses its effectiveness and the person no longer responds to its incentive power.

schedule of reinforcement: The frequency with which a reinforcement is given following a response; a strategy of behavior modification. An unpredictable schedule of reinforcement is more effective in maintaining new behavior than a schedule in which the person is rewarded every time.

schema: An elemental unit of mind; a mental representation of the outstanding and most essential characteristics of an object or event in a unique pattern.

self-actualization: The development of one's abilities.

sensorimotor stage: Piaget's first stage of cognitive development, occurring in the first year and a half of life; during this period a child moves from purely reflexive actions to actions deliberately initiated to achieve an effect.

sensory memory: A memory system that retains information for a very brief time, usually a fraction of a second. (Compare *long-term memory, short-term memory*)

seriation: The arrangement of a group of objects according to a quantitative dimension; an operation of the concrete operational stage.

sex role: The actions and feelings expected of a person in a society based on the stereotypical characteristics of a person's gender.

sex typing: The practice of promoting different attributes in boys and girls in accordance with the characteristics expected of men and women in that society.

shaping: A strategy of behavior modification that seeks to change undesirable behaviors one at a time rather than to change all undesirable behaviors at once.

short-term memory: A memory system that retains information for a brief time (typically thirty seconds), after which the information is either lost or transferred to long-term memory. (Compare *long-term memory, sensory memory*)

signal learning: Gagné's first learning type; it corresponds to classical conditioning. In signal learning, a stimulus acts as the sign for a reaction.

socialization: The process by which children learn the attitudes, values, and behavior that are commonly promoted in their society.

socioeconomic class: A concept referring to groups of people who share values due to similar vocations, incomes, and education.

soft sign: A neurological term referring to behaviors that are believed to reflect brain damage, such as perseveration, hyperactivity, impulsiveness, inattentiveness, and poor performance on mental tests. (Compare *hard sign*)

S-R bond: See *stimulus-response bond*

standard: An idealized representation of an idea or an act that an individual wishes to attain.

standard score (also called Z-score): A statistic that indicates how far an individual raw score is from the average score of the group, measured in standard deviation units. It may be positive (above the average), negative (below the average), or zero (equal to the average).

stanine score: A transformed score that has a mean of five and a standard deviation of approximately two.

stimulus-response bond (S-R bond): The association of certain stimuli with certain responses.

stimulus-response learning: Gagné's second learning type; it corresponds to operant conditioning. In stimulus-response learning, a stimulus provokes a deliberate and specific response from an organism.

streaming: See *tracking*

summative evaluation: Testing used to evaluate whether a particular subject matter was understood; summative evaluations usually refer to the final test at the end of a course. (Compare *formative evaluation*)

syllabary: A set of written symbols that stands for the sound of individual syllables in words. (Compare *logogram, pictograph*)

symbol: An arbitrary representation of a specific event or object, for example, the letters of the alphabet.

team teaching: The practice of using more than one teacher in a classroom, especially in classes that integrate students of varying abilities.

token economy: An economic system, often used in classrooms, in which students who engage in appropriate behavior are rewarded with tokens that can be exchanged for various privileges or objects.

tracking (also called streaming): The practice in school of grouping children according to ability.

transformed score: A score that expresses an individual's performance relative to others his own age or grade; obtained by manipulating a person's raw score.

undirected cognition: Spontaneous, undirected thought, for example, daydreaming and free association. (Compare *directed cognition*)

unit: A cognitive structure in mental activity. Schemata, images, symbols, concepts, and rules are units.

universal: An ability that develops as a matter of course in healthy children in any normal environment; for example, the ability to speak the language of one's community.

validity: An important criterion for a good test; a test is valid if it measures what it is supposed to measure.

verbal association: Gagné's fourth learning type; it involves the learning, through a coding connection, of a word that is associated with another word, as in learning a foreign language or mastering synonyms within a language.

Z-score: See *standard score*

acknowledgments and copyrights

of college classroom instruction as related to manifest anxiety. *Journal of Educational Psychology*, 1973, *64*, 25–132. Copyright 1973 by the American Psychological Association. Reprinted by permission.

12–1 *Social indicators, 1973.* Bureau of the Census. **12–2** *Social indicators, 1973.* Bureau of the Census. **12–3** Burnes, K. Patterns of WISC scores for children of two socioeconomic classes and races. *Child Development,* 1970, *41*, 493–499. Copyright 1970 by The Society for Research in Child Development, Inc. **12–4** Securro, S., and Walls, R. T. Concept achievement of culturally advantaged and disadvantaged children utilizing artificial and lifelike stimulus tasks. *Journal of Educational Psychology*, 1971, *62*, 531–538. Copyright 1971 by the American Psychological Association. Reprinted by permission. **12–5** Lesser, G. S., Fifer, G., and Clark, D. H. Mental abilities of children from different social class and cultural groups. *Monographs of the Society for Research in Child Development,* 1965, *30*(4, Serial No. 102). Copyright 1965 by The Society for Research in Child Development, Inc. **12–6** Adapted from Blank, M., Koltuv, M., and Wood, M. Individual teaching for disadvantaged kindergarten children: A comparison of two methods. *Journal of Special Education,* Vol. 6, No. 3, p. 215. Reproduced with permission.

13–2 Weikart, D. P. *Early childhood special education for intellectually subnormal and/or culturally different children.* Washington, D.C.: National Leadership Institute in Early Childhood Development, October 1971. **13–3** Adapted from Resnick, L. B., Wang, M. C., and Rosner, J. Adaptive education for young children: The Primary Education Project. In M. C. Day and R. K. Parker (Eds.), *The*

preschool in action: Exploring early childhood programs. Boston: Allyn and Bacon, 1977. **13–4** Resnick, L. B., Wang, M. C., and Kaplan, J. Task analysis in curriculum design: A hierarchically sequenced introductory mathematics curriculum. *Journal of Applied Behavior Analysis,* 1973, *6*, 679–710. Copyright 1973 by the Society for the Experimental Analysis of Behavior, Inc.

Boxes

Page 57 *Dick and Jane as victims,* Women on Words & Images, P.O. Box 2163, Princeton, N.J. 08540. **401** Copyright © 1973 by Wallace Tripp. From *A great big ugly man came up and tied his horse to me: A book of NO-sense verse.* Illustrated by Wallace Tripp, by permission of Little, Brown and Co. Drawing appears in full color in original source. **415** "Mairzy Doats" Copyright 1943 by Miller Music Co.; copyright renewed 1971 by Drake Activities Corporation; Al Hoffman Songs, Inc.; Hallmark Music, Inc. **465** Adapted from Clarizio, H. F. *Toward positive classroom discipline.* New York: John Wiley, 1971. **467** Adapted from Clarizio, H. F. *Toward positive classroom discipline.* New York: John Wiley, 1971. **475** Chart (abridged) on page 179 of *Looking in classrooms* by Thomas L. Good and Jere E. Brophy. Copyright © 1973 by Thomas L. Good and Jere E. Brophy. Reprinted by permission of Harper & Row, Publishers, Inc.

Pictures

Page 12 Susan W. Dryfoos/Monkmeyer. **14** Erich Hartmann/Magnum. **20** Bruce Anspach from Editorial Photocolor Archives. **23** Hugh Rogers/Monkmeyer. **27** Marcia Weinstein. **29** David Strickler/Monkmeyer. **42** Susan Ylvisaker/Jeroboam, Inc. **45**

(left) Harvey Barad/Monkmeyer. **45** (right) Marjorie Pickens. **49** Russell Abraham/Jeroboam, Inc. **53** Marjorie Pickens. **56** Blair Seitz from Editorial Photocolor Archives. **66** (top left) Doug Magee from Editorial Photocolor Archives. **66** (top right) Elizabeth Crews/Jeroboam, Inc. **66** (bottom left) Elizabeth Crews/Jeroboam, Inc. **66** (bottom right) Andrew Sacks from Editorial Photocolor Archives. **67** (top left) Russell Abraham/Jeroboam, Inc. **67** (top right) Marjorie Pickens. **67** (right center) Raimondo Borea/Editorial Photocolor Archives. **67** (bottom left) Sybil Shackman/Monkmeyer. **67** (bottom right) Charles Gatewood. **71** Charles Gatewood. **83** David Strickler/Monkmeyer. **89** James Carroll from Editorial Photocolor Archives. **90** Raimondo Borea/Editorial Photocolor Archives. **92** Marjorie Pickens. **94** Marcia Weinstein. **108** Bob Van Lindt/Editorial Photocolor Archives. **111** Raimondo Borea/Editorial Photocolor Archives. **113** William Simmons/Ford Foundation. **114** Virginia Hamilton. **115** Mike Borum/Image, Inc. **120** Sybil Shelton/Monkmeyer. **125** Ellen Levine from Editorial Photocolor Archives. **132** Blair Seitz from Editorial Photocolor Archives. **137** Marion Bernstein. **139** Doug Magee from Editorial Photocolor Archives. **140** Ken Karp. **143** Virginia Hamilton. **149** David Strickler/Monkmeyer. **155** Marjorie Pickens. **160** Rudolph Robinson from Editorial Photocolor Archives. **163** Ken Karp. **166** Eileen Christelow/Jeroboam, Inc. **170** Raimondo Borea/Editorial Photocolor Archives. **172** Marion Bernstein/Editorial Photocolor Archives. **180** Les Mahon/Monkmeyer. **185** Marjorie Pickens from *Beginning Experiences in Architecture,* by George E. Trogler, Van Nostrand Reinhold, 1972. **186** Marjorie Pickens from *Beginning Experiences in Architecture,* by George E. Trogler, Van Nostrand Reinhold, 1972. **188** James Carroll from Editorial Photocolor Archives. **193** Hugh Rogers/Monkmeyer. **195** Beryl Goldberg. **201** Suzanne Szasz. **206** Michael Meadows from Editorial Photocolor Archives. **215** Suzanne Szasz. **228** (top left) Marjorie Pickens. **228** (top right) Marjorie Pickens. **228** (center right) Marion Bernstein. **228** (bottom right) Marjorie Pickens. **228** (bottom left) Ira Kirschenbaum/Stock, Boston. **229** (top left) Virginia Hamilton. **229** (top right) Marjorie Pickens. **229** (bottom right) Suzanne Szasz. **229** (bottom left) Marjorie Pickens. **229** (center left) Marjorie Pickens. **231** Raimondo Borea/Editorial Photocolor Archives. **233** Virginia Hamilton. **235** Marion Bernstein. **236** Ken Karp. **239** George Gardner. **244** Marjorie Pickens. **250** Doug Magee from Editorial Photocolor Archives. **252** Ken Karp. **255** George Gardner. **267** Ken Karp. **271** Ken Karp. **275** Ken Karp. **285** Editorial Photocolor Archives. **288** Shelly Rusten. **291** Bill Grimes/Image, Inc. **292** Charles Gatewood. **295** Hugh Rogers/Monkmeyer. **300** Ken Karp. **309** Suzanne Szasz. **315** Mimi Forsyth/Monkmeyer. **318** Nancy Hays/Monkmeyer. **329** Nancy Hays/Monkmeyer. **330** Blair Seitz from Editorial Photocolor Archives. **333** Suzanne Szasz. **336** Harvey Stein. **346** Suzanne Szasz. **353** Charles Gatewood. **355** Beryl Goldberg. **356** Library of Congress. **360** Ken Karp. **363** Michael Hayman/Image, Inc. **367** Mimi Forsyth/Monkmeyer. **375** Michael Hayman/Image, Inc. **379** Hugh Rogers/Monkmeyer. **387** Marcia Weinstein. **393** J. Bruce Baumann/Image, Inc. **419** Harvey Stein. **420** Nancy Hays/Monkmeyer. **425** Cary Wolensky/Stock, Boston. **427** Hugh Rogers/Monkmeyer. **432** Harbrace. **433** Ken Karp. **440** Hugh Rogers/Monkmeyer. **443** Ken Karp. **444** E. and F. Bernstein Photos. **448**

George Zimbel/Monkmeyer. **449** Julie O'Neil/Stock, Boston. **451** Hugh Rogers/Monkmeyer. **452** Charles Gatewood. **472** Beryl Goldberg. **489** Charles Gatewood. **491** Harvey Stein. **495** Charles Harbutt/Magnum. **498** Doug Magee from Editorial Photocolor Archives. **499** Peter Vandermark/Stock, Boston. **504** Cary Wolensky/Stock, Boston. **507** George Gardner. **514** Ken Karp. **516** Shelly Rusten. **519** Charles Gatewood. **524** Charles Gatewood. **526** James H. Karales from Peter Arnold. **533** Marion Bernstein. **535** B. Kliewe/Jeroboam, Inc. **544** Sam Falk/Monkmeyer. **549** George Zimbel/Monkmeyer. **558** Eileen Christelow/Jeroboam, Inc. **566** (top left) Cary Wolensky/Stock, Boston. **566** (top right) Suzanne Szasz. **566** (center right) Wayne Miller/Magnum. **566** (bottom right) Ellis Herwig/Stock, Boston. **566** (bottom left) Clif Garboden/Stock, Boston. **567** (top) John J. Williams/Image, Inc. **567** (center right) Marcia Weinstein. **567** (bottom right) Jeff Albertson/Stock, Boston. **567** (bottom left) Don Fager/Image, Inc. **567** (center left) Norman Prince.

index

Page numbers in *italics* refer to illustrations; page numbers in **boldface** refer to the Reference List.

A